Advertising principles, problems, and cases

Advertising principles, problems, and cases

CHARLES J. DIRKSEN
Professor and Dean
Graduate School of Business
University of Santa Clara

ARTHUR KROEGER
Professor of Marketing
Graduate School of Business
Stanford University

FRANCESCO M. NICOSIA
Professor and Director, Consumer Research Program
Graduate School of Business Administration
University of California at Berkeley

1977

Fifth Edition

RICHARD D. IRWIN, INC. *Homewood, Illinois 60430*
IRWIN-DORSEY LIMITED *Georgetown, Ontario L7G 4B3*

Previous editions of this book were published under the title
Advertising Principles and Problems.

© RICHARD D. IRWIN, INC., 1960, 1964, 1968, 1973, and 1977

Fifth Edition

First Printing, March 1977

ISBN 0-256-01925-8
Library of Congress Catalog Card No. 76–47746
Printed in the United States of America

To: *Rita Dirksen*
     Julia Kroeger
     Marilu Nicosia McAllister

PREFACE

*I*n preparing this Fifth Edition of *Advertising Principles, Problems, and Cases,* the authors reorganized the book to provide a more logical development of the subject from the teaching viewpoint and to emphasize what advertising is, how it functions, and its advantages and disadvantages.

Francesco M. Nicosia, director of the Consumer Research Program of the Graduate School of Business Administration of the University of California at Berkeley, became a coauthor for the Fifth Edition and has been responsible for introducing additional concepts on the behavioral as well as the legal aspects of personal and mass communication.

This edition has been arranged in seven major divisions: Advertising Concepts; Economic and Social Issues; Preparation of the Advertisement; Advertising Mechanics; Media Mix; Research Techniques; and Advertising Management. More emphasis is also placed on social and economic aspects, buying behavior, and demand strategy.

The book includes 76 cases. Of these, 32 are new and a number of the 44 cases that were used in prior editions have been revised on the basis of recommendations received in order to strengthen them from the teaching standpoint. All of the cases are based on actual business situations that have actually faced advertising executives and the corporate name of the company is given in 44 of them. They are succinct enough in nature to be analyzed without an extensive amount of additional information.

Over 40 percent of the book consists of cases. While they do convey information, the authors recommend that they be used primarily as the basis for discussion. It is the decision-making process which can be developed through class case discussions that should be one of the major objectives of the use of this material.

Some instructors prefer to use cases as supplementary material to accompany one of the descriptive texts. Others prefer to rely on the text material. Regardless of what approach is adopted, it is always important to get students to learn as much as they can about types of organizations, advertising policies, merchandise assortments, and sales practices by visiting various companies.

There are several ways of approaching the class discussion of cases. One of these is to use the question(s) at at the end of each case as a starting point for the discussion. These questions point to some of the more significant problems presented in the cases and, at the same time, will allow a rather wide difference of opinion. Therefore, the questions can be discussed, pro and con, and, as an outgrowth of this discussion, students should be able to achieve a broad understanding of advertising. Another method of using cases is to disregard any questions offered at the end of the cases, and to proceed directly to locate, through class discussion, the issue or issues involved and to reach workable solutions to these issues. In this approach to case study, success will be dependent on the skill of the instructor in leading class discussion.

The general theory of advertising can be learned from textbooks. The nature of advertising practices, however, cannot be so easily covered by text material, but can better be reasoned out. For example, students should be able to readily develop the reasons why some products require dense distribution and national advertising, and others require only selective or representative distribution.

A student will realize that a housewife, who buys bread possibly two to five times a week, will not go very far out of her way to buy a particular brand she might prefer, when she can buy a second-choice brand at a convenient location near her home. From that conclusion, the student can reason out that a product purchased frequently, and without important product differences, must have dense distribution and extensive advertising if the market opportunity is to be maximized. When the student arrives at the conclusion by personal analysis, it means more to him or her.

Other generalizations about marketing practices can be reached by the same type of discussion. Why does a product which requires considerable sales effort carry a higher gross margin? Obviously, the rate of stock turnover will be lower, and the cost of greater sales effort must be covered. Why does impulse merchandise depend heavily on display and point of purchase advertising? The student should be able to reach the conclusion that such purchases on the part of the consumer are generally unplanned, and are likely to be made only on the reminder afforded by display and point of purchase promotional material.

These generalizations are typical of many that students can reasonably be expected to develop. And, it is the comprehension of points of this kind that actually develops an understanding of advertising. The authors believe that there is merit in having the students develop these generalizations (principles) from the discussions. A few examples of such generalizations are:

1. The market for a product is limited to those to whom it offers utility.

2. Cooperative advertising is adapted to products for which primary demand can be stimulated.
3. For a product of a highly individualized nature and for which strong buying motives can be stimulated, advertising may often be used as the sole method of sales promotion.
4. When a product enjoys brand dominance, the stimulation of primary demand may take the place of the stimulation of selective demand.

It is the opinion of the authors that the book is arranged in such a manner that instructors who do not use the case method will find there is adequate text material that can be used very effectively with the probing questions at the end of each of the 19 chapters.

We are indebted to Roy W. Brockman, C. A. Holcomb, and Lawrence C. Lockley for recommendations and the use of special material. We also wish to express our appreciation to John A. Dirksen and to our graduate students who assisted us in collecting the data for the cases. In addition, we wish to thank the American Association of Advertising Agencies, Inc., the Association of National Advertisers, Inc., many advertising agencies, and other companies for granting permission to use their materials and exhibits.

Finally, we wish to convey our thanks to Professor Charles Spindler and our colleagues at other universities for pertinent recommendations and testing of the text material and cases during the preparation of this Fifth Edition.

February 1977

CHARLES J. DIRKSEN
ARTHUR KROEGER
FRANCESCO M. NICOSIA

CONTENTS

3 Basic demand concepts   66

Market demand. Wants and needs. Sources of wants. Hattwick's "basic wants." Nature of habits: Dynamic qualities. Inherent drives and impulses. Impact of group membership. Psychological processes. Behavioral processes and management action: *Selection of appeals. Appealing to people who influence the decision to buy. Primary and selective demand. Combining primary and selective appeals. Primary demand advertising as a continuous process. The stimulation of primary demand. The stimulation of selective demand.* Highlights.

part two
Economic and social issues

4 The economic roles of advertising   125

Does advertising perform a function in the economy? Does advertising perform different functions in different sectors of the economy? *Competition. Price competition. Production costs. Overall product demand. Company images. Number of products. Cost of advertising. Product information. Allocation of capital. Distribution function. The question of causality.*

5   The social roles of advertising   154

Consumerism: *Background concepts. General considerations. Protection of consumer. Variations in personal values. Future of consumerism.* Advertising and social issues: *Waste in advertising. General social criticisms. Standard of living. Does advertising place an undue stress on material things? Does advertising cause people to buy goods they do not need?* Highlights.

6   Public and self-regulation in advertising   183

Self-regulation. Public regulation: *Local regulation. Federal regulation.* Summary.

part three
Preparation of the advertisement

7   Copy strategy and preparation   215

Setting objectives. Definition. Approach to writing copy. Important copy attributes: *Be brief. Be clear. Be apt. Be personal. Other methods.* The headline: *Types of headlines. Specific headline classifications. General recommendations.* Summary.

part four
Advertising mechanics

part five
Media mix

14   Other media forms   **434**

Direct advertising: *Use of direct advertising. Forms of direct advertising. The mailing list. Advantages of direct advertising. Limitations of direct advertising.* Outdoor advertising: *Types of outdoor advertising. Characteristics of the medium. Outdoor advertising rates. Public relations problems of outdoor advertising. Users of outdoor advertising.* Transit advertising: *Transit advertising and rates. Advantages of car cards. Disadvantages of car cards.* Point-of-purchase advertising: *Organization of the industry. Forms of point-of-purchase advertising. Use of point-of-purchase advertising. Considerations in creation and use of point-of-purchase advertising. Exhibits and trade shows.* Specialty advertising: *Advertising novelties. Calendars. Executive gifts.* Screen advertising: *Users of screen advertising. Features of screen advertising. Costs of screen advertising.* Directories. Sampling. House organ: *House organs for customers.* Packages, labels, and inserts.

part six
Research techniques

15   Research techniques   **475**

The need for research: *Advertising research.* General procedure in marketing research: *Planning the study. The preliminary investigation.* Execution of the research program: *Sources of primary data. Sources of secondary data. Methods of collecting primary data. Executing the collection of primary data.* Some special forms of research: *Motivation research. Use of mathematics in the decision-making process.* Testing advertising effectiveness: *Consumer jury test. The inquiry test. The sales-area or sales-result test. The systematic rating list, or checklist. Post-testing methods. Attitude and opinion testing.*

part seven
Advertising management

19 Organization for control 635

Location of advertising department within the company. Organization of the advertising department. Size of the advertising department. Why advertisers use agencies: *Selection of the agency. Working with the agency. Evaluation of agency performance.* The retail advertiser: *Retail advertising organization. Why retailers normally do not use agencies.* The advertising agency: *Definition. Agency organization. Types of agency organization. Agency jobs. Elements of agency service. Additional agency services. Sources of agency compensation. Agency recognition. The commission system. The agency industry.*

part one

Advertising concepts

1

THE ADVERTISING INDUSTRY

The word "advertising" is derived from the Latin word *advertere,* which means to turn (the mind) to. Broadly speaking, advertising does turn the attention of the public to a commodity or service, and in the broad sense it might be said that anything that turns attention to an article or service might be called advertising. In a more limited sense, however, advertising is usually considered as any form of paid public announcement intended to aid directly or indirectly in the sale of a commodity or service.

Definition

The American Marketing Committee on Definitions defined advertising as:

Any paid form of non-personal presentation and promotion of ideas, goods, or services by an identified sponsor. It involves the use of such media as the following:
Magazine and newspaper space
Motion pictures
Outdoor (posters, signs, skywriting, etc.)
Direct mail
Store signs
Novelties (calendars, blotters, etc.)
Radio
Television
Cards (car, bus, etc.)
Catalogues
Directories and references
Programs and menus
Circulars.[1]

---

[1] "Report of the Definitions Committee," *Journal of Marketing,* Vol. XIII, No. 2.

It is important to recognize that the costs of marketing may be reduced by greater efficiency in selling, in the selection of channels of distribution, in the use of advertising, and in improvements in packaging and shipping. On the other hand, these costs may be increased at least as much by increasing consumer services. More attractive packaging, the offering of a greater range of sizes, the offering of delivery service, the availability of return privileges, sales under credit terms—these and other services increase the cost of selling.

The woman who buys a package of breakfast food not only pays for the contents of the package but also for the box; the airtight wrapper; a part of the rent, of the labor and light, heat, and power of the retailer; the cost of delivery; the carton in which the packages are shipped; and even a part of the wages of the lumberjack who cut the tree and of the costs of the mill operator who converted it into pulp out of which the carton was made. The price the consumer pays is a complex of a thousand prices. There is room for many economies between the point of origin and the point of consumption.

It is, therefore, unwise to pick out advertising from the many factors which influence cost as a major determinant of price. As will be seen later, when advertising does not contribute more than its cost to marketing, it can rarely be afforded.

Development

Advertising as a business force is not a new tool, although it has seen its greatest development during the past 50 years. Almost since the beginning, men have used some form of advertising. Early in history, advertisements were cut in stone and placed in strategic locations so the people could see them. The town crier was an advertising man who broadcast his advertising copy by walking up and down the streets shouting information about the wares of his employer. Today, however, such media as newspapers, magazines, direct advertising material, outdoor signs, radio, and television are used to advertise products.

Advertising has been closely related to the long trend of rising standards of living in the United States. For products enjoying expansible markets, it has brought about both the economies of large-scale manufacture and of mass marketing. Thus it has been a factor in helping increase production and to decrease unit costs.

Advertising and a dynamic market

Fashion cycles, new ideas, and changing habits are three of the forces which make a market dynamic. However, what makes those forces formidable is the speed with which they spread and the unanimity with which they are adopted. Advertising is responsible in part for both the speed and the unanimity. It has developed a public, almost coextensive with the population, that reveals an amazing willingness to conform. This public wants to have, to do, and to be what is popular at the moment.

A manufacturer, whatever he may make, however basic and staple the product, or however well entrenched it may be in the market, can no longer settle down and let things take their course. He must hold himself ready to act, and to act quickly, interpret the signs, anticipate the attitude of the public, and analyze each new invention for its effect on his business. As an example, even a company like American Telephone and Telegraph continues to experiment, hoping that it will be able to anticipate each new invention.

Selling costs

Many people believe that advertising increases the retail price of the articles they buy. The question is not easily answered because the contribution of advertising to the efficiency of marketing will depend upon the conditions of demand and supply in a particular situation and upon the skill with which advertising is used.

Information and decision making

The behavior of any individual or organization throughout a day is marked by a stream of decisions concerning the many aspects of human life—work decisions, political decisions, religious decisions. Among the most basic choices are selling and buying decisions. How does each of us come to a decision? And, more precisely, what exactly is a decision?

Although decision making is certainly a complex process, its basic nature is rather simple. Herbert Simon, a famous psychologist, once defined a decision as the conclusion a person derives from some premises. These premises are essentially pieces or "bits" of information a person has available about a problem that he/she confronts. The problem may be how to spend the weekend, whether or not to go back to school for an advanced degree, or whether it is advantageous to postpone the purchase of a second car. For each problem, the decision maker may have available some information about it, e.g., the number and kind of alternative ways to spend the weekend, the costs and benefits of each alternative way, favorable and unfavorable past experiences, and so on. By utilizing this information, the decision maker may reach the conclusion that it would be best to stay home to do some gardening and reading rather than to take a ski trip or to have a date on Saturday and do some homework on Sunday.

The feature of importance to us in this definition is that the decision maker may have some information about the problem to be solved. One needs to ask: *Where does this information come from?* It may be derived from the individual's memory of personal experiences with a certain product, from recalling that a co-worker uses that product, and possibly from having read about it in a newspaper or magazine. All these and other sources provide bits of information that may be used in reaching a decision.

In the process of reaching a buying or selling decision, each individual or organization uses information about its internal needs and wants and may acquire further information about the situation and the available opportunities from external sources. The need to acquire information from the environment is not always very high in priority, and the acquisition itself may not be difficult. For instance, in a pastoral society a farmer tends to be very self-sufficient. He does not need to find out who sells the best tools, because he made most of them for himself during the long winter. He uses the seeds put aside last summer for sowing the fields, and his wife has worked hard at transforming the wool from their own sheep into blankets and clothing for the whole family. Yet in past and modern times, as soon as a society evolves from pastoral to more complex forms of organization, the need for information and the difficulty of acquiring it increase.

The demand for information and its supply

As a society grows in size, as cities are born, individuals and organizations tend to specialize in performing one or another role. One sees the birth of many specialized social roles: the soldier, the city clerk, the priest, and, among economic activities, the banker, the international merchant, the retailer, and the artisan. Through specialization, each individual is capable of contributing more to the social group. Concurrently, each becomes more dependent on the environment for the satisfaction of one's own needs and wants.

The advent of modern technology further increases the specialization of individuals and organizations. The seller becomes more and more removed from the final buyers of the products. Consider a lumber mill and some of its basic problems, the solutions of which require information: What type of lumber should it process? How should it be cut? What will be the demand for construction and for furniture? What will be the price of competitive materials? How much demand will there be for pulp to make newspapers, magazines, and books?

The same lumber mill also may need information for its buying decisions. For instance: What new machinery is available in the domestic and international markets? Are re-refined lubricant oils as good as virgin oils? Is it true that synethetic oils are better buys than virgin oils?

The individual consumer also experiences this same increasing need for information from the environment in order to make decisions. If one wants to sell an old car, should one trade it in, place a classified ad in the campus paper, or put a card on the bulletin boards at the dormatories and the student union? Why not keep it for another year?

In a postindustrial society, furthermore, as affluence spreads throughout society, more and more of the individuals experience not only discretionary income but discretionary time. This means that they can dedicate more of their energies to nonwork pursuits. At the turn of the century, the British miner worked from sunrise to sundown for six or more days a week. Consumption activities were necessarily limited not only by low income but by the small amount of time and physical energy available after work.

In affluent societies, consumer aspirations and expectations can and do increase in intensity and, above all, in number. Consumers seem to enjoy looking for new alternatives since they have the power to choose. The productive sector has been able to respond to these aspirations by increasing the number of alternatives offered. The affluent consumer faces a larger set of opportunities and seeks more information about these opportunities. Accordingly, the productive sector searches for ways to supply information about these opportunities.

All in all, as societies evolve from pastoral to more modern forms of organizations, there develops the formation of a demand for—and, correspondingly, the supply of—information. As a general assumption, the most important feature of this "market" for information in business is that the sending and acquiring of information implies costs. To sell a car, one needs to let potential buyers know it is for sale. Thus, the "managerial" question is: What is the best way of supplying potential buyers with this information? Should one place a classified ad in the paper or put cards on the bulletin boards? Each alternative costs both time and money. Any buyer must pay *time* and *money costs* in acquiring that information before purchasing a car.

Information is not a free good; it has never been free for either the sender or the seeker of information. This is true for any type of information, e.g., political, religious, and the like, including information about goods (products, brands, and services).

Information channels

Both individuals and societies have searched for ways to send and receive information. The simplest channel, of course, is casual, first-hand observation, such as when a woman sees a new style of hat in church or when a person strolling in the park observes a new type of shoe. Another channel is word-of-mouth, where information is exchanged within the family or among friends at school, work, or social situations. More than 30 years of basic and applied research show that this personal channel of communication is the most powerful in affecting political choice, farmers' choices of new farm equipment and farming practices, doctors' choices of new ethical (prescription) drugs, and a variety of consumer choices.

Another personal channel is available for sending or acquiring information; it consists of the salespeople working for manufacturers, banks, insurance companies, wholesalers, retailers, and so forth. By any yardstick, this is the channel that business firms rely on most in their attempts to direct information to intermediate and final buyers. By the early 1970s, for example, salaries and commissions paid to salespeople in the United States had already passed $50 billion per year.

Mass media, of course, are another major channel of information.

In early times, vocal cords and the ability to design symbols were the leading technology available to provide an information flow *from one sender to many seekers.* Town criers were used by city governments to announce political, religious, economic, and general news. They were also used by individual sellers in the open markets to attract the attention of passers-by to their merchandise. From ancient civilizations to medieval times, symbols and signs on the doors of retailers indicated the kind of products and services available within. They remained a popular mass medium until literacy no longer was reserved solely for the members of an elite based on blood or power.

Then, in the late 14th century, human inventiveness provided a new medium that was to become the most important commercial channel: the invention of the printing press. By the late 15th century, some periodicals and newsletters began to look more and more like present-day newspapers. By the early 1600s, these papers began to carry "economic" information in the form of advertisements. These ads publicized books, *brands* of toothpaste, coffee, and tobacco, adventure trips across the Atlantic, and theater presentations. Gradually, magazines were born and, with them, another channel became available for sending and acquiring types of information.

As societies evolved through industrialization, the old farmers' markets developed into more specialized forms for the exchange of information. Exhibits, shows, and international fairs become important channels, especially in the area of industrial activities.

With the results of the Civil War firmly directing this country toward industrialization, maturity in the advertising industry was reached in the 19th century. In the 20th, a new impetus came from the development of the broadcast media. The radio, and then television, established their individual functions in the mass communication system of this country.

A society's mass communication system and the advertising industry

While information is an input into the psychological process of decision making, different information may be sent and sought for purposes that cover a wide range of human life and behavior. The increasing complexity of modern societies makes it difficult for senders and seekers of information to communicate directly. The spontaneous and spectacular growth of mass media, especially in modern societies, reflects the efforts of individuals and organizations both to overcome the limitations and costs posed by personal channels and to complement and add to these channels' capabilities.

The mass communication system of a modern society carries an enormous *variety* of information—from local and national news to news about sports, political events, scientific developments, religious ceremonies, wars and crimes of all sorts, weather forecasts, legal trends, social and fashion news, and editorials. The total *quantity* of this information is very large. (It is a useful exercise for anyone interested in advertising to make a simple computation of how much information flows through the mass media daily, by counting, for example, the time and space allocated to nonadvertising topics.)

The information contained in advertising messages is only a subset of all the information flowing through a society's mass communication system. In fact, by any available yardstick, advertising information tends to be a small percentage of the total information exchanged through mass media. The advertising industry is only one small slice of the entire mass communication system.

The relationships between the advertising industry and the total mass communication system are numerous and complex and have not been studied systematically. Yet a major part of the costs of operating the mass communication system of our society is paid by those who send advertisements by way of this system. In the case of "commercial" television and radio, for instance, the major portion of the costs incurred in gathering, creating, and sending nonadvertising information is paid by the senders of ads. For print media also, only a small part of the cost is recovered by the subscription or newsstand price; most of the cost is again paid for by the advertisers. In the case of public television, most of its costs are paid by the taxpayer and by private foundations.

The main components of the advertising industry

The advertising industry is a social institution born to fulfill the human need to acquire and send information about the availability of products, brands, and services. It is highly complex and includes a variety of different elements.

The senders of advertising information

Practically all individuals and organizations have, at one time or another, sent or received some kind of advertisement through mass media. Students may use campus newspapers to search for a ride home for the next Christmas vacation, and they may pay a fee for inserting that ad. A look at classified ads in newspapers will give anyone an indication of the number of ads (and their costs) placed daily by people who wish to sell all sorts of things—from homes to cars, from refrigerators to dogs. Such nonprofit organizations as churches may advertise used pipe organs or furniture, or their search for a new minister. Local, county, state, and federal governments also may advertise. In fact, some estimates suggest that the federal government has, in recent years, become one of the ten largest advertisers in the United States.

There are no estimates of the number of nonbusiness firms that use a society's advertising industry, nor of the related advertising expenditures. There are, however, estimates of the advertising expenditures by business firms. The total cost of ads sent by business firms through all media in 1975 was about $28 billion. This annual estimate is compiled and updated by McCann-Erickson, an advertising agency, in its New York office and is published in *Marketing Communications,* a professional magazine.

Like individual consumers and nonbusiness organizations, business firms use ads for the purpose of informing consumers about the existence of some product, brand, or service; the special qualities this offering may have; the stores where it is available, and under what conditions it may be purchased. Recall that mass media are only one way for firms to send information to intermediate and final buyers; that sales people are used much more extensively to disseminate information; and that information is also sent via other channels, such as the copy on a package, or in the brochure placed inside the package. Fuller Brush uses sales people exclusively, and Hershey has never advertised its chocolate bars. The reasons for these sometimes large variations will be discussed in later chapters.

The advertising agencies

Relative to the very long history of advertising, advertising agencies are a recent component of the advertising industry; they were born, essentially, during the second half of the last century in this country. In the past three or four decades, they also have appeared in other countries and societies that have entered the era of postindustrialization (e.g., Western European economies and, very recently, Japan).

As their name implies, advertising agencies act in behalf of the senders of messages, especially business firms. The two key services that most of them tend to perform for their clients, the advertisers, are (*a*) the creation and development of ads, and (*b*) the selection and placement of the ads in the media form through which the ads can be sent most efficiently.

Both services are fundamental to the success of an ad or an entire ad campaign. Contrary to the popular stereotypes of "Madison Avenue," the performance of these two services requires a high level of creativity. It also requires production skills, an alertness as to what competitors do, an awareness of the ever-changing preferences of consumers, a willingness to take risks, and a great amount of just plain hard work. Like all other types of middlemen (and again contrary to another still-prevailing medieval stereotype) their average net profit is only about 6 percent of the "billings" (i.e., revenues).

Mass media

The mass media "carry" the messages from the senders to the audiences that those senders hope to reach. One way to classify mass media is by the technologies now available: print, broadcast, direct mail, and others (see Figure 1–1). Yet in affluent societies, within each type of medium there is an enormous range of differentiation, which is an indication that mass media must recognize the tremendous dif-

FIGURE 1-1
Advertising—estimated expenditures, by medium: 1950 to 1974 (in millions of dollars, except percents)

	1950		1955		1960		1965		1970		1974	
	Expenditures	Per cent of total	Expenditures	Per cent of total	Expenditures	Per cent of total	Expenditures	Per cent of total	Expenditures	Per cent of total	Expenditures	Per cent of total
Total	5,710	100.0	9,194	100.0	11,932	100.0	15,255	100.0	19,600	100.0	26,550	100.0
National	3,257	57.0	5,407	58.8	7,296	61.1	9,365	61.4	11,491	58.5	14,620	55.1
Local	2,453	43.0	3,788	41.2	4,636	38.9	5,890	38.6	8,109	41.5	11,930	44.0
Newspapers	2,076	36.3	3,088	33.6	3,703	31.0	4,457	29.2	5,745	29.3	7,910	29.8
National	533	9.3	743	8.1	836	7.0	869	5.7	1,014	5.2	1,165	4.4
Local	1,542	27.0	2,345	25.5	2,867	24.0	3,587	23.5	4,731	24.1	6,745	25.4
Radio	605	10.6	545	5.9	692	5.8	917	6.0	1,308	6.7	1,790	6.7
Network	196	3.4	84	0.9	43	0.4	60	0.4	56	0.3	70	0.3
Spot	136	2.4	134	1.5	222	1.8	268	1.7	371	1.9	380	1.4
Local	273	4.8	326	3.5	428	3.6	589	3.9	881	4.5	1,340	5.0
Television	171	3.0	1,025	11.1	1,590	13.3	2,515	16.5	3,596	18.4	4,850	18.3
Network	85	1.5	540	5.9	783	6.6	1,237	8.1	1,658	8.5	2,165	8.2
Spot	31	0.5	260	2.8	527	4.4	866	5.7	1,234	6.3	1,460	5.5
Local	55	1.0	225	2.4	281	2.3	412	2.7	704	3.6	1,225	4.6
Magazines	515	9.0	729	7.9	941	7.9	1,199	7.9	1,292	6.7	1,525	5.7
Weeklies	261	4.6	396	4.3	525	4.4	610	4.0	617	3.1	640	2.4
Women's	129	2.3	161	1.8	184	1.5	269	1.8	301	1.5	370	1.4
Monthlies	88	1.5	133	1.4	200	1.7	282	1.9	374	1.9	515	1.9
Farm, national	37	0.6	39	0.4	32	0.3	37	0.2	n.a.	n.a.	n.a.	n.a.
Farm papers	21	0.4	34	0.4	35	0.3	34	0.2	62	0.4	65	0.2
Direct mail	803	14.1	1,299	14.1	1,830	15.3	2,324	15.2	2,766	14.1	3,920	14.8
Business papers	251	4.4	446	4.9	609	5.1	671	4.4	740	3.8	915	3.4
Outdoor	143	2.5	192	2.1	203	1.7	180	1.2	234	1.2	335	1.3
National	96	1.7	130	1.4	137	1.1	120	0.8	154	0.8	220	0.8
Local	46	0.8	63	0.7	66	0.6	60	0.4	80	0.4	115	0.5
Miscellaneous	1,125	19.7	1,836	20.0	2,328	19.6	2,959	19.4	3,857	19.6	5,240	19.7
National	610	10.7	1,040	11.3	1,368	11.5	1,750	11.5	2,144	10.9	2,735	10.3
Local	515	9.0	796	8.7	960	8.1	1,209	7.9	1,713	8.7	2,505	9.4

Source: McCann-Erickson Advertising Agency, Inc., 1950–1965 compiled for Decker Communications, Inc., New York, N.Y.; in *Printer's Ink* (copyright). Beginning 1970, compiled for Crain Communications, Inc.; in *Advertising Age* (copyright).

ferences in the interests of individuals and organizations. There are specialized magazines for architects, for data processing directors, for doctors, dentists, and the like. There are magazines and periodicals that cater to the specific interests of different consumers: sports car enthusiasts, gardeners, fashion-conscious people, and so on.

In Figure 1–1 is given, in the aggregate, how business firms tend to choose different media for sending their ads. Note that contrary to popular stereotypes more money is spent on newspapers (i.e., retail advertising) than on television. Also, observe how direct mail advertising is a close third and how its importance has remained strong throughout the years.

The seekers of information

All consumers, individually or in organizations, need information for their decisions. Aware or unaware, they seek information. If they see an ad containing information about a product in which they are not interested, they may recall it for only a few minutes or days and then forget it.

The number of seekers of information at any point in time is very large. There are more than 200 million Americans . . . manufacturers . . . retailers—not to mention hospitals, schools, churches, government agencies, and other buyers. The critical economic problem the advertising industry must solve is not to convey information to all these individuals and organizations about all the possible offerings available on the market. To the contrary, the challenge is to convey information about new cars to those eight or nine million Americans who some forecasts say will buy this year's model. The challenge is to find out who those potential car buyers are, where they are, to which media they tend to expose themselves, and to talk about cars to *them* rather than to those interested in boats or trips to Europe.

Governments

An increasingly active and important component of the advertising industry includes all city, county, state, and federal governments of the country. These governments "manage" the behavior of the entire industry and of its components listed so far.

Government's management of the industry is accomplished through three main devices. First, *elected* officials pass laws that directly or indirectly may bear on advertising, such as antitrust laws. Second, *appointed* officials may issue regulations that concern the behavior of media, advertisers, and so on. For example, at the federal level such appointed officials are commissioners of the Federal Communication Commission, the Federal Trade Commission, the Federal Drug Administration, and many agencies. Third, courts at all levels of government establish rules of behavior that may bear not only on the behavior of the parties involved in a case, but on all members of the industry.

In earlier times, governments managed the advertising industry by indicating what kinds of decisions were *not allowed* by sellers, agencies, media, and buyers. For example, during the Prohibition era, ads about wine were prohibited. In recent times, governments have begun to manage the advertising industry by ordering specific behaviors (like the requirement that certain information about a product *must* be printed on its package).

In Figure 1–2 a graphic representation of the advertising industry is portrayed. On the one hand are the suppliers of information; on the other, the seekers of information. The advertising agencies and the mass media essentially function as mechanisms that bring together the supply of and demand for information. The interactions among these four components occur within the framework of laws, regulations, and court decisions.

The behavior of the industry and of its social managers (governments) reflects a multitude of environmental factors, especially the prevailing cultural, political, and social values of a society, and the norms of its social institutions, such as the family, the church, and the political party system. Of course, underlying all this, there are the basic economic facts of life—the number and type of natural resources and the quantity of each that provide both the means for achieving a society's goals and, concurrently, the upper limits to the satisfaction of these goals.

Information (ads) and economic goods

There are two additional components of the advertising industry not portrayed in Figure 1–2. The first concerns the type and quantity of information being sent and sought. The type of information that is of interest in business concerns the selling or buying of "economic"

FIGURE 1–2
The main components of the advertising industry

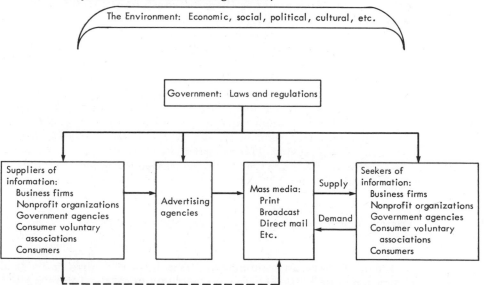

goods, that is, products, brands (in each product type), and services. The demand and supply of this information are *not homogeneous.*

To illustrate, on the demand side, seekers of information may be interested in different products, and those interested in the same product may be interested in different features or product attributes. Prospective buyers of automobiles, for example, differ in their interest in trunk capacity, performance, comfort, initial price, miles per gallon of gasoline, and so on. Accordingly, on the demand side, the ads of one manufacturer may convey information about the comfort qualities of its car, and the ads of another manufacturer may emphasize the high mileage per gallon quality of its car. Thus, the practical task assigned to the industry by society is, first, to recognize the fact that there are different demands for information by different market segments, and second, to find efficient ways to supply different information (ads) to the segments that want it.

This inherent heterogeneity in the demand for, and thus the supply of, information makes it necessary to produce and send a number of different messages. If all buyers of cars, homes, clothing, and other goods wanted exactly the *same* car, home, clothing, and so on, then the number of product features would be smaller and the number of messages also would be fewer. As affluent consumers have learned that they have not only the means but the right to express their individuality, different product features have acquired different importance for consumers. Accordingly, firms recognized this heterogeneity in the demand for information and had responded by creating new products and by product differentiation—e.g., by creating different brands—and by emphasizing the specific attributes that differentiate one brand from other brands.

In ancient times, only the elite of a society could afford to search for and acquire quality. Gradually, as affluence spread throughout society, an increasing number became eligible to search for and acquire qualities: different types of breads, meats, cars, clothes. This demand for an ever-increasing variety of products, brands, and services has led to an ever-increasing demand for different types of information.

At the same time, components of the advertising industry have adapted ecologically. Firms have provided an increasing variety of products, brands, and services. Witness the fact that the life cycle of any product has consistently decreased in the past two decades, and the number of new products brought to the market in each year is continuously increasing. The advertising industry has kept up by increasing the number and type of ads addressed to the different preferences of final buyers.

The advertising industry: Costs and benefits to society

One need not be an economist or an engineer to realize that a good choice depends on the relative costs *and* benefits of the different alternatives available. Suppose a consumer was considering purchasing one of two refrigerators: Brand A costs $400 and Brand B costs $500.

It would not be rational to choose Brand A only on the basis of knowing the cost of the two, for the benefits from each may vary. For instance, Brand B may come with a one-year warranty and may save about 33 percent in electricity per year, whereas the other refrigerator has only a 90-day warranty and offers no saving in electricity. If the relative importance of these two product features is high for the consumer, then the benefits from Brand B may more than compensate for its higher cost, and it is thus rational for the consumer to buy B even though its cost is $100 greater than A.

Most consumers use this simple commonsensical principle, whether they are aware of it or not. In economics and engineering, this commonsensical principle is called *efficiency*. That is, given two or more alternative choices, the costs and benefits inherent in each, and the preferences for different benefits, one will generally select the alternative(s) that will be judged to have the greater perceived efficiency.

This notion of efficiency in studying and evaluating the advertising industry in our economy and society is also of importance to consumers, industrial buyers, nonprofit organizations, regulatory agencies, lawmakers, and courts. What does the advertising industry do in the economy and society, and does the industry do it well, i.e., efficiently?

To answer this question one should identify and compute both the costs of the advertising industry and the benefits it provides for society. As for the benefits that the advertising industry brings to society, one should consider the following. First, throughout its history advertising has provided information to potential buyers about the availability and features of very many and changing types of products, brands, and services. Second, it pays the major part of the costs of some media, such as newspapers and magazines, and it pays almost the full costs of commercial TV and radio. Consequently, the entire institution contributes to the production and distribution of information of a nonadvertising nature. Furthermore, by making modern mass media economically viable, advertising contributes to the realization of a basic need of Western democracies: the freedom of the press (this from the written testimonies submitted to the Federal Trade Commission hearings of 1971 by N. Cousin, the former editor of the *Saturday Review,* and A. Heiskell, the chairman of the board of Time, Inc.).

A number of other benefits have also been suggested. For instance, the advertising industry contributes to economic development, lower prices, and greater competition. Some literature suggests that this industry has, in fact, negative "benefits" or effects on the economy and society—for example, by contributing to the moral decay of our society, by encouraging materialistic values, and, contrary to others' opinions, by raising prices and by creating monopoly power for the large advertisers. These and other issues will be discussed further in Chapter 4.

Consider the costs of the advertising industry. Before computing these costs, one should ask: Costs to whom? The computation may vary, according to whether the costs are analyzed on bases to the senders of information, to the consumers, or to the entire economy. In Figure 1–3a are listed data that may allow one to search for an answer to this question.

These data include the following: A time series started in 1929 records the total expenditures for advertising by senders of information (AE). Macro economists have measured the well-being of an economy by recording its gross national product (GNP), i.e., the value of all the economic goods produced and sold in the United States in each year. As for society, since all members of a society are consumers, one

FIGURE 1–3a
Time series: Advertising, the economy, and the household sector (current dollars in billions)

Year	AE*	GNP	PDI	PCE
1929	3	103	83	77
1930	3	90	75	70
1932	2	58	49	49
1934	2	65	52	51
1936	2	83	66	62
1938	2	85	66	64
1940	2	100	76	71
1942	2	158	117	89
1944	3	210	146	108
1946	3	210	159	149
1948	5	259	187	175
1950	6	286	206	192
1952	7	347	236	217
1954	8	366	256	236
1956	10	421	291	266
1958	10	449	317	290
1960	12	506	349	325
1961	12	523	363	335
1962	12	564	384	355
1963	13	595	403	375
1964	14	636	437	400
1965	15	688	472	430
1966	17	753	510	465
1967	17	796	545	490
1968	18	869	588	536
1969	19	936	630	580
1970	20	982	686	619
1971	21	1063	743	668
1972	23	1171	801	733
1973	25	1306	903	809
1974	27	1407	984	886
1975	28	1499	1077	963

* AE until 1974 from *U.S. Statistical Abstract 1975*. Years 1974 and 1975 from *Advertising Age*, October 25, 1975.
   Source: All but AE from U.S. Bureau of Economic Analysis, *Survey of Current Business*, January 1976. Note that all 1975 figures from this are preliminary and are subject to revision.

also may consider two well-established measures of consumer well-being: personal disposable income (PDI)—that is, the income received net of taxes—and consumer personal consumption expenditures (PCE).

Costs to the senders of ads

By looking at this data, insights can be secured into the cost of the advertising industry. Figure 1–3a gives the total expenditures all senders of ads have paid. Not infrequently, these expenditures are assumed to be the cost of the entire institution, but this assumption is obviously both incorrect and invalid.

To begin with, advertising expenditures (AE) represent only some of the costs born by all senders of economic information through mass media. For instance, firms also pay to communicate in a one-to-many fashion to their potential buyers by using such channels as product design, package and label design, or catalogs. These and other communication costs are not included in the time series AE. Furthermore, some business firms spend a greater amount to communicate via personal channels, such as sales people, than they spend on advertising.

By and large, the major part of advertising expenditures represent direct costs to business firms. These firms obviously are interested in knowing whether they spend too much, too little, or enough in sending ads to potential buyers, and they also are interested in knowing whether they should be spending more or less of their efforts in other activities, such as hiring more sales people, creating a new product or a new brand of an established product, changing production or data processing equipment to take advantage of new technologies, taking on the high risk of financing research and development activities, increasing wages and salaries to cut down absenteeism, or increasing the dividends to attract the money needed to expand production capacity or to change to more efficient equipment. There is no doubt that, as in all other human affairs, some firms may be spending too much and others too little in mass media advertising because it is not easy for any one firm to find out the right amount of effort to be spent on advertising.

Cost to the economy

Since AE represent some of the cost that firms, nonprofit and government organizations, and consumers have paid to send messages via mass media, it is valid to think of them as a partial measure of the cost the entire economy pays for producing and sending not only ads but the much larger set of noneconomic information through the mass communication system. In other words, AE can be used as an indication of how much the economy pays each year to meet its needs for information of all types.

As mentioned, an established measure of all economic activities in a country is the result of these activities: the gross national product (GNP). Thus, the cost of the advertising industry to an economy may be measured by the percentage of GNP that an economy allocates to its mass communication system

$$\left(\frac{AE}{GNP} \ 100 \ percent\right)$$

Figure 1–3b also shows how the cost of the advertising industry to the economy has varied since 1929. During the Depression of the 30s, the level of economic activities was low and, accordingly, the need for mass communication was very low (fluctuating around 2.3 percent). During World War II, most of the country's economic decisions were centralized and directed toward winning the war, and the economy's need for a mass communication system was at its lowest (1.3 percent).

The economy then geared up for recovery and expansion. More and

FIGURE 1–3b
Advertising as a "proportion" of the economy and of the household sector (in current dollars, in percentages)

Year	AE/GNP	AE/DPI	AE/PCE
1929	3.3	4.1	4.4
1930	2.9	3.5	3.7
1932	2.8	3.3	3.4
1934	2.5	3.1	3.2
1936	2.3	2.9	3.1
1938	2.3	2.9	3.0
1940	2.1	2.8	3.0
1942	1.4	1.8	2.4
1946	1.4	1.9	2.0
1948	1.9	2.7	2.9
1950	2.1	2.9	3.1
1952	2.0	3.0	3.2
1954	2.2	3.1	3.4
1956	2.4	3.4	3.8
1958	2.2	3.2	3.4
1960	2.4	3.4	3.7
1961	2.3	3.3	3.6
1962	2.2	3.1	3.4
1963	2.2	3.2	3.5
1964	2.2	3.2	3.5
1965	2.2	3.2	3.5
1966	2.3	3.3	3.7
1967	2.1	3.1	3.5
1968	2.1	3.1	3.4
1969	2.0	3.0	3.3
1970	2.0	2.9	3.2
1971	2.0	2.8	3.1
1972	2.0	2.9	3.1
1973	1.9	2.8	3.1
1974	1.9	2.7	3.0
1975	1.9	2.6	2.9

Source: U.S. Bureau of Economic Analysis, *Survey of Current Business,* January 1976.

more people began to enjoy the privilege once reserved for the few: discretionary income and discretionary time, and thus an expanding degree of consumption choices. As affluence spread throughout the country, as new technologies increased and affected both the factory and the family, and as new product, brands, and services were brought to the expanding industrial, institutional, and consumer markets, it would seem reasonable that the need for the economy's mass communication system would expand more than proportionally. This expectation seems to have been confirmed from 1944 to 1960, because the amount the economy spent for its communication system gradually increased to 2.4 percent.

Surprisingly, even though, by the 60s, although the economy's well-being and complexity was far higher than in 1929, the year of the previous highest expansion, the amount allocated to advertising did not reach the level of 1929 (3.3 percent). Even more surprising, though, is the fact that the cost of advertising to the economy did not continue to increase during the great expansion of the 60s, nor during the first half of the 70s. In fact, it steadily decreased! (Also note that this trend did not change even if "real" rather than "current" dollars were used.)

It is difficult to explain this decrease in the cost of the advertising industry to the economy. In fact, one would have expected that this cost would have increased for a simple reason: the number of senders of advertisements; the number of seekers of advertising information; the number of products, brands, and services that were advertised; and, most likely, the number of ads produced and sent through the communication system per year have increased continuously. The industry certainly provides much more information—economic and noneconomic—than in 1929, and yet it costs less to the economy.

Some possible explanations of why the advertising industry is now more "efficient" than ever have been suggested. First, it is likely that the higher efficiency may be partly due to the introduction of television. The cost of any one message produced and sent through this mass medium is high in absolute dollars, but since it can reach more people, television may be more efficient than other media (see Chapter 13).

A second reason for the increased efficiency of the industry may be due to better management decisions. For instance, consumer research can provide more relevant information on what product qualities different consumers prefer and what their readership and listening preferences are. Thus, the management of business firms and mass media cannot only avoid mistakes, but they can also relate to the needs of the final buyers more directly. Another possible reason is that final buyers, especially consumers, may be more inclined to respond favorably to ads. In other words, in recent decades many researchers have noted that several basic changes in the cultural values of society may increase the propensities to search for individuality via consumption activities. Katona and his associates have been recording for years an increasing level of aspirations and expectations in the consumers. Economists and lawyers also have noted the continuous shift from the "right to opportunities" to the "right to share the results." And consumer researchers have documented, in many instances, that consumers have learned how to exercise their right to consume by using the increasing amount of discretionary income *and* time which is available.

One must avoid the temptation, however, to imitate the critics of the advertising industry by accepting these and other reasons prematurely—some of the ideas suggested above have not yet been tested rigorously. Furthermore, it can be argued that the decrease in the advertising cost to the economy in the second half of the 60s is not real. During this period, a substantial portion of the GNP was devoted to war expenditures and to an increasing number of social services (e.g., medicare and education), where the need for ads may have been minimal.

According to this reservation, relating AE to GNP *net* of these war and social service expenditures would show that the cost of the industry has not decreased. At present, neither government agencies nor researchers have empirically explored this suggestion.

Cost to society

All members of a society are consumers. It is thus reasonable to measure the social cost of the advertising institution by relating AE to established measures of consumer well-being, namely, personal disposable income (PDI) and consumption expenditures (PCE). (Note that during the 70s approximately $1 to $2 billion in the reported AE concerned industrial rather than consumer advertising.)

Figure 1–3b gives how the cost of the advertising institution to consumers has varied since 1929. To begin with, this cost varies over time in a way very similar to the cost to the economy. Also, it has never reached the level of 1929. And, as in the case of the cost to the economy, it has consistently decreased since the mid-60s.

This empirical evidence would suggest that the social cost of the industry is decreasing. The meaning of this is that the industry is presumably becoming more efficient, and the reasons for this greater efficiency are as before. On the one hand, an increasing number of senders of ads have produced and sent to an increasing number of seekers of information a larger number of messages about an increasing number of products, brands, and services. Yet, on the other hand, the relative costs of these activities has decreased. In part, this greater efficiency can be explained by *(a)* improved technology of the mass communication system with the advent of television; *(b)* improved management decisions by senders and mass media; and *(c)* consumers' greater receptivity and ability to search for means (product, brands, and services) to express and realize one's personal dreams of a better life.

Here, too, of course, one should avoid the temptation of reaching conclusions. For instance, by relating AE to PCE it is assumed that all AE concern ads suggest that consumers spend more. This obviously is incorrect. Advertising also may inform consumers about the merit of savings. These include: bonds of the federal, state, county, and city governments and special public agencies; bonds of other profit and nonprofit organizations; stocks; banks, savings and loan associations, and credit unions; life and other insurance policies; and pension funds. Thus in principle one should relate only the cost of ads concerning spending (saving) with the amount spent (saved) by consumers before reaching conclusions.

Furthermore, the observed decrease in the cost of the advertising industry to the economy and to society must be discussed in the context of other economic and social issues. And, finally, one also must bring to the fore and carefully analyze another common assumption heretofore never examined: that advertising in the aggregate has a causal effect on the economy and on society.

It is always essential to distinguish very clearly between facts presented and personal preferences. Suppose, for instance, that one came to know, with absolute certainty, that the advertising industry is not only more efficient than it was in the so-called good old days, but, it also is the most efficient way to satisfy the need for information via mass media by any decision makers in this country. Yet, one must recognize that individuals differ from each other in terms of their personal preferences. Thus, some people may not like TV ads and the programs whose production is paid for by these ads. For these people, the fact that the industry is "efficient" is not very relevant.

At present, researchers do not know how to measure the intensity of people's liking or disliking of the advertising industry. Accordingly, society does not know the price different people would pay for changing or keeping the industry. There are a few examples that suggest the preferences and their intensity to the consumers.

In the mid-50s, *Reader's Digest,* the magazine with the highest circulation, was the only major magazine that still did not carry any advertisements. Increasing costs and decreasing profit returns, however, forced management to consider the only two alternatives: increase the price of the magazine or accept advertising. Management decided to let its readers decide by asking them which of the two alternatives they preferred. The clearcut answer was: Do not increase the price of the magazine; do accept advertising. In the election year of 1962, California voters were asked whether they wanted the development of pay television. A large majority voted no; apparently, they seemed to be able to get along with commercial television. During two long strikes by newspaper workers in large cities, citizens were asked what they were missing most during the strikes. Advertising was consistently cited as one of the most-missed items by the large majority of readers.

Classification of advertising

To understand advertising, it is important also to know something about the way advertising is classified. Advertising may be, and is, classified in many different ways by the people engaged in the field. Therefore, it is advisable to introduce some of the most commonly used terms at this point.

National, regional, and local advertising

Advertising reaches people through mediums, or media. Media are classified as national, regional, or local. The term "national advertising" usually is used to designate the type of advertising which is done by a manufacturer on a nationwide scale to stimulate the demand for his product among ultimate consumers. The advertising for automobiles, soft drinks, and food products appearing in such magazines as *Time* and *Reader's Digest,* and the advertising for electric razors and cosmetics appearing on the nationwide television networks, is national advertising. (See Figure 1–4 Ace Bowling Balls.)

FIGURE 1–4

If such advertising is confined to one region of the country, it is referred to as regional advertising. Whereas virtually all national advertising is done by the manufacturer, regional advertising may be conducted by the manufacturer, the wholesaler, or the retailer. A manufacturer of swimming pools, who operated only in the Pacific Coast states, might advertise his product in *Sunset* magazine (a regional magazine serving the Pacific Coast states) or on a network of television stations in the major Pacific Coast cities. Such advertising would be called regional advertising.

Local advertising is confined to one trading area or city, and usually is considered to be synonymous with the term "retail advertising." The advertising, familiar to all Americans, done by the department store in the city daily newspaper or on the local radio station is local advertising. The advertising may in fact be promoting the sale of nationally advertised brands of merchandise, but the stress is on the concept that the reader is to come and buy that brand in the advertiser's store rather than in some competitive store. Or the retailer may be attempting to induce the consumer to patronize his particular store and may not advertise any manufacturer's brands of merchandise. (See Neiman-Marcus advertising in Figure 1–5.).

Classifications based on audience to which directed

From the standpoint of the group, either the consumer group or the group that strongly influences the consumers, which the advertising is designed to influence, the following four classifications of advertising often are used.

→ *Consumer advertising* usually is restricted to that type of advertising, whether done by the manufacturer or a retailer handling the product, which is directed at the ultimate consumer—the individual who buys the product for himself or for use in his household. An advertisement for toothpaste appearing in *Parents' Magazine* and in *Better Family Living* would be an example of consumer advertising.

Industrial advertising is that advertising done by the manufacturers or distributors of industrial goods, designed to stimulate demand among the industrial buyers of such goods. The industrial goods might be raw materials, machinery, equipment, supplies, or fabricated parts. An advertisement for an electronic counter appearing in *Electronics* would be an example of industrial advertising. (See Figure 1–6.)

Trade advertising is that done by manufacturers to stimulate wholesalers and retailers to stock and sell the goods of the manufacturer. It is designed to obtain the aggressive promotion and sale of the manufacturer's line of products by the dealers who are logical outlets for such products. An advertisement appearing in *Chain Store Age* telling the grocer how much money he could make by stocking four new Gourmet Mixes would be an example of trade advertising.

Professional advertising is done by producers and distributors of products who are dependent on professional people to recommend, specify, or prescribe their products to the ultimate buyers or users.

FIGURE 1–5

I've always wanted one.

Price of unshown item? Whatever you want it to be. Neiman-Marcus. Dallas, Houston, Fort Worth. Bal Harbour, Florida. Atlanta in Fall '72.

Manufacturers of pharmaceutical products and building materials advertise to doctors and architects, respectively, not with the expectation that they personally will consume the products, but with the expectation that they will prescribe, recommend, or specify them to those individuals or builders who will buy the products on the basis of professional recommendations.

FIGURE 1–6
Example of an industrial advertisement

The only expense HP spared
in making these versatile counters...

... is yours.

Only Hewlett-Packard offers the versatility-economy combination represented by the new 5221A and 5216A Electronic Counters, using integrated circuits. Wide frequency range, high input impedance and sensitivity, long-life readout tubes with display storage, six measuring functions (in 5216A)...all this at prices as low as *one-half* that of comparable electronic counters available today.

The HP 5221A Counter has 0.1 and 1 second gate times (power line frequency time base), 1 meg/30 pF input impedance and an input signal sensitivity of 100 millivolts. It is the lowest cost frequency counter with a 10 MHz counting rate available. 4-digit readout is standard, 5 or 6 digits optional.

The HP 5216A Counter is an extremely versatile, 7-digit, 12.5 MHz counter for measuring frequency, time interval, period, multiple period average (in decade steps from 1 to 10^5), frequency ratio and totalizing. Gate times: 0.01/0.1/1.0/10 sec. Input sensitivity: 10 mV. Input impedance: 1 meg/50 pF. Time base: crystal with $< \pm 2 \times 10^{-6}$/month maximum aging rate. BCD output for operating data printers and other system elements. The price, even though the 5216A's frequency range is greater, is 30% below counters with similar functions.

Both counters feature HP's exclusive zero blanking, which makes reading easier and faster by suppressing any zeros to the left of the most significant digit. This unique benefit results from specially designed Hewlett-Packard proprietary integrated circuits used in both of the new counters.

Call your local HP field engineer for more details, or write Hewlett-Packard, Palo Alto, California 94304; Europe: 54 Route des Acacias, Geneva.

HEWLETT  *PACKARD*

Primary and selective demand advertising

Primary demand advertising is designed to increase the demand for a type or class of product, such as coffee, steel, cigars, or milk. It is usually done by trade associations or other cooperating industry groups; although, when a new type of product is introduced by one or several companies at approximately the same time, the individual firms often will use primary demand advertising to obtain initial demand for the product and get it established on the market. An example of this would be the initial advertising devoted to the promotion of color television sets, carried on for some years almost entirely by one firm (RCA); but later, when demand began to increase, carried on by a number of firms in the field. In contrast, selective demand advertising is designed to stimulate the demand for a particular brand of a product, such as RCA, Philco, or General Electric television sets.

Direct action and indirect action

Advertising designed to obtain some immediate response from the reader or listener is called direct-action advertising. Virtually all mail-order advertising is of this type, since it usually attempts to induce the reader to order the merchandise now. An advertisement that attempted to get the reader to send in a coupon for a sample of the merchandise would be an example of direct-action advertising. In contrast, indirect-action advertising is designed to influence the reader to have a favorable opinion or image of a brand so that when he does decide to buy that product he will buy the advertiser's brand rather than a competing one.

Product (and service) and institutional advertising

Most advertising, whether done by manufacturers of consumer or industrial goods, is done to increase the sales of a product (or service) or a specific brand owned by the manufacturer. Such advertising is called product advertising. However, some of the advertising done by such firms is not designed to promote specifically a certain product or brand of the manufacturer. Instead, it is designed to establish favorable attitudes toward the company as a whole on the part of present and potential customers, the general public or specific groups of people. It does not seek immediate action, but attempts to build up the reputation of the firm (by stressing the age and accomplishments of the firm, the skill of its employees, the extensive research carried on by the firm, the fine policies of the firm, and similar matters) so that consumers will trade with it rather than with other competing firms. This type of advertising is called institutional advertising. Some institutional advertising is used also for public relations purposes and for public service advertising, which involves sponsoring such public welfare activities as the prevention of forest fires, safe driving, and raising funds for various charitable programs. This latter type may also, on occasion, be defensive in order to dispel existing prejudices or to correct wrong impressions.

Miscellaneous classifications

Oftentimes, advertising is classified on the basis of the medium used, such as magazine advertising, newspaper advertising, outdoor advertising, radio advertising, television advertising, transit advertising (sometimes called transportation advertising), or direct-mail or specialty advertising.

Mail-order advertising is advertising in which the seller (the manufacturer or distributor) attempts to induce the reader to mail in his or her order for the goods advertised. This varies from national advertising, where the object is to persuade the consumer to buy the advertiser's brand when he or she goes into a store to buy that product, and from retail advertising, where the store attempts to induce the reader to come to that store to buy a particular brand of product, or to come to that store when he or she decides to shop for that line of goods.

Export advertising is that which appears in media that circulate in a foreign country. It is designed to stimulate demand among ultimate individual consumers or industrial consumers for the manufacturer's product.

These classifications are not mutually exclusive and much overlapping is involved, since many different bases are used for the purposes of classification. The advertisement of a manufacturer conducting a campaign for a new automobile via nationwide television networks might well be classified as national, consumer, selective, indirect-action, product, and television advertising all at the same time.

Highlights

The term "advertising" has two main meanings. It can be used to refer to the entire advertising industry or institution, and thus is a macro concept. It also can be used to refer to a specific management function in any organization that intends to send information to other members of society via mass media; in this sense, it is a micro, managerial concept.

In this chapter, besides considering the entire advertising industry, a few basic concepts and facts were introduced. As the size and complexity of a society increases, sellers and buyers find it more difficult to exchange information through personal contacts. Criers and symbols were one of the early mass media for ancient societies. Technological discoveries led to the birth of other mass media: the printed word and, more recently, radio and television.

Individuals and organizations experience both the need to send as well as to seek information to improve their selling and buying decisions. In any society one finds the existence of a supply and a demand for information. Advertising agencies work for the senders of information and principally (*a*) create the ads and (*b*) choose the media through which an ad has the greatest likelihood of reaching the individuals and organizations interested in that information. Mass media function as carriers of information, the majority of which is not advertising, for it concerns general news, political and religious events, and so forth.

The total cost of a society's mass communication system is paid to a large extent by the senders of ads. In the past and in the present, advertising expenditures have covered the cost of producing and sending ads as well as most of the costs of producing and sending other nonadvertising information.

The amount of advertising and nonadvertising information flowing through the mass communication system has increased, paralleling the economic and social growth of the country. Yet the cost of this information—as measured by the advertising expenditures of senders of ads—has not increased proportionally. In fact, the relative cost of the industry to the economy (AE/GNP $\times$ 100) and to consumers (AE/DPI $\times$ 100; AE/PCE $\times$ 100) has never reached the 1929 peak; and, since the mid-60s it has continuously decreased.

Questions

1. In what ways does advertising form a part of distribution?
2. How has the growth of mass production and mass distribution influenced the growth of advertising?
3. In your opinion, has advertising been an important factor in providing information for the products you purchase, such as:
   a. Clothing.
   b. Books.
   c. Stereo equipment.
   d. An automobile.
   e. Beer.
4. Do you think advertising will become more or less important to the economy in the coming decades? Why?
5. Bring to class six advertisements from your local newspaper, three which you consider to be examples of national advertising and three of local advertising. Explain the basis for your classification of these advertisements.
6. Bring to class two advertisements for the same product, one an example of primary demand advertising and the second an example of selective demand advertising.
7. What are some of the effects upon the nature of advertising which may come about because of the density of population in urban areas?
8. Contrast the significance of the use of advertising for industrial commodities versus ultimate consumer goods.
9. What do you believe will be the trend of the use of advertising in the next twenty years? Give your reasons.
10. Should advertising that may conflict with the national goals of the economy be curtailed?

SENECA CHEMICAL COMPANY
Use of advertising for recruitment

During the past few years the Seneca Chemical Company has found it difficult to induce the leading college graduates in business, engineering, and science to accept positions with the company.

The Seneca company has approximately 3,000 employees and maintains a well-rounded program of employee benefits, including vacations with pay, paid holidays, group insurance, an employees' retirement plan, and benefits which are similar to those prevalent in its industry.

The wage rates and average earnings of the employees compare favorably with those of other companies in the areas in which the corporation's plants are located. Seven of the company's ten plants are unionized, and contracts are in effect with local labor unions affiliated with the American Federation of Labor and the Congress of Industrial Organizations.

The chemical industry is generally highly competitive, and the Seneca company experiences competition in each of its product lines. This condition is especially pronounced in the sale of its mixed fertilizers, where the company's products are sold in competition with a relatively large number of producers.

The other principal products (superphosphates and industrial chemicals) are sold in competition with similar products and other products manufactured by other producers having the same end use. Competition in these lines has been, and it is expected will continue to be, substantial.

While Seneca had expanded its business over the last ten years, it had not strengthened its position in the chemical industry to the same degree that other chemical firms had done. The company executives were well pleased with the advertising and sales-promotional program and did not believe its failure to keep pace with competitors was due to poor marketing.

In this same period, Seneca's research program had been expanded with emphasis on these objectives: (1) the development of new products, (2) the improvement of existing products and processes, and (3) the development of new uses for existing products. The number of research personnel had been increased, and physical facilities had been expanded and enlarged.

After evaluating these and a number of other possible causes for Seneca's failure to maintain its position in the chemical industry, the executives came to the conclusion that the company was not getting the most qualified college graduates each year. Because of the excellent reputation of the company, to fill the various vacant positions the personnel manager had relied primarily on interviewing seniors on a limited number of campuses and conventional newspaper help-wanted advertising in the areas where the ten plants were located.

There were always an adequate number of young men applying for jobs with Seneca, so the personnel department had never made any concerted effort to attract college graduates. There was, however, a feeling in the organization that the men whom they had hired in the past ten years were not as well qualified as those they had hired in prior periods. No one in the Seneca organization had been too concerned about this because it was their belief that general world conditions had developed a tension among students that caused a certain amount of apathy and indifference on their part.

Seneca wanted to avoid a highly specialized training program because of the possibility of friction among the employees. For the same reason, the company did not want to offer concessions of any specific nature. Yet, because of the fact that there was a great potential in the industry, a young man with proper educational background could make very rapid progress.

Faced with the problem of recruiting the best-qualified college graduates and working within the policies set down by the executives, the personnel manager made a thorough investigation of the methods which other companies were using.

The majority of the companies used the conventional methods of recruiting. These included:

1. Interviews with college seniors on campus.
2. Recruiting advertisements in various educational journals and college publications.
3. Newspaper classified advertising.
4. Special letters addressed to selected lists of graduates.
5. Talks before fraternities, organizations, and other groups.
6. Personal contact with college placement officers, instructors, and deans.
7. Invitations to students to visit the offices and plants.
8. Special training programs in which the graduate would be assured of a limited promotion within the company.
9. General seminars of faculty and company representatives.
10. Sending financial reports and other company literature to the schools for student distribution.

In checking with the personnel director of an insurance company, the personnel manager of Seneca was told that this company had not been too successful with these methods. As a result, the insurance company and its advertising agency decided to use two mass-circulation magazines for recruiting advertisements. The company arranged its advertising schedule so that one-column recruiting advertisements appeared opposite the advertisements which were placed in the two magazines. Thus the company on one page told its general story to the public and in an adjoining column on a facing page told college graduates of the opportunities for them with the company. These magazine columns produced a large number of inquiries; the percentage of applicants joining the company as a result of this advertising seemed to be higher than the percentage of college graduates hired after interviews by the company's college recruiting team.

The insurance company director of personnel was so pleased with the results that he indicated that his company was planning to depend on media of the above type to recruit college graduates.

Case questions

1. To what degree can advertising be used to recruit college graduates?
2. When do you believe that it would be economical to use the type of media that the insurance company tried? To what do you attribute the successful use of mass-circulation magazines?
3. In your opinion, do college graduates put much emphasis on the classified section in which companies advertise for employees?
4. Indicate the types of appeal that a company should use in recruiting college graduates.

Case 1–2   **ATLAS HARDWARE COMPANY**
Considering advertising expenses

Atlas Hardware Company, a full service wholesaler, sold and distributed tools, builders' hardware, and a general line of shelf hardware, plumbing and electrical specialties to the retail trade. It distributed its merchandise to some five hundred accounts, and had a gross business of $2,500,000 annually.

The company had not done much advertising to the trade and to consumers but relied primarily on the manufacturers of the products it handled to build demand. As a result, Atlas had a tendency to charge to the advertising account a diversified list of items.

A new accounting firm had recently been hired, and, the senior accountant of the firm found in analyzing the records of the company that $52,963.86 had been charged to the advertising account in the prior year.

The following charges, shown on page 32, were included in the $52,963.86 advertising expenses:

1. Trade paper advertising . . . . $ 3,500.00
2. Purchase of mail-order list 250.00
3. Classified advertising for employees 835.00
4. Miscellaneous printing for personal calling cards,
    and the like 196.42
5. Photographers for publicity 112.35
6. Folders and brochures 1,897.45
7. Service club dues and expenses 562.32
8. Country club dues 1,200.00
9. Chamber of commerce dues 350.00
10. Christmas gifts to retailers 2,500.00
11. Postage on special mailings 475.00
12. Convention expenses 2,175.00
13. Subscriptions to trade magazines. 95.15
14. Printing and mailing of catalog 4,824.47
15. Entertainment of customers in homes of
    executives 3,175.25
16. Sponsorship of bowling team. 1,750.00
17. Promotional brochures for salesmen 1,115.45
18. United Fund donation 750.00
19. Ball-point pens with Atlas name on them 2,175.00
20. Advertisement in high school year book. 150.00
21. Premiums for Atlas salesmen for sales contests 5,000.00
22. Allowances to retailers for cooperating
    advertising 12,000.00
23. Political advertising. 750.00
24. Salary of advertising secretary 6,250.00
25. Special public service releases 875.00

$52,963.86

Case questions

1. Is it important for Atlas to have a strict interpretation as to what items should be charged to the advertising expense account?
2. Develop the criteria which Atlas might establish to use in the future in deciding which expenditures should be charged to the advertising account.
3. Should these criteria be the same for companies that rely on advertising for the major part of the sales effort?
4. Evaluate each of the above expenses and indicate whether or not it should be charged to advertising.

Case **EVALUATION OF MACRO CONCEPTS**
1–3
Case question

1. For the following statements on I, "Advertising, Communication, and Society" and on II, "Advertising, Information, and Competition" indicate in essay fashion to what degree society may or may not benefit through regulation.

I. Advertising, Communication, and Society

(The following two selections, A and B, are excerpts from N. Cousins, former editor, Saturday Review, *and editor,* World Review; *and A. Heiskell, chairman of the board, Time, Inc.)*

Advertising, as we have emphasized, is only one use of society's mass communication system, and it thus shares relationships of joint costs and benefits with other uses. For example, when postal rates go up, they affect not only the cost of ads but also the cost of all the information flowing through print media.

Cultures differ in the amount and kind of information that is allowed to flow freely throughout society. In the United States, a free flow has been generally encouraged.[1] For instance, second-class postal rates are seen as a subsidy to readers rather than to magazines and newspapers. Other channels of communication—from private conversations to speakers on soapboxes to TV networks—also can be and have been the subject of government encouragement and regulation. Regulation of any type of information flow faces many problems, which, as T. I. Emerson pointed out, "are not so much technical ones of method and efficiency in communication, . . . as they are questions of political and social control over the effects of communication."[2]

Emerson's point is obvious if we consider the regulation of political communication, such as the equal-time provision to which radio and television are subject. But it also applies to regulation of advertising. For example, social preferences regarding the free flow of information and free access to mass communications will affect the specific regulation of advertising. And social regulation of one use of the mass communication system will affect all other uses since all are related by joint costs and benefits.

It is not easy to visualize the interdependencies between advertising and other uses of a mass communication system, but the following two testimonies provide a feel for them.

A: First the testimony of Norman Cousins:

My purpose here is not so much to comment on the power of advertising as to ponder the implications of the fact that one of the tests of a free society is its attitude toward ideas. For ideas are a prime requirement for the growth and progress of any social organism that has to adapt to changing conditions. Obviously, every society—open or closed—is shaped by ideas. But the sources of ideas, the nature of ideas, the respect for ideas, and the way in which ideas are moved from one point to another, serve to define to what degree a society is open or closed. . . .

So far, these brief statements come under the heading of historical truisms. What is less self-evident, however, is the connection between

---

[1] Apparently there have been exceptions. In 1917, second-class mail rates were withdrawn by the government from *Appeal to Reason,* with a circulation of more than one million copies, apparently because of the paper's opposition to World War I. This paper subsequently died.

[2] T. I. Emerson, "Communication and Freedom of Expression," *Scientific American,* September 1972, p. 163.

advertising and ideas in an open society. My contention here is that advertising—more particularly, the creative skills and techniques it affords and puts to use—represents an increasingly vital part of the process by which ideas are circulated and put to work. Advertising has generally been recognized in terms of its ability to move goods. Its ability to move ideas is no less significant in any definition of its function in a modern and dynamic open society.

Some evidence. In 1962, President Kennedy believed it was in the national interest and the human interest to seek a treaty to limit nuclear testing. The President brought private citizens together for the purpose of persuading them to form a citizens' committee that would educate public opinion on the need for a treaty to seek this objective. The situation at the time was that more than two-thirds of the American people, judging by public opinion polls and tabulations of Congressional mail, had been led to believe that unlimited testing was essential to the national security and that there was little substance to the reports of dangers resulting from radioactive fallout. . . .

What was involved here was not just a challenge in mass re-education, but the fact of a stern deadline by which the re-education had to produce a visible result. The President had a timetable: A treaty would be proposed within three months; it had to be ratified within another three months. So long as public opinion was in such a predominantly negative condition, there would be little point in announcing a treaty and even less point in pressing for an early Senate vote. . . .

When the Citizens Committee considered its strategy for mobilizing public opinion, it realized it had to operate on many levels. It had to enlist the open and active support of leaders from all sectors of the national life. It had to get organizations behind it—business, labor, professional, religious. It had to fashion a solid base of scientific opinion. Finally, it had to mount a campaign in the general marketplace of public opinion. Resources were limited.

Given all these requirements and approaches, the Committee decided to put its main thrust into advertising. The approved program called for a series of prominent advertisements—in the nation's leading magazines and newspapers, in television spots, in organization journals. . . . The bottom line [of the ads] called for letters to Congress. And the letters came. They came in large numbers. . . . Within six or seven weeks, the clear preponderance of public support against any limitation of nuclear testing had diminished to the point where both sides were just about even.

It was at this juncture that the President publicly proposed a treaty. But he had a long way to go. He needed a working consensus before he could have any confidence in a two-thirds Senate vote. The advertising campaign continued. And the evidence of a growing consensus became apparent. As the Committee anticipated, *the opposition forces to the proposed treaty now began to use the same approaches* [stress added], mounting a mass advertising campaign in behalf of their own views. The effect was noticeable but not critical. In the end, the President's position was sustained.

What happened was the war of ideas became joined on the advertising battlefield [stress added]. The episode is worth recounting. . . . People can be persuaded but the techniques of persuasion are secondary to what is communicated. Given the proper material and the proper sponsorship, and skilled techniques, public opinion can be shaped by skilled advertising but it cannot be manipulated. . . . Whether we are talking about a labor union or a corporation eager to put its case before the public, or a minority group in quest of support, we have to recognize that advertising will be increasingly regarded as the most effective form for the communication of the message. But persuasion is not automatic. . . .

Advertising commands the attention more than that of any other form, editorial or commentary. But different sides and legions will turn to it—sometimes for opposite and competing purposes. Each will seek victory. There is no sure-fire formula for the use of words with maximum impact to insure such victory. But some things are clearer than others. Those who believe that advertising is a natural device for manipulation or distortion or exploitation are betting on a dubious proposition. Certainly, in any clash of ideas in which advanced advertising techniques are used on both sides, the appeal to good sense, supported by evidence, makes for a strong and often decisive difference.

What are the implications, in terms of national policy, of this major function of advertising as a vital instrument of ideas? First, policy-makers should recognize that advertising must be seen in a larger context than the commercial marketplace alone.

Second, it is the clear duty of government to establish standards for honest labeling, but it is the equally clear duty of government to regard advertising as an integral part of the consensus mechanism of an open society.

Third, just as the advertiser or the editor underestimates the intelligence of the reader at his peril, so government must not underestimate the ability of the average citizen to resist manipulation or exploitation. Nor should government underestimate the extent to which this fact is respected by the advertising profession itself.

Mr. Cousins' testimony underlines a basic feature of the United States mass communication system—its relative openness to diverse ideas. Note that *both* proponents and opponents of nuclear testing were able to use mass media to mount an advertising campaign. A similar openness to diverse political advertisements is visible during any presidential campaign.

But the openness of the media to political ideas extends beyond paid political announcements. During the 1960s, for example, Black Power, participatory democracy, civil disobedience, and other themes of the civil rights and antiwar movements received wide circulation through the mass media. In fact, antiestablishment groups and leaders received substantial coverage from national and local network TV, a medium that depends totally on advertising for revenue.

The next testimony, by Andrew Heiskell, chairman of the board of Time, Inc., publisher of *Time, Sports Illustrated, Fortune, Money,* and until recently, *Life,* discusses the main point of Cousins' presentation in more detail—namely, the relationship between advertising (the flow of economic information) and the flow of all other information in an open mass communication system.

Mr. Heiskell contends that the present advertising institution is basic to the maintenance of a free press and that other organizational designs for the flow of economic information cannot guarantee as free a circulation of all ideas and points of view. Toward the end of his testimony, Mr. Heiskell submits a particularly challenging hypothesis concerning social change. Free access to mass communications may, he argues, be eroded inch by inch. Taken singly, each limitation may appear harmless, even desirable; but their cumulative effects may not be noticed until it is too late. At that point, it may be impossible to recreate a free press.

B: Andrew Heiskell's testimony

I have been requested . . . to discuss the relationship of advertising revenues to the maintenance of a free press. I will confine my discussion to newspapers, magazines, and broadcast journalism—both the news and public affairs aspects of radio and television—those portions of the "free press" that are financed largely by advertising revenues. When I discuss the press collectively, I will be referring to each of these elements.

The relationship of advertising to the free press must form an important part of any thorough examination of the advertising industry. . . . In simple economic terms, advertising is the lifeblood of the press. Some $12 billion of revenues are provided to the various segments of the press by advertisers. Almost all of the revenues of commercial broadcast journalism and something like two-thirds of the revenues available to newspapers and magazines come from advertising dollars. I have no doubt that without those revenues the free press, as we know it today, could not continue to exist.

The free press has become such an integral part of our society and political system that we tend to take it for granted. We shouldn't. A few years ago, . . . a major survey of the world's press [was conducted]. That study determined that less than one-half of the world had a free press— that is, a press that was not controlled or substantially influenced by government or special interests. . . . The results of that study indicate that a free and unfettered press may be more fragile and more nearly unique than we like to think.

I think most of us would agree that the free press is necessary to the workings, indeed to the survival, of a democracy. An informed citizenry is possible only with an independent, multi-faceted, and competitive press. . . . The news media . . . make us aware of each other's problems and accomplishments. They are a part of the cement that holds this nation together. We have developed a system, largely financed by advertising, which does those things and which, I believe, does them quite well. I can think of no alternative means of financing that would allow us to do them as well.

The special role of the press has been encouraged as a matter of political and social policy throughout our history. "Congress shall make no law . . . abridging the freedom . . . of the press . . ." is the clear mandate of the First Amendment. But, an effective free press requires much more than the absence of government interference. It requires an affirmative commitment of our people and our government to an open society.

This, too, has become a fundamental tenet of our political system. Thus, our courts have developed a body of case law concerning libel which is carefully designed to maximize freedom of the press. Thus, Congress passed "The Newspaper Preservation Act" to improve the financial viability of the press. Thus, the Post Office has traditionally given special rates to newspapers and magazines. Thus, regulatory agencies, concerned with matters affecting the media, such as the FCC, have attempted to strengthen and encourage the independence of broadcasting and journalism. And, thus, the United States Senate's Subcommittee on

Constitutional Rights is these very weeks holding hearings on the problems of the relationship between press and government.

Of course, the press is not without its faults. We are frequently the subject of legitimate and valid criticism. There are, however, two criticisms—both frequently heard, both germane to the subject of this hearing, and both, I contend, quite inaccurate.

The first is the contention that the media have virtually unlimited and, therefore, potentially dangerous power to mold public opinion. Whether or not that criticism has any validity for advertising will be discussed later in this hearing in detail by those far more expert in the field than I. I address myself to this criticism only as it applies to the editorial content of journalism.

Opinions and beliefs are the product of society as a whole. News media play an important, but by no means a monopolistic role. Institutions such as schools, churches, business, and the family are vital and fundamental to the formation of the ideas and beliefs of an educated nation. Because there is such a diversity of means of communications in the country today, there is limited reliance on any one source. I think it is fair to say that the more active a citizen in the community, the more numerous are his sources of information and ideas. Such well-informed individuals are themselves usually an important means of influencing opinion in their communities.

A second criticism frequently heard and equally inaccurate is that advertisers, because they do provide the economic lifeblood of the press, exert considerable influence on the editorial content of the press. This is not so. The free press in America is indeed free. The multiplicity of advertisers, and, therefore, sources of revenue, makes control by any one advertiser or group of advertisers impossible. . . . I can speak best for my own company. We have always had a firm policy of keeping our editorial content entirely separate from advertising considerations and I know of no instance where an advertiser has been able to dictate the editorial content of our magazines. In fact, publishing and broadcasting are the only businesses I know that make a habit of criticizing their own customers. At times, advertisers have become so annoyed with us that they have withdrawn their advertising. Because we have so many different and competing sources of advertising revenues, we have always been able to ignore such withdrawals and most of those advertisers have eventually rejoined us.

Even in areas of great sensitivity for major advertisers, news coverage has been extensive and balanced. Ralph Nader is a household word and every American who knows how to read—as well as some who don't—are familiar with the Surgeon General's Report on smoking, because newspapers, magazines, radio, and television have told the public, in detail and at length, about both. . . .

The economics of the news media are of vital importance to the nation and the government. Because of economic pressures, only 37 U.S. cities have two or more daily newspapers in competition, whereas ten years ago there were nearly twice as many. So serious did Congress consider that matter that it passed special legislation, "The Newspaper Preservation Act," which permits papers to use joint facilities and combine certain commercial operations without concern for the antitrust laws. We have seen the disappearance of a number of great national magazines—most recently *Look* magazine. *Look* suspended publication this month in large part because its publisher saw no hope of economic survival in the face of the enormous increase in postal rates now being proposed.

At the time of its demise, *Look* had six and a half million subscribers, but this demand was not enough to overcome its economic problems. [*Life*, another well-known and highly circulated magazine, also stopped publication about a year after this presentation.]

In 1970, advertising revenue will provide some $12 billion toward direct support of the free press—about 1 percent of our G.N.P. Almost 100 percent of commercial television and radio broadcast revenues, of course, are derived from advertising. Some two-thirds of newspaper and magazine revenues are also generated by advertising. . . . The conclusion is inescapable that without these revenues the free press as it has evolved in America could not exist.

Advertising, of course, is more than a source of revenue for the press. . . . We in journalism have found that, in general, the public wants advertising. The old *PM* in New York, for instance, was originally published without advertising and financed entirely by circulation revenues, but soon found that its readers insisted on advertisements as a service. How else were they to learn about new movies, shows, and concerts, or the price of food at supermarkets, or clothing sales in the big downtown stores? . . . Last year slightly more than half of the $12 billion total spent on advertising in the press went into local advertisements—classified, retail and the like. . . .

Advertising, then, is a part of the service provided by the press and desired by the American consumer. . . . Is advertising the only way to support the free press as we know it? I must confess that I can think of none better. Consider the alternatives: There is the possibility of government subsidy. The danger inherent in such a situation, the possibility of control of content, is clear. In the American context, at least, the government has been kept out of the press and denied any power, economic or otherwise, that might lead to control.

Another possibility is that special interest groups who wish to reach and influence the public—such as political parties—might finance major organs of the free press. Such a situation—which exists in quite a few countries—seems little more desirable to me than the possibility of government subsidy. The press in this country has been a "fourth estate" and, if it is to continue to function as it traditionally has, it must continue apart from direct participation in the political process.

Another method of financing that has received considerable attention is greater payment by the consumer. In the first place, increasing reader costs for magazines and newspapers is probably not economically feasible. Time, Inc., studies show that higher subscription rates generally reduce circulation and, therefore, circulation revenues, by roughly the amount of the gain of the higher rates. In the second place, such a substitution would involve a very substantial amount of money for the individual reader. Without advertising, the annual cost of *Time* magazine would go from $15 to $45; the cost of a newspaper such as the *New York Times* would rise [from] 15¢ to 40¢ daily.

Those figures are misleading because they assume no change in circulation; but, as must be clear, all our experience indicates that circulation falls as prices rise. Since a sizeable portion of our costs are fixed and others are kept low by economies made possible through volume buying, prices for the subscribers who remained would rise, causing more subscribers to cancel, causing further rises, and so on. A *Time* magazine that goes to, say, 200,000 buyers would be a very different magazine and would play a very different role in informing the public, sparking discussion and inquiry, and in helping bind us together than the *Time* of today which is purchased by some 4.2 million people in the United States. Such a situation would limit access to news and information to the affluent. . . .

The broadcast industry faces similar problems. A nightly half-hour network news show costs in the neighborhood of $10 million a year. Even if the mechanical problems of billing and collecting from the public could be overcome, the cost of maintaining network news facilities would be enormous. All possible means of financing, then, would in some way diminish the present system.

We like to think of the free press in the abstract, but it does not exist in the abstract. It exists in the very real economic world with which all businessmen must deal daily. There are expenses and income and, to stay in business, the press must make a reasonable profit. Like many other industries, the great demand for capital has forced many publishing companies that were long privately held to "go public." That means that, over the long run, the press must achieve a profit margin more or less comparable with other investment opportunities.

The courts have recognized the special role of advertising as the economic lifeblood of the free press. Taxes which have singled out advertising revenues have been struck down largely on First Amendment grounds.

It is my firm belief that the greatest danger faced by the free press stems not from any deliberate or planned action by individuals or agencies in the government, but rather from a climate of indifference to what may appear minimal damage to First Amendment principles combined with expediency exercised in the desire to achieve what is often a good end. First Amendment freedoms always involve a process of balancing. In recent times, despite court decisions, there has been an alarming tendency on the part of some government officials and agencies to weight the scales against freedom of the press.

The desirability of convicting a criminal takes precedence over the protection from subpoena of a reporter's notes or a television producer's out-takes; the need for secrecy of state papers takes precedence over the press' duty to inform the public; the political gain to be made by attacking reporting takes precedence over the chilling effect of criticism by government officials; the need for state and local revenues to be gained from special taxes on advertising takes precedence over the dangers of hitting directly at the revenues of the press; the need to increase postal revenues takes precedence over the damage that a sudden large increase has on expenses, profitability and even the existence of a portion of the media.

Individual actions by individual agencies cannot be considered independently. They have a cumulative effect. That fact should be, but often is not, weighed in the decision-making process. I am a publisher and not a lawyer or constitutional scholar. Nonetheless, it is my view that, possibly as a matter of constitutional law, and certainly as a matter of public policy, First Amendment guarantees should extend to business and industry. I believe that any product which may be legally sold or traded in this country should have the right to publicly advertise itself. Indeed, if it does not have such an inherent right, it might as well not exist. I also believe that the various sections of the press should be able to decide for themselves the content of their pages—both editorial and commercial content.

Obviously, these First Amendment rights are subject to the same reasonable limitations that apply to any other exercise of freedom of speech and freedom of the press. I do not for a moment advocate the right of businessmen or advertisers make false or misleading statements. This commission must and should carry out its congressional mandate to regulate such advertising.

The free press in the U.S. does have its faults and we must continue to try to correct them. On balance, however, we have developed a press of high quality, free from control by government or special interest, and easily accessible to the public. In our highly complex, industrialized, and sometimes fragmented society, our many-faceted press both fills the needs of groups and individuals and provides one major force that holds a large and varied country together.

Competitive and diverse, the press provides an outlet for all shades of opinion and forms the marketplace of ideas necessary to the functioning of the democracy. That such a system is so rare indicates that we should take special steps to safeguard it. Advertising is an integral part of the system we have developed and any actions which affect advertising will affect the system itself.

Our form of government depends on carefully developed checks and balances, of which the press is a key element. As the power of government grows, and it does every day, it is important that the balance be kept by strengthening, not weakening, the free press.

II. Advertising, Information, and Competition

The next testimony, by H. Demsetz, professor of economics, University of California at Los Angeles, provides a more quantitative approach to the socioeconomic roles of advertising. Two features of this testimony are of special importance.

First, Professor Demsetz summarizes a new trend in economic theory: information is no longer viewed as a free good, but as a good that, like others, has its own costs, and for which there is a supply and a demand.[3] Second, he illustrates the applications of this new perspective to the study of the advertising institution. This perspective allows economists to raise new questions concerning the genesis and functioning of the advertising institution in an economy, and to undertake new empirical studies. Professor Demsetz reviews these studies in the context of previous theoretical and empirical work, especially earlier work on the relationships of advertising to industry concentration, profit rates, and price levels.

The testimony by Professor Demsetz

In 1776, a vintage year for great works, Adam Smith began his treatise on the *Wealth of Nations* with the sentence

> *The greatest improvements in the productive powers of labour, and the greater part of the skill, dexterity, and the judgment with*

---

[3] There has been an increasing interest on information in economics during the past three decades. The work presented by Professor Demsetz represents one of the several research interests that have emerged: For a review of all other developments, see J. Hirshlaifer, "Where Are We in the Theory of Information?" *American Economic Review,* May 1973.

which it is any where directed, or applied, seem to have been the
effects of the division of labour.

The quotation contains the key to understanding the main social function of advertising. Specialization cannot succeed without communication. In order to move closer to the life style to which we aspire, it is necessary to work and produce in a manner that is increasingly specialized, and this cannot be accomplished without increasing the resources we devote to communication.

The productivity increase brought about through specialization has allowed us to enrich our lives with product and travel variety, fewer work hours, and more time for leisure activities. Without the effective use of resources for communication, these forward strides would have been much more difficult. One of the important ways to use communication resources effectively is by advertising.

That advertising is primarily a method of communicating efficiently is revealed by the systematic variation in its use. Where customers are few, advertising expenditures tend to be small, and when products are new and less well known, these expenditures tend to be greater. For communicating with mass markets, the messages conveyed are appropriately nontechnical, whereas for buyers who are specialists, the messages are more like invitations to inquire further.

These variations in advertising efforts are not due to happenstance; there is a consistency across national boundaries[4] and through time that provides convincing evidence that the patterns we observe are due to the comparative advantage offered by advertising in solving certain communication problems. These problems are encountered more frequently when and where economies have become highly specialized in social organization. Since economic organization here has reached a higher degree of specialization, this helps to explain why advertising expenditure in the United States is a somewhat larger percentage of Gross National Product than it is in other industrialized nations.[5] As our economy continues to take advantage of specialization, we can expect to observe a slight upward trend in the fraction of our resources used in advertising. . . .

An economy built upon the productivity of specialized industries requires more than information about the availabilities and prices of products. Encouragement must be given to make product improvements and to avoid carelessness and deception.

The activities of labeling, branding, and advertising are important in establishing producer responsibility. Thus, suppose persons would like their cereal to contain more vitamins and minerals, and that they are prepared to pay the cost of adding these dietary supplements. . . . If each manufacturer is allowed to identify his product by branding and by advertising the vitamin-mineral content, . . . each will have an incentive . . . to promote an improved cereal. By the same token, producers of highly advertised brands, precisely because they are more easily identified and remembered, stand to lose a great deal if their products are

---

[4] On this, see the studies by the U.S. Federal Trade Commission, *Distribution Methods and Costs,* Part V, *Advertising as a Factor in Distribution* (1944); and N. Kaldor and R. Silverman, *A Statistical Analysis of Advertising Expenditure and of the Revenue of the Press* (Cambridge: At the University Press, 1948).

[5] Advertising outlays are slightly over two percent in the United States and slightly under two percent in the United Kingdom and Canada.

found to be faulty. Thus, branding and advertising greatly facilitate responsible decision making in an economy of specialists. Even the Soviet Union has found it desirable to reintroduce branding and advertising in its attempt to discipline managers and workers.

Most popular discussions of advertising give only lip service to its importance as communication. However popular are concerns about monopoly, fraud, and persuasion, and whatever element of truth these concerns may reflect, they can have relevance only to a very small fraction of advertising. The bulk of advertising activity is readily explainable as a response to the highly specialized economic activity which characterizes our society.

The cost of communicating would be significantly higher . . . and the main effects of a public policy seeking to reduce the use of resources in advertising would be undesirable. Exchange opportunities would be limited and specialized production hampered, with a resulting reduction in living standards; and resources would be diverted into less efficient selling methods. Even if some of the popular concerns about advertising do reflect real problems, these may be but a small price to pay for the considerable advantages offered to us by this method of communicating.

Studies of advertising undertaken by economists throw light on some of these popular concerns. Professor Lester G. Telser has studied the problem of advertising and monopoly.[6] His work seeks to discover whether there is a relationship between advertising intensity and the share of industry output enjoyed by the four largest firms in an industry. The degree to which output is concentrated in the hands of the four largest producers is a frequently adopted proxy for monopoly power.

Professor Telser has been unable to establish a significant correlation between *concentration ratios and advertising expenditures* per dollar of sales. There have been other studies of this problem. . . . Taken in total, the evidence argues strongly against any significant relationship between advertising intensity and industrial concentration. It is surprising to me that we should expect such a relationship. Indeed, advertising must be one of the main tools for upsetting established purchasing patterns, allowing new rivals, such as Toyota and Volkswagen, to compete more easily.

All firms have access to advertising, just as they have access to raw materials and labor. There is no more reason to expect the use of advertising to be a source of monopoly than the use of labor. The use of advertising, just as the use of labor, can be imitated by rivals. It may be the case that some firms have a particular knack for managing advertising, and others for managing labor, but such differences reflect competitive advantages and not monopoly.

There also have been some studies of *scale economies* in advertising, although it is not quite clear just what the policy implications of any conclusions about scale economies would be. If the per unit cost of advertising should fall as more messages are purchased, or more customers are contacted, or more dollars of sales are made, it does not follow that it would be wise policy to restrict advertising, for that would merely force buyers to bear less efficient communication methods.

Be that as it may, no broad assertion of scale economies in advertising can be supported by existing empirical work. Such is the conclusion

---

[6] See, especially, L. G. Telser, "Advertising and Competition," *Journal of Political Economy,* December 1964.

reached by Professor Simon in his survey of advertising cost studies,[7] and studies by Dr. Blank[8] and Professor Peterman[9] offer convincing evidence that television advertising rates do not generally favor large advertisers. The supposition that there exist scale economies or favored treatment in advertising seems to be incorrect, and so the argument that *advertising scale economies lead to monopoly,* an argument that is built upon illogical leaps of Olympian dimensions, is rendered irrelevant.

Professors Comanor and Wilson[10] have studied the relationship between profit rates and advertising in 41 industries. Their results suggest that a significant relationship exists between profit rates, measured from accounting data, and advertising intensity, measured by advertising expenditure per dollar of sales.

This finding is difficult to interpret. A similar relationship exists between research expenditures and profit rates, but hardly anyone would argue that research activity leads to monopoly power. Successful product development may simultaneously cause profit rates and advertising intensity to go up. Product failures are not long advertised. Air transportation continues to be advertised because it is successful, while railroads spend little to attract passengers because such traffic has proved unprofitable. Because of this we would expect to observe a correlation between profitability and advertising that has little to do with monopoly.

Moreover, it is not clear just why advertising expenditures per dollar of sales constitutes an appropriate measure of any supposed barrier to competition. A product which sells for a low price can exhibit a very high advertising intensity when such a measure is used, even though the total amount spent on advertising is small. There are many such commodities, and with respect to them it would hardly seem that the advertising expenditures of firms pose a serious obstacle to those who wish to compete. I quickly note that the same criticism can be made of Telser's use of advertising expenditure per dollar of sales in his study of industry concentration. Comanor and Wilson did include an alternative measure of advertising activity in their study advertising expenditures per firm. But this measure of advertising activity proved to have little relationship to profit rates.

The implicit value judgments contained in many studies of advertising, including that by Comanor and Wilson, should be noted. The premise is that advertising is unproductive. Hence, if advertising causes profit rates to be high, this represents a socially undesirable increase in the rewards to industries that use advertising. But advertising is a form of communication—it is a service, or a product, that serves useful social ends, and just as other products can be produced wisely and with good taste, so can advertising. A given physical product advertised poorly is not the same product if it is advertised well; poor advertising makes it more costly or painful to communicate and raises suspicions about the tastes of the manufacturer with respect to other properties of the product. We are quite prepared to say that the producers of well-designed

[7] J. L. Simon, "Are There Economies of Scale in Advertising?" *Journal of Advertising Research,* June 1965.

[8] "D. M. Blank, "Television Advertising: The Great Discount Illusion, or Tonypandy Revisited." *The Journal of Business,* January 1968.

[9] J. L. Peterman, "The Clorox Case and the Television Rate Structures," *The Journal of Law & Economics,* October 1968.

[10] W. S. Comanor and T. A. Wilson, "Advertising Market Structure and Performance," *The Review of Economics and Statistics,* November 1967.

products should be rewarded with higher profits; by the same token, well-designed advertising campaigns are deserving of higher profits.

In my final reference to empirical work, I would call attention to the forthcoming research of Professor Lee Benham.[11] Benham compares the prices paid for eye examinations and eyeglasses in states that prohibit the advertising of these services and products with prices in states that allow advertising.

This study directly confronts the notion that advertising adds to the cost of a product and therefore to its price. A significant difference in prices was found to exist after taking account of income and demographic variations among state populations. The prices for eye examinations and eyeglasses averaged $4.43 less in states allowing advertising. His work indicates that the use of advertising to convey information allows these services to be sold through larger commercial outlets at lower prices. Such outlets depend on being able to communicate with large numbers of prospective buyers, which advertising allows them to do at low cost. Where advertising is permitted, these firms can be successful in lowering product prices.

The underlying association between advertising and low prices observed by Benham should not surprise us any more than the relationship between the assembly line and low-priced model "T" Fords. Both techniques are geared to succeed only if mass markets can be tapped successfully, and this can be accomplished only if the real price faced by the buyer is lowered. The notion that cost and price can be kept lower by eliminating advertising ignores the impact of advertising on the size of the market to be served.

But in one respect, studies such as Benham's will tend to underestimate the benefits of communicating through advertising. In the absence of advertising, we might very well observe lower nominal prices, as popular notions would lead us to expect. But the real price must include the cost of acquiring information about the product and its producer. The consumer will bear a larger portion of this cost in the absence of advertising, and the information-gathering cost that he does bear may very well exceed that which would have been passed on to him through the product price if it had been advertised. The nominal price observed in a regime without advertising will be an underestimate of the true cost of the product to the buyer. With advertising, a significant portion of the communicating cost is contained in the product's price, but without advertising the cost of communicating may be hidden in the expenditures by consumers to acquire information about the product.

It is possible, even probable, that there do exist families of products in which advertised products sell for more than unadvertised. Advertised brands and the firms that produce them may be more reliable, and the expenditure made directly by the consumer to become acquainted with unadvertised brands may offset the advantage offered by lower prices.

More important than such price comparisons is the question of what advertising does to the entire structure of prices. An examination of the price structure with and without advertising would be of great interest. The Benham study is able to shed a little light on this problem because some states have been silly enough to forbid the advertising of eyeglasses and examinations.

Such controlled conditions are difficult to find in economies; conse-

---

[11] L. Benham, "The Effect of Advertising on Prices," *Journal of Law & Economics,* forthcoming.

quently, data bearing on this problem are not abundant. Theoretical work on the economies of information by Professor George J. Stigler[12] does suggest that if advertising is a low-cost method of communicating, then general restrictions on its use can be expected to result in a distribution of prices exhibiting a larger range and higher mean. Lower-cost methods of acquiring information reduce the cost of search to buyers, thereby encouraging them to search more for better combinations of price and other commodity characteristics.

The empirical work that I have been discussing does not lend support to the myth that oligopolists rely on advertising to keep out competitors and that the expenditures incurred to do so are passed on to the customers in the form of higher prices. No significant connection between advertising and oligopolistic structures has been uncovered, and industries that do advertise more intensely seem to be characterized by less stable market shares. What little work has been done on comparing prices for the same type of products suggest that the entire structure of *real* prices faced by buyers may be increased by arbitrary limitations on the use of resources for advertising.

Much criticism of advertising seems to be founded on two notions— that commodities possess intrinsic value and that persuasion through advertising is undesirable if not unethical. Neither of these notions can be justified. A glass of water at Niagara is hardly worth a glass of water in the Gobi Desert, and neither is an economist or lawyer. . . . There is nothing intrinsic about the value of the commodities and services that are offered to us. Their worth depends on how we perceive them and on the quantities available to us. . . .

Underlying the idea that commodities have intrinsic value is the belief that we are motivated by basic, stable, and simple wants. If man ever was so motivated, that primordial time, thank heaven, has long since passed. Only its ghost lingers to haunt discussions about advertising. We court new experiences while we strive for stability, we seek variety and new faces but hold on to old ways and friends, we desire to interact with others but carefully maintain the privacy of our homes. . . . Our wants are fascinatingly complex and sophisticated, not simple and basic. Professor Frank H. Knight writes: "What men want is not so much to get things . . . as . . . to have interesting experiences. . . . Most conscious desire is ultimately a wish to play a role, to be some kind of a person in some kind of a human world."[13]

New directions in these wants are difficult to decipher, and catering to them is not only a matter of the physical properties of commodities, which have little direct connection to social roles and states of mind. . . . We may like or dislike the complexity and dynamism of our wants, but if we are to form an intelligent policy toward advertising it is necessary to recognize them for what they are.

Virtually all of the specific forms in which our wants are expressed are learned. The complex process of want formation undoubtedly is affected by advertisers. Politicians, professors, and churchmen also play a part in this learning process. In a sentence, we are persuaded to most of the wants we hold.

Persuasion is an important element in all communication. At the

[12] G. J. Stigler, "The Economics of Information," *Journal of Political Economy,* June 1961.

[13] F. H. Knight, *Risk, Uncertainty, and Profit* (New York: Houghton Mifflin Company, 1921).

least, an attempt to communicate suggests that the other party would be better off taking note of the proffered information rather than turning to some other task or other information. . . . Information cannot be communicated voluntarily without persuasion, which is the only practical alternative to coercion.

Communication requires the attention of the listener. All teachers know how difficult that is to obtain, even when they have something to say. Listing the dry statistics of the American economy is a sure way to cut class enrollment. . . . I suspect that dry statistics on products would have the same effect. . . . However, it is a delusion to believe that persuasion would be missing from such advertising. The seller clearly would be implying that these physical characteristics are more important to the buyer than the infinite number of others that might be presented.

In this business of persuasion it is not at all clear that Madison Avenue has a special advantage. Advertisers enjoy neither the protection of Congressional immunity nor the privilege of academic freedom. More important, advertising is necessarily exposed to millions of people. Such exposure surely reduces the risk of serious misrepresentation. This cannot be said for personal selling techniques, whether practiced in an office on Pennsylvania Avenue, a classroom in Cambridge, or on the doorstep of a home.

But I think that the risk of serious misrepresentation in this nation is greatly exaggerated. We still have a society that tolerates healthy competition between those who wish to persuade us, and therein lies our most effective defense. We are exposed to a very large collection of persuaders, especially in the marketplace. . . . And the government is given free press coverage to present its case. . . . An expansive competition between those who would persuade us is what protects us from the excesses more characteristic of closed societies. If we have no confidence in ourselves when we are offered a great variety of options and suggestions, then how can we be confident of our decisions if we wear the blinders of censorship? . . . Since most men's wants and beliefs are learned, meaningful freedom must involve the right to choose between the offering of those who wish us to learn one life style rather than another, purchase this commodity instead of that, accept one suggestion rather than another. The free society keeps open the avenues of persuasion, and it encourages us to walk along these avenues. What threatens the free society most is the blocking of avenues of persuasion.

2

ADVERTISING AS A
MANAGEMENT FUNCTION IN A FIRM

The purpose of this chapter is to consider a second meaning of the term advertising, namely, a management function within any organization that sends information via mass media to individuals and organizations. The main concern here, therefore, is to understand how the rise of advertising fits not only within a firm's marketing department but also within the main corporate management goals and strategies.

Advertising also may be used by different types of organizations. These organizations may include a university that wishes to recruit promising graduate students, a church that wants to increase its membership, a group of citizens concerned with the environment that decides to inform the electorate about a referendum proposing some limits on the construction of nuclear plants, or a county that would like to see an increased utilization of its "production" of mental health services.

Information flows in a business organization

Recall that any decision is a conclusion derived from some premises, and that these premises are information "bits" about the problem to be solved by a decision. To understand the basic nature of advertising management decisions, to understand their major contributions to marketing management decisions and, ultimately, to corporate goals, one may look at a business firm as an organized set of information flows, some of which are internal to the organization, others coming from the outside environment into the firm, and still others flowing from the firm to the environment.

A business organization may be visualized as a cooperative arrangement among some basic groups of people. These groups are often called "vested-interest groups," for they participate in the activities of a firm only if their interests are satisfied. From a corporate management point of view, these groups are the "publics" of a firm. These publics include:

Suppliers of savings in the form of stocks, bonds, and working capital.

Suppliers of equipment, materials, and operating supplies.

Suppliers of human skills.

Suppliers of "revenues," i.e., the buyers of the goods produced by the firm.

Suppliers of general services, laws, and regulations.

The public at large.

Figure 2–1 represents graphically the communication problem that corporate management faces with respect to the first four publics listed above. The arrows may be read in two ways. First, the arrow moving from a public to the firm indicates the "contribution" that each public may give to a firm, and the arrow moving from the firm to each public indicates the "inducement" a firm may give to a public to obtain that public's contribution. For a firm to exist, then, it must obtain contributions from its publics by offering inducements to them to contribute.

As a general statement, the majority of individuals find that it would like to contribute as little as possible and receive as much as possible. For instance, when buying the stock of a company, investors contribute savings to that company and expect the best inducement,

FIGURE 2–1
A business firm as an organized set of communication flows

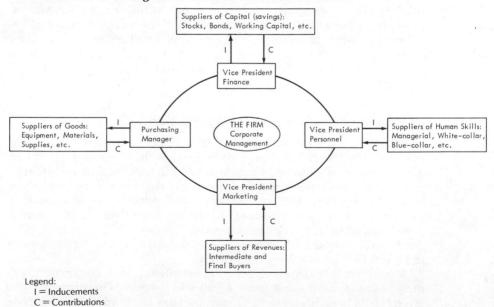

Legend:
  I = Inducements
  C = Contributions

i.e., the highest dividend and rate of growth. When buying a car, the consumer wants to pay the lowest price and receive the best inducement. The key job for corporate management is to understand these human interests and relate back to each group, explaining (*a*) why the inducement offered cannot be greater, and, concurrently (*b*) why the contribution requested is not smaller.

The arrows also can be read in another way—that is, as flows of communication from each public to the firm and vice versa. Since the nature of the inducements and contributions changes from one to another public, the content and purposes of each flow varies from one to another group. As a firm grows in size, it gradually develops "specialized departments," each concerned with understanding the needs of one public and explaining to this public the needs of the firm.

This specialization by communication processes for different publics is illustrated in Figure 2–1. The vice president in charge of personnel management specializes in the communication with the suppliers of human skills; the purchasing manager relates to the suppliers of equipment, materials, and supplies; the vice president in charge of finance communicates with the suppliers of financial resources; and, of course, the vice president in charge of marketing is responsible for communicating with the potential buyers of the firm's products, brands, or services.

The responsibility of these specialists to corporate management should be obvious. Their relationships with their publics must be efficient and effective in the sense that corporate management can, in fact, obtain a viable balance across the opposing interests of each group. The decisions of each department will be optimal only if each department manages the two-way communication flows efficiently and effectively.

What does this specialization in communication mean as far as the marketing department is concerned? And how does it help to understand the nature and role of the advertising department?

Marketing and advertising information flows

There are many types of audiences that make up the public of interest to a marketing manager. In business, it is actually rare that a marketing manager relates directly and only with the users of the firm's output. For instance, a lumber mill may cut lumber and build wooden pallets. These are sold to a local cannery for use in shipping its canned goods by truck to a large company operating cargo ships. This latter company is interested in the new technology of containerization, and it thus urges the cannery to abandon wooden pallets. In this situation, the marketing manager of the lumber mill must start some communication with the shipping company, for it is this company that must be sold on the advantages of wooden pallets over the new technology.

In general, a marketing manager may study the usefulness of establishing communication with several groups: (*a*) the immediate buyers of the firm's goods (e.g., DuPont may sell a synthetic fiber to both middlemen and to textile manufacturers); (*b*) the buyers from its buyers (e.g., DuPont may be interested in the middlemen and retailers who buy from a textile manufacturer); and, also, (*c*) the "final" buyers (e.g., the U.S. Army and individual consumers).

There is no general principle, because each situation demands different strategies. Figure 2–2 illustrates some typical situations. In the case of a packaged good, the manufacturer sells directly to retailers and is thus concerned with these firms and the final buyers as its two main audiences. In the other case, a manufacturer of household appliances sells to distributors, who in turn sell to retailers, who then sell to consumers. This manufacturer is therefore interested in establishing communication with these three audiences.

While this figure simplifies the number of means by which a marketing manager may communicate with audiences, it portrays personal communication through salespeople and mass media advertising (trade, national, and local). In an actual situation, other media are available—catalogs, trade shows, brochures, product and package design, and so on. Also note that the figure indicates only one means by which intermediate and final buyers communicate back to a manufacturer, by their purchases. However, an increasing means of securing information is through the use of marketing research, including trade, consumer, and advertising research.

Given the fact that advertising is only one of the means by which marketing management may communicate with its audiences, what tasks and responsibilities can be assigned to advertising management?

The contributions of advertising management to marketing and corporate management

From Figures 2–1 and 2–2 one can see that the main goal of advertising management is to help the overall communication program of corporate management and the specific communication program of the marketing department. The question, therefore, is what specific ways can advertising help management in its communication goals? What are these goals and what means are necessary to reach them?

From the viewpoint of corporate management, business functions, including advertising, must ultimately contribute—directly or indirectly—to some basic goals. Depending on the situation, corporate management may set short-term or long-term goals. For instance, in the short term, an advertising campaign may be developed to contribute to total sales or to total net profit; in the longer term, a series of campaigns may be expected to contribute to returns on investments or building a company image.

Confronted with the many inherent needs of a business, even the largest companies have limited resources and budgets. How can management allocate a limited budget to attain all the goals on an optimal basis? The principle is: Corporate management should allocate one dollar to the advertising department only if that dollar can contribute

FIGURE 2–2
Examples of information flows
A simple flow—a packaged good case

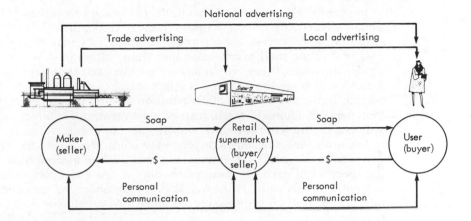

A complex flow—an appliance case

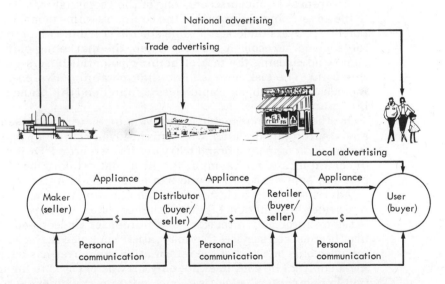

Source: Federal Trade Commission, Hearings, Fall 1971; written testimony by A. A. Achenbaum, senior vice president, J. Walter Thompson Co.

to sales, profit, or to whatever goal has been set more effectively than if that same dollar were given to the engineering department, to the materials management group, to the data processing center, or to the maintenance department, or to some other department.

In practice it is very difficult to measure to what extent advertising contributes to attaining corporate goals, especially because advertising does not and cannot always directly affect either returns, profit, or sales, for it is only one means of conveying information to intermediate and final buyers.

In general, there are great variations in the approaches and utilization of advertising by corporate managers. To begin with, variations exist across industries. For instance, sellers of raw materials such as coal or bauxite tend to advertise less than sellers of manufactured goods. Moreover, there are variations within each industry, for each firm tries to adopt the way that is appropriate to its technology, financial strength, and methods of distribution. In practice, it is dangerous to generalize from simple industrywide averages, for advertising is only one of the ways to assure viability for an organization.

From a marketing management viewpoint, the goals that can be assigned to advertising are numerous and depend almost entirely on the specifics of each marketing situation. A few examples should be sufficient at this point. If the marketing plan concerns introducing a new brand, and if it is necessary to assure that (*a*) all potential buyers become aware of the new brand, and (*b*) awareness be reached as rapidly as possible, then communication through mass media may turn out to be the most efficient way to reach these two goals.

Awareness is, of course, only one of the goals that may be assigned to the advertising. Suppose that the company wants to make sure that potential buyers understand some specific attribute of a brand of detergent, e.g., its ecological safety. Then, the marketing plan may assign to advertising the task of helping potential buyers understand this point. The task here is more than obtaining awareness; it now includes the goal that the audiences comprehend this brand's particular feature.

In other cases, management may want to relate to its present buyers and assure that the latter will remain loyal. Or it may want to get buyers of a competing brand to try out its own brand. Or it may want to communicate, for example, the idea that drinking beer can be a pleasant experience during the winter as well as in the summer.

Advertising may be instrumental in reaching the goal of sales, for it provides information. Like any other decision, buying decisions are based on information relevant to a purchaser's needs and the products, brands, and services that may satisfy such needs. But advertising provides only one part of the information any buyer has before making a choice. The consumer not only may be exposed to the information in competitors' advertisements, but to many other sources, ones that are often more powerful than those of the mass media. Among these, one of the most powerful sources of information is the buyer's own experience with the particular product, brand, or service being advertised.

This variety of influences on any purchase decision make it difficult to measure the results a marketing manager may obtain from the amount allocated to advertising. But even if these measures were relatively easy to make, there are still many alternative ways to communicate with intermediate and final audiences. Consider a few of these to appreciate how different firms utilize advertising.

A marketing manager may place emphasis on the firm's sales force as the principal channel of communication and spend 80 percent of the marketing budget on salaries and commissions to salespeople and other expenses and allocate only 20 percent on mass media advertising. Further, some proportion of the sales force can be used to communicate to intermediaries (e.g., middlemen and retailers) and the remainder to final users (e.g., industrial users or consumers). In this case, the manager may use some trade advertising directed at the intermediaries and some industrial advertising directed at the final buyers. Another firm, however, could direct all of its salespeople's efforts toward intermediaries and address all of its advertising to final users.

These different approaches exist even within the same industry. Consider the case of the cosmetics industry in Figure 2–3. Avon sends its salespeople directly to the final consumers on a 40 percent commission basis, and it thus uses very little communication with consumers via mass media (Avon's advertising budget is only 1.5 percent of its sales). But Revlon, however, follows a different strategy. First, its salespeople communicate only with retail store managers, and the commission or margin to these stores is in the 35 to 40 percent range.

FIGURE 2–3
The use of advertising and other forms of communication varies from firm to firm

The Cosmetic "Industry": Avon versus Revlon

	Avon	Revlon
Distribution	In-home (40% commission)	Stores (35–40% margin)
Advertising.	1.5% of sales	7.0% of sales

The Vacuum Cleaner "Industry": Electrolux versus Hoover

	Electrolux	Hoover
Distribution	In-home (30–35% commission)	Stores (20–25% margin)
Advertising.	Little or none	$1.5 million (Est. 1970)

The Home-laundry Product "Industry": Purex versus Major Laundry-Product Firms

	Purex	Major competitors
Advertising.	Relatively small	Major means of competition
Trade promotions	Heavy emphasis	Relatively minor

Source: R. Buzzell, "The Role of Advertising in the Marketing Mix," Marketing Science Institute, Cambridge, Mass., October 1971, Appendix.

At the same time, to communicate with consumers, Revlon uses advertising more intensively than Avon, at the level of 7 percent of sales. These large variations also are given in the other two illustrations in the figure: the case of a small home appliance, such as vacuum cleaners, and the case of home-laundry products.

All in all, what advertising should accomplish and how much one should spend on advertising varies from company to company. The answers depend on the overall marketing plan and how advertising fits into that plan.

The budget given to an advertising department is the result of various tradeoffs among different forms of communication available to a marketing manager. As Figure 2–4 illustrates, different firms spend different amounts for advertising, even when they are in the same industry. See, for example, the first column and compare the advertising budget of Lever Brothers with that of Procter & Gamble. The difference is not necessarily a question of size; rather, it reflects differences in company-specific situations and strategies (see the cases in Figure 2–3).

Figure 2–4 also reveals differences in how a company decides to use one mass medium or another and to what degree. For each company, the percentages show that while one spends relatively more on television, its competitor spends more on some other medium. Compare, for example, General Motors and Ford; R. J. Reynolds, Philip Morris, and Brown & Williamson; and so on.

In conclusion, the marketing manager expects advertising to contribute to sales by providing the appropriate information in the form that is understandable to those audiences that are directly (final buyers) or indirectly (intermediaries) interested in the firm's product or brand. Depending on the situation and the marketing plan, the specific goals of a complete advertising campaign may be, for example, the creation of *awareness* about a new brand or a new feature of an established brand; or the goals may be the audience *comprehension* of a new way to use an established brand, or the *liking* of certain features of a new brand. Other and challenging goals assigned to the advertising function include *changing the attitude* toward one's own brand to increase the probability that present buyers will *remain loyal,* or will *purchase more,* or will *purchase at other times.* Still another goal might be to persuade buyers of competing brands to *try out* the firm's own brand.

A marketing manager can use a variety of ways to communicate to the firm's different audiences. Advertising is only one element of the entire marketing mix. As in the case of corporate management, the marketing manager is faced with the problem of allocating the budget to each element of the marketing mix in an optimal manner.

The determination of an optimal allocation of a budget is not an easy task. In fact, different firms not only organize their marketing strategies in different ways, but a firm may find it necessary, over time, to change its approach, and utilization of its advertising. There are at least two compelling reasons for this: changes in the behavior of competitors, and, above all, changes in consumer preferences.

FIGURE 2–4
Leading national advertisers in eight media: 1974

Company	Total budget for eight media	Percentage of budget allocated							
		News-papers	Magazines (general)	Farm publications	Spot TV	Network TV	Spot radio	Network radio	Outdoor
1. Procter & Gamble	$246,433.8	0.7	4.1	0.7	36.0	59.1	0.1	—	—
2. General Motors	173,885.1	23.1	18.9	—	11.9	33.1	10.2	1.0	1.1
3. General Foods	146,465.0	5.5	8.4	—	33.4	52.2	0.4	—	0.1
4. Bristol-Myers	125,844.8	1.1	16.5	—	17.4	61.2	2.9	1.0	—
5. Amer. Home Products	123,424.4	1.3	4.0	0.3	26.2	64.3	2.8	1.0	0.1
6. Sears, Roebuck	106,031.6	1.5	11.9	—	22.9	39.7	23.6	0.3	0.1
7. R. J. Reynolds	100,883.8	48.7	28.9	—	1.4	5.4	0.2	—	15.4
8. Ford Motor Co.	97,755.4	14.7	11.6	1.6	20.8	40.9	6.7	2.3	1.4
9. Colgate-Palmolive	92,467.3	2.7	9.2	0.1	35.6	47.1	2.7	2.6	—
10. Sterling Drug	83,388.6	0.5	8.6	—	9.1	72.9	4.3	4.6	—
11. Philip Morris	77,516.4	28.6	35.5	—	8.9	9.2	1.3	—	16.5
12. Chrysler	75,381.0	26.0	12.7	0.9	14.6	29.7	14.6	1.3	0.3
13. Lever Brothers	70,559.2	3.9	3.7	—	40.8	51.3	0.2	—	0.1
14. Warner-Lambert	65,957.0	1.4	.9	—	19.0	73.9	2.6	1.7	—
15. General Mills	64,448.2	4.8	12.4	0.9	34.3	47.0	1.4	0.1	—
16. Ralston-Purina	63,749.8	4.7	9.1	0.9	23.2	59.0	2.5	—	0.6
17. Heublein, Inc.	63,140.1	8.3	14.4	—	37.8	28.3	4.0	—	7.2
18. Gillette	61,340.0	0.8	8.3	—	16.3	74.0	0.3	0.3	—
19. AT&T	59,593.2	8.1	24.6	—	26.5	31.3	8.1	0.6	0.9
20. Kraftco	56,330.6	10.0	21.0	—	23.4	41.3	2.6	1.2	0.5
21. Brown & Williamson	52,445.2	18.3	55.3	0.2	3.3	1.5	—	—	21.4
22. McDonalds Corp.	51,402.1	—	1.9	—	55.4	35.6	4.3	0.6	2.2
23. American Brands	50,577.1	29.3	48.7	—	3.6	9.9	—	0.1	8.4
24. Coca-Cola	50,323.5	6.8	1.2	—	43.1	34.4	12.6	—	1.9
25. Seagram Co., Ltd.	49,864.5	33.5	44.9	—	0.4	—	0.6	—	20.6

Source: *Advertising Age*, July 14, 1975.

Highlights

A few basic ideas about the nature and role of advertising have been developed in this chapter. Any organization needs to communicate to its principal publics. The marketing department generally is the firm's specialist in communicating to its potential intermediate and final buyers. The marketing mix represents the ways which an organization believes are the most efficient combination of means to communicate.

According to each firm and its specific situation, the goals assigned to advertising information may vary a great deal. They may range from creating simple awareness to favoring the formation of brand loyalty.

All available statistics point to the large variety of approaches to the utilization of advertising. There is a wide range in the amount spent on advertising from one industry to another and from one firm to another in the same industry. Moreover, these variations occur through time because of changes in production technology, in distribution methods, and in the buyers' preferences and behaviors. Finally, data show that even firms in the same industry allocate their advertising budgets among the available media in different amounts.

Advertising management fits within the communication program of the marketing department and, ultimately, within the overall communication strategy of corporate management. Ever-changing conditions call for changes in both communication strategies and marketing plans: The efficient advertising manager is the one who can consistently contribute most by providing the appropriate information to the appropriate audiences at the right time, within the firm's entire communication activities.

Questions

1. Is advertising only one element of the marketing mix? Why?
2. Why is it difficult to separate advertising's contributions from those of the other elements of the marketing mix and of the overall communication strategies of a firm?
3. Where should the responsibility of advertising strategies rest? With corporate management or with marketing management?
4. "Advertisers and advertising agencies should weed out those in their midst whose activities bring discredit upon advertising management and the entire advertising institution." Explain.
5. Assume that a manufacturer of a branded grocery product can use either salesmen or advertising to introduce its product. Which would you consider better? Explain.
6. To what degree can the overall selling functions be accomplished through advertising?
7. What are the necessary ingredients that a company's product should possess if the advertising of it is to be successful?
8. Indicate the reasons why some companies which sell almost identical products will use different advertising strategies.

9. Point out what you believe advertising can do for:
   a. A company manufacturing bearings which will be used in automobiles.
   b. A wheat farmer.
   c. A department store.
   d. An office furniture manufacturer.
   e. An attorney in general practice.
   f. A soft drink bottler.
   g. A manufacturer of air conditioning units for the home.
   h. A major bank with a full line of services.
   i. An automobile manufacturer.
   j. A manufacturer of typewriters.

Case **HIGHLANDS COMPANY**
2–1   **Evaluation of sales function**

Highlands Company is one of the leaders in providing environmental conditioning for the aviation and aerospace industries. Components and component systems for air conditioning and pressurizing various types of aircraft are designed and produced by one of the divisions of the company.

Highlands also is a developer and manufacturer of central air data systems which are used to sense the changes in aircraft's speed, altitude, and translates these data into various types of information for use by the pilot or autopilot in controlling the aircraft under flight conditions. In addition, Highlands manufactures miniature electronic analog computers, electrical static frequency converters, and a wide variety of electro-mechanical actuators and true airspeed and other flight instruments.

In its gas turbines and related turbomachinery division, the company manufactures gas turbine engines and other equipment used to produce pneumatic, hydraulic, and electrical power equipment for airborne and ground support starting, environmental control, and electrical systems; portable generator sets; and portable pneumatic power units for use in mining and oil field equipment. The company also produces heat transfer products, pneumatic valves, and storage vessels and valves for cryogenic fuels and liquids.

Sales

Sales for the company in the last fiscal year amounted to $319,-000,000. These sales were handled primarily through Highlands' own technical engineering sales staff to independent manufacturers supplying the aerospace industry, and to wholesale distributors who sold general hardware items and mill supplies. The company also sold directly to government agencies and to industrial companies.

Competitive conditions

In each of Highlands' product fields there is active and increasing competition from both large and small manufacturers, usually from different companies in each field. These competitive conditions, the dependence on government contracts, the requirement for continuing research and development costs as products are rendered obsolete by technological advances, the uncertainty of economic conditions and other factors inherent in the industry in which the company operates, makes it difficult to forecast what emphasis the company should use in its marketing strategy.

Advertising program

Highlands had limited its advertising because it was the opinion of the president that since the company's products were highly specialized it was unnecessary to invest major amounts in this form of promotion. He believed it was more advisable to invest funds that normally would be used for advertising into additional research and development. As a result, in the last five years, the company had spent an average of 0.004 percent ($1,200,000) for institutional advertising each year.

The marketing vice president, however, believed that the company should begin a more major institutional and product type of advertising program and recommended that the company should increase its advertising budget to 1 percent of sales ($3,200,000). He pointed out that in an analysis of his own and the salesman's time, the study showed:

1. Forty-five percent of their time was spent with customers and prospects.
2. Forty-two percent of their time was devoted to traveling and awaiting interviews.
3. Thirteen percent of their time was taken up with reports, office work, and the like.

Deducting Saturdays, Sundays, and holidays, and a two-week vacation period, there were 244 working days per year. On the basis of an eight-hour day, it gave the salesman 1,952 hours of working time per year.

With the number of accounts upon which to call, they were able to devote an average of only two days with each account twice a year. The vice president also indicated that there was an average of five persons in each organizations who had to be contacted.

As a result, he felt that they were not making the most effective use of their productive ability because they were devoting too much time to the dozen-and-one chores which could be more economically performed by advertising. In order to emphasize the importance of this, he broke down the sales function into the six basic steps of: (1) making contact, (2) arousing interest, (3) stimulating preference, (4) making a specific proposal, (5) closing the order, and (6) keeping the customer sold. He then analyzed each step as follows:

1. Making contact. Salesmen can make a few contacts each day; advertising can make thousands of contacts each day.
2. Arousing interest. Salesmen can arouse interest in a few prospects each day. Advertising can interest all of our potential prospects.

3. Stimulating preference. Salesmen can create preference in one place at one time. Advertising can be everywhere at once creating preference.
4. Making a specific proposal, and
5. Closing the order. These are the steps that, in our business, the salesman, and he alone, can do best.
6. Keeping the customer sold. This can be done more effectively by advertising because key men in industry change jobs, titles, and location at the rate of 50 percent per year in normal times and 63 percent per year in times of national emergency.

Using advertising to do steps 1, 2, 3, and 6 will free the salesman's time from these jobs in order for him to concentrate on steps 4 and 5. In this way a salesman can do a more effective job of performing the two steps for which he is best equipped.

Evaluation

The vice president indicated it was important to set up some method of rating the effectiveness of the increased advertising expenditure, and recommended that for each advertisement used during the next year, Highlands might make a study of a selected sample of the readers of the media used and assign weights to the four steps which he had stated could be more effectively performed through advertising.

The method suggested would include evaluating the competitive advertisements in each of the media used, and comparing these on a weighted basis. The weights assigned would be as follows:

Making contact.................. 4 points
Arousing interest .... 3 points
Stimulating preference .... 2 points
Keeping the customer sold....... 1 point

Among the individuals in the sample, they would be questioned on the above four areas. If 50 individuals in the sample indicated that they were contacted, 40 said that their interest in the product had their interest aroused, 25 said that the ad stimulated their preference, and 15 emphasized that the advertisement helped to keep them sold, then the rating for that particular advertisement would be:

$$50 \times 4 = 200$$
$$40 \times 3 = 150$$
$$25 \times 2 = 50$$
$$15 \times 1 = 15$$

Total points $\overline{415}$

By this type of comparison, the vice president of marketing believed that it would be possible to compare the effectiveness of the advertisements of Highlands with its competitors, and, also to show whether or not the advertising of the company was performing satisfactorily the functions which he believed could be done at a lower cost per unit than with sales personnel.

Case questions

1. Give reasons whether or not advertising can perform these sales functions for Highlands more effectively than the sales force.
2. Indicate the type of industry and other factors that must be considered.
3. What is your opinion of the approach for measuring the results?
4. Economically, the primary purpose of Highlands Advertising should be to educate and inform buyers. Comment.

Case **MAPCO, INC.**
2–2 **Appealing to the investment community**

MAPCO Inc., headquartered in Tulsa, Oklahoma, is an integrated energy and pollution control company operating the nation's largest liquefied petroleum (LPG) common carrier pipeline system and the world's first anhydrous ammonia pipeline. The company also produces and markets oil, gas, gas liquids, coal, liquid plant foods, sonic instrumentation devices, filtration equipment, and other water pollution control products. At present the company is concerned with developing an advertising program centered around an educational and name identification approach for the investment and business communities.

The company has four major divisions. The Production division engages in the acquisition, development, and production of oil, gas, and gas liquids reserves by either purchase or through an active exploration program, both domestically and internationally. The Mid-America Pipeline System is the nation's largest common carrier LPG pipeline, transporting propanes, butanes, and other liquefied gases, including anhydrous ammonia, from New Mexico and Texas to the Midwest. The Thermogas Division markets propane to the nation's farms, factories, and homes. The Coal division provides coal from the company's mines for power plants which, in turn, provide needed electricity.

Sales and revenues have risen rapidly for MAPCO during its 15-year history, and, in the last fiscal year, approximated $250,000,000. After-tax earnings also have grown and were over $40,000,000 in the most recent year. The company's common stock is traded on the NYSE and several other principal exchanges.

MAPCO Inc. is still a relatively young firm based some distance from the major financial markets. The company executives believe that it is important to place emphasis on name identification to help its financial officers attain good financing for the capital that they need to maintain growth.

The advertising program is straightforward. MAPCO runs weekly advertisements in *The Wall Street Journal* and monthly ones in *Business Week* and *Forbes.* Additionally, the program is run in Europe in

EXHIBIT 2–1

COAL RESERVES GROWTH

Coal may be the fuel of the future. MAPCO sold 2.2 million tons in 1973 and we're now building to meet announced plans to more than double production again by 1976.

More details are contained in our annual report. Write for it.

mapco INC.

1437 S. Boulder Ave.
Tulsa, Oklahoma 74119

NYSE Symbol
MDA

GROWTH... GROWTH... GROWTH...

... From a scrappy little pipeline company with $12 million in revenues in 1962 to a diversified integrated energy and pollution control company with sales of over $145 million.

There's more to MAPCO than its past. Get a preview. Write for our annual report.

mapco INC.

1437 S. Boulder Ave.
Tulsa, Oklahoma 74119

NYSE Symbol
MDA

MARKETING GROWTH

Despite energy conservation combined with warm weather, MAPCO's Thermogas Division prospered in 1973 and added over 3,500 new propane customers.
Watch the action.
Watch MDA.

mapco INC.

1437 S. Boulder Ave.
Tulsa, Oklahoma 74119

NYSE Symbol
MDA

LPG PROFITS

... start with lower shipping, handling and storage costs by using the Mid-America Pipeline System. Plan now to use "the underground highway that weather can't block". Call us, or write, and let us fill in the details for you.

**MID-AMERICA
PIPELINE SYSTEM**

A DIVISION OF

mapco INC.

1437 S. Boulder Ave
Tulsa, Oklahoma 74119
918 584 4471

**WORLD'S LARGEST
LPG PIPELINE**

EXHIBIT 2–1 (*continued*)

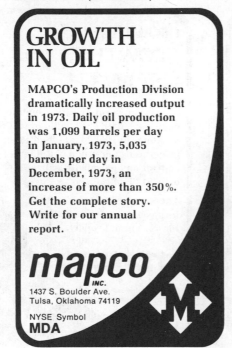

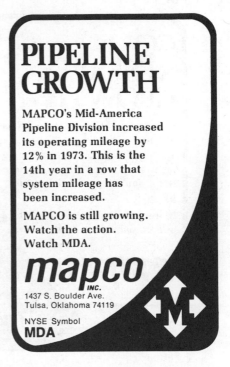

the *London Financial Times* and the *International Herald Tribune*. Some of these advertisements appear in Exhibit 2–1.

It is the objective of the company that this approach will make financial and business executives more aware of MAPCO. At the same time, MAPCO hopes it will help in attaining its financial needs and also to bring the name before individuals who are in a position to influence business deals and operations.

Case questions

1. How important is the use of advertising for MAPCO?
2. What other ways might MAPCO adopt to attain name identification?
3. Evaluate the advertising which MAPCO is using.
4. Why would MAPCO use the *Wall Street Journal?* To what extent would there be waste circulation?

Case **WINDSOR, INC.**
2–3 **Deciding on use of advertising**

Windsor, Inc., is one of the five leading United States manufacturers of high-quality bearings and bearing-using assemblies. Until a few months ago, Windsor had spent $2,000,000 each year on television, radio, and magazine advertising devoted to the ultimate consumer.

Originally, Windsor was engaged almost exclusively in the production and sale of miniature precision ball bearings manufactured to customer specifications. Over the years, due to standardization of product and changes in technology, Windsor began high-volume production of these ball bearings. During this period, it also broadened its bearing line through the development of new products. Although precision ball bearings of miniature and instrument size continue to represent Windsor's principal product line, the company now also designs, produces, and markets a broad range of larger-size ball and roller bearings and bearing-using assemblies. In addition, the company is using its technical capabilities in the precision field to design and produce bearings of commercial quality for industrial applications.

Products

Ball bearings constitute the principal portion of Windsor's production. A standard ball bearing is circular in shape and contains an outer race, an inner race, and, frequently, a retainer. The outer race and the inner race are concentric rings of different sizes. The balls rotate between the two races. The retainer is a device that fits between the two races and serves to maintain proper ball spacing.

The Antifriction Bearings Manufacturers Association's committee establishes standards of precision for the industry. When a bearing is described as a "precision" bearing, it means that it meets the ABEC* standards of precision. The description of a bearing as "miniature" means that its outside diameter ranges from 1/10" to under ⅜", and the description of a bearing as "instrument" means that its outside diameter ranges from ⅜" to 1".

In the bearing industry, certain categories and types of bearings, because of their wide acceptance, have come to be recognized as *standard.* In addition to producing "standard" bearings, a significant part of Windsor's business consists of the design, development, and production of "special" bearings which are designed to meet the particular needs and requirements of its customers. Windsor produces over 900 sizes and types of special bearings and bearing-using assemblies. Unit selling prices of these products range from $7 to $2,500. All bearings and bearing-using assemblies are manufactured by Windsor.

Windsor's principal product lines may be classified as precision bearings and products, and commercial quality bearings and products.

Precision bearings and products

A majority of the miniature and instrument precision bearings manufactured by Windsor consist of standard bearings. Applications for miniature and instrument precision bearings include aircraft

---

* American Bearing Engineers' Council.

navigation instruments, jet engine fuel controls, missile guidance and control systems, ground communication equipment, high-speed fans, dictation equipment, high-speed printers, peripheral equipment for computers, tape recorders, synchros, servos, potentiometers, miniature brake clutches, precision gear trains, high-altitude cameras, and high-speed dental handpieces.

Windsor develops and produces bearings and bearing-using assemblies of extremely high quality and accuracy, some of which have special configurations. The manufacture of these products may require tolerances as critical as 20-millionths of an inch. Windsor's experience in the field of application engineering has given it the capability to fill its customers' specific needs for bearings and bearing-using assemblies that have special performance characteristics.

Windsor's manufacturing process for precision ball or roller bearings involves approximately 50 operations consisting primarily of machining, heat treating, grinding and polishing the raceways from stainless or high chrome carbon steel or high-temperature alloy steel, and then assembling the complete bearing. Precise tolerances must be maintained throughout the manufacturing process, and continual testing and measuring are required. Some extremely high-precision bearings, such as those used in gyros for the aerospace industry, require up to eight inspection operations for each manufacturing operation. Windsor maintains a relatively high ratio of quality control or inspection personnel to production personnel.

Sales and distribution

Windsor has approximately 1,500 active customers, of which at least 95 percent are located in the United States and Canada. In the last fiscal year, the ten largest customers accounted for approximately 40 percent of net sales. The company's customers include a large number of major United States corporations in the aerospace, computer, office equipment, dental and surgical tools, industrial equipment, and automotive industries. However, no single customer accounted for as much as 6 percent of net sales.

Sales in the United States are made through 35 Windsor sales engineers and three manufacturers' representatives. Sales in Canada and Europe, which comprise the principal foreign markets, are made through six company sales engineers and four manufacturers' representatives. Foreign sales operations are conducted by the company's international sales organization.

Competition

Windsor has experienced a high degree of competition from four United States concerns and, on occasion, from several foreign manufacturers.

Two months ago, a new president of Windsor was appointed. In his review of the business expenses, he gave orders to eliminate all of the ultimate consumer advertising. It was his opinion that, because the bearings lost their identity in the product that the consumer purchased, this type of advertising was a total waste.

Case questions

1. How important is it to stimulate a demand for bearings with the ultimate consumer?
2. Is Windsor investing money in advertising? Is all money used for advertising an investment?
3. To what extent is Windsor wasting money by advertising?
4. Evaluate the objectives which Windsor has and the kinds of advertising that should be used.

3

BASIC DEMAND CONCEPTS

The managerial function of advertising is to provide information via various media to those individuals and organizations who may want it for their decisions. In this sense, advertising management is instrumental not only in helping to achieve the goals of the advertiser but, above all, in communicating with those who seek such information.

Like other forms of communication, the sender of an advertisement must understand the desires of the receiver(s) to communicate successfully. What are the needs and wants of the potential buyer? How do different buyers go about acquiring information, and how do they ultimately decide to buy? What leads buyers to switch products and brands? More specifically, what are the psychological, economic, and social processes that lead to the formation and change of demand for a product, brand, or service?

Although human wants are said to be insatiable, they are far from uniform. People want different things, and when they do want the same things, they may desire these things with different degrees of intensity.

One consumer wants an expensive car, whereas another prefers to spend the equivalent amount on a weekend cabin, to which he drives in a secondhand car. Another prefers to eat in exclusive restaurants, whereas another buys expensive clothes. Because of the range in preferences for products and services, consumers differ in their responsiveness to changes in price, to advertising appeals, to package improvements, or to any of the sales-promotional efforts used to increase sales.

Market demand

The two components which make up demand are desire and purchasing power. Both must act together simultaneously for a person to buy. In most cases, the desire for products is more active, but the inability to pay or the lack of purchasing power is generally the reason why a person fails to buy a product.

As a result, the desire which we have may not be satisfied, or we may substitute a lower-quality product for the one we want. In either instance, the psychological factor of "desire" was present, but the economic factor of "purchasing power" was lacking or inadequate.

Wants and needs

There is no sharp distinction that can be made between wants and needs. In many instances they fade into each other because the biological necessities for life are nonspecific.

As an example, we need air and food to live. On the one hand, air is so plentiful as to be generally classified as a free good. Yet, in flying at high altitudes, air must be provided at a high cost to preserve life. Neither is there one diet that will satisfy all individuals, nor is there any specific food that can be classified as a necessity for every person.

Sources of wants

Wants and needs are derived from many complex forces. Habit, custom, conformity, and distinctiveness are among these sources.

The demand for a new automobile might result from the need for more economical transportation. On the other hand, it might also be derived from the desire to keep up with our neighbors, or to be the first person with a new car.

In most cases, however, there will be an overlapping of a number of desires, and it may be difficult to isolate which specific one predominates.

Hattwick's "basic wants"

Melvin S. Hattwick, a psychologist, listed "eight basic wants in life," which, he said, were common to all inventories of people's wants and desires which had been made by psychologists.[1] They were represented as being those things which people desire most often and with the greatest intensity. They are:

1. Food and drink.
2. Comfort.
3. To attract the opposite sex.
4. Welfare of loved ones.
5. Freedom from fear and danger.
6. To be superior.
7. Social approval.
8. To live longer.

The basic wants were so named because they were believed to be based on "fundamental drives." It has been the opinion of some psychologists, which Hattwick shared, that people are born with the same

---

[1] Melvin S. Hattwick, *How to Use Psychology for Better Advertising* (New York; Prentice-Hall, Inc., 1950), pp. 18–21.

fundamental drives or wants and satisfy them in about the same ways. According to this view, drives easily are aroused by appealing to the "basic wants," and once a drive is set in motion, the person wants to satisfy it almost immediately. Hattwick also identified the following nine "secondary wants" learned by people through experience:

1. Bargains.	6. Dependability, quality.
2. Information.	7. Style, beauty.
3. Cleanliness.	8. Economy, profit.
4. Efficiency.	9. Curiosity.
5. Convenience.	

Nature of habits

Habit is a quality in a person that helps him to perform an act well or poorly in relation to his nature or actions. It is acquired by repetition and shows itself in facility of performance or in decreased power of resistance.

Fortunately for man, the problem of making decisions is eased by the fact that he has a habit pattern. The considerate man finds it easy to be thoughtful because he has acquired the habit of consideration. The safe driver finds it easy to be careful because he has acquired the habit of safety. The housewife finds it easier to fulfill her many obligations because she has acquired a number of habits in buying, cooking, and cleaning.

Because a child has not developed fully his habit pattern, notice how difficult it is for him to decide what toy he wants, what kind of candy he desires, and how slow he is to let another child play with a toy. If all our decisions were as difficult to make, our daily activities would be so complex that we would be weighted down by the burden of these decisions.

Habits are added to our nature and are related to human action either directly or indirectly. However, most habits are related directly with action because they are concerned with our powers to act. They help direct the powers of reason or the sense appetite to a specific type of action.

The most important natural cause of habits is human activity. It is by repetition that we acquire our operative habits. It is by repeatedly driving an automobile that we acquire the habits to make us skilled drivers.

The habits we acquire in this manner can be increased or decreased. The more frequently a person saves something each week out of his pay check, the stronger becomes his habit of thriftiness. On the other hand, the same man can lessen or lose his habit of thriftiness by acting contrary to it and ceasing to save.

In deciding on the marketing mix, therefore, it is important to know what the buying habits of the consumers are. Why do they buy a product? Where do they purchase it? How do they want to buy it? Do they want to pay cash or do they have the habit of buying on credit?

Do they want a 30-day open credit account, or do they want to buy it on an installment basis? Are they willing to make a substantial down payment? Do they want to buy the product in a drugstore or a supermarket? Will they see our advertisement on television? Do they read the daily newspaper? Will they see the advertisement in the morning or afternoon newspaper?

Dynamic qualities

Habits and customs are not static. The variety of drives which exist are of such a nature that it is not possible to predict how long a habit or custom will predominate. As an example, technological advances may change our mode of living, which may cause us to adopt different habits and customs.

No longer is a housewife considered lazy and inefficient if she serves her guests a dinner which she prepared by opening some frozen food packages. No longer is it considered essential for a girl to be thoroughly skilled in all phases of cooking before she gets married.

The do-it-yourself trend in the United States has increased the sales of a variety of tools and equipment. The demand for hi-fi sets was a factor in improving the sales trend for phonograph records. The increased demand for air transportation has resulted in a decreased demand for railroad passenger services.

How long will such trends continue? Have they become such an important phase of the American way of life that they will withstand the drives for other services? Will some other new development change our habits and customs?

Consumer behavior is inordinately complex. On the one hand, much of the consumer buying is so routine in character that the consumer buys more as a creature of habit rather than as a decision maker. Yet, when major purchases are made, the consumer must use "decision making" if for no other reason than to decide how to pay for the product.

Habit appears to dominate in the purchase of the items that are necessary to keep a normal household functioning. However, while these habits are being developed, "decision making" is more obviously at work.

At all times for major purchases, decision making takes place to a greater degree. In the purchase of a home or an electrical appliance, the consumer is generally influenced more by a pattern of motives instead of a single motive.

It is generally more economical for advertisers to use appeals to the consumer that will allow him to follow his established habit patterns than it is to try and change or develop new operative habits.

Inherent drives and impulses

Our wants are inherent and deep-seated. They can be positive or negative. They may lead to the motive, on the one hand, to buy a product, while at the same time be the reason for our not buying another article. They may lead to the motive to be "first," or to provide the reason why we refuse to be an innovator.

While these drives can be classified in a number of different ways, the following are among the important ones to consider. These are the drives for necessities, happiness, security, recognition, and emulation. Although the relative importance of each of these drives will vary among different individuals, nevertheless each person possesses these drives to some degree.

Drive for necessities. To sustain life is the first of the basic stimuli because man must satisfy his needs for food, clothing, shelter, and health in order to exist. Needs and tastes may differ between people in the same social strata, but the drive for minimum necessities is so great that man will generally give up other demands in order to get these essentials.

Environment is probably the most important factor in determining what these minimum requirements or standards will be. As an example, the nomads as they wander from place to place in search of their livelihood have evolved minimum standards which fall below the subsistence requirements of other ethnic groups.

Regardless, however, of what these standards may be, a person will labor to the fullest to get the necessities which make up his minimum requirements.

Drive for happiness. A second drive is the one for happiness. It is an inherent drive with which each of us is endowed. Man is made for happiness. Every perfectly designed item of nature strains for that fulfillment.

Happiness is the goal of all human activity. It is the common ground which all human desires, all human ambitions, meet. The salesman trying to meet his quota, the engineer building a bridge, the baseball player hoping to improve his batting average, the wife preparing the meal for her family—all are seeking for happiness.

Because the wants of man tend to be insatiable, no particular product can perfectly satisfy us. Not even health, strength, or beauty will satisfy all of our longings. Nor can even absolute power completely satisfy this want because it does not bring the peace which is a characteristic of happiness.

However, beneath the conflicting demands which man has, all men search for these things for one reason—they believe that the attainment of their desires will make them happy. Happiness is the ultimate end of all human acts.

Drive for security. A third drive is the one for security, and it will differ by the degree to which a particular person may think he needs it. Some men are more temperate than others. Some interpret security on the basis of an abundance of money. Others see it as the essence of an intellectual independence that can be achieved only by the spirit.

One man takes a job with a company because he analyzes the retirement plan and finds that it offers what he considers to be the highest in the industry. Another man studies the same company and concludes that his rate of progress will be too slow in the organization and decides to gain security through casting his lot with a company which may not even have a retirement program but in which he has an opportunity to earn a higher salary.

Although we do not interpret security in the same manner, experience shows us, however, that security ranks high among the various stimuli. At the same time, because we do not completely understand the meaning of security, there is bound to be some obscurity in how different persons react to this drive.

In the search for security, man must choose the way in which he is to attain it by his own actions. However, the impact of advertising may be such that it will greatly influence the security goals which are set.

Drive for recognition. The drive for recognition is another important stimuli because people are very much alike and desire to be recognized for what they have accomplished. They want to be given credit for their ideas and are disturbed when these are ignored.

Man is gregarious by nature, and much of his happiness is dependent upon his relations with other people. In fact, some men even dissipate personal fortunes in order to attempt to gain the esteem of their fellow man.

The prodigal man is a good example of this. He gives away his goods without prudence and deceives himself into thinking he can secure this recognition by getting people to look upon him as a generous man.

Again, in any group of men there must always be some who are willing to assume the duties of leadership. Frequently, the financial returns are below the levels paid by industry, by the honor and praise secured are great enough to offset any monetary loss.

In giving recognition to others, here are a few basic concepts to keep in mind:

Each person wants to feel important.

He wants recognition primarily by members of his own specific group.

He prefers to give advice in preference to receiving it.

He wants to feel that his ideas and suggestions are of the utmost importance.

He leans more towards people whose interests are comparable to his.

He wants others to judge him at a higher rather than at a lower level.

While he hates to be obligated to others, he prefers that those to whom he is obligated are outside of his own group.

He will accept flattery for only a limited time because he will soon recognize that it is insincere.

The object of giving recognition is the purpose accomplished by it. Just as the purpose of eating is for the maintenance of health, so the purpose of giving recognition should also be sound. It is not enough to provide a false type of recognition because the individual will react negatively towards it.

Drive for emulation.   A fifth drive is what usually is classified as the desire to equal or excel others. Generally, the others whom we wish to equal or excel are those in our own group.

In studies which *Fortune* and other organizations have made of executive behavior, it is interesting to note that when a man is promoted there is a strong tendency on the part of both the man and his family to upgrade the automobile, to move to a better section of the city, to join the country club, to buy a mink stole, or to take a European cruise in conformity with the activities of those at the new level which he has attained.

This same drive is inherent in our desire to accomplish more than our neighbor, to earn a higher wage, and to get a better home or television set. In some instances, the drive may even lead men to change jobs. As an example, ten mechanics who had worked for a company from five to ten years quit their jobs in a West Coast plant when they found out that new employees were being hired at the same pay scale which they received. As one of the mechanics stated: "The salary scale which the company pays is above the level which competing firms in the area are paying. I know it is going to be difficult to get a job at any higher wage than the company is paying me here. It is a matter of pride with me, and I prefer to get the same wage at another concern than to have these young guys in this plant earning the same rate that I do."

While the drive for emulation is primarily of an emotional nature, it has to be aroused in many instances through primary and secondary appeals. A picture of a person in an advertisement who is taking a trip invariably will result in some of his friends also taking a trip of some kind.

Impact of group membership

As a child becomes an adult, he or she acquires the ability to choose membership in those groups whose behavior and norms are the most attractive to him or her. Some of these groups are "aspirational" in the sense that, for instance, a teenage boy who wants to become a professional automobile driver begins to learn about car engines, reads sport car magazines, and associates with people who attend automobile races. In a word, he begins to absorb the norms and to practice the behavior of the group to which he wants to belong. Other groups are "face-to-face" types; for instance, a teenage boy is interested in music and joins the school band, and he shares with the other band members many other things in life, from reading certain magazines and buying certain records, to going with them to concerts rather than to sporting events.

Choice of group membership continues in adult life. Studies have documented how many doctors are hesitant to adopt new "ethical" (prescription) drugs on an individual basis. Scientific articles, brochures by the pharmaceutical houses, samples left by the "detail person" (salesperson) carry information that may not be adequate to influence their choice. Only conversations and consultations with other

doctors, and the opinions of those physicians whom they feel are to
be trusted, may lead to a decision to adopt and thus prescribe a new
drug. The same group decision process has been observed among
farmers in deciding whether or not to adopt new farm practices and
new farm equipment.

As an adult, the consumer also acquires the ability to choose between personal preferences and those of the group of which he is a
member. Of course, it does not have to be an "all or none" choice.
Charles Y. Glock, a social psychologist, has shown that for some products—especially those that are very socially visible—there seems to be
a greater influence of group norms, while for products outside this
category there is a tendency for personal preferences to prevail.

As an advertiser, one should not forget that these concepts are only
tendencies. Consider, for instance, the demand for beer. Some individuals like beer—it is thirst-quenching and it tastes good; but others
dislike it—it is fattening and it has a bitter taste. Concurrently, some
consumers drink large quantities of beer while others drink little or
none at all. The question for an advertiser is: Are a consumer's personal preferences stronger or weaker than what his friends do in
determining whether or not he will drink beer?

Figure 3–1 reports some findings by Charles Y. Glock in a simplified
manner. In the upper-left quadrant, consumers who are "heavy" beer
consumers are listed. Note that their preferences for beer are positive
and that their friends are also major consumers. In the lower-right
quadrant the opposite situation is given these consumers: they do not
drink beer, they do not like beer, and their friends do not drink beer.
In both quadrants, personal preferences and friends' behavior agree.

Evaluate the other two quadrants, those on the off-diagonal. In both
quadrants there is a discrepancy—a conflict—between the personal
preferences of consumers and the beer drinking of their friends. As
one can see in the figure, the behavior of a consumer's friends may
have a stronger impact on this consumer's beer drinking than his own

FIGURE 3–1
**Types of consumers: Amount of beer drinking influenced by consumers'
personal preferences and by friends' behavior**

Consumers' own personal preferences	Consumers' friends	
	Do drink beer	*Do not drink beer*
Do like beer	These consumers are heavy beer drinkers	These consumers are very light beer drinkers
Do not like beer	These consumers are moderate beer drinkers	These consumers do not drink beer

Source: Simplification of data by Charles Y. Glock, reproduced in F. Bourne (ed.), *Group Influence
in Marketing and Public Relations* (Ann Arbor, Mich.: Foundations for Research on Human Behavior,
1956).

personal preferences—consumers in the upper-right corner are light beer drinkers. But consumers whose friends drink beer are likely to be moderate drinkers, even though they personally do not care for beer.

These concepts and many others accumulated over the past three decades, both in survey and laboratory studies, are important for any communicator. Anytime one engaged in communication with an individual, face-to-face or via mass media, one must keep in mind that the audience is motivated by wants, desires, and aspirations that have a strong social origin. If one wants to understand the audience and be of service to them, and if one desires to influence them with ads, one must realize that they are social beings with varying desires.

The product, brand, or service called to people's attention is not limited to things with intrinsic chemical and physical properties. That which is offered must make sense in terms of the symbols—that is, social qualities—that consumers prefer. Modern consumers are concerned with social meanings and symbols.

In preparing an advertisement, therefore, a communicator must understand that the intended audience is made up of social beings, and that they tend to see the world, including the communicator's message, in terms of their own previous social experiences. Thus, if one were to advertise an expensive sports car, one should realize that the meaning of a sports car will vary with different audiences. For one market segment, driving a sports car is a vicarious way to experience the socially visible glory of being a professional driver; for another segment, it is experiencing in a sensual way the wind and the vibrations of the frame; and for yet another segment, it is an expression of still being youthful and of belonging to a society that cherishes youth. To the extent that it is economically feasible, the creation of different ads tailored to relate to these different meanings of a sports car may be advisable.

Psychological processes

There are different types of "psychologies" and, within each type there may be specific and sometimes conflicting theories. Although much of the research is still tentative and qualified, generalizations have emerged. Some of these are useful to advertising management, and a limited number of the major psychological processes and facts that are known to date are listed below:

(A) *A consumer perceives only a very small number of messages per day.*

This fact applies to any message from any source. As for advertisements, it is important to recognize misrepresentations that are publicized by some individuals and organizations. As an example, in written testimony submitted to the Federal Communication Commission, it was stated:

> Americans are drowning in commercials. Experts estimate that the average consumer is exposed to 500 to 1,500 commercial advertising messages

per day. Television alone accounts for a substantial portion of these messages. The average viewer, for example, watches an average of 200 commercials a day, 1,400 a week, 6,000 a month, 73,000 a year, or 4,891,000 a lifetime. A woman sees even more—approximately 5,423,900 commercials in a lifetime.[2]

The computations reported in the excerpt are based on estimates of the number of ads sent through mass media or, in the case of TV, the number of hours TV sets are on during an average day. Yet the use of the words "exposed," "watches," and "sees" suggests that the consumers do in fact "receive" and "perceive" all the ads in a given medium. This is incorrect, not only on the basis of common sense, but also in terms of well-known psychological precepts.

From a communicator's viewpoint, the relevant criterion is not the number of messages sent but the number of messages *received* by the people for whom they are intended.

As an example, Herbert Krugman, a psychologist, counted all the ads (one-page, four-color) that appeared in 47 major consumer magazines in 1970; the total was 20,374 ads. A national monitoring service has been measuring a variety of factors for years, including the number of readers of the ad-containing issue who saw some part of the advertisement which clearly indicated the brand name being advertised. Krugman matched his ads with this avilable measure and found that the number of such readers was 35 percent of total readership. He also found that the number of readers who read at least half or more of the words in the ads was only 8.7 percent![3]

And what about TV ads? Again quoting from Krugman, a cross-section sample was interviewed the day after an evening of TV programming. The viewers of prime-time programs were identified, and they were asked to recall the commercials on the show they had seen. On the average, only 12 percent of those *who had seen the show* the previous evening (a number smaller than the number of "sets on") could recall the commercials on the show. In a national sample, respondents were equipped with counters and asked to register, for half a day, every ad they saw. The modal group of counted exposures was between 11 and 20.

The above facts are typical of most messages sent via mass media, and, in fact, are one of the basic challenges to advertisers, advertising agencies, and media.

(B) *Physical perception.*

The reason why any consumer receives only a few of the messages sent via mass media is based on a commonsensical fact: individuals receive information from the environment through five senses. If an ad is not physically perceived by at least one of these senses, then it does not exist for the reader or viewer. If a consumer does not look at

---

[2] From a written statement by T. A. Weston, in behalf of the National Citizens Committee on Broadcasting, submitted to the Federal Communication Commission (Docket No. 19260), October 12, 1971.

[3] H. E. Krugman, written testimony to the Federal Trade Commission, *Hearings on Advertising Practices,* Fall 1971.

the page where the ad has been placed, he has not physically seen it. If a consumer is pouring a cup of tea and is asking a guest whether she prefers lemon or milk, then this consumer will neither see nor hear the radio or TV ad.

The physiological mechanisms making up the five senses are a marvel of nature. With relatively few exceptions, the five senses work very similarly for all persons. Human technology also has helped in making people similar in their ability to perceive physically; for instance, eyeglasses and hearing aids correct most of the deviations among individuals in physical perception.

The five senses also are physiological processes that translate the information contained in a stimulus into a language that makes sense to the brain. For instance, a person puts a lump of sugar in his mouth. As a stimulus, sugar has some information—e.g., its chemical structure. The taste buds have the ability to decode this chemical information—that is, to recognize it and thus distinguish it from that of a lump of charcoal powder—and then the ability to re-encode this chemical information into another language—electrical impulses that are sent to the brain. Since early infant training, most individuals have learned to associate the word "sugar" with the information sent to the brain. And, depending on family training, have learned to associate with this information pleasant or unpleasant feelings, thoughts, and even facial expressions.

From a communicator's viewpoint, one must appreciate some crucial implications of the role of physical perception. The properties of any stimulus can be usually measured in terms of the knowledge one has of chemistry and physics. In this sense, then, one can say that the information in a stimulus is objective. It also can be interpreted that the electrical impulses sent by the five senses to the brain contain objective information. Finally, scientists know that these physiological processes of decoding a stimuli's information, re-encoding it into another language, and sending it to the brain are extremely similar among human beings.

How then is it explained that the *same stimulus,* being processed by the *same physical perception* mechanisms, ends up having *different psychological* meanings? Why does the same food evoke different meanings for different people? And why does the same drink evoke different meanings for the same person in different situations?

(C) *Psychological perception.*

This is a complex psychological process, but its main nature and function for an advertiser are simple. One of the greatest poets of all time, Goethe, had already captured the core of this process 200 years ago by the simple phrase, "We see only what we know." Shakespeare recognized it 300 years ago when writing the opening part of Brutus's speech in the play, *Julius Caesar.* Therefore, the end result of the process of psychological perception can be described as a tenet: the psychological meaning of the "objective" information in any stimulus is "subjective."

Individuals decode objective information in terms of information they already have. The meaning of an advertisement, a package label, or a product design depends on the kinds of information the receiver uses in interpreting the physical and chemical properties of the advertisement, the label, or the design. The memory of a personal past experience with the advertised product, and even recalling simple hearsay stories from friends, are examples of information a consumer uses in interpreting an advertisement.

To appreciate the nature and consequences of the process of psychological perception is to appreciate the richness of persons, to be able to understand their meanings, and thus their wishes, desires, and, yes, their dreams. Above all, through this understanding the advertisers improve the method of communicating with potential buyers.

Even when perceived by the five senses, many messages are not perceived psychologically because they are not relevant to some consumers. Suppose one were to show the dots illustrated in Figure 3–2

FIGURE 3–2
What is the meaning of these dots?

to two groups of children. The children in one group are from a tribal society where no Euclidean geometry is taught; the other group is from the United States. Ask both groups what they see and record their answers. An examination of their answers will reveal that the first group of children has only a limited probability of attributing the meaning of a "triangle" to the stimulus in the figure, whereas the American group of children has a significantly high probability of interpreting the meaning of the stimulus as being that of a triangle. The subjective meaning of the "objective" information in the figure differs for the two groups, even though both groups have eyes—that is, they physically perceive in the same way. The American children use their previous knowledge (information stored in their minds) of Euclidean geometry in interpreting the dots in the figure and thus reach the psychological conclusion of attributing to the dots the meaning of a triangle. But the children in the other group do not have information in their minds about a triangle, and thus the dots are "meaningless." If the communicator wanted to convey the meaning of a triangle by sending the figure to the above two groups, he would achieve the purpose of his communication with the American children but would not do so with the other group. For this latter group, the stimulus has been physically perceived, but it has been *lost* through the process of psychological perception.

The second reason why a consumer receives only a few of the

stimuli sent by advertisers is because many stimuli are not perceived psychologically. The losses of the appeals of advertisements sent via mass media are partly due to the fact that many never reach the eyes or the ears of a consumer. Of those that are perceived physically, many are meaningless once they go through psychological perception—that is, from the point of view of the consumer, no information whatsoever has been received. All in all, physical and psychological perception processes operate upon the so-called objective information contained in any stimulus.

As mentioned, psychological perception is a complex process. Its results include not only the case of "loss" but also the lack of meaning of an ad. While the meaning intended by the communicator may, in fact, be received by the consumer, nevertheless another possible result of psychological perception may be that the meaning attributed to the ad by the consumer is different from, or even opposite to, that intended by the communicator.

Consciously or unconsciously, people actively look for information. They tend to see, hear, and sense what they want. They perceive whatever makes sense to them in terms of their own economic, psychological, and social wants, desires, and aspirations. Research in laboratory and real-life settings repeatedly has found that subjective meanings are usually determined by *motivated* perception. That is, the kind of information a person uses to interpret the meaning of a stimulus is related to that person's specific area of curiosity, interests, and feelings at the time a stimulus is perceived physically.

Consider an advertisement about a foreign car, which might emphasize only one attribute of the car: it delivers 30 miles per gallon under normal driving conditions. And consider an ad for an American-made mid-size car, also stressing only one attribute: it delivers 25 miles per gallon under normal driving conditions. Suppose a car manufacturer interviews a representative sample of consumers, measures the recall of the two car ads, and finds that, for a group of the respondents, the recall of the foreign car ad is much higher than that of the American car. Why might this difference be the result of psychological perception?

One of the possible factors for this difference may be due to "motivated" perception. One may, at first guess, think that, with gas prices being 60 cents per gallon or more, this group of consumers may find a difference of five miles per gallon between the two cars very meaningful, and they thus will tend to notice and remember (motivated memory) the foreign car ad more than the American one. This motivation might have two component drives. One is that these consumers may drive a lot. (In fact, if they drove the national average of about 10,000 miles per year, the cost difference between the two cars would amount to an average of only $40 per year.) The other motivational component may be related to the level of income of this group of respondents. That is, even if the respondents drove an average of only 10,000 miles per year, a saving of $40 per year may be very important if their income tends to be between $8,000 to $10,000 per year.

Now, after testing whether this is true, the company finds that a substantial number of the respondents are not in the above categories; that is, they actually drive about 10,000 miles per year and their income is in the $14,000 to $16,000 range per year. It thus is unlikely that amount of driving and amount of income are the motivational forces. But, then, what is the motivational force leading them to be more likely to perceive the foreign rather than the American car ad? The company continues its data analysis and finds that, on the average, these respondents tend to have a college education, are young, live in cosmopolitan areas concentrated in the North Central Atlantic states and on the West Coast, have white-collar jobs, and have traveled abroad. Concurrently, the company also finds different characteristics among those respondents who noticed and recalled the ad for the American car.

At this point of the analysis the company might draw some initial conclusions. For some audiences, the psychological perception of the foreign car ad is motivated not by the ad's manifest appeal to "saving," but by the latent psychological and social predispositions that find the "foreignness" of the car a meaningful symbol.

Consider another and common example of motivated perception. For more than two decades, findings have indicated that a large number of consumers who recall an ad for a product are consumers who bought that product before being exposed to that ad. A reason for this is that these consumers are familiar with the product and thus are more likely to notice its ads. But, more importantly, it is usually found that consumers actively seek out ads of the purchased product for "rational" motivational reasons. For example, it may be difficult for a consumer to know whether she has purchased the "right" product. That is (a) she recently bought an expensive vacuum cleaner, but she does not have the engineering expertise to judge whether it will last a long time without breakdowns; or (b) she does not know whether her co-workers approve of her new hairdo. Then, how can she find information that answers her doubts, thereby lessening her sense of uneasiness and perhaps even anxiety? In this situation, she is actively seeking supporting information. Consciously or unconsciously, she is motivated to look for such information, and while scanning the magazine in the dentist's office or looking at a TV program, she will notice and remember the ads about the product she purchased. This motivated perception—selecting out of many ads those that have relevance for her—is thus internally consistent with her goals and preferences and, accordingly, her behavior is rational.

Many messages never reach a consumer's senses. Those that are physically perceived undergo the process of psychological perception. Here the results of this process may be: (a) some messages do not make an impact for they have no meaning to some receivers; (b) some other messages are attributed a meaning different from, or even contrary to, the meaning the sender wanted to communicate; and, of course, (c) some messages are perceived as meaning that which the sender intended.

Now, what happens to those ads that are perceived "correctly" (i.e., from the point of view of the sender)?

(D)   *"Correct" perception of an ad's meaning does not necessarily change a consumer's predisposition toward the product, brand, or service being advertised.*

This concept may not be understood by advertisers. But it would be irresponsible for an advertising manager working for a firm, a political candidate, a hospital, the U.S. Army, or the U.S. Post Office to ignore current knowledge about what happens after a message has been psychologically perceived in the way intended by the sender.

To illustrate this fact about psychological processes, Chevrolet had an all-out campaign to overcome the rumor that the rear-end suspensions of the early Corvair were dangerous. (From an engineering viewpoint, they were not, and from a relative viewpoint, they were safer than those of a popular German car). To counter this rumor, Chevrolet introduced a new Corvair, with an entirely redesigned rear-end suspension system—in fact, a rather close replica of the one mounted in the powerful sports car, Corvette. But although a substantial number of people had psychologically "correct perception" of the new suspension, and some were even able to understand the campaign's engineering statements, consumers still felt uncomfortable about the Corvair and did not change their intentions to refuse to buy it. In fact, the Corvair eventually had to be withdrawn from the market, for neither advertising nor other communication procedures succeeded in changing a widely held negative feeling about the rear-end suspension.

Advertisers should recognize the difference between what is often called an "opinion" and an "attitude." A consumer may know the attributes of a brand, and may even like these attributes—that is, his or her opinion consists of "correct" information. Yet, this set of "knowledges" (an opinion) is not enough to create the desire to purchase the brand. Information about a brand does not mean that the consumer is motivated to do something about the brand. What is needed beyond information is a motivational drive—i.e., an attitude—that, if positive, implies a probability to buy the advertised brand.

Both an opinion and an attitude about a brand represent a mental picture of it—that is, some information about it. But the difference between these two mental states is that an attitude implies an affective motivational drive toward or away from the brand. *To create* a positive attitude in the consumer's mind, or to help a consumer *to retain* a positive attitude toward a brand are goals generally assigned to the advertising function. Yet, basic research indicates that achieving these two goals is much more difficult than making a consumer aware that the brand exists and then become knowledgeable of the brand's relevant features.

Suppose that an advertising campaign was aimed at a demographic market of one million people, that it reached 500,000 of them, that it succeeded in conveying the correct meaning to 250,000 of them, and that it has created a favorable attitude toward the brand in 125,000 people. The question now becomes: how many of these 125,000 will eventually buy the brand? And how much of it will they buy?

(E)   *A favorable attitude toward an entity does not necessarily lead to the purchase and use of that entity.*

Business experience and basic research indicate that it does not follow that all consumers who have a favorable attitude toward a brand will, in fact, buy it. Many psychological and social processes intervene between the moment a consumer forms a favorable attitude toward a brand and the moment that the consumer is ready to buy it.

The most obvious problem is that between the time a favorable attitude is formed and the time of purchase conditions may change. A psychological process such as forgetting may occur. It is also probable that, for some of the consumers, a process called "motivated forgetting" may take place. For instance, even though a consumer may have a favorable attitude towards a foreign car, over time he may become aware that he should be loyal to the United States manufacturers and, accordingly, should buy an American automobile. Essentially, this consumer is experiencing a conflict between two attitudinal drives. (Some would refer to this conflict with such terms as dissonance or incongruence, although these two terms have a rather different meaning in several branches of psychology.)

Consumers generally do not like to experience conflict, and may engage in all sorts of psychological and social activities to get rid of it. As mentioned, the consumer may gradually forget some of the features of the foreign car or, may gather information that suggests that he does not really care for such features. Someone else may rationalize away the conflict; for instance, he may be dating the daughter of a foreign car dealer and knows that the man is a good person, that he will get personal attention if the car ever develops trouble, and that, after all, the mechanics who work for the dealer need jobs.

But there is much more to it. As time goes by, the consumer may learn from friends that they had better experiences with another make of car, or may become impressed with a relative's car. On his way to work, he may find that a dealer selling another foreign make is having a week-long special—namely, a free air conditioner with the purchase of a car.

To put it briefly, as the motivation to buy a new car increases, or is intensified by an increasing series of breakdowns in his present car, he is constantly learning new facts about cars and clarifying his preferences and, possibly, even changing priorities. These and other changes may evolve with the 125,000 people whose attitudes toward a brand had become positive as a result of the brand's advertising campaign. Accordingly, a few or many of them may buy some other brand.

These examples point out some fundamental concepts about advertising management. Advertisements compete not only with the ability of consumers to avoid exposure to them but also how they will be interpreted. All advertisements also compete with ads of other brands.

They compete against the marketing mix of other companies—their pricing and promotional strategies, their superior product or package design, offers of better service by their dealers, and so on.

The ads compete with information coming through different channels and sources; research in political behavior; in doctors' choices of ethical (prescription) drugs; in consumer choices of breakfast foods, movies, and fashions; all confirming that some channels of information may have a higher probability to affect behavior than others. Word of mouth among friends, peers, and co-workers is one of the more powerful influences, for it is their norms, rewards, and sanctions that may be valued most.

As a result, the advertiser should study and understand what the needs, wants, desires, and dreams of potential customers are. Study and evaluate whether the firm's technical knowledge, production abilities, labor skills, and financial strengths can be put together to offer a product, brand, or service that appeal to consumers in terms of their own needs, wants, and dreams. If the answer is yes, then study and evaluate whether the firm's marketing system can present the product to the potential consumers as an interpretation of these needs. As discussed in Chapter 2, it is at this stage, communicating to the potential buyers the symbolic meaning(s) of the firm's product, that the contributions of the advertising department are important to the success of a campaign.

Behavioral processes and management action

There are many ways in which knowledge of behavioral processes and facts can help advertisers, mass media, and advertising agencies. Among these are the following three major areas: selection of appeals, selection of the people who have an influence on the decision to buy, and development of advertisements addressed to the demands of consumers.

It is important to reemphasize that marketing managers are ultimately interested in generating a demand for the output of their organization. Since any human action, including that of a purchase, ultimately is related to people's social and psychological activities, the formation of the demand for a certain product, brand, or service is the goal to which the understanding of human nature by the advertising department should contribute.

Selection of appeals

In its attempt to stimulate demand, advertising management must relate the firm's product, brand, or service to some specific need, want, desire, or aspiration. In advertising this relationship is established by choosing "appeals" or information that is relevant to one or more market segments. What stimuli will be most effective in evolving the desired response on the part of the prospect? Should it be one which appeals to only a limited segment of the market, such as the appeal in Figure 3–3?

One needs only to consider the appeals which are generally used to sell automobiles to appreciate how complex that may be. In selecting the appeals for advertising cars, the various companies have tried

FIGURE 3–3

This nice young man is a gambler. His $24,000 home is insured for only $15,500.

Good luck, nice young man.

Please. Don't take chances. Protect your home for all it's worth. Against loss by fire. Tornado. Burglary. Vandalism. And more. With a State Farm Homeowners Policy.

Naturally it costs money to increase your insurance as your home increases in value. But that's where State Farm has the edge on other insurance companies. State Farm offers a better deal than most. Same as State Farm does on auto insurance.

It's made us number one in both.

Whether you own or rent, it'll pay you to see your friendly State Farm agent about broad, low-cost coverage for your home and belongings. You can find him fast in the Yellow Pages. And maybe you'd better. Unless, of course, you have money to burn.

STATE FARM INSURANCE

State Farm Fire and Casualty Company
Home Office: Bloomington, Illinois

In Texas, savings on State Farm Homeowners Policies have been returned as dividends. In Mississippi, we offer a Comprehensive Dwelling Policy similar to our Homeowners Policy.

Courtesy State Farm Fire and Casualty Co.

to assess the importance of interest in engineering features, such as air-conditioning, safety, upkeep, economy, trade-in value, and the like. However, to know that a customer values comfort may not offer too much useful information. What is comfort? Is it the upholstery? Leg room? Head room? Good springs? Trunk space? Actually, the answer to the question should be centered on what different customers really mean by comfort.

Appealing to people who influence the decision to buy

Applied and basic research has shown that the decision to buy tends to be the result of a "group" process. In the industrial area, the purchasing manager of an organization is the person who may legally bind his or her organization to a purchase. But the object or service being bought must satisfy the needs of the users—the workers on the assembly line in the case of machinery or operating supplies, or the managers of various departments who need prompt and specific information about the possible acquisition of a new data processing system.

Sometimes, even the sales manager may participate in the purchase decision. For instance, the purchase of a component of the final item may help sales of the company's product, because the firm's own buyers believe that the component made by firm X is the best. Thus, the purchasing manager is under strong pressure to buy firm X's component rather than that from another firm. In very technologically advanced products, the people working in the R&D and engineering departments also may have an influence on the final choice of a vendor and product. Last, but not least, the finance department also may influence the purchase of the component, especially in cases involving large expenditures or when there is a decision to be made between purchasing or leasing.

A group decision also may exist in consumer marketing. The choice of a car may represent the results of a compromise among the different preferences of the various family members. Even the purchase of a brand of breakfast cereal or toothpaste may not necessarily be made exclusively by the housewife. She may act as the "purchasing manager" for her children and her husband, or she may act as the "coordinator" in deciding, for instance, which type of food should be served for dinner.

So the advertiser must determine not only who buys the product but also who influences the decision to buy. For some products, such as certain food items, the children's desires will be influential factors in the mother's final purchase. However, for other products, such as major appliances, it may be a joint decision of husband and wife, and the desires of the children will not even be considered. No sharp dichotomy of the influence can be assigned in general terms for all products. As a result, an advertiser is faced with the continuous problem of analyzing who influences the decision to buy in the ever-changing market environment in which his product is sold.

Primary and selective demand

In searching for ways to relate to the needs, wants, desires, and aspirations of potential buyers, the advertiser finds it useful to distinguish two types of demand: primary and selective. Which one is to be interpreted and stimulated depends on a variety of conditions concerning the potential buyers, the product, and the market.

Primary demand. As mentioned in Chapter 1, advertising designed to stimulate primary demand is that which attempts to interpret some economic and social psychological predispositions in order to stimulate eventually a demand for a *type of product.* For example, advertising which explains how a buyer may enjoy the comfort of an air-conditioner during the hot summer months, and how much healthier this buyer will be while working in an air-conditioned office or sleeping in an air-conditioned home, is advertising which attempts to interpret the predispositions of a buyer and eventually to create the demand for air-conditioners. This advertising emphasizes the desires and drives that will be satisfied by having such a piece of equipment installed in the home. In other words, primary demand advertising informs the potential customer how basic needs can be satisfied by a product and does not attempt to sell a specific brand. Figure 3–4 is an example of primary demand advertising.

Selective demand. Selective advertising is designed to stimulate the demand for *a particular brand, style, or model* of a type of product. In advertising air-conditioning equipment, the General Electric Company, if it were using selective advertising, would concentrate on those features of its brand that would persuade people to buy a General Electric model when they purchase an air-conditioner. The advertising usually point out those features of the brand that enable it to fulfill the customers' desires or needs better than any other air-conditioner on the market. It might stress the distinctive features and qualities of the brand that make it the superior product—that make it the best solution to the customer's problems or desires. Such features might be: more accurate maintenance of desired temperature in the house; smaller, more compact size and hence a better appearance; more economy in operation; better quality so it will last longer, or, require less maintenance; or its lower price.

In Figure 3–5, as an example, the Carrier Air Conditioning Company stresses the advantages of its product and does not try to build demand for air-conditioners in general. Its objective is to stimulate selective demand for its brand of products.

Combining primary and selective appeals

In practice, these two types of appeals are often combined in advertising. For example, although the main appeal of an advertisement might be primary (air-conditioners will give comfort, better health, make a more efficient worker, and so on), it might go on with a selective appeal by ending with "and the air-conditioner that will do this

FIGURE 3–4

DON'T FENCE ME OUT.

If you don't help your school officials
open recreation areas nights, weekends
and during the summer, nobody else will.

For a free button and information to help you, write: Fitness, Washington, D. C. 20203
PRESIDENT'S COUNCIL ON PHYSICAL FITNESS.

Courtesy President's Council on Physical Fitness.

job most effectively is the General Electric model, because it has the
most accurate temperature control, it is most efficient and economical
in operation, etcetera." This usually is done during the early period
after the product's introduction on the market, while it is still necessary to educate people to the want-satisfying qualities of a type of
product, but with enough demand already created that companies
attempt to obtain the major benefit of the demand they stimulate by
advertising for their own brand. However, even after a product has

FIGURE 3–5
The wall-to-wall air-conditioner

For wall-to-wall comfort.
Carrier believes a room air conditioner
should cool the room, the whole room,
wall to wall. With no frigid zones
or hot spots. That's the idea behind
our exclusive 18-way air flow control.
Another reason why more people
put their confidence in Carrier
than in any other make.

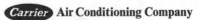

Carrier Air Conditioning Company

Courtesy Carrier Air Conditioning Company.

been on the market for many years, it may be advisable for firms to do some primary advertising to hold their product's share of the consumer's dollar against other and newer products that are appearing on the market. For instance, radio manufacturers might well do some primary advertising (use transistor radios while hiking, and so on) to show the want-satisfying qualities of radios. (See the Berry Doors advertisement in Figure 3–6.)

Primary demand advertising as a continuous process

It must be remembered that the stimulation of primary demand is, to some extent, a continuous process. For, although an extensive pri-

FIGURE 3–6
Contrast

Not if she has a Stanley-Berry Automatic Garage Door Opener!

Just a touch of the button—while sitting comfortably in your car—that's all there is to opening (or closing) your garage door the convenient Stanley-Berry way! Forget about wind, rain or snow. Wet feet, bruised knuckles and strained muscles are a thing of the past. And what a welcome sight on a dreary, dismal night to pull into your drive and have the garage door open and the light go on—all automatically! Don't wrestle another day! Have your Stanley-Berry Automatic Garage Door Opener installed now.

Portable transmitter and radio receiver are both completely transistorized and comply fully with F.C.C. regulations.

BERRY DOORS
DIVISION OF THE STANLEY WORKS
2400 E. LINCOLN RD., BIRMINGHAM, MICH. 48010

```
Berry Doors • Division of The Stanley Works
Dept. BHG-866, 2400 E. Lincoln Rd., Birmingham, Mich. 48010
Gentlemen: Please send me your descriptive literature on Stanley-Berry
Garage Doors and Automatic Openers.
Name_____
Address_____
City_____State_____Zip_____
```

Courtesy Berry Doors
Division of the Stanley Works.

mary advertising program for a given product may have stimulated a desire for the product among most of the present adult age groups and income brackets that constitute the potential buyers for the product at the time, there is a constant shift in the makeup of these age groups in the population. As teenagers, for example, move into the adult age group to become a part of the potential market, it may be necessary to educate them to the primary want-satisfying qualities of the product. Also, as people earn higher incomes and, hence, become potential buyers of a product for the first time, it may also be necessary to use primary advertising to stimulate their demand for the product. Similarly, changes in customs and buying habits of various groups may bring them into the market as potential buyers for a product.

The development of new uses for a product may call for the employment of primary advertising to point out these want-satisfying aspects of the product from this new viewpoint. Thus, for most well-established products, periodically at least, emphasis must be placed on primary appeal advertising. These types of constant changes in the composition of an advertiser's potential market are the basis for the saying among advertising people: "You advertise to a parade, not to an audience."

The circumstances or conditions in which primary or selective demand advertising may be effectively used vary somewhat, so the two should be analyzed separately. These conditions might be divided into three groups or categories: the conditions relating to demand; the conditions relating to the product or service; and the conditions relating to the market.

The stimulation of primary demand

There are many factors and conditions that may favor or hinder the advertising efforts of an industry or a firm aiming at stimulating primary demand for a generic product or service. For our purposes, these factors and conditions can be grouped as follows: those relating to demand; those relating to the product; and those relating to the market. Although there are interdependencies among these three groups, these will be considered separately.

Factors and conditions relating to demand. If a primary advertising campaign is to have any prospect of success, there must be strong basic drives or desires that can be satisfied by use of the product or service. The stronger these desires, the greater the probable response that can be obtained to any effective advertising that may be done. If the want which can be satisfied is that of sustaining life or securing happiness, for example, then the prospects for success in stimulating demand through the use of primary advertising are enhanced.

Of equal importance is the answer to the question of how well these wants are currently being satisfied by other products already on the market. If the consumer can satisfy his desires and wants easily and well with products currently on the market, and with which he is already quite familiar, convincing him of the desirability of changing to the advertiser's product will be more difficult than if this present need or want is not satisfied easily with products already available to him on the market.

As important as these two conditions is the closely related one of the strength of the appeal or appeals that can be used to promote the product. How strong an appeal can be associated with the product? And how strong is it as compared with the same or similar appeals associated with other competing products?

Another significant condition is that of the potential expansibility of demand for this type of product. Are the buying motives to which the advertising for this product is directed such that the amount purchased and consumed at any given price can be readily increased?

What are the basic trends of demand for products of this general type? The demand trend for some types of products may be increasing, while for others it may be declining. Many reasons can account for these trends, which are perhaps more basic than any promotional and selling activities of individual companies. Changes in the pattern of social life, changes in working hours and conditions, and similar deep underlying social, economic, and cultural changes will influence the trend of demand for various types of products. A favorable trend in basic demand greatly facilitates the possibility of using advertising successfully to increase the demand for a product.

Factors and conditions relating to the product. The most important condition is that the product have some significant advantage over alternative products in its ability to satisfy the wants and desires of the consumer. Unless the product can satisfy certain wants better, more easily, or for a lower price, it may be difficult to stimulate demand to a sufficient extent to make primary advertising feasible from an economic standpoint. Also, if the product has certain notable weaknesses or disadvantages, compared with alternative products, the task of stimulating primary demand will be much more difficult.

The outstanding characteristic of a product and its advantages over alternative products must be sufficiently great with relation to the price of the product or service. There must be what the prospective purchaser considers a reasonable relationship between the features and advantages of the product and its cost. For example, container companies attempting to stimulate primary demand for paper milk cartons when they were first introduced on the market had a product with significant advantages (less weight, elimination of bothersome return-the-bottle problem, elimination of glass breakage) but had extreme difficulty in stimulating demand for the paper carton among dairy firms because of the amount of cost differential.

Factors and conditions relating to the market. Several conditions of the market are significant in determining the probable success of primary advertising in stimulating adequate demand for a product. Can the prospects for the product be identified and are their characteristics known? Advertising must use the right media and appeals to be effective, and the right media and appeals can be selected economically only if the market is identifiable. Similarly, how many of such prospects are there? Do they have sufficient purchasing power to buy an adequate amount of the product?

On the basis of the number of prospects and their purchasing power, is it feasible to stimulate sufficient purchases to warrant the amount of advertising necessary to reach and influence these people? And is there sufficient margin between the cost of the product and its selling price to provide the funds necessary to support the amount of advertising that probably will be required?

Obviously, the above conditions are interrelated, and no one of them can be considered as an isolated condition. The significant characteristics and strength of appeals are related to the price of the product, and the price is related to and influences effective demand, and both influence the amount of advertising required. The importance of any of the above conditions will vary according to the circumstances surrounding any given situation, and in certain instances other factors may influence the feasibility of using advertising to stimulate primary demand. But these at least indicate the usual and more important factors and conditions that must be considered when analyzing the possibility of carrying out a successful primary advertising campaign.

The stimulation of selective demand

As in the case of primary demand advertising, a number of factors and conditions influence the probable success of a firm's advertising designed to stimulate demand for its particular brand of a generic product. It must be kept in mind that the opportunity to use advertising to influence selective demand profitably is dependent in part, in most instances, to the effect of advertising on primary demand. Hence, the conditions affecting selective demand must be considered against the background of the conditions influencing primary demand.

Factors and conditions relating to demand. One of the most important conditions which influence the opportunity to stimulate selective demand by company brand advertising is the trend of the primary demand for the type of product. If the primary demand trend is favorable, the probability of successful selective advertising is much greater than if the demand trend is adverse.

Another condition of considerable influence is the presence of strong basic buying wants or desires which the product is capable of satisfying, and the presence of strong emotional appeals that can be used to stimulate the potent basic wants and desires. It will be noted that these conditions of strong wants or needs or desires and potent emotional appeals which are used to stimulate demand are similar to conditions affecting primary demand. They are similar, but they are repeated here because they also are equally significant in influencing the opportunity to stimulate selective demand through brand advertising.

Conditions relating to the product. A brand of product that possesses some significant individualizing feature of real importance to customers has a much better chance of being advertised successfully than one without such features. The advertiser who can point out real discernible differences between his product and those of his competitors has much better possibilities for stimulating selective demand for his brand than does the company whose brand has no definite distinguishing features to differentiate it. At least it must be possible to convince the customer that the brand has distinctly superior and distinguishing features or qualities. Also, this factor influences the price differential obtainable, the gross margin obtained, and hence, the funds available for advertising the brand. Sugar is a prime example of a product with virtually no significant differences among brands, while cosmetic manufacturers have convinced the customer that there are great and significant differences among the products of different manufacturers.

Another condition of real significance in determining the opportunity for a firm to stimulate selective demand through the use of brand advertising is the importance to the potential customer of the hidden qualities of the product as compared to the importance of those external qualities that can be observed and appreciated by the customer by inspection. If there are such hidden qualities that are important to the customer, then the customer will tend to rely more heavily on the brand in buying, and so advertising can be used to build up the association of the brand with the desired qualities. But if, at the time of purchase, the customer can judge by inspection the attributes of the product important to him, then brand name is not so significant and the customer will not be influenced so much by advertising. The customer is prone to rely more on his judgment of those characteristics than on associations that might be built up in his mind by brand advertising.

Factors and conditions relating to the market. Of great importance in determining the ability to employ advertising effectively to stimulate selective demand for a firm's brand is the amount of money the company's program will make available for its advertising and promotion program. There always must be sufficient funds available. An inadequate campaign which cannot make an effective impression on the market will fail to get satisfactory results. The amount, obviously, depends on the number of units sold and the margin per unit, and which margin per unit is dependent in part at least on the effectiveness of advertising in stimulating the consumer's evaluation of the special and differentiating characteristics of the brand as produced by the advertising.

The effectiveness of the advertising in creating this evaluation on the part of the customer depends not only on the differentiating characteristics of the product but on the other conditions noted above. The amount of funds that will be available for advertising also would depend on other conditions, such as the amount and type of competition existing in the industry, the absolute amount of the price of the individual unit, the frequency of purchase of the product, and the number of customers for the product.

These probably are the most important of the conditions to be considered in attempting to ascertain whether or not advertising designed to stimulate selective demand is feasible. If all these conditions were favorable, advertising would undoubtedly be successful in stimulating satisfactory selective demand, if carried out well. But it is not necessary that all these conditions be favorable. A failure to meet one condition may be offset by great strength in one or more of the other conditions. It is basically the combination of the above conditions that is determining. Hence, judgment must be exercised in weighing the situation for any given product at a particular time to determine whether or not it seems to meet the conditions sufficiently well to make advertising worthwhile.

Highlights

In recent years, the behavioral sciences have provided some key insights into the nature of mankind and the processes that govern the behavior of the individual and groups. When applied to the behavior of buyers—individual consumers, families, and both profit and non-profit organizations—these insights are useful to advertising management.

The first and most important insight is that advertising cannot create "wants"; because "wants" are inherent, advertising can stimulate "latent" wants.

Advertisers should learn what people want and then offer the service or product that is needed. From this perspective, then, the role of the ultimate buyer in corporate and marketing decisions is fundamental. Figure 3–7 represents this principle graphically.

An organization should begin its analysis with the understanding of the buyer. It then organizes itself to provide a product, brand, or services whose qualities can be expected to match the demand of a large enough number of buyers to justify offering the product or service, or both.

The goal of advertising is to contribute to the solution of the man-

FIGURE 3–7
The role of the buyer in the management equation

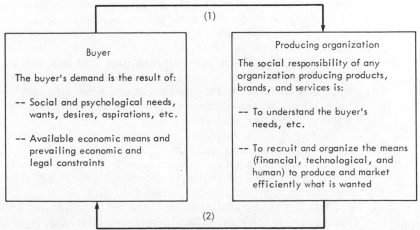

agement equation. This can be accomplished by understanding the needs, wants, and desires of the consumers to whom the production of the firm is directed. The "communication equation" to be solved by the advertiser is to relate the "qualities" of a product to the "qualities" of a market segment. In other words, to match the "attributes" of a group of consumers with the "attributes" of a product, brand, or service. Figure 3–8 gives a graphical representation of the communication equation.

In summarizing current knowledge of individual and group behavior, the psychological makeup of an individual is the result of a strong socialization process that begins immediately after birth and continues through life. The buyer is eminently a social person. The individual's memory, rules of behavior, and motivational forces are the result of his or her social life—of a daily stream of contacts within a

FIGURE 3–8
The role of the buyer in the communication equation

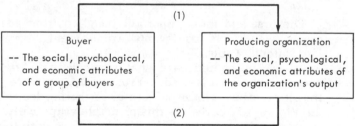

social environment, of attempts to adapt to the environment and to adapt the environment to one's own preferences.

The negotiations with one's own environment begin with the physical perception of the environment. Without physical perception, no environment exists. The process by which an individual gives meaning to any stimulus—psychological perception—is fundamentally simple. The interpretation of an "objective" stimulus varies between individuals. And, for the same person, it also varies according to the situation and over time. Whatever meaning an individual assigns to a stimulus, a stream of complex psychological processes may ensue. Formation and change of opinions and attitudes toward products, brands, and services is a continuous activity, constantly interacting with new infomation received or sought from other sources, such as mass media, salespersons, and personal relationships with relatives, friends, peers and co-workers.

Stimuli coming from all sources undergo a subjective process of psychological perception. For an advertiser, one of the most fundamental lessons based on current knowledge can be put this way: the "objective" knowledge we have about individuals is that they perceive their environent in a "subjective" way.

This increasing ability of buyers to see in a stimulus whatever they want to see is the most difficult and basic challenge to the advertiser.

But understanding and accepting this social psychological freedom of buyers is also rewarding, for it allows the advertiser to relate and to communicate the intended meaning of the message to the audience. In so doing, the communicator has a higher probability of having its audience become aware of the existence of a new brand. And the greater the understanding of the audience's needs and problems, the more likelihood of succeeding in stimulating not only curiosity and interest but also a favorable attitude, perhaps even a motivational drive to try the brand or to continue to use one's own brand rather than switch to a competitor's brand.

The advertising department that can understand and relate to the needs and wants of the intended market segment contributes to the success of the overall marketing program. Alone, however, the advertising manager cannot make up for poor marketing decisions in pricing, product and package design, inventory control, or choice of dealers, nor can he alone overcome the strengths of a competitor's marketing mix.

To the extent that corporate, marketing, and advertising management realize the dominant role of the buyer in their own decisions, the more successful they will be in stimulating demand and the clearer will be the issues bearing on the use of primary and selective demand appeals.

By dividing the potential market into segments, the advertiser can design the advertising, distribution, promotion, price, and even the product itself to appeal to those people who actually buy or are likely to buy the product. If one knows the composition of the market, he will better understand how his customers decide whether or not to buy his product and how he can influence that purchase decision.

For example, if the advertiser is promoting television sets, he could try to determine how such variables as age, sex, health, area of residence, home ownership, family income, recreational interests, marital status, and family size affect whether or not an individual would desire this particular set.

The concept of segmentation is widely used. If one checks on almost any consumer product, such as toiletries, automobiles, cigarettes, beer, liquor, or soap, one can probably figure out what segment the manufacturer is aiming at and how the advertising promotion and product itself have been designed to reach that segment. The shampoo market, for instance, has been divided by many factors, including: men and women; dry, normal, and oily hair; with and without dandruff; and natural and color-treated hair.

The advertiser can use the knowledge of the market in several ways: (1) to sell his product more effectively and (2) to develop a product to reach a particular market; and (3) to check on specific wants of the potential consumers of his product.

Having a target for advertising is a key reason to segment a market. Direct mail advertising, for example, enables one to focus on particular segments. One can choose from mailing lists that highlight almost any factor one desires, from geographic area to income, education, sex, and buying behavior.

Finally, advertising cannot create a want though it may stimulate a latent want. Essentially, the purposes of advertising are (1) to call attention to latent wants, and (2) to increase the urgency of recognized wants.

Questions

1. Define the terms "socialization processes" and "psychological processes."
2. Give a clear example of physical perception.
3. Develop a procedure by which you can prove the difference between physical and psychological perception.
4. Define "motivated perception."
5. Go to the library, search for books in basic psychology, and find examples of motivated perception and motivated forgetting.
6. While in the library, check out two or three books in cultural anthropology and search for examples of differences in the psychological meaning of so-called objective stimuli.
7. Some people living in the ghettos tend to buy luxury cars and other socially visible products. Why?
8. Bring to the class two magazine advertisements that you believe have utilized unusually effective appeals. Explain why you selected them.
9. Bring to class two advertisements you feel are using a weak or poor appeal. Explain the reasons for selecting them.
10. In most families, the housewife or mother does most of the grocery shopping and, hence, the actual buying of the product. However, many advertising people believe that for some of the items on her shopping list, she is strongly influenced in her selection of items or brands by other members of the family, so that advertising appeals should be selected to influence the husband or children. Do you agree? Why?
11. Name three products in the purchase of which you feel the children of the family have great influence on the mother's purchase. Explain why you selected them.
12. Which member, or members, of the family do you think have the most influence on the brand decision for the following: (*a*) automobile, (*b*) refrigerator, (*c*) automatic dishwashing machine, (*d*) coffee, (*e*) sofa, (*f*) bread?
13. In what ways do you feel the knowledge borrowed from sociology and cultural anthropology can be of help to the advertiser in selecting effective appeals?
14. By means of an example, illustrate the difference between primary and selective demand.
15. Under what conditions might an advertiser combine primary and selective demand advertising? Give an example.
16. It is sometimes said that the stimulation of primary demand is a continuous process, so advertisers should always do some primary demand advertising. Do you agree or disagree? Why?
17. Name two examples of products that you feel should be supported with strong primary demand advertising at the present time. Explain why you selected them.

18. Name two products that you feel are especially suited to strong selective demand advertising. Explain your selections.

19. Should the manufacturer of a small executive airplane stress primary or selective appeals in his advertising at present? Why?

Case 3–1 HAMMERMILL PAPER CO.
Use of consumer advertising

Hammermill is a diversified company engaged in five major market areas—fine and printing papers, industrial and packaging papers, converted paper products, wholesale distribution of paper and graphic art supplies, and converted forest products. In recent years, emphasis on the last four of these groups has decreased Hammermill's sensitivity to the cyclical fluctuations that characterize basic pulp and paper manufacturing. This emphasis is expected to continue in the years immediately ahead, although it also expects to grow in its traditional lines of top-quality fine and printing papers. In all its market areas, Hammermill plans to achieve a product mix which capitalizes upon the strengths of high product quality, technological superiority, and marketing expertise. The company's 34 manufacturing and converting locations, 36 wholesale distribution outlets, and a superior group of independent paper merchants provide a nationwide base for manufacture, distribution, and sale of high-quality products to serve diverse and growing markets.

Sales in 1974 were $607,488,000, compared to $477,890,000 in 1973, a 27 percent increase. Net income for 1974 was $35,482,000 or $5.18 per share, approximately twice as much as in 1973.

An unprecedented combination of factors contributed to this performance. For most of the year, Hammermill pulp mills and paper machines operated at virtually full capacity. The ending of price controls in March 1974 enabled Hammermill to realize much-needed price increases to offset higher raw material and operating costs. A favorable supply and demand balance enabled the company to schedule longer runs on paper machines and thereby gain manufacturing efficiency. Development of a more profitable product mix contributed also in a large measure to Hammermill's earnings improvement.

Advertising program

Hammermill's particular paper products are not specifically consumer products. The average person would find it difficult to find a box of Hammermill Bond stationery, or a small supply of its other grades of paper. Nevertheless, Hammermill has been advertising its products in consumer-oriented magazines since 1912, and the objective, simply stated, is to create brand awareness and brand preference for its products.

The company believes it has been meeting those objectives and today Hammermill Bond, for instance, is better known among the general public than its next nine leading competitors combined.

Hammermill's objective essentially is to reach those people who might now—or at some future date—be in a position to specify a particular grade of paper for business usage.

With this in mind, Hammermill has been using *Newsweek, Time* "B," *U.S. News & World Report, Business Week,* and *Sports Illustrated* magazines.

Paper is a relatively low-interest item. Accordingly, the company's strategy is not to discuss paper per se but instead to be the subject of good graphics. Readership scores on this series of ads indicate that the ads are quite appealing and, in fact, on a number of Starch Studies, its ads have had the number-one average cost ratio in specific areas.

In evaluating the ads (See Exhibits 3–1, 2, 3, and 4) Hammermill changed its message slightly in 1975. First of all, in an effort to tie in slightly with the nation's bicentennial, the company narrowed the scope of its subjects from "famous letterheads of history" to "revolutionary letterheads."

At the same time, in an effort to establish more awareness of the broad range of paper grades, it has begun referring to other grades which are produced and, at the same time, it changed from the Hammermill Bond logotype signature to the Hammermill Papers logotype signature at the end of each ad.

Origin of campaign

The origin of this particular campaign evolved a number of years back, when Hammermill first came up with the concept of "famous letterheads of history"—how letterheads for specific people, places, or events might have looked. The company produced a number of hypothetical letterheads and used them in sales promotion with its merchant salesmen distributing the letterheads to printers, advertising agencies, and other paper specifiers. The letterheads went over so well that the company subsequently conducted a contest in which it asked these people to submit their ideas of how letterheads for famous people might have looked.

The contest was a success and many of the letterhead designs submitted to Hammermill were then adapted and illustrated for use in the advertisements.

Several years later, although Hammermill believed that interest in "famous letterheads of history" had declined, it tried to find a vehicle for a similar contest. Accordingly, it conducted its "Hammermill Bond Revolutionary Letterhead Contest" in late 1974. The entries received in this contest and the letterhead designs that were submitted were so good that the company decided to continue its campaign and incorporated some of the designs into the current series of ads. Once again the readership scores confirm that this is a high-interest campaign, and that it is getting readership and that it is adding to the brand preference.

EXHIBIT 3–1

A good letterhead flags people's attention.

It's no surprise that the lady who created Old Glory would have a very creative letterhead.

She certainly knew how important it is to have a symbol that pricks up people's interest.

Of course, good letterheads start with the right paper. That's why you can't go wrong when you print your company letterhead on Hammermill Bond.

Because people recognize the Hammermill Bond watermark and the quality it stands for. Instantly.

They can see Hammermill Bond's richness. Feel its crispness. Hear it crackle to the touch.

Your company's letterhead will command a lot of attention when it's printed on Hammermill Bond.

When you're looking for quality, don't stop with the original. Water-marked Hammermill Xerocopy and Hammermill Electrocopy are made especially for plain paper copiers—to the same exacting specifications as Hammermill Bond.

Hammermill Paper Company, Erie, Pennsylvania 16533.

Whatever you have to put on paper, Hammermill has a paper to put it on.

HAMMERMILL PAPERS®

Courtesy Hammermill Papers

EXHIBIT 3–2

A good letterhead should make people take a second look.

When it came to righting a wrong, Lady Godiva wasn't one to hide behind a woman's skirts.

And her letterhead never lets you forget it.

A good letterhead is like that. It lets people see you for what you are, even before the letter itself says a word.

That should go for your company letterhead, too. And it will when you put it on Hammermill Bond.

Because people recognize the Hammermill Bond watermark and

HAMMERMILL BOND®

the quality it stands for. Instantly. They can see Hammermill Bond's richness. Feel its crispness. Hear it crackle to the touch.

Hammermill Bond. It reveals a lot about your company.

Ask your printer for samples of Hammermill Bond with matching envelopes.

Hammermill Paper Company, Erie, Pennsylvania 16512.

Courtesy Hammermill Papers

EXHIBIT 3–3

Your Humble Servant • Benjamin Franklin

A good letterhead helps others share your vision.

Nearsighted old Ben Franklin proved to be a lot more farsighted than most of his contemporaries.

While they looked at what the country was, he looked ahead to what it could become. As you can plainly see from his letterhead.

As a printer, Franklin would have known that great letterheads start with great paper. So it wouldn't surprise him to find how many company letterheads these days start with Hammermill Bond.

Because people recognize the Hammermill Bond watermark and the quality it stands for. Instantly.

They can see Hammermill Bond's richness. Feel its crispness. Hear it crackle to the touch.

Hammermill Bond—with matching envelopes. See if it doesn't revolutionize your letterhead.

When you're looking for quality, don't stop with the original. Watermarked Hammermill Xerocopy and Hammermill Electrocopy are made especially for plain paper copiers—to the same exacting specifications as Hammermill Bond.

Hammermill Paper Company, Erie, Pennsylvania 16533.

Whatever you have to put on paper, Hammermill has a paper to put it on.

HAMMERMILL PAPERS®

Courtesy Hammermill Papers

EXHIBIT 3–4

A good letterhead captures attention.

Until Washington crossed them up by crossing the Delaware and surprising them at Trenton, the Hessians were unbeatable.

And their letterhead is still pretty hard to beat.

Of course, good letterheads begin with the paper they're printed on. So it's no surprise that many of them begin with Hammermill Bond.

Because people recognize the Hammermill Bond watermark and

the quality it stands for. Instantly.

They can see Hammermill Bond's richness. Feel its crispness. Hear it crackle to the touch.

Hammermill Bond — with matching envelopes. It says a lot

HAMMERMILL PAPERS®

for the image of your company.

When you're looking for quality, don't stop with the original. Watermarked Hammermill Xerocopy and Hammermill Electrocopy are made especially for plain paper copiers — to the same exacting specifications as Hammermill Bond.

Hammermill Paper Company, Erie, Pennsylvania 16533.

Whatever you have to put on paper, Hammermill has a paper to put it on.

Courtesy Hammermill Papers

Questions

1. Evaluate the approach which Hammermill has adopted.
2. Should the greater emphasis be on primary or selective concepts? What conditions exist?
3. How important is the "habit" concept in problems of Hammermill paper?
4. Why does the consumer purchase Hammermill paper? Who is the main buyer of the product?

Case 3–2 **SUNKIST GROWERS, INC.**
Evaluation of consumer demand

In order to meet current and future needs, the Sunkist orange marketing plans have focused on three basic marketing goals:

1. Increase consumer and trade preference for Sunkist brand oranges.
2. Increase the differential between Sunkist grower returns and that of other California/Arizona growers.
3. Increase the overall consumption of eating oranges.

These goals reflect the continuing needs of the Sunkist grower, and are implicit in all marketing programs. It is important, however, that these goals be pursued in concert, in order to maximize returns to the grower.

Domestic consumer advertising objectives

Goals must be translated into specified and, when possible, measurable objectives to provide the necessary guidance for preparing effective programs. It is essential that the advertising objectives be in harmony with the objectives of the other marketing activities in order that the various programs work together to meet the marketing goals.

Several objectives have been established for consumer advertising:

1. Sustain current acceptance of the Sunkist brand as the best-quality eating oranges throughout the United States and Canada.
2. In areas where California/Arizona independents comprise the major competition, create an active consumer preference for the Sunkist brand.
3. In areas where Florida citrus is the most important competitor, establish Sunkist as the finest eating oranges available.
4. Increase consumer interest and desire to incorporate fresh eating oranges into their daily diet as an important, nutritious food item.

Domestic consumer advertising strategies

In order to accomplish the Sunkist orange consumer advertising objectives, the advertising should be formulated on the basis to two major strategy elements. The first is a creative strategy which delineates what should be communicated to the key audiences. The second is a media spending strategy that describes the geography, timing, and nature of the audience for advertising efforts.

1. Consumer creative strategies. The creative strategy acknowledges the need to formulate selling messages on Sunkist's behalf from three different viewpoints: to sell the Sunkist brand, to sell the characteristics of the navel orange, and to sell the current relevance of oranges as natural, nutritious food. At the same time, the creative strategy recognizes that each of these needs can be better accomplished when the claims are presented in the context of appetizing, mouth-watering visuals.

a. Sell the Sunkist brand. The degree to which consumers prefer Sunkist brand oranges has a profound effect upon the price they are willing to pay for the fruit, and thus upon returns. For Sunkist to secure the most advantageous prices the consumer must be made aware of the special steps Sunkist takes to deliver the best quality of oranges possible. The consumer must become willing to pay for that quality and must be encouraged to develop an active preference for Sunkist oranges. To secure active preference, advertising should convey specific claims that demonstrate Sunkist superiority.

These specific claims fall into two broad areas. First are those exclusive Sunkist activities, such as the higher standards for interior and exterior quality, the extensive inspection steps, and so forth. Second are those activities that can be preempted in the name of Sunkist. These would include the meticulous grading and the careful handling in the packinghouse, the special care and attention the grower gives to his groves, the dedication by nursery men to further improve the Sunkist varieties.

Since no independent shipper is making such claims, these can all become identified with Sunkist and add to the meaning of the Sunkist name on every orange.

b. Sell the characteristics of the navel oranges. Through research, consumers have indicated that approximately 79 percent of the oranges are bought to be eaten, approximately 9 percent are bought for juice, and approximately 12 percent are bought for either or both uses.

With fresh orange shipments in the United States running about 75,000 freight cars a year, Sunkist estimates that nearly 7,500 cars are consumed as juice. With Florida shipping some 30,000 cars, there are some 20,000 cars of Florida fruit purchased to be eaten. All California/Arizona oranges, navels and valencias alike, are better suited for eating than the Florida competition. But the navel has particular attributes that should be presented to the consumer. This is particularly true in the eastern half of the United States, where these attributes are most noticeable when compared to the predominate Florida fruit.

With these facts in mind, Sunkist's advertising should focus on the superior eating qualities of the navel and the careful handling and grading in order to preempt these appeals for the Sunkist brand.

c. Sell the current relevance of oranges as a nutritious, natural food. Of the last 20 years, the current period appears to be an excellent time in which to sell fresh oranges. Modern housewives and mothers are actively concerned about nutrition. The 1970 Psychographic Study of Attitudes about fresh oranges reflects a nearly universal appeal of fresh orange health benefits. A recent study completed by *Better Homes & Gardens* indicated that approximately three out of four homemakers go out of their way to see that all their meals are nutritious. In the midst of this growing desire for fresh, natural, nutritious food, stands the orange. The orange is refreshing, sweet, juicy, and easy to eat. It doesn't come in a cumbersome package, bottle, or box. It's simply an orange, a fresh, naturally nutritious, enjoyable fruit to eat.

   d. Sell the appetite appeal of the fresh orange. Each of the first three viewpoints can be significant for Sunkist. Yet each one starts from the point at which a consumer has some active desire for an orange. Recognizing this, the creative materials employed for Sunkist should combine specific rational selling messages with emotional, appetizing photography stages to generate the greatest primary demand for a fresh, refreshing, succulent orange. This approach has been employed in the television advertising for the last three years with excellent success. Research still indicates that such appetite-appeal photography heightens the viewer's desire for an orange, and thus provides a climate in which other specific claims can be even more effective.

   The creative materials should also provide a mixture of elements, focusing on various viewpoints. From these appeals the program can shift emphasis from brand to navel to nutrition as the local market and the seasonal opportunities suggest to be the most productive.

   2. Consumer media strategy. The media strategy should combine the economic advantages of the careful development of advertising weight, geographically and seasonally to increase demand where the greatest development potential exists, while maintaining demand in the remainder of the marketing area. The focus should be on key target audiences known to provide maximum sales opportunity.

   a. Utilize broad national programs, plus development market efforts. To maintain a strong level of demand for Sunkist fruit in the broad United States and Canadian markets, national advertising programs should continue to be used. In addition, greater emphasis should be applied to major markets which, in combination, represent the opportunity for significant growth in total revenue.

   b. Take advantage of seasonal opportunities. The winter and early spring months represent the period during which the greatest portion of orange sales occur. This is when one finds the greatest consumer interest, the greatest trade cooperation, and the best potential for displacing Florida in much of the country. It is also true that the consumers who start an orange habit during this period continue well into the early summer months. In the tracking studies of recent years, Sunkist has seen that higher levels of consumption gained during the early months persisted into June and July.

   c. Focus on key potential households. Research continues to indicate that children eat more oranges than do adults. And their influences leads to the fact that households with children consume more than twice as many oranges than do households with no children. Further, it has been amply demonstrated that strong marketing efforts can persuade both children and adults to increase their consumption of a particular product and to specify a particular brand. At the same time, the children do not make the food purchases themselves; mothers, as the shopping agent, generally do that. Consequently, mothers in these key households are an equally important target group for Sunkist. The program should seek to reach both the consuming children and their mothers. This audience combination should provide the most effective selling opportunity for Sunkist oranges.

General data and information

Market trend. While it appears that by 1978 the Florida crop may grow by 12 percent and its domestic fresh supplies by 37 percent, the Sunkist navel crop is expected to grow only 6 percent and the valencia crop looks to decline 10%. Therefore, a significant increase in domestic fresh sales would cause a particularly marked improvement in overall grower revenue from all sources.

Sunkist faces problems at the store level. In analyzing the domestic market situation, there are three considerations to review:

a. Competitive situation.

b. Consumer situation.

c. Trade situation.

a. The success of the Sunkist advertising has resulted in a competitive situation whereby other companies have utilized some part of the corporate name. In a theoretical sense it's legal, but in a practical sense the competition's strategy of living off Sunkist's name is questionable. Sun Treat, Sun Giant, Sun Rapt, to name a few, are using the "Sun" to capitalize on Sunkist's advertising effort. Tenneco also has "legally" duplicated the corporate logo.

b. The consumer situation witnesses a troubled consumer attempting to buy the essential needs with a shrinking dollar budget. The decisions at the store level are premised on alternative purchases. When the consumer evaluates the purchase of oranges, there are grocery purchases and alternative produce purchases and citrus purchases that could be made. These alternatives, considered in the decision process, are necessary to stay within a fixed food budget. If effective advertising helps to influence the decision in the home two actions should be considered. The first is Sunkist availability, and the second is in-store promotion either in the form of point-of-purchase materials or in better brand identification.

c. The trade situation ties in with the competitive and consumer situations. There is a growing number of retailers who believe that Sunkist is not worth a premium price. Yet, many retailers believe that Sunkist is worth a premium price for it's brand image and it's ongoing advertising effort.

There are also many new produce buyers and merchandising

EXHIBIT 3–5
Production and utilization projections—Domestic production and fresh utilization of oranges (in carloads)

Florida production is growing faster than that in California/Arizona.

	1973–74	1974–75	1976–77	*Percent change* 1976–77 *versus* 1973–74
Production				
Florida	334,000	346,500	373,000	+12
California/				
Arizona.......	95,365	91,654	92,578	− 3
Fresh utilization				
Florida	24,000	28,700	32,800	+37
California/				
Arizona.......	51,646	51,879	52,662	+ 2
(Sunkist)	(36,800)	(36,900)	(37,400)	+ 2

managers in the chains throughout the United States and Canada. Many of these may be looking only at cost efficiencies. This trade situation analysis dictates a need for a beefed-up trade advertising and promotion programs.

In summary, the competitive, consumer, and trade considerations, as presented, demonstrate a need for planned interrelationships. Sunkist has to convince the consumer to buy, through its effective ads, and must insure that the fruit is there when the consumer goes to buy it; also, Sunkist must make sure it's easily recognizable as "Sunkist" and not some other similar sounding brand. Additional data follow.

Conclusion

Factors favoring Sunkist's growth:

1. Heaviest orange users are the fastest growing segment of population—young families with children. They are educated, affluent, and careful about what they buy.

EXHIBIT 3–6
Sunkist economic situation

The growing cost of handling and marketing the fruit is not being offset by higher FOBs.

	1962–63	1972–73	*Percent change*
Navels			
Volume (Carloads)...................	12,291	17,186	+40
Domestic FOB.....................	$3.61	$3.58	− 1
Domestic on-tree return	$2.54	$1.87	−26
Valencias			
Volume (carloads)	12,238	17,750	+45
Domestic FOB.....................	$3.13	$3.41	+ 9
Domestic on-tree return	$2.06	$1.69	−18

2. Characteristics of Sunkist oranges have broad consumer appeal.
3. Sunkist brand is preferred by over 70 percent of consumers.
4. Sunkist has pinpointed regional areas of the domestic market which appear to hold particular potential for growth. Major gains may be achieved without involving entire market.
5. Current Sunkist commercials have secured good results and can be continued with minor changes.
6. Sunkist has successfully tested a development program utilizing heavy weights of advertising. In each of the two sets of test markets, the incremental revenue more than paid for the costs of the program and by substantial amounts.

EXHIBIT 3–7
Problems facing the Sunkist domestic orange franchise

1. The average sales value of a car of oranges in 1972–73 was little different than for one in 1962–63.

	1962–63	1972–73	Percent change
SK* domestic fresh volume (cars)	24,529	34,939	+42
SK domestic fresh sales ($000)	82,923	121,327	+46

* SK = Sunkist.

2. Competition for the consumer's dollar is great. In fact, approximately 3,000 new grocery store products are introduced in various areas of the country each year. In citrus, Florida is spending heavily in consumer media.

Florida Citrus Commission media expenditures (1973)

Network radio	$ 162,800
Spot TV	1,168,900
Network TV	6,995,700
Newspapers/Supplements	17,300
Magazines	410,600
Total	$8,755,300

3. On-tree returns are significantly higher on fresh utilization than on products.

On-tree prices, 1972–73 ($ per carton)

	Domestic fresh	Export fresh	Products*
Navels	1.96	2.78	.20
Valencias	1.80	1.63	.14

* 1971–72.

The California/Arizona orange grower is caught in a cost/price squeeze. Demand levels for fresh oranges must be raised over a significant portion of the business for the grower to earn a profit. This increased demand may result from a change in price, volume, or a combination of the two.

EXHIBIT 3–8
Income, costs, and production projection

California oranges, on-tree farm value and
income per acre (Valencias)

	1964–65	1971–72
On-tree farm value per acre	$638	$417
Cultural cost per acre	509	651
Income before interest on investment plus depreciation on trees............	129	−234

Potential Sunkist production
ranges (carloads)

	1974–75	1976–77
Navels		
High	36,700	37,700
Low.....	23,700	24,000
Valencias		
High	46,200	45,400
Low.....	28,000	27,400

Inflation is eroding the Sunkist advertising dollar. The advertising weight in 1972–73 had declined to 45 percent of what it was in 1968–69.

Sunkist domestic media expenditures—oranges

Year	Media budgeted (millions)	Percent of assessment income	$ per 1,000 population	1968 $ per 1,000 population	Gross potential messages*	Index of advertising weight
1968–69	$3.5	57%	$16.00	$16.00	192	100
1969–70	2.8	54	14.00	13.30	143	74
1970–71	2.4	49	11.00	9.90	118	61
1971–72	2.7	43	11.00	9.40	132	69
1972–73	1.8	30	8.00	6.40	86	45
1973–74	3.1	52	12.90	9.98	1.48	77

* Available budget/average cost-per-thousand Sunkist TV buys in million of household impressions.

EXHIBIT 3–8 (*concluded*)

Media costs will continue to rise.

Advertising media cost indexes

	Network TV	Spot TV	Spot radio	Magazines	Newspapers
1960	100	100		100	100
1965	137	128	100*	127	108
1970	172	159	110	143	118
1975	204	186	120	163	128

* 1966 used due to change in method of cost computation.

Case Questions

1. Should Sunkist use a different appeal for parents and children, such as an emotional appeal for children and a logical appeal for parents? Why?
2. To what extent should income figures be used in evaluating the buyers for oranges?
3. What changes in demand for oranges are likely to result as a result of the shift toward suburban living?
4. Are the number of people in an area an accurate index of its importance as a market for oranges?
5. What do you think of the marketing goals and advertising objectives as presented in the case?

Case **SCM CORPORATION**
3–3 **Setting marketing targets**

SCM Corporation is a diversified manufacturing company with sales in 1974 of $1.2 billion. Its products are used in many sectors of the consumer, industrial, and office markets in the United States and around the world.

Consumer products include Smith-Corona typewriters, Glidden paints, Proctor-Silex appliances, and Durkee foods.

Industrial products include chemical coatings, industrial and institutional goods, pigments and colors, metal powders, pulp and paper, organic chemicals, ceramic frits and industrial processing equipment.

Office products include SCM copiers, typewriters, telecommunications equipment for military and commercial users, and business forms and stationery.

Its six major lines of business extend from coatings and resins, the largest with sales of $312 million, to chemicals, sixth largest, with sales of $116.7 million. SCM's international sales have been increasing over the last few years. In 1974, as an example, 18.1 percent of its sales were outside the United States, compared to the 15.8 percent in 1973. Despite the growth, however, this is still a relatively small percentage for a company of its size, though the company believes that multinationalism is a sound concept.

Smith-Corona typewriter

In 1973, Smith-Corona planned to introduce a new portable typewriter product; this was considered a major development because the firm took the typewriter ribbon and put it into a cartridge. The cartridge could be changed in three seconds—and the typist's hands never touch the ribbon. The product concept represented the following, from a marketer's point of view:

1. The basic typewriter ribbon handling mechanism had to be redesigned. Many fewer parts were required in the new mechanism. This resulted in a more advanced, reliable machine.
2. A ribbon in a cartridge meant no more messy ribbon changes—the hands stay clean.
3. It meant speed in changing ribbons.
4. It meant simplicity—anyone could change it.
5. The cartridge concept permitted typing in a variety of colors—Smith-Corona made a wide choice of colors available.
6. New home typists could experience the quality results of typing with carbon film for important correspondence and easily switch back to the less expensive nylon ribbon for everyday use—both types would be available at no charge with initial typewriter purchase.
7. An erasure cartridge was developed—a quick way to take the mess out of correcting errors.

The objective and strategy which the company set are given below:

Smith-Corona
"CHRIS"
Consumer Creative Strategy

1. **Objective:**
   To announce Smith-Corona's invention of a totally new line of electric portable typewriters featuring the unique Coronamatic Ribbon Cartridge.
2. **Strategy:**
   a. *Target Audience*
      Parents of students aged 15–22.
      This group is judged to be largely in the 35–54 age group in middle to upper income households. (HH).
   b. *Buying incentive:*
      Smith-Corona has invented the totally automatic ribbon cartridge that lets you replace ribbons and change colors in seconds without ever touching the ribbon.
   c. *Tonality:*
      Introductory and important, with "new invention" flavor.
3. **Mandatories:**
   a. SCM tri-bar and logo must appear in all advertising in proportions dictated by the Corporate Handbook.
   b. Close-up demonstration of the typewriter and repetition of the cartridge replacement sequence and subsequent typing.

4. **Media objectives and strategy:**
   a. *Media objective*

   The prime media objective is to make as many potential consumers as affordable aware of the availability of the Smith-
   Corona.

   b. *Media strategy:*

   (1) *Target audience:*

   The 1972 W. R. Simmons study—"Selective Markets and
   the Media Reaching them"—dimensionalizes the size of
   the typewriter-owning households as shown below:

		Households	
		Number	Percent
		(millions)	U.S.
Own a typewriter		26.9	42.3
Acquired	in past year	2.7	4.3
	1 to 3 years ago	6.3	9.8
	3 years or less............	9.0	14.1
	4 to 10 years ago	9.4	14.9
	More than 10 yrs. ago	8.5	13.4
	4 years or more	17.9	28.2

   Thus, it is evident that during any given year, between 2
   to 3 percent of total U.S. households acquire a typewriter.
   This cannot be considered a mass market.

   However, the persons residing in the acquiring
   household can be described demographically as shown,
   based upon acquisition of 1) any typewriter within the
   past year and 2) a Smith-Corona typewriter—last purchase.

   It is interesting to note the differences in demographic
   profile between those households acquiring a typewriter
   in the past year versus those households that acquired a
   Smith-Corona as their last purchase.

   The Smith-Corona buyer tends to be less heavily
   skewed in the 35–49 year group vs. all others, and more
   heavily skewed in the 25–34 year group. The Smith-
   Corona purchaser is also better represented by the professional and managerial occupations, but less well represented in households with children 6–17 and with $15,000
   and over annual income.

   (2) *Reach versus frequency:*

   With the introduction of an exciting and beneficial innovation, Smith-Corona must disseminate its message to as
   many potential consumers as possible to make them
   aware of the availability of the CHRIS typewriter feature,
   stimulate interest in the product, and motivate a buying

Demographics	Acquired any typewriter in last year			Last brand purchased Smith-Corona		
	No. (millions)	Percent	Index	No. (millions)	Percent	Index
Age of head of household						
35–49 years.	1.5	54.8	191	2.0	35.9	126
25–34 years.	0.3	12.5	70	1.2	21.1	118
Occupation of household Professional;						
managerial	0.9	34.7	153	2.5	44.2	197
Clerical; sales	0.5	18.7	170	0.7	11.7	106
Education of household Attended/graduated						
college	1.2	42.4	165	2.5	43.9	171
Presence of children in household						
6–17 years	1.6	57.3	158	2.7	47.1	129
Race						
White	2.5	91.6	102	5.3	93.4	104
Household income						
$15,000 and over . .	1.1	39.9	207	2.0	35.3	183
$10,000–14,000 . . .	0.8	29.6	128	1.8	31.5	135
Locality type						
Metro suburban. . . .	1.1	39.1	112	2.4	42.5	120
County size						
A.	1.3	47.2	116	2.7	47.9	118

decision. Thus, reach becomes primary. However, to the extent affordable, attempts will be made to generate adequate levels of contact frequency against all consumers exposed to the CHRIS message.

(3) *National versus regional support:*
Advertising will be national to provide support for the nationwide introduction of the CHRIS typewriter feature. If, however, initial sales patterns indicate an inordinate skewing towards certain types of markets, specific areas may be singled out to receive heavy-up support for Christmas and graduation efforts.

(4) *Seasonality:*
The advertising effort will be confined to three key sales periods coincidental with back-to-school, Christmas, and graduation. If, however, dollars permit, supportive weight also will be scheduled between these periods.

EXHIBIT 3–9

Smith-Corona introduces the 3-second ribbon change.

Time it yourself on our new cartridge ribbon typewriter.

First it will amaze you. Then it will impress you.

The amazing part is that we succeeded in putting a typewriter ribbon in a cartridge for the quickest, simplest typewriter ribbon change imaginable. Also, the cleanest.

The impressive part is that Coronamatic™ Ribbon Cartridges come in nylon and carbon film (the kind usually available only with expensive office typewriters).

So in the same 3 seconds it takes to change a cartridge, you can now change to carbon film for typing that looks like printing.

It's like having two typewriters in one. One for day-to-day use. One for more professional-looking correspondence or reports.

And in case you make a mistake, we put a correction ribbon in a Coronamatic cartridge so you can correct errors, in seconds.

We also put an assortment of colors into the cartridges—so you can add a little (or a lot of) color to your typing if you feel like it.

Smith-Corona's new cartridge ribbon typewriters. In electric portable and office models.

Now you have a lot of reasons to <u>want</u> to change typewriter ribbons.

SCM SMITH-CORONA
SCM CORPORATION

Introductory offer: Participating dealers will give you an eraser cartridge, plus two film cartridges to introduce you to professional typing. This offer good on all new portable cartridge typewriters purchased before 10/1/73.

:01 Press cartridge release.

:02 Cartridge snaps out.

:03 Snap in another cartridge.

(5) *Recommended media:*

A combination of night network television and national magazines is recommended to introduce the CHRIS typewriter feature available on Smith-Corona typewriters.

(6) *Editorial environment:*

The selected media, in addition to reaching the desired target audience, must possess an editorial environment consistent with the image of Smith-Corona as the leading most prestigious and most innovative of all portable typewriter manufacturers.

(7) *Merchandising opportunities:*

Although media will be chosen based upon their ability to fulfill the objectives and strategy, wherever feasible, media which can stimulate the Smith-Corona sales force as well as the retail trade will be selected.

[The introductory spread advertisement is given in Exhibit 3–9.]

Case questions

1. How does one determine who the major decision maker is for the Smith-Corona typewriter?
2. As a result of the shifts which are now occuring in the distribution of the population among the several age groups, what factors will become more

and which less significant in influencing the buying habits for the Smith-Corona typewriter?

3. What demographic breakdown should be used for the Smith-Corona typewriter? Why?

4. Indicate the market targets that you would recommend for Smith-Corona and develop for the product the primary emphasis which should be used.

Case 3–4

LEVER BROTHERS COMPANY
Identifying the manufacturer

The Lever Brothers Company executives are faced with the decision of determining to what degree they should identify the name of the company with the variety of products which they advertise.

Among the major consumer products which Lever manufactures are the following: laundry detergents (Breeze, Rinso, Silver Dust, Cold Water Surf, Advanced All, Fluffy All, Wisk, Cold Water All, and Vim); all-purpose household cleaner (Handy Andy); fabric softener (Final Touch); Lux Flakes; Dove-for-dishes; Lux Liquid; Swan Liquid; Dishwasher All; toilet bars (Dove, Lifebuoy, Phase III, Lux Beauty Soap, Praise); toothpastes (Pepsodent, Pepsodent Floride, Super Stripe); Pepsodent Tooth Powder; toothbrushes (Pepsodent, Life Line, Life Line Professional); Pepsodent Antiseptic; and a number of food products, such as Imperial, Sof-Spread Imperial, Good Luck, and Golden Glow Margarine, Spry Shortening, Mrs. Butterworth's Syrup, and Lucky Whip Dessert Topping.

Lever Brothers Company is the second largest company in the industry and is also a leading member of the worldwide Unilever organization, which includes more than 500 operating companies. The company over the years has emphasized individual brand advertising. It has used virtually all media—magazines, newspapers, supplements, direct mail, radio, and television. Its largest expenditure goes into television because the executives believe this medium is very effective in reaching millions of people.

History

Greeting visitors at the entrances of Lever House and Lever Brothers manufacturing plants throughout the country is a stainless steel plaque stating the mission of the company as its founder, William Hesketh Lever, saw it: ". . . to make cleanliness commonplace; to lessen work for women; to foster health and contribute to personal attractiveness, that life may be more enjoyable and rewarding for the people who use our products."

The business began in 1895 when Mr. Lever opened a small office in New York City to handle the sale of Lifebuoy and Sunlight soaps, both then manufactured in England. Sales for the first year barely reached 50,000 cases. Manufacture of these products was started in the United States three years later, following the acquisition in 1897 of Curtis Davis & Company, a small soap concern in Cambridge, Massachusetts. In 1899, the sales office was transferred from New York to Cambridge, and the new company was incorporated in the state of Maine as Lever Brothers, Ltd. (Boston Works). The present name, Lever Brothers Company, was adopted in 1903.

Progress during the early years was steady but slow. Originally, only about 50 people were employed. The country was divided into 2 sales districts: the New England Territory, served by 12 salesmen working out of the Cambridge plant, and the so-called General Territory, which took in the rest of the country and was serviced first by jobbers and later by an exclusive sales agent.

These formative years played an essential role in the company's future success. One significant development was the establishment of a laboratory primarily concerned with testing the quality of raw materials. This was the forerunner of the present Research and Development Center in Edgewater, New Jersey, which serves as a continuous source of new and improved products.

In 1912, the company established a national sales organization and entered an era of rapid growth. Three still-famous products were introduced: Lux Flakes in 1914; Rinso, the first granulated laundry soap, in 1919; and, in 1924, Lux Toilet Soap, the first white, milled, perfumed soap made and sold in this country at a popular price. Supported by strong advertising and promotional campaigns, each moved into a position of market leadership. Sales soared to millions of cases! By 1929, the company had become the third largest manufacturer of soap and glycerine in the United States.

The growing demand for Lever Brothers products sparked a period of major expansion of manufacturing facilities. In 1930, the company constructed a major new plant at Hammond, Indiana. Another new plant was opened in Edgewater, New Jersey, in 1933, to manufacture shortening. Covo, a bulk shortening for commercial use, was produced at first; then, in 1936, Spry was introduced as a consumer product. These were Lever's first entries in the edible products field. In 1939, plants in Baltimore and St. Louis were acquired through purchase of the Hecker Products Corporation's soap interests. Among the products acquired was Silver Dust, a granulated laundry soap.

The end of World War II ushered in a new period of diversification and expansion of the Lever product line. This was achieved primarily through the purchase of other companies already established in related consumer goods fields. In 1944, Lever acquired the Pepsodent Company, a leading manufacturer of dentrifices, toothbrushes, and oral antiseptics, with a plant in Chicago. This established Lever Brothers as a major factor in the oral hygiene field. Four years later, the company achieved an important position in the food field through purchase of the John F. Jelke Company, a pioneer manufacturer of margarine and related food products. Within a few years, both Pepsodent and Jelke were completely integrated with the Lever organization and product lines.

During the early 1950s, the company again expanded its physical facilities and laid the groundwork for another period of growth.

Manufacturing operations were extended to the West Coast in 1951 with the opening of the Los Angeles plant. Two years later, a new plant was constructed at St. Louis to replace the Hecker Products facility acquired in 1939.

To meet the growing business needs of expanding operations, more office space and a more convenient business location were required. The company accordingly in 1949 moved its headquarters from Cambridge to New York City. Lever House, the new headquarters building on Park Avenue, was opened in 1952. Designed to provide ideal working conditions, the 24-story glass and stainless steel structure has received many awards for building excellence and is considered "one of the most significant buildings in the past 100 years of architecture in America." It has been called "the most honored office building in the world."

Of special importance to the company's growth in modern times was the opening in 1952 of the multimillion-dollar Research and Development Center in Edgewater, New Jersey. This scientific center united the research groups which had previously worked at separate plant locations and put at their disposal the facilities of a complete and modern laboratory. As a result of the steady stream of new and improved products that have come out of his laboratory in recent years, Lever Brothers has maintained a rapid pace for new product introductions.

Significant firsts have been scored by a number of its products in their respective fields. Notable among these are Imperial, the first premium margarine with the taste of the "high-priced spread"; Dove, a completely new type of beauty bar containing cleansing cream; Wisk, the first heavy-duty liquid laundry detergent; Lux Liquid, a pioneer liquid dishwashing detergent; White Lifebuoy, the first pure white deodorant bar; and Lux Beauty Soap, the first popular soap to offer consumers a variety of colors and the first to offer the sealed protection of an aluminum foil wrapper.

Another major development of recent years was the acquisition in 1957 from the Monsanto Company of the "All" family of controlled-suds powder detergents, which include Advanced All, Fluffy All, and Dishwasher All. The newest member of the "All" family is Cold Water All, introduced in 1963, the first nationally distributed heavy-duty liquid detergent that launders the entire family wash in cold water.

Other new products, all introduced since 1958, include Super Stripe Tooth Paste, which added a new visual appeal to dental hygiene habits; Life Line Toothbrushes; Lucky Whip Dessert Topping and Topping Mix; Mrs. Butterworth's Syrup, the original pancake syrup with butter in it; Golden Glow Margarine, a soft margarine containing liquid corn oil; Praise, a deodorant beauty soap; Pine Green Lifebuoy; Pink Dove; Vim detergent tablets; Warm Water Swan, a liquid dishwashing detergent; Handy Andy with Ammonia, an all-purpose liquid household cleaner; Cold Water Surf, a laundry detergent that works effectively in hot or cold water; Final Touch fabric softener; Dove-for-dishes, a new light-duty liquid; Phase III, a completely different toilet bar combining cream bar mildness and deodorant protection; and Sof-Spread Imperial, a soft margarine and companion product to Imperial Margarine.

In April, 1966, Lever acquired the nationally distributed Glamorene line of rug cleaners, cleaning appliances, and other household specialty cleaning products, which are sold through a network of brokers and in-store rental appliance franchises. Headquarters, research, and principal manufacturing facilities of the Glamorene Products Corporation, operated as a subsidiary of Lever Brothers Company, are located at Clifton, New Jersey. The Lever unconditional guarantee has become a trademark for quality products and dependable performance.

Case questions

1. What demographic target should Lever try to reach?
2. How might attitudinal segmentation be used in forming the target?
3. To what extent should Lever Brothers Company place emphasis on its company name in its advertising?

Case **TESORO PETROLEUM CORPORATION**
3–5 **Considering an appeal**

Tesoro Petroleum Corporation is an international integrated petroleum company and is primarily engaged in the following activities:

1. Exploration for and development and production of oil and gas reserves.
2. Refining and marketing of crude oil and petroleum products.
3. Transportation of crude oil and petroleum products and manufacturing and leasing of oil-field service equipment.

Tesoro's first decade ended in December 1974. During this period the company established its place as an important American energy company.

In its exploration for oil and gas reserves, its research included not only offshore United States and Alaskan sources, but also continued research in such countries as Indonesia, Trinidad, the Dutch sector of the North Sea, Canada, and Bolivia.

Refining

Tesoro owns and operates four crude oil refineries which on September 30, 1974 had an aggregate refining capacity of approximately 64,000 barrels per calendar day. Tesoro's newest and largest refinery was constructed in Alaska during 1969–70 and now has a capacity of approximately 38,000 barrels per calendar day. Its other refineries are located at Carrizo Springs, Texas; Newcastle, Wyoming; and Wolf Point, Montana. The shipments of the various products processed at its refineries have been as follows:

	Year ended September 30 (in thousands of gallons)				
	1970	*1971*	*1972*	*1973*	*1974*
Gasoline	49,148	67,117	91,317	105,226	159,065
Jet fuel	124,585	159,590	155,469	142,098	148,746
Intermediates	53,499	95,230	109,082	145,885	110,037
Fuel oil	112,255	154,512	169,120	226,284	392,794
Liquid petroleum gas	1,160	1,715	1,409	774	3,523
Other	—	—	853	790	—
Total	340,647	478,164	527,250	621,057	814,165

Transportation

Tesoro is an independent purchaser and gatherer of crude oil, condensates, and natural gas liquids from leases, resellers, and certain processing plants in the United States, principally in the states of Alaska, California, Louisiana, Montana, New Mexico, Oklahoma, and Texas. The crude oil, condensates and natural gas liquids so gathered and transported by its trucks and pipelines is delivered to its refineries and exchanged with or resold to other users. Volumes during fiscal 1974 represented by these commercial activities were approximately 70,000 barrels per day. An additional 20,000 barrels per day was transported by Tesoro's wholly owned subsidiary, Plains Pipe Line Company, an intrastate common carrier in Wyoming. The company also operates a total of 505 miles of various diameter pipelines in Louisiana, Texas, and Wyoming.

On June 27, 1974, the Tesoro Company acquired all of the capital stock of Eagle Transport Company, a Texas corporation. Eagle Transport's name was changed to, and now operates as, Tesoro Transportation Company. Tesoro Transportation is a petroleum and petroleum products, petrochemical, and various dry commodities transport operation, with intrastate authority in Texas and limited interstate authority to haul various products. Tesoro now owns or leases a fleet of approximately 180 petroleum transport trucks.

Equipment

Tesoro, through its subsidiary Land and Marine Rental Company, rents drill pipe, drill collars, blow-out preventers, and other oil-field service equipment to oil and gas companies and drilling operators in the Gulf Coast, Mid-Continent, West Texas, and Rocky Mountain areas, and in Alaska. Tesoro's subsidiary, Wheatley Company, manufactures specialized pumps and valves used primarily in the petroleum industry.

Coal

Tesoro Coal Company, a wholly owned subsidiary of Tesoro Petroleum Corporation, was formed in 1974 in order to help provide the

TABLE 1

Activities	Year ended September 30				
	1970	1971	1972	1973	1974
Oil and gas production					
Percent gross income	11.6	11.1	9.9	9.9	18.9
Percent operating profit	40.8	43.1	40.2	35.4	63.0
Refining and marketing					
Percent gross income	46.6	52.5	59.8	60.2	56.7
Percent operating profit	29.0	31.7	36.0	44.2	23.3
Transportation, manufacturing and leasing of oil-field service equipment, and other activities:					
Percent gross income:					
Transportation and marketing of crude oil and petroleum products	30.7	28.1	23.8	23.2	18.1
Manufacturing and leasing of oil field service equipment and other activities	11.1	8.3	6.5	6.7	6.3
	41.8	36.4	30.3	29.9	24.4
Percent operating profit	30.2	25.2	23.8	20.4	13.7

need for coal in the United States. In January 1975, Tesoro Coal Company had an estimated 900 million tons of coal reserves under option and is operating one underground mine to evaluate expansion potential.

Table 3–1 summarizes the percentage contributions to gross income and to operating profit of the activities for the five years ended September 30, 1974.

For fiscal 1974, gross income was $534.9 million, up 84.9 percent from $289.3 million in 1973. Consolidated net earnings increased to $60.9 million, a gain of 206 percent from the $19.9 million of last year. Primary net earnings per share increased to $5.76, a gain of 203 percent from $1.90 in 1973.

Marketing

Tesoro's major retail marketing activities are on the West Coast, Alaska, South Dakota, and Wyoming. Through its subsidiary Digas Company of Delaware, formed in February 1971, the company operates high-volume retail gasoline stations, the majority of which are in California. Of the Digas stations, 46 are located at Gemco and Memco stores owned by Lucky Stores, Inc. The company has an exclusive agreement with Lucky under which it has certain rights and obligations with respect to opening additional stations. Pursuant to this agreement and an agreement with Interstate Department Stores, Inc. (discussed below), the company opened ten stations in 1971, seven stations in 1972, eight stations in 1973, and five stations in 1974. The Lucky agreement expires in 1990, subject to earlier termination in respect of certain leases thereunder. The agreement contains certain restrictions on the Company, including restrictions on its right to open competing stations.

Interstate is presently being reorganized under Chapter X of the Federal bankruptcy laws. The agreement which Tesoro had with Interstate provided a right to operate stations and to open new stations at White Front stores owned by Interstate. Although the White Front stores have been closed, Tesoro continues to operate the 32 gasoline stations at those locations. These 32 stations account for approximately 34 percent of the total gasoline sold by the company.

Table 3–2 gives the gallons of gasoline sold by Digas stations and the number of stations operated for the last five years:

TABLE 2

	1970	1971	1972	1973	1974
Gallons of gasoline (000 omitted)	76,357	97,588	117,402	144,792	175,630
Number of stations in operation at end of year.	54	64	71	77	82

In addition to the stations operated by Digas Company of Delaware, Tesoro markets its products under its own brand and other company brands through 102 other gasoline stations and truck stops.

In Alaska, Tesoro, through its bulk terminals in Kenai, Anchorage, Valdez, Fairbanks, Tok, and Glenallen, markets brand gasolines, fuel oils, heating oils, diesel fuels, turbine fuels, and other petroleum products from its owned or leased outlets.

Tesoro is also engaged in wholesale and retail distribution of lubricants, fuels, and specialty petroleum products.

Through its subsidiary Tesoro-Europe Petroleum B.V., it markets light, medium, and heavyweight oil to industrial and retail customers and to governmental installations in Europe.

Tesoro's statement of consolidated earnings is given in Exhibit 3–10:

EXHIBIT 3–10

TESORO PETROLEUM CORPORATION
Statement of Consolidated Earnings

	Year ended September 30	
	1974	*1973*
Income:		
Gross operating revenues	$510,765,000	282,649,000
Equity in earnings of unconsolidated foreign investment (Note K).	22,241,000	5,526,000
Other	1,941,000	1,089,000
	534,947,000	289,264,000

EXHIBIT 3–10 (*concluded*)

	Year ended September 30	
	1974	*1973*
Costs and expenses:		
Costs of sales and operating expenses.....	436,431,000	249,171,000
General and administrative..............	8,763,000	6,174,000
Depreciation, depletion and amortization ..	12,344,000	7,884,000
Interest expense......................	6,844,000	2,849,000
Other	101,000	2,406,000
	464,483,000	268,484,000
Earnings before Income taxes and extraordinary item	70,464,000	20,780,000
Provision for taxes on income (note G)......	11,749,000	906,000
Earnings before extraordinary item..........	58,715,000	19,874,000
Extraordinary item—Tax benefits of net operating loss carryforwards..................	2,234,000	—
Net earnings	$ 60,949,000	19,874,000
Primary earnings per share (note C):		
Earnings before extraordinary item........ $	5.55	1.90
Extraordinary item.....................	.21	—
Net earnings......................... $	5.76	1.90
Fully diluted earnings per share (note C):		
Earnings before extraordinary item........ $	4.95	1.78
Extraordinary item.....................	.18	—
Net earnings......................... $	5.13	1.78

Case questions

1. To whom should Tesoro advertise?
2. Why or why not should Tesoro advertise its products?
3. Compare and contrast the buying motives for Tesoro's products to those of the buyer of men and women's clothing.

part two

Economic and social issues

4

THE ECONOMIC ROLES
OF ADVERTISING

A discussion of the possible roles of the advertising industry began in the late 1600s in England and, surprisingly, not much
has changed since then. It is somewhat arbitrary to distinguish
economic from social roles, but we shall follow this traditional distinction and, in this chapter, shall provide a summary of the main questions that have been raised about the institution's economic roles.

Does advertising perform a function in the economy?

For some people, the answer to this question is negative: in their
opinion, buyers and sellers do not need to acquire or to send information via mass media, and thus the economy does not need an advertising industry. There are at least three problems with this point of view.

First, as we have seen in Chapter 1, historical evidence suggests
that buyers (consumers and organizations) search for and use information and show interest in acquiring information at the lowest possible cost. Second, this viewpoint is at odds with the claim that buyers
should be given "perfect" information, because mass media provide
only one of the channels through which information may be supplied
to potential buyers. Third, throughout history sellers in different societies usually find it economical to send messages to potential buyers
through mass media.

But to some other people, supplying economic information to buyers through mass media is a useful function. However, some of these
people argue that the structure of the present advertising industry is
not adequate. For instance, the claim is often made that the advertising institution costs too much. Sometimes, suggestions are made about

changes in the industry that presumably would lead to lower costs. One example of such changes would be the formation of a central government operation which would accept only "classified" types of ads and would then distribute such ads (e.g., in a kind of catalog) to points of potential use (e.g., post offices).

These arguments are interesting if certain necessary conditions were satisfied. As an example, one cannot evaluate the efficiency of an economic activity unless its costs are compared with its returns. Thus it is not sufficient to say that advertising institutions cost too much, for one must specify the criterion or criteria used: i.e., too much with respect to what? Furthermore, we have seen that the cost of the advertising institution to the economy (AE/GNP) and to society (AE/-PCE) are lower today than they were in 1929 or in the early 1960s (Chapter 1, Figure 1–3b). As for the second argument, there is no doubt that the supply and distribution of ads via mass media might be done in a more efficient manner. The problem, however, is that no one has developed the details of a new organization of the industry, to compute the costs and returns, and finally, to compare these costs and returns with those of the current advertising industry.

Does advertising perform different functions in different sectors of the economy?

At the level of the entire economy, the advertising institution is essentially a mechanism that allows the demand for and supply of information to meet. We should expect that the importance of this mechanism may vary across different sectors in the economy. Some economists and public regulators have emphasized that advertising may have other economic roles than the simple creation and exchange of information. For instance, there has been a long tradition of research into whether advertising has different effects on sales and profits in different "industries."

The key problem with these empirical studies is their definition of industry—namely, they have accepted the definition used by the Standard Industrial Classification (SIC) and thus assumed that firms in the same SIC industry are, in fact, very similar to each other and very different from firms in other industries. As we have already seen, however, firms in the same "industry" may utilize various channels of communication in different proportions (see, for example, Chapter 2, Figure 2–3). This practical knowledge suggests that past and current statistical results may be simply spurious.

In recent years research has shown that the use of SIC definitions may be actually misleading if we want to ascertain the existence of the roles of advertising in different industries with respect to such criteria as sales and profits. To begin with, a distinguished econometrician, Dr. Frank Bass, and his associates have tested the assumption that firms in each SIC industry are similar to each other and different from firms in other SIC-defined industries. To test it, they used the same data used by the Federal Trade Commission to establish its policies concerning the possible effects of advertising on profits in 13 industries with a total of 97 firms. Although the statistical test of the assumption, that "firms' homogeneity within each SIC-industry, and firms' heterogeneity across SIC-industries" may disappoint federal regulators and others, they concluded that the assumption must be rejected. As a result, public policies based on this FTC study may be erroneous.

The SIC criteria establishing similarities and differences among firms used primarily the physical and chemical nature of the inputs utilized by each firm and the engineering nature of the firms' production technologies. But corporate and marketing decisions—from investments to selling and advertising decisions—are intrinsically behavioral; thus, the possible effects of advertising on sales, profits, returns, and so on may vary across industries and firms in relation to behavioral criteria, and may not be related to the physical, chemical, and engineering criteria used by the SIC.

To illustrate dramatically the large behavioral differences that exist in the world of business, consider Figure 4–1.

To begin, note that any combination of advertising, sales, and profit rates seems possible: consumer and industrial "industries" are mixed across the table, firms in the metal industry share the same rate of profit as a percentage of sales (6–8 percent) with the firms in the soft drinks industry; or firms in the appliance industry share the same rate of advertising as a percentage of sales (under 3 percent) with firms in the chemical industry—and so on!

Note, also, the differences among the industries listed along the bottom row of the figure. With the exception of the pharmaceutical industry, they all are consumer oriented and are heavy advertisers

FIGURE 4–1
Industries defined as being different by SIC are not different in terms of behavioral-managerial criteria: Advertising, sales, and profits

Advertising as a percentage of sales	Profit as a percentage of sales		
	Low (under 6%)	*Medium (6%–8%)*	*High (over 8%)*
Low (under 3%)	Tires (4)*	Metals (4)	Oil (6)
	Automotive (4)	Airlines (6)	Chemicals (4)
	Appliances (3)		
Medium (3%–10%)	Food (20)	Liquor (3)	Tobacco (6)
	Beer (4)		Paper (2)
High (over 10%)	Soaps (4)	Soft drinks (3)	Gum and candy (3)
			Toiletries and cosmetics (10)
			Pharmaceuticals (4)

* Number in parentheses indicates number of firms in this industry which were among the 25 largest advertisers (in their industry) in 1968 and also were listed in the *Fortune* 500.

Source: C. Ramond, "Measurement of Sales Effectiveness," in R. Barton (ed.), *Handbook of Advertising Management* (New York: McGraw-Hill), Ch. 22, pp. 22–26.

(their advertising as a percentage of sales is over 10 percent). Yet they differ substantially in terms of their profit as percentage of sales (from less than 6 percent to over 8 percent).

The author of this study, Charles Ramond, has also shown that there are major differences among the firms within the same industry. For instance, the four pharmaceutical companies in the high advertising/high profit percentages of sales in Figure 4–1 achieve different ratios of advertising to earnings. Similarly, Procter and Gamble, the largest advertiser in the United States, has an advertising/earnings ratio of only 1.00 to 1.49, whereas Colgate-Palmolive and Lever Brothers, its "smaller" competitors, who spend considerably less on advertising, have ratios of over 3.0.

All in all, the possible economic relationships between advertising and sales, profits, and earnings so far have not been conceptually stated appropriately by the typical econometric research.

Furthermore, not only corporate, marketing, and advertising managers but also the financial community and related federal agencies recognize the fundamental differences in the structure of firms —even those in the same SIC industries. These structural differences include those in the marketing mix, e.g., in the different use of the sales force, dealers, and advertising. Above all, they include differences in production costs, in R&D investment, and in the composition of their financial capital. Most likely, there are critical differences also in the social-psychological makeup of their managers and thus in the nature of the organizational decision processes.

If the people interested in studying the possible economic roles of advertising in the economy and in different industries fail to ascertain differences in kinds, then so-called quantitative studies of advertising's economic roles may give statistically significant results that are as meaningful as the total weight of a box containing tomatoes and potatoes. As one of the authors has written, "Armed with these figures, we could determine shipping charges, only to discover later that the box arrived at its destination with the tomatoes squashed and the potatoes rotted—a result presumably not desired by consumers, business, or public policy makers."[1]

Competition

The question, "Does advertising limit competition?" has to be considered from several viewpoints. If, on the one hand, we weaken the effect of competition through advertising, then we must submit to some other regulating device. And yet, can small and big firms exist in competition with each other? Do the major firms take advantage of the public?

In the decision against the Atlantic & Pacific Tea Company, the judge stated there was no evidence that the company had attempted to put smaller rivals out of business, but it had the economic power

---

[1] F. M. Nicosia, *Advertising, Management, and Society* (New York: McGraw-Hill, 1974), p. 238.

to do so. What the decision came close to stating was that A&P was required to compete, but it would become illegal if it competed successfully.

Certainly to gain the necessary economies in many industries requires "bigness." Bigness is essential for large-scale production in automobiles, steel, aluminum, and atomic power. Bigness is necessary for large-scale distribution of cigarettes, gasoline, and other low per-unit margin items. Bigness is necessary to have national distribution. Bigness is necessary to provide the funds for much of our basic research. Bigness is necessary to allow major changes in product design in a short-run period. Bigness is necessary to experiment with many new products. Bigness is more responsive to public opinion because the general concept of bigness tends to frighten the public.

In this economy with its tendency toward bigness, advertising is one of the forces which has been accused of weakening competition. And yet, with the ever continuing growth of business enterprises, with the development of national markets, with the need for greater efficiency at all levels, with the expanding markets, with the continuous search for new products (as an example, in the drug industry only 45 percent of the products now sold were on the shelves of drugstores eight years ago), with the greater investment needed to start a business with a capacity great enough to gain adequate economies, and with the greater knowledge which consumers have about all products, the use of advertising has had to evolve to meet conditions in the ever changing market.

The tendency toward bigness is a composite of many economic factors. This bigness has brought with it many social dividends. It also has driven out the less efficient firms. To what extent has this bigness weakened competition? Has it intensified the competition among a few? Will increasing the number of outlets intensify competition, or will it cause the greater number to be more willing to maintain the status quo?

One way or another, we must develop a consistent policy in regard to the growth of a business. Until we can decide on what we mean by bigness, we cannot decide on whether or not advertising is intensifying or weakening competition.

Price competition

The question, "Does advertising limit price competition?" is a difficult one to evaluate because of the complex price structure which we have in our economy and the variety of state and federal controls in effect. The degree to which a company may be able to control the market through such factors as product differentiation, brand name, company prestige, distribution economies, production economies, advertising appeals, and other methods of this type will vary from industry to industry.

In some areas of activity, such as in distribution of the services of utilities, regulations have been established to provide control of prices. In even such fields as law, medicine, accounting, and barbering, licensing arrangements have provided a means by which these groups have set prices for a number of their services.

The U.S. government has interfered with the market prices for all major agricultural products. In fact, such groups as agricultural cooperatives and other associations are partially exempt from the federal antitrust laws. The Robinson-Patman Act puts barriers in the way of price flexibility. The states have "unfair practices" acts which prohibit sales below cost.

In industries where there are a few dominant producers, such as automobiles, steel, and cigarettes, price and production policies initiated by one company may be followed by the others. When General Motors decided to manufacture a small car to be sold at a price of $3,000, Ford and Chrysler also decided to produce a comparable car. While there may be an attempt to penetrate the competitor's market through price-cutting, in all likelihood the costs for each manufacturer will be such that no company will have significant production advantages.

In retailing where industrial concentration is not so great, there is a greater tendency for price competition. At the retail level, for example, the price appeal is used extensively. However, where artificial price controls have been put into effect in any segment of the economy, they will intensify rigidity in prices whether they are placed at the retail, at the wholesale, or at the manufacturing level.

By and large, however, there is not enough evidence to indicate whether or not the use of advertising has been one of the basic causes in the inflexibility of certain prices. As an example, the lack of price competition in the cigarette industry results as much from such competitive factors as the necessity of getting cigarettes into more than 1.25 million retail outlets, the taxes levied on the industry, and the low per-unit margin, as it does from the extensive advertising that companies use.

Lee Benham has recently compared the prices for eye examinations and eyeglasses in states that prohibit advertising of these services and products with prices in states that allow advertising. After controlling for differences in income and demographic characteristics among state populations, Benham found that prices for eye examinations and eyeglasses averaged $4.43 less in states that allowed advertising. It would appear from this study that conveying information through mass media to a large number of potential buyers leads to a relatively greater sales volume, with ensuing lower unit costs and, through competitive pressure among advertisers, lower unit prices.

Production costs

In considering the question, "Does advertising decrease the production costs of goods sold?" it must be kept in mind that advertising is only one part of the marketing mix. It is also important to understand that the responsiveness of the consumer to an advertising appeal will appreciably affect the per unit cost. As an example, if a cooperative decided to spend $1 million in an advertising campaign to increase the primary demand for its product, the expansibility or inexpansibility of demand would have a direct effect on the per unit cost. The elasticity or inelasticity of demand would also affect the unit cost. Furthermore, these costs are going to vary even within a given industry. The used or unused capacity of a company also will affect these overall costs.

As a result, it is difficult to show that advertising can be credited with decreasing production costs. As Neil H. Borden stated:

> From an economic standpoint it is significant in these cases that the principle of decreasing costs does not continue beyond a certain point. Instead, a certain size of plant permits low manufacturing costs and, to attain a volume permitting this size of plant, competing firms may choose to use different marketing methods.
>
> From this discussion, it is seen that the answer regarding the effect of advertising upon production costs cannot be given categorically and simply.
>
> Where there is much affirmative evidence of striking economies in the costs of production which have attended the concurrent growth in the size of industries and in the use of advertising and aggressive selling, the sweeping claims sometimes advanced regarding production economies resulting from and maintained by advertising are not supported.[2]

On the other hand, some writers have credited advertising with lowering production costs through the process of increasing the demand for a product and thus making it possible for a company to operate on a larger scale, with resultant lower per unit costs. While there is merit in this viewpoint, nevertheless, the complexity of our economic system is so vast that it is difficult to pinpoint reduction in production costs to advertising through the use of any substantive data that are available.

Overall product demand

The question, "Does advertising increase the overall demand for products?" is one which becomes extremely complex to resolve. The demand trend of the product, the environment and social conditions, and the characteristics of the people in the market are only a few of the variables which must be controlled in order to determine what impact advertising has on the overall demand for products.

Most studies have indicated that advertising has accelerated the time in which products will be accepted. The demand for such products as television, automobiles, and appliances can be cited as examples in which advertising hastened expansion because favorable market conditions existed. On the other hand, in situations in which there was a declining demand trend, such as in men's hats, advertising was not able to reverse the trend although it was able to slow down the decline.

As a result, we might conclude that advertising can help to get

---

[2] Neil H. Borden, *Advertising in Our Economy* (Homewood, Ill.: Richard D. Irwin, Inc., 1945), p. 164.

products accepted more readily if the other conditions in the market are favorable. We do not have evidence, however, to show that advertising can reverse a declining trend unless there is a change in environmental, social, or other factors.

Company images

Another question deals with a problem that has been popularized to a great degree during the past decade: "Does advertising create company images which are misleading to the consumer?" In other words, can a company create and maintain an identity which is not consistent with the general policy of the organization? Can General Electric continue to use successfully the appeal, "Progress is our most important product," unless General Electric actually makes the necessary progress to justify such an appeal? Or can Westinghouse emphasize, "You can be sure if it's Westinghouse," unless it maintains high-quality standards? How long can Cadillac use the appeal of "Universal symbol of achievement" unless it actually continues to build an automobile that will justify this appeal? Will Maytag be able to emphasize its appeal, "The most service-free automatics made!" unless its product standards continue to justify it?

Is it true that all advertising to some degree is institutional advertising? As an example, how can a product be divorced from the company which makes it any more than the executives of the company can be divorced from their opinions? Is it true that one of the most important advertising functions is the establishment of identity? In other words, is it possible to separate the advertising from the company? How many companies actually know what product they are really selling? Are they selling a particular product, or are they selling something else? Is a company selling electric typewriters, or is it selling a more economical way of transcribing? Is the telephone company selling instruments, or a more economical way of doing something? Or is the company's image of even greater importance than the product?

In industry today, there is a growing belief on the part of many executives that the company image is becoming even more important to the total satisfaction the consumer derives from a product. As a result, the need to give a company a consistent identity appears to be more important. This identity, however, must be consistent in all aspects. As an example, a company cannot advertise its know-how for any period of time unless its product measures up to the required standards. Neither will a company find it economical to emphasize its progress unless it is actually a leader in the industry.

Number of products

The question, "Does advertising limit the number of products that will be offered?" is another one of the broad criticisms that is sometimes advanced. At the same time, other critics will point out that the use of advertising is the major factor in having such a great number of brands in the market. Furthermore, they claim that there are meaningless product differentiations which exist between these brands, and as a result, the consumer cannot make wise selections.

In evaluating the position of the two groups of critics on the number and variety of products offered, there is available data to substantiate either position on the question. On the one hand, wholesale druggists point out that as late as eight years ago, 55 percent of the products they now handle were not on the market; supermarket studies indicate that within the next eight to ten years, 50 percent of all the products they sell now will no longer be offered. The dramatic growth in the electronic and television industries which has resulted in many new products being manufactured are other examples which would seem to substantiate the fact that the use of advertising has not limited the number of products.

On the other side of the issue, however, the slowness of manufacturers in the automobile, steel, and other basic industries in making significant changes is used as a criterion to judge that the use of advertising has limited the introduction of significantly new products.

In certain industries, like automobiles, cigarettes, and steel, there is a tendency for concentration in the hands of a small number of large companies. As a result, these firms are in a position during a short-term period, within the scope of the competitive conditions which they face, to decide on the number and variety of products which they will manufacture.

The fact is, however, that the use of extensive advertising cannot by itself maintain a company's position in the market for the long-term period unless the other ingredients in the marketing and productive mix are properly allocated. As an example, did the use of advertising protect the automobile manufacturers from having to produce a small car? Or were these same manufacturers able to maintain the automobile as a symbol of prestige? Will the automobile manufacturers be able to continue to produce a small economical car and through advertising have it attain the prestige of the foreign cars?

In a free economy, because of the preponderance and the extent of the economic factors which influence the number and variety of products offered, the use of advertising will be only a minor aspect in limiting the number of products in a few basic industries.

Cost of advertising

The question, "Who pays for the advertising?" is one which critics point out to indicate that the sales price of goods might be lower if companies did not advertise. The cost of advertising, like all other expenses, is passed on to the consumer in one form or the other. However, the proper use of advertising can influence the unit sales volume and thus indirectly help to decrease the cost of production. In such instances, if the savings are passed on to the consumer in lower prices, the consumer will benefit even though he pays for the cost of the advertising.

It would be a mistake to assume that the above answer provides a sound solution to the basic problems indicated in the question. Such other points as the following are involved in the question: What is the result if the savings are not passed on to the consumer? What happens when the businessman does not properly appraise his market opportunities? What takes place when the firm does not effectively coordinate all other parts of the marketing program? What might happen to other sales costs if the use of advertising were decreased?

While these are only a few of the many questions which might be considered, the authors wish to point out that the cost of advertising is part of the sales cost and as such may be absorbed by our economic system in one of several ways. These include:

1. Advantages gained in production which may result in lower per-unit costs.
2. Advantages gained in distribution which may result in lower per-unit distribution costs.
3. Advantages gained in financing which may result in lower per-unit financial costs.
4. Advantages gained in general management relations which may result in lower per-unit managerial costs.
5. Advantages gained in price stability which may result in a decrease of the inherent dangers of cyclical influence.

From the cost viewpoint for the whole economy, therefore, the justification of the use of advertising depends on whether or not it performs its function more effectively than some other method.

Product information

The question, "Is advertising a satisfactory yardstick for the consumer to use in buying products?" is one which the critics frequently answer by showing a variety of advertisements which they deem misleading. Advertisements such as the following are among those which they claim show how ineffectively advertising can be used as a guide for buying:

1. And the two extra doors don't cost a thing.
2. Be slim this modern "hungerless" way.
3. Made of nonfattening vegetable flours.
4. The finest costs no more.
5. Regularly $95 and $115 suits hand-tailored from the finest imported worsteds—now—$39.95.
6. Now you can have the finest hand-detailed coat of 100 percent imported cashmere for only $39.95—other stores normally charge $89.95.
7. Best value mattress in 59 years for only $35.95.
8. Special purchase—save 60 percent and more.
9. We've sold hundreds of these chairs at $139.50—now a special purchase makes one yours for only $78.
10. It is kindest to your taste.
11. It kills germs on contact, by millions!

12. Can do 75 cleaning chores better, faster, easier than any other cleaner.
13. Helps solve nine major beauty problems.
14. It's as easy to paint your home as cutting your lawn.
15. You can't get a more expensive taste than with margarine.
16. Fades horrid age spots with one application.
17. The toothpaste for people who brush their teeth only once each day.
18. There are 500,000 special filters.
19. Drains all eight sinus cavities in four hours.
20. Shoeshine lasts 14 days.

While some of the above advertisements might be classified as misleading and others might not give the detailed information that some consumer wants, it should be kept in mind that the function of an advertisement is to stimulate demand. While in some instances this can best be done by using specific data about a product, nevertheless, in the majority of cases, some other appeal may do a better job of persuading the public.

As a result, it appears necessary for the consumers to use the other means which sellers offer, to supplement the data that is included in advertisements, if they want more detailed information. The fact that some of them may be willing to evaluate complex tests of articles does not mean, however, that all consumers desire the same type of information.

In most instances, the purchaser is satisfied to rely on either the reputation of the manufacturer or the brand of the product. Consequently, there is a lack of uniformity on the part of sellers as to the amount of detailed information they provide.

Allocation of capital

This question deals with capital allocation and is stated: "Are capital investments allocated uneconomically because of the use of advertising?" This is another one of those questions which deals with very broad economic concepts.

As to the question, therefore, of the part advertising plays in allocating investments in the economy, it is certainly true that whatever influence advertising has in helping a company succeed or in pointing out potential investment advantages, it is indirectly responsible for attracting venture capital to particular firms.

There is no concrete way, however, to place a universal value judgment on whether or not these activities are economically sound. It might be argued that in the patent medicine industry the use of advertising has played a major role in maintaining profits and, thus, indirectly attracting capital. While this may be true, is it the function of advertising to determine whether or not the manufacture of patent medicines is in the best interest of society? Is it not the responsibility of other groups in the economy to make this decision?

If these other groups decide that the patent medicine industry offers a satisfactory product, can it be said that because capital is attracted to the industry, it is not being used in the best interest of the economy?

By and large, therefore, the allocation of capital may be said to be only indirectly influenced by the use of advertising. And, as in evaluating any business investments, the investor is going to include in his analysis such other factors as market trends, risk elements, management's know-how, competitive conditions, and business conditions. In the final analysis, the flow of capital will be toward those industries where the risk and opportunities involved will be in balance insofar as the investor has the ability to judge.

Distribution Function

The question is: "Can advertising perform a phase of the distribution function more economically than some other method?" As the businessman looks at this question, he wants to know if the use of advertising will help him make a greater profit. The economist, on the other hand, although he is interested in the profit aspect, will also be vitally concerned with how advertising will contribute to consumption and how it will affect the whole economy.

In evaluating the effectiveness of advertising as an economic function, it must first be determined what the objective of the advertising is. This objective may be to shift the demand schedule to the right for a product, it may be to educate the public, it may be to keep the demand curve from shifting negatively, it may be to make demand less elastic, it may be to adapt the demand to the product, or it may even be to match the competitive advertising.

The advertising cost is part of the sales expense and, as such, it is hoped that it will be a cause and not a result of sales. Consequently, the effectiveness of the use of advertising must be judged on how well it performs a sales function.

As in all types of sales activities, the responsiveness to advertising will differ greatly with various products. For example, the sales of patent medicines are highly responsive to advertising. On the other hand, the responsiveness to advertising for the sale of major industrial equipment may be relatively low. The responsiveness to advertising will also vary during the life cycle of a product. The share of the market and the competitive position a company holds will sometimes be equally as important in determining the kind of responsiveness which will be secured. Both the long-term and short-term responsiveness will be other aspects which should be considered.

In judging the effectiveness of advertising, therefore, it is one thing to determine whether or not certain conditions exist in the market that would indicate the responsiveness to advertising. However, it is something else to measure the effectiveness of the use of advertising as compared to some other sales technique. While some excellent studies have been based on the incremental approach, there are such wide areas of responsiveness and economic activity that it has not been feasible to use control techniques that will give a satisfactory answer in all cases.

As a result, it has been necessary to deduce the effectiveness of the use of advertising from broad generalities which are based on general sales data. By and large, these studies have indicated that the use of advertising is, in most cases, an economical and effective sales tool.

The question of causality

There is no doubt that, at the micro-managerial level, it is usually difficult to disentangle whether the advertising dollar spent by a firm has in fact contributed not only to revenues but to profits and returns as well. As discussed in Chapter 2, many other decisions by a firm, such as pricing, selection of dealers, packaging, and so on, as well as decisions by competitors, also affect a firm's revenues, profits, and returns. And as discussed in Chapter 3, a firm's advertising is only one of the many psychological and social factors governing the buying behavior of consumers and organizations alike. At the same time, a number of recent and methodologically sound studies have ascertained that advertising by a firm can be a useful tool for marketing and corporate management. To cite only one example from industrial marketing, the Morrill study shows that a salesperson's call on a client tends to produce higher sales when the call is made on a client who is familiar with the salesperson's firm through exposure to the firm's advertising.

At the micro-managerial level, the question simply requires the use of common sense: i.e., some advertising campaigns produce results; others barely pay for their own costs; still others are not successful at all. But in this chapter we discuss questions at the macro level. That is, practically all of the questions discussed above concern the problem of whether the advertising institution is a cause of some event at the level of the entire economy or of its macro parts—an industry, the average price level, the average rate of profits, and so on.

A large number of empirical studies of whether advertising is causally related to profit, returns, concentration, monopoly power, and the like at the macro level have undoubtedly utilized inappropriate data and, as mentioned earlier, have neglected to account for differences in the behavioral characteristics of organizational decision making. More importantly, Richard Schmalensee has authoritatively dismissed many of these studies, for the reported statistical inference results were based on work that does not satisfy the necessary mathematical specifications of possible causal relationships.[3]

At the macro level, it will not be easy to ascertain whether advertising is somehow causally related to economic phenomena such as Gross National Product (GNP), Disposable Income (DI), or Personal Consumption Expenditures (PCE). Researchers are essentially deal-

---

[3] R. Schmalensee, *The Economics of Advertising* (Amsterdam, Holland: North-Holland Publishing Co., 1972).

ing with a classically difficult problem that faces all disciplines—in physics, chemistry, natural sciences and, of course, in the economic and behavioral sciences. To put it simply, the problem is the old one of the chicken and the egg: which comes first?

It is simple to realize that although the advertising institution may have an effect on the economy, the economy itself may have an effect on the advertising institution. Furthermore, as an economy comes out of a recession, buyers and sellers regain confidence. Consumers, firms, and other organizations begin to make buying plans and implement them, however cautiously. Similarly, sellers begin to increase their production runs in hopes that buyers will start placing orders. As the tempo increases, the need to send as well as to acquire information via all available channels (see Chapters 1 and 2), including mass media, naturally becomes greater.

One should not be surprised, therefore, to see that increases in economic activity go hand in hand with increases in advertising activity. In fact, the time series data supplied in Chapter 1, covering the period 1929–75, show that the correlation among such economic indicators as GNP, DI, and PCE are correlated with advertising expenditures at levels above 0.9! There are leads and lags, of course; for instance, GNP may change before or after changes in advertising expenditures. Nicosia has shown that advertising expenditures tend to lag behind changes in GNP, DI, and PCE during economic recoveries and that, during periods of prosperity, changes in the economy and advertising occur almost simultaneously.[4] Other studies tend to observe similar trends and support the thesis of the American Association of Advertising Agencies that advertising can help an economy to recover faster from a recession.[5]

But those persons who are interested in the economic roles of the advertising industry must be ready to think beyond the possible interactions between advertising and the economy. Although there are some reciprocal causal effects between the two, it is very likely that both advertising and the economy respond to changes in "antecedent" causes of an intrinsically cultural, social, and psychological nature. After all, buyers and sellers, individually and in organizations, are all human beings, immersed in a culture with its own values and living in social institutions each with its own norms, sanctions, and rewards. We shall turn our attention to this new perspective in the following chapter.

Questions

1   In the evaluation of the economic benefits of advertising, indicate the pros and cons of rising market share as a standard.

2.   A leading advertiser has stated: "Advertising is vital to our economic growth." Comment.

---

[4] Nicosia, *Advertising, Management, and Society,* Chapter 11.
[5] Ibid.

3. Some writers have pointed out that in our economic system much of our advertising costs should be viewed as economic growth costs. Comment.

4. In what ways does advertising increase the cost of distribution? Decrease the cost of distribution?

5. A leading economist made the following statement: "Since advertising is accompanied by rigid prices, it prevents the price mechanism from taking up the dynamic shocks in our system." Comment.

6. Select three companies in which you believe advertising costs may be viewed as being excessive. Give reasons.

7. What is the place of advertising in a capitalistic economy such as we have in the United States?

8. Is advertising necessary only in a "free economy" like the United States? Do countries like Russia need to use advertising?

9. Select three companies in which advertising budgets have been figured on a basis of sales and indicate the policy each company followed in its advertising program during recent cyclical changes. Have the advertising policies of these companies had any direct effect in minimizing the cyclical fluctuations?

10. A social worker recently stated: "Advertising has broken down competition." Comment.

11. To what degree can advertising either change or influence industrial investment plans?

12. Following a traditional regression procedure, Comanor and Wilson have estimated the effect that advertising may have on sales in different industries. One of their *typical* findings concerns the dairy products industry, that is, (*a*) a percentage change in price would cause no change in sales, and (*b*) one percentage increase in the advertising/sales ratio would cause an increase by 75 percent in sales. A discussant of these findings, Grabowski, has computed that, if such estimates were true, then a reduction of advertising expenditures for dairy products from, say, $80 million to $50 million would mean a decrease in sales of dairy products by two-thirds.

    Question: Does this and other estimates of consumer reaction to advertising make sense with respect to your personal experience?

13. Can we understand, explain, and predict economic relationships without taking into account cultural, social, and psychological factors?

Case **PROFESSIONAL ADVERTISING**
4–1 **Deciding on use of advertising**

Advertising by attorneys has been a rigidly observed taboo ever since the American Bar Association announced its first national code of ethics in 1908. Originally, the ad ban was intended to help restore dignity to the legal profession, which had been badly tattered by attorneys who put up large billboards or even hawked their services on the open streets with all the restraint of a snake-oil salesman. The prohibition on promotion never came under broad assault until 1975, when it was attacked by consumer groups, Government trustbusters and even some lawyers. So at the A.B.A.'s midyear meeting in 1976 in Philadelphia advertising—which was not even on the agenda a year earlier—was the premier topic. There was no way to avoid it. In June 1975 the U.S. Supreme Court threw out uniform minimum fees set by bar groups and ruled that attorneys—as well as doctors or other members of so-called learned professions—were not automatically exempt from antitrust laws. The court also held that the right of an abortion-referral agency to run informational advertisements is protected by the free-speech guarantee. In a talk to a lawyers' group, the deputy U.S. attorney spelled out a blunt warning: "An agreement to restrict advertising of legal service could be held to be a violation of the antitrust laws."

The Consumers Union, for one, agreed and sued the Virginia and California bar associations, claiming that restrictions against advertising are unlawful restraints of trade that keep the public in the dark about legal fees and lawyer qualifications. The consumer organization, which wants to publish a market guide to lawyers, also charged that the bar groups had violated its First Amendment right to print "important factual information." At the same time, individual attorneys in New York, Virginia, Wisconsin, and Hawaii went to court on their own behalf, arguing, among other things, that without ads a small practitioner was unfairly and illegally prevented from competing with larger, well-established firms. Moreover, the Federal Trade Commission filed a complaint attacking the American Medical Association's rule against doctors' ads, a move that seemed to support opponents of the lawyers' ad ban.

Mostly unbending.   Confronted with all this activity, the A.B.A.'s eight-member ethics committee in December 1975 proposed allowing all ads, except those containing "deceptive or unfair statements." Though noticeably more liberal on some issues in recent years, most of the A.B.A.'s 340-member house of delegates are all but unbending on professional style and propriety. The idea of advertising prompts nearly physical revulsion. The A.B.A. president told his colleagues he personally "recoils" from any ad. But he counseled that the organization was up against "a matter of constitutional law."

The delegates nonetheless adamantly refused to let lawyers give minimal information even to "bona fide consumer" groups. The old rules were broadened only to allow a listing of the lawyer's areas of specialization, his office hours, charges for the first consultation, and the availability of a full fee estimate upon request. Such information can be offered to the public only in bar-approved directories or a *Yellow Pages* ad that complies with local bar regulations on language and format.

Questions

1. Point out the advantages and disadvantages of allowing professional people to advertise.
2. Are there any specific situations when you believe professional people "should" or "should not" be allowed to advertise?
3. Are there any specific professional groups which "should" or "should not" be allowed to advertise?

Case   CHESHIRE COMPANY
4–2   Documentation of statements

Considering Regulations

Cheshire Company in recent years has expanded its business to include, besides the manufacture and sale of cigarettes, cigars, and smoking tobacco, a distilling operation and a snack food products business. As the Cheshire products were distributed in over two million outlets in the United States, it was necessary for the company to use extensive broadcast promotion to attain customer acceptance. The executives were concerned with the regulations which required the substantiation of advertising appeals.

Tobacco products

Cheshire's domestic tobacco business includes cigarettes, smoking tobaccos, and cigars. About 95 percent of Cheshire's net sales of tobacco products which consists of filter and nonfilter cigarettes, have been declining while total unit sales for the tobacco industry were relatively stable, although declining slightly. For several years up to 1968, industry sales of filter cigarettes grew rapidly, although this rate of growth has since leveled off. Cheshire's unit sales of filter cigarettes in 1968 represented only 11 percent of its total cigarette sales. At that time substantially increased emphasis was placed on the marketing of filter cigarettes, and by 1971 Cheshire had increased its unit sales of filter cigarettes to 58 percent of total sales. Its increased sales of filter cigarettes, however, have not been sufficient to offset the continuing decline in unit sales of nonfilter cigarettes, and even such increases in filter sales have leveled off in recent years.

Cheshire sells its cigarettes primarily in the U.S. market through distributors, and directly to chain stores and other large retail outlets. The market for cigarettes is highly competitive, and all companies advertise their cigarettes on an extensive basis.

The federal excise tax on cigarettes is eight cents per package of 20 cigarettes. In addition, the District of Columbia and the 50 states had cigarette taxes ranging from two to 18 cents per package of 20. There were also about 260 municipalities and counties collecting cigarette taxes ranging from one to seven cents per package.

Tobacco is an agricultural commodity subject to U.S. government controls. In the ten years ended in 1969 the average market price per pound of flue-cured tobacco increased from 60.4 cents to 72.2 cents, or 20 percent. From 1960 through 1968 the average market price per pound of burley leaf increased from 64.3 cents to 73.7 cents, or 15 percent. The average market price per pound of burley leaf in 1969 was 69.7 cents. The decrease in price in 1969 was attributed to a poor crop year for burley leaf.

The Federal Cigarette Labeling and Advertising Act, effective January 1, 1966, requires that packages of cigarettes distributed in the United States bear the statement: "Caution: Cigarette Smoking May

Be Hazardous to Your Health." A subsequent amendment, the Public Health Cigarette Smoking Act of 1969, requires that packages of cigarettes distributed in the United States bear the statement: "Warning: The Surgeon General Has Determined That Cigarette Smoking Is Dangerous to Your Health," and prohibits any other requirement of a statement relating to smoking and health on any cigarette package. The amended statute also prohibits radio and television advertising of cigarettes, and requires annual reports to the United States Congress from the secretary of Health, Education and Welfare and from the Federal Trade Commission on the lethal consequences of smoking, cigarette labeling, advertising and promotion, and recommendations for further legislation.

Distilling operations

Cheshire owns and operates three plants with a combined distilling capacity of 45,000 proof gallons of bourbon whiskey per day, and a bottling capacity of 17,000 cases of fifths per eight-hour shift, U.S. bonded warehouses with storage capacity of 900,000 barrels of whiskey, and two water reservoirs with 150,000,000 gallons total capacity. Cheshire sells its products through various distributors and state liquor authorities. The market for the products is highly competitive.

Food products

Cheshire also manufactures and sells crackers, cookies, and snack goods. Sales are made through distributors and directly to retail outlets, hotels, restaurants, schools, and similar customers. The market for all of these products is highly competitive.

FTC regulations

The Federal Trade Commission informed the advertising business that in its capacity as a "data book" it would demand detailed documentation for advertising claims related to safety, performance, efficiency, quality, or price. The reasons for the decision were as follows:

1. Public disclosure can assist consumers in making a rational choice among competing claims which purport to be based on objective evidence and in evaluating the weight to be accorded to such claims.
2. The public's need for this information is not being met voluntarily by advertisers.
3. Public disclosure can enhance competition by encouraging competitors to challenge advertising claims which have no basis in fact.
4. The knowledge that documentations or the lack thereof will be made public will encourage advertisers to have on hand adequate substantiation before claims are made.

5. The commission has limited resources for detecting claims which are not substantiated by adequate proof. By making documentation submitted in response to this resolution available to the public, the commission can be alerted by consumers, businessmen, and public interest groups to possible violations of Section 5 of the Federal Trade Commission Act.

Appeals used by a number of companies

Some of the broad appeals which the Cheshire Company executives decided to evaluate are listed below:

1. Anti-perspirant: "This will roll on more protection than you can spray on."
2. Tire company: "You get the best combination of advantages—traction, strength, and mileage. They all add up to the best value."
3. Aluminum wrap: "There is no wrap which will compare to ours because it is oven-tempered for flexible strength."
4. Household cleanser: "Wipes out household germs in 15 seconds."
5. Cereal: "The leading high nutrition cereal."
6. Cigarette company: "America's favorite cigarette break."
7. Cigarette company: "Has less tar than any other cigarette."
8. Cereal: "John Unitas caught the wheat germs from Mickey Mantle."
9. Toothache medicine: "Stops pain on contact."
10. Bourbon: "Professional tasters say our bourbon is the best."
11. Scotch whiskey: "It never varies."
12. Air Force recruitment: "Find yourself in the job of your choice." "Guaranteed."
13. Distilled dry gin: "World's driest gin."
14. Carousel projector: "We've made it the most for your money."
15. Balanced reducing formula: "Guaranteed to lose 5 pounds the first week or your money back."
16. Bath towels: "The finest bath towel that is made of the finest combed cotton."
17. Travel advertisement: "There are no strangers in paradise."
18. Avocado dip: "Try an avocado love potion—the love food."
19. National LP Gas Council: "Gas makes the difference. A juicy steak melts in your mouth."
20. Dry cleaning product: "Just spray it on and brush away the spot—lifts spots, soup to sauce."
21. Plastic baby milk bottles: "This bottle saved my marriage."
22. Computer company: "No other computer company has as much to offer."
23. Newspaper: "San Francisco has no city limit."
24. Crackers: Make your patio party perfect."
25. Gasoline: "Will hold exhaust emissions down, increase your gasoline mileage, keep your carburetor clean and keep your sparkplug from misfiring."

Case questions

1. Evaluate each of the above appeals and indicate how the various companies might document these statements.
2. Do you believe that advertisers should be allowed to use general "puffery" statements? Explain.
3. In the event that there are no reliable tests that can be developed, what approach should the advertiser use?
4. What various approaches might Cheshire use in evaluating the kinds of appeals which will meet FTC regulations?

Case 4–3   COD SEA FOOD, INC.
           Considering quality standards

Informing the Consumer

Cod Sea Food, Inc., is a supplier of fresh and frozen seafood. Its offices and shipping center are located in Massachusetts. Cod maintained rigid quality controls; however, because of recent problems in the industry, it became concerned as to what it should do in informing consumers that cod's products were safe. Cod recognized that there were inherent problems existing in the seafood industry that prohibited it from being able to test every item in order to be 100 percent sure that no contamination or impurity existed.

Business

Cod deals in approximately 125 types of fish and other seafood items, including most of the well-known forms of seafood, and a variety of gourmet and speciality items, such as lobster and lobster tails, scallops, shrimp, king crab, clams, and oysters. Cod does not process or cook any of the products it sells, although in some instances, at customer request, fish are cleaned or cut into portions before delivery.

Sales are made by Cod's ten salesmen to approximately 400 customers. Principal customers include several major supermarket chains, restaurants, hotels, country clubs, institutions, and steamships. No single customer accounted for as much as 10 percent of sales of seafood. Cod's five largest customers accounted for approximately 20 percent of its seafood sales.

Cod purchases most of its requirements of seafood directly from suppliers at the point of production or, in the case of imports, through brokers. Cod relies on local wholesalers only for regional varieties of seafood and to cover shortages which intermittently arise due to product scarcity or unexpected orders from customers. Certain varieties of seafoods are purchased in bulk frozen form and stored by Cod in its own freezers and in public warehouses for later sale.

Cod's sources of supply are primarily in Canada, Massachusetts, Washington, Florida, Japan, South and Central America, and the Caribbean area. From time to time Cod, along with most other suppliers of seafood, has encountered difficulty in securing sufficient quantities of certain varieties of seafood due to industry-wide shortages of fresh fish. The industry is currently experiencing such a shortage. The causes of these shortages have not been specifically determined. However, such shortages become most severe when weather conditions in catch areas or along transportation routes are particularly harsh.

Cod employs off-premises salesmen and performs the sorting, delivery, and other services which are not generally performed by wholesalers. Cod's salesmen telephone customers at prearranged times and receive orders for various quantities and varieties of seafood for delivery that day or the following day. The orders are filled beginning at 3:00 A.M. on the day of delivery and are delivered in the local area by its fleet of trucks and drivers. In addition, Cod has some customers with outlets spread throughout the continental United States, and deliveries to them are made by public truckers or by air or rail.

In recent years, as per capita U.S. consumption of both fresh and frozen seafood has continued to increase, there has developed a trend of sales in the industry toward frozen seafood products, and toward imported seafoods. Fresh seafood continues to account for more than 60 percent of Cod's sales; and sales of frozen seafoods, including certain shellfish and other specialty items, account for the other 40 percent.

Competition

The sale of seafood is a highly competitive business. Cod is one of the three largest in its area. While the company encounters competition from a large number of wholesalers and smaller companies specializing in one or two products, there are only a limited number in the area which handle the broad product lines maintained by the company and which provide the delivery and other service which is the keystone of the company's fresh seafood operations.

Government regulation

Cod's products, ingredients, and facilities are continuously inspected by the U.S. Department of the Interior and the Department of Agriculture. The company is also subject to regulations by state and local health agencies. The company has never had any sanctions or penalties imposed upon it by any such regulatory agency.

Ocean dumping

Many businesses—large, medium, or small—have some of their wastes dumped in the ocean. Up to now boats carried the waste outside the 12-mile legal limit to discharge this waste cargo. Informed sources state that regulations are being prepared to force these vessels further out to sea—even up to 100 miles.

Quality control

It was the opinion of Cod's executives that the company maintains the strictest quality control standards for its products of any of the firms in the industry. Yet, they realized that because of the many unforeseen problems that might occur because of conditions that could develop with the discharge of waste cargo in the ocean, it was not feasible for a firm the size of Cod to develop the necessary tests which could avoid future problems. It was also necessary for the company to handle a number of its tests on a sampling basis.

Cod also was faced with a competitive situation which results from the nature of the industry. Small distributors are in the industry and do not always maintain quality standards. The procedure for many of these distributors is to operate at the lowest possible level of the minimum standards set by the U.S. Department of the Interior and the Department of Agriculture.

Cod, on the other hand, has attempted to look at these standards as only a starting point, and has set its own quality standards above the ones established by these government departments. Yet, the executives recognized that because of the limited inspection staffs which the two departments have, Cod was checked only on two occasions in the last two years.

Questions

1. To what extent should Cod advertise to the consumer about its high quality standards?
2. Should Cod attempt to inform the consumers about the low quality standards of its competitors?
3. How can a relatively small company like Cod let the consumers know about the danger of ocean dumping and its effect on the seafood industry?
4. Do you believe Cod should make an effort to have the U.S. Department of the Interior and the Department of Agriculture establish more rigid standards for the seafood industry?
5. Is Cod obligated to let the consumer know that it uses the sampling procedure in conducting tests?
6. What can be done to alleviate the adverse publicity which the seafood industry received because of the banning of swordfish?

Case **KELLOGG COMPANY**
4–4   **Growth of a company**

Before Kellogg there was no such thing as a ready-to-eat cereal industry. But when W. K. Kellogg in 1906 toasted, packaged, and sold his first box of Sanitas Toasted Corn Flakes, a new idea in U.S. manufacturing was born and a new habit in U.S. eating came into being.

Also, that early box of corn flakes was the inspiration for pioneering several principles of advertising and merchandising that are now considered basic and taken for granted. A few of them are consistent advertising, test marketing, product sampling, packaging, and package display.

Today, the ready-to-eat cereal business in the United States alone amounts to nearly $700 million annually—of which Kellogg does almost half.

Early work in nutrition

Will Keith Kellogg and his brother, Dr. John Harvey Kellogg, worked together at the then well-known Battle Creek Sanitarium, in Michigan.

Dr. Kellogg had many new and radical ideas about food and nutrition, including many that are taken for granted today. The doctor figured that just about everything a body needed could be obtained from ordinary grains, nuts, and fruits—including coffee.

In working to make some of the grain foods more appetizing-looking and better-tasting, W. K. Kellogg had hit upon a way to "flake" hearts of wheat and, later, hearts of corn.

In 1906, W. K. Kellogg decided to devote the greater part of his time and effort to his new firm, the Sanitas Toasted Corn Flakes Company. A firm believer in the principle that if people tried a good product they would keep on buying it, W. K. Kellogg distributed four million sample boxes of Toasted Corn Flakes the first year.

By the end of 1906, its first year, the amount spent for advertising totaled $90,000, almost three times as much as the young company's initial working capital.

(It is interesting to note that within two years after Toasted Corn Flakes was introduced, there were 44 companies in Battle Creek imitating the product with their own versions. There was, in fact, an Indiana company that put on the market—it didn't stay there long!—a product called "Battle Creek Corn Flakes.")

Because there were so many imitations, W. K. Kellogg soon decided to feature his signature on each package and in the advertising—even though personal modesty argued against it.

Thus the line, "The package of the geniune bears this signature—W. K. Kellogg," became an important property of the company and contributed to its leadership.

However, though W. K. Kellogg never considered himself a merchandising expert, his basic sales premise included these three major basics:

1. That Toasted Corn Flakes should be sold as a delicious breakfast food rather than as a health food.
2. That it would "win its favor through its flavor."
3. That the W. K. Kellogg signature on every package would mark the genuine and original:
    —in making a good product and constantly trying to make it better.
    —in sampling it as broadly as possible.
    —in advertising extensively and intensively.
    —and in the principles of repetition and continuity in the advertising copy.

He believed in advertising broadly because, as he said, "Wherever you find people you'll find Kellogg's."

Early test market example

One of the food industry's earliest test market efforts can be credited to Kellogg's Toasted Corn Flakes.

The company bought $150 worth of newspaper advertising in Canton, Ohio.

It also had built an eight-foot papier-maché ear of corn and hired a man to get inside it and walk Canton streets.

On the strength of this test, the company "went national" (or relatively so) with that local campaign.

During the night before July 4, 1907, Mr. Kellogg was awakened with the report that his factory was burning.

He hurried to it. The ramshackle frame structure was a mass of flames—practically a total loss.

Before the day of July 4 was over, however, he had an architect come over from Chicago and start work on plans for a new factory.

By the time of the fire, not 18 months since the company was organized, it had spent approximately $300,000 in advertising.

With production completely halted by the July 4 blaze, the natural question in top minds of the company was, "Would that advertising expenditure be a total loss?"

Here is what Arch Shaw, company adviser, director, and major stockholder wrote to Mr. Kellogg: "The fire is of no consequence. You can't burn down what we have registered in the minds of the American women."

Within a few weeks, the boxes of Kellogg's Toasted Corn Flakes were rolling out of a new, more modern—and more fireproof—Kellogg factory! For nearly five years, Toasted Corn Flakes was Kellogg's one product.

In 1912, Shredded Wheat and Krumbles were added.

In 1919, All-Bran came into the line.

In 1922 the corporate name was changed to the Kellogg Company.

In 1927, the experimental lab brought to W. K. Kellogg two packages of a rather different-looking cereal.

He put sugar and milk on it, tasted it, and said, "You've got something there!" (That something was Rice Krispies, which were first marketed in 1928.)

In the early 1930s the Depression hit.

It will be remembered that after the market crash of 1929 pessimism stalked the land. Wall Street brokers jumped from tall buildings; apple sellers cluttered the street corners.

A "blues" theme song of the times was "Run for Cover. The Dam Has Broken."

W. K. Kellogg was not restrained by the prevailing fear. Instead he told his executives, "Double our advertising budget! This is the time to go out and spend more money in advertising."

As Horace B. Powell, of the W. K. Kellogg Foundation, reports it:

"Sales continued to accelerate, affected scarcely, if at all, by the Depression."

By 1940, the Kellogg Company had spent $100 million in advertising. The Leo Burnett advertising agency began working with Kellogg in the late 1940s. Burnett's first assignment from Kellogg in 1949 was on a product named Corn Soya. Unfortunately, the public never would learn how good a product it was; so after a matter of time, it quietly disappeared.

However, Corn Soya made one big contribution; it got the agency acquainted with the Kellogg people in Battle Creek.

And Kellogg awarded Burnett the other products in the line, which meant that it was in major-league television almost overnight—for Kellogg was one of the pioneers in that medium as it earlier had been in radio.

Let's look at the record

Since the early 1950s Kellogg has been a major user of both spot and network TV.

It is interesting to make a quick survey of some of the shows Burnett has worked on for Kellogg from the time it started working with them.

The first effort was Colonel Tim McCoy headin' up a rootin', tootin' Western on local TV in California for Kellogg's Corn Soya, NBC's "All-Star Revue," on which the top star was most frequently Jimmy Durante.

Then there was "Space Cadet," the mythical Project Mercury of the early 1950s for kids to watch which was presented live during three afternoons a week on the now defunct DuMont TV network.

"Mark Trail," adapted from the comic strip, was a radio show that Kellogg was sponsoring then, too.

The first national property for Kellogg was "Howdy Doody," on NBC-TV. Then late in the 1950s Kellogg pioneered a really new concept in TV: its syndication system, later called the Kellogg spotwork.

The big cereal company bought, financed, and produced an entire show, "Wild Bill Hickok."

An agency TV producer was sent out to Hollywood to supervise film production for both client and Burnett, and also to write and produce some of TV's earliest "integrated commercials." (These commercials used Guy Madison and Andy Devine, stars of the show, to sell the product, usually in settings related to the show story line.)

"Wild Bill Hickok" was the show that introduced Sugar Pops, Kellogg's first entry in the new presweet cereal field.

Kellogg commercials were spliced into the prints and shipped directly to the stations from the agency. Some stations refused to rerun the first 13 episodes right away. So hour-long features were bought on the open market, a print at a time, a subject at a time, cutting them down to 26 minutes, slapping in Sugar Pops, Rice Krispies, and Corn Flakes commercials, and racing them off to the stubborn stations.

"Superman" had been a Kellogg radio show, with Bud Collyer in the title role, in the 1930s. Burnett brought it to TV for the introduction of Kellogg's Sugar Frosted Flakes . . . and the same shows relinquished by Kellogg are still running, 14 years later, on stations all over the country—and still getting good ratings, too.

"Super Circus" was a Chicago institution starring another Chicago institution, blonde Mary Hartline. It had Mary and Cliffy the Clown, and Scampy, and ringmaster Claude Kirschner. An hour of wild and square confusion from the Civic Theatre every Sunday afternoon.

Arthur Godfrey and Art Linkletter were Kellogg salesmen on their own TV shows, Art on "House Party," Arthur on his own "Arthur and His Friends."

Col. John Glenn was a very successful contestant on "Name That Tune" during Kellogg's cosponsorship.

In the late 1950s the company bought into "What's My Line?" and stayed with it until late in 1965. It did the same with the "Garry Moore Show," a long and successful five-day-a-week strip on CBS. Both were long and happy associations.

Some shows hard to remember. There are some vehicles that are difficult to remember: "Hotel de Paree," "the Bucanneers," "The Deputy."

Then, moving miracles. Suddenly there was the Hanna-Barbera explosion of animated miracles: "Huckleberry Hound" and "Yogi Bear" and "Quick Draw McGraw."

"Woody Woodpecker" also contributed his animated art to Rice Krispies. Then the company moved along to a delightful live-action film series based on the "Dennis the Menace" newspaper cartoon. "Captain Kangaroo" began helping out with the preschool moppets; the company bought "Beverly Hillbillies" in the pilot stage; "My Favorite Martian" replaced Dennis; and "McHale's Navy" came in 1965.

Flashback: Start and growth

While Kellogg Company has been the leader of the ready-to-eat cereal manufacturers from the outset, it was not until about 1959 that Kellogg's share of market became greater than that of the combined shares of its two leading competitors, General Foods and General Mills.

It should be noted that the development by Mr. Kellogg of Corn Flakes started one of the greatest business revolutions in history: *the mass marketing of packaged food.* Until this happened, people generally bought their food items in bulk:—barrels of flour and sugar, sacks of grain, wheels of cheese.

Getting people to buy a cardboard box filled with light and airy and delicate-looking corn flakes was no easy task, and Mr. Kellogg finally, in desperation, invested the last dollar of his capital in national magazine advertising.

At the present time Kellogg Company and its subsidiary companies employ more than 10,000 men and women to produce and promote Kellogg products. It has 23 plants in 16 countries and a promising market for its product line in more than 150 countries. The packages are printed in many colors and many languages. Corn Flake cartons, for example appear in 12 languages.

Since cereals generally are eaten by the spoonful, it is hard to visualize how many families would be required to consume one billion pounds of cereal, which is about what Kellogg produces annually. Most of its products are consumed as breakfast food or as snacks, and many of them are used as ingredients in the preparation of other food.

While Kellogg's share of the ready-to-eat cereal market varies from country to country, it is estimated that the company produces nearly half of the cereals sold in world markets.

According to market research, about 60 brands of ready-to-eat cereal are now being marketed in the United States. In many cases, these products are sold in packages of various sizes designed to give consumers the cereal they prefer in the quantities they find most convenient.

The average family consuming cereal in the United States has about three different packages of cereal on the kitchen shelf most of the time.

Every year a score of new products joins the parade from the plant to the grocery shelf. This makes the cereal business a highly competitive one, not only in this country but in all countries where such products are sold.

The fact that ever-changing preferences on the part of consumers can motivate the sale of a variety of cereals is one of the chief reasons why the industry has prospered. During the last ten years, the annual per capita consumption of all ready-to-eat cereals has increased from 4.8 to 6.1 pounds in the United States. Comparable increases are on record in Canada, Great Britain, Australia, and many other countries. Australia is the one with the highest per capita consumption.

Generally speaking, the rate of demand for Kellogg's cereals has increased nearly twice as fast as the population in all countries where it does business.

For over 65 years Kellogg has been trying to convey to the public what it thinks is important about the nutrition, taste appeal, and convenience of its products. In its advertising, it tries to reach the younger children and teen-agers, as well as adults.

Marketing research shows that children and teen-agers consume about 50 percent of all the ready-to-eat cereal that is sold. Communicating the right sales messages to all age groups year after year with fresh impact is an absorbing task. Much depends upon the coordination of all aspects of promotion and distribution. Advertising has to do what it is supposed to do quickly, effectively, and with great frequency.

Advertising and promotion of Kellogg products

A packaged food business such as Kellogg Company depends on a completely integrated process of manufacturing, distributing, and selling of low unit-cost products to millions of people every day.

In such a business, the key to volume manufacture (and hence to low-cost manufacture) is to keep the stream of goods moving off the grocers' shelves and into the hands of the consumers every day of the year. The decision to buy or not to buy Kellogg products is made million of times each day by millions of people in thousands of stores. To maintain the constant high volume and low unit-cost it is necessary to continually remind consumers to buy Kellogg products and the principal means for keeping the Kellogg name in the mind of the consumer is advertising. This is especially true in the case of an institution such as Kellogg Company which distributes its products across the entire country.

From the beginning, Kellogg Company has advertised and promoted the sale of its cereal products through many advertising media. Mr. Kellogg recognized the importance of advertising and promoting, and among his early promotions was the use of his signature on the package to indicate a guarantee of quality. Today, consumers are constantly exposed to Kellogg products through newspaper, magazine, television, and other forms of advertising.

Product lines

Kellogg Company and its subsidiaries produce a variety of products on an international basis in keeping with the local customs. The following products are marketed by Kellogg Company in the United States on a nationwide scale:

Corn Flakes	Special K	Variety
Pep	Froot Loops	Corn Flake Crumbs
Krumbles	Product 19	Bag and Bake
Rice Krispies	Puffed Wheat	Croutettes
40% Bran Flakes	Puffed Rice	Pop-Tarts
Raisin Bran	Concentrate	Danish Go-Rounds
Sugar Pops	Puffa Puffa Rice	Salad Mixes
Cocoa Krispies	Apple Jacks	Assorted Individuals
Sugar Smacks	Handi-Pak	Self-Serve Bowl
Bran Buds	Jumbo	Packages
All-Bran	Request Pak	Frosted Mini-Wheats
Sugar Frosted Flakes	Snack-Pak	

Case Questions

1. How can the reasons for the purchase of cereal be classified?
2. What kind of buying behavior does the consumer have at present in the purchase of cereals? Will this remain the same or change during the next decade?
3. To what degree is the retailer responsible for selling Kellogg products?
4. How important do you believe the use of advertising was in the growth of the Kellogg Company? Give reasons.
5. In a recent year, advertising expenditures were estimated to be 12.6 percent of the total sales of all products for Kellogg, 9.3 percent for General Mills and 8.7 percent for General Foods. Comment.

Case *4–5*	**COUNTER-ADVERTISING** **Controlling product claims**

So-called counter-advertising to rebut controversial product claims made in commercials should be considered for television and radio. The Federal Trade Commission proposed that persons and groups be granted free, as well as paid- for, broadcast time to answer advertising claims involving such public issues as health, safety, and pollution. For example, the FTC would allow counter-ads to commercials advertising a company's antipollution efforts, those making autosafety claims, and food ads making nutritional claims.

The FTC statement was filed in response to a request for public comment by the Federal Communications Commission on its previously announced inquiry into the workings of the "fairness doctrine." The doctrine basically requires broadcasters to air positions opposing views broadcast on public issues. Among various problems the FCC wants to explore is how, and if, the doctrine should apply to commercials. So far, only cigarette commercials specifically have been ruled by the FCC to be under the fairness doctrine.

The FTC, whose proposal isn't binding on the FCC, likened the suggested counter-ads to the anti-cigarette commercials the FCC allowed. The FTC said such counter-ads also should be allowed to respond to advertising claims based on controversial scientific findings, and to ads that don't say anything about the negative aspects of a product. The FTC would leave it up to the FCC to decide when counter-advertisements should be permitted. But it suggested that the FCC allow open availability of commercial time for anyone willing to pay for counter-ads at regular rates, and that the FCC require broadcasters to provide some free time for counter-advertising.

Case questions

1. What criteria should be established to determine whether or not "counter-advertising" would be granted?
2. Who should decide as to whether or not this type of advertising will be done?
3. Comment on the pros and cons of this type of advertising.

5

THE SOCIAL ROLES OF ADVERTISING

*A*s mentioned earlier, it is somewhat arbitrary to try to separate the economic from the social aspects of human life, especially in modern societies like that of the United States. The purpose of this chapter, therefore, is to review those roles of advertising that current literature and research classifies as primarily social in nature.

We shall begin with an examination of the role of advertising in a social movement called consumerism. Over several decades this movement has captured the ever-changing issues of how the well-being of all consumers—i.e., society—may depend on the organization of a society's economic system, including that of its mass communication system and the advertising institution.

We will then proceed with an examination of some of the major social and cultural factors that underlie the issues emphasized by consumerism. Very little is known about these factors, especially as they may apply to the possible social roles of advertising. At present, different theories and speculations about these factors suggest that advertising may affect the well-being of society—all of us consumers —either positively or negatively. Advertisers should be familiar with such conflicting claims and theories, for it is this lack of knowledge that makes it difficult to formulate rational laws, regulations, and court decisions bearing on the performance of the entire advertising institution and on the decisions of advertising managers.

Consumerism

Consumerism has become an important issue confronting not only private managers but public policy makers as well. It has taken the form of the "consumer movement," a loose and changing grouping of people and voluntary organizations. There are different ideologies and

154

belief systems within the consumer movement, but for our purposes it is sufficient to say that one of the main concerns of the movement is the protection of consumers. This concern often is based on the assumptions that consumers are unorganized, ill-informed, even without purpose or direction, and perhaps unable to decide what is good for them.

Background concepts

Although some individuals think of consumerism as basically a phenomenon of recent origin, careful study of all available sources indicates that the origins of consumerism are lost in the dim past, as is true of so many facets of modern life. But it is undoubtedly safe to assume that some type of consumerism has existed as long as one man decided to "sell" one idea or product to another. However, the term "consumerism" is associated primarily with the last few decades.

Such literature as *The Affluent Society, The Waste Makers,* and *The Hidden Persuaders* contributed to the popularization of the concept. Also, on March 15, 1962, President John F. Kennedy sent Congress a message asking for the strengthening of programs for the protection of consumer interests. The President stated that the consumer had four rights as such: the right to safety, the right to be informed, the right to choose, and the right to be heard. He proposed increasing the staff of the Food and Drug Administration to provide greater protection from, as the President put it, thousands of harmful substances now contained in common household items. The Federal Trade Commission, he hoped, would have its duties enlarged to allow it to protect the consumer from unjust and concealed interest rates on small loans and on time payments. Attention should also be given to packaging, and to the enforcement of regulations to prevent misleading packages. Various steps were suggested but not outlined in any detail.

Important among the proposals was one which did not require legislative sanction: the appointment of a Consumers' Advisory Council. The council was appointed in July 1962. It was to report to the President's Council of Economic Advisors. Its duties were to examine and advise on issues of broad economic policy, on governmental programs protecting consumer needs, and on needed improvements in the flow of consumer research material to the public.

The work of the council, during the ensuing years, has been reinforced by the dedicated efforts of Ralph Nader, interested legislators, and other leading writers and individuals who have kept the surge of publicity about auto safety, product ingredients, and various consumer problems in the forefront. As a result it would appear that consumerism will influence corporate activity to an even greater degree in the years ahead.

General considerations

Although, as pointed out above, the consumer occupies the central position in the economic system, he has not always received the attention to which he is entitled. Our government has been slow to provide him with the protection which the economic system failed to afford him. Businessmen often have put more emphasis upon short-term rather than upon long-run results. When legislators show an interest in the consumer, they usually approach it on an individual basis. Consequently, the consumer's position in the economic system tends to be weak. Among the causes of this weakness are such ones as:

1. It is difficult for the consumer to judge the quality of the products in the market.
2. The information about the products that is offered may be misleading and confusing.
3. The number of brands of the various items complicates his selection to an even greater degree.
4. Some sellers suppress pertinent information about their products.
5. Conflicting claims about products add to the confusion.
6. There is a tendency for some sellers to try to get the consumer to purchase on the basis of emotion rather than on the use of factual data.
7. The consumer ends up by paying for a major share of the wastes involved in marketing.
8. Due to insufficient knowledge of consumer behavior, an accurate blueprint for defining products in terms of consumer choice is not available.
9. The consumer lacks the education and knowledge to judge what is the best buy.
10. It is too complex for the average consumer to evaluate the myriad conflicting claims of competing manufacturers.

Although the above list of criticisms is by no means complete, it includes a number of those which have been instrumental in spearheading "consumerism."

Protection of consumer

It would be naive to assume all businessmen are altruistic and virtuous. Much of the legislation which protects the consumer from adulterated and harmful products has been important to our public interest. The pure food and drug legislation, both national and state, has afforded protection in areas in which the consumer is particularly defenseless, and in which a small number of unscrupulous firms can cause great damage. Other legislation, such as the Wool Products Labeling Act, gives the consumer protection that he cannot himself provide, however vigilant and discriminating he may be. The ethical businessmen generally welcome such legislation, not only because it does afford the protection that the consumer needs, but also because it curbs unfair practices of competitors.

There are those, however, who believe that the consumer not only needs protection from the ills which he cannot determine or foresee, but also that he needs guidance in getting his money's worth. Implicit in this "Lo, the poor consumer" train of thought is the feeling the consumer is victimized by advertising and sales promotion and is, therefore, cajoled into buying more than he needs, into buying goods that merely pander to his whims, and into buying merchandise that is poor in quality and that is in poor taste.

Variations in personal values

In considering consumerism, we should be particularly careful to avoid attempting to project our own *value-judgments* into criteria for the guidance of others. Some families prefer to live in low cost housing in order to be able to drive expensive automobiles. Some individuals prefer to take a trip to Europe instead of maintaining insurance programs. Some people prefer playing golf to attending a football game. But each person has made a free choice of those gratifications which please him the most. The concept of "plain living and high thinking" is preeminently suitable for those who are attracted to it, but is not to be forced on others. It is impossible to designate one person's consumption pattern as foolish and another's as sensible.

Each individual must draw up his own calculus of values which may weigh pride and pleasure more heavily than frugality. As a result, any attempt to guide the consumer in getting his money's worth should curtail any attempt to project someone else's set of values.

Future of consumerism

Consumerism is here to stay. Tomorrow's consumer will be better educated, more affluent, and more critical. He will probably be less concerned with status symbols and more anxious to get information about the product. He will expect management to accept greater social responsibilities even if this results in a decrease in short-run profits. For managements who fail to measure up to the desired standards, there will be increased government regulations, consumer boycotts, and employee dissensions.

Nevertheless, the authors wish to emphasize that there is no immutability about taste. Freedom of consumer choice is more important socially and economically than is conformity to one set of criteria. What is waste for one consumer may be wisdom for another.

We live in a competitive economy. Business prospers as it offers consumers what they want. So long as consumer protection is confined to shielding the consumer from dangers that he himself cannot foresee or avoid, and to the enforcement of contracts, and the curtailment of fraud and deception, there is greater merit in allowing competition to enforce the meeting of the consumers' wishes with respect to variety, quantity and quality of goods and services.

It is the opinion of the authors that through the mass production and mass distribution methods the average American consumer has been able to secure a great variety of products. Nevertheless, because of these techniques, it is inevitable that the inherent dangers involved in large-scale production and distribution processes may result in defective products, and misleading marketing strategies.

Therefore, the authors recommend that:

1. More effective quality control procedures be established by manufacturers.
2. Improved communication methods be developed at all marketing levels.
3. Pricing strategy be set on an objective unit basis to allow the consumer to make more realistic comparisons.
4. Manufacturers take the initiative in setting standards for safety, service, and certification.
5. Better procedures be instituted whereby customer-seller-manufacturer complaints can be handled.
6. Warranties for products be simplified and the distribution link closest to the consumer be given greater autonomy in rendering the service on these warranties.
7. Business organizations support policies and programs aimed at giving consumers more information and protection.
8. The marketing and advertising strategies be reevaluated in order to mirror more effectively the evolving social and ethical norms of the younger generation.
9. Business make a greater effort to prognosticate the social problems of the consumer.
10. Finally, the credibility of business in the eyes of the consumers be reenforced.

Advertising and social issues

Advertising is one aspect of business that is most visible to everyone in a society. The manufacture of tools or clothing, the buying for retail organizations, and the planning done to staff and operate our corporations are all carried on in such a manner that the general public does not fully comprehend how they are administered. Except as a person's own work and the work of his immediate circle of friends become evident to him, his knowledge of business frequently comes from what he sees when he buys at retail or through individual salesmen, and from what he reads, sees, and hears of advertising. Although the combined advertising expenditures for American business is about 2 percent of the Gross National Product in the United States each year, advertising is so conspicuous to so many people that they may tend to judge all business by advertising.

In general, there is a feeling among some who disapprove of our free enterprise, capitalistic society that advertising is blatant, uneconomic, and antisocial, as though advertising alone were responsible for what they consider an undesirable state of affairs. However, analyses will indicate that many of these negative comments are basically criticisms of the American system of economic organization.

Waste in advertising

When people speak of waste in advertising, they do not generally refer to the offices of advertising agencies or the assignment to manufacturers' advertising departments of executives and clerical workers who possibly might be more productive assigned to other duties. When people speak of waste in advertising, they usually mean that more money is spent for advertising than they think is appropriate. This argument is advanced in spite of the fact that the percentage of Gross National Product devoted to advertising has decreased over the years. Sometimes an advertiser may invest more in advertising than might be necessary. Sometimes an expensive commercial picture is ordered when a photograph costing but a fraction of the artist's bill might have sufficed. Sometimes a manufacturer may allocate funds for advertising a product for which there is no ready market because suitable marketing research was not done. While the above examples indicate some waste, one can find some superfluous expenditures in almost all business activities.

Social waste is a difficult subject to interpret. The expenditure of a million dollars for advertisments in the newspapers of a particular trading area, as an example, may be quite conspicuous. But if the stores in the area can save a greater amount in payments to retail sales personnel, it is difficult to determine that there is wastefulness without research to substantiate it.

General social criticisms

When we evaluate social problems in relation to the use of advertising, we are even more in the area of value judgments. How can deficiencies in our social system be corrected? How can things be managed so that people will get more of the essential necessities without giving up too much of their basic freedom of choice and action? What part does advertising play in helping to accentuate or relieve those conditions?

We find that there is a tendency for the critics of advertising to base their allegations of its social value on such statements as:

1. Advertising makes false statements which confuse and mislead consumers, and often these statements are made by implication.
2. Advertising forces customers to want goods and services they really do not need.
3. Advertising promotes the use of products which are inherently harmful.
4. Advertising, as it is exposed to the consumer, lacks aesthetic attributes.
5. Advertising (particularly the television commercials) is forced on the consumer.

The truth or falsity of a statement is difficult to ascertain. Automobile tires are sold with the help of advertising. In general each manufacturer will emphasize certain features of his tires. At first glance, it might seem that one tire must be best, another second best, and another third best. But actually, testing laboratories find difficulty in making such clear-cut demarcations. One tire will give a "softer" ride; another will last longer; a third will "corner" better. Each manufacturer attempts to emphasize the characteristics that he believes interest the most people. The advertising appeals will state, "This tire will last longer on rough roads," or "This tire will make your old car ride like a new car." Even the U.S. Bureau of Standards, which spends millions of dollars each year attempting to help the federal government select the "best" buys, has a hard time making its selections.

Let us consider another situation. A manufacturer of cosmetics uses the appeal that his cosmetics will make a young woman more lovable and will attract young men to her. Certainly, in her fantasy life, the young woman will probably want to be lovable and to attract a young man. And certainly she will be more attractive in real life if she is well groomed than if she is not. We learn, from advertising, that a particular brand of carpet will make a living room more attractive, or that this new lighting fixture will make a hallway brighter. These, and many other similar statements, are true. They do not, however, say that they will accomplish the impossible.

People want to look better, eat better, live in better houses, drive better cars—in fact, improve all aspects of their standard of living. Merchandise which may satisfy, entirely or partially, the wants of the consumer may be sold more easily through persuading the prospect with the right appeal. One finds that not only in the advertising for dentrifices but also in sermons from the pulpit, in lectures from the rostrum, and in directives from the government similar tactics of persuasion are used.

Let us consider the next criticism, that advertising forces consumers to want merchandise they cannot afford. The ubiquity of advertising does not give it compulsive force. Indeed, advertising cannot move people in directions contrary to social trends. One of the reasons companies use marketing research is to find out how to advertise goods and services to coincide with the demand of the consumers. At a time when women used leg makeup rather than hosiery, manufacturers of hosiery advertised heavily to get women to wear stockings instead of leg makeup. But no movement contrary to the social trend was started. When men decided that they did not need to wear hats, the hat industry tried to use primary advertising to reverse this trend, but the results were unsatisfactory.

When electric ranges were first developed, they were advertised heavily by leading manufacturers of electric appliances. Women, according to various marketing research studies, were afraid that the change from gas cooking to electric cooking would impair their cooking skill. Although extensive advertising was done, it required 20 years to get women to start using electric ranges. Then, as more and more women used electric ranges, advertising helped to speed the acceptance trend.

Dr. Lawrence C. Lockley has said that advertising never brings about anything that would not occur without advertising, but that it does hasten product adoption and use. The number of instances which can be advanced to show that advertising has not been able to get consumers to buy products with a declining trend, or that advertising was not able to get consumers to adopt a product in advance of the time it seemed propitious, is great enough to dispel the belief that advertising has the ability to do more than advance effective suggestions.

Does advertising promote the sale of products which are harmful? There is a variety of legislation which is supposed to prevent the promotion of the sale of harmful products. There are many marginal questions here. Does one of the conventional shortenings build up the cholesterol content of the blood sufficiently to make it harmful to many people? We don't know. And in our confusion, we can find evidence suggesting that our conventional shortenings are entirely satisfactory. Are cigarettes harmful? Again, the evidence is not conclusive. So far as we can tell, smog is more harmful than cigarette smoke. And the studies attempting to show that cigarette smoking is harmful are not regarded as convincing by all statisticians. Are alcoholic beverages dangerous and immoral? Intemperately used, they are dangerous. Yet our one attempt to abolish them seemed to advance their use rather than restrict it. Again, conclusive evidence is not in.

Probably no product sold to the public causes more death and injury than the automobile. Yet few believe that it is immoral or that it should not be sold to the American public although federal laws now are requiring more safety and smog devices.

On the other hand, items whose disrepute is due to the adverse opinions of people who object to the American standard of living, or to the price system, should not, for those reasons, be banned!

Is advertising lacking in good taste? Laxatives, depilatories, liniments for aching muscles, and cemetery lots are all a part of the American scene. If the advertiser cannot advertise the goods and services that the American public openly buys, by what standard should he select what he is to advertise? Some radio and television commercials are obtrusive and irritating. If the public is offended by the appeals used, the advertiser may soon find out about their disapproval through his decrease in sales.

The first obligation of advertising is to communicate with the American public. Magazines, newspapers, television programs, and radio programs are molded to the public taste. Some people are more aesthetic and more sensitive than the general run of advertising readers, listeners, or viewers. If so, they may find some consumer advertising distasteful. That fact does not mean that the advertising now done is not gauged carefully to the level of most Americans. If it were not, it would indeed be wasteful.

Finally, we are told that advertising, particularly television advertising, forces its way into the American living room. Under our system of advertising, television comes to us without charge, at all times, and with a great variety of programs. Advertisers pay the costs of maintaining this service—evidently a service that the American public values—in order to advertise their products. The television viewer who is affronted by the television commercials is not obliged to keep listening to the commercials. If he wants to watch the programs, he may either submit to the commercials or he may turn the set off during the commercials. He is under no obligation to view the commercials or the television programs.

If he believes that the television service should be provided without the interference of commercials, then he must be willing to recommend that television programs be prepared at public expense and the taxpayer be assessed additional taxes to pay for this entertainment.

Some of the other social questions that are important are such ones as:

1. Does advertising contribute to a higher standard of living for society?
2. Does advertising cause people to place an undue stress on material possessions, to the neglect of their spiritual and cultural needs, their intellectual and aesthetic interests?
3. Does advertising persuade people to buy goods they do not need, that are not necessary for the satisfaction of the basic needs of life—food, shelter, and clothing?

Standard of living

Has advertising contributed to the ability of the masses to acquire and enjoy increased quantities and varieties of commodities? Most people would grant that advertising, through its contribution to more effective marketing and selling in the American economy, has made some considerable contribution to the present high standard of living of most Americans. It has undoubtedly been a contributing factor, along with many others, in developing in people the motivation to work harder in order to acquire some of the many luxuries and semi-luxuries made available by our productive economic system, and brought to the daily attention of people through advertising. The knowledge of such new products and improved products, and the potential enjoyment to be realized by their possession, has been brought to the attention of many individuals through advertising. Undoubtedly advertising has played a part in creating this desire among Americans to labor and to produce, and in turn to be able to acquire and possess and enjoy these goods and services which will lift their lives above the subsistence level.

The most exhaustive study that has been made of the economic effects of advertising reached the conclusion that advertising had made a major contribution to increasing the standard of living, as noted in the conclusion to the study:

> Advertising's outstanding contribution to consumer welfare comes from its part in promoting a dynamic, expanding economy. Advertising's chief task from a social standpoint is that of encouraging the development of new products. It offers a means whereby the enterpriser may hope to build a profitable demand for his new and differentiated merchandise which will justify investment. From growing investment has come the

increasing flow of income which has raised man's materials welfare to a level unknown in previous centuries.[1]

Today's economy is geared to a high level of consumption, and if high levels of production and employment are to be maintained, and the economy is to continue to grow, consumers will have to continue to maintain, if not increase, their standard of living with reference to material goods. Certainly advertising fills a considerable role in stimulating this continued high standard of living among most Americans.

This is especially true in light of the fact that a large portion of today's production is of goods not required to meet human physiological needs, but is designed to meet psychological wants. Potential consumers of such new goods, which might be considered luxury or semiluxury by many, must be "educated" to desire such products, if the economy is to function smoothly. One of the key influences in such education is advertising.

Does advertising place an undue stress on material things?

In light of the discussion in the preceding paragraphs of the role of advertising in contributing to and maintaining a high standard of living, it is obvious that advertising does stress to a considerable degree the consumption of material goods. Does this mean that there has been a decline in the stress placed on people's cultural and spiritual needs? Have people's interests in intellectual and aesthetic pursuits declined because of advertising, or are they less than they would be if we had no advertising? Has interest in literature, music, painting, sculpture, the theater, creative pursuits, and efforts on behalf of the poor, the ill, and the unfortunate decreased, or is it less than it would have been, because of advertising?

Such questions are difficult to answer categorically. However, many think a reasonable standard of living in material things is generally a prerequisite to a great interest in cultural activities and the arts. And they would also say there is not necessarily incompatibility between a high standard of living and a high level of cultural and spiritual life. Also, some would cite statistics on the number of books sold, the number of symphony orchestras in this country, the growth of attendance at art museums, and increases in similar activities as evidence that the level of cultural interest is higher in the United States than at any time in the past; although it may not be as high as the critics believe it should be, or as it might be.

And, even if people's cultural and spiritual life is not as "high" as the critics feel it should be, is this lower standard due to advertising? Does the stress on material things automatically rule out attention to the cultural and spiritual values of life? Many would agree with F. P. Bishop when he says:

> But in practice it is not easy to keep the conception of the ends of life separate from the problem of providing the means. Such is the constitu-

[1] Neil H. Borden, *The Economic Effects of Advertising* (Homewood, Ill.: Richard D. Irwin, Inc., 1942), p. 881.

tion of human life that the satisfaction of the higher desires is only possible by means of the relative satisfaction of the lower. Thus the gratification of the desire for knowledge is only possible in a society and, in a sense, by an individual, on condition that the more primary instinct to acquire property and secure the means of subsistence has been satisfied. Man does not live by bread alone, but without bread or its equivalent he cannot live at all; and a substantial minimum of material comfort and security is necessary before he can attend to the consideration of the true ends of life to the attainment of which material possessions should be no more than a means. Of course it is wrong for the philosopher in his study, adequately clothed and warmed and fed, and equipped with all the material adjuncts of *his* ideal life, to pour scorn upon others who may seem to be excessively preoccupied with material desires which do not vex him.[2]

Does advertising cause people to buy goods they do not need?

It is certainly true that much of the advertising of today is designed to sell new products that are not "necessities" at present. However, many of the products called luxuries or nonnecessities today become what people consider necessities for a reasonable standard of material living tomorrow, as was the case with the vacuum clearner and the electric refrigerator. Actually, much of the criticism of advertising on this score, of its selling people things they do not "need," is directed more at the fact that people buy things the critic does not think they should want. The question naturally arises as to who is to make the decision as to what people should want. Many believe it is the consumer himself who should decide what he wants and needs, and not the critics or a government agency or any other authoritarian body. If the consumer's freedom of choice in the marketplace is taken away from him, he might soon lose many of his other freedoms also. To some it would appear strange that the legislators, economists, political scientists, and historians who are so often the ones who feel the consumer should not be allowed freedom of choice, and the advertiser freedom of advertising, are the loudest in their demands for the freedom of speech to say what they think, and the freedom to protest the causes they do not happen to approve. Since advertising (so long as it does not violate standards of good taste, ethics, and so forth) is one form of free speech for the business community, it would appear reasonable that it be permitted, and that the consumer have the privilege of deciding what products he needs and wants, whether or not they happen to be what critics call necessities or luxuries.

Highlights

The list of the possible social roles of advertising in society that we have discussed is not exhaustive, and the examination of each role touched only on the main issues involved. In spite of the inherent

---

[2] F. P. Bishop, *The Ethics of Advertising* (London: Robert Hale, Ltd., 1943), pp. 34–35.

complexities, the entire problem of identifying and evaluating the social roles of advertising is fundamentally simple. The underlying issues are generally few and direct.

Probably the most important key issue is the difference in political ideologies held by members of society. At the risk of simplifying the range of current political ideologies, at one extreme we find a view that favors—in principle—a complete centralization of economic and social decisions. The specific criticisms of the advertising institution raised from the above viewpoint are not necessarily against the social need for some form of mass communication; rather, these criticisms are ultimately against the large degree of decentralization of the institution.

At the other extreme of political ideologies, the current tendency toward decentralization is seen as not sufficient at all. From this viewpoint, the social and economic organization of a society, including that of its advertising institution, should strive for complete decentralization. Each individual and organization should be free to send and seek any kind of information, with the courts presiding over the working of the system. Students of advertising must accept the fact that many specific issues about advertising tend to hide rather different—and often unreconcilable—beliefs of what is a good political organization of a society.

The other important key issue about advertising in society is, in many ways, the mirror image of the first. It deals with fundamentally different ways to perceive mankind and its place on earth. It involves differences in cultural values as well as in judgment. For the have-nots, to aspire to own a luxury car may be a concrete expression of their most noble desire to be integrated, to be members of a good society. And for a woman who wants a successful career, the purchase of more and better clothes and cosmetics may be a reflection of her desire to be a fuller participant in social life—for her it may not be materialism. Or, for some members of society, temperance, frugality, and concern for future generations may be the foundations guiding their behavior. From this point of view, many social and economic trends may be unacceptable.

Therefore, the productive private sector may face a dilemma whenever a particular group of values and beliefs is proposed as being superior to that prevailing in a free society. The private sector can survive—i.e., it can pay labor, vendors, capital, and taxes—only if it successfully identifies, interprets, and satisfies the prevailing economic, social, and psychological needs of consumers.

The differences in political ideologies and cultural values are translated into different and often contradictory judgments of what advertising should and should not do. This situation creates difficulties, not only for advertisers, advertising agencies, and mass media, but also for legislators, regulators, and the courts. But the situation is even more confusing for there is practically no empirical evidence of what the social roles of advertising actually are. For instance, recall from Chapter 4 that even the existence of a causal relationship between advertising expenditures and the Gross National Product, Disposable

FIGURE 5–1
The impact of cultural values and social institutions on the roles of advertising in an economy and in society

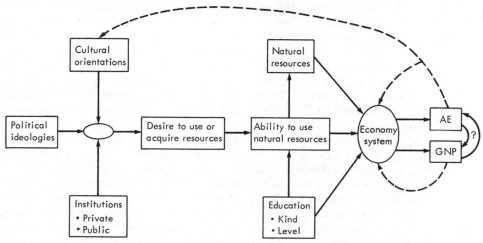

Source: F. M. Nicosia, *Advertising, Management, and Society* (New York: McGraw-Hill, 1974), p. 192.

Income, and Personal Consumption Expenditures is still to be empirically ascertained.

Figure 5–1 describes in detail some economic and social processes suggesting that current concerns with the advertising institution are misdirected. These processes point out that the main causes of what we observe in modern affluent societies are the existence of ample natural resources and the human willingness and ability to acquire and use natural resources for certain types of social and economic development. For instance, Brazil is one of the richest countries in natural resources, and Switzerland and Japan are among the poorest. Yet, the two latter countries have some of the highest GNPs and advertising expenditures per capita, while Brazil has one of the lowest.

All in all, the evidence bearing upon the possible economic roles of advertising in an economy must still be empirically determined. The evidence about the possible social roles of the advertising institution is practically nonexistent; in fact, in this area even conceptual clarity is lacking, for there exists an intertwining of concepts and personal values and judgments.

Private and social managers make decisions in the midst of this ambiguous situation. Clearly, they cannot possibly "maximize" the satisfaction of any one goal, for neither goals nor means are self-evident. At best, they can try to search for means and goals that by and large may be fair.

Questions

1. U.S. Public Health Service has estimated that in 1948 the average American threw away only two pounds of trash a day, but at present he discards over

five pounds—and the population has increased by over 30 percent in the same period. The waste ranges from orange peels and beer cans to junked appliances and abandoned autos. The Automobile Manufacturers' Association indicates that, nationwide over six million cars and 900,000 trucks are junked each year. Comment on what advertising executives can do to help resolve this problem.

2. Farm crops from citrus to cereals are annually dusted with about one billion pounds of pesticides. Such massive spraying effects the environment and human health. An estimated 75,000 acute pesticide poisonings occur each year. What can business do, through advertising, to control spraying?

3. List some marketing and advertising changes that are occurring and are likely to occur as a result of consumerism.

4. Which buying motives should be emphasized because of the increased consumerism movement?

5. For which of the following products and/or services would consumerism movements have greater impact? Give reasons.

a. Furniture.	f. Women's shoes.
b. Baby food.	g. Men's shirts.
c. Lamps.	h. Hospital services.
d. Short term loans.	i. Dishes
e. Drugs.	j. Television sets.

6. The state by protecting and enforcing competition will protect the interests of consumers. Discuss.

7. Who should be responsible for setting the standards for consumer goods?

8. Do you believe that the consumer movement will become a highly organized homogeneous course of action? Why? Why not?

9. Do you believe Congress should extend its jurisdiction to cover all clothing products under the Flammable Fabric Act which now makes sure that dangerous clothing is removed from the market?

10. It has been stated: "The consumer is king. What he wants, business will find it profitable to satisfy his demand." Comment.

11. Should legislation in protecting the consumer be directed primarily to regulating marketing and advertising? Discuss.

12. From the social point of view, how would you justify product differentiation which is the direct result of advertising? How might this vary if the economic point of view is emphasized?

13. Is advertising the cause of the American belief in the merits of a high-level consumption economy?

14. If advertising is as effective in causing America's preoccupation with material things as critics say, should not the critics use advertising to raise the spiritual, cultural, and social levels of our society?

15. A leading advertiser has stated: "Advertising is vital to our economic and social growth." Comment.

16. Some writers have pointed out that in our economic system much of our advertising costs should be viewed as growth costs. Comment.

17. Is it wrong for advertising to influence people to want so many luxuries and nonnecessities—things they really do not need to sustain life?

18. Select three companies in which you believe advertising costs may be viewed as being excessive, and give reasons.

19. What is the place of advertising in a capitalistic economy such as we have in the United States?

20. Is advertising necessary only in a "free economy" like the United States? Do countries like Russia need to use advertising?

21. Can a businessman divorce the interrelationships of ethical and economic issues in his advertising program?

22. To what degree can advertising either change or influence customer behavior?

Case **SOCIOECONOMIC CONCEPTS**
5–1 **Value conflict**

The outstanding feature of the American clothing economy during this century has been the gradual elimination of dress differences among the various socioeconomic groups. Clothing has become lighter in weight, simpler in style, more comfortable, and easier to care for. Certain items of the turn-of-the-century wardrobe are almost anachronisms. Today a skilled laborer may be required to wear a functional garment at his job, but his leisure-time wardrobe is as diversified as that of the average office worker. By the same token, a young secretary's style of dress is not too different from that of a young debutante's; while a Boston dowager may not even be as well dressed as the wife of a successful business executive. As for children, they are universally dressed in as little as the season permits, primarily with an eye to comfort, health, and easy care.

This equalization in dress habits is the result of interrelated social, technological, and economic changes, which were sharply accelerated during the last two decades, and which changed our society with previous periods and opened big new markets for types of consumer goods that were considered luxuries in the past.

It is a fact that, while total national clothing expenditures increased, they have not kept pace with the rise in consumer disposable income. The textile and apparel industries have referred to this trend as a loss of their "rightful share" of the consumer dollar and have geared their promotional programs to try to recover this share.

The concept of a rightful or traditional share is based on a static view of the economy and denies the existing competition among industries to sell consumers all kinds of traditional and new products through all sorts of advertising media and other marketing devices. Fiber producers and textile industries—suppliers to the apparel trades—realized that they, too, must enter the competitive promotional fray if they were not to risk even further loss of their potential markets to other consumer goods. Today, clothing is being promoted with comparable budgets and the same techniques as are cars, refrigerators, and myriads of electrical appliances.

The major economic and social factors that have broadened the market base for consumer goods and services of all kinds, and put clothing into competition with these goods for the consumer dollar are:

1. Advances in industrial technology which permitted mass production of erstwhile luxury items at prices the growing number of middle-income families could afford.
2. The tremendous rise in total consumer disposable income and average family income which supplies the purchasing power for the products of advanced technology.
3. The widespread improvement of family living standards, crystallized in the movement to suburbia and accompanied by increased ownership of homes, cars, and other durable goods.
4. The commitment of important percentages of family funds for the repayment of mortgages and installment loans on types of durable goods which establish "status" in the community.
5. The increase of leisure time due to shorter working hours and increased paid holidays and vacations.
6. The trend toward informal living, encouraged and influenced by conformity among peer groups in homogeneous suburban communities—expressed, as regards dress, in a trend toward casual clothes.
7. An expanding volume of "discretionary income" which permits a wide and unpredictable choice of spending or saving out of total income over and above income required for essential consumer goods.

These factors, combined with the postwar shifts in the age composition of the population (which expanded the clothing market for the very young and the very old faster than for the intervening age groups) caused the nation's clothing expenditures to lag behind expenditures for other consumer goods and services.

An examination of total and per capita trends in the production of major outerwear items for men and women reveals two fundamental changes in the character of their wardrobes: (1) There has been an expansion of so-called separates represented by skirts, blouses, and sweaters in women's wear, and by slacks, sweaters, and sport jackets in men's wear; while the market for traditional tailored clothing—dresses, suits, and coats for women, and suits and coats for men—has remained stable or declined. (2) The switch from "big ticket" items, represented by tailored clothing, to relatively "little ticket' items, represented by separates, made it possible to increase the average number of items in the typical wardrobe without any significant increase in per capita clothing expenditures.

The implications for retail selling efforts may require more individual sales transactions to sell a blouse or a sweater and skirt, than a dress or suit; or in menswear, a pair of slacks and a jacket, than a suit. Furthermore, the character of the separates items more frequently than not represents "trading down" from the traditional single item in terms of the sales check. There is much talk regarding the ability of the consumer to trade up on clothing, but a continuation of the trend toward substitution of little ticket items for big ticket items will only increase retail selling costs at the expense of profit margins.

Because of technological advances in the production of textiles and the competition which prevailed in the textile and apparel trades, among competing firms as well as with other industries trying to get bigger shares of the consumer dollar, consumer apparel prices increased less than the prices of all other consumer goods and service. While the potential purchasing power saved on clothing enlarged the funds available for the purchase of other goods, the textile industry suffered low profit margins, excess capacity, and eventual contraction to a capacity more closely in line with the size of the market.

Outlook for the industry

A survey of family expenditures made by the United States Bureau of Labor Statistics evaluated the impact of changes on clothing expenditure patterns. It was found that in comparable income groups: (1) homeowners spent less than renters on clothing, (2) families with very young children and older members spent less on clothing than those with young and middle-aged adults, and (3) suburban families spent less on clothing than urban families. The dominant features of the consumer economy during the past two decades included an accelerated trend toward home ownership, and a movement out of urban centers to suburbs. These factors, which tended to depress clothing expenditures, may be somewhat less important during the next decade because of offsetting developments.

In addition to the economic changes which are expected to stimulate clothing expenditures, there is a less easily measured factor which may well come into play. And that is the matter of "status symbols"—a psychological term which has been popularized as a result of the extension of market research to the investigation of consumer buying motivations.

Leading psychologists believe that, in a dynamic economy, status symbols tend to change whenever large proportions of the population acquire the currently popular ones. Since it is no longer as unique to own a home, a car or two, and a large number of other types of family goods, the leaders of change will be looking for other ways of differentiating themselves from the group.

There are also signs that the simple life—the backyard cookout, the informal open house, the universal acceptance of the "come as you are, we're not dressing" attitude—may become more elaborate as the young suburban families mature both chronologically and economically. More elaborate settings and more formal social mores may demand careful grooming and more selective attire.

In urban centers, too, there is a trend toward more selective attire for special occasions such as dining out, going to the theater, and entertaining, as people seek to enhance the flavor of such special occasions by dressing up.

However, for clothing to take on the major status symbol in the years ahead, it will be essential to expand the promotional programs in textiles and clothing and to gear the themes to the special psychological auras of different sectors of the clothing market. This should dispel the monotony of uniform glamour and help the textile and apparel industries, in the future, come closer to achieving their objectives of increasing clothing purchases than they have in the past, for the very simple reason that consumers are ready for a change of pace.

Case questions

1. How do you justify, on a basis of social values, the attempt of the clothing industry to get the consumers to look upon clothing as a "status symbol"?
2. Why do consumers fail to invest more of their disposable income in clothing?
3. When a declining trend exists for clothing, how can you economically justify the industry adopting a more extensive advertising program?
4. Would the standard of living be improved if the consumer spent more of his income on clothing?
5. When a conflict exists between social and economic concepts, how should the decision of whether or not to advertise be made?

Case 5–2 **VALUE ADDED BY ADVERTISING**
Considering important implications

The competitive enterprise system allows companies the right to produce and sell products which will satisfy the needs of the consumers. This right, however, has to be evaluated and controlled in the context of the conditions that exist in each situation. Some of the questions which arise include:

1. What is the importance of advertising in our economy?
2. To what extent should the decisions in the marketplace be the criteria used in determining whether or not certain products should be allowed to be sold?
3. How important is the concept of "freedom of choice" for consumers?
4. Will the product help the consumer attain greater total satisfaction?
5. How should new products be checked before they are offered in the market?
6. Should all manufacturers be required to inform the public in their advertising about the negative as well as the positive factors about their products?

The above questions are a few of the challenges which people in advertising must resolve as part of their social responsibility. Unfortunately, there are no easy solutions to these problems because a product that might be very worthwhile and valuable for certain groups could be harmful to other groups. As a result, the procedures to adopt for fulfilling this social responsibility are indeed quite elusive.

Consider the following two examples:

Example A. An advertising executive in addressing a college audience made the following comments about the value added by advertising:

> The concept of "Value Added by Advertising" is derived from the more general concept of *value.* While theories of value differ in detail, there is general agreement on the basic idea. Value may be summarized as follows:
>
> a.   Value is fundamentally a subjective quality, since it depends on the capacity or *ability of a good or service to satisfy human wants and desires.* For this reason a good or service has value only with reference to human beings and only from their point of view. This is another way of saying that value is not objective and that unless a product or service is wanted by someone it has no value whatever. Such psychological valuations cannot, however, be measured directly, at least with any existing techniques.
>
> b.   Since we cannot measure psychological value, a practical measure of the value of a product is its *value relative to other goods and services,* as expressed by the quantity of a given product which exchanges in the marketplace for different quantities of other products.

The total value of a product, as measured by its price, may be regarded as the end result of the process of "production," which is defined as the *creation of economic value by the addition of utilities* to goods. In a highly developed economic system such as that of the United States, it must be recognized that almost all products pass through several stages of production before they are finally consumed.

Products also pass through several stages of distribution before they are available at the proper times and places and are finally transferred to a consumer. The entire process of mining, manufacturing, and distribution (which includes advertising) must be included in the term "production," since at each stage a certain amount of *value is added* to the product.

The value added by advertising is that part of the final price of a product which can be attributed to the advertising stages of the process. Similarly, the value added by a given marketing institution, such as the retailer, is that part of the price which is paid for the contribution made by him. These values added result from the performance of *marketing functions,* which are just as truly productive types of work as are agricultural, manufacturing, processing or factory assembling activities.

Value added by advertising may be defined, then, as the dollar value of the functions performed in the marketing process. The value of advertising functions comprises a part of the total marketing functions, usually estimated at about one half of the total value of goods and services produced in the United States.

The most difficult part of the value added concept is its relationship with the concept of *cost.* In one sense, price and cost must be identical. What an article costs the consumer is its price. Similarly, what advertising costs the consumer is also the value added by advertising. Thus, in a functional sense, value added by advertising is the same thing as part of the "social cost" of distribution. At this point, however, the difference in attitudes toward advertising, manufacturing, and agriculture begins to appear. One seldom hears of the "social cost of manufacturing" or the "social cost of agriculture." The values contributed by these forms of production are clearly recognized, and increases in them are hailed as social benefits. If the share of Gross National Product going to advertising increases, however, it is frequently considered undesirable and wasteful.

Much of the well-known public antagonism towards advertising stems from failure to recognize its role in the production process. There seems to be a cultural lag between economic development and public attitudes; and since advertising has only come to be of great importance in the last 70 years, it is not surprising that it has not yet been accorded its proper place.

The basic assumption underlying the many attacks on advertising costs is what might be called the "constant margin assumption." The reasoning runs something like this: Total production should be measured by the physical volume of goods produced, fabricated, and marketed to consumers. A certain percentage margin is necessary for advertising costs. If this increases, the consumer receives no more value, because he receives the same physical goods; but he is forced to pay more. The cause for the increased margin must be inefficiency in the advertising, and advertising, therefore, costs too much.

One need not be an economic theorist to see the fallacy of the foregoing argument. In the first place, much of the increases in advertising expenditures is due to increased specialization in the economic system.

Our economy has undergone a dramatic and far-reaching change in organization—a change which continues and apparently will continue in the foreseeable future. The full development of the production system, the application of mass production techniques, and the movement towards automation, all operate to shift much of the burden of production from manufacturing to distribution.

Example B. A leading M.D. was asked the question, "What do you think of the newly advertised remedies on TV for bad breath?" His answer was as follows:

> It's sad to discover that a well-entrenched aphorism—a universally accepted tidbit of literary art—has at last bit the dust. Do you recall: "Even your best friend won't tell you"? In the past, think of the many completely oblivious to this personal failing: bad breath.
>
> But these days such blissful ignorance is impossible. Whether you turn on the TV for news, your favorite Western, or a spy show, you are bound to hear the forceful reminder (by implication) that your breath is bad. Unfortunately, my bad luck is to hear these harangues whenever I am preparing for dinner.
>
> You have bad breath! You have bad breath! These revelations are suddenly thrust on innocent, unsuspecting TV friends. These days they not only tell you; they shout it at you. It has gotten so bad that milquetoasts practice in front of mirrors so they can tell their bosses off.
>
> I do not minimize the discomforts sometimes caused by one whose breath is not as sweet as a child's. It can be a problem. But in answer to your question, I believe the problem of bad breath should be attacked

frontally by physicians and dentists. Removing the cause is often more important than experiments with various advertised agents. There's time for those later.

Here are some constructive points to remember:

People with chronic lung conditions and infections of the bronchial tubes (bronchitis, emphysema, etc.) have a tendency to have bad breath. Therefore, treat the underlying cause.

If you drink too much, smoke too much, it is not likely that your breath is sweet. Some patients with advanced kidney disease suffer from bad breath.

You may have no other reason for bad breath than food particles trapped between teeth causing decay and odor. Using the toothbrush after meals and finishing the cleansing process with dental floss is the best way to overcome the trouble. Are dentures clean? Do you make routine visits to your dentist or do you wait for a toothache to bestir you? It's possible that bad breath may be due to infection of your gums. Proper treatment will do much to improve the chronic complaint.

It is evident that mouthwash and gargles will be ineffectual unless you root out any infection like bad sinuses, tonsils, and adenoids.

It's not cricket to long for the good old days. But frankly, rather than have to listen to rudely overpowering TV commercials which deflate one's appetite like a pin in a balloon, I prefer the mildly Victorian approach. "Even your best friends won't tell you."

Case questions

1. How does advertising add value to the economy?
2. What value does the consumer receive as a result of advertising?
3. What economic value does the advertising effort actually have in order to get the consumer to purchase from one seller instead of another?
4. What social and economic value is there for advertising mouthwashes?

Case **UNITED FRUIT COMPANY**
5–3 **The use of a selective appeal**

Banana industry. The banana industry is highly competitive because bananas are produced on an extensive basis in both the Eastern and the Western Hemispheres. Asia was their original home, but they have been planted in many other warm parts of the world. The Hawaiian Islands produce a banana crop. In the continental United States, Florida grows small quantities of bananas. Some also are grown along the coast of the Gulf of Mexico.

The most important banana-producing region in the world is Central America. Mexico, the West Indies, Ecuador, and Brazil also have large banana plantations.

The bananas most commonly used as fruit in America are large, yellow, and smooth-skinned. They are known as Gros Michel, Valery, and Cavendish bananas, and there is no significant product differentiation regardless of the section of the world in which they may be grown.

Before 1860, most of the banana crop was consumed in the country where the bananas were grown. However, at about that time the first large commercial plantations were created. The activities required to build and operate these large plantations included the clearing of jungles and the building of roads and villages. As a result, only large companies with adequate financing were in a position to enter the banana industry.

The United Fruit Company was one of the major companies which concentrated its banana growing acreage in Central America. It was incorporated in 1899 and operated a steamship line to transport the crops to the United States. While market share varies from year to year, in 1975 Dole had about 45 percent of the market, Chiquita about 40 percent, and Del Monte about 14 percent.

Use of bananas. While generally the only part of the banana plant that is used is the fruit, people use the leaves of certain kinds of banana trees to roof houses or to make mats, bags, and baskets. Cooked bananas are becoming increasingly popular in the United States, where they are fried, made into fritters, cooked with ham and bacon, and used in pies, cakes, and bread. Banana flour also is coming into wider use. The banana is one of the few fruits that can be bought fresh and in good condition at all times of the year.

Imports. When the fruit is to be shipped for considerable distances, workers pick it green, a whole stem at a time, cut into clusters, and ship it in boxes. It is ripened at its destination market. The United States imports over 72 million bunches of bananas each year.

Competitive situation. No consumer franchises existed for bananas, and, typically, the brokers in a commodity market of this kind make their purchases on the basis of price rather than a consumer preference for a particular kind of banana.

Objectives. As a result of their analysis of the market, United Fruit Company executives set the following objectives for the marketing of bananas:

1. To reduce its costs per sales unit in order to compete effectively in a commodity business.
2. To create selective demand for its product.

Strategy. A cost improvement program was instituted to meet the first purpose. The second objective called for measures new to the company and unique in the banana industry. The first major step toward building selectivity centered on the product itself.

A comprehensive quality control program was adopted that included: (1) the planting of a new variety of banana more resistant to disease and wind damage, (2) a grading procedure which selected the best fruit, and (3) special packing and shipping methods to provide the bananas greater protection in transit.

The second step was centered on the methods to use to develop selective demand for United Fruit Company's product.

Execution. Consumer research indicated that United Fruit could fill a consumer need by providing a brand of banana with greater quality assurance. Specifically, 40 percent of all banana purchasers studied had purchased bananas at one time or another that looked good exter-

EXHIBIT 5–1

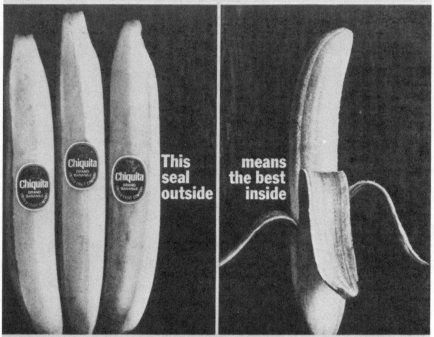

Courtesy United Fruit Company

EXHIBIT 5–2

The sign of a successful banana

That Chiquita Brand seal is a mark of achievement. Bananas that wear it have been rigorously inspected before they ever leave the tropics. Not just once, but six times. If a banana doesn't measure up, it doesn't make the boat.

Only after that are Chiquita Brand Bananas shipped. Shipped all the way from the tropics in strong, protective boxes. So when they arrive at your store, they're as sleek and golden and

tempting as bananas can be.
So to pick out the best of the bananas from the rest of the bananas, be sure to look for the seal on the peel.
It's the sign of a banana that's really a peach.

CHIQUITA BRAND BANANAS

THIS SEAL OUTSIDE   MEANS THE BEST INSIDE.

*Chiquita is a registered trademark of United Fruit Company

Courtesy United Fruit Company

nally, but when peeled were inferior. Research results also pointed out that the company had a strong property in "Chiquita" from the old radio jingle. While brand identification had been achieved by labels affixed to the banana, the company recognized that it had to do more than label the product to stimulate demand. The fact that United Fruit shipped its bananas up from the tropics in fiberboard boxes rather than on the stem appeared to be a demonstrable advantage because the shipment in the boxes subjected the fruit to less handling and bruising.

EXHIBIT 5–3

A television and print campaign was launched, promising "Chiquita bananas are shipped up in boxes to cut down on bruising." (See Exhibit 5–1.)

At the same time, the company continued its selective brand advertising campaign in national media. Among the advertising appeals used were those in Exhibit 5–2 and Exhibit 5–3.

Case questions

1. What are the conditions necessary in the banana industry, so a company can successfully use selective advertising?
2. Would it be economically advisable to emphasize primary appeals?
3. How important is "price" to the consumer in choosing between products like oranges, apples and bananas? Between different brands of bananas?
4. Evaluate the plan used and give any changes in it that the company should adopt.
5. What social value is there in advertising to create selective demand for bananas?

Case 5–4

GOLDEN HORN COMPANY
Evaluating use of advertising

Golden Horn Co. is engaged in the breeding, growing, processing, and marketing of poultry. Its activities consist of producing and hatching eggs, operating a feed mill, raising chickens, processing chickens in whole or cut in parts, and marketing chickens and feed. Its 25 distributors at the annual meeting requested that Golden Horn begin an advertising program to the consumer in order to help them capture a larger share of the volume of national and independent food chains.

Breeding

Golden Horn has a two-thirds interest in Yak Poultry Co., which is engaged in the business of producing eggs. Under the terms of the agreement Yak is obligated to sell and Golden is obligated to purchase the entire egg production. Golden purchases day-old breeder pullets and cockerels from approximately ten nonaffiliated primary breeders. One such primary breeder supplies approximately 50 percent of such breeder pullets, and another such breeder supplies approximately 50 percent of the breeder cockerels. The breeder flocks are sent to one of approximately 18 contract growing houses where they are kept for approximately 15 weeks. At such time they are transferred to one of approximately 12 contract breeder farms where they are kept during their entire productive egg-laying period (which period commences at about 26 weeks of age and may continue for 8 or 9 months). The contract growers are paid an average of 1.25 cents per chick housed, and contract breeders are paid approximately 12 cents per dozen hatching eggs produced. The contractors furnish all equipment, labor, and utilities while Yak's flocks are there, and supply the feed and technical assistance required. Yak's breeder flocks, which during the course of the year aggregate from 125,000 to 150,000 breeder hens in production at any one time, produce approximately 500,000 eggs per week.

Hatcheries

Hatching eggs are trucked by equipment from the contract breeder to the hatcheries where they are placed in incubators for 19 days, after which they are transferred to hatchers for two days. After hatching, the chicks are immediately delivered to grow-out farms. Golden currently purchases approximately 70,000 chicks per week from a nonaffiliated party.

Growing operations

Baby chicks are delivered by Golden to the contract growers, who furnish houses, equipment, labor, and utilities during the eight to nine week period necessary to raise the chicks to marketable size. Golden's personnel supervise the growing process and Golden furnishes feed, fuel, and medical supplies required during the growing period. Golden generally has an average of four to five million chickens on grow-out farms at any given time. Golden maintains approximately 220 broiler flocks which average 21,000 chickens per flock and the contract growers raise an average of four and one-half flocks per year. Each contract grower is paid on a performance contract under which the grower is guaranteed not less than $70 per thousand broilers started. At between eight and one-half and nine weeks the chickens are picked up and delivered to the company's processing plant.

Processing plant

The processing plant has a capacity on a one shift basis of approximately 500,000 chickens per week. The chickens, when delivered, are hung on overhead conveyors that carry them through the various processing steps, which include slaughtering, picking, eviscerating, chilling, grading, sizing, and packaging. The entire process takes approximately one and one-half hours. Golden sells both whole and cut-up chickens, with whole chickens accounting for approximately 75 percent of total sales. Chickens are delivered to distributors within 24 hours after processing.

Sales and distribution

During the last fiscal year Golden produced and sold approximately 22 million chickens. It sells its poultry to approximately 25 independent distributors. Such distributors resell products to major national and independent food chains and neighborhood food stores. During the last fiscal year the largest distributor accounted for approximately 21 percent of total sales.

Competition

The broiler industry is subject to intense competition. The severity of competition increases during periods of overproduction when the supply of broilers exceeds market demand. The broiler industry is also in competition with producers of meat and other fowl. Golden is also subject to certain seasonal fluctuations, whereby people tend to eat meat in greater quantities in the late fall and winter, resulting in a decline in the consumption and price of chicken. The primary areas of poultry production are Georgia, Arkansas, North Carolina, Alabama, Mississippi, and the Delaware-Maryland-Virginia area. Golden finds it difficult to sell fresh poultry on an interregional basis due to shrinkage, spoilage, and differences in shipping costs which prevent it from competing effectively outside of its region of the United States.

Evaluation of advertising

Golden's director of sales, John Aragon, was given the assignment to give a recommendation in regards to whether or not the company might find it economically and socially sound to begin a program of advertising. In his report to the directors he pointed out that the consumer, in making decisions to purchase, was faced with a number of alternatives. Generally, most of the decisions would fall into two categories: major purchases and minor purchases.

With major purchases there tended to be a gradual evolution which culminates in a concrete decision to buy the product. The stimulus to begin to evaluate the major product may be set in motion by both external and internal events. The washing machine may break down, a member of the family may be in an automobile accident, or the husband may be promoted to a new position. As a result, the consumer begins to question his friends about the product, checks the advertising more carefully, and visits the various stores to look at the models.

On the other hand, Mr. Aragon emphasized that in those purchases which would be classified in the category of minor decision making, the impact of advertising varies. Generally, however, advertising will place a minor purchase decision brand within the spectrum of what is acceptable. There is also the belief of many customers that one brand in particular is outstanding.

Recommendations

Mr. Aragon indicated that be believed Golden should advertise for the following reasons:

1. Advertising would provide a cumulative effect. Golden should not try to get immediate sales.
2. It was important from the social point of view to create a high degree of confidence in Golden's products.
3. Advertising would help develop a symbolic aura for Golden.
4. Although the purchase of Golden's products would generally be the minor decision type, for special functions the meat dish may actually become the equivalent of a major decision.
5. The emphasis of Golden's advertising should be centered on general reputation, quality, and value.

6. It is necessary to help the distributors gain a greater market share.

7. Advertising would be the most economical and fruitful method of giving the ultimate consumer information about Golden's products.

8. The consumer movement is going to continue at a faster rate and it is imperative for Golden to get involved in giving consumers product information.

9. Golden must keep abreast of the dynamic conditions in the broiler market.

10. Golden would have to make its products "familiar" before it could persuade the consumer to buy them.

Case questions

1. Evaluate the economical and social factors involved in getting the consumer to make decisions for:
   a. Major purchases
   b. Minor purchases

2. The average person, it is said, is exposed to 1,500 ads in a normal day. From the economic and social points of view, how can Golden justify spending funds for advertising?

3. How important is it for Golden to provide information to satisfy consumer needs for its products?

4. What effect would Golden's advertising have on the price which the retailers would charge?

5. From economic and social viewpoints, should Golden advertise?

6

PUBLIC AND SELF-REGULATION IN ADVERTISING

The functioning of any complex social group rests primarily on the integrity of each member of the group. Throughout history, however, it has been found that laws by elected legislators, regulations by public agencies whose officers are appointed, and courts' decisions may be necessary to insure a balance between the private and the public interests.

Like all other economic activities, the advertising industry has been the object of an increasing amount of social management by means of laws, regulations, and court decisions. This has been paralleled by an increasing amount of self-regulation by a variety of private groups, e.g., the Association of National Advertisers (ANA), the American Association of Advertising Agencies (AAAA), and the American Advertising Federation (AAF). The federal government, especially through the U.S. Department of Commerce, has also become active in this area by encouraging the advertising industry to be responsive to legitimate claims by various consumer organizations.

The tempo of public and self-regulation activities has increased enormously during the past decade not only through the design of public administration but also through the demands of business itself.

Self-regulation

Self-regulation by advertisers, advertising agencies, and mass media begins at the level of each individual firm. Each advertising decision directly or indirectly relates to a society's unwritten values and norms and its regulations and laws. Thus, each firm must insure that its advertising decisions satisfy these rules of behavior.

The large majority of advertising agencies tends to check formally the legality of these decisions by developing their own internal specialized legal staff. These specialized staffs are responsible for developing clearance and safeguard procedures. Figure 6–1 shows a form used by many advertising agencies to clear a TV ad prior to its production. By examining this form, the agency's lawyers have an opportunity to make sure that the actual product is being used in the ad and, if not, that there is an appropriate explanation. Other special procedures are followed in the case of "testimonials."

Legal clearance is also secured for ads to be sent via radio, newspapers, magazines, and other media. Clearance procedures are based not only on "legal" criteria but on principles of ethical conduct, such as those affirmed by the Creative Code as approved by the members of the American Association of Advertising Agencies.

Each mass medium will review ads from a legal point of view. Furthermore, each medium reserves the right to review ads in terms of its own criteria of what is acceptable and in good taste. None of the three national TV networks accepts ads for "liquor." Moreover, at each of the national TV networks, all ads and programs are reviewed by a special department, the Broadcast Standards Department.

Each seller has an obviously high interest in its relationships with its potential buyers. As discussed in Chapter 2, advertising is one of the ways by which such relationships can be established. Current social change suggests that corporate management should increase its involvement with the advertising function, not only in economic terms —i.e., the determination of the optimal advertising budget—but also in terms of the qualitative content of the firm's advertisements.

This increased involvement may require changes in the standard organizational structure of business firms in which the advertising department does not report directly to corporate management. Although such organizational changes may be difficult, top management may find it necessary to accept the view recently expressed by F. Stanton, the former president of a national TV network, that the responsibility of what is said in a company's advertisements rests directly on the shoulders of management, and nowhere else.

In addition to self-regulation at the level of each firm, there have been other forms of *group self-regulation*—for instance, that by specific industries. One of the oldest group efforts concerned with advertising self-regulation is the National Better Business Bureau, established in 1911. To increase the efficiency of this operation, a new organization was developed in 1970, consisting of local bureaus (the Council of Better Business Bureaus, Inc. (CBBB)) and the national bureau. The local bureaus investigate consumer complaints concerning local ads; furthermore, they actively check local ads and, if necessary, contact the advertiser and recommend corrective action. When deemed appropriate, the local bureaus may report their decision to local mass media, and these in turn may refuse further use of the objectionable ads.

The increasing changes in the economic and cultural fabric of the United States brought about by affluence have called for additional methods of self-regulation. In 1971 a new interindustry organization was developed. The first component of this organization was the Na-

FIGURE 6–1
Legal clearance of a TV ad prior to its production

TELEVISION COMMERCIAL TECHNIQUE CLEARANCE

DATE: _____

CLIENT _____ PRODUCT _____ JOB NO. _____

PRODUCTION HOUSE _____ FILMING DATE _____

The following questions with respect to the production of the above commercial(s) are to be answered by the agency producer, and the form signed by him and copies sent to:

1. _____

2. _____

3. _____

1. WILL MOCK-UPS BE USED?
   If yes, describe:
2. WILL ANY SPECIAL PROPS OR DEVICES BE USED?
   If yes, describe:
3. WILL ANY SPECIAL LIGHTING BE USED?
   If yes, describe:
4. WILL PRODUCT AND/OR PACKAGE BE COLOR CORRECTED?
   If yes, describe:
5. WILL PRODUCT BE STORED OR PREPARED FOR USE IN ANY WAY OTHER THAN IT WOULD BE BY CONSUMER?
   If yes, describe:
6. WILL THE PRODUCT BE PHOTOGRAPHED IN USE IN ANY WAY DIFFERENT THAN THAT USED BY CONSUMER?
   If yes, describe:
7. WILL A DEMONSTRATION, TEST, OR COMPARISON WITH OTHER PRODUCT BE USED?
8. (a) If yes, describe:
   (b) If yes, has such demonstration, test or comparison been incorporated into the commercial to be telecast?

Signed: _____
(Producer)

NOTE: TO BE SUBMITTED AFTER THE PRE-PRODUCTION MEETING BUT IN ALL CASES PRIOR TO ACTUAL SHOOTING. If the techniques outlined above are modified or changed substantially during the production session an appropriate amendment is to be filed.

---

tional Advertising Division (NAD) of the Council of Better Business Bureaus (CBBB). The second was a new independent National Advertising Review Board (NARB).

There are two main features in this latter organization. First, the membership of NARB consists of not only 30 representatives of advertisers and ten of advertising agencies, but also, and for the first time in the history of self-regulation, ten representatives of the public or nonindustry fields. The second innovation is that this new organization has some power to enforce its decisions concerning the appropriateness of advertisements.

The ways NAD and NARB function may be summarized as follows:

> The NAD will receive, evaluate, and act on complaints with regard to truth and accuracy in national consumer advertising. The complaints may come from any source—public, industry, or even government. In addition to handling complaints, the NAD staff will engage in monitoring to cover possible abuses on its own initiative. It also will render advisory opinions in advance to advertisers and/or agencies on planned advertising as a means of offering early guidance to help avoid problems.
>
> In the handling of complaints, the staff will seek to evaluate the merits of the issues raised. In most cases this will mean checking the representations made in the advertising with the available information on the performance of the product under accepted standards of truth and accuracy.
>
> If a complaint is considered justified, the staff will work with the advertiser and/or agency to seek an appropriate change in the advertising. The emphasis will be on a constructive resolution of the problem. If there is an impasse and the questionable advertising is neither altered nor withdrawn, the complaint will be appealed to the NARB.
>
> To expedite the appeals process, the chairman of the NARB will convene a five-man panel of the board to hear the specific case and reach a decision on behalf of the board. Each panel will include three advertisers, one agency, and one public member.
>
> The decision of a panel will be transmitted to the advertiser at the highest corporate level. If the advertiser refuses to cooperate with the NARB panel or does not agree with the decision of the panel that the advertising is in violation of NARB standards, the chairman of the NARB, after exhausting all procedures, shall inform the appropriate government agency. The latter shall describe the advertising and the questions raised and advise that the NARB file is available for examination upon request. The chairman shall make public the letter and any comments or position statement received from the advertiser.[1]

The NAD-NARB approach to self-regulation has been in existence for about five years (1971–76), and its public record can be examined. Figure 6–2 gives the total number of complaints received and handled by the first review process performed by NAD, and the sources of these complaints. It is interesting to note that of 917 complaints, only 172 came from private consumer groups, and even fewer (153) directly from consumers.

---

[1] From the written testimony to the Federal Trade Commission, *Hearings on Modern Advertising Practices,* Fall 1971, by H. H. Bell, President, American Advertising Federation (AAF).

FIGURE 6–2
Number and sources of complaints received and handled by NAD, 1971–1976

NAD monitoring	229
Local BBBs	221
Consumer groups	172
Consumers	153
Competitors	102
All other	40
Total	917

Source: John Crichton, "Report of the President," Annual Meeting. American Association of Advertising Agencies, May 1976.

Figure 6–3 illustrates the number of complaints concerning advertising to children. The role of advertising to children is not only an emotionally charged issue but, presumably, it should be of basic concern to all citizens interested in the appropriate socialization of children into adulthood. To this end, NAD created a Children's Advertising Review Unit two years ago. Here, too, it is interesting to note that, to date, only 47 complaints concern advertising to children. And once again, complaints from consumer groups and individual consumers make up only a small portion of the total.

Following the procedure outlined earlier, if a questionable advertisement is neither altered nor withdrawn, the complaint is appealed to the NARB. So far, a total of 26 ads have been reviewed by this organization. Of these, 14 complaints were upheld by the NARB—i.e., the judgment was against the advertiser.

In concluding this review of self-regulation, it also is important to recall that consumers and other seekers of information through the advertising institution are integral components of the institution itself. The performance of the institution depends in part on the active participation by consumer and organizational units. In a free society, each individual consumer carries the responsibility of fairness and

FIGURE 6–3
Number and sources of complaints concerning advertising to children received and handled by NAD, 1971–1976

NAD monitoring	32
Consumers	8
Consumer groups	4
Local BBBs	3
Total	47

Source: John Crichton, "Report of the President," Annual Meeting, American Association of Advertising Agencies, May 1976.

care in interpreting ads as well as the civic duty to report questionable ads to local, state, and federal agencies, and to interindustry organizations such as the local Better Business Bureaus and to national agencies such as NAD. In particular consumers have the right—and thus the responsibility—to organize themselves into voluntary organizations and participate in preventing false or misleading advertising.

In summary, self-regulation by individual firms, local Better Business Bureaus, and consumers is fundamental for the proper functioning of *local* advertising. At the *national* level, new groups, such as the NAD and NARB are strengthening the pioneering work started by the National Better Business Bureau. At present, it would appear, however, that self-regulation at the national level may be more effective than that at the local level. It is also important for consumers to recognize that another method of self-regulation is for them to write directly to a firm about ads which they believe are false or misleading.

Public regulation

Since the early experiments with democracy in ancient Greece, Western societies have recognized the potential conflict between the private interests of each individual and the interests of the public at large. Laws, regulations, and courts have essentially been the means of striking a balance between private and public interests. To achieve this balance is difficult, especially in complex societies like the United States.

Public management of the advertising institution by laws, regulations, and court decisions is certainly a challenging task, for, as we have seen, there is only limited knowledge of the economic and social roles of this institution. To appreciate the current complexities of public management of advertising, therefore, it is important to consider the distinction between local and national advertising regulation.

Local regulation

Recall that, by and large, federal laws and federal agencies do not have jurisdiction on "intra" state commerce. It follows, for example, that newspaper advertising by local merchants is, in principle, subject to regulation by city laws and city agencies. City governments do, in fact, regulate advertising by local firms in many direct and indirect ways. City ordinances, for instance, may establish limits to the number and size of store signs and billboards. On the basis of a recent interpretation by the U.S. Supreme Court, local courts may establish criteria of "decency" and thereby regulate the content of ads.

In general, however, city governments do not have the financial means and organizational ability to be active in regulating local advertising activities. Counties and, especially, state governments are in a stronger position. During the past decade, state laws have established offices responsible for the protection of consumer welfare, including protection from false, "misleading," and "deceptive" advertising. Frequently, these specialized offices have strong organizational ties with the state attorney general's office, which facilitates the administration of state laws.

One must be realistic in appraising the current potential of public regulation of *intra*state advertising. On the one hand, city, county, and state offices are responsible for covering all aspects of consumer well-being. In this context, we can see that advertising has received relatively less attention than problems in such areas as health and safety. On the other hand, the number of local advertisers is great and increasing; the cost of checking, assessing, and pursuing questionable ads is often prohibitive. In conclusion, then, it would appear that, for the short-run period, local regulation of advertising will depend largely on the quality of self-regulation by local firms, local Better Business Bureaus, and local consumer groups.

Federal regulation

In principle, federal laws and regulations by federal agencies apply to *interstate* commerce, and this includes national advertising. Federal laws and regulations, however, affect local regulations in many ways; for instance, many state, county, and city laws are, by and large, replicas of federal laws.

The current organizational setup of the federal government reflects to a large extent the historical effort of this country to move rapidly from an agrarian to an industrial society. The federal government is oriented toward the management of society's production problems: agriculture, commerce, labor, transportation, housing, and so on. But there is no U.S. Department of Consumer Affairs.

The spreading of affluence throughout the country, the increasing dominance of "consumption" activities, and the corresponding concern for consumer welfare has been met by the U.S. Congress with an assorted body of laws and agencies which lack cohesiveness at both the conceptual and implementation levels. It should not be surprising, therefore, that all too many federal laws and agencies may bear directly and indirectly on one or another operation of the advertising institution, often in ways that are sometimes confusing, even to the experts.

To illustrate the complexity of the ways in which federal laws and regulations may bear on advertising, consider the First Amendment of the U.S. Constitution, which protects freedom of speech. For several decades, the issue has been whether or not an advertiser is protected by this constitutional amendment because its interests are purely economic. Not until 1976 did the U.S. Supreme Court formally extend the protection of this amendment to advertising.

Beginning with the first law concerning the maintenance of competition in the country—the Sherman Act of 1890—advertising has become the object of social management through federal laws. As the body of federal laws—i.e., antitrust legislation—about competition has grown, advertising has become increasingly involved. And many decisions on antitrust matters by federal courts have applied directly to the workings of the advertising institution.

In more recent times, a rapidly growing amount of federal legislation aimed at the protection of the consumer has also come to bear on advertising. To name a few: the Automobile Information Disclosure Act (1958), the Fair Packaging and Labeling Act (1966), the Truth-in-Lending Act (1968), and the Fair Credit Reporting Act (1971).

The management of the advertising institution by the federal government has also been increased by another form of control—the creation of federal agencies to which are directly assigned the task of overseeing the proper functioning of different aspects of the institution. For instance, the creation of the Federal Communication Commission in 1934 allows Congress to guide the behavior of mass media. Similarly, the creation of the Food and Drug Administration and the progressive extension of its powers (the Food, Drugs, and Cosmetics Act of 1906, 1938, and 1962) bears directly on the information contained in labels by specifying not only what the labels *can* say but, following a more interventionist point of view, by specifying also what labels *must* say. The same power applies to mass media advertisements concerning the products under the jurisdiction of the FDA.

Founded in 1914, the Federal Trade Commission (FTC) has expanded its power to protect consumer interests at an increasing pace. The following list of examples of activities by the FTC during the last ten years gives some idea of the expanding jurisdiction of the commission:

1. In an action against a California-based enfranchiser of a hair-replacement system, the FTC has requested an injunction—a remedy it has not used for the past 15 years. The complaint charges the company with false advertising claims, failure to disclose possible medical risks, and use of "high pressure" sales techniques. An FTC spokesman indicates that use of injunctions will increase, especially where health and medical dangers to the public might exist. One reason for the revived use of the injunction is that, unlike consent or cease-and-desist orders, there is no longer delay while the administrative order is appealed through the courts. The protection given to the consumer is more immediate.

2. In another action, the FTC proposed that detergents carry warnings in advertising and on their labels (similar to cigarette package warnings). The warnings concern water pollution and would declare the quantity of "harmful" phosphorus in a given level of the product.

3. Another FTC proposal is aimed at getting new car list prices to reflect actual selling prices. It would require that "sticker" prices be no more than 3 percent higher than the lowest price at which most dealers' sales are made. Auto dealers and industry leaders oppose the regulation as an unworkable approach to the situation. They claim most consumers understand the list price is simply a starting point and also some cars must be sold at higher-than-average prices.

4. Cancellation of door-to-door sales is the subject of other regulation. It allows a three-day cooling-off period in which a buyer of goods or services worth $10 or more could cancel the purchase.

5. Greater protection of consumers who sign promissory notes in installment sales is the aim of another far-reaching FTC rule. It would

preserve buyers' claims and defenses in installment sales by (*a*) making any subsequent holder of a promissory note subject to defenses the buyer has against original seller, (*b*) barring agreements in which buyer consents to waive rights or remedies he or she may have, and (*c*) banning agreements by which buyer is prevented from making a claim or defense arising out of sale. The provisions would eliminate the traditional collection devices used by sellers, known as "confessions of judgment" and "wage assignments."

6. The new credit card law went into effect Janaury 25, 1971. It imposed limits on cardholders' liability and affected the way business by credit cards was transacted. This law affects the way credit card issuers, holders, retail stores, and others do business. First, issuers now have a system which enables the retailer to establish quickly and efficiently the identity of a cardholder. One of the results is that more of the expense for losses is shouldered by retailers who have the burden of ascertaining true ownership of cards. Some issuers find the cost of complying with the regulations and sending notices to cardholders is not worth the cost when compared to possible losses. Of course, the use of insurance protection will continue to be used by issuers as the best and safest way to guard against these "bad-card" losses.

7. Users of consumer credit reports (e.g., employers, insurance companies, retailers, banks, licensing agencies) now have legal responsibilities to the consumer. That's the impact of the federal Fair Credit Reporting Act, which went into effect April 25, 1971. A company *must notify* anyone turned down for employment, insurance, or credit because of an adverse report. It must (*a*) give the name and address of the credit bureau or consumer reporting agency making the report, and (*b*) tell the consumer of his right to request the specific information that was used.

8. The rights of financers holding consumer installment paper—already restricted by law in several states—now may be restricted nationwide. Purchasers of such paper have usually been considered "holders in due course"—with good title and no responsibility for seeing that the conditions of a sale were carried out. The Federal Trade Commission has come up with this new Trade Regulation Rule that would take away an important right from purchasers of consumer paper—their immunity from certain "defenses" and claims made by buyers against sellers.

The rule would require the face of any note drawn up by a retailer to contain a statement in ten-point boldface type. This would declare any third party buying the note is subject to legitimate claims that the consumer has which result from the original transaction. The rule also would forbid any agreement whereby the consumer waives any legal rights he has to make such claims. Finally, it would prevent a buyer from agreeing not to assert claims or defenses against the seller or the subsequent assignee of the note.

9. It is now illegal for a person to send unsolicited merchandise through the mails; if he does, he not only will lose the products but also faces heavy fines. The FTC enforces the new postal reorganization act passed in 1970. It labels as an unfair practice the sending of

unordered merchandise through the mails—with two exceptions: (*a*) free samples which are *clearly* and plainly *marked* as such, and (*b*) merchandise by a charitable organization asking for contributions.

10. Since manufacturers, either by themselves or through their dealers and trade associations, did not take action to control warranty coverage and administration, laws have been passed under which the various affected industries are finding it more complex to operate.

11. A company that manufactures drugs that doctors can prescribe is under a new regulation of the Food and Drug Administration. The regulation requires that any drug judged less than effective by the National Academy of Sciences contains the NAS findings in its advertising.

12. Any employer, retailer, or creditor which uses consumer reports in any way is now affected by the Fair Credit Reporting Act. The act imposes many new restrictions on all uses of such reports. One may be under a duty to tell applicants for jobs, credit, or insurance that he or she used a report and where it was gotten. One must disclose to the consumer the fact that an investigative report is being made. Disclosure must be made not later than three days after the date on which this report was requested. Such advance notice is required if the report concerns credit or employment for which the subject has applied.

The above list is certainly not all-inclusive. In addition to illustrating the wide jurisdiction of the FTC on consumer problems, the above list also illustrates the implicit lack of coordination among federal agencies. For instance, on the one hand the FDA requires manufacturers to list warnings and side effects on the labels of antacid products. On the other hand, the FTC argues that many people do not read labels (in itself a form of mass communication) and rely primarily on advertisements for their information. Since ads, especially broadcast ads, cannot possibly give all the medical information that can be printed on a label, the FTC argues that people may purchase and use these products—with possible adverse effects.

Similarly, the flurry of legislation concerning product safety and liability and the possible creation of new federal commission(s) may create further fragmentation of responsibilities and lack of coordination among federal agencies. A case in point concerns the so-called nonburning and self-extinguishing cellular (foam) plastics. Since their introduction in the mid-1960s, these plastics have been used increasingly in roof and wall insulation, furniture cushions and bedding, panels and siding, cabinets, chairs, tables, pipes and lighting, plumbing fixtures, and even in airplane interiors. Consumer acceptance was enormous. Yet, beginning in 1969, a number of accidents, with human deaths and large property losses, were assessed by courts as being due to the "flammability" of such plastics.

Until 1973, when the FTC filed a complaint, none of the following agencies, directly or indirectly involved, had intervened: the U.S. Department of Commerce; the U.S. Department of Health, Education and Welfare; the National Commission on Fire Prevention and Control; the National Product Safety Commission; the National Bureau of

Standards; and, of course, the American Society for Testing Materials and the Underwriters Laboratories, whose "scientific and objective" tests had declared these plastics to be "nonburning and self-extinguishing."

All in all, legislation and regulation of economic activities, including advertising—in the interest of the consumer—need a serious review. In a recent study for the National R&D Assessment Program of the National Science Foundation, R. Mayer and F. Nicosia surveyed 45 federal agencies, departments, commissions, and authorities, and they identified 25 main types of activities that bear on consumer protection and, directly or indirectly, on advertising. They were able to identify many cases of either duplication and lack of coordination or weak coverage.

Within this vacuum the FTC has developed a concern over the content of advertisements. Some success may have been achieved with respect to the definition of what is a *false* ad, or an ad containing false information. As for the commission's interest in defining "misleading" and "deceptive" advertisements, the early attempts were based essentially on ever-changing legal and cultural postures. In recent years, the commission has begun to appreciate the contributions that consumer psychology may make to such definitions. But it also has experienced two main difficulties. First, it has found that consumers are a heterogeneous lot and that, whatever the definitions of deceptive and misleading are, an ad may be deceptive for one consumer but not for another. (In consumer psychology, some researchers agree that the only objective knowledge we have is that a consumer's psychological reality is subjective!). Second, it has found that even well-known consumer researchers (D. Gardner, J. Jacoby, I. Preston, C. Small, and W. Wilkie, to name a few) tend to disagree among themselves about the possible ways for the commission to deal with the identification of what is misleading or deceptive and with the formulation of optimal policies concerning ads found to be misleading or deceptive.

For the near future, advertising management should expect an increasing amount of regulation by federal legislators and federal commissions, especially by the FTC, of what *can* be said in an ad and also of what *must* be said. In 1976, Greyser and Diamond summed up their experiences by pointing out that federal pressures on advertising management will be focused on the following areas:

> Advertising substantiation, whereby advertisers must have *advance* substantiation for the factual claims in their advertising.
>
> Corrective advertising, whereby those advertisers found guilty of false, misleading, or deceptive advertising must admit their guilt in a given amount of future advertisements.
>
> Broader interpretations of "deceptions" in advertising, including attacks on brand claims that are truthful but not unique to the advertised brand.
>
> Pressure for the mandatory inclusion in advertising of certain information, e.g., specific nutritional information in food advertising—i.e., a trend toward the so-called full disclosure.

Summary

The current regulation of advertising as outlined above may have limitations because government regulations may prevent, through holding back natural growth, the development of a proper balance in the economy. In a free economy, where the essential basic worth of the individual is stressed, businessmen like the acceptance that comes with observance of the rules of fair play.

It is the belief of the authors, however, that as society has grown more complex, government controls have had to play an even greater role, direct and indirect, in the checks on what might otherwise become abuses in advertising. Furthermore, we believe that advertisers should not attempt to resist all kinds of government control. The problem is to try to see that government provides the right kind of control over advertising and that it avoids those methods that are economically harmful. General recommendations in regard to regulations should include:

1. The preventive role and educational acts of the Federal Trade Commission should be emphasized.
2. Both government and business should make every effort to meet their mutual obligation to "satisfy the public."
3. The distinction between the control of advertising itself and false advertising should be kept sharp. Advertisers should consider extending a program of voluntary grade labeling for established and common consumer goods, to help reduce socially wasteful advertising costs.
4. Government agencies, in enforcing controls, should differentiate between *cause* and *effect.* (The amount of the advertising budget may not be the reason a company has gained market control.)
5. Advertising should not have the kind of barriers placed against it that would limit its functions of communication and stimulating demand in our fast-changing dynamic economy.
6. The various agencies should penalize false advertising, but not advertising per se.
7. Government agencies should attempt to regulate more on a case-per-case basis instead of an industrywide approach because of the variations in conditions which exist in the different markets.
8. Since technology and automation are here to stay and will continue to increase, it would appear to be more realistic to use the best possible tools at our command to satisfy the consumer. This would include the use of advertising as a tool of education and communication.
9. There is no way to eliminate all competition and maintain free competition.
10. It should be kept in mind that much of the criticism of advertising comes from persons who favor control of production and consumption. Since such control attempts to regulate consumption, the importance of advertising under such controls would tend to decrease.

11. Advertising cultivates or stimulates the tastes of consumers; it does not create them.
12. It is not unethical for an advertiser to stress the advantages of his product without pointing out the disadvantages. It is unethical, however, for an advertiser to communicate what he knows to be untrue.
13. Ethics of advertising are complex and must be considered from various points of view.
14. It is essential to place intellectual honesty as the important element of management-consumer relationships.

Questions

1. Two consumer researchers, Jacoby and Small, would define an ad as "deceptive" if there is a deliberate attempt to manipulate the consumer by the sender of the ad; and an ad as "misleading" if the seeker of information misperceives the ad because of his/her own perceptual processes. Discuss.

2. In mass communication research, it is known that the sender's meaning of an ad will be misperceived by a substantial number of receivers. Some of these misperceptions may bring harm to these receivers. Is this a sufficient ground for the FTC to declare an ad unlawful? Should consumers in a society that has invested billions in education be held responsible for their own misinterpretations? Discuss.

3. The FTC currently maintains that if a sufficiently high number of receivers misinterpret an ad, the ad should be judged misleading and withdrawn. What is meant by "a sufficiently high number of misinterpretations?" Should this be 2, 5, 10, or 16.52 percent, or what percentage of the total number of people who have received the ad in question? Explain.

4. Discuss the following comment: "Many people complain that current TV ads are dull and seem to appeal to the lowest common denominator of intelligence. This will turn out to be a self-fulfilling prophecy if the FTC should decide that even a small number of misrepresentations, say 5 percent, is sufficient to declare an ad unlawful."

5. Who should be responsible for setting the standards regulating what can be said in an ad?

6. Discuss the following comment: "Some consumer activists argue that advertising makes people buy things they do not want. But, in the recent case of *Virginia State Board of Pharmacy* v. *Virginia Citizens Consumer Council,* some consumer activists have argued that consumers have the right to have drug prices advertised by pharmacies. There is a fundamental inconsistency, perhaps even a double standard, in these two claims."

7. Two brands are exactly equal in terms of their physical, chemical, and engineering characteristics. They differ, however, in terms of the consumers' perceptions of the psychological and social needs that each brand can satisfy. The advertising of the two brands tries to differentiate them in terms of their ability to fulfill such psychological and social needs. Should the FTC declare such ads unlawful?

8. Legislation and regulation aimed at protecting the consumer should focus mainly on advertising, because this is the most powerful source of consumers' dissatisfaction. Next in importance would be all other marketing

decisions. Production, engineering, and R&D decisions should be next. The FTC budget should be allocated with this priority in mind, i.e., advertising, other marketing decisions, and so on. Do you agree with this priority?

9. Self-regulation by business firms and industry groups is bound to be the best way to improve the working of the advertising industry, because it tends to reflect more faithfully the preferences of each local community of consumers. Discuss.

10. Do you believe that the majority of consumers are willing to spend their time on the identification of questionable ads and questionable advertising practices? Explain.

11. Would you be willing to offer some of your free time to the local Better Business Bureau? Explain.

12. Does a seller have the right to tell all the weaknesses about the products of competitors? Is there any restraint from the ethical point of view that is required? What steps can be taken to integrate advertising into our industrial system? Is this primarily an economic and social problem, or is it one of an ethical nature as well?

13. For many years, critics have voiced criticisms about television commercials. To what extent should the FTC adopt a program of controlling these commercials?

14. In a recent speech, a public official stated the following: "We should place a greater control upon advertising because advertisers are now paying a major share of the cost of producing the various television programs, magazines, newspapers, and other media that, in my opinion, the freedom of the press no longer exists." Evaluate this statement.

15. Give the advantages and disadvantages of the government not placing any control over advertising.

16. What are the obligations of the advertiser in advertising his product?

17. It has been stated, "Because of the unwillingness to change and of the inclination of advertisers to behave in a socially irresponsible way, the government has found it necessary to institute regulations and controls—not because these are necessary in all cases, but by default." Comment.

18. Assume that you go to a drugstore and you ask for a brand of aspirin. The clerk hands you another brand and tells you that his brand is exactly the same as the brand you requested but, because it is not advertised, he can sell it to you at a lower price. Is this ethical? Would your answer be the same if the salesperson in a clothing store made the same comment about a suit you were planning to purchase?

Case   **CIGARETTES**
6–1   **Control of Advertising**

The production of cigarettes in the United States has been controlled by six firms which account for more than 99 percent of the total output. These firms are the American Tobacco Co., Brown & Williamson Tobacco Co., Liggett & Myers Tobacco Co., P. Lorrilard & Co., Philip Morris, Inc., and R. J. Reynolds Tobacco Co. Out of these six corporations five are U.S. based; the sixth firm, Brown & Williamson Tobacco Co., is a subsidiary of a British corporation.

During the first half of the 20th century these companies faced a relatively stable environment. This was true with respect to consumption, trends, pricing, behavior, and product developments.

The per capita consumption was continuously rising between 1900 and 1950. During the period, advertising became the basic means of competition. The ability to provide major advertising expenditures determined whether or not a company could enter the industry.

As far as the products of the industry were concerned, few significant changes occurred up until the 1950s, although many different brands of cigarettes were introduced. The major important change before the 1950s was the introduction of blended tobacco cigarettes in the early 1920s. Profits in the cigarette industry were also higher than they were in other manufacturing industries.

This state of affairs changed in the early years of 1950s as medical researchers began to correlate a relationship between smoking and health. These reports dramatically changed the working environment or conditions of the industry, constituting a threat to the successful merchandising of the products. As a response, filter brands were introduced and promoted. Such brands became popular in a short time, and by 1959 the filter brands had increased their market share to 51 percent from less than 1 percent in 1952.

There seems to have been a widely shared opinion in the late 1950s that the introduction of filter brands would be sufficient to restore the stability of the industry.

However, in the 1960s major changes in the industry were continuing to take place. This is illustrated by the change in market share among companies for 1960, 1969, 1974, and 1975. (See Exhibit 6–1.)

One of the main reasons for this shift was the issue of tobacco and disease. Some companies were able to capitalize on the health safety features of their cigarettes.

An important development in this context was the appointment of ten scientists in 1962 to a committee on tobacco and health by the United States Surgeon General. The task of this committee was to make a comprehensive review of all available data on smoking and its effects on health. The report was published in January 1964. As a result of the serious warnings in the report, there was a decline in cigarette consumption by 2.5 percent for the year. In previous years consumption generally increased by the same percentage.

Legal actions that followed the Surgeon General's report

The above report was followed by studies by Congress, the Federal Trade Commission, and the Federal Communications Commission. As a result of these studies, such requirements as placing a warning on cigarette packages (1966 and 1970), the permission to include contents of tar and nicotine in advertising (1966), and the banning of cigarette commercials on TV(1970) were adopted. Moreover, a rule was issued in 1967 that TV channels broadcasting advertising for cigarettes had to give free time for antismoking messages.

In its annual report, when the publication of the report of the U.S.

EXHIBIT 6–1
How the companies rank (estimated domestic consumption of cigarettes as a percent of the industry total)

	1960		1969	
	Market share	Rank	Market share	Rank
Company				
R. J. Reynolds Tobacco Co.	32.6%	1	32.0%	1
American Tobacco Co.	25.7	2	21.0	2
Liggett & Myers Tobacco Co.	11.7	3	6.9	6
P. Lorillard & Co.	10.9	4	9.2	5
Brown & Williamson Tobacco Co.	9.4	5	15.7	3
Philip Morris Inc.	9.3	6	15.1	4
All others	0.4		0.1	

	1975		1974	
Company	Market share	Sales in billions of cigarettes	Market share	Sales in billions of cigarettes
R. J. Reynolds	32.5%	193.6	31.5%	185.9
Philip Morris	23.8	141.7	23.0	135.7
Brown & Williamson	17.0	101.3	17.5	103.3
American Brands	14.2	84.5	15.0	88.5
Lorillard	7.9	47.6	8.2	48.4
Liggett & Myers	4.4	26.2	4.7	27.7
All other	.2	1.1	.1	.5
Total	100.0	596.0	100.0	590.0

surgeon general was completed, P. Lorrilard & Co. mentioned 1964 as "the most disconcerting year in the company's history." In response to this situation the company stated as one of its goals "to prepare a solid base for future operations in the new climate."

I. Actions taken by companies to overcome difficulties

A. Research on the relationship between smoking and disease.
B. Increase development of new products.
C. Self-imposed constraints on advertising.
D. Price increases.

   A. Medical research financed by the industry had already begun in the 1950's. However, in 1964 the Tobacco Industry Research Committee offered the American Medical Association a grant of $10 million, which was about $2 million larger than the total amount given in the prior five years.

   B. The product developments were concentrated on efforts to reduce the content of those smoke ingredients which were supposed to be hazardous. Filter brands was one improvement in this respect in the

1950s. The significance of these brands was even more pronounced in 1969 when they constituted 77 percent of the market. The extra-long brands were introduced in large scale during 1967 and reached 10 percent of the market the same year.

C. The self-imposed constraints on advertising came into effect by the establishment of the Cigarette Advertising Code in 1964.

The code restrained advertising basically in the following three respects:

1. Promotional activities should not deliberately be directed to or designed to appeal to persons under 21 years of age.
2. Advertising which referred to health issues should not be used unless the administration of the code had determined its significance for the advertisements.
3. Advertising which referred to the removal or reduction of ingredients in the smoke should not be used unless the administration of the code had determined its significance for the advertisement.

II. Action in market other than the United States

Operations abroad afforded an opportunity to reach American servicemen overseas and foreign consumers. The shipment of cigarettes to the first group increased considerably by the mid-1960s mainly because of the enlarging United States involvement in South East Asia. Servicemen constituted a goal target for sales expansion on two grounds: (a) their type of mission increased the likelihood of smoking; (b) they were not exposed to anti-smoking messages to the same extent as their counterparts in the United States.

The foreign group of consumers had for quite some time attracted U.S. cigarette producers, and as the domestic market declined the efforts in foreign markets increased. The main reason why growth in sales could be expected abroad was that per capita consumption was substantially below the United States level.

Most recent developments in the industry

The cigarette companies are waging a multimillion-dollar marketing campaign that arises from a shift in strategy. Cigarette manufacturers are reemphasizing "full flavor" brands. This approach suggests that for the tobacco companies, at least, the anti-smoking lobby may have lost some of its clout, though supporters of new, tougher restrictions on cigarette sales think they will get additional backing from the new Congress.

In 1975, also, Reynolds added a full percentage point to its market share during the cigarette industry's worst year since 1969, when unit sales declined for the first time. In 1975 industry sales inched up only .09%m or six billion cigarettes, to 596 billion. Of the country's six major producers only Reynolds, which increased its sales by 7.7 billion units, and its nearest rival, Philip Morris Inc., posted sales gains.

A massive infusion of advertising dollars enabled Reynolds top

brand, Winston, to hang onto its position as America's favorite cigarette, despite a continuing threat from Philip Morris' Marlboro, which
has been nipping at its heels for the past six years. Reynolds also
scored heavily with a concept of segmented marketing, which helped
it achieve gains for Vantage (lower—not lowest—in tar and nicotine)
and More, a long (120 mm), thin, high tar and nicotine filter cigarette
wrapped in brown paper, which represents the industry's first successful national introduction of a new brand since the ban on broadcast
advertising five years ago.

In 1974 and 1975, advertising budgets have been markedly increased for the five major Reynolds brands: Winston, Salem, Camel,
Vantage, and Doral. Total advertising dollars—$85 million in 1973—
were boosted by $17 million in 1974 and $12 million more in 1975.

Additional concepts

The Federal Trade Commission questions if health hazard warnings in the cigaret industry's outdoor ads measure up to the requirements of a 1972 settlement order.

The dispute over the size of warnings in outdoor ads is considered
by FTC staffers as the most significant issue which has been raised
about current cigaret advertising. The court action claims that the
warnings fail to comply with an agreement which provides for notices
that are "clear and conspicuous." FTC wants the court to assess penalties which could range up to several million dollars and would go into
a fund for development of anti-cigaret educational messages.

During the negotiations between the commission and the cigaret
companies, the advertisers pointed out that the settlement calls for
type sizes no smaller than two inches high. FTC took the position that
regardless of type size, the requirement is not met unless the warnings
are sufficiently conspicuous to be read by motorists as well as pedestri-
ans.

FTC's action in October 1975 accused each of the six major companies of failure to include warnings in vending machine materials, but
FTC announced that it was allowing an additional time to seek agreement on the size of warnings in outdoor ads.

The amended complaint also claims all six companies failed to
provide sufficient space between the lines of warnings statements in
print ads, and that three companies—Brown & Williamson, R. J. Reynolds, and Liggett & Myers—failed to put the proper space between
the warnings statements and the enclosing rule of the warning box.

Also in the amended complaint; FTC charges that R. J. Reynolds
omitted warnings from a direct mail circular (a letter inviting consumers to write in for sample cigarets), and that American Brands
omitted the warnings from a tobacco product called Fridays.

Case Questions

1. To what extent should the Government regulate the cigarette industry's
   advertising?

2. Should the cigarette industry be curtailed from using appeals which are truthful yet may be deceptive because the omission of facts bearing upon them may create false impressions?
3. When might a company in this industry use a "new" statement for a product?
4. To what extent are legal ramifications implicit in every facet of cigarette advertising?

Case **POPULAR RECORDS, INC.**
6–2 **Misleading advertising**

The Federal Trade Commission issued the following complaint against Popular Records, Inc.

The respondent, Popular Records, Inc., is a corporation which, for some time, has been engaged in the advertising, offering for sale, sale, and distribution of phonograph records and record-vending racks. The respondent has maintained a substantial course of trade in interstate commerce, as "commerce" is defined in the Federal Trade Commission Act. Furthermore, Popular Records, Inc., has been in substantial competition with corporations, firms, and individuals in the sale of phonograph records and vending racks of the same general kind and nature as those sold by Popular.

In the course and conduct of its business, Popular Records, Inc., has made various statements and representations concerning its products and methods of conducting business, for the purpose of inducing the sale of its phonograph records and vending racks, which have been false or misleading. These statements have been made by means of advertisements published in *The Wall Street Journal,* a number of local newspapers in areas where the respondent does business, and by means of letters, brochures, and other promotional material mailed to prospective purchasers.

Among some of the typical statements and representations made are the following:

(1) By newspaper advertisements:

DISTRIBUTOR
MALE OR FEMALE
FULL OR PART-TIME

Earn extra money in your own business. No experience or personal selling necessary. Requires only few hours a week spare time to service CHOICE BRAND RECORD DISPLAYS, located by us in food markets, drugstores, etc. Cheap record racks are rapidly being replaced by SENSATIONAL CHOICE BRAND SELF-SERVICE RECORD DISPLAYS. Store makes money, so do you. Excellent profit . . . but this is NOT A GET RICH QUICK SCHEME, as we are a highly respected record company rated in Dun & Bradstreet. Must have car and minimum of $975 for record inventory, displays, store accounts, and advertising material. Write for local appointment, include phone number.

CHOICE RECORD DIV.
POPULAR RECORDS, INC.

(2) By letter:

. . . this is an ideal opportunity for you to own . . . a full-time, high-profit, volume business. . . .
. . . Choice Brand Record Displays, located by us in high-traffic retail stores. . . .
. . . keep your racks filled with fast moving record selections.

(3) By promotional brochure:

HERE'S THAT ONCE-IN-A-LIFETIME OPPORTUNITY FOR Unlimited Success on A Limited Budget.

Make more money in less time than you thought possible.

YOU CAN SERVICE 5 RACKS IN ONLY 5 TO 6 HOURS A WEEK and Pocket Tremendous Profits.
5 to 6 hours a week servicing your locations can bring you clear profit you never dreamed of making in so little time with so little effort. . . .
It won't take long to learn this money-making business and once you do—the sky's the limit.

CHOICE UP-TO-DATE RECORDS SOLD AT YOUR LOCATIONS. . . .
Customers will quickly discover that the newest hits from stage, screen, etc. . . . are always available at *your* Choice racks.

Popular Records can bring these superb recordings to music lovers everywhere at prices far below those being charged for records of comparative value.

If you cannot service "Fast-turnover" "High-profit" locations—DO NOT APPLY.

Q. HOW DO I KNOW THAT YOUR COMPANY IS RELIABLE?

A. We are listed by Dun & Bradstreet. . . .
. . . we give the public a truly fine $4.98 Hi-Fi value for the really sensible price of $1.98.
In response to inquiries induced by such advertisements, letters, and literature, the respondent or its employees, agents, or representatives call upon members of the public initiating such inquiries; and then make oral representations repetitive or elaborative of and in addition to those contained in the aforementioned printed materials.
Through the use of such statements and representations, the respondent has represented, directly or by implication, that: (1) the respondent's newspaper advertisements constituted offers of employment, (2) a highly profitable business could be obtained for an investment of $975, (3) all money invested by a purchaser of records and racks was secured by the stock purchased and that a full refund of the investment would be made by the respondent upon the return of the stock, (4) weekly net profits of $50 to $100 and more could be easily obtained by the purchaser for his investment of $975, (5) the respondent implied that he has negotiated contracts with The Great Atlantic & Pacific Tea Company, The Kroger Company, Safeway Stores, Inc., Sears, Roebuck & Company, Peoples Drug Stores, Inc., and other large and reputable food, drug, and general merchandise companies and stores, by which it was agreed that the

respondent's distributor in a given area would install vending racks with phonograph records in such companies' "high-traffic" retail stores located in the area, (6) the purchaser would be the sole distributor of the records in a defined geographical area, (7) a portion of all the records sold by the respondent to a purchaser were "hit" tunes currently being sold throughout the nation, (8) the records sold by the respondent had a retail value of $3.98 or more each, (9) the purchaser's opportunity for expansion, with concomitant earnings of incredible amount, was limited only by the industry of the purchaser and the size of the trading area wherein he would be the distributor, and (10) the respondent's integrity was avouched by the fact that they were listed in *Dun & Bradstreet Reference Book*.

These statements are false, misleading, and deceptive because in truth:

1. The respondent did not offer employment to persons answering the advertisements. The purpose of the advertising has been to obtain leads to persons of established finances in order that a concentrated effort might be made, through personal solicitation, to induce them to enter into contracts for the purchase of phonograph records and vending racks.
2. Seldom, if ever, has an investment of $975 in the respondent's phonograph records, vending racks, and plan of merchandising resulted in the establishment of a highly profitable business.
3. Money invested in phonograph records and vending racks was not secured by stocks. The maximum amount returnable to an investor who wishes to terminate his contract is limited by contract to $360 for each unit investment of $975.
4. Seldom, if ever, have net profits of $50 or more weekly been realized by purchasers of Popular Records, Inc.'s phonograph records and vending racks costing $975. Net profits at certain rates cannot be expected by the purchaser from the beginning of operations or at any other time.
5. Popular Records, Inc., the respondent, does not have contracts with the Great Atlantic & Pacific Tea Company, The Kroger Company, Safeway Stores, Inc., Sears, Roebuck & Company, Peoples Drug Stores, Inc., or other large food, drug, or general merchandise companies or stores, whereby agreements had been reached which would permit purchasers of the respondent's products to place vending racks and records on store premises. Invariably, store locations were not determined until after contracts for the sale of records and racks by the respondent had been negotiated, and then the purchasers learned that locations were available only in independently owned restaurants, drugstores and variety stores not having the high-traffic and sales potentials promised by the respondent.
6. The respondent breached promises made to purchasers of their products to preserve sales territories for the sole and exclusive distributorship of purchasers.
7. Few, if any, records available from respondents at the time of the initial sale thereof to purchasers, or later, contained what the consuming public considered to be current "hit" tunes.
8. Most of the records sold by respondents could be obtained from retailers selling records in competition with the respondent's customers in the same trading area for $1.98.

9. Seldom, if ever, has the purchaser of Popular Records, Inc.'s products for the $975 investment found that his return therefrom warranted any effort to expand his operations.
10. The respondent's listing in *Dun & Bradstreet Reference Book* signified nothing more than it had a certain credit rating and a certain estimated financial worth.

The use of these false, misleading and deceptive statements by the respondent has had the tendency to mislead members of the purchasing public into the erroneous and mistaken belief that these statements were true and into the purchase of substantial quantities of its phonograph records and vending racks. As a consequence thereof, substantial trade in commerce has been unfairly diverted to the respondent from its competitors. These acts and practices of the Popular Records were and are to the prejudice and injury of the public and of the respondent's competitors, and constitutes unfair and deceptive acts and practices and unfair methods of competition, in commerce, within the intent and meaning of the Federal Trade Commission Act.

Popular Records, Inc.'s reply

1. We deny the charge that our newspaper advertisements constituted offers of employment as alleged in the complaint. In all our advertisements we used such phrases as: "your racks," "your investment," and "your own business." Such statements clearly indicate that the individuals who would apply are not to be employees of the company but are entering into a business of their own.

2. We believe that a highly profitable business can be obtained for the investment of $975. The two tables given below show that according to generally accepted standards of "highly profitable business" individuals have established very profitable businesses. As is shown by the first chart, 70 percent of those who have invested $975 in the business, for the purchase of our records and record racks, are making a return of 21.7 percent on their investment. Over half of the people are making a return of 53.5 percent. Because of this, we believe that a highly profitable business can be and usually is established by those who invest $975 in this business.

3. To the complaint that the investment was not completely secured by stocks and that the maximum amount which the individual could get for the return of all the stock was $560, we reply: (a) that the most he can hope to recover is $560. (b) In the newspaper advertisements and other promotional material, the purchasers are told that the $975 investment covers not only the stock of records and vending racks but also displays, store accounts, and advertising material. We do not allow any allowance for the return of these. (c) There is an expense for closing the accounts when an individual returns the stock which he purchased from us, and the individual helps to cover this expense by receiving a slight reduction in the amount of money which we will allow him for the return of his stock. (d) There is a loss of good-will when one of our distributors withdraws his racks from a store. In order to insure that the individual will not enter the business unless he fully realizes what he is getting into, we assess him for a small penalty fee as compensation for the loss of good-will which he has caused us. We have found that it is extremely difficult to get the racks reinstalled in stores from which they have been removed. (e) Because the racks are usually damaged in use, we seldom allow more

Return in investment on Popular Records Inc.'s $975 investment package

Percentage of individuals who make the stated net profit or more	Average net profit earned per week	Average net profit earned per year	Less labor expense of $520 per year	Percentage return on invested capital— annual net profit less expense divided by $975
100..............	$ 1	$ 52	loss	0.0
95..............	5	260	loss	0.0
85..............	10	520	$ 0	0.0
70..............	15	780	260	21.7
50..............	20	1,040	520	53.5
30..............	25	1,300	780	80.0
20..............	30	1,560	1,040	107.0
15..............	35	1,820	1,300	133.3
10..............	40	2,080	1,560	160.0
5..............	45	2,340	1,820	187.0
2..............	50	2,600	2,080	222.0

Percentage of individuals who make the stated net profit or more	Average net profit earned per week	Average net profit earned per year	Less interest expense of $60 per year*	Earnings per hour of work—net profit less interest expense divided by 260 hours†
100..............	$ 1	$ 52	loss	$0.00
95..............	5	260	$ 200	0.77
85..............	10	520	460	1.77
70..............	15	780	720	2.77
50..............	20	1,040	980	3.77
30..............	25	1,300	1,240	4.77
20..............	30	1,560	1,500	5.77
15..............	35	1,820	1,760	6.77
10..............	40	2,080	2,020	7.77
5..............	45	2,340	2,280	8.77
2..............	50	2,600	2,540	9.77

* Interest expense of $60 is based on 6 percent interest on $975 for a period of one year: $975 X 0.06 = $58.50 plus $1.50 = $60.00

† The 260 hours is based on the average number of hours worked by each person per week times the number of weeks in a year, 52.

than $30 per rack, while the cost of each of the five racks to the purchaser is $50.

4. We grant that no one has earned $100 per week on an investment of $975 and only about 2 percent of the people make more than $50 a week. However, as can be seen from the preceding charts in section two, very good profits can and are obtained by individuals who have made the $975 investment.

5. Although it is true that no prior contracts with large and reputable food, drug, and general merchandise companies and stores have been

made by which it was agreed that Popular Records' distributors in a given area would install vending racks in such companies' "high-traffic" retail stores, we do not believe that such a representation was ever made. We did make contracts with these and other stores after negotiations on the contract with the distributors had begun. We could not make the contract with the stores until service could also be promised because, among other things, if we could not service the stores, they would want to commit the floor space our distributor needed for other uses. Because the best locations in a trading area were often in local, fairly small establishments, we often chose to get contracts with these smaller companies. The teenagers make up a large percentage of those who buy our records, and because they usually shop at these smaller stores, these locations are often the choicest spots available. It is also important to keep in mind that we did not claim any specific sales potential, and most of the locations which our distributors set up have a turnover which is fast enough to make a good return for them. Furthermore, the turnover at these locations is at least up to the average record turnover in the surrounding area.

6. When a purchaser was not the sole distributor in some defined geographical area, it was usually due to changing conditions in that area. For example, population increases, inadequate saturation of the sales potential within the market area, etc. allow us to expand with other distributors at no detriment to the old distributor. In any such case, before we accept another distributor to service the same area (using different stores), we give the old distributor a chance to expand or improve his service so that the new distributor would not be necessary. Finally, it should be kept in mind that since most of the customers of our records (a) do not go shopping specifically for the records and (b) the customers of one store where the Popular Records racks are installed do not generally shop at the other stores where they are installed, sales of the original distributor were not affected.

7. Although it is true that there are similar records being sold by retailers for $1.98 or less, it is our opinion that these records are inferior to the ones which we are offering for sale. Our records are technically superior to most $1.98 records. The quality of the records which we sell is usually associated with $4.98 hi-fi records. Also, the talent which is on our records is superior to the talent which is on most $1.98 records.

8. Some of the reasons why only a very small percentage of people have made an investment of a second or third $975 are (a) many individuals do not have another $975 which they have free to invest; (b) most of our purchasers handle their own racks and they are satisfied with the present results which they are getting; and (c) most of our purchasers use this investment only as a source of marginal income and, therefore, do not want to spend more than a few hours a week in this type of work.

Case questions

1. What legislation empowers the Federal Trade Commission to make a decision regarding a "misleading" advertisement?
2. How would you define "false" and "deceptive" advertising?
3. Has Popular Records been deceptive in its advertising?
4. To what degree should controls be set for protecting the consumer in advertising of this nature?

Case	**HEALTH CARE, INC.**
6–3	**Considering use of advertising**

Health Care, Inc.'s primary business is the ownership and operation of eighteen acute-care hospitals in the United States. In addition, Health Care operates a central medical laboratory, provides inhalation therapy equipment, services, and personnel training, and other ancillary services to hospitals.

As a result of the decrease in the rate of occupancy in eight of its hospitals, to an average rate of 65 percent or lower, the directors were considering whether or not they should adopt a "professional" type of advertising program in the areas where their hospitals were located.

It has been the policy of Health Care's management to expand the scope of the services it offers for health care in the communities it servces, through increased services, expansion of existing facilities, and acquisition of additional acute-care hospitals.

Hospitals

Health Care's hospitals are classified as investor-owned hospitals, as distinguished from "nonprofit" hospitals operated by tax-exempt organizations or governmental agencies. All of its hospitals are acute-care facilities and, except to a minor degree, do not provide for extended care. During the last fiscal year, it derived more than 95 percent of its revenues and income (before incomes taxes) from hospital operations.

All of Health Care's hospitals are accredited by the Joint Commission of Hospital Accreditation of the American Medical and American Hospital Associations.

Rate of occupancy

On the basis of figures contained in the guide issue of *Hospitals,* the journal of the American Hospital Association, the average of occupancy of proprietary hospitals during the latest year for which such figures are available, was 74.6 percent nationally. The average occupancy rates of the company's hospitals were as given in Exhibit 6–2.

It was the opinion of the directors that the services in all of its hospitals were comparable and that their administrators were competent in handling the details.

Medical staff

Approximately 3,400 licensed physicians and surgeons are members of the medical staffs of Health Care's hospitals. Many of these physicians and surgeons are also on the staffs of other hospitals. Patients are admitted only upon request of the members of the medical staff. The physicians and surgeons are not employees of Health Care and any of them may terminate his connection with the hospital at

EXHIBIT 6–2

City	Percent of occupancy	City	Percent of occupancy
A	75	J	63
B	84	K	76
C	66	L	65
D	62	M	60
E	82	N	79
F	78	O	81
G	64	P	63
H	73	Q	83
I	87	R	64

any time. Rules and regulations concerning the medical phase of each hospital's operations are adopted and enforced by its medical staff. Such rules and regulations provide that the members of the staff elect officers, who, together with additional doctors selected by them, constitute the medical executive committee of the hospital which, subject to general control of the hospital's board of directors, supervises all medical and surgical procedures and services through various subcommittees.

Medical laboratories

Health Care's hospitals operate the medical laboratory through its laboratory division. In addition to its hospital laboratories, it operates a central medical laboratory which provides specialized services for the company's hospital laboratories in the area, and, to a limited extent, performs specialized laboratory analyses for clinics and physicians not having qualified personnel or specialized equipment available. The central medical laboratory is divided into biochemistry, toxicology, microbiology, serology, and hematology departments and is equipped for automated biochemical analysis.

Inhalation therapy services

Inhalation Therapy Services, Inc., a wholly owned subsidiary of the company, provides inhalation therapy equipment, services, and personnel training. Inhalation therapy involves the use of intermittent positive-pressure breathing machines and other devices to aid in the treatment of pulmonary emphysema and related respiratory conditions.

Competition

In the areas in which Health Care operates, there are other acute-care hospitals which provide services comparable to those offered by Health Care. Some of these hospitals are owned by governmental agencies and others by tax-exempt entities supported by endowments and charitable contributions, which support is not available to Health Care's hospitals. A number of the larger hospitals employ interns and resident physicians who are available to assist in the treatment of a patient. Such services are not provided by Health Care's hospitals.

The occupancy rate of a hospital depends upon the utilization of the facility by doctors on its staff. Any doctor may terminate his connection with the hospital at any time. Health Care endeavors to merit the continued support of the doctors on the staff of a hospital and to attract other qualified doctors by a program which includes the improvement and modernization of its facilities and equipment and, in addition, the enforcement of high ethical and professional standards.

Government regulation

The operation of hospitals and medical laboratories is subject to compliance with various federal, state, and local statutes and regulations. The regulatory agencies administering such statutes and regulations have the power to fix standards of care and service and to determine the adequacy of facilities and the qualification of management. Health Care's hospitals must also comply with the requirements of municipal building codes and local fire departments. Health Care's present facilities hold all required state and local licenses and permits. Expansion of hospitals generally requires the approval of local hospital planning councils.

Medicare, Medicaid and other insurance

Health Care receives payments for services rendered to patients from private insurers, the federal government under the Medicare program of assistance to indigent patients. Under the Medicare and Medicaid programs Health Care is reimbursed for the reasonable direct and indirect costs (as defined by the program) of the services furnished, plus a return on equity. However, Medicaid reimbursement is limited to retail billings. Claims for payments under Medicare, Medicaid, and Blue Cross are subject to audit by agencies administering the program, and portions of the amounts claimed are withheld pending such audit and final settlement. Health Care computes the amount to which it will be entitled from these sources, and, for accounting purposes, establishes a reserve equal to the difference between the charges billed to these programs and such computations.

Employees

Health Care employs approximately 4,750 persons of whom approximately 50 percent are nurses or other licensed technical personnel engaged in hospital and laboratory work. Labor relations have been satisfactory. Approximately 90 percent of such persons are full-time employees.

Its hospitals, like others, experience a relatively high rate of turnover of employees and difficulty in employing and retaining an adequate number of nurses, technicians, and other employees.

Advertising policy

One of the directors at the annual meeting of the board stated as follows:

> I recognize that the operation of a hospital is a professional endeavor and that any advertising to get business is frowned upon by the Joint Commission of Hospital Accreditation of the American Medical and American Hospital Associations. Yet, when I see our census (occupancy rate) in eight of our hospitals below the "break-even point" I am convinced that we should be allowed to let the people know that our services are superior to those offered by some of our competitors.
>
> I made a point to visit the competition in three of these cities and I found that their occupancy rates were above 75 percent in each case, yet, the services which were offered to the patients, I believe were inferior to what we offered. The rates were all comparable, and, as a result I concluded that if we could let the people know about some of our innovations we could increase our census above the break-even point.
>
> It is also my opinion that we could really bring down this astronomical cost of hospital care for the patient if we would take the leadership in promoting our hospitals and get our census up close to the 90 percent level.

Case questions

1. Why do you believe it has been the policy of professional groups (lawyers, accountants, and doctors) to refrain from advertising?
2. Do you believe this general policy should be changed? Give reasons.
3. To what degree should hospitals be competitive in seeking patients?
4. As a media representative would you accept advertising from Health Care, Inc., which indicates how its services are better than those of the other hospitals in the area? Why or why not?

Case   **AMERICAN TELEPHONE & TELEGRAPH COMPANY**
6–4   **Considering Telephone Hour**

Walter Straley, an A.T.&T. vice president, made a speech, in accepting an award of the American Symphony Orchestra League—an honor resulting from sponsorship of the "Telephone Hour," which presents musical documentaries.

Mr. Straley said what he had to say better than anyone could interpret it. Moreover, he said it with grace and rare style. His statements follow, in excerpted form:

> I could offer the not unusual public relations rationale that being aware, as we are, of the significance of the cultural community and its influence upon our corporate well-being, that we seek through this medium your goodwill, and this, of course, would be nonsense. We are glad to have it,

if we have it, of course, but we will continue to merit your goodwill only by keeping your telephone working for a fair charge and fixing them promptly when they do not. . . .

To level with you, the "Telephone Hour" is mostly a corporate whim, and as a more or less responsible Bell System organization man, I am grateful beyond words that we allow ourselves the indulgence in it. The "Telephone Hour" as a part of our advertising program is difficult—nay, impossible—to justify. It costs a good deal and is clearly a Nielsen rating failure.

The present youth of our country will, I suppose, ultimately control our corporate destiny. Yet, our audience is heavily weighted with people past 50. A reputable public relations analyst showed me irrefutably recently that we could reach the same opinion-forming group and millions more of it with National League football and "I Spy," and I am sure he is right. . . .

Excepting the shows themselves, there really isn't very much about the "Telephone Hour" which seems really reasonable, and this, I think, makes it unreasonable, and I am very glad of that, for too much reason is not sweet, and corporate life is filled with reason.

Obviously, we cannot permit ourselves much of this cultural frivolity, and I hasten to assure our stockholders among you that we take in dead earnestness through other means, of course, our marketing responsibility to use sex, success, and other love in appropriate advertising lures to secure longer long-distance calling and passionate accommodations to our rainbow-hued array of extension telephones. I am grateful that you honor this single idiosyncrasy, and I am hopeful that your recognition will not, however, cause the whole thing to seem logical, for I am delighted with the illogic of it. . . .

Other advertising

When Governor Edmund Brown, Jr., was secretary of state, he said a ban on advertising by state-regulated public utilities would save Californians $200,000 a day in reduced rates. Spokesmen for the major utilities disputed Brown's figures.

Brown said public utilities spent more than $73 million on public relations and advertising, although none faced direct competition. He cited Pacific Telephone as an example, claiming it spent $30 million a year on advertising and sales. "Where else can you go to obtain telephone service other than to Pacific Telephone," Brown said.

A vice president of PT&T in Southern California said Brown was giving out "bad information." "We only advertise in three categories. The first is to inform the public about our services, the second is to promote the use of those services, and the third is to recruit workers." He said Pacific Telephone spent $8 million specifically on advertising last year with the balance of the $30 million going to tell customers how they could get maximum service at minimum cost.

"Utility rates are actually lower because of advertising," the vice president claimed. He said a "direct distance dialing" campaign saved the company $1 million a year for each 1 percent of the population that used it.

Case questions

1. Point out the economic advantages and disadvantages of not controlling the amount of the expenditures for advertising which is done by public utilities.
2. To what extent should public utilities have their advertising controlled?

part three

Preparation of the advertisement

7
COPY STRATEGY AND PREPARATION

*I*n the prior chapters, emphasis was placed on the important aspects of demand creation and the techniques of product identification. It was pointed out that the attention of the prospect must be attracted and drawn to the product or service to be sold. Interest in it must be aroused and, after one is induced to desire it, this desire must be converted into a buying decision.

Setting objectives

Before the copy can be prepared, however, it is important to evaluate the overall marketing objectives to be sure that they are in harmony with the economic and social aims of society. If the company, as an example, has a marketing objective to increase its market share by 10 percent by selling to a new market segment, then the decision as to the degree to which the company believes it should concentrate its advertising on this demographic group will have to be made before preparing copy. At the same time, the social implications should also be checked to determine if there are conflicts which might exist. Consider a cigarette company that decided to increase its market share by concentrating more advertising on the 18 to 30-year-old market. The social implications of the marketing objectives and the morality of advertising cigarettes to the above market segment should not be overlooked.

The authors have found that preparing copy by objectives is an effective base from which to develop practical advertising appeals. Such a procedure accommodates the correlation of the copy to the overall marketing program and, at the same time, assists the copywriter in presenting the material in clear and concise terms.

Before going into the details of preparing an advertisement, it is advisable to discuss briefly the objective(s) of the individual advertise-

ment. That is, what must the individual advertisement accomplish to
be an effective one?

Various advertisers will describe somewhat differently the specific
objectives. Some will divide the requirements into gaining attention,
arousing interest, obtaining readership, stimulating desire, establishing conviction, and securing action. Others will express requirements
for effective advertisement in terms of obtaining initial attention of
arousing and holding interest, and of creating an effective and lasting
impression on the audience that will result in current or future favorable action.

Although the ultimate objective of the advertisement may be to
obtain action in the form of a sale or to create a lasting "brand image"
in the mind of the potential buyer, these ends obviously cannot be
achieved unless the immediate objectives of having the advertisement
noticed and read are achieved. That is, unless the advertisement attracts the attention of the potential customer and holds that attention
(by arousing and maintaining interest) long enough to have the advertisement read and understood, the ultimate goals cannot be achieved.
Hence, in preparation, these immediate functions of the advertisement must be kept in mind and planned in such a manner to achieve
these specific purposes. For example, the headline, the layout, the
illustration (including the use of color), and/or the typeface used,
among other aspects, should be planned with the primary objective
of attracting the initial attention to the advertisement, but in such a
manner that this initial attention will aid in arousing and holding
interest and creating a favorable lasting impression.

It is also important to keep in mind that in writing copy which is
to appear in newspapers, magazines, and other publications of this
nature, a somewhat different approach is used from that used in preparing the script for radio and television.

The script for radio advertising must put primary emphasis on the
audio aspect. In television advertising, on the other hand, the script
should complement the picture and, at the same time, appeal to the
sense of hearing of the viewer. Television advertising appeals to both
sight and sound.

Furthermore, the commercials on radio and television are of a temporary nature, because the listener or viewer cannot bring them back.
The advertiser has to decide on the degree of repetition he wishes to
use. With a printed advertisement, however, the reader decides how
many times and to what degree he wishes to read it.

Definition

Copy includes the word messages, whether for print, radio, or
television. In the printed advertisement, it consists of the printed
words except, perhaps, for those words forming part of the registered
trademark. In other words, copy is defined here as the word message
of the advertisement.

For example, in the March 1976 issue of *Sports Illustrated* appeared a Dodge Charger advertisement. The headline was: "Get hooked on the looks and sold on the price." Following this was the copy:

> At today's prices, a lot of people would consider themselves lucky to get an ordinary-looking car for under $4,000, let alone a great-looking Dodge Charger. That low price includes a lot of standard features you've come to expect in Charger. Like carpeting, soft vinyl-upholstered seats, disc brakes, and an Electronic Ignition System. Charger can also give you something else you might not expect. Surprisingly good fuel economy. Even with an optional automatic transmission. Charger's six-cylinder engine got 23 MPG on the highway and 16 city in EPA estimates. (Your mileage may differ, depending upon your driving habits, the condition of your car, and optional equipment. In California, see your Dealer for engine availability and mileage results.)
>
> Here's "The Clincher." "For the first 12 months of use, any Chrysler Corporation Dealer will fix, without charge for parts or labor, any part of our 1976 passenger cars we supply (except tires) which proves defective in normal use, regardless of mileage." The owner is responsible for maintenance service such as changing filters and wiper blades.

Approach to writing copy

Before any copy is written, the copywriter should answer five basic questions, "What am I advertising or selling?" "To whom am I advertising or selling?" "How can I best convey this message, or concept, to my reader?" "Where and how is the product being sold?" "When will the product be purchased and used?" The answers to these questions provide the basic idea for the copy.

"What am I advertising or selling?" The copywriter must determine what there is in the product or service he is selling that appeals to a desire of the potential buyer. At first glance, it might seem obvious that he is selling a certain product, such as a typewriter, hi-fi set, soft drink, or face cream. In actuality, though, he is not selling the product but what the product can do for the prospective buyer. For the buyer is not interested in the product as such, but in what the results will be if one buys and uses the product. So the advertiser of a TV dinner would not sell a unit with so many well-cooked, well-flavored items, but a quick, easily prepared meal, proficiency as a hostess, a quick nourishing meal when you are on a camping trip, and the like. Similarly, in the case of the soft drink one sells the refreshment provided during a break in the workday, or after a hard tennis match. The advertiser of a jar of face cream does not sell the ingredients, but a lovely skin or the way to become a beautiful person and be popular. And the advertiser of a typewriter may be selling a more efficient means of communication.

In each case, the advertiser is selling something of self-interest to the buyer, and showing how the product will satisfy or gratify that desire or self-interest of the buyer. So the advertiser of life insurance shows how insurance is a way to educate the buyer's children, provide security for his wife, or provide travel and enjoyment in old age. Even in advertising oranges good health may be emphasized. So copy should generally sell something that the product will supply or accomplish, and that the customer wants or needs.

"To whom am I advertising or selling?" The copywriter must ascertain who are the prospects for the product, what their wants are, who influences the prospects in making their decisions to buy, and what the wants of these people are. In addition to determining who the prospects are, the copywriter must determine what these prospects will consider as evidence that will make them buy the product.

"How can I best convey this message, or concept, to my reader?" Having decided on the prospective customer, the wants and motivations, the want-satisfying qualities of the product, and how these will satisfy the desires and self-interest of the prospect, the copywriter must decide how best to bring these two—the product and the prospect —together. In other words, one must decide on the best way to get the appeal across to the prospective customer.

"Where and how is the product being sold?" Is the product being sold through supermarkets? Is the product dependent upon having it "pulled" through the channels of distribution, or does it need to be "pushed" through the channels? Generally speaking, at one end of the spectrum the "patent medicines" have to be pulled through the channels which result in placing the greatest emphasis on the "appeals" to the ultimate consumer. At the other end, shopping goods may have to be pushed through the channels to a great degree, which necessitates placing more emphasis on appeals that will help the consumer identify the brand.

"When will the product be purchased and used"? It is usually more effective to correlate the advertising to the period when the consumer is primarily interested in purchasing it. As an example, major purchases of jewelry items will be made prior to Christmas when some jewelry stores realize more than 70 percent of annual sales. It is therefore important to correlate the appeal to the time of the year in which the consumer is going to purchase the item.

Important copy attributes

The copywriter should keep the overall plan of the advertisement in mind when considering the actual wording to be used to convey the want-satisfying qualities of the product to the prospect, and then to show how it will satisfy his desires. One must also keep in mind the medium in which the advertisement is to be used. That is, if the particular advertisement is to appear on a billboard along a highway, the copy must be brief and concise; whereas if it is to appear in a monthly magazine which will be in homes for some months and be read at leisure, the copy does not have to meet the same rigid restrictions as to length and brevity.

If the copywriter is preparing copy for radio, he or she must keep in mind that the ear cannot assimilate as much material as the eye and that the message is very fleeting. If one is writing copy for television, he or she has to develop the script in a manner similar to that of a person writing plays for motion pictures. In other words, the copywriter should visualize the scenes and write the script for what the characters are to say, with instructions to the technicians and performers who are responsible for producing the television commercial.

The matter of special functions to be accomplished by the advertisement also must be kept in mind by the copywriter. For example, if an attempt is to be made to induce immediate action and sales, one may wish to include specific suggestions in the copy about when the product is available, the price, terms of sale, or other special conditions. Good copy should be brief, clear, apt, interesting, and personal. To write copy of this nature, it is important to keep the following observations in mind.

Be brief

A copywriter must write briefly, yet effectively. Therefore, read the rough draft slowly. Study each sentence. Consider its meaning and importance. Eliminate unnecessary words; weigh each word. At times one word, if properly selected, can be made to take the place of several without weakening the sentence. A sentence with slight alterations can frequently be made to take the place of two, sometimes of several, sentences, and occasionally an entire paragraph can be cut.

Some individuals believe that no one reads long advertisements. Certainly an advertisement should never be longer than is necessary. However, if the success of the advertisement is jeopardized by dropping even one word, then that word should be included.

Two men spoke at Gettysburg. One of these men spoke for two hours, and very few persons could quote a single sentence from his talk. The other man spoke about 300 words. That address, 300 words, has become one of the nation's recognized literary gems. This speech of Abraham Lincoln's is an excellent example of what advertising copywriters should understand by brevity. Be brief, but leave nothing worthwhile untold.

Be clear

When advertising lacks clarity, it will be ineffective. Even a slight vagueness will cripple advertising copy. The authors' analysis of several thousand pieces of advertising discloses that most frequently clarity is clouded by one or more of the following three faults: (1) the use of words whose meanings are not understood by the prospect, (2) the incorrect selection and use of words, or (3) ambiguous phraseology.

Local tradition, habit, custom, and nationality are among the factors that play a part in determining the manner in which copy will be interpreted. Some people in some sections of the country still believe that white eggs are superior to brown, while the reverse is believed by persons in other sections. Manufacturers of certain products have found it necessary to package identical products under several different labels so as to meet the copy emphasis that must be used to satisfy the wishes of their customers in different sections of the country.

Be apt

Copy must be apt—it must fit the needs or wants of the prospects. The influencing power of copy depends greatly on the correlation that exists between the desire of a prospect and the quality or feature of the product. The ability to show this relationship is the art of making copy apt.

To write copy that is apt, a copywriter must continuously study human nature. While the appeal to vanity and pride in personal appearance may influence some people, nevertheless the consumers' ever changing method and mode of living and financial condition may make other appeals more important.

If the product is to be sold to a manufacturer, study the needs of manufacturers. If automatic equipment is to be advertised, the manufacturer will be interested in knowing that one man can do as much work with this piece of equipment as ten men could do with some other product. Such information will be apt because the cost of labor is an important problem with the manufacturer. Another manufacturer will be interested in knowing that the equipment can be adjusted readily, that is strongly built, and that it is easy to purchase parts.

In the sale of baby food, the copy should be so written that it will appeal to mothers. The mother's pride in the health of her child and her natural concern for the baby's general welfare must be studied if the copy is to be apt. To be apt, copy must be specific. Generalities create vagueness.

In Figure 7–1, A.T. & T. uses an illustration and copy that may be difficult for the reader to correlate with its line of products although it possesses a strong attention-attracting device.

Think of the copy as speaking to one specific individual; think of one man or one woman; think of a girl getting dressed for her first date; think of a woman preparing a meal for her children; think of the product that flashes through their minds. Think of that momentary flash, followed by a warm feeling of approval. It comes, it goes, but it has registered. That friendly thought has been stored away; it will rise to the surface again when the occasion demands. There is a predisposition there in favor of the product, a preference for a specific product.

The art of writing advertising copy that is apt is the art of putting into words that which creates in the minds of prospective purchasers a desire to possess the article, in which the need of the prospects will be satisfied by a feature or quality in the product.

To write interesting copy, one must share the problems and hopes which are those of the prospects. To be genuinely human is to be emotional. Emotion or feeling is a most vital feature in good advertising copy. People want to learn about individuals who live on their street; men and women who had to work hard in their childhoods;

FIGURE 7–1

And we were glad to share them—with hundreds of people from over 40 nations who visited us last year to learn about the telephone business.

They came from places like Chad, Dahomey, Malawi, Togo and Bechuanaland; and from France, Germany, Japan, India and Australia.

All these people had one thing in common. They wanted the latest information about modern telecommunications and we gave it to them. They saw how our fast nationwide switching system works. Learned how scientific breakthroughs are converted into better means of communications. And studied the day-to-day work of our operating companies.

We're glad to do everything we can to help people improve their telephone service as we keep improving our own.

We may be the only telephone company in town, but we try not to act like it.

They came to get our trade secrets

AT&T
and Associated Companies

Courtesy American Telephone and Telegraph Company

folks who are human enough to have budget problems and know what it is to make a small income go a long way. They are the kind of people the public understands.

Customers enjoy being told of a girl who prepares a special meal because her boyfriend likes it that way. They like to hear about a dad repairing a toy for his son with a tool he purchased at the hardware store. They respond to the little boy who cried every time he played with his friends until a tonic improved his health.

The reason the boy on the street enjoys football is that he knows about it. He knows the names of the players. He is interested in football because it is constantly being interpreted to him in an interesting way. Copywriters are dealing with human nature, not dead commodities. They are interpreting worthwhile commodities to the prospects.

Be personal

Copy should be written from the prospect to the product, not from the product to the prospect. Visualize this scene: A city street is lined with people out to greet a new President; they crowd along the sidewalk; they stand on window ledges, boxes, and anything that will raise them above other spectators. Finally, he appears. The crowd shouts its greeting. The President rides in his car with head uncovered. How dramatically he picks out one group along the curb, smiles, and raises his hand unmistakably to them. Then his eye alights on a party nearby. He greets them all along the route. He picks out a definite face or particular group of faces when he bows to return a greeting. The President has left the impression of having addressed them personally, man to man! He is remembered because he was personal.

The great temptation that confronts copywriters is to preach to the prospects. The difference between the personalized advertisement and the group preachment may be seen in the following copy:

A. *Group-appeal copy:*
    Consumers know it is necessary to select carefully a good brand of coffee.
A. *Personalized-appeal copy:*
    Find out, at no cost, how really good caffeine-free coffee can be!
B. *Group-appeal copy:*
    Here is America's first forgettable tire. Forget it for 40,000 miles.
B. *Personalized-appeal copy:*
    Brace yourself! You will get a 40,000-mile guarantee.
C. *Group-appeal copy:*
    Our machine is an incredible vacuum cleaner.
C. *Personalized-appeal copy:*
    Take over the controls of the vacuum cleaner that floats on its own air stream and . . . . .

Personalized copy is centered on the prospect. What is the first thing one looks for when you examine a picture? How often will you buy a picture of a group unless you recognize one of the faces as either your own or the face of some friend? The same personal factor measures a person's interest in an advertisement. Personalized copy, therefore, presents something of interest to the reader. The two personalized steps in effective advertisements are illustrated in the following examples:

Do you need money? Write for this booklet.
Cool off with this fan.
Guard your health by washing with this soap.

In each of the foregoing statements, two elements are present. The first, the idea of interest to the reader, serves as the entering wedge for the second idea, the use of a specific product.

The real salesman counsels—he shows ways of doing something better—he imparts suggestions which will be to the prospect's advantage. As a result, companies encourage that their salesmen are practical counselors.

The personalized advertisement is developed from an idea within the scope of the reader's personal interest. It may be taken from the physical qualities or the satisfaction derived from the product. To get the reader to appreciate what the product may mean to him, advertising seeks to awaken his imagination.

Every interpretive approach translates a statement of fact into one that means something to the prospect in his own sphere of thought. It matters not what the product is; one can, by visualizing the wants of the prospect, develop a personal copy theme. The correct theme may appear frequently to be deeply hidden; but, in fact, it is often a situation so obvious that it is easily overlooked.

Other methods

Emphasis also may be secured through a number of mechanical devices, as well as through direct description, description by effect, by detail, by analogy, by suggestions, and by narration.

Direct description tries to picture the article in words. It endeavors to describe the product in such a way that the reader can see it as vividly as if he had it before him. Direct description is important where the satisfaction it may give already has been established.

Description by effect gives the effect of using the product, or tells what the product will do, as in the following examples:

Serve Hostess Fruit Pies—made with more fruit filling than crust—

Now you can fly . . . for $25.

Feel this fresh all day long!

You cannot brush bad breath away—reach for Listerine!

When it is important to emphasize what the product will do, a description by effect can be employed to advantage.

Description by detail is useful in the advertisement of products for which primary demand already has been stimulated, because it permits emphasis to be directed to a distinct useful feature of the advertiser's particular brand of product. In describing by detail, points of difference between the advertised product and competitive ones should be chosen. Where little difference exists, any detail which has not been emphasized previously may serve the purpose.

Description by analogy draws a parallel between the idea to be conveyed and one that is already established. A well-chosen analogy, metaphor, or personification has strong descriptive power. For example: "Mennen presents a 'Swaddling Powder' as new as your baby. . . .

Once upon a time . . . mothers swaddled their new-born babies in soft silks and linens. Today—you can wrap your baby in even greater luxury and in the newest protection of New Mennen Baby Powder." A precaution to observe, however, in using this device is to be sure to base the analogy on an idea which is well known, and not to use an analogy that is far-fetched.

Description by suggestion starts the thought process and then lets the reader's imagination finish it. It plays on his emotions, his recollections, and his imagination; the advertisement need say very little to suggest a great deal.

Epigrammatic copy is a higher form of description by suggestion, implying its entire meaning in very few words. Of all the forms of suggestion, it is the most subtle. "The office safe isn't" and "It's a wise hammer that never loses its head" are examples of this type of copy. Epigrammatic copy is terse and succinct. It may lack conviction but is rich in suggestions. Because it is subtle, its point may be too vague for its readers to grasp.

Description by logic depends on facts to prove why a prospect should purchase the product. It is not what the advertiser says but what the facts show; not what he thinks but what the evidence is. The facts may be secured from impartial tests; they may be established through satisfaction of customers expressed in testimonials and endorsements, through samples, trial offers, and guarantees; or they may be demonstrated through logical argument based upon other facts especially compiled.

In addition to the aforementioned kind of descriptive copy, there is another type called the narrative form. Generally it is written in the first person and has both sincerity and convincing qualities. Because it seems to come from a specific person, it carries its point directly and vividly. Narrative copy can assume the form of monologue, of dialogue, or even be in the third person.

The story in narrative copy should get under way immediately, for the entire effect depends on getting the reader absorbed in its action. This may be accomplished by opening in the middle of the conversation. The prelude may be disposed of either by omission, if it appears self-evident, or by caption, by illustration, by explanatory note, or by doubling back after the start of the copy, like a motion picture which has a scene cut in, showing what happened prior to the opening of the story.

The story should illustrate a definite point, and once it establishes this point, the scene should be shifted to the prospect. A good transition is a delicate piece of copy craftsmanship which draws the reader into the advertisement quite naturally while his interest in the story is at its height. The last step of the narrative copy is to tell the prospect what he should do.

The headline

The headline is that part of the copy which has been made to stand out in the advertisement by the size or style of type in which it has been set, the prominence of its location, or the white space surrounding it.

The function of a headline is to attract the favorable attention of prospective purchasers and to interest them so that they will read the advertisement. Subheadlines are subordinate headlines. They are used in a wide variety of ways and for many reasons, such as to complete the meaning of the headline, to bring out related but additional or different appeals, or to break up lengthy copy.

It is not possible to say that the headline is more important than the illustration, or that one is subordinate to the other. As an example, in a recent advertisement of a large oil company, the principal illustration was the picture of a mushroom and a toadstool standing side by side in their native habitat. The caption read: "Which is the mushroom and which is the toadstool? Would you eat one to find out?" The copy brought out the point that if it was foolish to take a chance of being poisoned by eating mushrooms when they could not be identified simply by looking at them, it would be equally foolish to buy and use oil of unknown lubricating qualities.

Without the headline, this illustration, the picture of the mushroom and the toadstool, was meaningless. The headline, "Which is the mushroom and which is the toadstool? Would you eat one to find out?" is almost as worthless if used alone. When used together, they make a forceful comparison.

It is questionable whether the writer of this advertisement got the idea for the illustration or the headline first. It is quite probable they came simultaneously. His visualizing efforts perhaps drifted toward apt comparisons, and knowing of the close physical likeness of toadstools and mushrooms, he recognized a similarity in the difficulty people have in telling them apart and the difficulty they have in differentiating between brands of oil.

When a salesman tells a customer about the merits of his product he already has the ear of his prospect. While there are a number of factors that might prevent him from closing the sale, he does have the attention of the buyer.

In advertising a product, however, the advertiser does not have this exclusive attention. The television program, the music on radio, the articles in the magazine, and the news in the newspaper are generally more important to the prospect than the advertisement. These special features are the reasons why people watch television programs or purchase newspapers and magazines. As a result, it is necessary to attract the prospects from their prior interests for a long enough period to get them to listen to or read a message. It also becomes important to distract them in such a manner so that whatever attention-attracting device is used will lead logically ino the message and will appeal to the prospect.

Types of headlines

Headline appeals may be classified into two broad categories, direct or indirect. The direct-appeal headline attempts to use a primary sales feature of the product for both the attention-attracting device as well as the sales appeal. An indirect-appeal headline attempts only to stop the reader and to get him to read or listen to the body of the appeal.

An example of the direct appeal is found in Figure 7–2. Mennen points out: "MENNEN SPEED STICK. It actually builds up a resistance to odor." This is direct selling emphasizing one of the main features of the Mennen Speed Stick.

An example of the indirect approach is the Blue Cross Advertisement in Figure 7–3. "This is all the profit we need." This appeal doesn't sell anything other than a general interest concept.

In deciding whether to use the direct or indirect appeal, one should analyze the product to determine what specific advantages it has over those of competitors. If these advantages are such that lend themselves to a direct appeal, then, as a general rule the advertiser is more likely to make the sale if he uses this approach. There is always greater danger of attracting the attention of those who may not be interested in the product if the indirect selling appeal is used. There is also the additional danger of antagonizing even the actual prospects if the indirect approach results in their believing they are misled in reading the copy.

Specific headline classifications

Among the ways in which headlines may be classified are the following:

1. Directive.
2. News.
3. Slogan.
4. Rational.
5. Curiosity.
6. Emotional.
7. Gimmick.

It is difficult to make sharp distinctions between the classifications because there is overlapping in the divisions, and a given headline or appeal may embody two or more of the above types.

The *directive approach* is used more often in retail advertising. The objective with this appeal is to get the prospect to act now. An example of this is found in the Whirlpool advertisement in which it gives the telephone number to call in an emergency:

"IN CASE OF EMERGENCY CALL (800) 253–1301"

A *specific news* item headline is given by *Datsun* in an advertisement:

"HOW TO BUY A SMALL CAR"

How important is this news item in getting prospects to read the body of the text? Will this news item attract the people who buy cars? Does the news item drive home the selling points? Does it attract attention

FIGURE 7-3

THIS IS ALL THE PROFIT WE NEED.

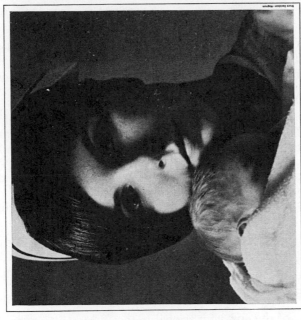

It better be.

We don't make a nickel of the other kind. But when 63 million people know they can enter hospitals and simply present their Blue Cross cards, we think our business is a rip-roaring success.

And that's exactly what Blue Cross is. People who never know when they might need a hospital's services, so they all put a little into big emergency funds called Blue Cross.

When the need comes, the money is there.

Making sure that your hospital bill gets paid and that you and yours are well cared for is what Blue Cross management does.

Now, with all that to do, you might well ask why we also take the time to advertise. Our answer is this. One-third of America already has Blue Cross.

We feel that the other people have a right to know about it.

BLUE CROSS®

Courtesy Blue Cross.

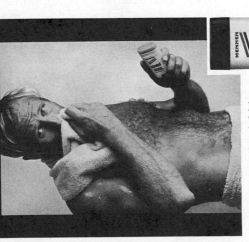

MENNEN
Speed Stick

It actually builds up a resistance to odor.

This deodorant's special bacteria-fighting ingredient builds in a resistance that lasts even through a hot, soapy shower. You don't have to settle for protection against odor anymore.
Now you can build up a resistance with...Mennen Speed Stick

FIGURE 7-2
Courtesy The Mennen Company.

while starting to sell? These are some of the questions that should be considered whenever an appeal of this kind is used.

The Bank of California incorporates its *slogan* in the headline:

"COME TO THE BANK FOR ACTION"

It should be kept in mind that when a slogan is used, it should embody the most significant message of the advertising campaign, and that if the theme of the advertising changes, the slogan also should be changed.

The *rational appeal* is an important approach to consider using because prospects have a tendency to envision themselves as being intelligent individuals and desire to rationalize their decisions. DEN-TU-CREME uses this approach in its headline:

"ARE YOU SPENDING MORE THAN 45% SECONDS CLEANING YOUR DENTURES? IF YOU ARE, YOU'RE WASTING YOUR TIME."

Institute of Life Insurance uses the *curiosity appeal* in:

"WIFE INSURANCE IS FLOWERS ON HER BIRTHDAY, RIGHT?"

The danger of the curiosity appeal is that it may attract readers who are not interested in the product, and, it is also difficult to correlate the "sales" message to this type of headline.

Foster Parents Plan, Inc., used the *emotional appeal* effectively with the headline: "You can dry his tears." This type of headline is effective in situations where we wish to attract the readers through the sense appetites.

While the *gimmick approach* is somewhat similar to the curiosity approach, it is one that goes beyond mere curiosity by presenting an appeal that is completely an attention-attracting appeal. Dayton uses this appeal—"$2 against your life. . . ."

General recommendations

In the final analysis, the suitability of the headline rests upon its ability to get the prospect into the main copy in a positive frame of mind.

There are four major characteristics in most good headlines: (1) brevity, (2) clarity, (3) aptness, and (4) interest.

Brevity. A caption that is not brief and concise fails to perform its first and most important task. Each advertisement has been prepared to attract the favorable attention and hold the interest of the reader. This means that each advertisement is silently but skillfully attempting to attract the eye of the prospect. The reader, on the other hand, may not be particularly interested in the advertisement—to him it may even be an intrusion—he knows what he wants and where to find it. In his own opinion, his time is both limited and valuable. Recognizing this picture of the competition and handicaps that confront an advertisement, it is important that the headline be sufficiently short to be read at a glance.

Clarity. Little advantage will be gained from the use of a headline sufficiently short to be read at a glance if its meaning is not clear. It is important that the advertiser state his headline in a clear and concise manner so that it will appeal directly to the prospect. Unless this is done, there is danger of a vague headline attracting the attention of persons who may not be in the market for the product, but missing those who should be reached.

Aptness. Aptness is developed by showing that the product advertised has the particular feature or quality that fills or satisfies the prospective purchaser's needs or wants. Attempts to prepare cute or clever advertisements may result in vague and irrelevant headlines that are not appropriate. Such statements as "Why not?" or "Would you?" do not particularly mean anything to anyone. The caption "We announce" is vague and has little meaning, for who cares for what anyone else wishes to announce? "Look at this offer" is entirely too vague. Tell the prospective purchaser what the offer is, and if it is sufficiently enticing, he will stop and read the advertisement.

Interest. There is perhaps no easier way to make a headline interesting than to make it speak directly to the individual reader in a personal manner. This does not mean that one must eliminate the necessary dignity that an advertisement should possess.

When preparing a headline do not address the prospect like a man giving a talk by saying, "Ladies and gentlemen." The use of the word "you" usually will help make the headline personal. An interesting headline is a sincere and personal message prepared for an average prospect.

There are several things that may nullify a prospect's interest in an otherwise interesting headline—seeming exaggeration, insincere or misleading statement, and antagonism. Whether the caption should be a declaration, question, command, or a part of an unfinished sentence in the form of a phrase will depend entirely on the objectives of the specific advertisement.

Below are listed several captions and illustrations which have been used successfully in advertisements:

1. Tire advertisement:
    Illustration: An automobile tire superimposed on a man's hand gripping into the soil.
    Headline: "The Armstrong grip."
2. Cough medicine advertisement:
    Illustration: Young mother giving little boy a spoonful of medicine.
    Headline: "For fast relief of cough and cold miseries."
3. Shampoo advertisement:
    Illustration: Mother and daughter, both with beautiful hair, very similar in appearance.
    Headline: "Now! Wash those years right out of your hair!"
4. Advertisement for long-distance telephone calls:
    Illustration: Young woman beaming as she listens on telephone;

while a question mark appears in another equal-sized panel next to her.

Headline: "Can you picture the other half of this long-distance call?"

5. Camera Advertisement:

Illustration: Charming young couple sitting on park bench, the man giving instructions to smiling policeman holding camera.

Headline: "Just press the button, Chief—it'll come out fine!"

6. Advertisement for hearing-aid glasses:

Illustration: Young girl talking to her grandmother, who is wearing a pair of glasses.

Headline: "Grandma, did God give you new ears?"

7. Advertisement for encyclopedia:

Illustration: Two women and a man listening attentively to a man talking at a party.

Headline: "When you talk . . . do people listen?" (Copy theme: people listen to you if you have a command of words.)

In each of the above advertisements, the headlines are brief, clear, apt, and interesting. At the same time, an inherent personal appeal also is present. The chief weakness of many headlines is that they are not specific and, as a result, may not attract the right prospect.

Summary

There is no easy road to copywriting. It is an exacting activity which requires the ability to use basic human appeals and to recognize the differences that exist in the writing style that should be used for the different products and media.

Good advertising strategy makes the copy conform to the advertising plan. All necessary provisions should be made so the reader will be put to the least amount of trouble. Frequently the reader is told to ask for a product "at your dealer" when the goods may not be stocked in his store. Instructions should be precise and complete. All questions which might possibly arise should be anticipated. "Get the summer catalog: out soon" leaves the reader wondering when it will be out, where he can get it, whether he will have to pay for it. "Go to your dealer—there is one in every town" is less effective "Go to the dealer that shows this sign" or "For sale ——" (where the local address can be given in the advertisement).

An advertisement can at times be closed with a suggestion such as: "Some day soon when you're feeling adventurous, match your mood with a drive in the new Plymouth; the car is ready for inspection at Plymouth showrooms." "If your background qualifies you to work in any of these areas, we would be pleased to hear from you." This gentle suggestion is a refined type of closing, stronger than the implied, but possessing a courteous, gracious charm which is effective with some people and necessary in advertising some products.

The closing part of the advertisement generally should help to overcome the tendency to procrastinate. The reader may be quite sincere in believing that he will carry out the suggestion contained in the advertisement the next time he is in the market for the advertised product. However, as soon as he turns from the one advertisement to the next advertisement or story, he starts to forget the message. The best way to be certain he does take the desired action is to urge him to do so immediately—now.

Although many devices exist for inviting action or for assuring early attention by means of urge lines, the concluding message in advertisements still offers opportunity for further improvement. The urge line may tell how restricted the offer is, for example: "Since the number of albums available for this special offer is limited, orders will be filled in the sequence received, and this offer may be discontinued at any time. We sincerely urge you to mail the coupon now" or "Stocks limited! Act now!" Or it can stress the value of that which is being offered; for example: "If you act now—this coupon is worth $4.55." "Buy now for extra values." The urge line can reiterate the convenience of acting and the subsequent satisfaction, as "Get a jar of Kava today and prove it tonight" or "Start feeding your pet Puss 'n Boots today. In just three weeks—or even less—see if you aren't delighted with an amazing improvement in her health, appearance, energy."

It is also important to recognize that one must differentiate between execution of copy in print and broadcast. With print copy you can come back and view it at a later time. Broadcast provides a fleeting impression. The depth of that impression may determine its effectiveness.

Although radio and television are fluid media, they are dissimilar. If, as an example, the television sound part of the commercial is about the same as the radio commercial except that it has visual aids, then there is probably too much in the television audio phase because the pictures are not doing the job that they should be accomplishing. Television is a medium of demonstration while radio is a medium of imagination.

Yet, in preparing radio or television commercials, one should keep in mind that these medias serve primarily relaxation and entertainment functions. Consumer needs, as well as competitive product situations are constantly changing. As a result, the focus will change and require different media or different times. The suspense show has certain characteristics, the dramatic and variety shows have others, which may require correlating the commercials to the nature of the programs because the audience have a tendency to judge them in the context in which they are viewed or heard.

When writing copy, try always to use the present tense. Keep in mind the illusion that you are using the appeal for the first time—it will almost add news value to the statement that the Eastman Kodak

Company manufactures Kodaks! Keep constantly in mind the prospect's likes and dislikes; write about these things as the situation may require, but never allow any other point to dominate the advertisement. Visualize the product as an article which the reader needs and stress how it will benefit him. Speak to the consumer as a friend, an unbiased authority, in order to create the atmosphere of word-of-mouth comments so that he will relax and accept the recommendations.

While new copy slants are constantly being sought by advertisers, one will find that frequently these innovations will be short-lived. The important aspect to keep in mind is that the advertisement should be unified and where possible it should concentrate on one main idea.

Questions

1. Indicate how you would use a specific strategy and translate it into dynamic advertising for print media for the following products:
    a. Bell & Howell 16 mm movie camera.
    b. Polaroid camera.
    c. Cross pen and pencil set.
    d. Norelco electric shaver.
    e. Firestone tires.
    f. Book club.
    g. Prudential Life Insurance.
    h. Ford Pinto automobile.
    In what manner would you translate differently if broadcast media were being used?
2. Many companies do not actually know the product they are selling. Explain.
3. Compare a letter to your parents asking for money with the copy in an advertisement.
4. Select five advertisements from any current magazine and comment on the copy in regard to: clarity, aptness, interest, and personalization.
5. Select from any current media two advertisements in which the headlines are satisfactory; select two in which you believe the headline might be improved. Rewrite these and give reasons why you believe they are better.
6. What are some of the major advertising problems involved in getting the attention of the prospect?
7. Differentiate between preparing copy for print media and the script for broadcast media.
8. When might it be advisable for an advertising copywriter to leave out some of the basic information?
9. Indicate when you believe *humor* can be used successfully in advertising. Contrast the use of humor in print and broadcast media.
10. In what ways may the scripts for radio and television be the same? In what ways may they differ?
11. A leading advertising executive made the following statement: "The major emphasis today is on arresting and visual concepts, jarring headlines, terse copy, elimination of the secondary, sharp focus on a single selling point." Comment.
12. Copy writers were advised to adopt the following strategy: "Get the attention of the customer any way you can and then embark on your selling

story!" Today the advice is frequently given, "Your attention getter today has to make our selling point." Comment.

13. How might an advertiser get the appeal to radiate from the culture into the product?

14. Give some of the consumer resistances that a copywriter should keep in mind in writing copy.

15. A regional distributor of Freeze Dried Coffee has decided to sell the product on a national basis. Develop a slogan which you believe could be used successfully in both print and broadcast media. The distributor wishes to emphasize that the quality of his product is superior.

Case **SPALDING**
7–1 **Evaluating a comparison appeal**

Bristol-Myers invests heavily in Datril to make it the "fastest selling non-aspirin pain reliever" as it goes after leader McNeil Laboratories' Tylenol in a hard-hitting comparative ad campaign.

General Mills revised a *Total* Cereal comparison TV spot. Quaker Oats objected to a comparison of *Total* and Quaker's 100% Natural Cereal on grounds that it was deceptive and misleading to the public.

California Raisin Advisory Board advertised "Sweets make her [child shown in ad] happy. But too many sweets make you unhappy."

Hobart Corporation with its ads for Kitchen Aid dishwashers stated, "Guys who fix dishwashers buy Kitchen Aid for themselves"; this referred to the results conducted by "an independent research firm" which showed that repairmen selected Kitchen Aid as their number-one choice when asked "which dishwasher they'd buy for themselves."

Nissan Motor Company for the Datson B–210 claimed, "No car in America gets better mileage. . . ."

Lanvin-Charles of the Ritz in its advertising emphasized "Liquid Revenescence is the most famous, most luxurious daytime moisturizer ever created . . . there is no other moisturizer that can even be compared to it."

Johnson & Johnson stressed "combing out tangles after shampooing used to hurt me. But now Mommy uses Johnson's No More Tangles. Thank you Mommy."

The above appeals are only a few examples of the use of competitive advertising appeals. In some instances, a direct frontal approach is used without any equivocation in listing the pros and cons of the comparison of the products.

On the other hand, a subtle approach is used that does not name the competition, but points out, "We are number two, so, we have to try harder," or, "we are the only hometown owned bank in the area."

Rising consumerism has restored more of the competitive nature to markets. And, yet, it is essential to consider when it is advisable to use competitive strategy, and, when and where it can be used most effectively.

The $250,000 challenge

Spalding developed a campaign centered around a Golf Ball Distance Test which was conducted by Opinion Research Corporation. The test made is given in Exhibit 7–1. As a result of the test, Spalding developed the $250,000 Challenge campaign. A typical ad used in the campaign is shown in Exhibit 7–2.

EXHIBIT 7–1

A Golf Ball Distance Test
Conducted for
Spalding

by

OPINION RESEARCH CORPORATION
PRINCETON, NEW JERSEY 08540

June 20, 1974

This presents results of a golf ball distance test conducted for Spalding in April and May 1974.

Objective. The overall objective of this study was to test the hypothesis that the Spalding Top-Flite golf ball travels farther than major competitive brands when struck by "average" golfers.

Findings. Under the test conditions described herein, the Spalding Top-Flite golf ball does travel farther than any of seven other major competitive balls tested.[*]

Definitions:

a. An "average golfer" is defined as a man with a handicap of at least 6 but no more than 20, or a woman with a handicap of no more than 30. (Women were included in the test.)

b. "Major competitive balls" were defined as seven specific products that comprise the greatest share of the premium pro shop golf ball market—
   Blue Max
   Golden Ram SS4–90
   Omega
   Royalist +6
   Titleist–90
   Titleist DT
   Wilson LD–90

c. "Distance" is defined as the combined distance a specific golfer hits a specific ball with a five iron and the club he normally uses off the tee. Flight and roll are included.

Statistical analysis

In all, 210 golfers participated in the test. (Of these, approximately 15 percent were women.)

"Successful" participation required that no more than four unmeasureable balls be hit. This qualification eliminated 44 participants and left us with a base of 166 "qualified" data sets. Of course, the number of successful hits of any *one* ball was something less than 166.

---

[*] The basic study involved 11 balls—the 8 "test" balls, plus the experimental Spalding balls. For this report, the existence of the nontest balls is ignored.

EXHIBIT 7–1 (continued)

Results were as follows:

Ball	Number of observations	Mean distance (yards)	Standard error of mean
Top-Flite................	135	370.5	6.5
Titleist DT	122	362.3	5.9
Omega.................	135	361.5	6.0
Blue Max	137	359.7	6.4
Royal +6	131	358.0	6.5
Titleist–90..............	126	356.9	6.5
Wilson LD–90	126	356.4	6.6
Golden Ram SS4–90......	131	355.1	6.2

These data are *indicative* of a clear win for Top-Flite since the difference between Top-Flite and the second ball (8.2) is greater than the difference between the second ball and the eighth (last) ball in the test. However, the results are not subject to statistical validation at this point. This comes from two factors—

1. The standard deviation of our samples is large. This was expected and comes from using a wide range of golfers in the test. (One man hit one ball a combined total of 573 yards—some women and older men were under 200 yards for individual balls.)
2. These are highly correlated observations. The differences *among* golfers were far greater than those *within* golfers. For example, the man who hit one ball 573 yards (two shots) hit all balls over 400 yards; but a woman hitting one ball under 200 yards, hit no balls over 250 yards.

Therefore, it became desirable to move on to a more sensitive test—one that took into account the high intercorrelation among the observations.

In brief, in this test we looked at *pairs* of balls hit by individual golfers and determined the *difference* in distance hit. We then computed the mean difference and the standard error of the mean of the difference and applied a conventional test to determine if the mean difference differed significantly from zero.

A problem arises quickly here in that additional observations are lost since we are now looking at people who have hit *two* specific balls successfully.

Results were as follows:

Top-Flite and:	Observa-tions	Mean difference (yards)	Standard error of difference	t	p
Titleist–90	103	+13.3	2.9	4.58	0.001
Golden Ram SS4–90....	109	+11.5	3.1	3.69	0.001
Royal +6	106	+10.1	2.8	3.61	0.001
Titleist DT	101	8.4	2.8	2.93	0.01
Wilson LD–90	104	8.7	3.1	2.75	0.01
Omega...............	113	4.5	2.4	1.86	0.06
Blue Max.............	114	3.5	2.9	1.21	—

To explain, the probability (*p*) of observing difference such as those due to chance is about one in a thousand for the Titleist–90, the Golden Ram SS4–90 and the Royal +6. For the Titleist DT and the Wilson LD–90, it is about one in one hundred, and for the Omega, about one in 20. By commonly accepted

EXHIBIT 7–1 (*continued*)

statistical standards, we can say that the distance achieved by the Top-Flite is "significantly" better than that for any of these balls.

> But, a problem arose at this point; we cannot point to a significant difference in performance between the Top-Flite and the Blue Max.

A review of the data showed an interesting situation. While the mean value of all readings for Top-Flite was 370.5 yards and that for Blue Max was 359.7 yards (a difference of 10.8), the mean difference observed from those hitters who successfully hit both balls was 3.5.

Further investigation showed the probable source of this problem—those who had successfully hit the Top-Flite but not the Blue Max averaged almost 400 yards on their Top-Flite performance. On the other hand, those who successfully hit the Blue Max, but not the Top-Flite, averaged about 350 yards on their Blue Max shots. In other words, the specific players who successfully hit both Top-Flite and Blue Max excluded strong hitters of Top-Flite and weak hitters of Blue Max.

As statisticians, we are not permitted to leap to conclusions, but we were faced with two obvious explanations—

1. People who can successfully hit both Top-Flite and Blue Max are, systematically, unable to hit the Top-Flite as far as those who can hit the Top-Flite but not the Blue Max. (While this seems improbable, it is one possible explanation of our data.)
2. We have encountered a statistical anomaly . . . a chance occurrence that would not recur in a repeated test.

The obvious technique to determine which of these conclusions is correct is to conduct an additional test.

The results of this test, conducted only between Top-Flite and Blue Max, are as follows.

```
Golfers . . . . . . . . . . . . . . . . . . . . . . 42 (40 qualified)
Pairs . . . . . . . . . . . . . . . . . . . . . . . 79
Mean difference. . . . . . . . . . . . . . . 9.3
Standard error of difference . . . . . . 2.93
t . . . . . . . . . . . . . . . . . . . . . . . . . . . 3.17
p. . . . . . . . . . . . . . . . . . . . . . . . . . . 0.01
```

There is less than one chance in 100 of observing this difference by chance. Therefore, we can say that the Top-Flite travels significantly farther than the Blue Max.

Ball acquisition and handling

Using Opinion Research Corporation's National Probability Sample, 15 locations in the 48 contiguous states were selected. A resident interviewer was contacted in each location and instructed to visit the golf professional at the nearest "large, private country club" and to purchase 16 dozen golf balls from him—two of each of the test brands (including Top-Flite). Payment was in the form of an exchange—an equal number of new Top-Flite balls were presented to the professional in payment.

Most pros did not have all the balls in question in stock so other shops in the area were visited until the sample was complete. Some balls without good national distribution were obtained in less than 15 locations.

In general, we may say that the balls tested were representative of shelf stock from pro shops around the country.

EXHIBIT 7–1 (*continued*)

Ball handling. Packages from all sources were separated into 11 stacks by brand (type) of ball. Each worker was assigned a brand of ball. Processing involved the use of indelible opaque marking pen to obliterate any identifying marks on the ball and to indicate a code letter. The code letters were assigned by random drawing. Once each ball had been marked, the balls were assembled into sets for the test. Each set included one of each of the test balls. The set was placed in a plastic bag and sealed at Opinion Research Corporation.

Since the balls of each type were thoroughly mixed at each stage of the process, the sets of eight balls that were made up can be assumed to contain representative samples of the pro shop shelf stock of each type that is available.

As will be shown in more detail below, each golfer participating in the test used one set of balls. Therefore each ball in the test was struck by only one golfer—once with a five iron and once with the club he normally uses off the tee.

All balls used in the test were returned to ORC for safekeeping. At some future time after acceptance of this report, the balls will be released to the client for such nondestructive testing as he might wish to undertake. (The balls should be maintained in tested condition until such time as a new test is conducted to replace this one.)

Procedures for the supplemental test

In the supplemental test only Top-Flite and Blue Max balls were tested. Unused sets of balls from the first test were broken open and the Top-Flite and Blue Max balls removed. This provided us with approximately 100 balls. An additional two dozen of each brand were acquired from a local pro shop to supplement this number. The new balls were marked as before and the full supply of each ball was then carefully intermingled.

Sets of balls were made up including three balls of each type. Since it is important to our test procedure to be able to identify specific pairs of balls, each ball in this test was given an identifying number from 1 to 6 with the Blue Max balls given odd numbers and the Top-Flite balls being given even numbers. In this way the pairs to be measured were predesignated. As before, the sets were sealed at ORC. And the used sets are currently in storage in our office.

The measuring grid

A drawing of the measuring grid is provided on the next page. In essence it is a cross hatch pattern of 10-yard squares 280 yards long by 80 yards wide. The first cross hatch is at the 80-yard line. The key measurements for the grid (indicated by asterisks) were made by professional surveyors before the actual grid was laid out using four-inch plastic tape.

The use of the grid made possible rather precise measurements of the distance the ball traveled. Since the horizontal elements of the grid gave us distance from the base line, and the vertical elements gave us the deflection from the center line, a simple trigonometric calculation gave the exact distance from the hitting point to the point at which the ball was measured.

Recruiting procedure

Golfers were invited to participate by interviewers stationed at local country clubs and/or public courses (with preference given to the members of the clubs which provided the range). In order to participate, a male golfer had to have a handicap of at least six but no more than 20. The female golfer must have had a handicap of no more than 30.

On completion of the test, each participant received a certificate good for a

EXHIBIT 7–1 (*continued*)

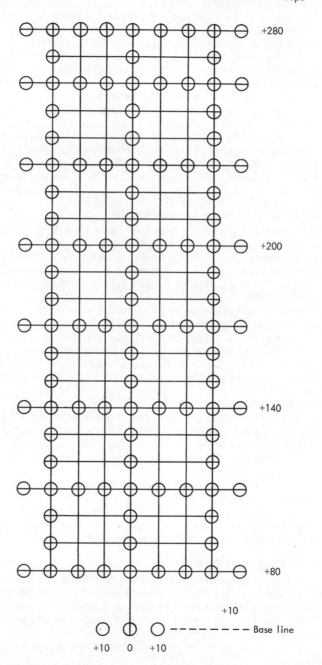

EXHIBIT 7–1 (*continued*)

half dozen balls *of his choice* at the pro shop of the course whose range we were using.

No respondent was permitted to participate more than once. If he missed the grid with four shots, he was excused and the data are not included in this study. However, he still earned his certificate.

Range procedures. Golfers would appear at the range according to the appointments set up in the recruiting process. Each golfer would first sign in with the range officer, providing his name, address, age, handicap and frequency of play. He would then be read the detailed instructions he was to follow in the test. A copy of these instructions is appended.

The golfer was provided with range balls with which to warm up before actually participating in the test. Once he was ready to start, he would be shown the base line and his designated hitting area, and a bag of test balls would be broken open and dumped on the ground before him. He would then proceed to hit each ball with his five iron (one golfer insisted upon and was permitted to use a seven wood). After each ball was hit, the range crew would make the necessary horizontal and vertical measurements and pick up the ball. The hitter would wait until given a signal by the crew before hitting the next ball. Since the balls were hit in the order in which they fell on the ground, this was essentially a random order and no other control over the order of hitting was employed. (Records were kept concerning the order in which the balls were hit.)

Once the entire set of balls had been hit with the five iron, the balls were retrieved and returned to the golfer so that he could hit a second time, this time, using the club he normally uses off the tee. Provision was made for replacing badly cut balls, but this proved to be unnecessary during the course of this test.

A ball that ended its roll outside the grid on either side would not be counted. However the grid was considered endless on its long axis. Balls hit beyond the grid were measured.

Additionally, "ground balls" were omitted from this study. These include any male shots that struck the ground before the 80-yard marker and any female shots considered ground balls by the range officer.

At the close of each hitter's activity, the record sheet and the balls were returned to the range officer and verified. At that time the set of balls was sealed into a new bag and numbered with a number corresponding to that of the hitter.

Test conditions

In reviewing this record of test conditions, the reader should keep in mind the fact that the statistical test used for this study involves the measurement of the difference between the distances a single golfer hits a specified pair of balls. In all cases, the conditions under which a golfer hit any pair of balls were essentially the same. Therefore, the fact that range conditions were not identical is irrelevant for purposes of this study.

The main study was conducted in Scottsdale, Arizona, using two country club ranges—

1. Camelback Country Club—a large, open range, watered regularly, with a somewhat elevated tee area and a slight downward slope. The test occupied about two-thirds of the range. At times the other third was in use for regular practice, making it difficult to retrieve mis-hit test balls.
2. Century Country Club—a smaller range, not watered regularly, with no tee elevation and essentially flat. The test occupied the entire usable range.

Temperatures ranged from the 60s in the mornings to the high 80s/90s in midafternoon. Air was still in the mornings, with a breeze (10+ mph) starting about

EXHIBIT 7–1 (*concluded*)

noon. The prevailing wind was at the golfers' back at Camelback and from his right at Century.

Relative humidity was quite low (20 percent or less).

Active dates for the 122 golfers at Camelback were April 24, 25, 26, 27, 28, 30; at Century (92 golfers) one less day was used, with testing starting on April 25.

Supplementary test.   The supplementary test took place at Golfcrest Country Club, Pearland (Houston), Texas, on May 29 and 30, 1974.

The entire range was used. Golfers hit from a somewhat elevated driving area toward a range containing many slight rises and depressions. The range was watered regularly and the grass was cut quite short.

Temperatures for the Pearland test were in the high 80s and low 90s. A stiff breeze blew all of the time, crossing the range from left to right.

Relative humidity was high (70 percent or more).

EXHIBIT 7–2

$250,000 says Top-Flite® is The Longest Ball.

Only The Longest Ball would make this challenge: $250,000 to the first of these: Titleist, Royal +6, Blue Max, Wilson LD, Titleist DT or Maxfli that can beat Top-Flite in a truly meaningful distance test. No machines. No gimmicks. Just men & women golfers with a wide range of handicaps, hitting woods and irons until Opinion Research Corp., an independent testing firm, determines the conclusive winner.

Top-Flite already won a test like this using hundreds of golfers and beat the other leading balls by 8 to 13 yards! Now Top-Flite challenges them again, one-on-one, in the same kind of test.

TOP-FLITE:
beat Titleist by 13.3 yards
beat Royal +6 by 10.1 yards
beat Blue Max by 9.3 yards
beat Wilson LD by 8.7 yards
beat Titleist DT by 8.4 yards

The distance measurement is a "tee to green" combined total distance of two-shots—the first off the driver, the second off the five-iron. Test conducted by Opinion Research Corp., Princeton, N.J.

All balls tested will be purchased from pro shop inventories as of April 1, 1975 in various regions throughout the U.S., and must meet U.S.G.A. specifications. Challenge expires August 31st, 1975. For complete details write to Spalding, Dept. TFC, Chicopee, Mass. 01014.

Case questions

1. Evaluate the effectiveness of using comparison appeals. Are there any specific products for which this type of appeal will be more effective?
2. What about the reaction to this approach from the various demographic groups who purchase golf balls?
3. List five other appeals which Spalding might have used and compare the effectiveness of these to the "companion" approach in this case.
4. Which demographic groups will be reached more effectively with "comparison" appeals?

Case **SPEIDEL**
7–2 **Deciding on buying motives**

Speidel, a division of Textron, Inc., was founded in 1932 as the Speidel Corporation through the merger of three companies which were then owned and operated by the Speidel brothers. Mr. Paul Levinger, president of Speidel, assumed his position in 1961, having been with the company since 1934.

Speidel is the leading watchband manufacturer in the United States, and since 1965 has been the distributor for British Sterling, a line of "quality" men's toiletries.

In May 1964, the Speidel Corporation was acquired by Textron, Inc., a diversified manufacturing company. Although Speidel is a division of Textron, Inc., the actual operation of the company remained the same as before the Textron acquisition.

At its beginning in 1932, Speidel occupied two floors in the Providence, Rhode Island, building which now, with other buildings in the area, is owned and occupied completely by Speidel.

Speidel has had many firsts in the industry. It was primarily responsible for getting the retailers to take the watchbands from under the counters and display them in attractive cabinets on the counters. It developed a beautiful package for the bands, which played a major factor in developing the bands as gift items. In 1940, it introduced the first ladies' expansion bracelet, the "Mignon."

In 1946, Speidel used full-page advertisements in *Life* and the *Ladies' Home Journal*—the first full-page national advertisements ever run for watchbands. In the spring of 1948, Speidel decided on a more spectacular approach and bought a portion of "Stop the Music," one of the more successful "giveaway" programs on radio. In 1949, the company became a pioneer television advertiser as sponsor of the first network television show to originate in California. Speidel was one of the first national advertisers to shift the major portion of its advertising budget into television.

Another of Speidel's most important breakthroughs was the development of the Twist-O-Flex watchband in 1959. The Twist-O-Flex is a band that conforms not only to the shape of the wrist but also flexes in any desired direction. This band almost revolutionized the watchband industry and even further solidified Speidel's position as the country's leading watchband manufacturer. (See Exhibit 7–3.)

EXHIBIT 7–3

Courtesy Speidel, a division of Textron, Inc.

Speidel has relied heavily on advertising to build its market and, as early as 1947, it was spending $500,000 annually on advertising. The advertising budget now averages over $5 million, which includes the expenditures for British Sterling.

Speidel has attempted to see that through the combination of qual-

EXHIBIT 7–4.
A partial list of the shows sponsored by Speidel since 1948

1. STOP THE MUSIC—1948–50
    (A nationally famous radio program)
2. THE ED WYNN SHOW—1949
3. SATURDAY NIGHT REVIEW—1950
4. WHAT'S MY NAME?—1950–53
5. MASQUERADE PARTY—1952
6. NAME THAT TUNE—1953–54
7. MAKE ROOM FOR DADDY—1953–54
    Danny Thomas
8. THE SID CAESAR SHOW—1954–55
9. THE BIG SURPRISE—1955–1956–1957
10. DOWN YOU GO—1956
11. THE ARTHUR MURRAY PARTY—1957
12. FESTIVAL OF STARS—1957
13. THE PRICE IS RIGHT—1957–60
14. AMERICAN BANDSTAND—1959
15. THE JACKIE GLEASON SHOW—1960
16. THE DEAN MARTIN SHOW—1960
17. THE ASPHALT JUNGLE—1961
18. TARGET, THE CORRUPTERS—1961
19. NAKED CITY—1961
20. SURFSIDE SIX—1961
21. CONCENTRATION—1962
22. THE PRICE IS RIGHT—1962
23. HAWAIIAN EYE—1962
24. SUNSET STRIP—1962
25. BEN CASEY—1962
26. THE DEFENDERS—1962
27. WHAT'S MY LINE—1962
28. THE ELEVENTH HOUR—1962
29. THE JACK PAAR SHOW—1963–1964–1965
30. PASSWORD—1963
31. THAT WAS THE WEEK THAT WAS—1964
32. GOLF CLASSICS—1964
33. PEYTON PLACE—1964–1965–1966
34. ALFRED HITCHCOCK—1964–65
35. HUNTLEY-BRINKLEY—1964
36. THE MAN FROM U.N.C.L.E.—1965
37. DANIEL BOONE—1965
38. THE LONG HOT SUMMER—1965
39. THE PATTY DUKE SHOW—1965
40. SHENANDOAH—1965
41. RUN FOR YOUR LIFE—1965–66
42. PLEASE DON'T EAT THE DAISIES—1965–66
43. THE VIRGINIAN—1965–66
44. WACKIEST SHIP IN THE ARMY—1965–66
45. NBC TUESDAY NIGHT AT THE MOVIES—1965–66
46. I SPY—1966
47. LAREDO—1966
48. HAWK—1966
49. GREEN HORNET—1966
50. CBS FRIDAY NIGHT AT THE MOVIES—1966

EXHIBIT 7–4 (*continued*)

51. WALTER CRONKITE—1966
52. BIG VALLEY—1966
53. FUGITIVE—1966
54. ABC SUNDAY NIGHT AT THE MOVIES—1966
55. BATMAN—1966
56. JERICHO—1966
57. LOST IN SPACE—1966

ity control, engineering, and effective advertising the name Speidel would be synonymous with quality and a name to be trusted.

Typical appeals are such ones as:

1. The Speidel Millionaires
    Obviously Speidel—Obviously Superior
2. Speidel Twist-O-Flex has become synonymous with quality metal watchbands.
3. Speidel improves on perfection with Romunda.
4. Speidel has spent hundreds of thousands of dollars researching, testing, and perfecting Romunda.
5. These new sophisticated Speidel minatures are the result of Speidel's continuing effort to bring women—in watch bracelets—the same fashion excitement they seek in other accessories and clothes.
6. Speidel's products are being presold on many popular network TV shows.
7. Did you know that Speidel products now account for more than 10 percent of the business of many jewelers who carry them?

A list of the shows which Speidel has sponsored in given in Exhibit 2.

Case questions

1. What are the important buying motives of the ultimate consumer for watchbands?
2. To what extent are these of a primary nature? Of a selective nature?
3. To what degree do you believe the demand for watchbands would be expansible? Inexpansible?
4. Indicate whether or not these motives are primarily of a direct or derived nature.
5. What impact will the increase in sale of Digital watches have on Speidel's market?

Case **REEB**
7–3   **Meeting new challenges**

Reeb is a manufacturer and marketer of a wide variety of grocery products as well as chemicals and industrial products. It is faced with

selecting copy strategy for its various product lines for the current
year in the face of the Federal Trade Commission's objective of advancing consumer interests in terms of nutrition, product information, safety, quality, and value.

Products

Grocery products traditionally have been the Reeb's principal business and account for over 75 percent of consolidated net sales. Reeb's
grocery products are sold primarily to chains, wholesalers, and other
distributors of food products. It maintains a network of 12 distribution
centers throughout the United States, each of which carries an inventory of most of the company's grocery product items. Technical research, market research, test marketing, advertising, and promotion
are important to growth through new products and continuance of
well-established products. Reeb extensively advertises its grocery
products, with an emphasis upon television. The company maintains
a fulltime sales force in the United States of about 400.

Cereals. The company manufactures and sells both hot and ready-
to-eat cereals in the United States and in foreign markets. Hot cereal
products, most of which are sold under the Reeb brand, include regular and quick-cooking oatmeal, instant oatmeal, enriched cream of
wheat, and rolled wheat cereal. Several new flavored varieties of instant oatmeal have been introduced in recent years. Principal ready-
to-eat cereals are sold under the following names: King Kong, Energy,
Ringo, Wheat-O, O-Puff, and Duol.

Reeb also manufactures prepared pancake mixes, frozen foods and
other mixes, and table syrup under the Lucky brand, as well as pie
crust and other mixes under the Delco brand. These products are
marketed primarily in the United States and Canada.

Frozen waffles are also manufactured and sold under the Lucky
brand. Frozen pizza and related products are sold under the Delco
brand. Distribution of frozen products is concentrated in the United
States and Canada.

Cookies and crackers. Reeb manufactures and sells cookies and
cracker products under the Deluxe name. In an effort to improve the
results of its cookie and cracker business, Reeb discontinued its high-
cost store delivery system and now sells through distributors.

Pet foods. Reeb manufactures and sells a broad line of dog and cat
foods. Principal brand names are Doggie for dog foods and Cattie for
cat foods. The dog food line includes canned, dry and semimoist products, and the cat food line consists of canned products in the United
States and of canned and dry products abroad. Pet foods are sold
abroad either under the above brand names or under local brands.

Institutional and other foods. Institutional foods include many of
the Reeb's regular grocery products suitably packaged for restaurants,
hotels, hospitals, schools, and the vending trade.

Chemicals. Reeb manufactures and distributes chemicals, which
are produced from agricultural by-products, and are used in the refin-

ing of petroleum and in the manufacture of a wide range of products, such as plywood, rubber, plastics, and foundry molds. Chemicals are sold directly to manufacturers and through distributors, principally in the United States and Europe.

Industrial products

The company manufactures and sells to industrial markets certain grain products, such as industrial flour sold to millers and corn grits sold to the brewing industry.

Raw materials and supplies

Raw materials used by Reeb for its grocery products include oats, wheat, corn, rice, sugar, meat by-products, and fish, most of which are purchased on the open market. The raw materials for its chemical products include corncobs, oat hulls, and bagasse. The company purchases the major portion of its packaging materials, such as containers, labels, and shipping cases, from outside sources.

Regulation

Production and distribution of most of Reeb's grocery products are subject to the Federal Food, Drug, and Cosmetic Act and to various state statutes regulating safety and labeling of products.

The Federal Trade Commission (FTC) has initiated a study of the economic structure and effectiveness of competition in the breakfast cereal industry. At the request of the FTC Reeb is furnishing information in connection with the study. Recent press articles indicate that FTC economists have prepared a report critical of profits and advertising expenditures in the cold breakfast cereal industry.

Reeb also is participating in government hearings, investigations, and conferences which have the general objectives of advancing consumer interests in terms of nutrition, product information, safety, quality, and value. Reeb is unable to predict the effect of these trends on its business, but believes that its positive attitude toward consumer interests and the nature of its product lines are compatible with these objectives.

Deciding on strategy

As a result of the increased emphasis on consumerism and the fact that it was complex to evaluate on a truly scientific basis the nutritional benefit which the consumers derived from the grocery products line, Reeb's executives believed that it was essential to decide whether or not the copy strategy which had been used should be changed.

The executives were particularly concerned with the cereal advertising. They had found that placing emphasis on nutritional, health, and testimonial appeals had proved to be successful. They had also utilized the fewer calories appeal on various occasions and had found this to be successful.

Some of the general copy appeals which had been suggested for the current period, included:

a. It's the real food.
b. Breakfast delight.
c. Start the day right.
d. How to get a great shape and be right.
e. The cereal of the stars.
f. Eat up, America.
g. Keep young and fit with Reeb.
h. You can maintain a busy schedule with Reeb.
i. The easiest-to-digest breakfast.
j. The cereal that is all wheat.
k. Reeb can give you the edge.
l. Want to lose pounds fast?
m. How to be sure you get enough nutrition.
n. Star athlete says, "Win with Reeb."
o. "Mom, get me a package of Reeb."
p. How to fight the bulge.

Questions

1. How can Reeb develop a selective copy strategy?
2. To what extent should Reeb expect to adopt a primary advertising copy strategy to counteract some of the pending regulations?
3. Some children play an important part in the decision as to which cereal to purchase. How important are the concepts of health, nutrition, etc.?
4. Evaluate the suggestions of the advertising department and develop a copy strategy for Reeb's cereal products.
5. How important would the use of the "natural food" be for Reeb?

Case   **RINGLING BROS.–BARNUM & BAILEY**
7–4   **COMBINED SHOWS, INC.**
         Deciding on copy

History

The Company traces its history to the circus organized by P. T. Barnum in 1871 at a time when the American circus was emerging from a period of inactivity during the Civil War.

In 1881, James A. Bailey, who had operated a circus for some time prior to 1873, combined his circus with Barnum under the name "P. T. Barnum's Greatest Show on Earth, Howe's Great London Circus and Sanger's Royal British Menagerie." In 1888 the name of the circus was changed to "Barnum & Bailey's Greatest Show on Earth" and Bailey became sole owner of the circus after Barnum's death in 1891.

In 1882, five Ringling brothers—Al, Otto, Alf T., Charles, and John —introduced their first show entitled "The Ringling Bros. Classic and Comic Concert Company," and by 1890 the Ringling brothers' circus had become a serious competitor of the Barnum & Bailey circus. After a period of intense competition and the death of Bailey, the Ringlings in 1907 acquired the Barnum & Bailey circus from Bailey's estate. After operating the two circuses independently until 1919, the Ringlings combined the two circuses. The resulting circus was incorporated in 1932 as "Ringling Bros.–Barnum & Bailey Combined Shows, Inc." (sometimes referred to herein as "Former Ringling Bros.").

John Ringling, the last surviving brother, died in 1936. Shortly after his death, operation of the circus was taken over by John Ringling North and his brother, Henry Ringling North, sons of Ida Ringling, the Ringling brothers' only sister.

In October 1967, Roy Hofheinz, Irvin Feld, and Israel S. Feld founded Hoffeld Corporation under the laws of the state of Delaware for the purpose of acquiring all of the outstanding capital stock of Former Ringling Bros. In November 1967, Hoffeld acquired all the stock for $8,000,000 in cash.

Hoffeld held the circus as a wholly owned subsidiary corporation from November 1967 until December 31, 1968, at which time Former Ringling Bros. merged with and into Hoffeld and the name of the Company was changed from "Hoffeld Corporation" to "Ringling Bros.–Barnum & Bailey Combined Shows, Inc."

General

The principal business of the Company is entertaining "children of all ages" through the staging of circus performances in various cities throughout the United States and Canada. Shows are staged two or three times a day and performance time is between 2½ and 2¾ hours. Admission prices range from a low of $2.00 to a high of $7.50 and vary depending upon the location and arena in which the circus is performing. In every city, at certain performances, reductions from regular price are given to children under 12 years of age.

In 1971, for the first time in its 101-year history, Ringling Bros. operated two separate but comparable circuses called "Ringling Bros. –Barnum & Bailey Red Unit" and "Ringling Bros.–Barnum & Bailey Blue Unit." The Red Unit toured for 47 weeks before returning to winter quarters in Venice, Florida. The Blue Unit toured for 36 weeks. It is anticipated that the Blue Unit will tour for 40 to 42 weeks or longer in subsequent years. With the addition of the Blue Unit, each circus will now play a two-year itinerary, visiting approximately twice as many cities as played in the past. Under this new arrangement a completely different circus will be shown in every city in successive years. Each unit stages two or three shows per day during the touring season except during those days when the circus is traveling. The shows include a variety of traditional circus acts and five theme production number extravaganzas.

Acts

Forty to fifty acts are presented in each circus performance and are supplemented by numerous clown routines. With the exception of wild animal, high wire, and specialty acts, performances are staged simultaneously in three rings. The circus includes traditional circus acts, such as clown acts, high wire and trapeze acts, a variety of animal acts, teeterboard and perch acts, and various other acts, such as jugglers, unicyclists, tumblers, horsemen, and so on. Each act performs for a period of two to twelve minutes, and performers frequently participate in more than one act.

The quality and variety of the acts are important features in the business of Ringling Bros., and new acts must be found annually in order to keep performances fresh and interesting to the public. To insure a variety and quality of new acts, the circus is continually on the outlook for new talent. Many trips a year, ranging from two days to three months, are made abroad to book acts. Last year, as an example, approximately 50 to 60 circuses were visited in Europe, Mexico, and other parts of the world. In addition, the talent search is extended to circus schools which are part of the cultural mores of many Eastern European countries. Of the 275 to 300 performers comprising the circus casts, approximately 150 are citizens of foreign countries, principally European. Many acts are family units in which the father or mother is responsible for training the children in circus routines.

Pursuant to the terms of an agreement between Ringling Bros. and the American Guild of Variety Artists, all acts perform under contract with the company. These contracts range from one to five years, and, as a minimum, guarantee the act one season of work. Frequently, Ringling has an option to renew performers' contracts for periods of one, two, or three additional seasons, in most instances under the same terms and conditions as included in the original agreement. All foreign acts, to qualify for acceptance under the company's agreement with the American Guild of Variety Artists, must be classified "unique" and the quota of foreign performers may not exceed 55 percent of the total performers of the circus.

Production numbers

In addition to the acts, each circus performance includes five production number extravaganzas. These numbers combine musical selections with a parade of circus performers in various costumes built around a central theme. For example, one of the production themes two years ago featured a trip to the moon by a performer-astronaut, and included the complete cast dressed in a wide variety of lavish costumes utilizing many different floats and sets. Other theme productions include an aerial ballet and an elephant spectacle.

Discussion of production numbers begins in the March preceding the calendar year in which the numbers are to appear. Themes are suggested, discussed, and finally chosen, after which costumes are designed and ordered from the circus costume manufacturer.

Music for the production numbers, as well as music for the acts, is provided by the circus band, comprised of the circus bandmaster and traveling musicians, augmented by local musicians.

Concessions

In addition to paid admissions, Ringling Bros. also derives revenues from a variety of concessions. The company has an agreement with a concessionaire for the sale of program books, food, (snow cones and candy floss) and circus novelties. The company's concessionaire also operates a food service on the circus trains and a restaurant which is located at the circus winter quarters in Venice, Florida, from which the company also derives some revenue.

Many of the arenas played by the circus have their own concessions, such as hotdogs, soft drinks, popcorn, and the like, which are normally sold by the arena's concessionaire with no payment to the circus for these sales. However, the company's concessionaire is usually afforded the opportunity to vend program books, snow cones, candy floss, and circus novelties in most arenas. Ringling Bros. also derives income from the sale of advertising space in its program books.

Royalties

Ringling Bros. also receives revenue from theater and television reruns of the motion picture entitled "The Greatest Show on Earth." The company recently entered into an agreement with an independent firm to design products and license the use of the circus name. The agreement covers a broad variety of products, including toys, childrens' books, food, clothing, and so on. While no licensing agreements have yet been signed, negotiations are substantially completed for 17 agreements covering numerous products bearing two-year terms and providing the company with an aggregate guaranteed minimum compensation of approximately $100,000 against a percentage of sales of licensed products.

Television program

Pursuant to an agreement with the National Broadcasting Company, a one-hour television program is scheduled featuring highlights of the circus. This show, packaged in full by the company, is hosted by a prominent show business personality and features approximately 35 minutes of circus performances.

Arenas

The circus has operated indoors in arenas or auditoriums since the "big top" was discontinued in 1956 in Pittsburgh, Pennsylvania. Ringling Bros. enters into contracts or leases with the various arenas for the dates during which the show will be played. Typical arrangements provide the arena with either a guaranteed minimum rent against a percentage of the gross revenues derived from ticket sales (excluding admission taxes) by the company from the engagement, or a fixed rental without a percentage.

Most contracts bear one-year terms, although arenas customarily reserve circus dates many years in advance. The longest single engagement of the circus has been at Madison Square Garden, New York City, where one of the units annually plays six consecutive weeks. The company also entered into an agreement with Houston Sports Association, Inc., providing for a 13½ week circus engagement in the Houston Astrohall.

Transportation

The principal means of transporting the circus between cities is by Ringling's own trains. The company presently owns two trains, one for the Red Unit and another for the Blue Unit. Twenty cars are assigned to the Blue Unit and 24 to the Red Unit. The Blue Unit uses fewer cars because of the purchase by the company of four "piggyback" cars which are used with the Blue Unit train and can carry greater loads of material and equipment than the customary type of equipment. The circus enters into agreements annually with a number of railroads which agree to move the circus trains from location to location. The railroads furnish engines, cabooses, and crews, and coordinate the scheduling and logistical work with a representative of Ringling Bros. Prior to entering a city, the circus advance agent has arranged for water and sanitary facilities, siding facilities, and has attended to the myriad of other details which must be observed before the arrival of the circus train.

Advertising and promotion

The circus uses all media in its advertising campaign, including television spot commercials, radio, billboards, newspapers, magazines, and direct distribution of literature. Approximately six to eight weeks before the circus arrives at any given community, representatives of the circus's advertising staff, supplemented by local advertising agencies and public relations firms, commence advertising for the circus performances. Advertisements for a particular city are carried in media up to a radius of 100 miles from the arena. Two clowns are sent in advance of the circus as part of the promotional efforts, and bus cards and press manuals are also utilized. Approximately 10 percent of the expected revenue in each community is reserved for publicity.

The name "Ringling Bros.–Barnum & Bailey Circus" and the service mark, "The Greatest Show on Earth," are featured in all advertising and no individual performer or group of performers are named as stars or featured attractions. In prior years the company relied substantially on advertising and promotion efforts of outside independent promoters. The company now assumes all advertising and promotional activities for 31 engagements and supervises such activities for the other 13 engagements.

Competition

Although there are other circuses operating throughout the United States, Ringling Bros. is the largest, employs more performers than any other circus, and guarantees the longest continuous period of employment. Other entertainment and recreation attractions may be considered competitors of the circus as they compete for leisure-time dollars. Management believes the loss of any act would not cause a serious disruption in its performances and believes further that it will be able to compete successfully with other entertainment and recreation attractions by continuing to offer a variety of fresh acts, productions, and other attractions.

Case questions

1. Assume that you are asked to prepare the copy for the local media in your city advertising the appearance of Ringling Bros. How would you proceed in solving the following problems:
   a. To whom would you direct the appeal? Why?
   b. Would the market targets be the same in each city?
   c. To what extent would you vary the appeal in the following media: television and radio spot commercials, newspapers, and billboards?
   d. What impact will population trends, productivity, income and expenditures, size of families and households, and education have on the market targets which Ringling Brothers may have to reach in the late 1970s.

8

IDENTIFICATION METHODS

*I*n order for a company or organization to get its advertising message to potential consumers, it is essential that some means be used that enables the prospect to identify the advertiser's product. Without such identifcation the prospect will not be able to know what to ask for, nor whether or not the goods offered are the same as those which were advertised.

Since the beginning of commerce, makers of goods have placed upon their products identifying marks or brands. The early Greek potters used marks, trade guilds had guild marks, and public houses and business establishments used identifying signs from the earliest times. Although historically these identification marks, such as trademarks and brands, were used largely for the purpose of identifying the manufacturer or source of origin of the product (so that he could be held responsible in case of poor quality or fraudulent practices), today their primary significance is as a means of attracting and building patronage. The trademark and brand name are devices to aid consumer memory, to make resale easy, and to facilitate the customer's selection of the particular manufacturer's product that has been presold through advertising or other promotional means.

Importance of trademarks

In an average year there will be 30,000 trademark applications filed at the U.S. Patent Office. Of this number, registrations will be issued to more than two-thirds of the applicants.

With the more important role trademarks are playing in marketing, some companies employ proper use campaigns through their house organs, advertising, information manuals, and press mailings. Some such corporations are: E. I. du Pont de Nemours Company, Inc.; Standard Oil Company (N.J.); Ortho Pharmaceutical Corporation; Johnson

& Johnson, for Band-Aid brand trademark; Chesebrough-Pond, Inc., for Vaseline.

A similar approach was taken in the modernization of trademarks by the following companies: Allis-Chalmers Manufacturing, in their stylized A-C monogram; Cities Service Company, in their new CITGO brand; Crescent Macaroni & Cracker Co., for its Crescent and Star cookie line; Weyenberg Shoe Manufacturing Co., in PORTAGE PORTO PEDS and MASSAGIC shoes brands; and in the new symbols adopted by the Oppenheimer Fund (four-hand clasp), New York Life Insurance Co., American Business Press, Inc., West Baltimore Building Association, Beau Brummel Ties, and the National Broadcasting new log.

Some basic definitions[1]

Patent: Applies to new and useful inventions or discoveries or improvements. Owner has exclusive rights for 17 years from date of issue whether or not he actually uses or takes advantage of the patent himself.

Copyright: Protects the owner against others copying "artistic creations" such as books, articles, music, paintings, and drawings. (Advertisements can be admitted to copyright, particularly if they show a degree of originality or artistic and literary merit.) Copyright is effective upon publication with copyright notice. Protects against copying by others for 28 years and can be renewed once for a similar period.

Trademark: A word, symbol, or device used to identify a manufacturer's goods or services and to distinguish them from those of others. Must be in use in interstate commerce before it can be registered with the Patent Office. The certificate of registration remains in force for 20 years and may be renewed without limit for additional 20-year periods. Registration accords a degree of protection against another's use of the same or similar mark if confusion is likely to exist, but in itself does not give exclusive ownership, as does a patent or copyright. Patent and copyright could be considered a reward for something done, whereas trademark rights have to be earned, as shown later in this report.

Service mark: Applies to the advertising of services rather than products. Includes marks, names, symbols, slogans, and other distinctive features that distinguish the services of one company from those of another (Greyhound).

Certification mark: Used by persons other than the owner of a mark to certify geographical origin, grade or quality, material, mode of manufacture, or other characteristics of goods or services (Underwriters' Laboratory Seal).

Collective mark: A trademark or service mark used to indicate membership in a union, association, or other organization (Shriners' emblem). Also to identify goods or services of a collective group (Sunkist).

Brand name: Synonymous with *Trademark.*

Trade name: (also known as *commercial name*): Many people assume that "Trade Name" and "Trademark" are synonyms. In rare cases they are (Johnson & Johnson), but in general usage the terms are quite different. A trademark is the brand of a product; a trade name is the name of the company that makes it (Cadillac-General Motors Corporation). A

---

[1] Reprinted with special permission of Charles A. Holcomb, of the Kudner Agency, Inc., New York, and the American Association of Advertising Agencies.

trade name cannot be registered as such, although the trademark itself may be a part of the company name.

Principal Register: As its name suggests, this is the trademark register that affords greatest protection and should be used wherever possible.

Supplemental Register: This accords less extensive rights, although it accepts a broader variety of marks. Marks which are nonregistrable on the Principal Register, for instance, because they are descriptive, may be acceptable on the Supplemental Register if they have or may have possible trademark significance, i.e., be capable of distinguishing the applicant's goods or services. To be acceptable the mark must be used exclusively for at least one year before application. A supplemental mark which has been used exclusively for five years may be promoted to the Principal Register by affidavit showing such exclusive use. Distinctive slogans may be registered but may not qualify if used solely in advertising.

Secondary meaning: This is an important ingredient in the trademark mix. The term generally is used with reference to words that are descriptive of some characteristic of the product, but have been used so extensively as a trademark by a single company that they have come to be generally recognized as such (Holeproof hosiery, Nu-Enamel paint). The same principle applies to place names and family names (Waltham watches, Ford automobiles). To begin with, they are not good trademarks because by their very nature they do not belong to any one business concern. But long-continued, exclusive use by a single company can given them an additional (secondary) meaning. If this happens they are entitled to protection as trademarks. There is no inflexible rule to use in determining whether a secondary meaning has been acquired. The Patent Office or courts decide each case on its own merit. However, the exclusive and continuous use for five years may under the law be accepted as prima facie evidence that the mark has become distinctive. (Depending on circumstances, a shorter period may be acceptable.)

House mark: A primary mark of a business concern producing a variety of products usually used in association with another or secondary mark (Du Pont—primary; Lucite, Dacron, Zerone—secondary).

Coined word: An invented or manufactured word, i.e., the product of a person's imagination, having no previous meaning (Kodak).

Generic term: Used to designate a general type, class, or name of a product (electric shaver, aspirin). Such a term cannot serve as a trademark for that product. But it can be perfectly satisfactory as a trademark for another *type* of product.

Descriptive: A word or term which describes one or more characteristics of a product, e.g., what the product is, what it is made of, or what it does. Descriptive marks cannot be registered (unless secondary meaning has been established).

Suggestive mark: Suggests rather than describes one or more of the characteristics of the product it is to identify (Ivory soap, Arrid deodorant). Is registrable.

Arbitrary mark: Connotes nothing about the product (Camel cigarettes, Shell oil).

Laudatory term: Word or words that indicate general superiority (premium, blue ribbon, supreme). Such words usually make weak trademarks because they lack distinctiveness, being used by many companies for a variety of products.

Infringement: The use by one of a mark which is so similar to the existing mark of another that confusion is likely to occur.

Dilution: The use of another's mark in a manner which tends to deprive it of distinctiveness. For instance, the slogan, "Where There's Life—There's Bugs," was held to be a dilution of the beer slogan, "Where There's Life—There's Bud."

Abandonment: A trademark is ordinarily considered abandoned after two consecutive years of nonuse unless there is no intent to abandon it and good reason exists for failure to use it.

Trademark registration

Contrary to popular impression, registering a trademark does not confer the status of ownership, as does a patent. Trademark rights are recognized at common law as property rights, aside and apart from registration under the trademark statutes. Such rights come from priority of use, continuous use, and due diligence in proper use and protection. You might say registration is like a birth certificate: it merely provides official recognition of what has already been created. But it is a constructive step toward protection. It puts all on notice that the trademark has been registered; no one can plead ignorance of your claim. It means that in all probability any case involving it will be tried in a federal court, and that the burden is shifted to the other party who must prove that the registration is invalid or that you do not own the trademark. Two very important points should be understood: (1) a trademark applies only to the specific article of merchandise to which it is affixed, and (2) "mark" is a common legal synonym for "trademark," and it may apply to a picture, device, or other symbol as well as a word.

The purpose of a trademark is to protect the owner from unfair competition and the public from being deceived. The legal attitude toward it is based on the principle that a man cannot sell his own product under the pretense that it is the goods or services of some other firm. Therefore, he cannot be permitted to use names, marks, or letters by which he may make purchasers believe the goods he is selling are manufactured by some other company.

The party first to use a trademark in the United States is considered its owner for that class of commodity. Common law, founded on custom and usage, works to prevent unfair methods of competition. Our trademark laws represent an accumulated body of legal acts tempered and revised by the courts to meet changing requirements. The present federal trademark act, the Lanham Act, was passed in 1946 and went into effect in 1947. This act probably represented the most drastic change of all inasmuch as it opened up new areas for trademark registration by creating the Supplemental Register. Note the point made earlier for the two registers in the section on basic definitions.

Registration gives a trademark the following advantages:

1. The burden of proof in litigation is placed on the other party if it did not register its mark.
2. It helps to prove the exact nature of the trademark in case a question should arise as to whether or not there is an infringement by a second mark.

3. It gives federal courts jurisdiction in action against infringements. An injunction issued by this court is enforceable anywhere in the United States; that of a state court in only one state.

4. Domestic registration is now necessary in only a few foreign countries. These countries require that the trademark be registered in the United States first before accepting registration under their respective laws.

When a man sells merchandise under his own name, he may experience difficulty in protecting that name if a second person with the same name enters the same type of business. Even in cases of serious misuse of a family name, the courts have allowed a person to use his own name, while they will generally stop the use of a trademark in similar circumstances. The second party may not necessarily have to stop using that name, as the courts may only compel him to use his name in connection with a distinguishing mark. This distinguishing mark may consist merely of a line of copy to point out the difference, as:

Henry Ford
(Distinct from Ford Manufacturing Company)

or

Smith Manufacturing Company
(Not connected with original Smith)

In view of these facts, it is important to distinguish between a trademark and a trade name. In advertising, words used for trademark purposes often are spoken of incorrectly as trade names. Though this practice is a common one, it is incorrect.

State registration

It is not necessary to register a trademark in any state in order to use the mark within a particular state. While each state has its own trademark laws and procedures, trademark rights are a matter of common law, and neither state nor federal registration takes precedence over the facts of priority of adoption and use.

However, state registration may be valuable because some state trademark laws impose criminal penalties for deliberate and knowing infringement of locally registered marks. State trademark procedures usually permit registration without previous official search for conflicts or prior use. The cost of such registration is nominal.

Nonregistrable marks

Following is a broad picture of what the Patent Office will not accept for registration. It does not include certain exceptions,[2] but is an indication of what to avoid when creating a new trademark.

---

[2] For instance, trademarks used during the ten-year period prior to 1905 may be continued for the same class of goods. For example, there exist some 30 registrations for the Red Cross name or symbol which is not now registrable.

1. A mark which so resembles another existing trademark for the same or similar goods as to be likely to confuse or mislead purchasers.
2. Anything merely descriptive, geographically descriptive, or deceptively misdescriptive.
3. Generally, marks which primarily are surnames since others having the same name are entitled to use it. Unusual surnames may be registrable but difficult to protect.
4. Anything contrary to good taste or public policy: (*a*) immoral, deceptive, or scandalous matter; (*b*) anything that disparages persons, beliefs, institutions, etc.; (*c*) flags or other insignia of the United States or any state, municipality, or foreign nation; (*d*) name, portriat, or signature of any individual now living, except with his written consent.

Trademark in conflict

A mark is considered in conflict if it is ruled that there is too great a similarity to another trademark in look, sound, or meaning. The question always comes up when registration is applied for. And it is the basis for infringement actions.

Conflicts occur in three areas: identical (or substantially identical) products, the same class of product, and completely unrelated products. The following examples are typical.

Identical items. Lemon-Up was held to sound too much like Seven-Up, as was Nidol analgesic too much like Midol.

Trademarks can conflict because of similar meaning even though quite different in appearance and sound. Hence, Canned Light paint was considered too much like Barreled Sunlight. For the same reason, I Wanta for biscuits was turned down because it conflicted with Uneeda (the marks also looked somewhat alike). On the other hand, Hava for biscuits was approved.

No conflict was found between Easy-Carve and Morrell E-Z Cut—both for boned hams; Milk-O-Seltzer and Alka-Seltzer; Omicron watches and Omega; or Canadian Crown whiskey and Canadian Club.

Same class of goods. "Same class" is broadly interpreted. It includes products which in the mind of the buyer might come from the same source represented by the owner of the original trademark, whether or not such is the case. It has even been applied to goods because they are sold in the same type of outlet, although of a different character.

Sweetheart paper towels and tissues was held to conflict with Sweetheart soap; Quick Tea conflicted with Nestle's Quik powdered cocoa; Jantina shoes with Jantzen beachwear; Comet floor wax with Comet cleanser; Buffagum antacid, analgesic chewing gum with Bufferin.

However, no conflict was found between Rose Hall and Robert Hall—both clothing; nor Goldenrod shelled pecans and Goldenrod ice cream; nor E-Z Krinkles raw potato product and Krinkles breakfast cereal.

Unrelated products. In general, it is unusual and difficult to prevent the use of a conflicting trademark in fields completely outside the activities of the original owner—even if such protection is wanted. However, there are exceptions. Kodak, for instance, was refused registration for something as far afield as cigarette lighters; Johnny Walker was enjoined for cigars—more evidence of the strength of these marks!

Each question of conflict is decided on its own merits by the Patent Office or court. Rulings are a matter of judgment, and, as the earlier examples show, it is not always easy to follow the line that separates the sheep from the goats. The deciding factor is the degree of confusion which is, or might be, caused by the mark in question.

The Seven-Up Company once sued a competitor using the mark Fizz-Up for its lemon-lime drink. Evidence offered by the plaintiff included a public reaction survey in which approximately 25 percent of the persons interviewed indicated some degree of confusion because of the similarity between the marks. The court held this was sufficient to warrant infringement, and the injunction was granted. (The fact that Seven-Up had become an extremely well-known mark probably also played a part in this decision.)

Another factor is the trend of the courts to prevent a newcomer from exploiting the reputation already established by another firm's trademark. This is sometimes known as the "free ride" doctrine which, while not universally accepted, is gaining judiciary support.

It is obvious that the questions of conflicts is strictly a legal one. But the Trademark Committee can help by submitting alternate suggestions for marks in case a search invalidates for registration the number-one choice.

Requirements for a good trademark

It is difficult to select a good trademark. Every effort should be made to develop a strong one with unique identity and broad protection. A coined word, such as Kodak, is a strong mark, well identified as Eastman's property. Examples of marks difficult to protect are such nondistinctive words as Gold Label, Superior, and Premium. The owner of a Blue Ribbon trademark, for instance, was not able to prevent the use by another company of Blue Ribbon as a trademark for a closely related product. The court pointed out that Blue Ribbon was registered over 60 times in the Patent Office for all kinds of goods; hence, it could not recognize "a large measure of distinctiveness" in the name. To some degree this also applies to the design. Common shapes slow up quick identification. In one year alone 429 circles were registered in the Patent Office, 293 oblongs, 272 ovals, and 123 squares.

When challenging another's adoption of the same mark, the owner of a weak mark may be offered only limited relief by the courts, such as merely preventing its use by another on goods that may be practically identical. If you are creating a new trademark, why start with that handicap?

Distinctiveness is the prime ingredient in a trademark. Over a half-million trademarks have been registered at the Patent Office. Replacing those that for one reason or another are dropped from the registers are some 20,000 new ones each year.

Yet these are only those used in interstate commerce. Each state has its own registrations. And there is a large body of locally used trademarks that are not registered anywhere. Worse yet, any of these state and local marks may prevent registration of a new mark at the Patent Office on the basis of prior use. There are many trade and private sources available for trademark search in addition to the files at the Patent Office. (The U.S. Trademark Association publishes a list of 125 principal reference sources.) *Printers' Ink* maintains what is said to be the largest file of slogans.

What are the characteristics that make a trademark strong and distinctive? It should be instantly recognized, easily remembered, and able to be reproduced effectively in any size, color, or medium. It should be dissimilar from other marks in appearance, sound, and meaning. It should resist time changes. It should have no unpleasant connotations and be suitable for export commerce. Do not worry about relevancy. A trademark becomes accepted as a symbol, and eventually the public reads no meaning into it except that of brand identification. What, for instance, could be less pertinent than Frigidaire kitchen range, Hotpoint refrigerator, Chock Full O'Nuts coffee? Actually, the more apt a trademark seems to be, the harder it may be to protect.

Classifications of trademarks

Coined word. Coined words make good trademarks if easy to pronounce and remember. They may be meaningless—Raytheon, Yuban, Zonite. Or suggestive—that is, the mark suggests a feature benefit or function of the product itself: Certo, Kleenex, Zerex. Mechanical means of trying various combinations of prefixes and suffixes with pertinent roots can be helpful in searching for a suitable mark. Misspelled common words: Arrid, Kromekote, Ennds (if not merely descriptive) are included in this category. Through popular usage, some trademarks in a sense have been coined by the public: Coke, Bud, Luckies.

Abritrary. This includes the large number of trademarks where an existing word or symbol is selected arbitrarily, without relevance to the product: Camel, Arrow, Admiral. Others might be termed "semiarbitrary" in that they aim to establish a favorable impression of the product—a connotation of quality, prestige, economy, or whatnot: Pall Mall, Prudential, Partner's Choice. When combinations of common words are used, this line should be pursued with caution lest the mark becomes descriptive.

Pictorial. Good, if distinctive and kept simple, because it has strong identification and recognition values: Log Cabin, His Master's Voice, Four Roses. Often capsules a sales message: Bon Ami, Shaw-Walker. Characters make strong trademarks with added merchandising values. Many types are used. Distinctive people: Old Grand-Dad, Quaker man, Chef Boy-Ar-Dee, Campbell kids. Mythical: Green Giant. Historical: G. Washington, Lincoln, Webster. Animal: Elsie, White Owl, Hartford Stag.

Geographical. Usually will be refused for registration if the name denotes merely a place of origin rather than the brand of a specific owner. Thus Grand Rapids for furniture, Herkimer County for cheese would not be acceptable because the localities are well known for those products. However, secondary meaning established by long use makes Waltham and Elgin OK for watches, Paris for garters.

Surnames. Family names generally may not be registered as trademarks, since others with the same name are entitled to use them. However, many surnames have acquired trademark status through historical association by the public with specific products: Whitman, Gillette, Wrigley. Full names of individuals—baptismal plus surname—are entitled to registration if used as trademarks: Elizabeth Arden, Robert Hall, Fanny Farmer.

House mark. This is an overall trademark used by a company with multiple brands. It may be used as the brand name of various items that make up the company line (Toastmaster appliances) or used in connection with the individual brand marks (Westinghouse Laundromat washing machines, Westinghouse Magnalux electric lamps). Many house marks are contractions of the company name (Sunoco, Nabisco, Alcoa) or initials (GE, RCA, A&P). Before adopting a mark consisting of initials, consideration should be given to the difficulty people have in remembering arbitrary letters and numbers. Such combinations are almost certain to resemble other trademarks, and it may take a long time to make them distinctive and recognizable as referring to specific products and companies.

In choosing a new trademark one thing is certain: the more descriptive it is, the harder it will be to protect. If it is "merely descriptive," it cannot be registered in the first place. If it is "highly suggestive" (this distinction is made by the Patent Office), it may be registrable. If it has trademark significance, it may be registered on the Principal Register. Or one may have to settle for a listing on the Supplemental Register, hoping that it can be transferred to the Principal Register later.

It sometimes happens that individuals concerned with the selection of a new trademark will fall in love with a word that is descriptive enough to be difficult to protect. It should be pointed out that the risk of losing exclusive rights—especially after years of promotion—outweighs almost any advertising or sales advantages of such a mark. One might say this is a case where "it is better never to have loved at all than to have loved and lost."

Loss of trademark

Exclusive ownership rights in a trademark can be lost for several reasons. The trademark may be abandoned voluntarily or through neglect. The last can happen when goods withdrawn from the market are reinstated after a lapse of several years, or when the sale of a business fails to assign trademark rights. Dilution can lead to the loss of trademark rights, as can failure to maintain the quality requirements of the licensee. Rights can be lost by adverse decisions on conflict or prior use.

But a principal reason for the loss of trademarks is that they become generic. Some were descriptive (shredded wheat, dry ice, milk of magnesia, mineral oil), others semidescriptive or suggestive (cellophane, escalator, zipper). Some were meaningless when introduced (aspirin, kerosene, celluloid); but eventually all got into the language as common words.

Cellophane lost out largely because it was introduced as a new *type* of product. By the time competitive products were on the market, "cellophane" was the only name by which this type of product could be identified by the public. The court ruling (1936) is significant: "It therefore makes no difference what efforts or money the du Pont Company expended in order to persuade the public that 'cellophane' means an article of du Pont manufacture. So far as it did not succeed in actually converting the world to its gospel, it can have no relief."

This is the same philosophical rock on which Thermos was wrecked, the difference being that Thermos had been established as a trademark for half a century and was widely known. In fact, it was so well known that according to the trial court it finally became generic in spite of frantic efforts by its owner to protect it. The judge felt that the company itself contributed to the consequent loss of exclusive ownership. From the beginning the advertising objective was to popularize the term Thermos bottle. The company's 1910 catalog states that "Thermos is a household word." In the recent trial, the court pointed out that, intentionally or not, this was "an encouragement for generic use of a synonym for *vacuum insulated*."

This line was pursued vigorously by the company until 1923 when it brought a trademark infringement action against the W. T. Grant Company. It won—on a technicality—but the judge who decided the case expressed the thought that Thermos might have become the name of the product, hence invalid as a trademark.

With this warning, the company charged its advertising policy by associating "vacuum" or "vacuum bottle" with Thermos. It also began to police the misuse of the trademark by others. But at the trial, the judge found that the number of such protests from 1923 to the early 1950s was "infinitesimal" compared to the great number of generic uses that had appeared in print during the same period. He ruled that the company had failed to use reasonable diligence in protecting its mark.

About 1954, the company intensified its protecting measures. The name of the company was changed to include the word "Products." Again, to strengthen the brand connotation, the line was diversified to include such items as camp stoves, tents, bottle openers—all labeled as Thermos products. Policing activities were stepped up.

But such measures were ruled too little and too late. Referring to them, the judge said, "The plaintiff's extraordinary efforts, commencing in the middle of the 1950s and carried on into the time of the trial, came too late to keep the word "thermos" from falling into the public domain; rather it was an effort to pull it back from the public do-main—something it could not and did not accomplish."

Thus, the American Thermos Products Company lost its exclusive trademark rights. Aladdin Industries, against whom the infringement action was taken—or anyone else, with certain restrictions—is now free to use "thermos" for vacuum bottles.

What steps to take in protecting a trademark

Set up a trademark committee. Establish the responsibility for the many steps in trademark procedures, from creation of a mark through the continuing "due diligence" necessary to maintain its exclusive brand status. Create a "strong" mark. See earlier notes on how and why.

Meet basic requirements. The trademark must be placed physically on the product, its container, point-of-sale displays closely associated with the product, or tags and labels attached to the product. The more types of exposure, the better. The product must be sold or transported in interstate commerce before federal registration is applied for. Principal Register offers more protection than Supplemental Register.

Use properly in advertising. A trademark is an adjective. Do not use it as a verb or noun. A trademark is not a *thing* or a *kind* of thing. It is a *brand* of a thing. To maintain this proprietary status (the objective of all protective measures), the trademark should always be associated with the generic name of the product. Ask for "Wamsutta sheets." Do not use as a possessive. Say, "The wonderful smoothness of Wamsutta sheets," not "Wamsutta's wonderful smoothness."

Sometimes the combination of trademark and product is cumbersome, especially when repeated several times. But how much repetition of the trademark is really necessary? One mention in the copy (plus logotype or prominent display element) may be enough. Repeating the brand name is good in broadcast media, but can easily be overdone in print.

How should the trademark be shown in print? There is no hard and fast rule about this. The legal objective is to make it distinctive from common words. This can be done with quotes, italics, boldface type, and so on. But it should start with a capital letter—it is a proper name.

Cap initials and lower case is by far the most popular treatment. Some advertisers like to see the trademark name stand out from the rest of the text matter by running it boldface, all caps, or reproducing the trademark itself, if distinctively lettered. While this might have some legal advantages, they could well be outweighed by marketing disadvantages—a jumpy layout and interruption of fast, smooth reading. This, of course, does not apply to the use of the trademark as a display element.

Nor is there a mandatory way to show that the trademark is registered. Trademark law gives three choices:

1. Registered in U.S. Patent Office
2. Reg. U.S. Pat. Off.
3. "R" in circle.

Most popular use by far is the "R" in circle positioned close to the trademark. It not only satisfies legal requirements, but is easiest to handle mechanically. However, several other types of notification are in common use. Eastman Kodak for many years has used simply "trademark" with Kodak. Some companies asterisk the trademark, referring the reader to a footnote showing trademark ownership.

Do not show a trademark as registered before it is actually so registered. This can be considered by the courts as a purposely false claim of registration; trademark suits have been lost because of it. "Trademark applied for" is not recommended. Prior to registration, many companies simply use the notation "Trademark" or "TM."

Avoid statements that, while designed to enhance exclusive rights, may have just the opposite effect. For instance, the Whosis Company advertises its Yanko bottle opener with such phrases as, "If it isn't a Whosis, it isn't a Yanko." Or, "Get the genuine Yanko." This not only misuses the mark as a noun, but implies the existence of more than one Yanko bottle opener.

There is no rule that specifies how many times the notice of registration should appear in an advertisement. Some companies have definite policies about this—to use it the first time that trademark is shown, to use it only in display or logotype, or to use it wherever the trademark appears. However, the objective is to make clear that the trademark is registered, and there is not much point in overdoing it or setting up arbitrary specifications that may diminish the sales impact of the advertisement.

In addition to protecting the trademark in product or corporate advertising, many companies run special advertisements for the sole purpose of identifying their trademarks—Coca Cola, du Pont, Ethyl, Eastman, to name a few. Some car campaigns run over an extended period; others are of the one-shot variety. This is not only beneficial from a merchandising viewpoint but could be helpful in a legal action in showing "due diligence" in protecting a trademark.

Police misuse of trademark. A trademark is valuable property—a visual symbol of a company's or product's reputation. If the owner is to maintain exclusive rights to it, he must do everything possible to prevent or correct misuse in print or broadcast media.

The law makes it very clear that trademark rights are lost by acts of omission as well as commission. Whether the misuse is innocent— due to ignorance or apathy—or deliberate infringement, prompt action should be taken by the trademark owner.

The most common cause of trouble is the trend of a trademark to become generic. Once the public thinks a word is the name of a thing rather than the brand of a thing, it gets into the public domain. For words mean what people understand them to say.

Keep records. Proofs of advertising should be maintained in the trademark file (one for each mark), showing first use of the mark and enough subsequent evidence to demonstrate consistent use. A brief history of how the trademark came into being and pertinent data covering earliest plans for marketing should be filed to establish priorities. Copies of labels, invoices, and shipping documents should be in the files to support the first use of the mark in commerce. Of great importance is a record of all policing correspondence as well as notes on actions taken. All decrees and judgments of the Patent Office and courts should be bound together. Registration, renewal dates, and other legal specifications should be preserved in the trademark file.

If possible, apportion sales figures for various trademarks; they could be important in assessing damages. For instance, one company was awarded $239,000 when another firm's mark was found to infringe on its well-known trademark.

Watch those licenses. Licensing the use of a trademark carries with it two responsibilities for the owner. First, he must make sure the standards of quality of the licensed product are consistent with the quality which is assured by the reputation of the original trademark. This applies especially where several companies are licensed. The following agreement is typical: "The Creslan trademark may be used only in accordance with the provisions of a trademark agreement with American Cyanamid on fabrics the quality of which has been approved by American Cyanamid in writing as having met its standards of quality."

Second, licensing must be carried out in such a way that the trademark continues to indicate a single source of goods. The owner must make sure his trademark is not misused, either through generic designation or promotion (intentionally or not), as a mark of quality. For instance, from a current ad, "Dacron is du Pont's registered trademark for its polyester fiber. Du Pont makes fibers, not the fabric or dresses shown." Nor should it be used by the licensee in a manner that could be construed as unfair competition. This is a matter of original contracts and rigorous supervision.

If these many protective steps seem burdensome, keep in mind the fact that someday your company may have to take the risk of proving in court that it has taken every reasonable measure possible to protect its trademark. U.S. courts decide nearly 1,000 trademark cases annually!

Questions

1. Why is it important for an advertiser to be able to identify his product?
2. What is a trade name? A brand name? A trademark? Give an example of each.
3. What are the important conditions a trademark must satisfy in order to be registered?
4. What are the main advantages of having your trademark registered under the Lanham Act?
5. Should a trademark be registered in every state? Why or why not?
6. What are some of the important requirements for a good trademark?
7. How may a trademark be "lost"?
8. What steps should be followed to protect a trademark?
9. List what you consider three very good trademarks and three you consider weak. Give reasons for your selections.

10. Give what you consider would be a satisfactory trademark and brand name for the following products:
    a. Sweater.
    b. A new brand of soup.
    c. A ball-point pen selling for $1.95.
    d Hair tonic.
    e Toothpaste.
    f. A special wafer for acid indigestion.

11. The manufacturer you represent distributed an inferior branded product during the war. This impression has been left with the buying public, and your sales have dropped to 25 percent of what they were prior to the war. What action would you recommend that this manufacturer take, and why?

12. Comment on the following statement: "Doctors and nutrition experts always have known that skim milk retained the life-giving proteins and minerals in milk after the fats were extracted. Thus 85 percent of the very small demand for fresh milk was on doctors' orders for people who could not use the fat content but who needed the other factors in milk. The hundreds of millions of gallons of skim milk annually left behind during cream and ice cream production had to seek a market in very low recovery products like cheese, animal feed, and even, experimentally, a synthetic cloth. To seek a market in skim milk and very low recovery products, a company used a simple little word—'SLIM.'

    "The public can be told that something is good for its health, but it takes a word that appeals to the weight-consciousness of people to get the fire started."

13. Indicate how you believe the cases listed below should be decided.
    a. A number of cases involving attempts by business firms to protect their business reputations and trademarks were taken before the courts.
       Perhaps the most significant cases have been those relating to product simulation problems, where the courts have attempted to apply the principles set forth in the 1964 Supreme Court decision in *Sears, Roebuck & Co.* v. *Stiffel Company* and *Compco* v. *Day-Brite Lighting Inc.* There the Supreme Court indicated that while state law could not prevent the imitation of the appearance of a product, it could require copiers to identify their products as their own.
    b. In a case before the Court of Appeals for the Seventh Circuit, the owner of the trademark DUM-DUMS for a peculiarly shaped lollipop sought an injunction against a competitor marketing under the mark POP-POPS a lollipop which duplicated plaintiff's. The defendant's managing partner testified that in designing the packaging he tried "to get as close to (plaintiff's) as I thought good ethics and good taste would allow me to."

Case **THE COCA-COLA COMPANY**
8–1   **Value of trademarks**

In the Mishawaka opinion, Justice Frankfurter observed that "If it is true that we live by symbols it is no less true that we purchase goods by them." He could have added that there is scarcely a social custom,

or a generally recognized rule of conduct, or a basic principle of literature, law, or philosophy that is not frequently associated with, or interpreted by, or made more effective through, some well-known symbol.

At the top of the list, the *Cross* of the Christian Church before which
billions of people have bowed in the last 1,900 years.

The Sickle and the Crescent, emblem of the faith of 250 million
followers of Mohammed who twice a day turn their faces toward
Mecca to offer up a prayer.

The Golden Bough, with its countless suggestions of superstition,
of fear, of spiritual yearning, and of tragic ignorance.

The *Red Cross,* with its promise of relief and of mercy.

The *flag* of every country, with all that each means to the citizen
or subject in terms of patriotism, national ambition, and desire for
security.

The *Lion* of Great Britain, the *Bear* of Russia, the *Lily* of France,
the *Eagle* of the United States, the G.O.P. *elephant,* the Democratic
donkey, and the picture of *Uncle Sam,* each synonymous with a whole
library of human history and human experience.

The blind goddess balancing the *scales* of justice, the *laurel wreath*
on the brow of the victor, the *crown* of royalty with its uneasy glory.

No wonder the Egyptians and Chaldeans imprinted a sign on their
bricks, or that the Greeks marked their pottery, or that the artisans
who built Solomon's Temple left their characteristic sign on it, or that
the Romans and Etruscans made symbols familiar companions of the
work of the craftsman. Admittedly, the beginning of commercial symbols is hidden in the long past, but they are of "ancient lineage" and
boast a "long pedigree."

In the use of trademarks the businessman has merely imitated
what all have done in all fields of activity. An illiterate person went
into the leather business and made an "X" as a substitute for his
signature, and the combination of this "X" and the man's name came
to be "Mark Cross," the best known of all of the manufacturers of
leather goods.

A bookkeeper in a drugstore searched for a name for a new beverage, wrote the compound word "Coca-Cola" in a flourishing script, and
gave to commerce the mark which was to travel oftener and farther
than any other word mark known to man.

"His Master's Voice," "Kodak," "Smith & Wesson," "Ivory Soap,"
"Winchester," "Frigidaire," "Old Dutch Cleanser," "Waltham," "Arm
& Hammer," "Steinway," "Coca-Cola," and "Green's Fuel"—these
trademarks and 400,000 more chaperone 50 million shoppers daily in
the marts of trade in North America. At least 850 of these marks now
serving our economy have been with us continuously for more than
50 years.

Much has been written about the legal characteristics having to do
with "The Value of Trademarks from a Merchandising Standpoint,"
but before this boon to the trader came of age in the sight of the law,
it had established itself with the manufacturer and merchant. The
law concerns itself with brands because of their availability and their
special usefulness in expanding and conserving consumer goodwill.

Prior to the Middle Ages, these marks served only to identify the product of the particular workman or of his group.

The 12th and 13th centuries discovered new reasons for putting the marks on manufactured products. Merchants marked their wares to provide evidence of ownership in case of shipwreck or loss. The guilds required their members to place the adopted seal on the output of their labor to fix responsibility for faulty work. These brands were the fore-runners of the merchant's and the manufacturer's marks of today, but at that time the one served only as evidence of title to property and the other insured the liability of the careless craftsman. Here we come upon the basis of the modern theory, that a trademark distinguishes the origin or ownership of goods—the manufacturer's mark pointing to the origin and the merchant's mark connoting ownership.

In England such marks had become quite common as early as Edward III. Notable among these were the swan marks, the printers' and publishers' devices, the cloth marks, and the marks in the cutlery trades.

Not until 600 years later did the businessman in the Western world wake up to the selling qualities of brand names and marks, and these names and marks acquired stature only with the arrival of the power machine. When factories began to turn out goods in volume they generated the necessity for mass consumption, since the mill had to find more and more buyers if it was to keep on running.

The trademark of the 20th century has matured into an indispensable servant of the production and distribution of goods, a direct response to a practical need, a utility in great demand in this latest phase of the industrial revolution.

Charles Holcomb has described trademarks as "The cornerstone of the multibillion-dollar advertising business, the foundation of marketing policies in consumer goods industries, a powerful influence on the buying habits and cultural pursuits of people all over the world, and a force to be reckoned with in evaluating the state of our competitive economy."

Edward S. Rogers considered the marks a necessary support of a free economy; observing that " 'free enterprise' rests on the practice of identity and personal responsibility on the part of the producer for the goods he sells," which are documented by his marks and brands. He did not believe "we can have competition if we do not distinguish the competing goods and give the purchasers a chance to choose between them. . . . Trade-marks stake the reputation of the seller on the character of his goods," and underwrite his responsibility to the purchasing public.

Wherein does society at large share in the economic gain which flows from a wide and intelligent utilization of marks and brand names by manufacturers and sellers for goods?

In some sense a brand serves as a guarantee of the quality of the goods to which it is attached; but it is not so much a legal warranty as it is a moral representation that the goods are of equal merit to those purchased before under the same name, and that their identity is vouched for by the owner of the mark.

These symbols also act their part in advertising. The highly profitable service that commercial marks are performing for American business is in the field of institutional and merchandising publicity, whose intention is to enlarge and intensify mass goodwill, with bigger sales as the ultimate target. When properly cast in advertising, the mark becomes a lodestone, an effective psychological pull that brings buyers to the owner's place of business. The trademark has been called the "silent salesman," but in fact it speaks with decisive voice everywhere in our commercial life.

The dealer, the distributor, and the factory look to advertising to bring customers. The nexus—the spark of the advertising matter—is the trademark. It is the reflector of reflectors of the goodwill, the popularity of the merchandise, and the reputation of the company. As the institution and its product acquire a good name, the mark somehow gathers to itself this public approval and becomes a magnet to would-be buyers.

Responsible management and quality product are cornerstones of sound public relations; but the third element must come into play before that valuable intangible asset known as goodwill can be crystallized, consolidated, and turned into dividends. This goodwill expresses itself in the fact that the firms holds its customers—plus the favorable report these customers circulate about it in the community. This expectation that former customers will also be future customers may for a particular company acquire a huge value. The goodwill of The Coca-Cola Company has for long been worth several times as much as all of the tangible assets it owns.

Advertising has been relied on primarily to carry the message for Coca-Cola to its dealers, consumers, and potential consumers. The trademark "Coca-Cola," since 1886, has dominated this advertising in whatever media it appeared and whatever form it took. What the Coca-Cola business has done has been repeated in one degree or another by every other successful business that looks to the public for customers. Everyone recognizes the essential part played by advertising, but not everyone appreciates the work done by the trademark, especially in getting sales and holding fast to customers. A trademark will bear endless repetition without holding fast to customers. A trademark will bear endless repetition without becoming stale and without losing its selling power with the marketgoers. Wherever a mark appears in a paper, in a magazine, or on a poster, it should be given a prominent place. It rates a high seat, and it can use profitably all of the light, color, and sparkle you can give it.

The grade labelers, the consumers' leaguers, and the innocent tools of the promoters of state socialism are striving to discredit trademarks and brand names in the minds of the public. Their argument implies that our shoppers are incapable of choosing intelligently between competing goods and that our marks and brand names are a hindrance to smart purchasing. They would place all of us in the hands of a government employee who would tell us where, when, and what to buy, through grade labels which are to be substituted for human experience and individual preference as the one basis for the buyer's choice.

No mark can possess a character superior to the goods it sells, and the reputation of both mark and goods must be supported by true worth. Thus supported, a mark acquires a just fame and becomes a real convenience to the buying public, a sign they can trust, a badge of a successful business. The dealer and the distributor share with the owner the impressive merchandising advantages of the mark, the consumer favor that follows it, and the selling power of the goodwill it symbolizes.

Case question

1. Evaluate the importance of trademarks in our present merchandising strategy.

---

*Case
8–2*
HUNT–WESSON FOODS, INC.
Developing of brands

Twenty years ago most housewives had never heard of tomato sauce. Today, 28 million of them—more than 50 percent of the home-makers in the United States—use it regularly.

What happened? It started in 1943, shortly after Hunt Brothers Packing Company merged with ValVita Food Products. Searching for a product with potential mass appeal, the company chose tomato sauce (then often described as "Spanish Style"), a minor commodity product sold primarily in California, New York, and the Gulf states and almost totally unknown in the middle regions of the country.

The company poured millions of dollars into a nationwide cam-paign that introduced tomato sauce as a recipe ingredient for meat, fish, and spaghetti dishes. Working chiefly through full-page, four-color ads in consumer magazines, the company enticed the housewife with large, colorful photographs of food, then showed her how to du-plicate the results. It created a market where none had existed—a market which it proceeded to dominate (today the company continues to sell more tomato sauce than all its competitors combined).

What is particularly fascinating about the tomato sauce campaign is the thinking behind it. For here was the outgrowth of a marketing philosophy that played a major role in transforming Hunt Foods and Industries, Inc., from a small, local cannery (1943 sales: less than $10 million) into a diversified, nationwide industrial complex with sales of over $500 million. In 1964, all of the company's food operations were consolidated under the Hunt-Wesson Foods Division. In 1966, this business was established as a separately incorporated subsidiary un-der the name "Hunt-Wesson Foods, Inc." Today, this company ac-counts for over 70 percent of Hunt Foods and Industries, Inc., sales.

To understand that marketing philosophy, it is important to understand Hunt-Wesson's attitude toward advertising. To Hunt-Wesson, advertising is not an expense but an investment, an indispensable tool for selling Hunt-Wesson products and building a reputation for the company and its brand names. But indispensable as it is, advertising is still just one ingredient in the marketing mix. Director of Advertising Fritz Ohliger explains it this way: "Advertising is one means of communication—one link in a chain of sales motivators. There are so many factors that convince people to buy or not to buy: price, packaging, point-of-sale material. If you stopped to think about it," he says, "you could make up a list of 20 or 30 factors that affect sales—like, 'How good is your distribution system?' 'How effective are your salesmen?' 'What's the competition doing?' Any one of these could help counteract a bad advertising campaign or help ruin a good one."

"Then of oucrse, there's your most important factor," Ohliger says, "and that's quality. All your advertising and pricing and packaging, all your skills as a salesman aren't going to do you one bit of good if your customer doesn't think your product is first rate, if he doesn't come back for more. So, at the heart of this philosophy is an insistence on quality."

Hunt-Wesson advertising itself is a notable example of this desire for quality. "The look of quality has always been a primary requirement," says Ohliger. "Fine illustrations and reproduction, clean layouts, full-page color advertising with appetite appeal and with very strong impact. In order to achieve this look, we've always gone first class. The best photographers. The best copy. The best engraving and printing. We'll produce a dozen ads, go right down the line on them, test them thoroughly, then use only the best ones."

Right from the start, Hunt-Wesson's quest for strong advertising impact has guided a choice of large circulations and dominant schedules. In 1947, when the company began advertising nationally, it bought 52 successive full-page color ads in *Life*. All 52 ads concentrated on the same product: tomato sauce. This was a new approach—a kind of strategic bombing designed to build sales volume and brand franchises quickly. Hunt-Wesson intensfied the advertising even further by concentrating virtually all its fire on certain "spearhead" items (sauce, paste, catsup). These items, Hunt-Wesson figured, had the greatest growth potential; they were economical, they could be used by broad segments of the population, and they were in categories where there was no single dominant national franchise.

Here then were several radical departures from what was considered sound marketing strategy. Other canners were spreading out their advertising, distributing it among various products in their lines, and continually trying to add more products to those lines. Hunt-Wesson, on the other hand, was eliminating a number of low-volume items and focusing production and promotion efforts on the spearhead products.

This business of bucking tradition is nothing unusual for Hunt-Wesson. Throughout its rapid climb, the company has flouted old bugaboos. Take, for instance, Hunt-Wesson's approach to the relationship between advertising and distribution. According to some experts, when you promote a new product you start with regional advertising and expand it as brand strength develops. Yet, in promoting tomato sauce, Hunt-Wesson let advertising precede a product into an area; that is, the company advertised the product nationally before it achieved national distribution and thereby created a demand that expedited wider and faster distribution.

Many of Hunt-Wesson's marketing innovations have, by now, become standard practice in the industry—but not for Hunt-Wesson. It is constantly changing, constantly shifting to meet specific product needs. What has remained constant is the overall philosophy and the overall goal: to develop strong consumer brand franchises, franchises which Hunt-Wesson regards as "our real earnings and our real assets."

The development of Hunt-Wesson's brand franchises has been entirely compatible with the narrow focus on spearhead products. The spearhead ads have helped to sell immediate use of the product; at the same time, they have added, bit by bit, to the total public personality of the Hunt brand. As people have become familiar with the widely advertised spearhead products, the name "Hunt's" has transmitted a stronger quality image. In this way, the spearhead products have paved the way for the others and for new products yet to come.

Today, Hunt-Wesson has some of the nation's most successful food products: Hunt's tomato sauce and tomato paste are the largest selling brands in the U.S.; Wesson is the top nationally distributed vegetable oil; Hunt's catsup and Hunt's peaches both rank among the best sellers. Snowdrift is one of the leaders among solid vegetable shortenings; and Ohio Blue Tip matches are strong number two sellers in their field.

Some of these brands were nurtured and developed by Hunt-Wesson. Others are comparatively new arrivals in the Hunt-Wesson family (arrivals who share one common trait: strong, quality brand names). Hunt-Wesson magazine ads currently appear in consumer magazines and in hotel, restaurant, institutional, bakery, and professional magazines. Hunt-Wesson has always relied heavily on national magazines because of appetite appeal possible with quality, full-color reproduction and because of the large female audience of such publications. Television, radio, and newspapers also have been used effectively, particularly in regional advertising campaigns designed to supplement the national magazine coverage.

There is a tendency among advertising and marketing people to feel that the longer the list of magazines you are using for a given product, the better the campaign. The attitude at Hunt-Wesson tends to be the converse. It is convinced that the concentration of an advertising message in a few magazines has a greater refect than simply the sum of the number of impressions. It likes to dominate an audience . . . to bring its message home to them with real power . . . to convert them to Hunt-Wesson. For example, it will run an advertisement for a single product in every issue of a monthly magazine, in every issue of even a weekly magazine. And what is more, it will regularly run more than one advertisement for a single product in the same issue of the same magazine. Hunt believes that the advertising dominance will be reinforced by the power of reaching the consumer with as much frequency as the particular magazine provides—be it monthly or weekly. Further, it reasons that the added power upon the consumer's mind of more than one ad per issue will drive home its message much more forcefully than will a single impression each time.

Hunt-Wesson was a pioneer in the use of the broadcast medium and especially television at the time when it was particularly exciting because of its novelty. In fact, in 1950, Hunt's Tomato Sauce was the first product to be advertised five days a week on a single network. During the next ten years, however, broadcast dollars were concentrated in local television. But it did not use local television in the usual way. Many advertisers will run campaigns of moderate weight in a relatively large number of markets. In an effort to find the best way to use the medium, Hunt-Wesson has always run long-term campaigns of extremely heavy weight—that is, a very intensive schedule of commercials—in a relatively small number of markets. Its philosophy of dominance comes into play once again, because Hunt-Wesson believes that the power stemming from concentration of its messages against a few number of consumers would tend to impress more efficiently Hunt-Wesson's communication in their minds. And Hunt-Wesson is not afraid to repeat the same message by using the same commercial once it finds the one that best communicates its message.

Hunt-Wesson Foods, Inc., products include: Hunt's (tomato products, fruits, and vegetables), Wesson and Snowdrift (vegetable oils, mayonnaise, and shortenings), Pride of the Farm and Snider's catsup, Blue Plate (mayonnaise, margarine, salad dressings, preserves and jellies, and coffee—all distributed primarily in the South), and Ohio Blue Tip Matches.

Case questions

1. Why, in your opinion, does Hunt not use a single brand name for all of its products? Give the advantages and disadvantages of such a policy.
2. In some instances Hunt does not identify itself with the products in its advertising. Why is this policy followed?

Case 8–3 **ROBERTS, INC.**
Considering brand policy

Roberts, Inc., manufactures lines of domestics, consisting of blankets, towels and other bath fashions, sheets, and bedspreads. It also sells rugs and carpets through its RC Division.

Approximately 60 percent of Roberts' sales are made under its own brand name *Robo*. The remaining 40 percent of sales are made in quantity to chain stores, department stores, and other retail outlets for marketing under their private labels.

Sales under the brand name *Robo* have declined 5 percent during the past year where the sales to the chain stores and other outlets have increased 6 percent. Roberts' vice president of marketing believes that the customers are beginning to recognize that the chain stores are handling the "Robo" line at substantial discounts under private brands. Since Roberts sold the products to the chain stores at a price differential of 7 percent, the vice president was concerned about the inherent dangers if this trend of declining sales under the "Robo" brand continued.

Roberts' central marketing division

The central marketing division, with headquarters and principal showrooms in New York City and district offices in nine other major marketing centers, places its principal marketing emphasis on Robo brand products which are sold primarily to leading department stores in major metropolitan areas and also to distributors, for resale to other retail accounts located in secondary markets. The division's marketing program emphasizes related product selling through "One Vision" promotions of matched and coordinated sets for bedroom and bath. Special store fixtures, developed by Roberts, Inc., are supplied to retail department stores which set up "Robo Shops" within their own domestics departments for operation by store personnel.

The company's merchandise is displayed on these fixtures, and a cooperative advertising and display program featuring the company's seasonal products is employed. These shops have been installed in over 125 leading stores throughout the country and have resulted in a sales increase in past years of Robo's highly styled and most profitable merchandise. The division carries substantial stocks of finished merchandise at the mills and also operates warehouse "Service Centers." In addition to direct sales to retailers under its own labels, Roberts sells a broad line of domestics in quantity to leading mail-order and retail chains, buying groups, and jobbers for resale under their private labels. Private label sales are made principally by the central marketing staff, and two private label customers accounted for approximately 12 percent of Roberts' volume.

Blankets. Roberts manufactures regular and electric blankets of wool, acrylic fibre, rayon, cotton, and blends of these materials. Blankets, including automatic rifles and shells, account for approximately 28 percent of the company's sales. Roberts has a line of printed blankets and, in addition, has developed improved finishes for synthetic blankets.

Towels and bath fashions. Roberts' marketing emphasis on style and fashion has been particularly effective in its lines of towels and bath fashions. Printed towels have grown in popularity and now represent an important and profitable portion of the towel volume. The overall product line was strengthened by the addition of other bath fashions consisting of bath rugs, shower curtains, and lid covers. The latter articles which are purchased from outside manufacturers are coordinated with towels and are styled by Roberts exclusively for its distribution. The addition of these bath fashions has given it the advantage of offering coordinated styling for all textile products normally used in a bathroom. Towels and other bath fashions account for approximately 24 percent of Roberts' sales.

Sheets and bedspreads. Roberts also manufactures and markets a quality line of fitted and hemmed combed-cotton bed sheets and pillowcases. The line is marketed in white, solid colors, stripes, and printed patterns which coordinate with the printed patterns of the Roberts' other domestics. Roberts Inc., also manufacturers and markets a wide variety of woven bedspreads both under the Robo label and private labels of chain stores, mail-order, and other bulk customers. The bedspread mill is equipped to manufacture yarn-dyed box-loom and jacquard spreads, plain piece-dyed spreads and colonial and heirloom styles, both in spread and coverlet sizes. Matching draperies for bedrooms and bath are fabricated from the same materials and sold with the spreads as matched sets.

Screen printing. The use of matching and coordinated printed patterns on bedroom and bath products has made an important contribution to Roberts' development of fashion in domestics. These patterns are printed principally by a silk-screen process requiring skilled techniques.

RC marketing division

The RC marketing division is responsible for styling and marketing rugs and carpets manufactured by Roberts. The division's sales, which during the last five years have increased from approximately 26 percent to 30 percent of the company's total volume, are made to four principal types of outlets: department stores, furniture stores, carpet specialty stores, and interior decorators.

Advertising

Roberts uses national advertising in leading home furnishings and general media, and offers a cooperative local advertising program and promotional help at point of sale Robo customers.

In the advertising copy, Roberts stresses quality products, advanced styling, and points out the widespread acceptance by leading department and specialty stores in the United States.

Case questions

1. What are some of the inherent problems that Roberts will face if it continues to sell 40 percent of its products under private brands?
2. To what degree is the "brand" important to the ultimate consumer in the purchase of Roberts' products?
3. How can Roberts build the "Robo" brand loyalty and still sell to chain stores who will sell under private labels?
4. Point out whether or not Roberts will be able to sell the products under the "Robo" brand at a higher price than what the company charges the chain stores. Is this a satisfactory policy?
5. Give the broad strategy which you believe Roberts should adopt.

part four

Advertising mechanics

9

LAYOUT TECHNIQUES

A layout is a working drawing or blueprint for an advertisement. It is a pencil-sketched plan showing the sizes, positions, and color-weight values of the different units that make up the completed advertisement.

An architect draws the plans for a house for the purpose of showing the contractor in detail exactly how the house is to be built, how the rooms are to be arranged, and where the windows, doors, and stairways are to be placed. Both the contractor and the owner of the house will study the plans to be sure that the house, when completed, will meet with final approval. A layout bears the same relationship to an advertisement that the architect's plan does to a finished building.

Purposes of a layout

There are three fundamental reasons for making a layout.

The actual drawing of the layout enables the advertiser to visualize in detail exactly how the completed advertisement will look when published. As one gets farther into the work of making layouts, it may be found that what was believed to be a very clever layout idea may be confronted with unexpected difficulties. As a result, changes in the mental picture may have to be made before it can be transferred to paper.

The second purpose for making a layout is to give the printer a picture of the completed advertisement. If properly prepared, the layout will give the printer the location of each unit in the advertisement. He can measure the layout and find just how high and how wide each panel of type should be; he can see, from the layout, the exact location of every unit by measuring the distance from margins and other units. A properly prepared layout with complete marginal notations and copy will save misunderstanding between the advertiser and printer, and result in the advertiser getting a printed advertisement that is a sound reproduction of the visualized idea.

The third function of a layout is to have something concrete to submit to the client. In many instances, it is necessary to get approval from several officials of the client company before the advertisement can be run. Carefully prepared layouts always make this task easier.

The basic principles of layout

To develop a layout, the following six points should be considered: (1) first impressions, (2) atmosphere, (3) artistic design, (4) variety, (5) space division and balance, and (6) unit placement.

First impressions

The appearance of an advertisement makes the first impression on a reader. If this first impression is favorable, the reader's attention may be held and he will read the advertisement.

This generally can be accomplished somewhat more effectively by having all the parts of the layout organized in such a way that they will point toward one specific objective.

As an example, in an advertisement in which the headline stated here was a new wall paint, each part of the advertisement pointed to this basic concept. On the other hand, in an advertisement for an electrical cooking unit, the basic appeal was that this appliance cooked everything better. However, the individual parts pointed to a number of other appeals, such as where the product might be purchased, how the busy housewife could use it, and how the product could be washed. As a result, the first impression was like looking at a smorgasbord.

In Figure 9–1 Vickers created an interesting first impression by the manner in which the dynamic small character was used in the layout to get across its message.

Atmosphere

It is in the layout that one should try to highlight that intangible—atmosphere. In many instances it is the atmosphere in the advertisement that attracts the reader's attention.

In automobile advertising, as an example, emphasis frequently is placed on atmosphere. In checking various media, one will see advertisements during the fall months illustrating cars being driven through the open country with fall-colored foliage scenes. In the winter, cars are shown in snow scenes; in the spring, the advertisers will attract prospects with illustrations of picnics and fishing trips. An intriguing atmosphere carried properly into the layout will do much toward creating interest.

FIGURE 9–1

We're the little company that's selling gas. Real fast.

Vickers

VICKERS PETROLEUM CORPORATION. A SUBSIDIARY OF VICKERS ENERGY CORPORATION. A SUBHOLDING COMPANY OF ESMARK.

Artistic design

It is important that the layout be arranged so that the reader will be able to follow the appeal that is used. If the headline states that this is the most reliable television set, then each part of the layout should be arranged in a manner to develop this theme. If the appeal used is that ready-mix cake can be made with the ingredient, the proper arrangement of the step-by-step procedure will provide the type of orderly layout needed for artistic design. Proper arrangement is the basic quality that will make an artistic layout.

Variety

One of the ways to attract the attention of readers is to make use of the principle of variety. By varying the approach from the standard form, an advertisement will stand out, and a higher readership rating may be attained. Variety may be secured in a great many ways, such as by using different color combinations, leaving more white space, providing contrast, varying the direction of the pointing devices, using different typefaces, and utilizing different proportions for the parts of the layout. (See Clairon advertisement in Figure 9–2.)

Space division and balance

While it is difficult to give an exact definition for the division of space, it is, however, this proper dividing of space that satisfies an indefinable inner sense of proportion and causes the reader to be pleased with the harmonious structure of the advertisement.

Among the divisions into which artists classify themselves are two—conventional and modern. The conventional artist lays out his picture on the canvas before starting to paint, for the purpose of getting satisfying proportions. His layout dictates to him where certain objects must be located in order to get a pleasing effect in his finished picture. He paints to obtain realism—to portray his object or scene graphically. He accepts the law of space division as fundamental, but does not make it his first and only consideration.

The modern artist accepts the law of space division not only as a fundamental rule of art but as the principal objective of the finished picture. Modern artists do not, strictly speaking, attempt to paint realistically or to portray their objects faithfully. They divide the space on their canvas for the purpose of producing a picture which is ostensibly a pattern or design created by the objects and the spaces between the objects.

The division of space leads into a wide variety of complicated designs or patterns. However, at present it is more important to consider the fundamental divisions and their comparative values in order that the different units (illustration, headline, copy, trademark, signature, and so on) may be placed and divided effectively.

Examine Illustrations 1 and 2 in Figure 9–3. Number 1 is divided at the center by a vertical dotted line. Number 2 is divided into equal

FIGURE 9–2

Anytime...but not just for any man!

Cologne:
$5.00 and $8.00
After Shave:
$4.00 and $6.00

Available only at fine drug, department and men's stores.

Courtesy Clairon Division

parts by a horizontal line. Both spaces have been cut exactly in half, leaving two equal divisions of space. This is the least complex of any possible division. Such divisions, which are equal, have a tendency to be uninteresting and monotonous. Monotony may result from equality or uniformity. As an example, if one part of an electrical cord is broken, a person's attention generally will be attracted to that spot. One

FIGURE 9–3
Space division illustrations

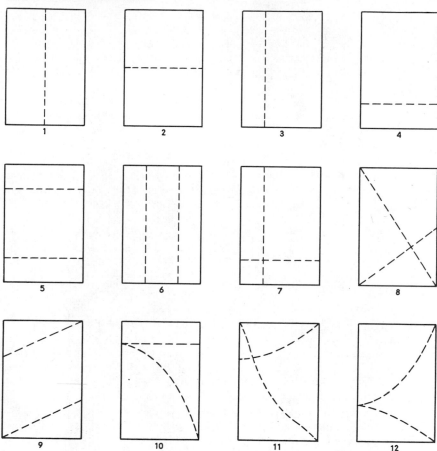

could take a hundred individuals past a fence with a broken picket, and if they remembered having seen the fence at all, the one fact that would stand out would be the broken picket. Thus, to avoid monotony or sameness, it is usually better not to divide the space into equal parts.

Illustration 3 presents a simple, yet graphic picture of life's great drama. Men, animals, and other creatures of nature do not attack a foe of equal strength. They are constantly seeking the more timid and weak as an antagonist. Illustration 3 depicts inequality—the struggle for life in a simple form. It illustrates a dramatic, unequal, interesting situation. The smaller space battles against the larger space for its place. One might visualize an illustration similar to a large boy fighting with a small youngster. One's natural tendencies and inclinations are to sympathize immediately with the smaller boy. A situation of this kind is interesting and stimulating. These situations are the kind that generally will attract attention.

Illustration 4 gives a dramatic situation similar to the one found in Number 3, except in the fourth drawing a horizontal dotted line is used to make the division, while in the third a vertical line is used. American United Life Insurance Company used this method of space division in Figure 9–4. This situation creates an impression of a large object crushing a smaller one. A comparative analysis of the mental reactions to these kinds of space divisions usually indicates that while Illustration 4 may not create the interest that Illustration 3 does, it is nevertheless superior in attention-attracting qualities to either Illustrations 1 or 2. Illustrations 5 and 6 are similar to 3 and 4, except that each has been divided into three spaces instead of two. These divisions give dramatic situations which, for attracting interest, are probably greater than those found in 3 and 4. The three spaces enlarge the field of activity and enable one to get greater variety. The vertical spaces will, of course, get different reactions than the horizontal.

Illustration 7 gives a more complex division of space. None of the four spaces is equal in area. It broadens even further the possible fields of activity which enable a layout man to produce greater variety. It has the advantage of oblongs, both horizontal and vertical. The intersecting point of the two divisional lines also results in an "X." This provides another device for attracting attention. In Figure 9–5, the Carrier Air Conditioning Company advertisement utilizes this principle on an effective basis.

Illustration 8 provides a space divided into four unequal parts, three of them forming triangles of different sizes. The division is brought about by two diagonal lines crossing each other, producing the "X." The crossing of two opposed diagonal lines is symbolic of crossed swords, and creates the atmosphere of duels, battle, and the like. This dramatic action attracts attention and creates interest.

Illustration 9 is another of the many possible uses of diagonals. This is similar to Illustration 5, but possesses an appeal with greater dynamic force than straight horizontals. Here one gets the feeling of the power required to pull something uphill and the effect of coasting down at a high rate of speed.

Illustration 10 portrays a combination of straight and circular lines bringing about two curved space divisions. Curves create soft fluid designs, lacking in force and directness when compared to straight lines, but making up for this deficiency in beauty.

In Illustrations 11 and 12, the divisional lines are curved. It is the opinion of many artists that straight lines are masculine in feeling and curved lines are feminine. Men usually are attracted by advertisements that go straight to the facts in a logical manner; beauty in advertising is not as important to men as it is to women. Women, on the other hand, are usually attracted by advertisements that tend toward the artistic and consider logic and facts as secondary. It should not be overlooked, however, that curved divisions of space develop an atmosphere of ease and quiet, while divisions of space made by straight lines create a feeling of power, speed, and excitement. Gordon's gin uses curved lines in Figure 9–6 (page 288) to create a feeling of love and softness.

**FIGURE 9–4
Space division (4)**

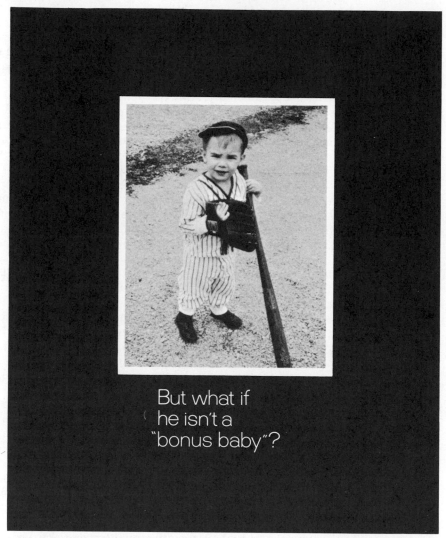

But what if
he isn't a
"bonus baby"?

Let's face it, not every youngster can earn a fortune in the major leagues. Or even win a college scholarship. But as a college graduate, chances are he'll earn $100,000 to $200,000 more, in his lifetime, than a high school graduate.

So play it safe and prepare for the expense of his college education now, with the help of American United Life's Sentinel policy. By the time he's ready for college, your Sentinel policy can be worth more cash than the total you've paid in premiums. And you'll have life insurance protection all the while.

Talk with your A·U·L agent. He'll show you how a Sentinel policy can guarantee your child's education, even if you're not here to see him graduate.

American United Life
FOUNDED 1877

The Company with the Partnership Philosophy
AMERICAN UNITED LIFE INSURANCE COMPANY
FALL CREEK PARKWAY AT NORTH MERIDIAN
DEPT. S-47, INDIANAPOLIS, INDIANA 46206

Courtesy American United Life Insurance Company

FIGURE 9–5
Space division (7)

We can take about 10 pounds off our
air conditioners. But we won't.

That's the way we like them
and build them. Heftier. Stronger.
Carrier uses heavier components,
thick Weather Armor® coating,
more insulation. So they'll last longer,
run quieter. Maybe that's why more
people put their confidence in Carrier
air conditioning than in any other make.

Carrier Air Conditioning Company

FIGURE 9–6
Space division (curves)

How the English keep dry.

GORDON'S
DISTILLED
LONDON DRY
GIN

Gordon's Gin. Largest seller in England, America, the world.

PRODUCT OF U.S.A. 100% NEUTRAL SPIRITS DISTILLED FROM GRAIN. 86 PROOF. GORDON'S DRY GIN CO., LTD., LINDEN, N.J.

Unit placement

After the space has been divided, it is necessary to determine how the different units of an advertisement will be placed within these spaces. The units themselves, or the white spaces between them, should, by their position in relation to each other, create a pattern or design which will be attractive.

The selection of particular units for specific spaces in the advertisement is of importance because the advertisement must have the appearance of being clear and easy to read. If not properly located, the shapes and color-weight values of some units may have an effect of blocking the vision.

Because it is difficult for the eye to obtain a photographic impression of a complete scene or entire subject at a glance, it is advisable, whenever possible, to locate the units in the layout so that they will be seen in the order of their importance.

Path of the eye: Illustration 1 in Figure 9–7 shows the normal path traveled by the eye when looking at an advertisement. Notice that the eye enters the page on the left near the top and passes down and across the space in the form of an arc, leaving the space on the right side near

FIGURE 9–7
Illustrations

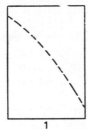 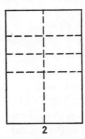 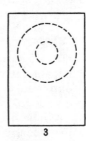

1   2   3

the bottom. Although the eye will follow this particular path under normal conditions, it can be diverted by pointing devices, barriers, and the like.

Various tests indicate that the eye wanders while following the natural course. There is a place, however, along the path where more will be seen at a short distance from the path than at any other point. In other words, it can be said there is one place that is more likely to be explored by the eye than any other. This point is called by some the optical center; by others it is known as the focal point; and by others it is referred to as the visual point.

In Illustration 2, the focal point is slightly above the center of the space. Usually it is located, for all practical purposes, by dividing the upper half of the space into thirds and then drawing a vertical line dividing the spaces equally. The focal point will be at the center of the intersection of the vertical and horizontal lines.

At this point, the unguided eye generally will wander. It has been found through experimentation that an area around this point, about one-third of the width of the space, has the greatest potential for advertising purposes.

Examine Illustration 2. If the space were six inches wide and nine inches high, the optical center would be approximately two inches in diameter. From this optical center area there is a gradual but declining value. The second most valuable area surrounds the optical center and is called the "field." The field can be estimated to include a circular space which in the overall width (including optical center) is about five-sixths of the width of the space under consideration. As an example, if the space under consideration were six inches wide, the field, including the optical center, would be five inches in diameter. All space not included in the optical center and field is called the fringe.

Generally, the unit which has been designed for the purpose of creating interest, should be placed in the optical circle. However, when conditions exist which may make it impractical to do this, it is then advisable to place the unit as near the focal point as possible. Location for all other units should be selected according to the order in which it is desired they be seen or read. Copy panels should be located also with this thought in mind. Trademarks and slogans usually are placed in locations to complete the pattern, for ordinarily they are not an important part of the sales appeal. The firm's name usually comes at the bottom or end of the copy unless, for cause, it is placed elsewhere.

When a coupon is used, it is generally placed in one of the lower corners. To spur a prospect to act, it should be made easy for him to clip the coupon. As a result, the outside corner of the page is used because it requires only two cuts, one vertical and one horizontal. Some advertisers even use a triangle-shaped coupon because it requires only one diagonal cut.

There are certain situations, however, where it may not be possible to place the main appeal near the optical center. In cases of this kind, some pointing device may be used to guide the eye from its natural course to another path or route so that the reader will be more likely to see and read the basic appeal.

Pointing devices.   Many techniques can be used to guide the eye, such as arrows, rising smoke, trailing vines, pencils, and other devices.

In a recent soup advertisement, the pointing device employed to carry the eye from the headline to the product was a cluster of peapods on a leafy stalk. The lower pod was open and displayed a row of peas, slanted conspicuously toward the bowl of steaming soup. It formed a pointing means, and yet, because it fitted into the complete advertisement, was not readily recognized as such a device.

A soft-drink distributor used an illustration of the beverage being poured from the bottle as a pointing device. A ribbon on a package, a man pointing to a product, different intensities of colors, a curving highway, or a wire stretching from a pulley are a few of the devices which can be used.

Background unit.   One of the ways to place a product in the foreground and make it stand out is to place a background behind it. When this is done, it creates a third dimension. This illusion may be created by leaving white space around an illustration which becomes as much a background as the picture of distant hills or mountains.

A background which creates a third dimension has the advantage of making the advertisement stand out in bold relief, bringing it out into the foreground in front of other units, and thereby giving it display prominence.

In an advertisement of batteries for portable television sets, a battery was placed in the immediate foreground, standing out against white space. Back of the battery was a picture of three persons on the beach viewing a television program. The scene was a little grayer than the illustration of the battery and was vignetted into the white space at the bottom. Superimposed on this background, in an upper corner, was the company's trade name. In this advertisement, the treatment of the background harmonized with both the copy idea and the scheme of the design.

A television advertisement for a color television set also made a similar use of backgrounds to help illustrate visually what the product does. The theme of the campaign was "The Theater of the Home." The illustration depicted a scene of a show in color.

Reasons for dual background. Below are listed several reasons for using a dual-purpose background. These do not represent all the reasons, nor do they indicate that any one of these is more important or valuable than another. However, they indicate a number of instances in which a dual-purpose background can be used effectively:

1. To show uses of the product or to form a pattern, thus uniting a number of small illustrations in a decorative design that does not detract from the boldness with which the main illustration or picture of the product is to be treated.
2. To make specific appeals to various occupational classes by using scenes behind the product that will interest each group—an office building, golf course, fishing stream, hunting scene, a factory, and so on.
3. To contribute to or symbolize an atmosphere of luxury, refinement, and strength.
4. To construct an allover pattern either of the product or trademark against which an illustration or copy can be made to stand out.
5. To suggest what is likely to happen if the product is not used—the skeleton is an effective device to use as background for an insurance policy, a sheet of fireproof wallboard, or a set of automobile tires.
6. To place a trademark or some other unit in the distance so that it does not cut into the scene depicted.

Questions

1. "The worst thing about today's cult of creativity in advertising layout is that it puts the emphasis on spectacular individual ads instead of campaign success." Comment.
2. "Many of the bad layouts in print media today can be blamed on broadcast media." Discuss.
3. It has been stated that original layout forms come from creative thinking, not from previously conceived formulas. Comment.
4. Explain what is meant by the focal point and select an advertisement in which this has been used effectively.

5. Select an advertisement from a magazine in which the main appeal was not placed in the optical center. Explain why.

6. Where is the best location in the layout to place a coupon in the following cases:
   a. Full-page advertisement.
   b. Upper one-half page advertisement.
   c. Column advertisement near the gutter corner.

7. Select and clip from some newspaper or magazine an advertisement which, in your opinion, has made good use of the focal, field, and fringe spaces. Make a layout of that advertisement showing, with light circles and optical center, the field and fringe. Make a second layout using a different arrangement of the parts. Indicate whether or not you believe there is improvement.

8. Select and clip from some publication the advertisement that in your opinion excels all others in "favorable attention-attracting" and "interest-creating" qualities. Base your judgment upon the ability of the advertisement's caption, illustration, and general typographical apperance to "attract favorable attention" and "create interest." Before making your selection, be sure you understand what is meant by the terms "attracting favorable attention" and "creating interest." The quality of the copy is not to be considered. Make a layout of this advertisement, exact in size and similar in color-weight values; letter in the captions and signatures—the lettering to be similar in style, size, and weight; try to make illustrations recognizable.

9. It has been stated that in a layout pattern, one element must dominate in order to get the reader's attention. Comment.

10. How can the layout express the ideas of the advertiser?

11. Indicate some of the methods for securing distinction in a layout.

12. What information do you need before a layout can be started?

13. Point out the layouts you would recommend for the following products for print media:
   a. Retail discount house.
   b. Swift's Premium franks.
   c. Salem cigarettes.
   d. Dial soap.
   e. Bulova watch.
   f. Shrimp cocktail.
   g. Hathaway shirt.
   h. Coca-Cola.
   i. Leslie salt.
   j. New York Life Insurance.

14. Indicate how layouts would vary between the following media: Newspapers, magazines, trade publications, direct mail, transit advertising, and outdoor.

Case   **ANALYSES OF ADVERTISEMENTS**
9–1   **Considering layout principles**

In Exhibits 9–1 through 9–5 evaluate the advertisements on the bases listed on page 297.

EXHIBIT 9–1

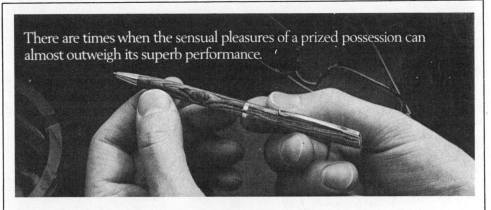

There are times when the sensual pleasures of a prized possession can almost outweigh its superb performance.

Executive Timber by Hallmark.

Executive Timber is wood, carefully and expertly crafted into superb writing instruments.

Take the pen in your hands. Feel the heft of it. The warmth of it. Roll the barrel between your fingers. Note the subtle texture of the grain, enriched by fine Swedish oils.

Because no two grain patterns are precisely alike, every pen and pencil in the Executive Timber line is unique. You will own an original. One of a kind.

Executive Timber. A distinguished gift. An intensely personal possession. So carefully created Hallmark gives you a lifetime guarantee against even the slightest mechanical defect.

Executive Timber is for the person who likes the feel of wood —the warmth of wood—and the naturalness of wood.

There's walnut, richly grained and deep in color, from the timberlands of North America.

There's teakwood, as robustly colorful as the teakwood that graced the majestic sailing ships of the 1800's.

There's wenge from the African Congo—perhaps the most distinctively grained wood in the world.

There's cordia, hard and finely-textured, from the East Indies.

And rosewood. And tulipwood. Both imported from the rain forests of South America.

Each of these woods has its own personality. Its own grain pattern. Its own color. Its own texture. And for the discerning craftsman, each of these exotic woods has its own distinctive musk.

The pen writes as comfortably as it feels. Glide it over a sheet of fine paper and notice how the tungsten carbide point leaves a smooth, single-width marking.

A sealed cartridge resists the possibility of leakage—even if you are 30,000 feet up and traveling at 650 miles an hour.

For those reasons and more, every Hallmark Executive Timber product carries a lifetime guarantee against even the slightest mechanical defect. This guarantee is backed by every store that sells Executive Timber. The promise is simple and clear: any mechanical defect will be promptly corrected at no cost to you.

Executive Timber. A distinguished gift. A prized possession. Perhaps the most prudent purchase you will make this year.

Pen and pencil set $30. Pen $15. Pencil $15. At fine stores where quality writing instruments are sold. Hallmark Cards, Inc., Kansas City, Mo.

"When you care enough to send the very best"

EXHIBIT 9–2

EXHIBIT 9–3

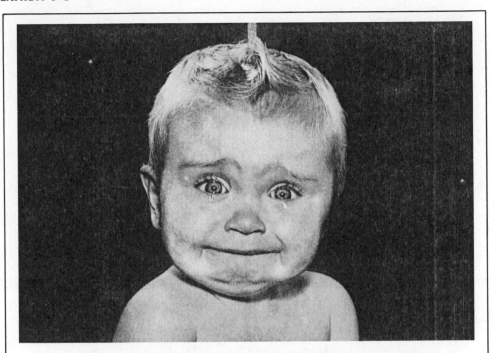

By the time he's out of 8th grade America will be out of oil and gas.

Impossible?

No. It's fact. The latest U.S. Government figures indicate our proven reserves will only last:

OIL	12 YEARS
GAS	12 YEARS
URANIUM	30 YEARS
COAL	500 YEARS

These frightening numbers reveal our energy problem. And the solution. Today we use oil and gas for 75% of our needs. And coal for only 17%.

Can there be any question about what we must do? We must conserve. We must use precious oil and gas for those things only they can do. We must...make a national commitment to coal.

What is a "national commitment" to coal? It means recognizing coal as our primary energy fuel. It means converting its power to energy that can substitute for oil and gas. It means a crash program to develop economical liquefaction and gasification of coal.

It does *NOT* mean coal without regard for the environment. It means reasonable regulations to protect the land, air and water and encourage the use of coal.

We must eliminate environmental extremism. We can tolerate neither those who would destroy the environment nor those who would be unduly restrictive.

It means, in short, a National Energy Program based on a foundation of Coal and Conservation.

Many are puzzled by what is happening in America. As a people we have some unique characteristics, among them ingenuity and a desire to get the job done. Yet, when it comes to solving our energy problems, we've been chasing our tails.

A simple review of our energy fuel assets—and a recognition of the peril of dependence on foreign oil—must lead those who govern and all thinking people to the obvious conclusion that Coal and Conservation is the answer to our near-future energy problems.

It's elementary...even for an 8th grader.

The call to greater energy independence **COAL AND CONSERVATION!**

American Electric Power Company, Inc.

Appalachian Power Co., Indiana & Michigan Electric Co., Kentucky Power Co., Kingsport Power Co., Michigan Power Co., Ohio Power Co., Wheeling Electric Co.

EXHIBIT 9–4

Three kinds of gas for your kind of car.

Unleaded.

Beginning with the 1975 models, all cars manufactured in this country will require unleaded gas, the cleanest of all automobile fuels. Generally, cars that run on regular will perform equally well with unleaded gasoline. Cars requiring premium, however, will not be able to use unleaded.

Regular.

Most of the cars manufactured today are geared to run on regular, the most economical of the three fuels. If regular gasoline is recommended for your car, continue to use it, but keep in mind that in most cases your car will perform equally well using an unleaded fuel.

Premium.

The premium user is pretty well locked in. If your car is designed to run on premium, the high performance fuel, it *requires* premium. The use of a lower octane fuel can cause serious damage to your car's engine.

We're selling all three.

Some oil companies have stopped selling premium. Not Vickers. We're going to continue to offer you whatever kind of gas you need — regular, unleaded or premium — because we know the right kind of gas is the key to your car's performance. So, keep us in mind. We're the little company that's *still* selling all three kinds. Look for the "V" — the Vickers sign.

We're the little company that's selling all three kinds of gas.

EXHIBIT 9–5

We're the little company that's selling all three kinds.

Some of those other oil companies are out there thinking they don't need to sell premium gasoline anymore. But not us. When you're the 29th largest oil company in the country, you don't *stop* selling anything. You keep right on giving your customer the kind of gas he needs.

Yes, Vickers is going to sell all three kinds of gasoline. Regular. Unleaded. *And* premium. So whatever kind of car you drive, keep us in mind. Just look for the V — the Vickers' sign.

1. Favorable attention-attracting qualities.
2. Interest-creating qualities.
3. Effectiveness of layout to direct the eye.
4. Use of contrast, proportion, balance, and unity.

Case 9–2 **EVALUATION OF DIFFERENT LAYOUTS**
Preparing layouts

1. Make two thumbnail sketches of the advertisements for each of the exhibits in Case 9–1.
2. Rearrange the units in your sketches in several ways.
3. Compare your recommended sketch with the original advertisement and give reasons why you believe your layouts are better or worse.

10

ADVERTISING PRODUCTION

T he continued breakthrough in new production technology for print media includes the dramatic techniques that the *Wall Street Journal* began using on November 20, 1975. On that date the *Wall Street Journal* was sent by satellite from its Chicopee printing plant in Massachusetts to its new Orlando plant in Florida. A total distance of 44,000 miles. Hovering thousands of miles over the equator, the Westar I satellite electronically received and then sent a full page every three minutes.

New techniques

This communications system, designed by the American Satellite Corporation, was another breakthrough in publishing for *The Wall Street Journal* that added to a list of firsts, beginning with automatic typesetting in the 1950s and microwave transmission in the 1960s.

The time saved with satellite transmission allowed its Orlando plant to make faster delivery in Florida and nearby states. Its subscribers were able to act on and use the in-depth business coverage even sooner. It also provided better, faster, and more efficient service for the advertisers.

During 1975 a number of newspapers also changed from hot metal and time-honored skills of typographers, engravers, and stereotypers and began printing from cold type as a result of modern technology that advanced newspaper production into the world of electronics.

In these cases, printing from lead and zinc became a part of the past, pushed aside by computerized photocomposition. It was like stepping from the horse and buggy into a jet-powered 747.

What are the changes?

The reporter has relegated his old Underwood to newsroom history and uses a sophisticated IBM Selectric typewriter to prepare news copy scanner-ready with coded instructions to a computer.

An editor reads the copy then codes it for storage in the computer. The editor's soft-leaded pencil has been replaced by the Selectric in the preliminary editing step.

Copy now is sent to the production floor—not to be received by a copy-cutter who in the past would deal it out to a bank of linotype operators for setting in hot metal, but to a copy control operator who feeds it into a scanner, which is an optical character reader, from where it goes to storage in a complex computer system.

In the newsroom the editors and copy readers sit in front of visual display terminals (VDTs) complete with sophisticated keyboards with which they call up the news story from computer storage for screen display. Copy deletions, additions, and the final copyreading and editing are done on the display terminal. The editor keyboards the headline on the story and orders it back to storage in the computer to be "called out" when all stories on the page are completed.

The editing and computer instructions ended, electronic wizardry transfers the printed copy to a photo negative. The automated conversion from negative to glossy print follows and the news story is ready for page makeup.

The compositor, with a page scheme prepared by an editor, pastes up the page with the printouts of all the news stories, headlines, and whatever glossy photos are indicated. Next comes the conversion of the paste-up page. This is done by means of an electronic process that transfers the page image to a thin plastic plate. The plate goes to the press deck and is wrapped on the cylinder of the web press.

With the start of the presses, the newspaper is conveyed to a highly mechanized mail room, bundled, and dispatched to awaiting trucks, delivered to the newspaperboy and then to the reader.

Physical changes in the newspaper plant are as revolutionary as the computerized production lines.

In the newsroom the VDT-equipped desks have replaced the familiar horseshoe-shaped copy desk. Copy readers have set aside the standard tools of the trade—heavy pencil, ruler, scissors, paste pot. In exchange, however, they brought back a long forgotten headpiece—the green eye shade to accommodate editing on the video screen.

The composing room is no longer recognizable. Linotypes are gone. The turtles and page forms in which pages were laid out in lead type and zinc photo reproductions are no more. The stereotype department, with its huge tanks of melten lead used to convert the flat page forms to mat and then to curved plates of lead, also has been emptied. The engraving section is no longer one having massive caldrons of etching acids and bins of abrasive red powders and great tanks of water; it is now one of streamlined electronic wonders.

General factors

Although these new production techniques offer special advantages to advertisers, the preparations of advertising for broadcast and print media is a complicated activity because it calls for the efficient utilization of the specialized talents of a number of individuals. Here the usual problems of communication, timing, planning, decision making, and human relations assume a new dimension of challenge.

Illustration appeals

The appeals used for illustrations are similar to the ones used in the copy and the other parts of the advertisement. A few of the appeals around which the illustration may be built are such ones as appeal to the emotions or instincts, or to appetite, comfort, danger, health, love, pleasure, pride, ambition, responsibility, safety, service, testing, testimonial, and economy.

On the other hand, the advertiser may decide not to use any of the above appeals but to place his emphasis on some specific idea about the product. As an example, some companies will show the product alone with the objective of getting the prospects to recognize the package.

Methods of illustration

Among the methods of illustrating an idea are the ones listed below. It would be incorrect to say this is a complete list or that one of these methods is better than another. The use of each technique is dependent upon the objective of the advertiser.

However, such methods as using an illustration of the product alone, placing it in a setting or scene, showing the product in action, giving the result of the use of the product, comparing it to the product of a competitor, using symbolic concepts or placing emphasis on detail are some of the more important ones.

There is growing evidence, however, that consumers are getting tired of many of the symbols of rising aspiration appeals that have been used and are demanding more rational strategy. As a result, it is now even more important for the illustration to be developed in correlation with the current economic and social setting.

As an example, in visualizing the illustration the overall appeal should be focused on one sales point which can be reinforced by an exciting headline, succinct copy and convincing visual concepts. All of these parts must also be considered as a unit.

Setting for envisioning

As a result of the greater emphasis on the use of broadcast media and the shifts in stress on various social values along with other dynamic changes in the past decade, there has evolved a more complex combination of circumstances that require new insights into the process of visualization.

The changing cultural patterns have brought about a different interpretation of conformity to characteristic goals and institutional means. The reluctance of society to measure success in terms of heavy emphasis on financial attainment is also but one example of a symptom of this attitude.

Yet, at the same time there is the inherent drive on the part of the consumer to have an identity. The dynamism in society, however, makes this more and more difficult to attain. The demands on the individual by an affluent society, the outgrowth of leisure as a problem in society, the stress on large-scale organizations, and the decrease in individuality have lessened the chance of developing this unity of personality.

National advertising market

The segmentation of the market that has taken place has also eroded what was at one time considered to be a national advertising market. National advertising is now frequently designed and placed on a regional basis with the retailer and distributor having an ever growing voice in the process. This has resulted from a number of factors which include:

1. Increased cost of network advertising.
2. Failure to develop a yardstick to measure adequately the national advertising.
3. Desire on the part of large distributors to participate in the advertising planning.
4. Need to use specific appeals for different sections of the country.
5. Use of spot advertising on a basis that is as effective as network promotion.
6. Availability of special regional and metropolitan rates for media.
7. Segmentation of market potential.
8. Potential of correlating advertising to meet needs of various markets.
9. Decline in expenditures for advertising as a percentage of Gross National Product.
10. Sophistication in media selection.

Clues to preparation

In selecting the procedures which should be used in formalizing the overall advertising appeal there are many facets which should be included. It is also important not to underestimate the complexity of the total situation. Keep in mind that no detail is ever too small to be considered.

Some of the questions that might provide an insight into the clues for firming the approach are the following:

1. Who makes the decision as to the class of product to purchase? (primary appeal)
2. Who makes the decision as to the brand to buy? (selective appeal)
3. Who influences the buyer?
4. Where will the product be purchased?

5. When will the buyer purchase the product?
6. How will the buyer arrive at the decision to purchase it?
7. What type of budget is available to stimulate demand?
8. Will the appeal have to differ for the various market segments?
9. Are there any contradictions about the product characteristics that need to be overcome?
10. How do customers relate to the product?
11. What kind of self-enlargement or self-expression might result from purchase of the product?
12. How can the communication be best advanced? Will it be confined to a verbal expression? A pictorial approach?
13. Are there any incongruous or inappropriate presentations for the product?
14. What media are available for the presentation and can the same appeal be used in all of them?
15. Is the approach geared for short-term or long-term goals?

It would be incorrect to say that this list of questions is complete. Nevertheless, they give some indication as to the complexity of what is involved in broad visualization.

Consider the Vicks VapoRub advertisement in Figure 10–1. The mother probably makes the decision as to the product and brand which will be purchased. When the youngster comes down with a cold, the child becomes the influential factor. As a result, the decision to show the benefits derived from the use of the product becomes an effective appeal. This appeal can be dramatized in a number of ways and can be used both in broadcast and print media. It is also an appeal that will reach the segment of the market in which families have children. On the other hand, there is the danger of getting some negative reaction on the basis that a product that can be used by youngsters will not be strong enough for adults.

Another approach that is of interest is the one found in Figure 10–2. Again, this advertisement not only uses illustration effectively to dramatize the general appeal, but also pinpoints rational factors that are of importance to the potential consumer.

General suggestions

In evaluating some of the different procedures in envisioning an idea for the advertisement, it is important to determine not only what the product is technically but also how the consumer sees it. The concept of the "psychological environment" includes the notion that what people "see" depends not only on the appeals used, but, also on such factors as the type of persons they are, the environment in which they live and the ideology which they have. People "see" things in the way their culture and the particular social group in which they move have induced them to visualize these things.

As a result, each appeal has certain advantages. In a television advertisement, several devices may be used, each serving its own pur-

FIGURE 10–1

Sniffles,
congestion,
coughs,
tears...
so sick
with
a cold!

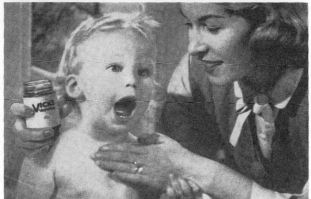

Comfort your baby with soothing relief that acts faster, works longer than aspirin or cold tablets

ATOM TRACER TESTS PROVE VAPORUB ACTS IN 7 SECONDS, WORKS 10 HOURS

Your loving hands massage Vicks VapoRub over chest, throat, back—and right before your eyes, the stuffiness starts to clear, the cough calms. That's because soothing vapor medications reach cold-infected nose, throat, and chest in just 7 seconds . . . keep working for 10 hours—startling facts discovered by laboratory atom tracer tests. Medical literature shows that pills and tablets which go through stomach and bloodstream act slower and for shorter periods. And VapoRub relieves stuffiness, coughs, congestion . . . symptoms aspirin does not help. For sniffles, sneezes, as well as croupy coughs . . . for grown-ups and children—use VapoRub for every cold. Use as a rub, in steam, in the nose.

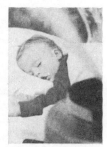

Doctors prescribe medicated steam for colds and croupy coughs. To make steam most effective, add VapoRub to bowl of boiling water or vaporizer, as directed.

VICKS VAPORUB ®

WORLD'S MOST WIDELY USED COLDS MEDICATION

Courtesy Vicks Chemical Company

FIGURE 10–2

The shortest distance between two points is experience.

Point one is oil or gas buried under tons of earth. Point two is the consumer. Getting from one to the other can be a shaky process. But, C-E Natco experience in action can make that trip one straight, smooth line.

We bring nearly half a century of experience to every job we do. Like separating, heating and removing impurities from oil and gas streams. Fabricating water conditioning equipment to meet water flood, disposal and pollution requirements. Giving new life to dying wells with custom-blended chemical treatments. We can do it.

From the drawing board to the field, C-E Natco experience in action is your straight line from production to profit.

E=E NATCO PROCESS EQUIPMENT
COMBUSTION ENGINEERING, INC

Experience in Action. Worldwide.

C-E NATCO / COMBUSTION ENGINEERING, INC / P.O. BOX 1710 / TULSA, OKLAHOMA 74101 / TELEPHONE (918) 663-9100

pose; thus, the person who failed to use the product may dramatize a situation while another person who did use the product may show the benefits derived. In print media a package may be placed with a before-and-after scene.

While the combinations are extensive, the following points are some which might be considered in deciding on the appeal to use:

1. A single sound appeal is better than a poor one supported by medi-
   ocre ones.
2. Continuity in a series of advertisements can be secured by employing the same technique of visualization in each advertisement,
   and allowing the ideas to provide distinctiveness.
3. The test of an appeal is whether or not it conveys the idea which
   underlies the advertisement.
4. The illustrations, script, text, and so on should complement each
   other.
5. People like to look at illustrations. As a result, good illustrations
   will arouse interest.

Mechanical techniques

Because by its very nature advertising is also dependent upon the
mechanical means by which the message will be presented in a sound
and economical manner, the authors have included a limited number
of the basic introductory highlights and principles. An understanding
of this material will indicate some of the nomenclature that is essential in considering the recommendations of the production staff.

Printing

Although a number of new processes have been developed, these
new techniques are generally adaptations of one of the three basic
printing processes. These three processes are called: letterpress printing, intaglio printing, and lithographic printing. Letterpress printing,
or relief printing, is transferring to the paper from a raised surface.
Intaglio, or rotogravure, printing is transferring to the paper through
an etched or depressed surface. Lithographic, or planographic, printing is transferring to the paper from a flat surface which has been
specially treated. The three processes of printing are shown in Figure
10–3.

Lithographic printing may be either direct or indirect. Indirect
lithography is referred to as offset lithography. The main difference
between direct and offset lithography is that in direct lithography the
plates touch the paper. In offset the plates do not touch the paper but
deliver the ink to an intermediate cylinder which is covered with a
thin sheet of rubber. It is this thin sheet of rubber that prints off, or
offsets, the ink on the paper. The upper cylinder carries the paper
receiving the impression and the lower shows the printing plate in a
magnified cross section (line and Ben Day).

Type measurement

The point system is the standard method of measurement used by
printers for type, rules, and borders. The basis of the point system is
the "point." A "point" is approximately 1/72 of an inch in height.
There are 72 points to the inch. Only the height of type is measured

in points; the width is not measured by points and will vary depending upon the face of type used. When type is spoken of as 6-point and 8-point, it means that the body—not the face—of the letter is 6/72 or 8/72 of an inch high. The height of the face is usually less than the height of the body. The face of an 8-point capital M for example is only about 6 points high, the other 2 points being taken up by the shoulder.

FIGURE 10–3

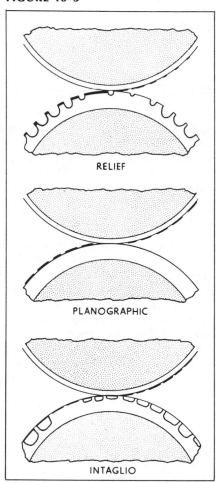

RELIEF

PLANOGRAPHIC

INTAGLIO

Em

The em is the name of the unit of measurement used by printers in computing the amount of composition in a column, page, or booklet. Printers at times estimate the cost of composition by the thousand ems of type set. The em represents a square of the size of type measured; thus, measuring 6-point type the em is a square 6 points wide and 6 points high. In 12-point type it is 12 points by 12 points; the size of the em will vary with the size of the type.

The advertising man will not generally use the em in the manner in which it is explained above. There is, however, another use of the term "em" with which the copy writer must be familiar. The 12-point em, also called a pica em, is sometimes used as a measurement of width, 1/6 of an inch square. When the width of a column is stated to be a certain number of ems or picas, 12-point picas is usually meant. Thus, if a column is said to be 12 ems or picas wide, the column is 2 inches wide. In referring to measurements of this kind, however, it is better to say 12 picas than 12 ems, to avoid the possibility of any confusion.

Leads

A "lead" (pronounced *led*) is a thin strip of metal used for spacing between lines of type so as to give the printed matter a more open appearance. Leads are not as high as the type and, therefore, do not print on the paper. They vary in thickness as 1-, 2-, 3-, and 4-point leads. Type with a lead between the lines is known as leaded. Leaded type matter is generally recognized as containing 2-point leads between the lines. It is always well to specify the amount of leading. Specify 1-, 2-, or 3-point lead; then there can be no misunderstanding as to the amount of white space that is desired between the lines. When no leads are used, the type matter is said to be set "solid."

When a lead is spoken of a 2-point or 4-point, the measure refers to the thickness and not to the length.

Amount of leading

The amount of leading that is advisable depends upon the size and style of type, length of line, and sometimes on the character of the advertising copy. Very small type such as 5- and 6-point should generally not be leaded more than 1 or 2 points under any circumstances; 8-point type usually does not require more than 2-point leading; 10-, 12-, and 14-point type may be leaded with 2-, 3-, or 4-point leads, depending upon the amount of white space desired. Boldface type requires more leading ordinarily than lighter faces. However, leading should be used principally as an aid to legibility.

Classes of type

For practical purposes the various styles of type are divided into two classes: "display type" and "body type." Display type is heavier in the face than body type and is used where emphasis is needed in an advertisement, as, for example, in captions, subcaptions, prices, signatures, addresses, and so on. Body type is used in setting those portions or units of an advertisement that do not require display, such as the body or text matter in an advertisement.

Display type

Display type is made in a series of sizes ranging ordinarily from 6-point to 72-point. There are usually 13 sizes within this range. These are : 6-, 8-, 10-, 12-, 14-, 18-, 24-, 30-, 36-, 42-, 48-, 60-, and 72-point. Some type faces, however, are made in additional sizes. There are also some type faces that have display sizes larger than 72-point. The foregoing division refers to the standard metal type faces. There are other types which are made in sizes much larger, but these type faces are generally used for printing large posters, handbills, and the like.

Width of display type. Display type is made in four widths of faces. These four widths are known as extra-condensed, condensed, medium or regular, and extended. It is advisable under most circumstances to use the medium width of face because it is more legible. The condensed face is not as wide as the medium and is used when a caption is long and the space to be occupied is narrow. Because of the extreme difficulty in reading it, the extra-condensed faces should not be used except in narrow panels. The extended faces should be generally used where a wide measure be filled with a few words.

Display type requirements. Effective display type should possess the following characteristics: (1) the type should be legible, that is, it should be easy to read; (2) the lines of the face should be such as to make the letters easily recognized at a reasonable distance; (3) the type should be attractive, should draw attention by reason of its beauty and simplicity; and (4) type should have sufficient strength in its lines to impress its identity on the reader without sacrificing anything to beauty. In most cases, the face should be strong enough to afford plenty of contrast to body matter.

Text or body type

Type for text or body matter should have one important quality, that is, legibility. Generally, either Old Style Roman or Modern Roman will fit the requirements for text or body matter. If at any time these two faces are not available, pick a face that has their general characteristics for legibility.

Faces of type

While legibility is generally the most important single factor which should be considered in a choice of a type face, there are other factors which should also be evaluated. As an example, one of the other more important factors is color or weight. Some faces print very dark and some print very light; between these two extremes are a whole series of different degrees of lightness or darkness which can be attained by the careful selection of a type face.

In selecting a type face, there are thousands of type faces from which to choose and additional ones are being developed each year. However, there is no reason to know the names of all of these because each printer has only a limited number of type faces, depending upon the kind of equipment and facilities he might have. As an example, Lanston faces are made by the Lanston Company and are for use on the Lanston Monotype machine. This is also true with the Ludlow machine and some of the other kinds of monotype equipment.

Some of the other major type manufacturers are: American Type Founders, Neon Type Foundry, Mergenthaler Linotype Company, Baltimore Type and Composition Company, Bauer Type Foundry, Inc., Los Angeles Type Foundry, and Intertype Corporation.

Regardless of which of these companies designs and manufactures the type face, the faces of type may be divided into two major classes. These are the old-style group and the modern group.

The old-style group was designed originally in the 15th century to duplicate the writing in Italian books. As a result, these faces have a rich look because the serifs (strokes which finish off the letters) are slanting and the loops of the letters are not mathematically correct. The large curves in the capital letters also change from thick to thin on a gradual basis. Some of the faces of type which have old-style faces include: Garamond, Cheltenham, Caslon, Goudy, Kennerley, Hess, Old Style, and Cloister.

The modern group was started in Italy by Giambottista Bodoni in the early 19th century. It was based not on handwriting but upon what Bodoni believed would make a legible type.

As a result, the serifs are not slanting but are at right angles to the stroke, the loops are closer to being mathematically correct, and the contrast between the thick and thin strokes is pronounced instead of on a gradual basis as is the case in the old-style group.

During the ensuing years, many imitators have copied and adopted the kind of typography which Bodoni developed. Among some of these are such ones as: Bookman, Bodoni, Century, Clearface, Scotch, Perpetua, and Modern Roman.

There are a number of type faces, i.e., Futura, Franklin, and Gothic, which have no small finishing strokes or serifs. These type faces without serifs provide a clean-cut appearance which can be used effectively to display modern styles.

While the above broad classification of type faces might seem to indicate that the job of finally deciding on a specific face is an extremely complex one, it is not as difficult as it might appear.

In the first place, the selection of type is a matter of common sense, and by answering such questions as the ones listed below, the advertiser will, with the help of a printer, be able to resolve which of several faces of type will be best suited for the job. These questions include:

1. What is the size of the advertising space?
2. Is the advertisement appealing primarily to women or men? (If it appeals primarily to men, the type should generally create a more rugged appearance.)
3. What faces of type are generally used in the publication in which the advertisement is to appear?
4. In what manner can harmony be secured through the use of a special type face?

5. What are the type faces with which the readers of the advertisement are familiar?
6. How are the different type faces correlated to the subject matter of the advertisement?

Finally, in selecting a type face it is well to keep in mind that when there is any doubt in the matter, it is generally better to use the standard faces. These standard type faces are more legible, and the readers are usually more familiar with them.

Lines of type per inch

Another problem in selecting type is to determine the amount of type that can be set in a given space. Figure 10–4 gives the number

FIGURE 10–4
Lines of type per inch

Size of type	Set solid no. of lines	2-point leaded no. of lines
5-point.............	14	10
5½-point...........	13*	9*
6-point.............	12	9
8-point.............	9	7*
10-point...........	7*	6
12-point...........	6	5*
14-point...........	5*	4
18-point...........	4	3*

of lines of various sizes of type that will set within an inch. The asterisk (*) means that the size of type does not divide evenly into 72 points (number of points per inch) and that a fraction of a line is left over.

Use of small type for body type

Small type should not be set in lines which are too wide. It is extremely trying to the eye to follow line after line of small type across a wide page. It is generally advisable not to set the following sizes of type in measures wider than indicated below:

> 5-point not over 10 picas wide
> 5½-point not over 10 picas wide
> 6-point not over 12 picas wide
> 8-point not over 16 picas wide
> 10-point not over 22 picas wide

Twelve-point type or larger can usually be read with ease in lines of any reasonable length.

Measuring advertising space

Two units are used in measuring advertising space in publications: (1) the column inch, and (2) the line. A column inch is a space 1 column wide and 1 inch deep—not a square inch. It must be borne in mind that a column is not an exact unit because different publications have different column widths.

The "line" is actually an agate line and is equivalent to a space 1/14-inch deep and 1 column wide. It is derived from the agate size of type. There are 14 agate lines to the inch. When one speaks of a 100-line advertisement, it is necessary to divide 100 by 14 in order to determine the column depth in inches. The "column inch" and the "line" are units used for measuring the depth of advertisements. Publications may use either of these two measures for quoting prices for space.

Engravings

Relief printing plates

There are three main kinds of relief printing plates: (1) line engravings or zinc etchings, (2) halftone engravings, and (3) wood engravings. Line and halftone engravings are classed as photoengravings or process engravings. Photoengraving is a process by which a design or image is transferred, by means of photography, to a metal plate by having portions of the surface etched or cut away by chemical and mechanical actions.

The general principle of making photoengravings for printing purposes is to put a design or image on a metal plate and to cut away—by hand, by machinery, or with acid—such portions of the plate as are not to appear in the finished illustration. This leaves the design standing in bold relief.

Line engravings or zinc etchings. Line engravings, often called zinc etchings, can be made by the photoengraving process from any drawing or print that consists of distinct lines, dots, or masses of solid black such as pen, crayon, or charcoal drawings. Each line, dot, or solid mass in the drawing is represented by a line, dot, or mass of exactly the same shape and relative size on the printing surface of the plate. The best copy for the zinc etching process is made with black ink on a white surface. Illustrators generally use India ink for their drawings, as it produces clear black lines even when drawn fine. Grey or shaded effects must be obtained by numerous lines or dots placed closely together, but each line or dot must be a distinct black character in itself. Strong red, dark green, or dark blue lines or dots can be reproduced. However, these colors are considered poor copy by the engraver because they are not sufficiently intense to photograph clearly.

Combination line and halftone plates. There are advertisements which, by their very nature, demand illustrations which can only be produced by combining line engravings and halftones in the same plate. As an example, it might be necessary to use several products in which it is desired to reproduce exact photographic likeness. In order to get the desired atmosphere around these photographic illustrations, it might be easier to use pen-and-ink drawings and then combine the halftone with the line engraving. These combinations also can be satisfactorily used in a variety of situations, such as in fashion drawings and ornamental decorations in which photography might be inserted for background effect.

The Ben Day process. Many mechanical methods have been devised for the purpose of reproducing shaded effects and backgrounds in extended areas of space. One of these mechanical methods is that known as the Ben Day process. Through the use of the Ben Day process, tints are transferred from a celluloid film to the surface of paper, metal, or lithographic stone. By means of this process, line spaces can be given the necessary highlights which will give the appearance of halftones. A wide variety of textures and designs may be secured with the Ben Day process.

Electrotypes. Electrotyping is a process by which type forms and engraved plates are duplicated. The original line engravings and halftones have a limited life when put on the printing press, and eventually must be replaced. To save this expense, it is often advisable to make electrotypes and use these on the printing press, saving the original engravings which are more costly. It is also desirable to have more than one engraving of an individual illustration.

In electrotyping, an impression of the type form or engraving is made in wax or other material, and on this impression the metal is deposited by an electrical process, thus making an exact reproduction of the original. Unlimited numbers of electrotypes may be made from an engraved plate without injury or wear to the original.

Plastic plates. Plastic printing plates are made from a granular plastic material. They can be made in large quantities at a relatively low cost and are not so expensive to mail as electrotypes. They are quite durable, are not easily scratched, and require less ink than metal plates.

Mortises. A mortise is a hole cut through, or a notch cut in, the edge of the plate to permit the insertion of type matter. The first type of mortise is known as an inside mortise; the notch on the edge of the plate is called an outside mortise.

When a drawn border is used to add to the effect of an advertisement, the border is usually engraved on the plate, and the part intended for the type is mortised out. In advertisements carrying coupons, the electrotype often is mortised out so that different identifying characters, such as box or street numbers, may be inserted.

Matrices or "mats." Matrices or "mats" as they are called, are a cardboard-like composition material on which has been impressed, under high pressure, a faithful reproduction of the original plate. The original plates and electrotypes cannot be bent without damage. They are made for "flat bed" presses. However, newspapers and other media often use rotary presses. Therefore, when rotary presses are used, the plate must be capable of being curved so that it can be fitted on the rotary press. National advertisers also find it more economical to have matrices made and sent to the newspapers instead of plates.

Color

The vivid reproductions that can now be secured through the use of color combinations have resulted in getting advertisers to use color more extensively in their advertising. However, the media charge a premium when color is used.

With so many advertisers using color in some publications, a black-and-white advertisement will sometimes prove to be a real contrast and may get a higher readership rating.

Selection of colors

Decide on the purpose of the design and choose the colors accordingly. Choose colors that have proper association. In choosing colors, be prepared to make some sacrifices. The combination that has the greatest legibility may not be the most pleasing (black letters on yellow have the greatest legibility).

If one desires a pleasing combination, it may be necessary to sacrifice distinct legibility (yellow and blue combinations are generally preferred).

As a single color, blue is the favorite with men and red is the favorite with women. For example, in choosing a color for advertising a refrigerator, note that while red is the favorite with women, it may have the wrong association. The ideal dominant color to use might be blue. It has the proper association and ranks second with women and first with men.

Remember that colors may look totally different under artificial illumination than when viewed in daylight. At night, dark blues and purples may appear nearly black, red and yellow may appear more yellow, and yellow will be added to greens. Use large light areas in illuminated advertisements, and remember that value difference between letters and background is of utmost importance for legibility.

As a general rule, complementary color combinations are more satisfactory to use for television and outdoor advertising. They are the most attractive combinations and are preferred by the greatest number of people.

Color process

When the four-color process is used, a separate halftone plate is made for the three primary colors—yellow, red, and blue—and also one for black. (See Figure 10–5.) In the three-color process (which is seldom used) no black halftone plate is needed, and in the two-color process work, any two colors can be used.

In making the plates which are used for the color process, a photo-

FIGURE 10–5
Reproducing the full-color illustration

There are many advantages in using four-color reproductions for advertising purposes. Among the more obvious is the ability to show the product, or person, in "living color"! But beyond this there is a further advantage in that a color illustration not only has variations in lights and darks (which do show up in a black and white) but also a variation in intensity of color which produces much more depth than can possibly be achieved in black and white.

It is possible to take a color photograph and by color correction create a negative which will give a passable print. In general, this process does lose a great deal of the sharpness of detail found in the original.

To produce the full-color illustrations as are typically used in magazines today, four plates must be made. This process is known as four-color lithography. A color print or transparency is broken down by means of a camera and halftone screen into the three primary colors, red, yellow, and blue. A new negative is produced for each of these separate colors and one for black is also made to enhance the detail.

Panel A shows the black-and-white illustration produced by the use of a color-corrected negative.

Panel B shows a proof of plate created from the negative made for the yellow color.

Panel C shows how the plate carrying the red color tones will appear.

Panel D shows the result when the yellow color plate is over-printed by the red color plate.

Panel E shows how the plate carrying the blue tones appears when printed alone.

Panel F shows the three primary colors combined by overprint-ing the blue plate on the red and yellow proof.

Panel G shows the black plate alone.

Panel H shows the completed four-color reproduction when the plate for black has been over-printed on the three primary colors.

Note the resulting depth of contrast, vividness and depth shown in this illustration as compared with the color-corrected black-and-white reproduction illustrated in Panel A.

In the four-color lithography process it is possible to achieve almost every conceivable color hue and value. It requires the skill of a trained camera technician and color-dot etcher, and is, there-fore, considerably more expensive than black and white.

This is the process which makes possible the excellent color reproductions which we see every day in our magazines and in other advertising material.

Panel A

Panel B

Panel C

Panel D

Panel E

Panel F

Panel G

Panel H

graphic method of color separation is used. The colored illustration is photographed with different filters in order to get the negative from which halftone plates are made. When these plates are printed in their respective colors and superimposed in the proper manner, the same colors in the original illustration will be reproduced.

Use of color

The use of color in all advertising media will continue to grow because:

1. The mechanical techniques in the reproduction of color in all media have improved.
2. Color provides a more accurate picture of how the product actually appears.
3. It can be used in an effective manner to get greater sales results.
4. It will attain generally higher readership ratings.
5. The additional cost of using color is not excessive in relation to the results which can be secured.

Questions

1. Briefly describe the illustrations you visualize which might have the best impact for the following products, and give your reasons:
   a. Ban Roll on.
   b. Excedrin Pain Reliever.
   c. Mazola Corn Oil.
   d. Zenith Chromacolor Portable TV set.
   e. Purina Dog Chow.
2. A large paper manufacturer used the same illustration of a girl examining a new type of paper in *Life, Reader's Digest, Time, Business Week,* and *Fortune.* Evaluate this policy.
3. Indicate some of the points to keep in mind in selecting an illustration if the advertisement is to appeal primarily to teen-agers.
4. In what way will the advertising appeal and the media affect the typography that should be used in the advertisement?
5. Select advertisements from current newspapers or magazines in which the following production techniques were used:
   a. Halftone.
   b. Line engraving.
   c. Silhouette finish.
   d. Color halftones.
6. Indicate when a company should use the four-color process in its advertising.
7. In the selection of color combinations, does it make any difference whether the advertisement is pointed to men or women? Explain.
8. Select from a newspaper or a magazine advertisements in which the illustrations that were used have appealed to the negative, obstacle, and positive aspects of the prospect's wants. Indicate whether or not some other appeals might have been more satisfactory.

9. Select three advertisements in which there are no illustrations. Give possible reasons in each case why no illustration was used, and indicate several illustrations that might have been used.

10. Continuity in a series of advertisements can be used by employing the same method of visualization in each advertisement and allowing the ideas to provide distinctiveness.

11. Explain how a person's background might affect how he would interpret an illustration used in an advertisement.

12. In the production of print and broadcast advertising what can be done to avoid the problems of which the consumers frequently complain. These include: intrusiveness, exaggeration, high-pressure selling and offensive advertising.

13. Point out what techniques might be used to get the consumers to have a positive conscious impression towards the advertisements to which they are exposed.

14. Interview a number of retailers and manufacturers in your area. Ask them to show you how they prepare their advertisements for both print and broadcast media. Also visit the advertising department of your local newspaper and ask the manager to give you the details of the production techniques used.

15. Write a brief statement of what you would tell an artist of the visualization you interpret for the following:

    a. *Automobile battery:* Where the good ideas on starting, start.
    b. *Trucking company:* We move families, not just furniture.
    c. *Home air conditioning unit:* It is so compact your neighbors won't even see how comfortable you are.
    d. *Soft-drink company:* Open a bottle and springtime breaks loose.

Case **ORAL B COMPANY**[1]
10–1 **Suggesting illustrations**

The executives of the Oral B Company requested that its advertising agency prepare an advertisement which was to appear in a 1977 issue of *Reader's Digest.*

The Oral B toothbrush was placed on the market in 1949 by a young San Jose, California, dentist. Since the end of World War II, he had pondered the need for a brush which could not only clean teeth but could cleanse and stimulate an area equally important to sound dental health—the gums. What he wanted was a "mouthwash" rather than a toothbrush. Hence, the name "Oral B."

Digesting complaints about existing brushes and suggestions for improvement solicited from dentists and dental schools, he proceeded to redesign a product which had not undergone a basic change in 150 years. By mounting 2,500 (three times the usual number) flat-trimmed, medium-soft synthetic bristles on a straight handle, he produced a remarkable brush. It could reach easily into heretofore inaccessible crevices and could clean teeth more effectively. The same

---

[1] Used with permission of Clark Lawrence, President, Long Advertising, Inc.

brush could also massage gums without injury to delicate tissues. This was a vital point in tooth care which had never before been emphasized to the public. It was this feature which established Oral B as a new standard in toothbrush design.

Initially, the young San Jose dentist had a small supply of the brushes made for some of his patients and a few fellow dentists, who were enthusiastic. As a result, they began prescribing the new brush for their own patients. Requests became so numerous that it was decided to manufacture them in quantity.

Detailing by mail

The fledgling company was on the threshold of a highly competitive field, operating on a very limited budget, and the new toothbrush was just catching on with dentists. Long Advertising, Inc., was then contacted, and a modest advertising program was directed toward the dental profession. This effort included informative folders, catalog sheets, letters, a heavy detailing operation, and attendance at as many dental conventions as the time of Oral B sales representatives would permit. Using prescription pads bearing the product name, dentists began sending patients to drugstores for the new Oral B toothbrush.

Dentists force distribution

Consequently, wholesalers began to stock the product, and druggists, who normally would be reluctant to add a new product to the thousands already in stock, began to display and sell Oral B. From the start, a policy was established to win over the druggists as well as the dentists. This was done by establishing a fair-trade price which provided an ample profit on each sale. Another attractive feature was the small quantity which druggists could purchase, which contrasted with other similar products. The small compact displays took up very little room and sold rapidly, keeping inventory at a minimum. Thus, with simple methods and minimum expense, Oral B successfully moved into the toothbrush market through the side door.

Advertising starts with the dental profession

In 1950, a small advertising campaign was launched in state dental journals, and even more emphasis was placed on attendance at all major dental meetings. As sales rose sharply, exhibit booths were maintained at all major conventions. In 1967, over half a million professional samples were sent out to dental hygienists, assistants, dental students, and dentists. Scholarships and grants to dental colleges and the American Dental Association are also a part of the Oral B Company's continuing cooperation with the profession.

In 1951, the dental journal program was expanded to include national coverage, a step which combined with dental and drug detailing to bring about three results: (1) a sharp incense in sales, (2) the interest of larger wholesalers, (3) the appearance of major competition.

Since 1951, nearly all major toothbrush manufacturers have entered the market with some version of the soft-bristle brush. However, with the advantages of being first with the brush, plus marketing lead time and strong professional support, the original promotion plan was continued and intensified.

Consumer advertising initiated

Starting in 1952, consumer advertising got a modest start after a careful survey among dentists to confirm the hope that they would approve this step. Most dentists questioned were enthusiastic, and so a consumer campaign was launched. Every precaution was taken to keep the dentist and his philosophy clearly in mind while developing the consumer approach.

Although national magazines have been the backbone of the consumer program, radio, television, and newspapers also have been used effectively to achieve special marketing objectives. The policy has been to evaluate all major media annually and make changes whenever greater advertising effectiveness would result.

While the Oral B toothbrush has moved up to the number-one position in California (the nation's top drug market) and the West, and joined the top three brands in drugstore sales nationally, the Oral B Company learned these valuable lessons:

1. Good distribution can be achieved without huge cost. The device in this case was seeking sales for a good product through dental prescription.
2. Ethical groups (dentists, in this case) are not so opposed to consumer advertising as is often supposed. They object mainly to misleading and fraudulent claims, but will back an educational approach placing them and their profession in a good light.
3. The low-pressure, ethical type of approach in both trade and consumer advertising can get good results, even in a highly competitive field.

Current promotion plans call for adherence to the policies which have served so well in the past. This includes effective soft sell, relying on advice of the dentist as final authority, avoiding exaggerated or otherwise questionable statements, and a strong program of dental contact through attendance at more than 70 dental conventions annually.

Case questions

1. Suggest five illustrations to accompany the following copy A or copy B in a full-page advertisement which was to appear in an issue of *Reader's Digest*.

COPY A.   The right brush protects your gums, too!

Take the guesswork out of choosing a toothbrush and ask your dentist about Oral B. This brush does something about the fact that over 37 percent of all tooth troubles start with gum troubles.

The gentle message of 2,500 smooth-top Oral B fibers stimulates circulation to help you keep gums firm and healthy. The same flexible fibres polish teeth and clean hard-to-reach crevices.

Insist on Oral B for the entire family.

COPY B.   The 2d best thing you can do for your teeth

First visit your dentist regularly. Second, use the best toothbrush you can buy.

Ask your dentist about Oral B. Let him explain how effectively it protects gums as well as teeth. Oral B has three times as many smooth-top flexible fibers, to massage gums gently, clean teeth thoroughly. The double action of Oral B is the best mouth care you can have between dental checkups. The Oral B habit is easy to acquire. And so pleasant! Try Oral B today!

2. To whom should Oral B direct its appeal?
3. What should Oral B Company try to attain through its illustration?
4. Should the illustration be used to bring out special features in the toothbrush?
5. What should Oral B emphasize in the illustration of its product?

Case
10–2

CREATING ILLUSTRATIONS
Preparing descriptions

For each of the five advertisements in which the copy is given below, write a description of the kind of illustration you believe should be used to accompany the copy.

COPY A.   Magnavox
(this advertisement is to appear in *Reader's Digest*)

Turn your TV into the most exciting home video game ever.

Serve . . . return. You move to the net for a volley and, when your opposing player rallies, you stroke the electronic ball past him . . . for a point!

This is Tennis, played on the all-new Odyssey, the most-exciting home video game you can get for your own TV.*

Odyssey is high-speed action—and reaction—with realistic sound and on-screen scoring (Model 200).

You control the flight of the ball and pace of the games; games that are fun for the whole family: Tennis (singles and doubles), Hockey and Smash.

Put TV's fun and excitement on your side of the screen. Get—and give—Odyssey.

For the name of your Odyssey dealer, call 800-243-6100, toll-free. (In Conn.: 1-800-882-6500.)

ODYSSEY®
All new from Magnavox.

COPY B.   DeBeers
(this advertisement is to appear in *Ladies' Home Journal*)

You once said "I do." Now you can say "I'm glad I did."

The eternity ring.

Back when you got married, a wedding band told of that special, hopeful love of youth.

The diamond eternity ring tells of something even more special, more hopeful, for it symbolizes a love that's known the years.

The tradition of the eternity ring goes back centuries . . . to ancient Greece, where it first reflected eternal love.

Given on an anniversary or at the birth of a child, it takes its place alongside the engagement ring and the wedding ring, on the same finger, in the same spirit.

Because it's a man's way of telling his woman that if he could, he'd marry her all over again.

Your jeweler has a selection of eternity rings to choose from . . . full circles of diamonds or half circles, set in white gold, yellow gold, and platinum.
DeBeers Consolidated Mines, Ltd.

COPY C.   Manpower
(this advertisement is to appear in *Time* magazine)

Ready vacation replacement
skilled, experienced, specially trained office help
Call for the GIRL IN THE WHITE GLOVES from MANPOWER
The very best in temporary help

COPY D.   FMC
(this advertisement is to appear in *FORTUNE*)

Are we letting our fresh air slip through our fingers?

We don't have to. Methods for controlling many types of air contaminants are available and effective.

For example, an FMC process, incorporating use of hydrogen peroxide, is ridding communities all over America of their most troublesome odor problems—those caused by sewage. FMC is a world leader in the manufacture of peroxygen chemicals.

FMC also has a recently patented process for removing sulfur dioxide from utility and industrial power plant stack emissions. This advanced process permits use of high-sulfur coal, our country's most abundant reserve of fossil fuel.

Tell us your needs. FMC serves worldwide markets for environmental equipment, food and agricultural machinery, material handling, power transmission, industrial and agricultural chemicals. FMC Corporation, 200 East Randolph Drive, Chicago 60601.

FMC

COPY E.   Cluett, Peabody & Co. Inc.
(this advertisement is to appear in *Ladies' Home Journal*)

She started slowly.

First we let her check all Daddy's shirts for the "Sanforized" label.

Then she could go to the store and do the same thing when Mommy shopped for blouses.

After a while she even bought a fitted sheet.

See, everybody in our family follows these two rules:

You can't be sure the fabric won't shrink unless you see "Sanforized." You can't be sure of top wash and wear performance unless you see "Sanforized-Plus."

But I think Melissa's going to be the best shopper of us all.

Last week she was looking for some new blue jeans.

And the salesgirl said, "Well, they aren't actually labeled 'Sanforized.' "

Melissa bit her.

"WE'RE RAISING MELISSA TO BE SUSPICIOUS!"

part five

Media mix

11

MEDIA DECISIONS

Once the advertising strategy has been decided upon, the advertiser faces the important problem of bringing his message, or advertisement, to the attention of the appropriate prospects. It is obvious that the finest advertisements can be of no value to the advertiser unless they are seen and read, or seen and heard, by the potential buyers or users of the advertiser's product, service, or idea. If enough money were available, one approach would be to place advertisements "everywhere" and present them to everyone who might be a prospect, so that no matter where a potential prospect turned he would be exposed to the firm's advertising message. However, the amount of money that can be spent for advertising any product or service is limited, so this suggestion is not economically feasible. Hence, it is important to the advertiser that his advertising be placed where it will reach the largest number of real prospects, and influence them most effectively at the minimum cost. This task of deciding on the proper placing of the advertisement is called the selection of media.

Definition

An advertising medium is the means or conveyance by which the sales message is carried to prospective customers. A newspaper is a medium, as are magazines, streetcar cards, poster boards, matchboxes, television, radio, and the like.

Generally, no single medium will suffice in reaching all potential customers and, as a result, it is often necessary to use a combination of several media in an advertising campaign.

Types of media

The major types of advertising media can be divided into the 12 principal classes, which are listed below:

331

1. Newspapers
   a. Metropolitan
      Daily
         Morning
         Evening
      Sunday
   b. Rural
2. Magazines
   a. *Consumer*
      (1) General
      (2) General with specialized interest
      (3) Women's magazines
      (4) Home and shelter magazines
   b. Industrial and trade
   c. Service and professional journals
   d. Technical journals
   e. Farm publications
3. Television
   a. Network
   b. National spot
   c. Local
4. Radio
   a. Network
   b. National spot
   c. Local
5. Direct mail
6. Outdoor advertising
   a. Billboards
   b. Signs
7. Transit advertising
8. Motion pictures
9. Point-of-purchase displays
10. Specialty advertising
11. Containers
12. Miscellaneous (programs, directories, timetables, house organs, annuals, menu cards, registers, and the like)

Advertising expenditures in major classes of media

Some idea of the overall significance of the various classes of media can be gained from the allocations of total advertising expenditures as shown in Figure 11–1 for the years 1974 and 1975.

Selection of media

The problem of selection of the best medium or media for a particular advertiser will vary greatly, depending on the particular situation and circumstances in which he is conducting his individual business.

FIGURE 11–1
Advertising volume in the U.S. in 1974 and 1975 (76 ad volume may top $31 billion)

	1974		1975		
Medium	Millions	Percent of total	Millions	Percent of total	Percent change
Newspapers					
Total	$ 8,001	29.9	$ 8,450	29.8	+ 6
National	1,194	4.5	1,200	4.2	+ 1
Local.	6,807	25.4	7,250	25.6	+ 6
Magazines					
Total	1,504	5.6	1,475	5.2	− 2
Weeklies.	630	2.3	605	2.1	− 5
Women's	372	1.4	375	1.3	+ 1
Monthlies	502	1.9	495	1.8	− 1
Farm publications	72	0.3	75	0.3	+ 4
Television					
Total	4,851	18.1	5,325	18.8	+10
Network	2,145	8.0	2,325	8.2	+ 8
Spot	1,495	5.6	1,645	5.8	+10
Local.	1,211	4.5	1,355	4.8	+12
Radio					
Total	1,837*	6.9	2,020	7.1	+10
Network	69*	0.3	80	0.3	+16
Spot	405*	1.5	440	1.5	+ 9
Local.	1,363*	5.1	1,500	5.3	+10
Direct mail.	3,986	14.9	4,125	14.6	+ 4
Business publications. . . .	900	3.4	920	3.3	+ 2
Outdoor					
Total	345	1.3	340	1.2	− 1
National	225	0.8	220	0.8	− 2
Local.	120	0.5	120	0.4	0
Miscellaneous					
Total	5,284*	19.7	5,590	19.7	+ 6
National	2,760*	10.3	2,875	10.1	+ 4
Local.	2,524*	9.4	2,715	9.6	+ 8
Total					
National	14,755	55.1	15,380	54.3	+ 4
Local.	12,025*	44.9	12,940	45.7	+ 8
Grand Total	26,780*	100.0	28,320	100.0	+ 5.8

* Revised
Source: *Advertising Age,* December 29, 1975, p. 34.

A small manufacturer of an industrial product that is a component
or fabricated part of one particular industry in a field with only one
trade publication would have a relatively simple media selection
problem. He would use the trade publication going to the people in
that particular industry, and his problem would be to decide on the

size and frequency of his insertions. In addition, he might, and probably would, use direct-mail advertising.

In contrast, a large manufacturer of a nationally distributed consumer product that is widely used by many types and classes of people faces a complex problem in selecting media. He could conceivably reach a large share of his potential market through any one of the major mass media—television, radio, newspapers, magazines, and outdoor advertising. And even after he determines the basic type of media to use, he has a problem of selecting the specific class of individual publication or station within the type. For instance, should he decide that magazines are his best medium, he must decide whether to use general magazines, general magazines with special interest, women's magazines, or home and shelter magazines. And if he decides to use home and shelter magazines, he must decide whether to use *Southern Living, Better Homes and Gardens, House Beautiful, Ladies Home Journal, Good Housekeeping, American Home,* or *Home & Garden.*

It should be apparent from the above discussion that there is no simple formula or rule for solving the problem of the selection of media. Each advertiser faces a unique situation with respect to his particular market and marketing program. Each type of medium possesses certain characteristics, advantages, and weaknesses from the individual advertiser's standpoint. Hence, in general, it can be said there is no medium that is the best for all similar firms. The individual advertiser must determine on the basis of his specific needs in a given situation which medium or media are best for him.

Factors influencing selection of media

A number of factors influence the decision of the advertiser and must be considered in the selection of media. The most significant of these factors are: (1) the product, (2) the potential market, (3) the extent and type of distribution, (4) the objectives of the campaign, (5) the type of message or selling appeal, (6) the budget available, (7) competitive advertising, (8) and the character of the media: (*a*) circulation or coverage, (*b*) the audience reached, (*c*) relative cost, and (*d*) miscellaneous factors. These factors will be discussed individually in the following pages, but it should be kept in mind that in many cases it is the combination of these factors that determines the selection of media, and not any one individual factor taken by itself.

The product

The characteristics of the product exert an important influence on the decisions involving which media shall carry the advertising message. Certain consumer products of an intimate nature may find it difficult to employ certain of the mass media without encountering the danger of antagonizing large portions of the public, including those who are potential customers, although in recent years most media are becoming extremely liberal in their criteria for accepting advertisements. Certain individual media will not take advertising for certain specific classes of products. For example, some family-type magazines do not carry liquor or cigarette advertising, and at present TV does not accept "hard liquor" or cigarette advertising. Restrictions also may prohibit use of certain media by advertisers of specific items. The general character of the product may also strongly influence the type of media used. That is, if the product has a certain personality or image, certain media may be appropriate to maintain or develop that image; whereas other media may tend to diminish or distort this personality or image.

Similarly, product personality would influence very strongly the decision as to the class of broadcast program or magazine selected to carry the advertisement.

The potential market

The characteristics of the potential market are of primary importance in influencing the selection of media. Since the principal object in selecting media is to find a vehicle that will carry the advertiser's message to the potential buyer most economically and effectively, it is quite apparent that this statement is true. It is evident that one of the first aspects of the selection of media is the proper identification of the potential users of the product or service, or in other words, the market. The marketing research studies conducted by the advertiser should have collected data regarding the nature of the market and a profile of potential users. And considerable data is available on the audiences reached by the various types of media and by the individual media within these types. However, it will be found that it is usually quite difficult in practice to match closely the market the advertiser's research has delineated, and the audience reached by any of the media, particularly in the case of mass media.

If the advertiser's product is one which goes to a limited and easily identified segment of the market, the problem of media selection may not be too complex. For instance, if the product is one sold only to poultry raisers, or to yachting enthusiasts, or to superintendents of hospitals, there will be one or only a limited number of magazines reaching the bulk of members of these groups, and the magazines normally are subscribed to only by prospects.

However, for most products, the market is not so easily identified and is not such a specific segment; and the media reaching prospects also reach many somewhat similar people who do not fit closely the profile of the advertiser's market. Most mass media reach a rather diversified group of consumers and, hence, involve a considerable amount of waste circulation for any particular advertiser. The individual media do, of course, reach somewhat different groups of consumers. In the case of newspapers, the audience will vary with the editorial and news policy of the paper. Although television and radio for the most part are also mass media and reach a broad spectrum of consumers, the individual stations in some instances do vary in the audience they attract. The general character of the programs presented by the station is a determinant of the type of audience it attracts. Some radio stations emphasize symphonic and classical music, high-quality plays, and educational programs; some feature popular music; some stress news; others will strive to cover a wide range of popular programs. Each may attempt to attract a somewhat different audience, and often will conduct studies of the character of its audience in order to provide the advertiser with the information to match against a profile of his potential customers.

Some magazines are also more selective in the audiences they reach. The trade and professional journals reach rather specific and specialized audiences. There are consumer magazines that go to groups interested in specific hobbies or sports or other special interest groups. Others appeal especially to women, to homeowners, to youth, to specific racial groups, or to certain religious groups.

Outdoor advertising is basically selective from the standpoint of geographic location only, although the specific location of posters within a city may enable some selectivity with respect to income groups.

In summary, it is evident that since the advertiser wishes to reach his prospective customers most efficiently, his problem is to identify them as accurately as possible in order to select a medium that will carry an effective message to them most economically.

Extent and type of distribution system

Another factor that must be considered in the selection of media is the extent and the type of distribution the advertiser has for his product. Generally speaking, there is no point in advertising a product to consumers and creating a desire to buy the product if it is not possible for the interested consumer to find the product in the outlets where he normally shops. There is little point in the advertiser's using national media if he does not have national distribution. Hence, an advertiser with regional distribution will generally not use national network radio or television. However, in some areas, regional networks are available. He may be able, in a number of magazines, to buy the regional editions if the regional edition coverage conforms quite closely to his distribution pattern. Generally, an advertiser with regional distribution will use various combinations of local media, such as newspapers, spot radio and television, outdoor, and car cards. The same is true for an advertiser who has national distribution, but whose distribution varies widely in intensity. He may find it better to use local media so that he can exert more intensive advertising effort in those areas with the best distribution coverage.

Even on a local basis, the distribution pattern may influence media selection. An advertiser with good outlet coverage within a large city may have rather weak distribution in the suburbs and surrounding area, and find that some of the local media such as particular radio and television stations have a large share of their audience in the outlying suburbs. In this case, the advertiser might decide that the purchase of time on these stations would involve too much waste circulation to make them effective media from a cost standpoint.

The objectives of the campaign

This factor, the objectives of the campaign, is in some respects quite closely related to the preceding factor. For, in those cases when the advertiser uses a medium to advertise to consumers in an area where retail distribution is not adequate, so that he can use the effect of the advertising to obtain distribution, his decision on media selection is influenced both by his distribution pattern and the objectives he has in mind. His decision on media is influenced by what he hopes to achieve with this particular campaign of advertising. Where the objective of the advertising campaign is primarily to influence consumers, the factor of the potential market is of primary importance. In those cases where the objective is to gain distribution in an area where distribution is weak or where the advertiser now has no distribution, the advertiser must consider the media which will be of maximum value in achieving the dual purpose of influencing the consumer and the potential dealers. In some instances, advertisers have used costly television spectaculars because of the impact on dealers, realizing that, although the program will obtain a fairly good consumer audience, it is not the most efficient medium for reaching the potential customers. Also, in some cases an advertiser may use a specific medium solely for its impact and effect on dealers. In the case of products for which the dealer is very important in the ultimate sale to the consumer, and far more significant than the influence of consumer advertising, the advertiser may select media primarily for the effect they will have on dealers and their support of his product. In this instance, the objective of influencing dealers will be the prime factor in the selection of the medium to use.

The objectives of the campaign also influence media selection from a somewhat different standpoint. An institutional advertising campaign may be run in different media than would a product advertising campaign for the same company. Some large companies sponsor high-quality television programs to carry primarily institutional messages, whereas they do not use this medium for their regular product advertising. A firm carrying on what Neil H. Borden classifies as public service institutional advertising might well use a general interest magazine to carry such an advertisement, although it would not find such magazines a good medium for its product advertising.

In a similar vein, firms sometimes wish to create a better climate or market for their securities, and run advertisements in media reaching security analysts, brokers, bankers, and other financial people who are of influence in this field, although such media do not reach the potential buyers of their product.

Also, if the objective of the advertising is to create a certain image of the product in the minds of consumers, the media selected should have the status or personality to help develop and sustain that product image. Certain magazines are prestige magazines, and products may gain some reflected prestige by appearing in advertisements in such magazines. Similarly, certain television programs are prestige or "highbrow" in nature and, therefore, would tend to increase the effectiveness of advertisements designed to enhance the image of the product.

These illustrations should suffice to indicate that the specific objective of an advertising campaign will be of great influence in the selection of the media to carry the particular message.

The type of message or selling appeal

The type of message or appeal believed most effective in selling the product or service will, in many cases, dictate the type of media used to carry the advertising campaign. For example, if it is believed that fine color illustrations are significant in the effectiveness of product advertising, then magazines may be the first choice as a print medium, since their quality of color reproduction is generally superior to that in newspapers. If the feeling of timeliness and newsworthiness is an integral aspect of the appeal, newspapers, radio, and television are particularly appropriate media. For this reason, they are often used in advertising the introduction of a new product, a new model of a product, or a special promotional offer. If demonstration of the product in use is of particular value, television is the especially appropriate medium. If the product is one requiring a rather detailed explanation or long directions, print media have the advantage over broadcast media. If the product sells to a mass market and is so well known that the main objective of the advertising is to keep the name and package before many people, outdoor advertising would be an appropriate medium, with its advantages of large size and excellent color reproduction. Should the strategy of the appeal involve the desire to inspire confidence in the product and its quality, the advertiser might well select those magazines that have developed a high degree of reader confidence in the accuracy of their editorial content, such as *Sunset* and *Good Housekeeping* (which also has its respected Seal of Approval).

The budget available

Another factor that must be considered in planning the selection of media is the amount of funds available for advertising. For instance, a product might be one for which actual demonstration would be highly desirable, as would the prestige of a quality network television program at a prime evening hour, but yet the advertiser would be unable to sponsor (or even cosponsor) such a program because its cost exceeded his total advertising budget. Or the advertiser might believe it most desirable to use a four-color, full-page advertisement in *Reader's Digest,* not only to reach desirable prospects, but also to influence the trade, yet finds that his budget does not permit the use of this magazine. In the last case, his budget might be sufficient to enable him to buy, say, one four-color page ad in *Reader's Digest,* but he might feel that this would be of insufficient impact to accomplish his purpose, and that he could not afford the minimum effective schedule of advertisements. Thus, the advertiser must turn to a medium in which he can get sufficient participation or a sufficient schedule of insertions to achieve an effective program.

Competitive advertising

The pattern of competitive advertising in the various media is frequently a factor that should be considered in planning the media strategy. By analyzing the expenditure pattern of competitors in the various media, the advertiser can determine the relative evaluation of the different media by these competitors. Advertisers normally will place considerable weight on the fact that successful competitors place the bulk of their advertising in particular media. It is assumed they have done so on some sound bases, not only of evaluation of the product and the market, and other pertinent factors, but also of successful experience over time with these media.

Hence, unless there are good reasons to select other media, many advertisers normally will follow the industry pattern. In some cases, however, the advertiser may decide it is advisable to depart from the industry pattern. One of these cases often occurs when the advertiser's budget is so much smaller than that of the competition that he feels his advertising would be overwhelmed in those media being used by competitors. In this case, the advertiser should carefully analyze the possibilities of using alternative media that would reach his audience and in which his smaller expenditures might give him a dominant position for his product line. For example, the advertiser might, on the basis of other factors, have decided that magazines would be the preferred medium, but evaluation of competitors' advertising showed they all placed the bulk of their advertising in these same magazines and took a heavy schedule of dominating space. The advertiser might decide that his infrequent small-space advertisements would exert little impact. As an alternative, he might use outdoor and transportation advertising for his advertising program. However, the advertiser should be certain that the alternative media he selects do provide a satisfactory means of reaching his audience with an effective message.

The characteristics of the media

The preceding sections have discussed those factors involved in media selection that are of a rather broad marketing nature and involve the general strategy of media selection. In the following several sections, the discussion will consider factors that bear more specifically on the nature of the media themselves.

Circulation or coverage

The advertiser must consider the circulation or coverage of the media being considered in his media strategy. In the case of magazines and newspapers, this is a very clearly defined concept—the number of copies of the publication that are delivered to people, either to regular subscribers (usually by mail in the case of magazines, and by delivery boys in the case of newspapers) or by newsstand or street sales. Or in the case of some trade magazines of the controlled circulation type, the circulation is the number delivered to their lists of recipients. The advertiser is interested not only in how many copies are distributed but also in how closely this distribution fits the pattern of his distribution geographically, and how closely the type of people receiving it fit the profile of his buyers and potential buyers.

Reliable data on the circulation of most magazines and newspapers is provided by the Audit Bureau of Circulations (ABC). For the controlled circulation trade magazines, data is provided by the Business Publications Audit of Circulations, Inc. (BPA). In the case of broadcast media, the above concept of circulation is not considered applicable. (The usual basis of considering coverage of broadcast media is the audience, which will be discussed in the following sections).

One concept used today is that of the number of radio or television sets owned. One aspect of sets owned is in terms of the number or percentage of homes having at least one set in the home, while another aspect of sets owned is from the standpoint of the total number of sets owned by consumers in the geographic area being considered. In most areas of the United States at present, virtually all homes own at least one radio and one television set. As a result, the more significant factor is the multiple ownership figure.

Currently, the average radio ownership in the United States is more than three sets per home and approximately one and one-half television sets per home. This multiple ownership is particularly significant in the case of radio. With this great number of radios, 230 million in households and 91 million in automobiles and public places, the listening habits of Americans have changed. Instead of the family listening to the radio set in the home, as is still largely true in the case of television, each member of the family listens to his or her own set. This is particularly true in the summertime, when car radios and portable sets are used most extensively because of the pattern of living occurring during that season.

The audience reached

A factor that has become more significant in recent years is the number of people actually reached by a medium. More consideration is being given to the concept that the most significant aspect of coverage from the advertiser's viewpoint is in terms of the total audience potential, indicated not by the number of copies of a print medium circulated or number of radio or television sets owned, but by the total number of readers of the print medium or total number of sets tuned in, in the case of radio and television.

With regard to print media, this total audience potential is measured by the circulation of the medium multiplied by the average number of readers per copy. This factor has been stressed particularly by the magazines, many of which have conducted comprehensive studies to determine the total readership of their publications, both by those within the home receiving the copy and the pass-along readership by people outside the subscriber's or purchaser's home. This total readership figure in some cases varies appreciably even for magazines with comparable circulation. One other additional value of these readership studies conducted by or for the magazines has been the information they have provided on the characteristics of the readers of the magazines.

These data can be of great value in ascertaining how closely the readership characteristics parallel the profile of the advertiser's potential buyers. In the case of the broadcast media, the audience concept is normally expressed in terms of total number of sets tuned in to the particular station or program. Normally, this measurement is done with reference to a particular program, a portion of a program, or a time period, rather than a general one for a station or network as a whole. Here again in evaluating particular programs or time periods, the advertiser should not be dominated by the total audience rating alone, but should, to the extent possible, also consider the characteristics of the audience being reached. For example, an advertiser whose potential market was of a certain sophisticated nature, might well consider a program with a rating of 12 featuring a symphony orchestra superior, for his purpose, to a western program with a rating of 20.

It must be kept in mind in considering this factor that the audience of the different types of media cannot be compared directly because of the differences in the kind of advertising message reaching the consumer and the somewhat different terms in which audience is measured. The potential customer views (or watches and/or listens to) television, listens to radio, reads magazines and newspapers, and sees and reads outdoor and car-card advertisements. Hence, they are receiving different forms of communication in somewhat different circumstances. In most magazine readership studies, anyone who has read one item in a given issue is defined as a "reader" in measuring the total audience, which in a sense implies he has been exposed to all the items in a magazine. In the broadcast media, the audience is the number of sets turned on at a particular time. In the case of outdoor advertising, the audience is defined in terms of the people who pass the location of the billboard during a period of time from a direction enabling them to see the advertisement; and in car-card advertising, the number of passengers who rode in the vehicle during a given period of time. Thus, it is obvious that the audiences for different types of media are not directly comparable.

It should also be noted that the advertiser must use extreme care in using audience studies even when using data concerning only one type of medium. This is true because various studies measuring the total audiences of magazines may use different techniques and definitions of what constitutes a reader, and different studies of radio listening and television viewing use different techniques for measuring the audience of a particular program or station. Hence, the person evaluating media must be aware of these differences in the data being used.

Relative cost

The relative cost is another factor which influences the selection of media. As noted earlier, the total budget available and the ability to do an effective job of advertising with that budget in a particular type of medium is significant. When the type of media has been determined, then the cost factor becomes a matter of the relative cost of the individual media. In the case of newspapers, this relationship is determined by the use of the milline rate, and in the case of magazines, the cost per page per thousand.[1]

In the case of radio and television, when data are available, the comparison can be made on the basis of the cost per commercial minute per thousand listeners or viewers. However, it should be stressed that relative cost is only one factor to consider, and that usually many other factors will be more significant than this matter of relative cost. But in those cases where several media appear approximately equal on the basis of all other criteria used, then the advertiser probably would select the medium which is most economical on the cost comparison basis.

Miscellaneous factors

Several other factors sometimes enter into the selection of media, but are not of general enough significance to warrant lengthy discussion, although they may be of great importance in individual situations. For instance, in some cases the interest and confidence the readers have in a publication can be of real importance to the advertiser. This may be particularly true in the case of some trade papers, when no readership studies are available and where the quality of the editorial material may influence the attentiveness and care with which the editorial material and the advertisements in the magazines are read, and the influence they may have on the readers. The editorial content should be studied carefully to see if it provides a good atmosphere for the advertiser's particular product and advertisement.

The advertiser must also check on the availability of the time he desires, in the case of radio and television. In network television, for instance, there are only so many prime hours of broadcasting time. If the particular time or program the advertiser desires is not available, he obviously is precluded from using that medium in that manner. The same might be true in the case of spot commercials at certain times of the day.

When considering magazines, the advertiser might well check on the mechanical requirements, including such items as the use of color, the availability of bleed pages, the closing date for the advertisement

---

[1] Explained in more detail in Chapter 12, on newspapers and magazines.

to be in the hands of the publisher, the ability to handle inserts, the possibility of securing certain preferred positions in the publication, and the amount of premium charged for such preferred positions.

In some cases, the advertiser may also be influenced in selecting media by the amount of merchandising aid and assistance the media will provide for the advertiser in working with the trade in the area involved.

Responsibility for selection of media

A brief note regarding the question of who assumes the responsibility for the selection of media may well be in order at this point. The overall decisions for the general types of media are the responsibility of the top management people responsible for planning the marketing and advertising strategy and program of the advertiser. Since the question of the media to be used is so significantly influenced by the decisions on other aspects of the total marketing program, in terms of the objectives established, the funds provided, and others, the decision must be made by management people at this stage of the planning. The marketing and advertising executives should, of course, avail themselves of all the specialized knowledge the media people in the advertising agency possess, regarding the qualities, coverage, costs, etc., of the various media in arriving at their decisions as to the basic pattern of the media to be used.

Once the basic decisions as to types of media to be used have been made by management, the detailed decisions concerning which particular stations, programs, magazines, or newspapers should be made by the technically competent people in the media department of the agency (or company, if the advertising is handled entirely by the company itself).

Use of computers in selecting media

In the last few years, several of the large national advertising agencies have been devoting a great deal of effort and considerable sums of money to the development of a more scientific approach to the selection of media. Much of this effort has been directed to the development of mathematical models that will be applicable in making decisions regarding media, along the same general lines that models are being developed in many areas of business activity to aid in the decision-making process. Once the model has been developed, the use of high-speed computers enables the mass of relevant data to be processed, thus obtaining the media and media schedules that best fit the criteria laid down by the media people.

Several different approaches have been used in these programs. In at least one case, the system is primarily the adaptation of linear programming to media scheduling. Other organizations have developed somewhat different systems and programs. The general concept is to develop a model which includes all possible pertinent data relative to the media selection decision. Among the data incorporated in

the model are all available information on the media themselves
(such as rates, audience size and composition, duplication and accumulation among media), data on consumers and their buying habits
(such as demographic data on consumers, purchase rates, brand share
figures, any data available on probable consumer rates of brand
switching), and any data on the effectiveness of advertising in influencing the consumer (such as effect of repetition or number of
exposures, size of advertisements, and probability of switching
brands).

A general decision system is also developed. The data and decision
system are the inputs for the computer. The computer will then select
the media or media schedule that would give the optimum results for
a given expenditure of funds.

To date, limited information is available on the various applications of media models and computer use to media selection. The firms
using such an approach apparently are pleased with the results to
date, although granting that much data on consumers, their buying
habits, and reactions to varying types, amounts, and frequencies of
advertising are still lacking. In the present state of the use of models
and computers, it should be noted that the computer merely processes
the data and the decision system that the operator feeds into it, albeit
much faster than could be done by humans (and in some cases the
bulk of work is so great it probably could never be done except with
the use of computers). The media people must still tell the computer
how to do its work and make its selection. However, this quantitative
approach to media selection and scheduling holds much promise, and
will quite probably become a much more significant factor in the
whole area of media selection in the years ahead.

Summary

In the selection of media, the following questions are among the
more important ones which the advertiser should consider:

1. Does the medium reach the right audience?
2. Is the environment of the medium one that will produce interest
   and confidence in the products which are advertised?
3. What is the image of the medium in the minds of the prospects?
4. What is the purchasing behavior of the media audience?
5. What type of exposure can the advertiser hope to secure in the
   media?
6. How many people does it reach?
7. What is the accumulation of audience members by successive
   programs or issues of the printed publication?
8. How much duplication is there among the different media?
9. What will be the cost of reaching prospects in the different
   media?
10. What merchandising services are provided by the media?

11. How is the distribution of the product correlated to the circulation of the media?
12. What data are available to judge the media?
13. Will the budget of the advertiser justify the use of the media?

Since media charges generally represent the largest expenditure in the advertising budget, and the success of a campaign rides on sound media choices, advertisers increasingly are concerned with objective methods of evaluating media in their selection.

Questions

1. Would you agree with the authors' statement, "There is no simple formula or rule for the selection of media"? Why?
2. State in general terms the objective desired in the selection of media for an advertising campaign.
3. What is the significance of the changes that have taken place in advertising expenditures in the various media in 1974 versus 1975, as shown in Figure 11–1?
4. Give an example of a product being advertised in a particular magazine because of the nature of the product and the appeal used.
5. Give examples of advertisers using certain media because of the characteristics of the potential market.
6. Discuss the influence of the advertising budget on the selection of media.
7. How might the amount of competitive advertising influence your selection of media? Give examples.
8. Why do advertisers distinguish between the "circulation" of a medium and its "audience"? Under what circumstances do you think this distinction is important? Give examples.
9. Is it possible to compare one medium with another on the basis of cost? Explain.
10. What influence has the widespread use of computers had on media strategy?
11. If you were selling space for *Reader's Digest,* what data would you want before contacting a space buyer for a food account? For an automobile account?
12. An FM radio station in a metropolitan area, a "good music" station, stresses in its advertising that, although its audience is rather small, it is highly selective. It says most of its listeners are in the upper income brackets, and are two-car families, and hence its advertising cost per prospect is low. If you were the Cadillac distributor in that city, would this station be a more effective medium than the television station that reached almost everybody in the city? Why?
13. A salesman for space in *Playboy* magazine tells you that more women read his magazine than read either *Glamour* or *Vogue.* Assuming he is correct, would you, as advertising manager for a manufacturer of expensive, fashionable women's apparel, switch your advertising from *Glamour* and *Vogue* to *Playboy?* Why or why not?
14. A salesman for magazine space tells you, "Many people recall the magazine advertising campaigns for Volkswagen and Avis Rent-a-Car, but do

they recall any television campaigns as well? No! This is because print advertising is more effective and is remembered longer than broadcast advertising." Do you think this is true? Discuss.

Case   **GARRARD (Division of Plessey Consumer Products)**
11–1   **Planning Media Strategy**

Garrard has continued to be ranked number one in recognition by consumers of its brand of turntables, brand preference and intention to purchase. It was the only name in turntables that the consumers knew until recent years (see Exhibit 11–1).

One of its best products is the Garrard ZERO 100 automatic transcription turntable. The price list of the Garrard automatic turntable is given in Exhibit 11–2.

In deciding on the media for the current advertising campaign, the company believed that it should place special emphasis on the ZERO 100. While some of its competitors used television advertising, Garrard placed greater emphasis on stereo and audio magazines, such as *Audio, High Fidelity Magazine, Modern Hi-Fi, Stereo Guide, Stereo Review,* and *Gramophone*. It also used general specialty magazines, which included *Playboy, National Lampoon, New York Times Magazine, Scientific American, New York,* and *Opera Review,* and *Rolling Stone.*

Garrard ZERO–100 automatic transcription turntable

Incorporating practically every known plus feature in one automatic turntable, the new Garrard ZERO–100 unit introduces for the first time in an automatic a zero-tracking-angle device on the arm which causes the head to maintain practically perfect tangency to the record groove at all diameters. It is well known that a minimum tracking angle is one of the desiderata in any record-playing mechanism, but on all conventional arms, the tracking angle will vary from a value of as much as +4 deg. at the outer grooves to −1 or −2 deg. somewhere between the start and finish, then rise again to a value of perhaps +1 or +2 deg. at the innermost grooves.

Arms have been introduced that corrected this problem, but they were only for single-play turntables—never before on automatics. The importance of a near-zero tracking error is attested to by the number of such arms that have been on the market in the past and which no longer are. A little study of the problem of perfect tangency will convince anyone that a solution by the "parallelogram" types were not successful is that the increased number of bearings caused too much friction. Now, with the availability of improved types of free-rolling bearings, the same principle has been worked out with complete satisfaction.

EXHIBIT 11–1

Admit it.
It's still the only name in turntables
that <u>everybody</u> knows.

Not so many years ago, Garrard was the only name in turntables that *anybody* knew. There was simply no other quality product on the market.

Since then, a number of excellent turntables have made a name for themselves.

However — and this is the point we're trying to make — the balance of power hasn't changed all that much.

Can you name *another* brand that your mother, your grocer, your insurance man and your cab driver would instantly recognize today?

You know you can't. Garrard is still the only truly popular, universally respected name in its field.

Don't take our word for it, though. Ask the professional opinion surveyors. Their recent studies prove conclusively that Garrard remains

the best-known brand, regardless of age group.

In a recent nationwide survey of college students, Garrard ranked number one in brand recognition, brand preference and intention to purchase. Among adults, in a separate survey conducted by Psychology Today, it also ranked number one in brand recognition and approval, preference, and intention to purchase.

Add to that Garrard's current advertising campaign in Playboy, National Lampoon, Rolling Stone, The New York Times Magazine, Scientific American, New York and Opera News. Plus, of course, Stereo Review, High Fidelity, Audio and all the newsstand buying guides. Then draw your own conclusions.

Which brand is easier to sell? The one they *all* know or the ones they don't?

Garrard

Division of Plessey Consumer Products 100 Commercial Street, Plainview, New York 11803

EXHIBIT 11–2
Garrard Automatic Turntables (price list)

Turntable	Price	Base	Base price	Dust cover	Dust cover price	45 RPM automatic spindle	Spindle price
Zero 100c.........209.95		BW20	14.95	D20	7.95	LRS100	4.50
Zero 92...........169.95		BW20	14.95	D20	7.95	LRS100	4.50
82 ....119.95		BW20	14.95	D20	7.95	LRS100	4.50
70M..............109.95		Incl.	—	D10	7.95	LRS50	4.50
70 .... 89.95		BW10	9.95	D10	7.95	LRS50	4.50
62 .... 69.95		BW10	9.95	D10	7.95	LRS50	4.50
42M.............. 69.95		Incl.	—	D10	7.95	F45	2.75
42C 59.95		Incl.	—	D10	7.95	F45	2.75
40B 49.95		BW10	9.95	D10	7.95	FLRS35	2.75
Zero 100SB........209.95		Incl.	—	Incl.	—	—	—
86SB 159.95		Incl.	—	Incl.	—	—	—

A simple list of all the ZERO–100 features should serve to spotlight the changes that have been incorporated in this model of the Garrard.

> 15-deg. vertical tracking angle adjustment.
> Sliding-weight stylus-force adjustment—easily adjusts as little as one-tenth of a gram.
> Magnetic and antiskating control.
> Spring-loaded tonearm safety restrictor (lock).
> Long-taper variable speed control.
> Illuminated stroboscope with two bands of lines, one for each speed.
> Rotating manual spindle
> Proven "Synchro-Lab" motor—a combination of induction and synchronous types.
> Lightweight, balanced, full-diameter platter.
> Safe two-point record support.
> Handsome combination of chrome, brass, and plexiglas for tonearm mounting.
> Adjustments for arm lowering position, lifting height, and lifting-height restriction.

All of these features combined into one automatic turntable make news, even though some are found on other units. Only in the ZERO–100 are they all put together. Taking them individually, the vertical tracking-angle adjustment is a simple lever which has two positions marked "M" and "A." In the "M" position, the cartridge is tilted slightly so it is at the proper 15-degree angle for the third record of a stack of six, the maximum number that may be stacked on the machine.

The stylus-force adjustment is by means of a sliding weight on the arm, which is first balanced with the weight at "O" and then the

weight is moved to the desired stylus force. A movement of 1-⅛ in.
varies the stylus force by only one gram, so an accurate setting can
be made to any desired amount up to three grams, or even down to
one-quarter of a gram.

The antiskating control involves no mechanical linkage to the arm.
A simple slide on the fixed arm mounting serves to place a shield
between a fixed magnet and one mounted on the movable gimbal
which supports the arm. Separate calibrations are provided for conical and elliptical styli.

While most turntables have a lock to hold the arm on its rest, it is
usually a solid one, and lifting the arm could cause damage when it
is supposedly locked. On the ZERO–100, the lock is sufficently firm, yet
if the arm is lifted when locked, a restraining spring gives slightly to
remind you that it was locked, suggesting that you release it.

The variable-speed device on modern turntables usually employs
a tapered spindle on the motor shaft against which the idler wheel is
moved up or down to provide the speed change. If the taper is steep,
the idler contact with the shaft can vary, causing an unwanted wow.
In the new Garrard, the tapered shaft is long, with a gradual taper that
ensures good contact and allows a more accurate setting of the speed.
The two speeds are indicated by a built-in stroboscope—a series of
lines in the usual fashion, but placed on the underside of the platter,
illuminated by a neon bulb, and viewed by a series of mirrors from
the top of the unit. The two bands of lines allow accurate setting for
either speed.

The rotating manual spindle is now common on high-quality turntables and is now a part of the Garrard. The "Synchro-Lab" motor, a
unit which employs both an induction section and a synchronous section, makes the best of two worlds—quick starting and constant speed.
The platter is nonferrous, and is a lightweight conponent with a full
rubber surface for the disc, providing damping needed to support the
entire record surface.

In the ZERO–100, Garrard retains the reliable two-point support for
the stack of records. Once the stack is placed on the automatic spindle,
a plastic clip steadies the stack, yet allows the bottom record to drop
gently to the platter on a cushion of air.

The tonearm pivot mounting uses a gimbal for the two bearings,
and it is in a strong plexiglas structure which mounts the antiskating
magnet. Another magnet is mounted on the gimbal, and a shield may
be interposed variably between the two magnets to adjust the amount
of compensation applied. An indicator on the shield shows the settings
suggested for both conical and spherical styli, with the calibration
such that the setting is made to the value of stylus force applied by
manes of sliding weight on the arm. The arm structure accommodates
a variety of adjustments for setdown position and for lifting height,
together with another to permit adjustment of the amount of lift so
as to clear records remaining on the spindle.

The speed control remains similar to that on the SL-95 series, in
that the control has four positions—one for 45 rpm. seven-inch records, and three for 33⅓, with setdown positions for 12-, 10-, and 7-inch

discs. Under the knob is the vernier speed adjustment, which provides approximately 3 percent increase or decrease in the normal speed.

The operating controls also are similar to the SL-95B—three tabs: automatic start, stop, and reject; manual motor start; and cue, for lifting and lowering the arm.

Performance

The ZERO-100 performed as follows: wow measured 0.08 percent— that is in the band from 0.5 to 6 Hz. Flutter, in the band from 6 to 250 Hz, measured 0.03 per cent, both of which are excellent. The variable-speed control gave a range of a little better than +3 per cent on 33⅓ rpm, and a little less than that on 45 rpm. No change in speed was noted over a line-voltage range from 85 to 135 volts, but the expected change came when the line frequency was varied, due to the synchronous section of the drive motor.

While the skating of the arm should be much less pronounced with the near-zero tracking error, it can be shown that some skating tends to exist, but the amount is certainly less than that with conventional arms. This is probably the reason why the magnetic antiskating feature works so well. There is a difference in the sine wave shown on the scope when the antiskating compensation is set properly. Similarly, using the same cartridge on a conventional arm and on the ZERO-100 arm, a difference could also be observed on the scope. For all performance measurements, a Stanton 681-EE cartridge tracked perfectly at ½ gram, less that the pressure Stanton recommends. At 1 gram, it was less sensitive to floor vibrations, and a 1½ grams, not at all. Signal to noise ratio measured 41 dB unweighted, or, with the standard "A" weighting, 56 dB, using the CBS BTR-150 broadcast test record, which also supplied the 3000-Hz signal for the wow and flutter measurements. Arm resonance was measured at just under 10 Hz, and the change cycle required only 10 seconds from the completion of the last groove on one record to the setdown on the outer grooves of the next. Thus the Garrard ZERO-100 is one of the finest in a long line of automatic turntables which have been around for over 50 years. And as usual, each new model contains improvements over its predecessors, with constant research which strives to better performance, appearance, and reliability.

Case question

1. What media should Garrard use in its current advertising campaign?

Case **TROPITONE FURNITURE COMPANY**
11–2 **Use of media**

The Tropitone Furniture Company, a Florida manufacturer of high-quality aluminum frame patio furniture, is faced with the decision of firming the timing of its advertising program to achieve a more balanced sales mix between contract (hotel, motel, resort, restaurant, and club) markets and residential markets.

Since consumer (residential) media usually cost considerably more than trade/professional media, another objective was to do it as economically as possible without ballooning the budget.

Tropitone is what is known in the trade as "high-end" (top-quality) merchandise, with individual pieces ranging from $50 to $250. As a result the target residential audience was upscale (higher income, more education, and culture and travel oriented).

Buying Patio Furniture

The prospect of fuel shortages and higher costs of vacationing are giving many would-be travelers a new interest in making their own backyards and patios more attractive, more comfortable and enjoyable this summer.

Landscaping with new shrubs, flowers, and ground cover, and adding decks, canopies, and in some cases pools will be more in evidence. But perhaps the most frequent improvement will show up in the form of beautiful and inviting outdoor furniture arrangements that add a new dimension in family living space, plus a relaxed and informal area for entertaining friends.

Moving up to top-quality outdoor furniture often takes the residential buyer into new and unfamiliar territory. "First of all, we're talking about relatively expensive items," says James Baker, president of Tropitone Furniture Company. "Top quality furniture—something with style that will hold up well for five to seven years in heavy use, with practically no maintenance, and a lot longer with a little care—is going to cost anywhere from $50 to $250 per piece."

The higher price, Baker points out, generally results from higher grade materials and better construction. "For example, top lines use much thicker tubing, and the tubing bends are made more carefully, without flattening. Frames are welded together rather than riveted. Strapping is usually solid extruded virgin vinyl, with mildew inhibitors and ultra-violet stabilizers added. And the best finishes are used, usually pigmented plastic compounds that are applied in dry powder form by an electrostatic process and melted on to form a coating that's four to six times thicker than paint.

"When the homeowner looks at furniture like this, one really has to start thinking like the owner of a hotel or resort, because now one isn't just buying something to sit on . . . but making an investment."

For that reason, Baker points out, there are a number of considerations that become important to the purchase decision, which might not have seemed so important with lower-priced furniture.

"Delivery time is one good example," Baker says. "Most residential buyers are surprised to learn that the better grades of patio furniture are practically always made to order and not sold from dealer inventory. Delivery takes anywhere from six to 12 weeks, depending on which manufacturer is selected and when. This means if one wants to enjoy furniture in June, you can't wait until June to order it—March would be about the latest date."

Since most quality furniture is built to withstand rugged commercial use, Baker explains, most residential buyers will have their furniture for many years and probably will want to add to it in the future. "It's very important to select styles and colors that will stay in the manufacturer's line for a long time. If one buys a fad style or a strange color combination, it may not be possible to get additional pieces several years later because this particular style or color is no longer available.

"When one finds a style, ask how long that style has been available and how consistently it has sold across the country. Tropitone's Leilani series, for example, has sold well for 20 years now, and the Tropi-Kai and Pagoda series have been in the market for more than ten years. It's a good bet that durable designs like these will be around for a long time to come."

This doesn't mean that new styles should be avoided. Some new styles will become lastingly popular. Here, the best test is the manufacturer's past record. If the company already has a number of enduring styles, chances are good that their newest designs will have some staying power, too.

"In terms of color, Tropitone found that the most continuously popular finishes are white, light yellow, light green, and light blue." "Other colors—and right now it's the strong, intense basic colors—come into fashion for awhile then disappear. No furniture manufacturer can afford to keep offering colors that aren't in fashion, but they'll always have the traditional best sellers."

Another thing the customer should do, Baker advises, is to buy extra glides and matching touch-up paint from the manufacturer at the time the furniture is purchased. "The best furniture generally has nylon glides under all chair and table legs, because end caps of wood or metal usually wear out too fast. But when the furniture is used on flagstone or concrete patios, even nylon will wear out long before the furniture itself. Chairs and other pieces that are moved around a lot may go through several sets of glides in their lifetime."

Matching paint is a good idea, Baker says, not only to repair accidental nicks and scratches on the furniture, but also to create matching accessories. "Many homeowners like to add color-coordinated planters, lamps, wicker birdcages and other items to their furniture grouping as an extra decorative touch. A few cans of spray paint will open up lots of possibilities."

Buyers of premium grade patio furniture often prefer designs with rigid, welded frames rather than folding frames.

"Hinged fittings and joints can often be points of weakness," Baker explains. "With rivet hinges, the kind most often found in outdoor furniture, the rivet has a habit of enlarging its hole, working loose and falling out . . . especially when the furniture is frequently folded, repositioned, and moved around. Rigid frames usually last a lot longer."

The problem is aggravated where hinges are made with steel rivets, he points out, especially if the environment is salt air, as found at any sea coast area. "Salt air works to create an electrolysis wherever the steel meets the aluminum, dissolving the metals and leaving a white powder oxide residue," he says. "Rigid, welded frames avoid these problems.

"If the furniture will have to be stored seasonally," Baker says, "the buy should look for rigid furniture designed for stacking. Wherever more than two or three pieces are to be stored, stacking often gives even better storage capability than folding furniture because the stacking is vertical. Additional chairs don't gobble up more floor space."

When it comes to patio tables, Baker suggests using acrylic tabletops that look like glass but provide much more safety at about the same cost. "Plain glass is fragile and dangerous, and tempered glass can shatter under the right conditions. Cast acrylics, on the other hand, have 15 to 20 times the impact strength of glass, and can even support the weight of an adult standing on the table top."

Items that will be rolled about, such as serving carts and chaise lounges, should be equipped with large wheels four to six inches in diameter, he says. "These larger wheels may look a bit awkward at first, but they make moving a lot easier, especially over the rough planks, cobblestones, or pebble beds so often found in pool or patio areas. They also smooth out the ride, which is particularly important for serving carts.

"Before you make the final selection," Baker says, "don't forget to ask how your furniture will be protected in shipment. This is only good business on your part. Practically all furniture is delivered by common carrier, which means the handling is beyond the control of the manufacturer. Scratches, dents, and outright breakage are not uncommon. Protective wrapping or padding should cover all parts that are vulnerable to shipping damage, even though the entire piece may be enclosed inside a carton. This, of course, should be done at no extra cost to the buyer."

Advertising concepts

Since Tropitone had long been used and seen at such prestigious resorts as the Makaka Inn, the Newporter, Caneel Bay, Dorado Beach, even the MGM Grand, the products have had good exposure to a sizable cross-section of the potential consumers.

As a result, there appears to be merit in building upon that exposure by tastefully suggesting that if Tropitone was chosen for the best of resorts and hotels, it deserves consideration for the best of homes.

To reach the upscale residential market, Tropitone developed a campaign of fractional-page units in which the size, shape, and layout of each ad dominated the page. This space efficiency provided enough budget savings so that the company able to use top publications like *New Yorker, Sunset, Palm Springs Life, Better Homes and Gardens,*

EXHIBIT 11–3

Caneel Bay,
Dorado Beach
and home.

Tropitone outdoor furniture is seen in the nicest places. Not the least of which ought to be yours. And not terribly expensive. Seven handsome styles. Eighteen smashing colors. One dollar the catalog. Tropitone Furniture Co., Inc., P.O. Box 3197, Sarasota, Florida 33578 or 17101 Armstrong, Santa Ana, California 92705.

Tropitone Furniture Co., Inc.

Chicago, Dallas, Miami, New York, Santa Ana, San Francisco, Sarasota, Seattle, Houston, Los Angeles

EXHIBIT 11–4

Caneel Bay,
Dorado Beach
and home.

Tropitone outdoor furniture is seen in the nicest places. Not the least of which ought to be yours. And not terribly expensive. Seven handsome styles. Eighteen smashing colors. One dollar the catalog. Tropitone Furniture Co., Inc., P.O. Box 3197, Sarasota, Florida 33578 or 17101 Armstrong, Santa Ana, California 92705.

Tropitone Furniture Co., Inc.

Chicago, Dallas, Miami, New York, Santa Ana, San Francisco, Sarasota, Seattle, Houston, Los Angeles

EXHIBIT 11–5

Furniture for the Great Outdoors

Like yours.

People don't go on vacation to stay inside, so it makes sense to invest in outdoor furniture that adds comfort and style—without subtracting from profit.

And that's why Tropitone makes sense.

Tropitone's new Tenicote® finish is a lot thicker and tougher than paint. Frames resist bending, loosening or corroding because the heavy-duty aluminum is welded together—not bolted. And the vinyl straps are extra thick and specially fastened, so they last longer than a single season.

If you've already discovered that cheap won't do—or don't want to waste money finding out—write for our new 48 page color catalog.
Tropitone Furniture Co., Inc.,
P. O. Box 3197, Sarasota, Florida 33578 or
17101 Armstrong, Santa Ana, Calif. 92705.

This is part of Tropitone's Cantina line—one of seven exacting collections of outdoor furniture, available in 18 absolutely dynamite colors!

BUSINESS REPLY MAIL
NO POSTAGE REQUIRED IF MAILED IN THE UNITED STATES

First Class
Permit No. 160
Sarasota, Fla.

tropitone
Tropitone Furniture Co., Inc.

P.O. Box 3197
Sarasota, Florida 33578

House Beautiful, and *House and Garden,* with the objective of enough frequency to make a continuing impression. (See Exhibits 11–3 and 11–4.)

To maintain a strong position in the contract markets, Tropitone use 4/C half page spreads plus an unusual die-cut insert in order to increase coupon return. (See Exhibit 11–5.)

Along with this kind of advertising Tropitone sent spring and fall "Story-starter kits" to editors of 60 trade and other publications, plus home furnishing editors of 270 major daily newspapers in order to expand the editorial exposure and reinforce the impressions made through advertising.

Case question

1. Develop a "time" schedule for the media you would recommend for the Tropitone Furniture Company.

Case **PHILLIPS-VAN HEUSEN CORPORATION**
11–3 **Developing media factors**

The Phillips-Van Heusen Corporation has had an interesting history and has been responsible for many of the innovations in the men's furnishings industry.

Phillips-Van Heusen came into existence as a result of the merger of two companies: D. Jones and Sons, founded in 1859 (who operated a chain of factories in Lebanon County, Pennsylvania), and M. Phillips and Sons, founded around 1887 (who at first operated a small plant located at the corner of Center and Norwegian Streets in Pottsville, Pennsylvania). In 1907, D. Jones and M. Phillips joined forces, and the new firm became known as Phillips-Jones Corporation. In July 1957, this name was changed to its present one, the Phillips-Van Heusen Corporation.

To understand the development and growth of Phillips-Van Heusen requires some knowledge and background of the evolution of men's shirts during the first half of the 20th century.

Around 1840, or just prior to the Civil War, the era of the starched collar, front, and cuff gave rise to the dickey bosom. The dickey bosom, with separate detachable cuffs, was an innovation in itself. Even the well-dressed gentlemen of that era, with a good supply of this separate bosoms and cuffs, had need for only a very few shirts. A further innovation was to have the necktie or bow tie sewn right in as part of the dickey bosom, so that the whole neck ensemble was of one piece. By 1850, this style of dress had all but vanished. However, its influence has persisted right up to the present day, and a shirt with a bosom and cuffs of a different color from the body is still sold as an item of high-fashion men's wear.

By around 1890, the collar-attached shirt began its rise in popularity. Ar first, its use was restricted to what would now be called a work shirt for use in factories and mills. As this era progressed, a man wore either a work shirt with an attached collar or a neckband type shirt which required a separate white stiff collar. Usually the neckband shirt was colored, striped, or some fancy type of patterned design. All-white shirts did not become popular until after the First World War, when fine broadcloth fabric began to be imported from England. Following the armistice in 1919, almost five million men who had the experience of wearing collar-attached military shirts were mustered out of the armed forces. The old-fashioned neckband shirt was definitely on the wane in popularity. As with other changes in popular taste, many old established companies refused to see this oncoming trend and suffered accordingly. One of the exceptions was Phillips-Van Heusen, the first major brand house to make and feature collar-attached dress shirts.

The year 1920 was a historic one for the Phillips-Van Heusen Corporation, as well as for the menswear field as a whole, for it was then that Phillips-Van Heusen brought out the Van Heusen collar and, as *Time* magazine stated recently, "revolutionized the entire dress shirt industry." The product was named for its inventor, John M. Van Heusen, who discovered and perfected a method for weaving cloth on curve and who applied this discovery to the manufacture of men's collars. By the use of this curvilinear cloth, he was able to achieve a graceful fold line, avoiding the unsightly gaps that occur when a straight piece of cloth is forced into a curve. In addition to this curving process, Van Heusen also perfected a method whereby a man's collar could be woven entirely in one piece, whereas normally, men's collars are manufactured from three separate pieces of cloth—a top and bottom piece of fabric with a liner between them. Thus was born the Van Heusen Century, the soft collar that "won't wrinkle ever."

Those men who still desired a neckband type shirt could wear a collar with the *look* of the old stiff formal collar, but which had all the *comfort* of a soft collar. Thus, 40 years ago, the Van Heusen brand name came into existence. It was some time before this, of course, that Phillips-Van Heusen began its expansion into other areas of the men's furnishings field. As far back as 1912, Phillips-Van Heusen became the first major brand manufacturer to produce men's sport shirts, and even earlier, around the turn of the century, they began to manufacture and produce pajamas. This was followed over the years by the addition of the other product lines that today make up the Van Heusen roster—1937, Van Heusen neckwear; 1950, Van Heusen handkerchiefs; 1951, Van Heusen swimwear and beachwear; 1956, Van Heusen sweaters; 1959, the company entered into retailing by acquiring a large chain of fine men's stores in the northeast; 1961, Van Heusen slacks.

By 1939, Phillips-Van Heusen had fallen from a once highly respected position as an industry leader to a low point in the company's history. Beginning in 1929 and throughout the Depression, the company had been in a steady decline. Promotion was spotty, sales slumped, distribution was careless, and little thought was given to the types of outlets that were carrying the Van Heusen line. Prestige dropped to a low ebb; the company had lost about $1 million and was operating at a deficit.

In 1939, Seymour Phillips became president of the company, and through his leadership revitalized the company so that it regained its former position as an industry leader. Since 1939, the company has never failed to show a profit. A high point on this road back was the winning of the coveted Army-Navy "E" award during World War II. Van Heusen was the first company in the industry to achieve this distinction.

Among Mr. Phillips' first steps as president was the improvement of the styling, quality, and durability of the Van Heusen products. To insure a continuing high standard of quality control, a testing laboratory was established in the Bronx, New York, plant.

Distribution was completely overhauled. The 11,000 accounts of *all* types then on the books were slashed to 1,000, and the job of rebuilding distribution with class menswear and department stores was begun.

In 1939, the advertising budget was $9,775. Under the leadership of President Phillips, this amount was systematically increased until the year 1949, when it passed the $1 million mark. It now surpasses $2 million.

Phillips-Van Heusen today employs over 3,000 people at its 12 factories and depots in Illinois, California, Washington, Georgia, Pennsylvania, and Arkansas. Last year's sales were over $55 million.

Advertising and sales promotion

In 1908, when national advertising in the United States was practically unknown, the Phillips-Jones Company ran a one-column, three-inch ad in the *Saturday Evening Post* for its Princely and Emperor shirts. Small and almost insignificant by today's standards, this advertising was, nevertheless, quite revolutionary for its time. This was an era when few manufacturers could envision the potential of brand advertising and brand selling.

The advertising department together with Van Heusen's advertising agency is responsible for a complete advertising and sales promotion program which includes everything from television commercials to packaging. The preparation of a Van Heusen national advertising campaign begins a full 12 months in advance. The first step is a preliminary meeting between the advertising director, the general merchandise manager, and the various merchandise and sales department heads. The purpose of this meeting is to select the promotions that are to be advertised and promoted nationally. The advertising director then meets with the agency's creative group to determine specific advertising concepts. The full-time job of organization and layout of the campaign then begins. There are many more meetings, and each progressive step is cleared with the merchandising and sales departments to minimize errors and eliminate possible deviation from the original concept.

The agency then prepares roughs or storyboards of the proposed ads and commercials, and presents these together with media recommendations to a special advertising executive committee consisting of the advertising director and representatives of Van Heusen's top management team. Once approval is obtained, the agency proceeds with the preparation of the finished commercials and places orders for the desired time and space.

All this effort finally culminates at a general meeting of the entire Van Heusen selling force, which assembles to view for the first time the merchandise and the advertising they will be working with during the coming months.

This presentation is made twice yealy—one presentation for the spring–summer and another for the fall–winter season. Each complete campaign is geared to the specific season in question and to the specific merchandise to be brought forth that season.

The Van Heusen sales promotion program is an extension of its national advertising and is based on the promotional themes or ideas developed for that national advertising. Sales promotional material is prepared simultaneously with art and copy from the campaign used, and is modified and tailored to serve the needs of local retail selling. This is a completely integrated advertising-sales promotion effort starting with Van Heusen selection of media, deciding on the appeal, and continuing right through to the all-important point-of-sale materials.

Case questions

1. What are the major factors which Phillips-Van Heusen should consider in selecting its media?
2. Analyze the Phillips-Van Heusen product line and marketing situation as it relates to the major factors that influence the selection of media.
3. What particular media would be most effective for the Phillips-Van Heusen corporation?
4. Which of the factors discussed above seem most important to Phillips-Van Heusen in selecting media?

Case **PINDAR COMPANY**
11–4 **How diminishing returns affect selection of media**

Pindar Company is a leading manufacturer of sleeve-type bearings and bushings for use principally in the automotive industry. Its products also are used extensively in the aircraft, farm equipment, diesel engine, and locomotive industries.

The principal products of the company are:

1. Bearings, bushings, and related products. Lined bearings and lined, plain, and graphited bronze bushings are manufactured in a wide variety of types and sizes for use as original equipment and for replacement purposes in internal combustion engines and in many other applications. Rubber-and-metal bearings are manufactured for use primarily in automotive chassis applications.

2. Electronic components and devises.   Artifically grown piezoelectric crystals are produced and sold for use in phonograph pickups, microphones, headphones, hearing aids, sonal and underwater listening devices, and other acoustical products. Analyzing and recording instruments, including direct-writing oscillographs, amplifiers and strain, surface and general purpose analyzers, are manufactured for industrial and research use.

The customers of the company include manufacturers of automotive original equipment, aircraft engines and equipment, railroad locomotives, engines and engine parts, agricultural machinery and equipment, and electrical machinery and equipment. The company sells directly to manufacturers, as well as through distributors, wholesalers, and jobbers of automotive parts and electrical products.

The following tabulation gives the percentages of total sales represented by sales to the principal classes of customers:

Manufacturers of:	Percent of total sales
Automotive original equipment	31
Aircraft engines and equipment	15
Railroad locomotives	5
Other engines and engine parts	11
Agricultural machinery and equipment	10
Electrical machinery and equipment	9
Distributors, wholesalers, and jobbers	19
Total	100

A major portion of the total sales of Pindar has been made to a relatively small number of customers. In the past year, sales to the three largest customers (manufacturers of automotive vehicles) accounted for 25 percent of total sales, while sales to the ten largest customers accounted for 46 percent of the volume. Sales outside of the United States amounted to 3 percent of total sales.

The bearing and bushing business is highly competitive. Pindar's competitors include not only other independent manufacturers of bearings and bushings but also certain manufacturers of equipment using such items who produce substantial portions of their bearing and bushing requirements. Automotive manufacturers will also sell bearings and bushings for replacement through their own outlets.

As a result, because of the intense competition, the advertising manager of Pindar had followed the policy of dividing his advertising budget so that the leading industrial magazines would be included for each of the major customer classifications. For every classification, he used three or more magazines.

It was his opinion that while such a policy resulted in some duplication of the reading audience, nevertheless Pindar was able to make a greater impact on its potential customers by advertising in the most important specialized magazines for the various groups. In the selection of the magazines for the automotive classification, as an example, he divided his budget in automotive trade publications as follows:

Publication	Percent of advertising budget
A	40
B	30
C	15
D	15

The representative of *Publication A* was dissatisfied with this division because his magazine was recognized as the leading publication in the industry. To show the Pindar advertising manager how he might be able to make his advertising dollar more effective, he prepared a chart (Exhibit 11–6) on "How the law of diminishing returns affects advertising media." He pointed out that it is uneconomical, under average conditions, to select more than one or two publications to cover the important potential buyers, because, as was indicated in the chart, the number of additional readers becomes smaller as each successive publication is added, and the cost of reaching these extra readers becomes proportionately higher.

He believed that with a limited budget, to divide an advertising schedule between the number one and two magazines in any industrial field resulted in too thin a coverage to obtain good returns from either publication. It would only be when two trade magazines had practically equal circulation, market coverage, editorial acceptance, and space cost that a split schedule on an alternate-month basis would deliver as much, or more, effectiveness than a full schedule in one magazine. It would have to be a very exceptional situation, in his

EXHIBIT 11–6
How law of diminishing returns affects advertising media cost for each additional publication

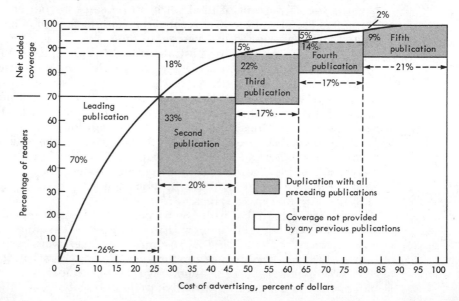

opinion, that would justify a policy whereby a company would adver-tise in more than the two leading publications.

Pindar had followed for the last ten years a policy of using the same copy for each of its principal product categories in the industrial magazines which were used for that specific line.

As an example, in the media selected for the automotive classifica-tion the advertisements featured an illustration of an engineer looking through a microscope examining a bearing with a headline, "A Pindar Engineer is Your Best Friend." The copy then stated that no other sector of the industry rendered equal service and know-how.

During the past year the advertising manager had received some negative feedback from a number of purchasing executives who said that it was annoying to them to see the same advertisement time and time again in several different industrial magazines. It was their con-tention that repetition turned them off and that no industrial ads were so brilliant and intellectually acceptable that they justified this exces-sive repetition. It was also their opinion that this practice of repetition resulted in significant diminishing returns because it discouraged them from reading any of Pindar's advertising.

Case questions

1. Evaluate the advertising policy which the advertising manager of Pindar has been using.
2. On what hypotheses do you believe that the representative of *Publication A* developed the chart for the "law of diminishing returns"?
3. What policy should Pindar follow in deciding on the number of trade maga-zines to use?
4. What should be the policy of Pindar in repeating the same advertisements in several different industrial magazines?
5. Would this law of diminishing returns operate the same way for TV, radio, and outdoor boards if similar studies were made for those media?

12

NEWSPAPERS AND MAGAZINES

*I*n the preceding chapter the authors discussed some of the significant factors involved in the selection of media. In this, and the following two chapters, the salient features of the most important media will be discussed briefly. This chapter will include the publication media, newspapers and magazines; chapter 13 will cover the broadcast media, television and radio; and chapter 14 will cover other media forms.

Newspapers

The position of the newspaper as an advertising medium seems secure. The newspaper has for many years been the leading medium in terms of advertising revenue. In 1974, advertisers spent $6,807,-000,000[1] on newspaper advertising, over 25 percent of all advertising dollars. About eight of every ten adults will read a newspaper on any given day. As of January 1, 1976, 1,756 daily newspapers were published, with a combined daily net paid weekday circulation of approximately 6,655,431.[2] Of these, 340 were morning newspapers, with a daily circulation of 26,144,966,[2] and 1,449 were evening newspapers, with a circulation of 35,732,231. There were 641 Sunday newspapers, with a circulation of 51,678,726.[2] In addition, there were 8,804[3] weekly newspapers, most of which are published in small towns.

Classification of newspapers

Newspapers are usually classified as morning and evening daily papers, Sunday papers, the Sunday supplements, weekly or rural papers, shopping news, and specialized newspapers.

---

[1] *Advertising Age,* September 15, 1975, p. 51.

[2] *1975 Editor & Publisher Year Book,* pg. 5.

[3] *1974 Ayer Directory of Newspapers, Magazines & Trade Publications,* pg. viii.

Daily papers. Most daily papers are evening papers, carrying news of that day's important national and local events, including business, entertainment, financial, social, and sports activities. Usually they have a larger relative readership by women than men. The morning papers usually have a wider geographical circulation (covering more of the suburban areas around the city) than do evening papers. They carry the news of the preceding day, with news coverage comparable to evening papers, and have a larger male readership than female. Individual circulation and reading audience characteristics should be studied carefully by media department executives, however, rather than selecting papers purely because they are morning or evening.

Sunday newspapers. One of the main characteristics of the average Sunday newspapers is its bulk. It has special sections with longer articles of specific class interest; the circulation of Sunday newspapers is ordinarily greater than that of dailies. Although the rates are higher, the per unit cost may be lower.

In using Sunday newspapers, the advertiser should check circulation figures to be sure this edition reaches the desired market. Since only 5.25 percent of the 10,800 weekly and daily papers publish a Sunday newspaper, this edition usually has a wider and more extensive circulation.

The Sunday supplements. Some 300 newspapers also have magazine supplements, or Sunday magazines, which they publish or distribute as a part of their Sunday papers. There are two kinds of Sunday newspaper magazines. The first type is the independent Sunday magazine, individually edited and published by a particular newspaper. There are approximately 90 such magazines. The second type is the syndicated magazine, which is distributed to many newspapers although it is centrally edited and published. These magazine sections use smoother paper stock than the rest of the paper and provide for superior color printing.

Some newspapers also have comic supplements that appear in the Sunday editions. These comic sections usually are edited and published on a syndicate basis, and the printed copies sent out to the subscribing newspapers. The advertiser can reach all the papers on the list of any syndicated comic supplement by placing one insertion order and preparing one set of plates.

The weekly newspaper. The weekly newspaper usually serves a small community and, on the average, has a circulation of only about 3,000 copies per issue. Because they serve a local and homogeneous population, and cover thoroughly the news concerning the local people and their problems, they usually have a very high readership —considerably above that of the average metropolitan daily paper. Thus, although their advertising rates usually are higher than daily papers on the basis of circulation, the thorough reading and longer life of the weekly may well justify such higher rates. As a rule, the bulk of their advertising comes from local advertisers.

The shopping news. In some respects, the shopping news is not a true newspaper. As a rule, such papers carry very little news of the type characteristic of the newspaper, and have a limited amount of editorial matter. Some publish a considerable number of pictures and stories of local events to increase readership and interest, although, for the most part, they carry only advertising. They are usually distributed free on a controlled basis, with the publisher determining to whom the paper will be distributed. Usually the publisher attempts to deliver copies of his shopping news to every dwelling unit in the shopping district of the area he serves.

Specialized newspapers. Although these papers are either dailies or weeklies, they usually are classified separately because they have a unique feature for newspapers due to their high selectivity in terms of type of audience. They serve special groups of people who usually have some close and common bond of interest. For example, some are published for certain religious or racial groups, or in a foreign language. Others are designed for specific labor or trade groups, for a specific political party, or to cover special fields of business, such as finance. Many are published by high schools and colleges for the students and staffs of their respective institutions.

Appeals

Newspapers are read hurriedly and have a short life, although they reach all classes of people. An advertisement in a newspaper is usually read but once, with the average reading time estimated to be less than 30 seconds. In this short space of time, the appeal must stimulate the reader into action. As a result, since one of the functions of this type of advertising is to produce immediate sales, the copy appeal is based generally on quantity, quality, and/or price.

On the other hand, the purpose of general or national advertising in newspapers is to create goodwill and acceptance—first for the product itself, and then for the merchants who sell it. Such copy generally should be direct and terse, because the average newspaper reader is not going to spend much time reading the advertisement.

Flexibility

Daily newspapers have great flexibility for an advertiser. The advertiser can reach his audience daily, if he wishes. It is possible to concentrate the sales efforts during the most profitable season, and then to thin out his efforts during slack periods. Copy can also be inserted, withdrawn, and changed within a few hours before the newspaper is printed.

Because of this flexibility, copy can be correlated to recent important news or local events. A sudden storm might necessitate a change in the advertisement a department store was planning, or the announcement of the passing of a new city ordinance might provide an appeal which would be more effective than one that had been planned for an advertisement.

In addition to this flexibility of timing, the newspaper also has the advantage of great flexibility from a geographic standpoint. That is, the advertiser can place advertising in only the particular area or areas he desires to reach. He can also adjust the amount of advertising he desires to use in a particular market to meet his particular needs.

The newspaper has people on the staff who can help the small retailer or local business firm who wishes to advertise with them. The services may include planning the advertising, writing the copy, preparing the layout, and providing illustrations. These services are available for all local advertisers, but are used primarily by the small retailers, since larger firms usually will have their own advertising departments or may use local advertising agencies.

Many newspapers also conduct research studies, the results of which can be helpful to local retailers as well as to national advertisers. These studies may be general compilations of pertinent data relative to the population and buying power of a trading area. Studies are also made of the newspaper readership and the coverage it provides of the population of the market area. Other studies sometimes made include surveys of consumer buying habits and brand purchase studies.

Many of the larger newspapers also provide merchandising aids for national advertisers. Frequently, this involves attempting to obtain more retail cooperation in displaying the products of the advertiser, using the point-of-purchase display materials provided by the advertiser, encouraging retailers to place advertising to tie in with the advertising of the manufacturer, or to push retailer use of the cooperative advertising allowances of the manufacturer.

Classified and display advertising

The advertising appearing in newspapers is divided into two major categories—classified and display. Classified advertisements are the small statements of fact that appear in special columns which have been set aside for that purpose. The columns are headed according to the class of advertisements appearing in them and from this get their names, classified advertisements. Display advertising, on the other hand, includes all advertising matter not included in the classified sections.

Advertising space and rates

Newspaper advertising space is sold by the agate line or column inch. The agate line is one-fourteenth of an inch deep and one column wide. The width of the column differs according to the publication, but is usually about two inches. The column inch is one inch in depth and one column wide. A column inch contains 14 agate lines. A flat rate is a rate of so much per agate line, regardless of the amount of space used or the frequency of use. Most newspapers also have a contract rate, in which the cost per line decreases as the number of lines used in a year increases, or with the frequency of insertion.

Preferred positions

Newspaper advertising is ordinarily sold by the publisher on a run-of-paper or ROP basis. Run-of-paper means the advertisement will be placed in the position in the paper that is most satisfactory to the publisher. The publisher naturally will attempt to use good judgment in placing advertisements, since he desires that the advertiser obtain the best possible results from his advertising. However, except for certain special pages, such as amusement pages, the newspaper representative will not make definite commitments as to the exact placement of advertisements at the time the advertiser places the insertion order.

If the advertiser definitely wants a special position in the newspaper, he can obtain it (assuming it is available), if he is willing to pay extra for it. Oftentimes, however, it is possible to obtain a specially desired position without paying extra by merely indicating on the insertion order "run ROP, this particular position requested." Then, if the advertising makeup man finds it feasible, he will give the advertiser this preferred position at no extra charge, although the publisher still has the right to run the advertisement where he desires.

If the advertiser insists on a special position, he may secure it in most papers by paying extra for it at a preferred or full position rate. An example of a special position often offered by papers is "full position," which provides reading matter all across the top and down one side of the advertisement, or places the advertisement at the top of the column with reading matter down one side. Such full position commonly costs from 25 percent to 50 percent above the ROP rates. Another commonly offered special position, for a usual rate of 10 percent to 20 percent extra, is known as preferred position. This guarantees reading matter all along one side of the advertisement. There are other special positions available in most newspapers. These often include pages 2, 3, and 4, and the sports, society, or women's page.

Readers

Some publications allow advertisers to set their copy in the same type style as the news matter. This gives the advertisement the general appearance of being a regular news story. Advertisements of this sort are run next to news columns. These advertisements are usually followed by the word "Advertisement" in small type. A higher rate is usually charged for this privilege. Some newspapers refuse to accept this type of advertisement.

Local and national (general) advertising

The two principal classes of newspaper display advertising are designated by the terms "local" and "national," or "general." Local or retail advertising is that done by an advertiser when he sells directly to the consumer through one or more local retail stores which he alone owns and controls. National, or general, advertising is that placed by an advertiser—not a local or retail advertiser, but usually a manu-facturer—advertising his brand of merchandise.

Most newspapers have a different set of rates for the two above classes of advertising, with the general or national rate usually ave-raging from 35 percent to 50 percent higher than the local or retail rates. Also, the national advertiser usually is charged a flat rate, whereas the retailer is offered a contract rate, with discounts for quan-tity and frequency of advertising.

The justification for this difference in local and general rates ad-vanced by newspapers is that the sale of general or national space involves high commissions or brokerage fees and other costs. Much national advertising space is sold through publisher's representatives who receive a 15 percent commission. Also, most national advertising is placed by advertising agencies who also receive a 15 percent com-mission for their work in creating and handling the advertising they place in the newspaper. In addition, the newspapers have extra costs in handling the national advertising which originates out of the city. This double system of rates has long been the subject of discussion and debate, but it still persists. It has caused advertising agencies placing national advertising, as well as national advertisers, to use all legiti-mate methods to take advantage of the lower local rates.

Special and color rate differentials

Newspapers in most cases also vary the rates charged for different types of advertising. For instance, the rate charged for political adver-tisements is usually different from that charged for an advertisement of a general nature.

Newspapers also charge extra rates for the use of color. In recent years, the use of ROP color in newspaper advertisements has devel-oped rapidly, and most daily and weekly papers now will provide color. Some provide only black and one color, some black and two colors, and a few provide black and three colors. Usually there is a minimum size space required if the advertiser wishes to run a color advertisement, the minimum commonly being 800 to 1,000 lines. Color advertisements above the regular rate for black alone will in most instances amount to the following: 25 percent for black and one color, 35 percent for black and two colors, and 45 percent for black and three colors.

The national advertiser who desires color reproduction comparable to that in good magazines can obtain such in most newspapers by the use of preprint color. This involves the advertisement printed on large rolls by a firm specializing in color printing, shipping the printed rolls to the various local newspapers which print the black impression, cut the roll to page size, and insert the preprinted advertisement in the paper. This normally requires a full-page ad, and costs the advertiser the paper and color production costs plus the regular space rate in the newspaper. There are several types of preprint production, varying somewhat in the special technique involved in the printing and inser-tion in the local paper.

The milline rate

When selecting advertising media, it often is necessary to compare the rates of several newspapers. Assume that the rates of two newspapers are to be compared. Each charges 50 cents per line. One paper has a circulation of 50,000, while the other has a circulation of 45,000. The rates are the same, and if all other points are equal, the one with a circulation of 50,000 is a better buy than the one with 45,000 circulation. However, in actual practice, the rates per line will be in odd cents, and the circulation figures will be complex. Therefore, in order to compare the rates of different publications, the milline rate is used. The milline rate of a publication is the rate per line per million circulation. This can be figured in two ways.

Example:

A publication has a rate of $1 per line, and its circulation is 500,000. $1 divided by 500,000 equals $0.000002 multiplied by a million equals $2. $2 is the milline rate.

The above method involves the use of small fractions. The following method eliminates the small fraction or large decimal:

$$\frac{1,000,000 \times \$1}{500,000} = \$2 \text{ milline rate}$$

In figuring the milline rate of the newspapers listed above with circulations of 50,000 and 45,000 and a line rate of $0.50, the following procedure would be used:

$$\frac{1,000,000 \times \$0.50}{50,000} = \$10 \text{ milline rate for newspaper}$$
$$\text{with circulation of } 50,000$$

$$\frac{1,000,000 \times \$0.50}{45,000} = \$11.11 \text{ milline rate for newspaper}$$
$$\text{with circulation of } 45,000$$

Advantages and disadvantages

The advantages of using newspapers include: (1) they provide intensive coverage of the cities and surrounding area; (2) they have geographical selectivity; (3) they are very flexible, and copy can be tied in with latest developments; (4) they are relatively low cost in comparison to other media; (5) they reach all economic classes; (6) they can be tied in with the sales appeals in specific localities; (7) they can be used effectively in a cooperative advertising plan; (8) they can emphasize the local news appeal; (9) they can be used even when the advertising budget is quite modest; (10) they can be used on a daily basis; (11) they appeal to the entire family; (12) they are one of the media in which great numbers of people look for information about merchandise which they are about to purchase; (13) they await the convenience of the reader to read; (14) they are the major local medium for which readers pay; (15) they can be used effectively for test campaigns and to check results; and (16) they are *news* papers.

The main disadvantages of using newspapers are: (1) for products purchased by a restricted class, there is considerable waste circulation; (2) the paper and printing techniques may make them unsatisfactory for products which require special color and other mechanical features to show qualities of the products; (3) they are read hurriedly and the impact of the advertisements may be relatively brief; (4) there are complex difficulties in selecting a satisfactory schedule of newspapers in a campaign and in deciding which newspaper to use in a specific market; (5) there are so many advertisements in some newspapers that it is easy for an advertisement to get buried; (6) when an extensive list of newspapers must be used, it may be more economical to use the "low cost per-thousand" broadcast media for continuity; (7) there is overlapping of newspaper circulations in many sections of the country; (8) many newspapers employ publishers' representatives to represent them nationally, which results in the national advertiser having to place his advertising through an intermediary.

Magazines

Whereas newspapers as a rule reach the people in a city or shopping area, most magazines reach a particular segment of the national market. They normally select special interest groups and design their editorial content for such groups. Virtually any segment of the population can find one or more magazines to appeal to its particular interests.

Influence of magazines

There are more than 9,000[4] periodicals published and distributed in the United States. The total per-issue circulation of all the members of the Audit Bureau of Circulations is about 235 million.

Nearly seven of every ten adults who are 15 years of age and over in the United States are regular magazine readers. Over eight of every ten U.S. families are magazine-reading families. Magazines are read regularly by 85 million adult consumers. Magazine advertising expenditures were $2.47 billion in 1974.[5] Magazines exert their influence in two ways—through their editorial content and through their advertising. So closely are the editorial and the advertising pages welded in magazines, that it is difficult to divorce one from the other. They combine to make a total effect.

Classification of magazines

The more important classifications used for magazines include the following: general consumer, women's magazines, shelter magazines, industrial, trade, service, professional, technical journals, and farm publications. This classification could be much more detailed, since, for instance, Standard Rate & Data Service divides consumer maga-

---

[4] Statistical Abstract of the United States, 1975, p. 5.

[5] *Advertising Age,* September 15, 1975, p. 51.

zines into some 50 classifications, business magazines into 159 classes, and farm publications into 11 classifications. There is no need to give all these classifications here, but the detailed breakdowns possible indicate the high degree of specialized interests served by magazines, and the fact that many consumer groups and virtually every professional, industry, and trade group has its own special magazine. In the following paragraphs, a few of the most important classes of magazines will be discussed briefly.

General consumer magazines. These magazines are edited to appeal to the general consumer, rather than to any special interest segment of the population. Generally, they tend to be read by higher income consumers, who buy them either for entertainment or information, or both. The editorial content of these magazines consists of fiction, articles, pictures, and special features that are selected to appeal to the so-called general reader.

Women's magazines. There are several different classes or categories of magazines published primarily to appeal to women. These include women's fashions, women's service, romance, society, dressmaking and needlework, and home service. The women's service magazines and home service, or shelter, magazines are probably the most important classes. The women's service magazine is an important source of fiction and information about family and personal problems as well as fashion news, with most of the editorial material featuring information about the family, home, and housekeeping. Thus, the publications are aimed at reaching and influencing millions of housewives who do a large part of the buying for the household and who also influence the purchase of many other items bought by the family. The women's service magazines include such leading publications as *Good Housekeeping, Ladies' Home Journal,* and *McCall's.*

The other important class of women's magazines is the so-called shelter group. These are magazines similar to those discussed above, except that they concentrate their editorial appeal almost entirely on the home, covering the areas of food preparation, home building and remodeling, home decoration, and gardening. Good examples of this category are *Better Homes and Gardens, The American Home,* and *Sunset* (which also includes a strong section on travel).

Business publications. Approximately 2,400 business magazines are listed in Standard Rate & Data Service. The Audit Bureau of Circulations classifies this large number of publications into four categories, which for our purposes are more meaningful than the 159 classification groupings given by Standard Rate & Data Service. The four ABC categories are: industrial publications, which are published for all kinds of industry; institutional papers, edited for clubs, colleges, hospitals, hotels, schools, etc.; professional publications, published for architects, artists, doctors, engineers, lawyers, professors, and so on; and merchandise publications, which go to retailers, wholesalers, and other types of distributors.

Some of the features of these publications should be noted briefly. They have very high selectivity, going to groups that are specifically interested in the particular field or subject covered. The publications usually have a good knowledge of their readers in terms of positions held, type of firms by which employed, and interests. The magazines usually contain editorial matter of a rational nature, often quite technical, and usually of a type designated to help the reader to do a better job, to familiarize him with new developments in the field, to give the features of new products being introduced, and to tell how products and services might enable the reader to increase his returns from his business or profession. Because the copy of advertisements run in these magazines usually attempts, like the editorial content, to tell the reader how to increase his profits or income from the use of the advertised product or service, the advertisements have very high readership. These magazines usually have small circulations, and their advertising rates on a per page basis are low. In many cases, subscriptions for these magazines are paid for by business firms, and the copies are routed to several members of the firm for reading.

Some of these publications attempt to reach all of a certain type of reader in many or all industries, and are called horizontal magazines. Examples would be *Purchasing,* which is designed to reach purchasing agents and others interested in purchasing in all industries, and *Sales Management,* which reaches sales executives in all industries. Other publications are designed to reach all levels of readers within a single industry or field, such as *Modern Textiles Magazine, Appliance Manufacturer,* or the *American Drycleaner,* and are called vertical magazines.

Farm magazines. As indicated by their category title, these magazines are edited for the farm market or specific segments of that market. Some are edited to reach the general farm market, such as the *Farm Journal* and the *Progressive Farmer.* However, more of them are designed to reach particular segments of the farm market, such as those edited for the fields of dairy farming, livestock, poultry, or fruits and vegetables, with examples being *Hoard's Dairyman, Breeder's Gazette, American Poultry Journal,* and the *American Fruit Grower.* Within these detailed classification groupings as given by Standard Rate & Data Service, there are very specialized publications. For instance, in the poultry class there is a magazine, *Turkey World,* aimed at those specializing in turkey raising, and within the fruits and vegetables class there is a magazine, *California Citrograph,* aimed at citrus fruit growers.

In some cases, farming magazines are selective on a geographical basis rather than (or in addition to) a specific interest basis. For example, the Cowles Publishing Company, Spokane, Washington, publishes the *Idaho Farmer,* the *Washington Farmer,* and the *Oregon Farmer,* each magazine edited to cover the agricultural interests of the particular state, with the bulk of subscriptions going to that state.

Advantages and disadvantages of magazines

Advantages. Magazines offer high selectivity, national and local coverage, use of excellent mechanical techniques, prestige, longer life, and a relatively low cost.

Whether an advertiser wishes to reach executives, homeowners, farmers, men, women, college students, teen-agers, or any other specific group, there will probably be several magazines available for him to use. For business groups, there are such publications as *Nation's Business, Fortune, Forbes,* and *Business Week;* for literary groups, such magazines as *Harper's* and *Atlantic Monthly;* for parents, such magazines as *Hygiene* and *Parents' Magazine;* for juvenile groups, *Seventeen, Boys' Life,* and *Scholastic;* for fraternal groups, such magazines as *Rotarian, Christian Herald,* and *Columbia;* for farm groups, such magazines as *American Pigeon Journal* and *Successful Farming.*

Another advantage which magazines have over newspapers is that an advertiser can get national circulation. Since magazine circulation tends to follow population trends, for most general products the circulation of the national magazine may be closely correlated to the advertiser's market.

A third advantage is that, because of the higher quality of paper in magazines, it is possible to use a variety of colors and mechanical techniques. Illustrations may be done in opaque and transparent watercolors; photoengravings and four-color halftones are some of the other methods which can be used effectively.

A fourth advantage is that advertising a product in such magazines as *Vogue, Good Housekeeping, Esquire,* and *Town and Country* helps to enhance its prestige and, at the same time, provides a means by which the manufacturer can prevail on local dealers to make use of the national advertising in local tie-ins. Point-of-purchase displays, window displays, and local advertising are a few of the methods a retailer can use to point out that a product the store sells was advertised in a national magazine.

A fifth advantage is that magazines have a longer life than most other media and are read more thoroughly. A magazine usually will be picked up to be read a number of times by the subscriber as well as by members of the family.

A sixth advantage is that magazines provide a low per-unit cost of reaching potential customers. Even a small company may find that by properly choosing a magazine that will reach its selective group of customers, this medium will be an economical one to use.

There are several other advantages in addition to the six discussed above. The great strength of magazines lies in their believability, acceptance, authority, and editorial vitality. Magazine readers come more from the prosperous and middle-income class home and represent above-average prospects for nationally advertised products. Magazines have extensive "pass-along" or "secondary" readership. The loyalty to some magazines is so great that they may create in the minds of their readers a feeling similar to belonging to a special, select class. Magazines may also reach buyers who are out of range geographically as well as buyers who are hard for the salespeople to approach.

Disadvantages. One of the main disadvantages in the use of magazines has been the necessity of buying space and preparing copy for the advertisement well in advance of the date on which it is to appear. In some cases, weekly magazines require that the plates for the advertisement be in their hands seven weeks prior to publication date in the case of four-color advertisements. After this closing date, no changes in the advertisement or cancellation of space may be made.

Many magazines are making all possible efforts to shorten this period between closing date and publication date, but it is still in most cases such a period of time as to constitute a timing disadvantage for the advertiser. This was apparent in the 1974 advertising of the United States automobile manufacturers when instituting their "discount" sales programs. Because of timing, for one reason, all advertisements were on television, none in magazines, a medium normally used extensively by automobile firms.

A second major disadvantage of magazines is that of waste circulation if the advertiser does not have complete national distribution, or has wide differences in distribution and sales strength in different markets of the country. That is, magazines as a rule did not possess geographical or market selectivity. This weakness is still true in many cases. However, a number of magazines now issue regional editions of their magazines, so that an advertiser can advertise in only those regions of the country which he desires, or can advertise different products in different regions. They have 10, 26, 59, and up to 70 regional and local editions; a number have from 10 to 20 major market editions; some have editions defined by metropolitan market areas, and some have up to 50 test market editions.

Approximately 60 consumer magazines which do not publish regional editions attempt to reduce their territorial selectivity weakness by providing for split-run insertions of advertisements. This split-run system means that by making special arrangements (and paying for extra production costs involved) an advertiser may advertise different products in different regions of the country to fit his needs, or two different advertisers can run advertisements for their respective products in different regions. Each advertiser would pay for that share of the magazine circulation delivered into his region.

In rare instances, a consumer magazine will limit the geographic area it serves. For example, *Sunset* (one of the leading shelter magazines), accepts subscriptions essentially only in the far western states and in Hawaii. Even in this restricted area it publishes three regional editions, with a large share of the editorial matter changed for each edition. However, it is still true that for the most part magazines do lack the geographic selectivity possessed by other media.

There are several other limitations in addition to the two discussed above. Closely allied to the disadvantage of a lack of geographic selectivity is the need to use an appeal in the advertising that is broad enough to be satisfactory in every section of the country (or of the region) and yet specific enough to persuade the prospects to act. Since in many instances there are significant differences in demand and in conditions in different markets, this is often a serious handicap to the copywriter. Since magazines are as a rule published weekly or monthly, the advertiser cannot communicate with his buyers as frequently as he can with newspapers, radio, or television. Also, the cost of mechanical preparation of advertisements for magazines, especially for four-color advertisements, can be quite high.

Special services provided to advertisers

As is true of newspapers, magazines do offer some special services to advertisers. Some of the magazines have specialists in merchandising in certain fields of retailing, such as food, drug, appliance, or department stores. Many offer merchandising material such as display and special letters to dealers at cost to aid in tying in the product at the point of sale with the magazine advertising. Some magazines will provide help to the advertiser and his advertising agency in handling the sales force, broker, wholesaler, and retailer meetings at which the advertiser's national advertising and sales program is explained and sold to the trade. Several of the fashion magazines publish advance editions for the trade to help coordinate the selling programs of the stores with the national advertising in the magazines. Most publishers conduct considerable research in the areas of readership, brand preference, consumer attitudes, and general market conditions, and provide the results of such studies to advertisers and potential advertisers. Some magazines also will provide aid to advertisers in running test programs by publishing advertisements in only the copies going to the test markets.

Space rates

Magazine advertising space generally is sold by the page or fraction of a page, although in some cases it is sold by the agate line. Many magazines quote rates for one page, one-half page, one-fourth page, and one-eighth page, and some quote rates for full, two-third, and one-third pages. For advertisements of less than one-half page, most magazines will require the advertisement to be in multiples of 14 agate lines. Some magazines also sell "junior" units which have editorial material above and along one side. These units are usually offered as junior pages and half pages, the junior units containing about 60 percent of the number of lines in the regular units.

Rates are quoted on two bases: flat and open. Flat-rate magazines charge the same rate regardless of how much space the advertiser uses during the year.

Discounts. Open-rate magazines, on the other hand, will charge on the basis of the volume of space used and/or the frequency of insertions of advertisements during the year. Monthly magazines will often quote a discount for 6 advertisements run during a year, and a still larger discount for 12 advertisements run during the year. Weekly magazines in many cases will quote a successively larger discount for advertisements inserted 13, 26, 39, or 52 times during a period of 12 months. The Standard Rate and Data Service provides rate and circulation information about magazines as well as about newspapers.

Other factors influencing rates

Several other factors besides the amount of space and frequency of insertion influence magazine rates. As is indicated in the schedule above, magazine-rate quotations normally refer to the rates for black-and-white printing, and color rates normally are quoted separately for each multiple of colors offered by the magazine. Also, as is true of newspapers, most magazines make an extra charge for certain preferred positions. Because of the greater attention-getting value of the cover pages, they are particularly desired by advertisers. Although the premium charged for these preferred positions (cover pages) varies by magazines, the following example would be fairly typical. The second cover (inside front cover) and the third cover (inside back cover) are required to be in four colors, the rate for which is usually about 40 percent above the black-and-white page rate, but it is often the same rate as for a four-color page in the magazine. The fourth, or back cover, usually must be in four colors and will carry a premium charge of from 25 percent to 40 percent above the regular four-color page rate. In consumer magazines, the first, or front, cover is not sold to advertisers, but trade and industrial magazines often sell space on the front cover to advertisers, usually at a premium rate somewhat higher than the fourth-cover rate.

Most magazines which make bleed pages available also charge a premium of about 15 percent above the regular rates. A bleed page is one on which the advertisement is printed fully to the outside edge of the page, with no margin. Another position for which special rates are applicable is the center spread, which consists of the two facing pages in the exact center of the magazine. On these two pages, the printing can be done on a single sheet of paper, and the advertisement can run across the gutter—the usual margin space between the pages—without a break. Usually the rate for the center spread is the same as for two facing pages in four colors, regardless of whether or not the advertiser uses four colors in his advertisement.

Another basis for a rate differential is the use of inserts. In many magazines, if the advertiser desires to have a distinctive advertisement, he can elect to use special stock for printing it instead of the regular paper stock used by the magazine. To do this, the advertiser has his advertisement printed and forwards it to the magazine, which inserts it in the publication. This permits the advertiser to make his advertisement as distinct as he desires in terms of paper stock, colors used, and printing process. The distinctiveness of such inserts usually results in great attention and impact for the advertisement. If the paper stock is quite different than the usual magazine stock, the magazine will often tend to open at the insert, giving it even greater attention value.

Cost comparisons

As is the case with newspapers, it is often desirable in the case of magazines for the advertiser to compare the rates and cost of the media. In newspapers, the unit of measurement used is the milline rate. In magazines, the basis of comparison is the "cost per page per thousand," based in large part on the fact that the most common unit of space for which magazine advertising rates are quoted is a page or fraction thereof, rather than the agate line as for newspapers. The two figures used in computing the cost comparisons for magazines are the one-time insertion cost of a black-and-white page advertisement and the net circulation of the magazine.

The formula for the cost per page per thousand circulation is:

$$\frac{\text{Page rate x 1,000}}{\text{Circulation}} = \text{Cost per page per 1,000 circulation}$$

For example, if the rate for magazine X is $12,500 per black-and-white page, and the net circulation is 2.5 million, the cost per page per thousand would be $5, computed as follows:

$$\frac{\$12,500 \times 1,000}{2,500,000} = \$5 \text{ cost per page per 1,000}$$

As was noted in the preceding chapter on selection of media, many advertisers today analyze carefully the figures for audience, or readers, of magazines (as determined by marketing research studies) as well as the net circulation figures. In such cases, the advertiser may well compute a cost per page per thousand readers, using the same formula as above, except that total audience or readers would be used in place of circulation in the denominator of the formula.

In many cases, the advertiser is interested in reaching a particular identifiable group of readers of the magazine, specially in the case of the business publications where the circulation is usually broken down by special groups. When such is true, the advertiser often compares costs on the basis of the number of real potential prospects reached by the media. To do this, he takes the figure of real prospects in the circulation or readership, and by substituting this figure for net circulation computes an effective cost per page per thousand. It is obvious that this is a more meaningful figure for the advertiser when it is possible to identify clearly the real prospects among the circulation or audience of the magazines being compared.

The warning indicating the care that must be taken in the use of cost comparisons for selecting media should be repeated here, particularly in the case of cost per page per thousand circulation. This figure does not indicate how many people will read a particular advertisement, or how many real prospects will read the advertisement. The cost per page per thousand will vary widely among magazines. Usually, the greater the selectivity of the magazine in terms of the interests of its readers, the purchasing power they represent, or the positions they hold, the higher its cost on a page per thousand basis. For instance, the cost per thousand rate for *Barron's* is about 6.5 times higher than for *Reader's Digest* while for *Fortune* it is about 8.1 times that of *TV Guide*.

In attempts to justify their particular rates and cost, magazines today use a number of different bases for indicating the quality and/or quantity of their circulation and audience. In addition to quantity of readership, they conduct studies to indicate the quality of readers, the amount of time the reader spends with the magazine, the number of different days he reads in it, the length of time he keeps the magazine in the home, and the confidence he has in the editorial and advertising material appearing in the publication. Such data should be studied carefully by the advertiser along with the comparative cost ratios.

Statistical reports

Magazine publishers offer a wide variety of different types of statistical reports. These analyses give detailed information on income of readers, percentage of different kinds of advertising carried, circulation according to market areas, and other such factual evidence.

Among the more important independent studies is the Starch Advertisement Readership Service which points out such data as number of readers, age of readers, occupation, reader duplication, and to what extent the advertisements in the magazines checked were seen or read thoroughly.

W. R. Simmons & Associates also makes an extensive analysis in its annual audience report, "Study of Selective and Mass Markets and the Media Reaching Them."

Audit Bureau of Circulations

During the early days of advertising, the circulation figures issued by some publishers were open to question. Unreliable statements were made and affirmed with such glibness that advertisers could not rely on the circulation figures. This condition placed a handicap on the publishers who sought to give only the exact figures of their circulation, as well as on the advertisers and agencies attempting to use the figures in planning the selection of media. As a result, the Audit Bureau of Circulations (ABC) was established in 1914 under the sponsorship of advertisers, advertising agencies, and publishers of newspapers and magazines, all of whom were anxious to protect themselves against the publishers whose circulation figures were not dependable. The membership of the board of directors of the ABC consists of representatives of advertisers, advertising agencies, and publishers of newspapers and magazines, with the buyers of advertising space having a majority on the board. The Audit Bureau of Circulations will not accept for membership and audit any publication that has less than 70 percent paid circulation. (Those magazines distributing the bulk of their circulations on a free or controlled basis may become members of the Business Publications Audit of Circulation, which audits the controlled and paid circulation of its member publications.)

The Audit Bureau of Circulations makes independent audits of the circulations of its member newspapers and magazines. In the case of newspapers, it reports the net paid circulation for three geographical areas: the "city zone," the "retail trading zone," and "all other."

Its statements of circulation also indicate the breakdown by "street-vendor sales," "dealer sales," "carrier-delivered circulation," and "mail subscriptions." This information is of interest to advertisers, since a high home-delivered subscription circulation is considered an indication of continuing readership by entire families. Its reports also indicate what share of the subscription list is "in arrears" (overdue in payment for the paper or magazine) and what share of the circulation was obtained by means of special inducements (such as contests and premium offers). Both these items are of interest to advertisers as reflecting on the desirability of the circulation.

In addition to auditing the circulation figures of member publishers and certifying to their accuracy, the ABC also establishes standards for reporting on circulations and serves as a clearing house for circulation reports. Approximately 90 percent of the daily newspapers in the United States and Canada belong to the organization. ABC has also influenced those publishers not members, since advertisers have become skeptical of circulation figures not certified by some accredited agency. As a result, many nonmembers now issue sworn statements of their circulation figures, compiled in a manner similar to that of the ABC. This organization has had a most beneficial effect in the advertising field.

The *Verified Audit Circulation* verifies the validity of circulation figures by statistical sampling procedures which determines the accuracy of circulation lists, receipt of the publication, and qualification of recipients.

The Advertising Checking Bureau, Inc., provides a checking service on whether or not the ads actually appeared in the newspapers as ordered. This checking-proof service is available for more than 95 percent of all daily newspapers circulation in the United States, as well as for many weekly newspapers.

Standard Rate and Data Service

The Standard Rate and Data Service provides detailed information about the various major media. It offers rates and data information for daily, Sunday, and weekly newspapers; business publications; consumer magazines and farm publications; spot radio; spot television; national radio and television; films for television; transportation advertising; and Canadian media.

With the exception of the data for weekly newspapers, the bulletins for the other media are published on a monthly basis. The weekly newspaper bulletin is published in March and September.

The content of each of the ten Standard Rate and Data Service publications is arranged in such a manner as to provide the important data for buyers of advertising time and space.

Questions

1. Why do you think newspapers are the leading medium in terms of advertising revenue?

2. If the circulation of the three newspapers were approximately equal, should it make any difference to an advertiser whether he uses a morning, evening, or Sunday newspaper? Explain your answer.

3. Newspapers usually quote a lower rate for retail advertising than for national advertising. Do you think this practice is justified? Why or why not?

4. Give examples of three products that you think could justify paying the premium for preferred position in the newspaper. Why?

5. Check the advertisements in your local newspaper for a week. Give reasons why certain advertisers and certain product advertising seem to be concentrated on certain days of the week.

6. In some cities, most supermarkets run their big one and two-page "special" advertisements on Thursdays, and so most national advertisers of food products schedule their advertisements for Thursday to reach all the people who will be reading the paper for the supermarket specials. The advertising manager for a new food product with a limited budget decided to run his small-space ads in the paper on a day other than Thursday, when he said the competition for readership would be much less severe. Comment.

7. Do you think the adoption of regional editions by magazines is a threat to newspapers in competing for advertising? Why?

8. For what types of products do you think the newspaper is a better medium than magazines? Magazines than newspapers? Why?

9. The rates for television advertising are normally reduced during the summer months. A magazine is considering reducing its rates for summer months about the same relative amount. Is this a sound move? Why?

10. What is the difference between vertical and horizontal industrial magazines? Under what circumstances is this difference of significance to an advertiser?

11. In theory the cost per page per thousand gives a basis for comparing magazines. Is it sound to select magazines on the basis of the lowest cost? Explain.

Case **HARAPAHOES, INC.**
12–1 **Considering use of newspapers**

Harapahoes, Inc., is engaged in the manufacture and sale of linoleum, asphalt tile flooring, corks, corkboard insulation, and cork-type covering. It also manufactures felt-base rugs and flooring. During the last fiscal year it had sales of $80 million.

The company had limited its use of newspaper advertising to 10 percent of its annual advertising budget. The percentage breakdown for the Floor Division media was as follows:

Magazines	50%
Television	20
Radio	15
Newspapers	10
Direct Mail & Other	5
Total	100%

The company today is made up of the Floor Division, the Building Materials Division, and the Industrial Division.

Floor Division. From its origin in 1920 the Floor Division expanded rapidly. Within 15 years it became Harapahoes' highest sales volume division, and it still is. According to the company, several new ideas introduced in 1938 were important factors in the Floor Division's consistent expansion: published price lists, a wholesaler-retailer distribution system whose pattern is still followed, and national advertising. The company reports that there are two major markets for the Floor Division's product line, and that considerable homogeneity exists within each: (1) the residential market. Customers are interested in Harapahoes' linoleum for use in their homes. (2) the commercial market. Customers are business and professional men. In such a market Harapahoes' linoleum is considered as a means of improving the appearance and services of stores and offices.

As might be expected, there is a corresponding split in the division's sales and advertising programs: One major effort is directed to the residential, the other to the commercial market.

Underlying all Floor Division advertising is the conviction that people buy floor covering only after deliberate, rational thinking. Linoleum, for example, is not a snap-judgment item; often it is purchased as part of a costly remodeling or redecorating project. Altogether, according to company executives, Floor Division advertising should be calm, believable, and editorial in nature. Incidentally, Harapahoes' advertising director tests the "editorial nature" of each proposed Floor Division ad by asking himself, in effect, this question: If the logotype and sales plug were deleted, would the ad be informative enough and provocative enough to make a good editorial feature in the magazine for which it is scheduled?

Early in 1976 Harapahoes and its advertising agency had occasion to review and evaluate the Floor Division's campaign. It had been appearing in national magazines for several years, with illustrations and copy based on testimonials obtained from successful users of Harapahoes' floors.

Although the Floor Division's sales curve had been healthy during the testimonial campaign, the company evaluated its advertising as only a "pretty fair effort." Letters of inquiry traceable to it were disappointing in number. Results in general seemed neither good nor bad. Further, satisfactory testimonials were becoming scarce. The client and its agency, therefore, decided that they must change—and improve—the campaign. In evaluating the campaign of one of its competitors, the company found that the two campaigns were similar in several respects. Each was aimed at a specific market and showed the application of linoleum floors. Both were major advertising efforts, involving the consistent use of full-page, full-color ads in national magazines, but the competition put more emphasis on newspapers. Harapahoes also observed that the two campaigns differed sharply as to their basic themes:

1. The Harapahoes ads had been built around statements from satisfied users. Illustrations and copy featured the interiors of existing establishments.

2. In contrast, the competitor's campaign featured *ideas developed by extensive research.* Each advertisement showed a variety of new "ideas for homeowners" and offered, at a nominal charge, pamphlets giving further details.

The Harapahoes Floor Division concluded that an honest contribution of ideas—really helpful ideas, and a variety of them—would be the key to successful advertising.

The new campaign began with research in building design. Ideas were gathered from many sources: designers, associations, equipment manufacturers, and food merchandising experts. Information was then checked with officials of the National Association of Architects. Finally, ideas reached the drawing board stage, to serve as the basis for designing a complete interior. Each business classification featured in the commercial campaign was to be selected with an eye to its potential as a market for Harapahoes' floors. Late in 1976, the Floor Division's advertising department made out a production schedule, allotting time for creative work, illustration, and production of the ads.

Selection of media

One of the company's executives questioned the 50 percent of the budget that was being spent for magazines and indicated that he believed the company's major competition was probably getting more mileage by allocating about 45 percent of its budget for newspapers.

He stated that the consumer could be influenced to a greater degree if the name of the local distributor was associated with *Harapahoes.* He also believed that it would be possible to develop a rather extensive cooperative advertising program with the dealers if the newspapers were used to a greater degree.

In further emphasizing the reason why he believed the company should allocate more of its budget for newspapers, he stated:

1. Newspapers are the most widely consumed form of communications in the United States, with over 60 million copies distributed daily and over 50 million on Sunday. Over 80 percent of all adults read some newspapers during the average day.

2. Newspapers throughout the years have received a larger share of the country's total advertising investment than any other medium.

3. Their major advantage to advertisers stems from the fact that they are *news* papers and people read them to find out what happened today.

4. Newspapers form a perfect environment for the *news* advertising which we are planning for the current campaign.

5. Our Floor Division depends upon "merchandisability" to sell its products, and local retailers favor using this medium. As a result, we should get better sales effort from the dealers if we allocate more of our budget for newspapers.
6. We will be able to make a deeper penetration of individual markets.
7. ROP color is now available in most papers, and while the quality of reproduction is not as good as what we get in magazines, it is more than adequate for our product.
8. Newspapers will have greater flexibility and we will be able to tie in the appeal to the local news.
9. The people we are trying to reach with our advertisement can be reached more directly through the newspaper.
10. We will be able to use more specific appeals in the newspapers.

Case questions

1. Evaluate the reasons that the Harapahoes executive gave as to why newspapers should be used to a greater degree.
2. What would be the disadvantages of Harapahoes putting more emphasis on newspapers?
3. The company spends 6 percent of sales on advertising. How much would you allocate to newspaper advertising? Give reasons.

Case
12–2
UNITED STATES STEEL CORPORATION
Selecting magazine media

United States Steel carries on a wide variety of advertising and sales promotion programs, including product, merchandising, and corporate campaigns involving different media, such as magazines, radio, motion pictures, exhibits and displays, direct mail, creative sales aids, merchandising kits, and product literature of all kinds.

The advertising director decided that there would be merit if a humorous approach would be used in providing the quality and dependability of United States Steel pails and drums.

Working with King Features Syndicate, Inc., he had Jimmy Hatlo of the famous "They'll Do It Every Time" cartoon prepare the four cartoons in Exhibits 12–1, 12–2, 12–3, and 12–4.

Case question

1. Indicate in what magazines you believe these advertisements should be used.

EXHIBIT 12–1

EXHIBIT 12–2

EXHIBIT 12–3

EXHIBIT 12–4

Case
12–3 **ROTHESAY, INC.**
Using bleed ads

Rothesay, Inc., manufactures quality clothing which sells in the higher price ranges for ready-made clothing. The product line includes men's suits, sport coats, outer coats, slacks. Rothesay also manufactures men's and women's raincoats as well as a limited line of women's dresses and sportswear.

Rothesay products are sold to over 4,750 independent retail specialty and department stores in all 50 states as well as to the company's own stores. Sales of $225 million in the last fiscal year to independent retailers account for 80 percent of total wholesale sales, with the balance representing sales to Rothesay's own stores.

The company's manufacturing operations are conducted at factories located in southern, midwestern and eastern states. Wool fabrics and blends of wool and polyester are the principal raw materials with silks and cottons also used to a lesser extent. Approximately 38 percent of the fabrics used are imported and the balance is supplied by domestic mills.

Retail stores

Rothesay operates 135 retail stores for men and women in 45 metropolitan areas throughout the United States. The stores are operated under separate established local names. However, all merchandise carries the Rothesay brand labels.

These retail stores sell clothing manufacture by Rothesay as well as clothing, furnishings, sportswear, hats, and shoes purchased from other manufacturers in order to balance the selections of quality clothing.

Competition

The business in which Rothesay is engaged is highly competitive, both on the wholesale and retail levels. While it is recognized that no manufacturer of similar clothing accounts for more than a small percentage of the total amount produced by the entire industry in the United States, Rothesay would be considered to be one of larger manufacturers.

Advertising

The company has placed emphasis in its advertising on the media of television, radio, newspapers, and magazines. In its magazine advertising, however, the marketing vice president was concerned about a number of recent studies that showed the Starch readership scores for Rothesay's ads were relatively low, compared with other advertisements appearing in the same publication.

In attempting to determine the reasons for this he evaluated a number of research studies that had been made. In one of these reports he found that "Bleed Ads" received higher Starch rating for "Noted Scores," "Associated Scores," and "Read Most Scores" by above 35 percent over "Non-Bleed Ads." The same difference seemed to exist regardless of whether the ad was a black-and-white one or a four-color one.

As a result, he recommended that the company should begin to use bleed ads for its magazine copy. When the advertising director received this suggestion he told the vice president that for advertising quality clothing, bleed ads would detract and might have a negative impact on the readers.

It was his contention that one needed to use extensive white space along with glamorous settings to convey the appeal which Rothesay should use. He indicated further that bleed ads were more effective for sale merchandise and for low-price items.

In his report he also pointed out that in the magazines that Rothesay used there was usually an extra charge that was assessed. Included in his list were the following magazines:

Name of magazines	Charge for bleed pages
Esquire	Full rate plus 10%
Playboy	plus 10%
Sports Illustrated	plus 15%
Penthouse	No extra charge
Gentlemen's Quarterly	plus 10%
National Lampoon	plus 10%
New York Magazine	plus 15%
Time Magazine	plus 15%

Case Question

1. Should Rothesay use bleed ads in its magazine advertising?

Case 12–4 **DFM COMPANY**
Deciding on appeal characteristics

The DFM Company is engaged in the production of rock products, chemicals, cement, and lime. It also develops and produces space launch vehicles, space craft, electronics, and nuclear systems.

In planning its advertising strategy for its commercial products, the company is concerned about integrating the appeal characteristics for its print media campaign to attract the most effective readership for its advertising.

Commercial products

There are three major divisions in the commercial products. The Cement and Lime Division produces cement, industrial lime, and refractories. The Chemical Division manufactures printing inks, concrete additives, and industrial sand. The Rock Products Division produces crushed stone and sand and gravel for use in construction.

Cement and lime division

Cement. The Cement and Lime Division manufactures and sells portland and masonry cements, high-calcium and dolomitic lime, and refractory products. The early use of portland cement was principally to make concrete for applications where compressive strength and durability were primary requirements. In recent years, however, lightweight concretes, prestressing techniques, and improved methods of casting have made portland cement concrete of increasing interest to architects and builders. Masonry cement is used to make a mortar for laying brick and other masonry units.

As of the end of the current year, the division's plants had a combined annual rated capacity of 25,000,000 barrels of cement. Utilization of that capacity amounted to approximately 90 percent.

The Division sells cement in 32 states and the District of Columbia. Major metropolitan markets include New York, Philadelphia, Baltimore, Washington, Richmond, Jacksonville, Birmingham, Memphis, Tulsa, Oklahoma City, Denver, Kansas City, Minneapolis-St. Paul, Detroit, and Pittsburgh.

Approximately two-thirds of the division's portland cement shipments were made to ready-mix concrete plants, with most of the balance divided among concrete product plants, building material dealers, and contractors.

The normal marketing area of a cement plant is limited by transportation costs, mill prices, and other competitive factors. However, improved distribution techniques for portland cement, such as the use of distribution terminals, combined rail-truck movements, and water transport have in recent years opened new markets to many of the division's plants. The division currently operates 15 storage and distribution terminals.

A research and development laboratory is under construction, which will be devoted to the development of improved and new processes and products, as well as to providing technical assistance to customers.

Lime and refractories. Lime and refractories are also produced by the division. These products include grain line, which is sold to municipalities and industries for water and waste treatment; high-calcium and dolomitic fluxing lime for the steel industry; and dead burned dolomite and synthetic magnesite for the steel and basic refractories industries.

Chemical division

Printing inks. The Chemical Division is a leading producer of printing inks, other than newspaper ink. Its products include letterpress, lithographic, flexographic, gravure, and screen inks. Thses inks are supplied throughout the world to commercial printers, publishers, and printers of packaging materials, and are used on labels for cans and jars, soap and bread wrappers, cigarette packaging, record jackets, magazines, milk and frozen food cartons, paper cups, and cellophane and polyethylene wrappers.

It also produces a line of varnishes, various chemical products used by lithographers in platemaking and in pressrooms, and a complete line of organic pigments. It is also a major producer of colorants for the printing ink, plastics, and rubber industries.

Silica sand

The Silica Sand Division quarries sand and refines it for industrial uses. The sand is used by the foundry industry in preparing molds and cores. The Division also markets substantial quantities of refined silica sand for use in the production of glass.

Rock products division

The Rock Products Division produces crushed stone, sand and gravel (construction aggregates), primarily for highway and other heavy construction, and also produces agricultural limestone. The Division operated over 100 quarries and sand and gravel pits in midwestern and eastern states, and has pursued a continuing program of developing new raw material reserves located near areas of new highway and other major construction. The Division considers its raw material reserves fully adequate for its business.

Aerospace division

The Aerospace Division's principal activities include the design, development, and production of missiles, space launch vehicles and spacecraft, electronic and nuclear products, the modification of aircraft, and the production of components of various defense products. The Corporation serves as systems manager of major defense and space programs, with responsibility for the integration of the activities of many companies contributing to a single system.

Net sales for the last year of the various divisions are given in Exhibit 12–5.

EXHIBIT 12–5
DFM net sales (in millions—19—)

Commercial products:	
Cement and Lime Division	$100
Chemical Division	85
Rock Products Division	50
Total Commercial Products	$235
Aerospace	250
Total Net Sales	$485

The marketing vice president who had recently been hired from another company to head this position at DFM was responsible for making the final decision in regard to the advertising program that should be adopted.

In discussing the approach to follow, he emphasized that it was his opinion, based on his past experience, that it was essential to use multipage ads in advertising the kinds of products that DFM sold.

He stressed the fact that multipage ads received high readership regardless of what appeal was used. In industrial print media, he stated, "a one-page ad does not attain a readership rating as high because of the great number of advertisements that appear in the various publications." He, therefore, recommended that the number of advertisements be decreased, and that in the future all advertisements be multipage ones.

The account executive of the advertising agency which had handled the DFM account for the past ten years did not agree with this approach. He believed that the emphasis on the appeal characteristics which the agency had used in the past would be more effective, and that, while multipage ads had merit, it was more important to have the "right appeal" in the "right media" at the "right time."

The agency representative went on to state, "Our studies underscore the appeal characteristics that DFM should use are centered around: (*a*) copy containing specific product information; (*b*) illustrations picturing product in use; (*c*) headlines emphasizing what product will do. We have also found that the readership secured through multipage ads includes a high percentage of readers who are not potential customers."

The DFM marketing vice president responded to this analysis as follows: "The product characteristics for our commercial products are not different enough for us to use the approach you recommend. Unless we can come up with some significant differential, we need to get broad readership regardless of whether or not there may be a high amount of waste circulation."

Case question

1. Evaluate the approach that DFM should adopt.

13

TELEVISION AND RADIO

T he two broadcast media, television and radio, have many
similarities, so they will both be discussed in this chapter. Both
broadcast via the public airwaves and operate under a license
from the Federal Communications Commission. They both present
programs and commercials on a similar time basis, and sell the same
general classes of time: network, national, spot, and local. Both have
national organizations of stations (networks) to provide for simultaneous broadcasting. And both have the same trade association, the
National Association of Broadcasters.

However, since they also exhibit some marked differences, they
will be covered individually, albeit with some cross-references as material is analyzed and developed.

Television

Advertising volume

Television has exhibited the most rapid growth of any advertising
medium. In approximately 25 years the total advertising expenditures
have gone from zero to $4,851,000,000 in 1974.[1] Since a major portion
of this is national advertising, television is now the leading medium
for national advertisers. The expenditures for network television
(which gives simultaneous coverage of the national market)
amounted to about 44 percent of total television advertising. The
amount spent on national spot television (national advertisers using
individual stations to reach specific markets) represented about 31

---

[1] *Advertising Age,* September 15, 1975, p. 51.

percent of the total. Expenditures for local television (use of local stations by retailers) amounted to 25 percent of the total.

Number and types of stations

The basic unit in the television field is the individual local station. At the beginning of January, 1976 there were 513 commercial VHF (very high frequency) stations and 197 commercial UHF (ultrahigh frequency) stations or a total of 710 commercial television stations.[2] This represents a dramatic growth when it is recalled that commercial television stations did not actually start operations until the end of World War II. In 1947, the five stations that had been licensed by the Federal Communications Commission when World War II started, finally began broadcasting.

In addition to the 710 commercial stations, there were 155 noncommercial UHF stations and 97 noncommercial VHF stations operating at the beginning of January 1975, or a total of 252.[3] However, since these last do not carry advertising, they need not be considered at any length here. But it should be noted that the programming may have a distinct influence on some segments of the potential listeners for commercial stations and, hence, in one sense cannot be totally ignored by the commercial stations and the networks.

Networks

At the present time, most of the commercial VHF-TV stations are affiliated with one of the national television networks. These three are the American Broadcasting Company (183 primary affiliated stations and 67 secondary), the Columbia Broadcasting System (197 stations), and the National Broadcasting Company (213 affiliates). A fourth network, the United Network, was established and operated briefly in 1967, but failed after only a few weeks of operation. Each of the three networks also operates a radio network. There are also 20 commercial regional television networks.[4]

The networks provide a means for national advertisers to reach a national audience, since the network normally has an affiliate in each major market area. They have negotiated affiliation agreements with the stations to give a good coverage of the national market, and have arranged for facilities with the American Telephone and Telegraph Company (coaxial cables and microwave relays) which enable the stations affiliated in the network to be interconnected for simultaneous broadcast of programs and commercial announcements. The networks also provide the facilities for originating programs, and in some instances, producing the programs. They also have the organization and facilities to handle the sale of network programs and time periods to advertisers and advertising agencies.

---

[2] Reprinted, with permission, from the 1976 *Broadcasting Yearbook,* p. A–2.
[3] Ibid., p. A–2.
[4] Ibid., pp. D–18, D–25, D–27, D–28, D–33.

The network, which enables the advertiser to reach the national market through television, can charge a sufficiently high rate to the advertiser to permit the hiring of the best of talent and the production of expensive programs, which would be impossible for the individual station from an economic standpoint. Since the cost of such expensive programs and talent is spread over the entire national market, the cost to the advertiser of reaching a thousand viewers can still be a reasonable one when he uses the network setup.

Community Antenna Television (CATV) is becoming a more important segment of the field. It enables homes in poor receiving areas, or where there are no local stations, to get TV reception. It uses a master antenna to receive signals from television stations located at some distance, and distributes the signals to the subscriber homes by cable. There now are approximately 3,000 such systems, with approximately 8.2 million subscribers. It is strongest in rural and mountain areas where few stations are available and where regular television reception is poor

TV receiving sets available

As mentioned earlier, of prime importance to the advertiser is the number of TV receiving sets in the homes of potential customers (or in public places) that can receive the advertising message as it is broadcast by the stations and networks available. (Although a number of sets in various public places enables people to view television, it is believed they constitute a minor segment of the TV viewing audience today and will for the most part be omitted from this discussion.) As of January 1976, in the United States, it is estimated there were a total of 71,500,000 "TV households." That is, approximately 97 percent[5] of all U.S. households have at least one TV set available for viewing advertising broadcasts by the above television stations.

More than 45 percent of households own two or more sets; more than 68 percent own one or more color sets; 86 percent can receive UHF signals; and 15 percent are CATV subscribers. There are over 120,000,000 TV sets in the United States, 57,000,000 of which are color sets.[6]

Types of TV advertising

Television advertising is commonly classified as network, national spot, or local advertising.

Network advertising. This is using the facilities of one of the three networks in which the program and commercial are produced, or originate at a central station, or studio, from which the broadcast is sent out to the other stations of the network. This obtains wide and simultaneous coverage of the country with a single telecast.

Several of the advantages to the advertiser in using network adver-

---

[5] 1976 Ibid., p. A–2.

[6] 1976 *Advertising Yearbook*, p. A–2.

tising have been alluded to in the previous discussion. Often they permit the production of top-quality shows which attract large audiences and enhance the prestige of the advertiser, both with the consumer and the trade. The networks usually have the best hours for broadcasting on the stations in the network. The arrangements for network advertising are much simpler than for spot campaigns, and the cost is lower on a network basis than it would be for the same time bought from the individual stations involved. Even though the network time cost is high, it may actually be quite economical on the basis of cost per thousand viewers, assuming the distribution of the advertiser's product parallels fairly closely the pattern of the network stations.

There are some weaknesses of network advertising which the advertiser must consider with respect to his individual needs. Some stations in the network may be relatively weak in their market areas. If the advertiser has weak distribution in some areas, he may not gain full benefit from some of the stations included in the network. The show that carries a commercial must be the same for all markets, whereas the tastes of people do vary by areas of the country. Programs vary widely in their popularity in different parts of the United States. The advertiser usually must make fairly long and costly commitments on network advertising.

National spot advertising. All nonnetwork broadcasting and advertising, that which originates in the single station broadcasting it, is called spot broadcasting and spot advertising. Any such nonnetwork advertising paid for by a general (national) advertiser is "national spot" advertising. The advertiser who uses national spot advertising may use the sponsored program approach or the announcement approach. He may have a program filmed or taped and then have it used on selected individual stations in the various markets he wishes to reach at the time he selects in each market. Or the advertiser may prepare his commercial announcements and have them aired during participation shows or during station breaks on the stations and at the times he buys. In either event, he can buy the stations he desires in each market and the times he desires on each station (subject, of course, to the availability of the desired times).

It is obvious that this procedure has certain real advantages for the advertiser. In the terminology used with regard to print media also, spot advertising is highly selective. The advertiser can choose exactly which markets to cover with his advertising and can omit all others. He can also select different programs for different markets if such procedure is believed to be desirable, and he can schedule his program or announcements for what he considers the best time of day and the best day of the week for each. The advertiser can also, of course, vary the commercial announcement itself for each market, should he so desire, including the appeal used and the personality delivering the advertising message. If the advertiser has a line of products, he can also advertise different products in various local markets as deemed desirable.

The other main advantage of spot advertising is its flexibility. The advertiser can gear the amount of advertising he places in any market to what he believes the current situation there demands. He can meet varying seasonal needs easily with spot advertising. It is possible to run intensive campaigns in each individual market as he introduces a new product or special promotion there. The advertiser can vary the type and amount of advertising in terms of both time and market. He can adjust all facets of his program to meet the conditions of the individual markets. In a sense, spot television advertising fits the adage so often used with respect to newspaper advertising (as contrasted with national magazines not having regional editions), "All business is local."

Local. Local television advertising is done primarily by retailers. It may utilize programs produced and sponsored by a retailer, or, it may be a network show which is sponsored in part by a local advertiser. It may be a syndicated series which a retailer sponsors. Much of local advertising consists of spot announcements, and much of it is cooperative advertising which is sponsored by the retailer but paid for in part by the manufacturer.

Planning uses of TV advertising

In planning for use of television as an advertising medium, the advertiser must consider several general aspects. Among these are: the type of program he will sponsor or use as a vehicle for his advertisement (if any); whether he will use spot announcements or sponsor a program; and the day and the time of day he will utilize the medium.

The advertiser must consider whether to use a regularly scheduled national show, to share a program by cosponsoring or using alternate sponsorships, or a participating program. And he must decide what type of program or show he will sponsor (comedy, drama, sports events, and the like). He will try to select a program appropriate to the product, that will attract the largest possible audience of potential customers, and that will also influence his dealers and sales organization favorably.

The advertiser must also decide whether to sponsor a program or use spot announcements. There are several advantages to sponsoring a TV program. He can conceivably tailor it to fit his special desires. Sponsoring a good-quality, popular program gives prestige to both consumers and the trade. Often the program and its stars can be used effectively as a merchandising device. Also, the advertiser can control the placement or timing of his commercials, and can integrate them into the program if he so desires. Due to high costs, advertisers will often cosponsor a program or sponsor it on alternate weeks.

As noted earlier, the spot announcement approach gives the advertiser much more flexibility. He can run a "saturation" campaign, concentrating his expenditures in a short time period, or in certain areas. He can run a very strong introductory campaign for a new product, and then change to a normal sustaining campaign later.

Due to the high costs of one-sponsor shows, and the risks involved in selecting a popular show, fewer advertisers are sponsoring programs; instead, they are either buying participations in a number of programs or using the spot announcement approach.

The current trend in programming is for networks to plan the pattern of the programs on their networks, particularly during the prime evening hours, in an attempt to obtain the largest possible audience in competition with the other networks. This approach is called the "magazine concept," with the network or station planning the programs (like the magazine plans the editorial material in its publications) and selling only spot announcements. The advertiser controls merely the advertisement itself.

Another trend which is evolving is a reduction in the number of half-hour series shows. Instead, there are more lengthy shows, many of them movies and specials. The networks believe the longer programs—60 to 90 minutes are the best approach for the time from 7:30 P.M.to 11:00 P.M. They feel the longer shows give more time for plot development, which enables them to hold an audience for the whole evening, especially if they follow the long programs with a movie. Also noticeable is the tendency to use shows that appeal to a broad cross-section of audience, particularly a large share of the younger audience, where much of the buying power is concentrated.

The TV audience

Obviously, when the advertiser considers television as a medium for his advertising, he is interested in the questions of size and composition of the audience he can reach.

The average American home views TV for a total of six hours and 56 minutes a day, according to A. C. Nielson statistics.[7] Figure 13–1 gives an idea of the general composition of the audience by time of day and days of the week. The average successful prime-time television show will reach 32,000,000 people. A "smash" may reach 40,-000,000 or more people. An estimated 73,000,000 people watched the 1976 Super Bowl football telecast. (A one minute announcement in that event commanded the medium's highest unit price, $230,000.[8])

Measuring the TV Audience

Several methods of measuring this audience of individual stations and of specific programs have been developed and are being used currently. They are all based on the same general basic concept. That is, all systems use some method of contacting a sample of television homes to determine their viewing habits, at what hour the television set was turned on, and to which program or station it was tuned. This data collected from the sample is then expanded to give figures for the total statistical universe or market for which the specific study is being made. Hence, figures on viewing habits are estimated for the particular city or market or for the whole United States, and for all viewers or viewers of a particular station or a specific program.

---

[7] Reprinted, with permission, from the 1976 *Broadcasting Yearbook*, p. A–2.

[8] 1976 *Advertising Yearbook*, p. C–300.

FIGURE 13–1
TV audience composition*

Day Part	Percent of U.S. homes using TV	No. of viewers per 1,000 homes	Percent of audience per average minute			
			Men	Women	Teens	Children
Mon.–Fri., 10 A.M.–1 P.M.	24.5	1,368	19	56	6	19
Mon.–Fri., 1–4:30 P.M.	33.2	1,406	17	59	8	16
All nights, 8–11 P.M.	63.2	2,032	34	42	11	14

* Audience estimated from *Ayer Media Facts,* 1975, pg. 8.

A number of different measures of the television viewing audience ordinarily are used. The *sets-in-use* (sometimes called "households using television") measure is a figure showing the percentage of all homes in the sample (city, market, or country) in which the television set was turned on at the time the measuring was done. For example, if the measurement was made of the U.S. audience at 8–8:30, Saturday night, and 50 percent of the sets included in the sample were turned on at the time, the national figure for sets in use would be 50 percent. For the United States, that would mean that 50 percent of the sets, or approximately 31.5 million sets, were turned on.

Another very important measure used is the *program rating,* or the percentage of all homes in the sample involved tuned in to the particular program being rated. In the above example, if 15 percent of all sets in the study were tuned in to the program X, the program *rating* would be 15 percent, or, as usually expressed, 15.

The *share-of-audience* is a frequently used measure of comparison. This is the percentage of those homes having the television set turned on that are tuned in to the particular program being measured. In the above hypothetical illustrations, since 15 percent of the stations were tuned to program X, and 50 percent of all television households had sets turned on, the *share-of-audience* would be 15/50, or 30 percent. The *total audience,* a measure also used, is the total number of homes the study indicates is listening to the program. In the above case, it would be 15 percent of the total U.S. TV homes, 63 million, or approximately 10 million homes.

Audience composition is also an important measurement. This refers to the distribution of the audience by demographic factors.

A number of different techniques or methods are being used currently to obtain these measurements of the size of television audiences. One method involves placing a recording device on the television set in a carefully selected sample of television homes. An example of this is the *audimeter* method used by the A. C. Nielsen Company. The audimeter records on a continuous basis the time the set is turned on, to what station it is tuned, and the time the station is tuned in and out. In this way, an accurate measure is obtained of the time a set is turned on, the program to which a set is tuned, and what dialing and shifting of stations is done during the commercials

on the station break. The sample of homes can be drawn scientifically
from the entire population of television homes and then expanded to
the total universe. Accurate trends of the above type of information
can be obtained, since the same sample is used over a period of time.
The chief criticism of this method is that it measures only that the
set is turned on, and gives no indication of who was viewing the program or whether they were viewing and listening during the commercials. Also, it gives no indication of whether viewers can identify sponsors or the message carried by the commercials. Recordings are made
on a two-week basis, but reports to clients are not made until approximately three weeks after the end of the two-week measuring period.
This method is rather costly, and occasionally mechanical failure of
the audimeter eliminates a few members of the sample.

A second method of measurement is the *coincidental telephone*
method. This involves telephoning a sample of homes during the
broadcast to determine whether or not the television set is turned on
and, if so, to what program and station the set is tuned. With this
method, it is possible to ask additional questions, such as who is viewing the program, the product advertised, and the sponsor of the program. This method is used extensively for measuring local market
areas. It has the following advantages: it is fast, since ratings can be
supplied the day following th broadcast; it is relatively inexpensive;
it does not rely on the accuracy of people's memories; it can check on
actual viewing and people's awareness of the advertiser and the product or service or idea he is advertising. The chief disadvantage of this
method is that it can include only households having telephones. In
addition, it is used only in large cities and is limited in the hours
during which calls can be made to approximately the span, 8 A.M. to
10 P.M. It obtains information at only the instant the telephone call is
completed. As in any telephone interviewing, the number of questions
must be limited, and it must be assumed the respondent is giving
accurate information.

A third method of measurement is the *roster-recall* method. This
technique consists of having personal interviewers call at homes to
show the respondents a roster, or list, of the stations in the area and
the programs being broadcast. The interviewees are asked to indicate
which stations and programs they recall having watched. Usually, the
interviews include only a few hours of programs and are conducted
shortly after the broadcasting period involved. This method can include all homes, including nontelephone homes, and has the usual
advantages of personal interviewing. On the other hand, its use is
restricted normally to larger cities, it does depend on the accuracy of
the interviewee's memory, and it is subject to possible bias in that the
interviewee may check more of the better programs in order to make
a favorable impression on the interviewer.

The *diary* method consists of giving to a selected sample of television people or television homes a diary form requesting them to keep
a record of all their viewing of television programs. They are asked
to record their viewing at the time it takes place to minimize dependence on memory. This method can cover viewing time outside as well

as in the home, and can supply information about viewers similar to that obtained in the methods using the automatic recorder and the roster-recall. It is also a relatively low-cost technique. The usual criticisms of this method are based on the question of the accuracy with which people will keep such a diary.

Since these methods vary considerably in the techniques involved, it is not too unexpected that their results in program ratings sometimes vary considerably. There is much discussion regarding the accuracy of the ratings and the amount of influence they have on the programs that are sponsored on television, particularly on national networks.

The program rating figure is the most widely publicized and used of the measurements discussed above. However, the advertiser should exercise care in the use of the program rating figure. This figure does not give consideration to the average number of people who may be viewing the program on each set, nor does it provide information on the composition of the viewing audience.

And, to the advertiser, even more important is the question of whether or not the people actually viewing the program are potential users of his product. Also, he is highly interested in knowing whether or not the viewers are actually viewing his commercial message as well as the program itself, and how many saw, understood, and were influenced by his commercial. Hence, it is obvious that the advertiser should not be ruled by a program's rating, although trends in program rating may well be very important to him. He should also use the other reports on television audiences offered by some of the research services, and study the local market reports to ascertain the variations in viewing by area.

Cost of television advertising

The advertiser who sponsors his own program on television has two basic cost elements—program costs and time charges. The television advertiser also must pay such expenses as those required for studio rehearsal time and production. The cost of an individually sponsored program can be very high. In a few instances, a single hour and one-half spectacular has cost a sponsor over a million dollars for the program alone. Many of the regular network shows cost up to $100,000 per broadcast for the talent alone.

This factor has led to the increased use of alternate sponsoring and cosponsoring of programs, and, more recently, wide use of the scatter plan—buying participations in a number of different network programs or station break periods.

Rate structure

Television rates for programs are quoted on the basis of time periods and vary according to the time of day involved. The usual time periods are one hour, a half-hour, a quarter-hour, ten minutes, and five minutes. In some cases, a one- and one-half hour period will be sold for special shows, or spectaculars, and for unusual events, longer periods may be arranged and shown. The periods of one minute and less are called announcements, and are placed at the breaks between programs or in participating programs. The units of time for announcements are one minute, 30 seconds, 20 seconds, and ten seconds. The basic rate which the television station charges for its time periods is set according to the time of day the program is shown or when the commercial announcement is given.

Typical time divisions and schedules of charges for participating announcement programs and spot announcements are given in Figures 13–2 and 13–3. It will be noted that stations vary their rates, depending on the time of day or night and the program involved, reflecting the normal difference in the size of the audience attracted at that hour by the different programs. In Figure 13–2, it is seen that the station charges a high of $1,500 for a 30-second announcement after some shows at 6:00 to 8:00 in the evening, to a low of $50 for 10:00 to 1:00 A.M. Also to be noted is the program rate of $3,600 for one hour. Figure 13–3 shows for a different station the variation by class of time, length of announcement, and frequency.

The national and regional television networks set their rates on the basis of the time of day the program is shown, the number of stations of the network which the advertiser includes, and the amount of time for which the advertiser contracts in a given period. The average 30-second announcement on prime-time network TV now costs $30,-000. The higher rated spots cost $50,000, the lowest about $20,000.[9] One of the major TV network's one-hour basic rate for its 214 stations is $166,415. However, actual rates for the network for one hour of time are quoted as a percentage of this basic station rate, and vary from 18 percent to 67 percent of the basic rate, depending on the time of day and the season of the year.

Some examples of the cost of one minute of network television commercial time on well-known programs might be of interest. One minute of commercial time on the average professional football game broadcast costs $65,000; on National Collegiate Athletic Association games, $50,000; and on the 1975 Super Bowl game, $225,000 (an estimated 71,260,000 people watched the game). One minute of commercial time on a World Series baseball special broadcast costs $82,000. An idea of relative costs involved is obtained when it is noted that approximately 41.5 percent of TV households are reached by a Superbowl game, or an advertising cost of approximately $8 per thousand households; whereas the average Monday night professional game reaches 21 percent of households at a cost of $4.75 per 1,000; and the World Series delivers 30 percent of households at a cost of about $4 per thousand.[10]

A 30-second announcement on individual TV stations costs up from $6,000 in major markets to as low as $5 in the very small markets.

[9] Audience estimated from *Ayer Media Facts,* 1975, p. 8.

[10] Reprinted, with permission, from the 1976 *Broadcasting Yearbook,* p. A–2.

FIGURE 13–2

NEW YORK *

New York-Northeastern New Jersey—Cont'd

WNEW-TV
NEW YORK CITY
(Airdate April, 1940.)

Metromedia Television

METRO TV SALES
(NoB)   TvB

Media Code 6 233 0650 3.00
Metromedia Television, Division of Metromedia, Inc.,
205 E. 67th St., New York, N. Y. 10021. Phone
212-535-1000. TWX 212-867-6978.

1. PERSONNEL
Vice-Pres. & Gen'l Mgr.—Lawrence P. Fraiberg.
Vice-Pres. & Gen'l Sales Mgr.—Charles T. (Budd) Meehan.
National Sales Manager—Lawrence Maloney.

2. REPRESENTATIVES
Metro TV Sales.

3. FACILITIES
Video 37,100 w., audio 5,500 w.; ch 5.
Antenna ht.: 1,330 ft. above average terrain.
Operating schedule: 7:10-1:30 am Mon thru Fri;
8.25-1:30 am Sat; 7:40-1:00 am Sun. EST, DST.

4. AGENCY COMMISSION
15% to recognized agencies on net time charges only;
no cash discount.

5. GENERAL ADVERTISING See coded regulations
General: 2a, 5.
Rate Protection: 12k, 14h.
Basic Rates: 40a.
Cancellation: 70a.
Prod. Services: 87a, 87b.
Orders received more than 28 days in advance of start
are subject to reconfirmation 28 days prior to start at
the rates in effect on date of initial broadcast.

6. TIME RATES
Eff 9/4/72—Rec'd 10/17/72.

8. PARTICIPATING ANNOUNCEMENT PROGRAMS
Rec'd 2/11/74.
30 SECONDS

	Section		
MON THRU FRI, AM:	I	II	III
Underdog—7-7:30 am	250	150	100
Flintstones—7:30-8 am	250	150	100
Bugs Bunny—8-8:30 am	250	150	100
Flying Nun—8:20-9 am	250	150	100
Hazel—9-9:30 am	150	100	75
Mothers-In-Law—9:30-10 am	150	100	75
I Love Lucy—10-10:30 am	150	100	75
Green Acres—10:30 11 am	150	100	75
Andy Griffith—11-11:30 am	150	100	75
Midday-Alive—11:30 am-1 pm	150	100	75
Movie Matinee—1-3 pm	200	150	100
Casper—3-3:30 pm	760	600	400
Huckleberry Hound—3:30-4 pm	700	600	400
Bugs Bunny—4-4:30 pm	1000	900	700
Lost in Space—4:30-5 pm	1000	900	700
Flintstones—5:30-6 pm	1000	900	700
I Love Lucy—6-6:30 pm	1000	900	700
Bewitched—6:30-7 pm	1200	1000	850
Mission Impossible—7-8 pm	1500	1300	1000
Dealer's Choice—8-8:30 pm	1000	900	700
Merv Griffin—8:30-10 pm	1100	900	700
10 O'Clock News—10-11 pm	1250	1050	850
One Step Beyond—11-11:30 pm	900	700	500
11:30 Movie—11:30 pm-concl.	300	250	200
Various—approx 1 am	100	75	50
SAT:			
Daktari—7-8 am	170	100	75
Western Movie—8-8:30 am	170	100	75
Rifleman—9-9:30-10 am	200	150	100
I Love Lucy—10-10:30 am	200	150	100
Ebony Affair—10:30-11 am	200	150	100
Soul Train—11 am noon	500	35	300
Creature Features—noon-1:30 pm	500	400	300
Eastside Comedy—1:30-2:30 pm	500	400	300
Shirley Temple—2:30-4 pm	500	400	300
Big Valley—4-5 pm	750	600	450
Bewitched—5-5:30 pm	750	600	450
Ghost & Mrs. Muir—5:30-6 pm	750	600	450
*Weekend Playhouse—6-8 pm	1500	1250	1000
TBA—8-10 pm	1500	1250	1000
10 O'Clock News—10-10:30 pm	1250	1050	850
Black News—10:30-11 pm	1250	1050	850
11 pm Feature Film—11 pm-concl.	300	250	200
Various—1 am approx	100	75	50
SUN:			
Daktari—7-8 am	100	80	50
Wonderama—8-11 am	900	800	600
Flintstones—11 am noon	1300	1000	800
Eastside Comedy—noon-1 pm	860	650	500
Five Star Movie—1-3 pm	750	600	500
Metro Movie—3-5 pm	750	600	500
Saint—5-6 pm	750	600	500
*Weekend Playhouse—6-8 pm	1250	1050	850
Lawrence Welk—8-9 pm	1500	1250	1000
10 O'Clock News—10-10:30 pm	1250	1050	850
Sports Extra—10:30-11 pm	1250	1050	850
Gabe—11-11:30 pm	400	350	250
David Susskind—11:30 pm-1:30 am	400	300	200

(†) Price for special negotiated separately.
(*) Sold in combination with Sunday Weekend Playhouse. Rate buys two exposures.

10. PROGRAM RATES
Mon thru Fri 5 pm-1 am; Sat 1 pm-sign-off;
Sun noon-sign-off. 1 hr........................ 3600

FIGURE 13–3

6. TIME RATES

AA—Mon thru Sun 6-10:30 pm.
A—Mon thru Fri sign-on-6 pm; Sat & Sun 5-6:30 pm; Mon thru Sun 10:30-11 pm.
B—Mon thru Sun 11 pm-sign-off; Sat & Sun sign-on-5 pm.

7. SPOT ANNOUNCEMENTS

	1 Pl	3 Pl	5 Pl	10 Pl	15 Pl
CLASS AA					
60 sec	235	205	175	145	115
30 sec	135	115	95	80	65
20 sec	115	100	85	70	55
10 sec	90	80	70	55	40
CLASS A					
60 sec	110	95	85	70	55
30 sec	65	55	50	40	35
20 sec	50	45	40	30	25
10 sec	40	35	30	25	20
CLASS B					
60 sec	55	50	45	35	30
30 sec	35	30	26	22	20
20 sec	30	26	22	19	15
10 sec	25	22	19	15	12

8. PARTICIPATING ANNOUNCEMENT PROGRAMS

	1 Pl	3 Pl	5 Pl	10 Pl	15 Pl
CLASS AA					
60 sec	250	230	210	190	160
30 sec	145	135	120	110	90
20 sec	125	115	100	90	75
CLASS A					
60 sec	125	110	95	80	65
30 sec	75	60	55	45	40
20 sec	60	50	45	35	30
10 sec	50	40	35	30	25
CLASS B					
60 sec	65	60	50	40	35
30 sec	40	35	30	25	20
20 sec	35	30	26	22	18
10 sec	30	26	22	18	14

9. PACKAGE ANNOUNCEMENT RATES
ROS
75% of the applicable time classification fixed-position rates.
ROS rates apply only to schedules with a weekly minimum of 7 spots. ROS spots will be shown at station's discretion.

10. PROGRAM RATES
Mon thru Sun 6-10:30 pm, 1 hr.................... 1300

FIGURE 13–4

TELEVISION

SPORT EVENTS – AVERAGE RATINGS AND VIEWER COMPOSITION

	TV HH Rating	Audience Composition				% of Total Men Viewers of T/C		
		Total Men '000	% of Adult Viewers	Total Women '000	% of Adult Viewers	18-34 (U.S. = 39%)	35-49 (26%)	50+ (35%)
FOOTBALL								
NFL Superbowl	41.6	24,240	61%	15,410	38%	36%	28%	35%
ABC NFL	21.2	11,930	63	7,020	37	38	31	31
CBS-NFL	14.1	7,870	66	4,140	34	35	29	36
NBC-NFL	13.4	7,540	66	3,930	34	36	27	37
College Bowl & All Star	21.6	12,630	60	8,500	40	32	27	41
NCAA Reg Season	12.2	6,250	63	3,640	37	36	25	39
BASEBALL								
World Series	30.7	15,610	54%	13,130	46%	29%	27%	44%
All Star Game	23.8	13,260	60	8,940	40	35	22	43
Regular Season	9.0	4,310	59	3,030	41	28	20	52
HORSE RACING								
Kentucky Derby	16.5	6,730	45%	8,230	55%	20%	24%	56%
Preakness	14.9	7,620	56	6,090	44	39	18	43
Other Racing	5.2	1,560	46	1,850	54	19	29	52
BASKETBALL								
NBA Regular Season	9.3	4,930	67%	2,410	33%	47%	25%	28%
NBA Playoffs	13.5	6,670	61	4,330	39	41	26	33
NBA All Star Game	12.6	6,350	60	4,150	40	52	22	26
ABA Playoffs	4.3	1,380	57	1,050	43	36%	37%	27%
BOWLING								
Pro Bowl. Tour	9.0	3,940	51%	3,850	49%	31%	26%	43%
Brunswick Open	6.0	2,140	40	3,180	60	43	11	46
AUTO RACING	7.7	3,280	54%	2,780	46%	37%	26%	37%
GOLF								
CBS Golf Classic	4.1	1,760	57%	1,350	43%	26%	26%	48%
Tournaments	8.6	4,200	55	3,380	45	28	22	50
TENNIS								
CBS Tennis Classic	4.5	1,980	54%	1,690	46%	36%	26%	38%
Alan King Tennis	3.6	1,250	52	1,140	48	22	40	38
Family Circle Tennis	4.1	1,590	46	1,840	54	33	19	48
World Champ Tennis	4.7	2,090	59	1,460	41	38	26	36
Wimbledon	4.5	1,720	49	1,770	51	35	21	44
BOXING								
Madison Sq. Garden	5.1	2,720	65%	1,470	35%	35%	16%	49%
MULTI-SPORTS SERIES								
American Sportsman	9.4	4,560	61%	2,860	39%	40%	24%	36%
ABC WW Sports	11.6	5,520	59	3,760	41	40	25	35
CBS Sports Spectacular	6.4	2,970	54	2,490	46	35	25	40

Source: Nielsen

1975 NETWORK TV COSTS – 30 SEC. ANN.

		1st Qtr.	2nd Qtr.	3rd Qtr.	4th Qtr.
PRIME (Inc. Movie)	Est. cost	$29,000	$30,000	$24,000	$37,000
	Avg. Rtg.	20.2	15.9	13.4	19.4
	CPM HH	$2.10	$2.75	$2.61	$2.64
DAYTIME	Est. cost	$5,000	$5,200	$4,600	$5,700
	Avg. Rtg.	7.8	6.6	7.3	7.5
	CPM HH	$0.94	$1.15	$0.92	$1.05
EARLY EVENING NEWS	CBS Est. Cost	$11,200	$12,800	$9,500	$16,000
	Avg. Rtg	15.5	11.7	10.5	15.7
	CPM HH	$1.05	$1.60	$1.32	$1.41
	NBC Est. cost	$15,000	$15,000	$11,000	$13,500
	Avg. Rtg	13.8	12.2	9.5	14.6
	CPM HH	$1.59	$1.79	$1.09	$1.28
	ABC Est. cost	$10,000	$10,500	$8,000	$12,000
	Avg. Rtg	11.5	9.2	8.0	12.2
	CPM HH	$1.27	$1.67	$1.46	$1.36
TODAY SHOW	Est. cost	$6,000	$6,350	$6,350	$6,350
	Avg. Rtg.	5.2	5.4	4.4	6.2
	CPM HH	$1.68	$1.72	$2.11	$1.42
AM AMERICA	Est. cost	$1,500	$1,500	$1,500	$1,500
	Avg. Rtg.	2.5*	2.5*	2.5*	2.5*
	CPM HH	$.88	$.88	$.88	$.83
TONIGHT SHOW	Est. cost	$12,300	$13,700	$13,000	$14,300
	Avg. Rtg.	9.1	8.9	9.5	9.4
	CPM HH	$1.97	$2.25	$2.00	$2.10
LATE EVENING MOVIE	CBS Est. Cost	$6,900	$8,000	$7,200	$8,200
	Avg. Rtg.	7.4	6.1	6.1	6.6
	CPM HH	$1.36	$1.91	$1.72	$1.72
ABC WIDE WORLD OF ENTERTAINMENT:					
WIDE WORLD MYSTERY	Est. cost	$6,250	$7,500	$6,750	$8,000+
	Avg. Rtg.	5.8	5.4	4.9	5.6
	CPM HH	$1.57	$2.03	$2.01	$1.98
WIDE WORLD SPECIALS	Est. cost	$6,250	$7,500	$6,750	$8,000+
	Avg. Rtg.	4.6	5.4	6.6	5.0
	CPM HH	$1.98	$2.03	$1.49	$2.21
MIDNIGHT SPECIAL	Est. cost	$5,000	$5,300	$5,300	$5,300
	Avg. Rtg.	5.0	4.0	3.4	3.5
	CPM HH	$1.46	$1.93	$2.28	$2.09
TOMORROW	Est. cost	$1,650	$1,650	$1,650	$1,650
	Avg. Rtg.	2.6	2.8	3.0	3.3
	CPM HH	$.93	$.86	$.80	$.69

*As estimated By ABC network. (1st Qtr. Actual Rating 1.6) ABC guaranteeing equivalent of 3.0 Rating.

Source: ABC, CBS, and NBC as of January '75.

Discounts

As a rule, television stations offer a cumulative quantity discount rate based on the number of time units the advertiser uses during a given period. Common patterns are to quote discounts based on cycles of 13 times, 26 times, 39 times, 52 time periods, and so on. And in the case of 60- and 30-second announcements, 20-second station break spots, and 10-second IDs, discounts often are given based on the quantity bought during a week. Some offer lower summer rates (June through August).

Advantages of TV as an advertising medium

The obvious and chief advantage of television as an advertising medium is that it makes full use of both sight and sound. Print media rely on sight only, and the ability of the potential customer to read the advertisement.

TV can attract the attention and interest of the potential customer through both sight and sound in combination. In addition, it has a great advantage of being able to use motion. This permits the actual demonstration of the product in use to be made by a living salesman. Since the salesman can discuss and explain the use of the product and its advantages and features as he demonstrates it in use on television, the commercial is the nearest thing to personal selling that can be achieved in advertising or promotion.

Also, while the commercial is on the screen, there is no competition from adjacent editorial material, as is true of print media. And it permits the use of the human voice, which many consider more effective for numerous purposes than the printed word because of its intimate nature. Television also permits the use of color, which can add greatly to the effectiveness of the advertising, and permits the commercial to do an excellent job of package identification.

Another important advantage of television, although not inherent to the medium, has developed. Because of its tremendous popularity, it has proven to be a true mass medium. Since 97 percent of all homes have television receiving sets, and the average home has a set turned on over six hours a day, the advertiser using television can reach almost all the people in all parts of the United States with his message. As a result, many advertisers of widely used items employ television as a medium even though they make little use of the demonstration advantage of television, but do basically much purely reminder type advertising. Closely tied in with this factor of television's effectiveness in reaching and influencing such a large proportion of the people is the advantage of television advertising's effectiveness in influencing the trade.

Television also has the advantage of being relatively selective and flexible in several ways. By the selection of type of program, the advertiser can gain a relatively selective type of listening audience. Also, the selection of time of day and of the week permits a certain selectivity of audience. He can select only those markets and areas in which he wishes to advertise and those stations he wishes to use. The television advertiser can use as much or as little time as he desires. He can use spot television to run seasonal advertising programs, and can run saturation programs for special occasions such as promotions or introduction of new products. The advertiser also can use different appeals in various local markets as he deems desirable, and, in the case of spot television, can make his message timely.

Limitations of television

As is true of all advertising media, television does have certain limitations or weaknesses. The advertising message lasts only as long as it is being presented on the receiving screen. If the prospect is not viewing or listening at the exact moment the advertisement is presented, the message is gone forever and wasted as far as that prospect is concerned. This is quite a contrast to print media, where the message may be available to the prospect over quite an extended period of time.

Also, since in most markets several television stations are broadcasting at the same time, the message of any advertiser can reach only that portion of the total viewing audience tuned to a particular station at that time. And, in the case of announcement advertising on station break time, his audience may be further reduced, because many viewers may be twirling the tuning knob, selecting a new station for the next time period. Even during sponsored programs, viewers may leave the set during the commercial to do other things, thus missing the commercial message.

The cost of good programs is very high, eliminating this form of television advertising as a medium for many smaller advertisers. Also, the advertising message must be brief.

Another problem or handicap in the use of television is that of different time zones existing in the United States. A program broadcast on the East Coast at the prime time of 8:00 P.M. would be heard at 5:00 P.M. on the West Coast, during the childrens' hour, if broadcast simultaneously on a national network. To compound this problem, various areas of the country have different daylight saving practices. Advertisers can and do overcome this timing problem by using electrical transcriptions or delayed broadcasts. Possibly a greater time handicap is that there are only so many desirable hours available on a television network, so that the number of advertisers who can use desirable time is limited.

Radio

The organization of the radio field

As is true with television, the advertiser considering the use of radio as an advertising medium is interested in the facilities provided for broadcasting and receiving his advertising messages. Similar to television, three segments of facilities are of interest to the potential advertiser. These are the individual stations, the network system, and the number of receiving sets owned.

Number of stations. The basic unit in the radio field is the individual local station. At the beginning of January 1976, there were 4,463 commercial AM radio stations licensed, 2,767 commercial FM stations, and 804 noncommercial FM stations.[11]

The networks. As is true in television, many of the leading radio stations are organized into networks. These were formed early in the history of radio to provide programs to the affiliated stations in local

---

[11] Reprinted, with permission, from the 1976 *Broadcasting Yearbook,* p. A–2.

markets covering the country, which could be broadcast simultaneously by telephone cable. This enabled advertisers to broadcast their advertising messages to most parts of the country through one organization, as is done in television today. There are four national networks and 53 regional radio networks.

Before television reached its present great popularity, the radio networks were important, and most radio advertising was network. Since the present wide viewing of television, the radio networks have declined in relative importance, and only a small percentage of radio advertising is network, compared with national spot and local.

For selected years the expenditures for the three types of radio advertising have been as shown in Figure 13–5.

FIGURE 13–5

	National network	National spot	Local	Total
1945	125,671,834	76,696,463	99,814,042	
1950	124,633,089	118,823,880	203,211,000	
1955	60,268,000	120,393,000	272,011,000	
1960	35,026,000	202,102,000	385,346,000	
1965	44,602,000	247,942,000	535,238,000	
1966	47,217,000	284,522,000	580,220,000	911,979,000
1967	47,600,000	289,800,000	602,200,000	946,600,000
1968	54,750,000	342,200,000	733,400,000	1,130,300,000
1969	50,900,000	349,600,000	799,900,000	1,200,400,000
1970	48,800,000	355,300,000	852,200,000	1,252,800,000
1971	55,100,000	378,000,000	954,600,000	1,387,700,000
1972	65,000,000	384,300,000	1,098,400,000	1,547,700,000
1973	59,400,000	382,800,000	1,213,400,000	1,655,600,000

Source: Reprinted, with permission, from the 1975 *Broadcasting Yearbook.*

Sets available. According to latest estimates, there were 413 million radio sets,[12] or over 1⅞ sets for every man, woman, and child in the United States as of January 1975. The average American household has 5.5 radios. Almost every household owns at least one radio.

Of the 413 million sets, 299 million are in households, while the remaining 114 million are in automobiles and public places.[13] (Estimates are that 95 percent of automobiles have radios.)

Literally millions of people own either regular portable radios or the small transistor radios which they carry with them in their pockets. Thus, the average American is physically in a position to listen to radio at almost every hour that he or she is awake. In the average week, over 95 percent of all persons 12 years old and over are reached by radio. Although the amount of family listening to radio in the

---

[12] Reprinted, with permission, from the 1975 *Broadcasting Yearbook,* pp. C–289, C–290.

[13] Reprinted, with permission, from the 1976 *Broadcasting Yearbook,* p. A–2.

evening has declined drastically since the advent of television, the great number of sets of various types in use indicates that the average American, as an individual, still spends considerable time listening to radio.

Radio programs. The advertiser using radio must decide whether or not to use a sponsored program. However, in recent years, with the television's taking over the main big-show entertainment aspects of broadcasting, the number of sponsored programs has declined drastically. Although many of the comments made earlier about the advantages of the sponsored show on television are true of radio, it must be remembered that the sponsored radio show does not carry the same amount of prestige today that it did in the past. Also, the radio show is much less costly to produce. Production costs are much lower than for television shows, because they are much simpler to produce, usually calling for less expensive talent, much less rehearsal time, and do not call for the staging and costuming required on television.

Today the majority of advertisers using radio do not use sponsored shows. Most radio stations and the networks have adopted what is often referred to as the "magazine format" of programming. That is, the network or stations plan the programming for the day and week to develop a listening audience for the station, much as a magazine develops a particular editorial content to appeal to a certain audience. This involves the use of many participation programs, with the station responsible for the production of the program. A large portion of the programs in radio today consists largely of news and music, following a planned general format. The advertiser's commercials are interspersed in the participation shows or inserted in the station breaks, as is done to a more limited extent on television.

Audience measurement in radio. Basically, the same general approach is used in the measurement of the radio audience as is used in television—that of determining the percentage of a sample of homes listening and applying this percentage to determine the number of homes in the universe that are listening. In doing this, radio uses the same four techniques for determining listenership as are used to determine viewing in television. However, there is one additional serious problem in the case of radio. As noted earlier, a very large share of the radio listening is done outside of the home (while driving in automobiles, at the beach, or on picnics in the case of portables, and at various times and places with the use of transistor sets), and it is difficult to measure the actual amount of such listening. This audience can be measured by the use of personal interviews and diaries, but it still makes extremely difficult the accurate determination of the size of the radio audience.

The cost of radio advertising. As is true of television, the advertiser using radio as a medium must consider two basic elements of cost— time charges and program costs. However, unlike television, studio rehearsal time and production expenses are relatively low, particularly today when few of the high-salaried performers are employed in radio. In the case of sponsored programs, the advertiser will find the same time unit structure on radio as in television. If he decides

FIGURE 13–6
Three-class time breakdown (usually used for program time purposes)

Class AA: 6 A.M. to 10 A.M. and 3 P.M. to 7 P.M., Monday through Friday.
Class A: 10 A.M. to 3 P.M. Monday through Friday; 6 A.M. to 7 P.M., Saturday.
Class B: 7 P.M. to midnight, Monday through Saturday; 7 A.M. to midnight on
           Sunday.

to use the announcement approach rather than a sponsored program,
he will have basically the same selection as in television, except that
he may find available a somewhat wider choice in short commercial
times. Radio time charges have continued to decrease in many areas
as station owners have tried to meet the competition of other media,
especially television. Spot announcements, cooperative sponsoring of
special programs, special concessions, and other inducements have
been used. Some local stations will run ads for local direct selling
organizations on a "commission" basis, with no set charge, but with
so many cents or dollars for each item sold as a result of the radio
advertising.

Radio stations today generally set their rates on the basis of three
classes of time. The periods indicated in Figure 13–6 are typical of the
classification definitions.

A typical table of time charges for programs follows:

FIGURE 13–7
Station time rates

	1 hour	½ hour	¼ hour	10 minutes	5 minutes
Class AA	$265.00	$160.00	$110.00	$90.00	$55.00
Class A	225.00	135.00	95.00	75.00	45.00
Class B	155.00	90.00	65.00	50.00	30.00

Discounts

13 consecutive weeks	5%
26 consecutive weeks	10
39 consecutive weeks	15
52 consecutive weeks or more	20

A sample of the costs for announcements can be obtained from
Figure 13–8.

Selecting the program and station

Although in general the discussion of television program selection
holds true for radio, it should be stressed that since relatively few
advertisers sponsor programs today, this problem does not have the
importance in the radio field that it does in television or did formerly
in radio. However, if the advertiser using radio does wish to sponsor
a program, the same concept of selecting a program that will appeal
to his potential customers is the dominating consideration. For in-

FIGURE 13–8
Spot announcements / regular announcements (rotate 6:00–10:00 A.M. and 3:00–7:00 P.M.), annual frequency

Times per week 1 minute	1–25 times	Class AA 26– 103 times	104– 155 times	156– 311 times	312– 467 times	468 or more times
1 time	$110.00	$99.00	$93.50	$88.00	$85.25	$82.50
5 times	104.50	94.05	88.83	83.60	80.99	78.38
10 times	99.00	89.10	84.15	79.20	76.73	74.25
15 times	93.50	84.15	79.48	74.80	72.46	70.13
20 times	88.00	79.20	74.80	70.40	68.20	66.00
25 times	82.50	74.25	70.13	66.00	63.94	61.88

30 second

1 time	100.00	90.00	85.00	80.00	77.50	75.00
5 times	95.00	85.50	80.75	76.00	73.63	71.25
10 times	90.00	81.00	76.50	72.00	69.75	67.50
15 times	85.00	76.50	72.25	68.00	65.88	63.75
20 times	80.00	72.00	68.00	64.00	62.00	60.00
25 times	75.00	67.50	63.75	60.00	58.13	56.25

1 minute — Class A

1 time	60.00	54.00	51.00	48.00	46.50	45.00
5 times	57.00	51.30	48.45	45.60	44.18	42.75
10 times	54.00	48.60	45.90	43.20	41.85	40.50
15 times	51.00	45.90	43.35	40.80	39.53	38.25
20 times	48.00	43.20	40.80	38.40	37.20	36.00
25 times	45.00	40.50	38.25	36.00	34.88	33.75

30 second

1 time	54.00	48.60	45.90	43.20	41.85	40.50
5 times	51.30	46.17	43.61	41.04	39.76	38.48
10 times	48.60	43.74	41.31	38.88	37.67	36.45
15 times	45.90	41.31	39.02	36.72	35.57	34.43
20 times	43.20	38.88	36.72	34.56	33.48	32.40
25 times	40.50	36.45	34.43	32.40	31.39	30.38

1 minute — Class B

1 time	35.00	31.50	29.75	28.00	27.13	26.25
5 times	33.25	29.93	28.26	26.60	25.77	24.94
10 times	31.50	28.35	26.78	25.20	24.42	23.63
15 times	29.75	26.78	25.29	23.80	23.06	22.31
20 times	28.00	25.20	23.80	22.40	21.70	21.00
25 times	26.25	23.63	22.31	21.00	20.35	19.69

30 second

1 time	30.00	27.00	25.50	24.00	23.25	22.50
5 times	28.50	25.65	24.23	22.80	22.09	21.38
10 times	27.00	24.30	22.95	21.60	20.93	20.25
15 times	25.50	22.95	21.68	20.40	19.76	19.13
20 times	24.00	21.60	20.40	19.20	18.60	18.00
25 times	22.50	20.25	19.13	18.00	17.44	16.88

Note: 20-second announcements—80% of 1-minute rate.
10-second announcements—50% of 1-minute rate.

stance, a number of advertisers still sponsor sports contests on radio, since it is believed they attract a large listening audience with certain characteristics and can, therefore, be a very effective vehicle for many products. Because of the emphasis on the so-called magazine format approach and the heavy emphasis on news and music, the advertiser must decide what type of participation program attracts the best audience for his product.

The criteria for selecting the station are the same in radio as in television. Probably the main difference is that there are many more radio stations than TV stations, and so the alternatives are increased. Too, with the greater number of stations, including commercial FM stations, and their attempts to develop special audiences through their programming, it may be possible in some cases for the advertiser to obtain a station appealing more specifically to his segment of the market, giving him greater selectivity of audience.

Advantages of radio

The chief feature of radio as an advertising medium is that it depends solely on the spoken word. Thus, the listener can hear the programs and the commercials while doing other things, such as driving a car or doing housework. It does not require the effort and concentration required by other media. And the human voice is probably the most natural way for people to communicate with each other. The human voice has a warmth and persuasiveness in conveying a message that can be most effective. It permits the listener to develop his own image of the program or store or setting, and to involve himself in the situation in his own preferred way, since he does not see the setting or action or announcers. In many instances, such mental imagery can be much more effective than any actual setting and performance.

Also, radio can and does reach almost everybody. As noted earlier, virtually every home and most automobiles have radios, and many individuals have a portable set, so that most people have sets available to them at almost every hour of the day. Thus, people can listen to radio at almost any time and any place, regardless of their other activities. Hence, radio can reach a mass market. With the great number of sets in the hands of the population, the potential audience of radio is greater than that of television, all magazines combined, or all newspapers combined.

Radio is a selective medium in the sense that the advertiser can advertise in only those markets he desires. He can vary his messages, and the intensity of coverage of different markets to meet local conditions. He can obtain also, by proper selection of programs, time of day, and stations, selectivity of type of listenership. In the case of FM radio with its features of high-fidelity music reproduction and static-free reception, stations often develop quite a selected segment of the market with excellent musical programming.

Radio is also flexible and timely. The advertiser can run as many commercials in an area or during a time period that he believes to be desirable. And news events and special occurrences can be aired on radio almost as soon as they happen. For this reason, many people listen to radio habitually "to keep up with the latest news." This same effect of timeliness can be brought into commercials when announcing special promotions or the introduction of a new product.

As a result of the lack of concentration required in listening to radio, it is probable that a larger percentage of listeners hear the radio commercials than is true with television viewers. A study conducted by the authors indicates this may well be so. In this study, made in a metropolitan area on the West Coast, 52 percent of the respondents indicated that during the television commercial they regularly left their television sets to do other things, such as to make telephone calls, work in the kitchen, or get refreshments. Of this same group who responded, only 27 percent said they left their radio sets during the commercials.[14]

Radio advertising is much less costly than most of the advertising media. A single 30-second announcement on a station in a large metropolitan market will cost usually less than $300. On a national network, such a 30-second commercial announcement will cost the advertiser from $650 to $2,200, depending on the network, the time of day, and number of times the announcement is run.[15] As a result, the advertiser can reach a market with a budget much smaller than is needed for television.

Disadvantages of radio

As is true of other media, radio has real weaknesses as an advertising medium. Like television, the message that radio delivers is a perishable one. If the person is not listening to the advertiser's message at the time it is broadcast, it is gone forever. Also, as is true of television, with the great number of television and radio stations on the air, the advertiser's message can reach only that share of the population listening to his particular station at the time of the broadcast.

The advantage of being able to listen to radio while doing other things means that many people are hearing the radio program only as a background effect, and are not listening attentively. Hence, although they may be listening to the music, they may not actually grasp the content of the advertising message delivered between musical numbers.

Radio is the one medium in which it is impossible to illustrate the product, so it is not a good medium for products which must actually be seen by the potential customer. However, for many products, a verbal description can still be a very effective selling device.

Radio also poses the problem of selecting the station and program

[14] C. J. Dirksen, *Listening Habits of TV and Radio Audiences in Santa Clara County* (Santa Clara, Cal.: University of Santa Clara Press, 1957).

[15] Reprinted, with permission, from the 1975 *Broadcasting Yearbook,* pp. D–22, D–25, and D–27.

that will obtain the desired number and composition of audience the advertiser desires.

Questions

1. Do you believe television is a better medium for advertising certain types of products than others? If so, give examples and explain why this is true.

2. Does the present wide use of color television add to its suitability for more types of products than when it was "black and white"? Explain.

3. Describe briefly various measures of the television viewing audience that are frequently used. Which do you consider best? Why?

4. What do you understand by the term "magazine concept" as applied to broadcast media? What is its significance to the advertiser on television and radio?

5. Television and radio rates to advertisers are normally established on a time-period basis—Class A, Class B, and so on—although the size of the audience within that time period may vary considerably. Would it be better to set rates on the basis of program ratings? Why?

6. Why is the advertiser so interested in the television program on which his advertisement appears?

7. What is a participating program? What are its significant features from an advertiser's standpoint?

8. What are the important factors for an advertiser to consider in determining whether or not to use radio as an advertising medium?

9. Is it possible to use television and radio to reach particular consumer groups or market segments effectively? Explain.

10. How would you use television and radio, on an effective cost basis, to reach farmers? Businessmen? Housewives? Teen-agers?

11. With virtually every American home having at least one television set, and most of them having color, do you believe it possible for radio to compete successfully with television for the advertisers' dollar in the future? Explain.

12. Watch your television programs from 7:00 to 10:00 P.M. one evening. List all ads appearing during that time. In your opinion, how many and which ones utilized effectively the features of television as an advertising medium? Explain.

13. Listen to your favorite radio station for one hour. List the ads you heard. How many utilized effectively the features of radio as an advertising medium? Explain.

Case 13–1 KAJD

KAJD is a VHF American Broadcasting Station located in a major midwestern city with a population of 1,500,000. The executives of the station are concerned by the fact that its local advertising revenue makes up only 15 percent of its total revenue. As a result, they believe it is important for them to begin an advertising campaign in order to try to increase the amount of local advertisng revenue to about 25 percent of the total overall volume.

Business of the company

KAJD is at present exclusively engaged in and derives all its revenue from television broadcasting. According to both industrywide television rating services, the station ranked second in share of television homes in its respective metropolitan area and market during the last television season.

The television broadcasting industry

Structure. Television broadcasting in the United States basically consists of networks and stations. A network provides programs to its affiliated stations and sells the programs, or commercial time in programs, to national advertisers. There are three major networks: CBS, NBC, and ABC. Each provides programming for about 75 of the 120 hours per week broadcast by the average affiliated station. The remaining programs by an affiliate are either produced by the station or acquired from other sources.

Television stations are either network affiliates or independents. An affiliated station has a contractual arrangement with a network whereby the affiliate has first call on the network's programs in its community. The vast majority of commercial stations are affiliated with the major networks. Independent stations are not affiliated with a major network on a regular basis and must produce or acquire virtually all their own programming.

Television stations are either Very High Frequency (VHF) stations, which transmit on Channels 2 through 13, or are Ultrahigh Frequency (UHF) stations, which transmit on channels 14 through 83. For technical reasons, a VHF station can be received over a broader area than a UHF station. Moreover, in most markets in which there are both types of stations, VHF stations have an additional but decreasing advantage arising from the inability of most older sets (those marketed prior to April 1964) to receive UHF signals.

Sources of revenue. The principal source of revenue for a television station is the sale of time to advertisers. A time sale may involve all or part of a program, or spot announcements within or between programs. For the affiliated station, there are four types of revenue:

Network. Payments by a network to a station for broadcasting network programs which have been sold by the network to agencies representing national advertisers.

National spot. Payments for time sold by the station or its sales representative directly to agencies representing national or regional advertisers. The time sold may be a program but usually is a series of spot announcements, generally either between programs or within the station's own programs. Most national sales contracts are short-term, often covering spot campaigns running for 13 weeks or less.

Local. Payments for time sold by a station's local sales force to local advertisers or agencies.

Other. Payments by advertisers for items other than time, such as programming, talent, and production costs. This is not a major source of revenue for most stations.

A television station charges rates which are primarily determined by the estimated number of television homes it can provide for an advertiser's message. The estimates of the total number of television homes in the market and of the station's share of those homes are based on one or both of the industrywide television rating services. A station's rate card for national and local advertisers contains a detailed schedule of prices which takes into account, in addition to audience delivered, such variables as the length of the unit of time and the quantity purchased. The rate that serves as the basis for payments by a network to an affiliated station is largely determined by the proportion of homes it delivers to the network in relation to the total homes delivered by all the network's affiliates.

Competition. The television broadcasting industry competes for the time of viewers with other leisure-time activities and for advertising dollars with all other media. Within its coverage area, a television station competes with other television stations and with other advertising media serving the same area. The outcome of the competition among television stations for television dollars in a market depends on share of audience, on price and on the effectiveness of the sales effort.

New sources of competition include pay television (Pay TV) and community antenna television (CATV). CATV systems carry television broadcast signals by wire or cable to subscribers who pay a fee for this service. (See "CATV.")

Programming (KAJD)

KAJD serves the needs of its area audience by providing a balanced schedule of entertainment and informational programs, including news and public affairs. The ABC network programming carried by KAJD includes comedy, drama, music, sports, news, special events and documentaries and constitutes about 60 percent of the programming broadcast. In addition, KAJD provides local programming which is attuned to local and area needs. Such local programming is either purchased from other sources or is produced by the station. Emphasis is placed on locally originated news and related informational programs. KAJD has three locally produced half-hour news programs and several five-minute newscasts each day.

Editorials on both national and local issues are developed and written and are presented at least three times a week. News documentaries and discussion programs on area problems are presented from time to time. KAJD subscribes and adheres to the Television Code of National Association of Broadcasters. This code contains program and advertising standards on such matters as morality, taste, deception, and commercial content.

Network affiliation. KAJD has a standard affiliation contract with the ABC Television Network. The contract provides that the network will offer to the affiliated station a variety of network programs, sponsored and unsponsored, with respect to which the station has the right of first refusal before any other television station in its community.

The station also has the right to reject or accept the programs offered.

KAJD is compensated by the network for commercially sponsored network programs which it carries. The amount of compensation is determined by a formula which applies a series of percentage adjustments to the station's network rate as set forth in the contract. The station's network rate may be reduced during the term of the contract only if the rates of the ABC affiliates in general are reduced.

Besides providing an important source of income, the network affiliation is advantageous because, generally, network programs have a degree of public acceptance which increases the salability to national and local advertisers of time adjacent to such network programs. Although FCC regulations prevent network contracts from having terms of more than two years, such regulations permit successive renewals.

Sources of operating revenues. The following table shows the approximate percentage of contribution to the company's operating revenues (less agency commissions) by source for the fiscal year:

Network advertising.	21%
National spot advertising.	60%
Local advertising	15%
Miscellaneous revenue	4%

The executives believed that it would be more effective if they could increase the local advertising to 25 percent of the total revenue and have the approximate contribution to the station's revenues as listed below:

Network advertising.	16%
National spot advertising.	55%
Local advertising	25%
Miscellaneous revenue	4%

Color television. KAJD transmits network color programs and originates film, tape and live color programs from its own studios. The company believes that color programs have greater appeal and that color advertising has greater effectiveness than black and white. Although the company's station and the industry in general do not charge a premium for telecasting in color, the company anticipates that the greater effectiveness of color, combined with the expected growth in the number of homes with color sets, will tend to increase overall industry broadcast revenues.

Company's competition. KAJD operates in a competitive environment described under "The Television Broadcast Industry," which, generally is applicable to the industry.

All VHF channels allocated to the market are occupied. Three UHF channels allocated, an all-UHF market, also are occupied. All such VHF and UHF channels have been on the air for more than seven years. The company anticipates continued vigorous competition from its VHF competitors and from its two UHF competitors.

Federal regulation. The company's television broadcasting operations are subject to the jurisdiction of the FCC under the Communications Act of 1934, as amended. The act empowers the FCC, among other things, to issue, revoke or modify broadcasting licenses, to assign frequency bands, to determine the location of stations, to regulate the apparatus used by stations, to establish areas to be served, to adopt such regulations as may be necessary to carry out the provisions of the act and to impose certain penalties for violation of such regulation.

Broadcasting licenses may be granted for a maximum period of three years and—upon application and in the absence of conflicting application (which would require the FCC to hold a hearing), or adverse findings as to the licensee's qualifications—are renewed without hearing by the FCC for additional three year terms. The company's renewal application has always been granted without hearing for the regular term.

The act prohibits the transfer of a license or the transfer of control of a licensee without prior approval of the FCC. No license may be held by a corporation of which more than one-fifth of the capital stock is owned of record or voted by aliens or their representatives (one-fourth in the case of a parent of a licensee corporation), or which is subject to alien management, ownership, or control to the degree specified in the act.

Under FCC regulations, a license to operate a television or radio station will not be granted to any person (or persons under common control) if such person directly or indirectly owns, operates or controls another station of the same type covering substantially the same area. In 1964, the FCC adopted more restrictive rules relating to the overlap of service areas of stations under common control.

Case question

1. What type of advertising program might KAJD adopt to increase its volume of local advertising revenue?

Case   **BEAUREGARD COMPANY**
13–2   **Preparing a TV spot commercial**

The Beauregard Company operates one of the largest restaurant chains in the United States. As of January the current fiscal year, the Beauregard chain included 750 restaurants, of which 350 were operated by the company and 400 were operated by licensees.

Beauregard's restaurants have been established primarily on the basis of serving motorists with food of an assured quality. Most of the restaurants are located on highways or main roads leading into urban areas, and most are designed to provide both table and soda fountain services.

Because of the location of the restaurants and the eating habits of motorists, most of the restaurants have a substantial mid-afternoon and late evening business, in addition to the normal breakfast and luncheon business. While the company's business is largely seasonal, the decline in the volume in the North in the winter is to some extent offset by increased business in the Southern and Western areas.

The restaurants vary in size and type from complete-menu dining room establishments, some of which serve liquor, to counter-type walk-up milk bars and curb-service operations. Seating capacities range up to 300 people, although the standard restaurants built in recent years have seating capacities for 100 people.

In order to maintain high standards of quality and uniformity, in its own and licensed restaurants, Beauregard has evolved a system of plants, commissaries, and distribution centers strategically located throughout its chain, in which it manufactures or processes for distribution to all of its restaurants about 750 different products. Under the supervision of trained chefs, the commissaries prepare many of the foods which are supplied to the restaurants. The products include a wide variety of canned, packaged, or frozen foods, meats and baked goods, also ice cream, fountain supplies, candies, pastries, soups, and paper goods and service supplies. Beauregard supplies standardized menus on a cyclical basis.

Although some of the restaurants are located in large cities, most of the 750 restaurants are located on highways or on main routes leading into urban centers.

The standard form of operator's agreement under which the licensees are licensed to operate under the Beauregard name provides for use by the licensee of the Beauregard name and the various trade names, designs, advertising, and architecture and other similar features.

The operator's agreement contains provisions requiring the licensee to conform to standards established by Beauregard as to quality of commodities and service, quality of equipment, furnishings and design, maintenance of the building and premises, and other provisions for the protection of the interests of the Beauregard Company.

In line with Beauregard's aim "to provide the public good food at reasonable prices and assure them what to expect from a Beauregard restaurant," the company undertakes a major institutional advertising program. In the last fiscal year, Beauregard spent $5 million for institutional advertising, of which the independent operators contributed about 20 percent of the amount on a voluntary basis.

Advertising

Of the $5,000,000 invested in advertising, the company had spent about 50 percent on 30-second spot commercials which were placed primarily on television stations throughout the United States during the months of March through October each year.

Beauregard's vice president of marketing became concerned about a recent increase in rates which the television stations in 90 percent of the company's market areas announced for the coming year. As a result he decided that the company should consider the advisability of using 10-second instead of 30-second commercials.

In his analysis he pointed out that while the cost of a 10-second commercial averaged about 50 percent of a 30-second commercial, Beauregard would be able to place about twice the number of 10-second commercial than if it continues to use the 30-second one.

He also believed that since the company was using television spots primarily for institutional advertising, that the memorability of the sales message could be enhanced more effectively with more 10-second spots. Studies which he had made also indicated that unless the advertising budget was dramatically increased, the number of impressions would decrease because of the complex problem of continuing to deliver these advertising impressions on the target audience. In his report, he went on to say that in the past advertisers have concentrated efforts on increasing the effectiveness of the advertising: making the message more meaningful, relevant, persuasive.

But to date advertisers have not really addressed the question of memorability. Even if one accpets, for the sake of argument, that day-after recall is some measure of memorability, albeit an imperfect one, the advertisers have certainly not succeeded in creating more memorable advertising.

Since 1965, norms for 0:60 and 0:30 commercials tested among women have shown very little change, very little improvement. If commercials are going to be seen less frequently, and the time elapsed between impressions is going to get longer, then one must work to make the sales message of commercials remembered longer.

Memory is that faculty which enable the consumer *to preserve for future* use the knowledge which is acquired. The advertiser knows a lot about making effective commercials, but has very little research to guide about what makes advertising stick in the memory. However, examination of empirical evidence and application of theories of learning suggest several characteristics that make commercials *memorable:*

1. *Make it simple.* Learning time depends on the *quantity of material:* the simpler the material, the faster it is absorbed. Some people believe that a message that is simple and quick to absorb is also remembered for a *long time.* This is not to argue for empty or inane commercials, but for the careful selection and portrayal of one or two salient features, rather than a hodgepodge of features.

2. *Proceed from known to unknown.* It is easier to associate with the familiar than with the strange. A message that is consonant with previous impressions is more easily memorized than a new message. A message that invites vicarious participation by the viewer helps the process of learning.

There is a special benefit in sticking with the known. The existing slogan, the present demonstration—the present advertising campaign. Don't change strategies, and don't change the familiar elements of the campaign. Make fewer commercials, and run them for a longer time. Frequent change of commercials may add novelty and excitement, but one will not be getting the benefit of familiarity that leads to high memorability of the advertising.

Make it live. A vivid impression is better retained than the run-of-the-mill. Strong, clear, intense, bright portrayals make for vividness.

4. Use the right length. The length of TV commercials has historically been determined by convenient pricing rather than effectiveness. One bought the least demanding but economical unit of time, not the most memorable.

Recall testing suggests that there is little to choose between the scores for 60- and 30-second commercials. One knows that if it can be said in 60 seconds, it can also be made into a 30. One may be able to strip every 30-second commercial to the core of the message, and say it in ten seconds.

But sometimes a message cannot be said in 30 or even 60 seconds. Then one has to take the time, and make it as long as it has to be.

5. The mnemonic device. One of the most important characteristics of memorable commercials is a mnemonic, which is something intended to assist the memory. It can be a sound, it can be written words, it can be something visual—real, or symbolic—or a combination of all these things. It is called an "advertising property," or a "branding device."

The trick is that it must trigger brand name and consumer promise in a flash. It is "A burr that clings to the mind." Consider Commander Whitehead. He first appeared in 1951 in print and on TV in 1957. Is there anyone who does not associate the commander with Schweppes? Yet he has been absent from the scene for three years.

Remember the perking coffee pot and its perky music? That's Maxwell House. It appeared first in 1956 and last in 1965.

If a crown popped on someone's head, would that make one think of Imperial Margarine? It has been around since 1964.

The Green Giant has been ho-ho-ho-ing since 1959, and is still going strong. The Pillsbury Doughboys have been around since 1966—both great mnemonic devices.

The Tiger in Your Tank was around for only a few years after 1964. But it swept the world for Esso with McCann.

When one succeeds in creating a burr for a product, preferably something that can be embedded in the mind's eye, one has found a way of making commercials remembered better and longer.

Coming: the 10-second commercial. Having to get along with fewer TV impressions because of higher costs will exert inexorable pressure for greater frequency, one way or another. This may lead to shorter-length commercials—twenties, fifteens, tens. As was suggested earlier, the shorter length is not going to doom effectiveness; on the contrary, it may stimulate one to focus campaigns more sharply on the most important points.

Case question

1. Prepare a 10-second commercial for Beauregard restaurants.

Case   **RADEK, INC.**
13–3   **Deciding on the use of television advertising**

Radek, Inc. one of the leading department stores in a midwestern city, is considering the advisability of putting a major percentage of its advertising budget into television advertising.

The Radek store had used a few spot announcements, as well as special programs, like its competitors, but the amount spent on television had never exceeded more than 2 percent of the annual advertising budget. In the past, Radek's advertising had been concentrated in newspapers, radio, and direct mail.

It was the opinion of the general manager of the store that television would now be a preferred medium for promoting merchandise in its market. He recommended that the advertising department apportion 35 percent of the current budget for this medium.

Radek's yearly sales averaged about $35 million, and the company budgeted 2.75 percent of sales for advertising. Of this amount, the company had been spending about 65 percent for newspaper advertising, 15 percent for radio advertising, and the remaining 20 percent for direct mail and all other forms of advertising.

The general manager, in recommending a greater emphasis on television, pointed out some facts about the medium.

Home audiences

In Radek's trading area 45 percent of the TV sets are owned by the top-third income group. In the middle economic group, ownership is 39 percent, and 16 percent in the remaining economic third. As a result, television advertising could reach all segments of Radek's market.

Television results

It was the opinion of Radek's general manager that the response to television advertising was superior, as indicated by the results shown by local advertisers who have used the medium. The examples covered products or offers in different classifications of advertising: high-priced products, medium-priced products, low-priced products, and free offers (booklets).

High-priced products

Air-conditioning unit. A 12-week local spot campaign at a time and film production cost of $12,700 brought in approximately 800 inquires for a $400 air conditioner. These inquiries resulted in $160,000 worth of business.

Low-priced products

Product with dual adult and juvenile market. A test survey was conducted one month before the product was advertised on TV, and again

EXHIBIT 13–1

	Before campaign	*13 weeks after start of campaign*
Percentage naming advertised product	12.2	23.4
Men	17.4	21.6
Women	10.5	22.2
Children under 18	41.7	62.5
Percentage naming advertised product as last brand bought	1.6	5.0
Men	1.4	2.3
Women	1.4	5.3
Children under 18	8.3	12.5

after the schedule had been on TV for 13 weeks. Five hundred television families were visited, and one member in each family was asked what brands or makes he cound name and what was the last brand purchased. Increased mention of advertised product and increased sales showed that the five-a-week TV spot had had major impact. (See Exhibit 13–1).

Free offers

Cookbook offer. In a given month, thirty-three 40-second free-cookbook offers following an 80–second film playlet in two markets brought in 55,276 requests. Cost of the TV spots was $7,265.43. The unit cost per request was 13 cents. The printed media offer cost, on the other hand, $92,687.77 and brought in 36,541 replies at a unit cost of $2.54 per reply.

In another instance, an advertiser desiring response in order to distribute a booklet about a vacation resort found a careful analysis of inquiries from various media—newspapers, magazines, and television—to reveal the following cost-per-inquiry comparison: television, 27 cents; printed media, 62 cents.

Retail advertising

Radek's advertising manager argued that he was well aware of the impact of television for national advertising, but he did not believe that it could do as good a job at the retail level as could be accomplished with newspapers. He said that the newspaper is the best medium of advertising in which great numbers of people, as a matter of custom, look for advertisements of merchandise or service which they are about to purchase.

He also mentioned that the newspaper is the local medium which is sure to reach daily the interested attention of an audience in excess of the circulation for which the advertiser pays. The newspaper's advertising rate is based generally upon copies sold rather than upon the number of readers. On the other hand, he stated, "that a television

EXHIBIT 13–2
TV rates in Radek's market

ANNOUNCEMENT CLASSIFICATIONS

Most announcements are assigned two prices. Announcements offered at the higher price (fixed rate) may be purchased on a fixed position non-preemptible basis. When purchased at the lower price (preemptible rate) advertisers may be preempted on 2 weeks' notice.

PARTICIPATING ANNOUNCEMENT PROGRAMS

When network or local programming delays the News, Weather and Sports block (including announcements) or other regularly scheduled 10-10:30 pm programs and announcements, regular rates will apply except in instances when the start of the News, Weather and Sports block (including announcements) is delayed until after 10:30 pm.

	Fixed	Pre-empt
CBS News—7-8 am Mon thru Fri.		
1 min.	22	18
30/20 sec.	14	10
Channel 3 News At Noon—noon-12:30 pm Mon thru Fri.		
1 min.	120	110
30/20 sec.	72	66
Dialing For Dollars/Early Show—3-5 pm Mon thru Fri.		
1 min.	90	80
30/20 sec.	54	48
Perry Mason—rotating 10:30-11:30 pm Sun & Mon.		
1 min.	90	80
30/20 sec.	54	48
It Takes A Thief—9-10 pm Mon.		
1 min.	130	120
30/20 sec.	80	70
Late Show—rotating Tues thru Sat.		
1 min.	54	46
30/20 sec.	32	28
Wackiest Ship in the Army—11:30 pm-concl Sun.		
1 min.	12	10
30/20 sec.	8	6
Channel 3 News At 6—6-6:30 pm rotating Mon thru Fri.		
1 min.	230	200
30/20 sec.	138	120
Thursday & Friday Night CBS Movie, rotating.		
30/20 sec.	200	186
Theatre 3—8:30 pm-concl Sat.		
1 min.	300	240
30/20 sec.	150	120
Channel 3 News At 10—10-10:30 pm approx rotating Sun thru Fri.		
1 min.	220	190
30/20 sec.	132	114
Munsters—5-5:30 pm Mon thru Fri.		
1 min.	120	100
30/20 sec.	72	60

PROGRAM RATES

AA—Daily 6:30-10 pm.
A—Daily 10-10:30 pm; Sat & Sun 6-6:30 pm.
B—Mon thru Fri 5:30-6:30 pm; Sat & Sun 5-6 pm; daily 10:30-11 pm.
C—Mon thru Fri 11 am-5:30 pm; Sat & Sun 11 am-5 pm; daily 11 pm-concl.
D—Daily sign-on-11 am.

	1x	52x	104x	156x
CLASS AA				
1 hr.	1300	1170	1105	1072
1/2 hr.	780	702	663	644
CLASS A				
1 hr.	1000	900	850	825
1/2 hr.	600	540	510	495
1/4 hr.	400	360	340	330
10 min.	320	285	270	260
5 min.	250	200	190	180
CLASS B				
1 hr.	800	720	680	660
1/2 hr.	480	432	408	396
1/4 hr.	320	288	272	264
10 min.	260	234	221	215
5 min.	240	190	180	170
CLASS C				
1 hr.	650	585	553	536
1/2 hr.	390	351	332	322
1/4 hr.	260	234	221	215
10 min.	185	167	157	153
5 min.	130	105	100	95
CLASS D				
1 hr.	420	378	357	347
1/2 hr.	252	227	214	208
1/4 hr.	168	151	144	139
10 min.	125	113	106	103
5 min.	90	81	77	74

SPOT ANNOUNCEMENTS

AA—Daily 6:30-10 pm.
A—Daily 10-10:30 pm.
B—Daily 6-6:30 pm & 10:30-11 pm.
C—Daily 3:30-6 pm & 11 pm-midnight.
D—Daily sign-on-3:30 pm & midnight-sign-off.

CLASS AA	F	P	Q	I	R
30/20 sec.	190	160	140	120	100

F—Fixed position.
P—Preemptible on 2 weeks' notice.
Q—Preemptible on 1 week's notice.
I—Immediately preemptible.
R—Immediately preemptible without notice.

	60 Seconds			30/20 Seconds			10 Sec	
	F	P	I	F	P	I	F	P
A	145	125	110	87	75	66	52	—
B	95	80	70	57	48	42	30	25
C	85	70	50	51	42	30	26	21
D	50	35	20	30	21	15	15	11

Announcements between rate classifications take the rates of the higher classification except:
3:30 pm Mon thru Fri, takes Class D.
6:30 pm & 10 pm take the following rates:

	M	T	W	Th	F	Sa	Su
60 sec F	115	115	115	115	115	115	—
P	100	100	100	100	100	100	—
30/20 sec F	75	75	75	75	75	75	—
P	60	60	60	60	60	60	—
10:00 PM:							
60/30/20							
10 sec F	150	150	150	150	150	150	150
P	130	130	130	130	130	130	130

F—Fixed position.
P—Preemptible on 2 weeks' notice.
I—Immediately preemptible.
The following programs rotate horizontally and vertically:
Late News—Sun thru Sat.
Dragnet—5-5:30 pm Mon thru Fri.
Tonight—Mon thru Fri.

message must be received within a fleeting moment. An advertisement in the daily newspaper lives for many hours—and sometimes for days."

The women's market

The advertising manager also believed that television did not penetrate the major important women's market. He stated that there are two major markets: housewives devoting full time to running a home and raising children, and working housewives with a full-time job who run their homes after business hours. More than half of the working housewives are in the 25 to 44 age group and are considered by many to be among the most desirable prospects. These women cannot be reached by daytime TV. About 90 percent work in business or industry an average of 40 hours a week. Their evening TV viewing has to be selective, because evenings are spent catching up on the many household duties. Daytime TV cannot reach many widowed, divorced, or separated women who must also work. There are almost five million women who fall in this category, along with the six million single women who work during the day and cannot be reached by daytime TV.

Cost

The advertising manager stressed that television is an expensive medium for retailers and presented the rates in Exhibit 2 for the local station to indicate the significance of this (see Exhibit 2).

The data for the county in which the Radek Department Store is located is given in Exhibit 3.

EXHIBIT 13–3
TV market area for department stores

Total households	275,200
TV households	262,900
Consumer spendable income	$2,724,275,000
Total retail sales	$1,712,387,000
Consumer spendable income per household . . .	$10,378

Case questions

1. Do you believe the Radek Department Store should invest 35 percent of its advertising budget in television advertising? Why or why not?
2. If the company decided to use television, what type of programs should it use and at what hour of the day should it advertise?
3. Assume that the company apportions 35 percent of the budget to television, how should the rest of the budget be divided?
4. Evaluate the points which the general store manager and advertising manager give for the two media.

Case **GLAMOR, INC.**
13–4 **Television merchandising**

Glamor, Inc., is engaged in the design, manufacture, and distribution of a wide assortment of hair care items and accessories, including hair curlers, hair rollers, wave and pin-curl clips, chignons, hairnets, combs, and barrettes. At the present time, the company's line of prod-

ucts, including variation of size, decoration, and color, consists of over
400 items. During the last year, various types and styles of hair curlers
and rollers accounted for approximately 85 percent of the company's
dollar sales volume, and various types and styles of barrettes, novelties, and other items accounted for the remaining 15 percent.

The higher cost of professional hair care and the widespread marketing and use of home permanent kits in recent years have broadened the market for the company's line of hair care and hair accessory
items as more women have become aware of the simplicity, effectiveness, and economy of styling and curling their own hair. Women who
do receive regular professional hair styling may also use the Glamor,
Inc.'s, hair care items for nightly pinups and day-to-day styling as a
means of complementing and caring for the professional styling. In
addition, the company believes the increasing teen-age awareness of
style and appearance has been an important factor in its sales growth.

Periods of general business recession have not noticeably affected
the company's business in the past. It is the opinion of management
that during recession periods more women style their own hair in
order to save the higher cost of professional hair styling.

Each year, the company generally produces new styles in certain
lines, which it categorizes as its seasonal lines. As new hair styles have
come into vogue, the company has developed or adapted different lines
of hair accessories to complement such stylings, thus broadening its
line of products beyond that of the standard type hair accessories.
Changes in women's hair styles have had no material adverse effect
on the company's business, since its basic product of hair curlers and
rollers is used regardless of hair style. Hair styles requiring medium
length to long hair are most favorable to the company's business in
that a limited number of hair styles may be employed with short hair
and, hence, a fewer number of hair care and accessory items. Medium
length to long hair may be styled in a number of different ways, using
many different types of hair accessory items.

Glamor, Inc., for the most part, designs its products and manufactures them from the raw material into the finished product. It also does
its own packaging and ships to its customers. The principal raw
materials used are plastics, aluminum, wire, brushes, cards, and cartons. Sources of such materials are many and varied. None of the raw
materials used is in short supply, and the company does not see any
difficulty, in the foreseeable future, in obtaining sufficient raw materials at competitive prices.

During the past several years, Glamor has developed self-service
combination merchandise racks, both counter and floor, designed
primarily for self-service stores. These racks, which hold a wide assortment of the company's products, have been found useful in introducing such products to new retail outlets. As new products are introduced, the company adds them to its combination rack assortment. It
has been Glamor's experience that after introduction of the company's
products by means of combination racks, many retailers have devoted
regular counter and retail space to such items.

In order to broaden its line of hair care items, the company has placed on the market bobby pins, wave nets, slumber caps, and bandeaus, which are manufactured by other firms on a purchase order basis, packaged in the company's cards and containers and sold with its regular line of products.

The volume of net sales has increased steadily over the past 12 years. Sales for the past year amounted to about $15 million.

Distribution

The company's products are sold throughout the United States and in Canada, and in a number of other countries. The United States is divided into ten sales areas, each area served by several company salesmen. Changes in retail merchandising in recent years have widely increased the number and type of retail outlets for the company's products. Initially, the company's line of hair care items was sold almost exclusively in variety stores. Food stores, department stores, drug stores, discount stores, and mail-order houses are now equally important outlets. The company sells its products to approximately 4,000 jobbers who, in turn, each sell to a large number of retail outlets, and to approximately 500 chain store systems, having approximately 40,000 retail outlets.

Advertising

Glamor had concentrated its advertising in trade journals, women's magazines, and in *Reader's Digest.* However, one of its major competitors began to use daytime women's shows on television with theater audiences so that samples could be distributed in the audience while the commercial was being aired.

During the commercial lead-ins, the hostess of the show explained that the audience had been invited to try the competitor's products, and then asked the home viewers to try the product. In some markets, the competitor distributed these samples through drug and food stores.

It was the opinion of the executives of Glamor that this competitor had made significant market gains as a result of using television. They recommended, therefore, to their advertising director that he should point out to them what kind of merchandising service they might expect to receive from television stations. The advertising director gave the following report.

A-D's suggested merchandising activities

Television campaigns. Television networks and stations place considerable emphasis on assisting advertisers throughout their television campaigns. It is their belief that any advertising campaign can be a great deal more effective with proper merchandising assistance.

Product sales will fall short of their *potential goal* if the key people behind the scenes are not properly prepared. These key people must be fully aware of the campaign. Salesmen and retailers should have the full story to insure an adequate supply of stock and be given that extra "boost" to stimulate interest and demand.

Our product, like every product advertised, requires special attention for its specific needs. With a fresh approach, television will tailor a merchandising plan designed to fit our needs.

As a television advertiser, we will have the advantage of full assistance from their merchandising departments. The following activities are merely suggested ideas:

In-store spectacular. Many television stations will offer animated displays to be used in stores at the advertiser's discretion. These displays will be designed exclusively for our product. Fully animated, these displays are effective tools for product sales. They are designed, constructed, installed, and serviced at no cost to the advertiser.

Counter cards. As an added help in emphasizing the campaign and pointing up sales, an attractive counter card tying in campaign and product will be produced in quantity for distribution by sales representatives to stores that stock our product.

Sales meetings and brochures. When advisable, they will prepare a sales brochure to include various advertising tools—advertisers' campaign, success stories, map of coverage area, etc. They will be glad to discuss plans for a television representative to speak to the sales staff, highlighting the important facets of their campaign. This meeting can be either at the regularly scheduled sales meeting or perhaps it might be held in the TV studios.

Nightletters. When time is essential and an extra plus is needed to help kick off an important TV campaign, a night letter or telegram to the right person can be very valuable in increasing distribution and opening the door for the local sales representative.

Mailers. There are various forms of effective mailers which can be sent to key buyers, to people of the advertiser's choosing. A mailer sent at the proper time can play an important role in announcing or reminding the right people of your product's television campaign.

Contests. We can partake in various contests which can be of tremendous benefit; a contest will stimulate viewership, create added attraction to the product, and provide an emphasis on the product's advertising messages.

Personal appearances. Special activities, such as store sales, product introductions, and sales meetings can be highlighted with the appearance of the television personality that gives our product's commercials.

Trade ads. In further support of our campaign, an ad can be placed in trade publications, thus giving added reminder to key buyers about your television campaign.

Gimmick attractions. There is an inexhaustible list of special gimmick attractions available. Favors, imprinted messages, promotion pieces, etc., can be cleverly used to attract attention. These can be as store giveaways or sent to key people people of the advertiser's choosing.

Glamor, Inc., had spent $1,500,000 for advertising in the prior year and had decided to increase this to $2,500,000 for the current year.

Case questions

1. What are the advantages of television as a medium for Glamor, Inc.?
2. What merchandising services are beneficial enough to Glamor to warrant the use of television advertising?
3. Should Glamor use television in place of some of their magazine advertising?

Case   **SPOT TELEVISION AND RADIO**
13–5   **Planning using spots**

1. A leading detergent manufacturer had selected as the central appeal for its TV and radio spot advertising the following central theme (the product is purchased and used primarily by women for washing dishes): "It softens your hands as no other detergent can. You can discard your expensive hand lotions the day you begin using this detergent."

That company planned to spend $2 million in spot TV and radio advertising during a six-month period, emphasizing the above appeal.

2. A major cereal company had selected for its TV and radio spot advertising appeal: "Get the energy of champions with the breakfast of the stars." This cereal is one that appeals to children because it is sugar-coated. The company had allocated $1.25 million for TV and radio spot advertising for a six-month period.

3. An international soft-drink beverage company budgeted $2 million for spot TV and radio advertising for a six-month period and decided to emphasize the appeal: "Get that special refreshing sensation."

The soft drink is sold in bottles and easy-opening cans and is purchased by children, teen-agers, and most other groups.

Information in regard to market coverage, time periods, and costs is given for spot television and spot radio commercials in Exhibits 13–4 and 13–5.

Case question

1. For each of the companies listed above, develop a six-month budget in which you indicate how the allocations for spot TV and spot radio commercials should be used. The products are sold on a national basis in all markets of the United States.

EXHIBIT 13–4
Spot television (TV market coverage)

The number of TV households tuning at least once a week to one or more stations originating in a given TV market. Below is shown the percentage of U.S. TV households viewing stations in each group of markets. The top 10 markets combined cover 38 percent of the United States; the top 20, 50 percent, and so on.

Time periods

The time periods used in this section are defined as follows:

Prime evening—7:30–11:00 P.M., Monday to Sunday
Early fringe—5:00–7:30 P.M., Monday to Sunday
Late fringe—11:00 P.M.–sign-off, Monday to Sunday
Daytime—Sign-on to 5:00 P.M., Monday to Friday

Note: Ten- and 20-second commercials are available during all time periods for network and independent stations. Sixty-second commercials are available only on independent stations during prime time when sponsored network programs are broadcast. Central Time Zone classifications are one hour earlier, local time.

EXHIBIT 13–4 (*continued*)

TELEVISION

U.S. TELEVISION STATISTICS

SET OWNERSHIP (Nielsen Est. as of Sept. 1974)			STATION FACILITIES (FCC as of April 1, 1975)		
					Licensed + Operating
Total TV Homes	68,500,000	100%	Commercial TV		698
(Est. 9/1/75)	(70,100,000)		VHF		507
			VHF		191
Homes with:					
Color TV Sets	46,850,000	68%	Educational TV		221
B&W only	21,650,000	32	VHF		89
			UHF		132
2 or more Sets	28,360,999	41			
One Set	40,140,000	59	Total TV		919
CATV*	8,619,000	13			
UHF*	61,197,000	89	*Arbitron Est., Nov. '74		

COVERAGE OF U.S. TV HOMES BY ADI MARKETS
1974 – 75

Rank	Market (ADI)	TV Homes	% of US TV Homes	% of Mkt. ADI TV Homes With:* CATV	Color	Multi-Set	UHF
1.	New York	6,192,900	9.0%	6%	62%	55%	84%
2.	Los Angeles	3,545,700	5.2	11	78	48	91
3.	Chicago	2,772,100	4.0	2	69	54	95
4.	Philadelphia (Wildwood)	2,239,000	3.3	14	70	56	95
5.	Boston (Manchester, Worcester)	1,673,700	2.4	6	67	50	93
6.	San Francisco	1,635,600	2.4	24	70	41	91
7.	Detroit	1,504,900	2.2	1	71	57	95
8.	Washington, D.C.	1,282,400	1.9	7	70	52	92
9.	Cleveland (Akron, Canton)	1,274,700	1.9	11	75	52	94
10.	Pittsburgh	1,069,800	1.6	25	70	49	89
MARKETS 1–10		**23,190,800**	**33.9%**				
11.	Dallas-Ft. Worth	1,045,800	1.5%	7%	74%	48%	90%
12.	St. Louis	917,200	1.3	1	65	47	89
13.	Minneapolis-St. Paul	871,200	1.3	3	70	39	83
14.	Houston	857,500	1.3	4	72	44	95
15.	Miami (Ft. Lauderdale)	838,900	1.2	2	76	53	87
16.	Atlanta	818,500	1.2	8	70	45	93
17.	Tampa-St. Petersburg (Sarasota)	801,200	1.2	11	75	47	94
18.	Seattle-Tacoma	768,400	1.1	20	73	39	83
19.	Baltimore	735,700	1.1	2	65	62	92
20.	Indianapolis	721,700	1.1	10	76	42	89
MARKETS 1–20		**31,569,900**	**46.2%**				
21.	Hartford-New Haven	637,500	0.9%	1%	69%	47%	93%
22.	Cincinnati	628,300	0.9	3	73	56	93
23.	Kansas City	627,700	0.9	8	71	47	91
24.	Milwaukee	620,200	0.9	2	74	52	94
25.	Portland, Or. (Salem)	607,900	0.9	12	75	41	83
26.	Sacramento-Stockton (Modesto)	604,700	0.9	17	77	37	93
27.	Denver	594,900	0.9	4	73	47	83
28.	Buffalo	578,400	0.8	14	69	48	90
29.	Providence	576,800	0.8	1	72	41	88
—30.	Nashville (Bowling Green)	542,500	0.8	7	61	42	77
MARKETS 1–30		**37,588,800**	**54.9%**				
31.	San Diego	517,300	0.8%	28%	79%	45%	94%
32.	Memphis	507,400	0.7	8	63	40	79
33.	Columbus, Ohio	507,000	0.7	10	74	41	89
34.	Charlotte (Hickory)	502,400	0.7	8	66	40	92
35.	Phoenix (Flagstaff)	496,900	0.7	7	75	44	89
36.	New Orleans	476,400	0.7	3	71	53	93
37.	Louisville	465,300	0.7	6	65	39	93
38.	Oklahoma City	458,000	0.7	7	74	26	84
39.	Greenville-Spartanburg-Asheville	454,600	0.7	8	65	38	80
40.	Charleston-Huntington	442,600	0.6	32	62	33	82
MARKETS 1–40		**42,416,700**	**61.9%**				
41.*	Dayton	431,700	0.6%	8%	77%	49%	95%
42.	Albany-Schenectady-Troy	430,800	0.6	11	65	49	91
43.	Grand Rapids-Kalamazoo	426,100	0.6	9	67	41	89
44.	Orlando-Daytona Beach	425,500	0.6	20	75	43	88
45.	Wilkes Barre-Scranton	406,900	0.6	46	77	37	98
46.	Harrisburg-York-Lancaster-Leb.	399,900	0.6	35	77	45	96
47.	San Antonio	396,300	0.6	14	66	39	87
48.	Birmingham	395,500	0.6	7	65	39	92
49.	Norf.-Port.-Np. News,-Hamp.	389,200	0.6	2	65	51	89
50.	Toledo	389,100	0.6	20	74	48	95
MARKETS 1–50		**46,507,700**	**67.9%**				
	1–75	54,488,900	79.2%				
	1–100	59,544,600	86.5%				
	1–150	66,057,000	96.0%				
	1–206	68,771,000	100.0%				

*Based on Winter 1974   Source: Arbitron

EXHIBIT 13–4 (*continued*)

TELEVISION

TV HOUSEHOLD RATINGS AND MEN/WOMEN VIEWER RATINGS

PROGRAM TYPE		TV Households Rating	'000	Men Ratings 18+	18-34	18-49	25-54	55+	Teens 12-17
MORNING (M–F)									
Today	7:30-8:00AM	6.2	4,250	2.3	1.3	1.2	1.4	4.9	8
	8:30-9:00AM	6.2	4,250	2.1	7	1.3	1.4	4.5	9
CBS News	7:00-8:00AM	2.1	1,440	1.1	4	7	8	2.3	*
DAYTIME (M–F)									
Drama		8.3	5,690	1.4	1.2	1.1	1.0	2.3	1.3
Quiz & Aud Part		7.0	4,770	2.0	1.5	1.5	1.4	3.6	1.5
All 10:00AM-4:30PM		7.5	5,120	1.8	1.4	1.3	1.2	3.0	1.5
EARLY FRINGE (M–F)									
Informational	6:00-7:30PM	13.7	9,360	9.2	5.3	6.2	7.4	16.1	3.5
EVENING (SUN.–SAT.)									
General Drama		18.2	12,490	10.6	9.5	9.5	10.5	12.8	10.2
Susp. & Myst.		18.7	12,810	13.2	11.6	12.3	13.6	15.0	8.8
Situation Comedy		22.9	15,720	15.0	11.7	12.8	14.3	19.1	14.0
Western Drama		19.3	13,210	12.6	10.1	10.7	11.2	17.6	9.9
Feature Film		20.3	13,930	14.6	15.3	15.6	15.8	13.0	13.0
All 7:30-11:00PM		19.4	13,290	13.3	12.1	12.7	13.7	14.7	10.8
LATE NIGHT (M–F)									
Tonight	(NBC)	9.4	6,440	5.1	4.9	4.8	5.1	6.0	1.7
Tomorrow	(NBC)	3.3	2,260	1.2	1.2	1.2	1.4	1.2	*
Late Movies	(CBS)	6.6	4,520	3.9	4.7	4.3	4.4	2.6	2.6
Wide World Myst	(ABC)	5.6	3,840	3.3	3.9	4.2	4.3	1.3	2.4
Wide World Specials	(ABC)	5.0	3,430	2.6	3.0	2.9	3.2	1.9	1.0

PROGRAM TYPE		Working Women	18+	Women Ratings 12-24	18-34	18-49	25-54	55+	Children 6-11
MORNING (M–F)									
Today	7:30-8:00AM	3.0	4.8	1.6	2.6	3.7	4.7	6.3	3
	8:30-9:00AM	1.7	4.7	1.2	1.9	3.1	4.1	7.7	4
CBS News	7:00-8:00AM	1.3	1.7	6	8	1.0	1.0	3.3	6
DAYTIME (M–F)									
Drama		2.9	7.4	3.5	6.9	7.0	7.6	8.2	8
Quiz & Aud. Part		2.5	5.4	2.5	3.9	4.3	4.9	7.3	1.6
All 10:00AM-4:30PM		2.6	6.1	3.0	5.2	5.4	5.9	7.6	1.3
EARLY FRINGE (M–F)									
Informational	6:00-7:30PM	8.7	10.5	4.3	6.3	7.2	8.5	17.0	3.7
EVENING									
General Drama		13.6	15.2	12.4	15.0	14.3	14.6	17.1	11.3
Susp. & Myst.		13.9	14.6	10.4	14.4	14.0	15.0	15.4	8.3
Situation Comedy		18.3	19.2	15.6	16.6	17.1	18.3	22.3	16.3
Western Drama		12.4	15.3	9.6	12.4	12.6	13.8	20.8	16.0
Feature Film		14.6	15.4	13.6	17.6	16.9	17.2	12.6	10.5
All 7:30-11:00PM		13.9	14.9	11.7	14.8	14.5	15.2	15.5	11.1
LATE NIGHT (M–F)									
Tonight	(NBC)	5.8	6.4	3.1	6.0	6.2	6.9	8.2	5
Tomorrow	(NBC)	1.5	2.1	5	1.0	2.0	2.4	2.4	*
Late Movies	(ABC)	4.2	4.3	3.2	4.9	4.7	4.6	3.8	1.2
Wide World Myst	(ABC)	3.3	3.6	2.7	4.5	4.1	4.0	2.7	1.1
Wide World Specials	(ABC)	3.2	3.7	2.0	4.1	3.9	4.3	3.3	7

*Less than 0.2 Rating.

Source: Nielsen Nov. '74

TV VIEWER COMPOSITION BY AGE

PROGRAM TYPE		No. Men Viewing (000)	% of Total Men Viewing 18-34	18-49	25-54	55+	No. Wom. Viewing (000)	% of Total Women Viewing 18-34	18-49	25-54	55+
MORNING M–F)											
Today	7:30-8:00AM	1,510	22%	41	32	50	1,920	20%	47	51	39
	8:30-9:00AM	1,390	14	40	36	56	1,450	15	41	45	49
CBS News	7:00-8:00AM	730	15	98	38	53	1,260	18	37	31	57
DAYTIME (M–F)											
Drama		920	33%	50	40%	42%	5,170	35%	59%	54%	33%
Quiz & Aud.Part		1,330	29	47	37	47	3,930	27	49	48	41
All 10:00AM-4:30PM		1,150	31	48	37	45	4,490	32	55	51	37
EARLY FRINGE (M–F)											
Informational	6:00-7:30PM	6,000	23%	44%	45%	46%	7,680	23%	42%	42%	48%
EVENING (SUN.–SAT.)											
General Drama		6,950	36%	58%	55%	32%	11,070	37%	58%	51%	34%
Susp. & Myst.		8,820	35	61	57	30	10,670	37	59	54	31
Situation Comedy		9,760	31	56	53	34	13,990	33	55	50	35
Western Drama		8,250	32	55	49	37	11,190	30	51	47	41
Feature Film		9,560	41	69	60	24	11,280	43	68	59	24
All 7:30-11:00PM		8,690	36	62	57	29	10,880	37	60	54	31
LATE NIGHT (M–F)											
Tonight	(NBC)	3,330	38%	62%	56%	31%	5,010	33%	56%	53%	36%
Tomorrow	(NBC)	790	41	67	66	25	1,560	34	58	60	33
Late Movies	(CBS)	2,540	48	72	63	18	3,130	43	68	56	26
Wide World Myst.	(ABC)	2,150	47	83	73	11	2,620	47	71	58	22
Wide World Specials	(ABC)	1,690	47	73	68	20	2,680	42	65	61	26

	Total Men (000)	Men 18-34	18-49	25-54	55+	Total Women (000)	Women 18-34	18-49	25-54	55+
Population Base in U.S. TV Homes	65,280	25,920	42,420	36,130	17,250	73,040	27,520	45,130	38,470	21,810
	100%	40%	65%	55%	26%	100%	38%	62%	52%	30%

Source: Nielsen Nov. '74

TELEVISION

FACTORS FOR CONVERTING TV HOME RATINGS TO MEN/WOMEN VIEWER RATINGS

PROGRAM TYPE		Base: TV HH GRP's	Men Conversion Factors 18+	18-34	18-49	25-54	55+	Teens 12-17
MORNING (M–F)								
Today	7:30-8:00AM	100	37	21	19	23	79	13
	8:30-9:00AM	100	34	11	21	23	73	15
CBS News	7:00-8:00AM	100	52	19	33	38	110	9
DAYTIME (M–F)								
Drama		100	17	14	13	12	28	16
Quiz & Aud. Part.		100	29	21	20	20	51	21
All 10:00AM-4:30PM		100	24	19	17	16	40	20
EARLY FRINGE (M–F)								
Informational	6:00-7:30PM	100	67	39	45	54	118	26
EVENING (SUN.–SAT.)								
General Drama		100	58	52	52	58	70	56
Susp. & Myst.		100	71	62	66	73	80	47
Situation Comedy		100	66	51	56	62	83	61
Western Drama		100	65	52	55	58	91	51
Feature Film		100	72	75	77	78	64	64
All 7:30-11:00PM		100	69	62	65	71	76	56
LATE NIGHT (M–F)								
Tonight	(NBC)	100	54	52	51	54	64	18
Tomorrow	(NBC)	100	36	36	36	42	36	6
Late Movies	(CBS)	100	59	71	65	67	39	39
Wide World Myst.	(ABC)	100	59	70	75	77	23	43
Wide World Specials	(ABC)	100	52	60	58	64	38	20

PROGRAM TYPE		Base: TV HH GRP's	Working Women	Women Conversion Factors 18+	12-24	18-34	18-49	25-54	55+	Children 6-11
MORNING (M–F)										
Today	7:30-8:00AM	100	48	77	26	42	60	76	102	5
	8:30-9:00AM	100	27	76	19	31	50	66	124	6
CBS News	7:00-8:00AM	100	62	81	29	38	48	48	157	29
DAYTIME (M–F)										
Drama		100	35	89	42	83	84	92	99	10
Quiz & Aud. Part.		100	36	77	36	56	61	70	104	23
All 10:00AM-4:30PM		100	35	81	40	69	72	79	101	17
EARLY FRINGE (M–F)										
Informational	6:00-7:30PM	100	77	91	31	46	53	62	124	27
EVENING (SUN.–SAT.)										
General Drama		100	75	84	68	82	79	80	94	62
Susp. & Myst.		100	74	78	56	77	75	80	82	44
Situation Comedy		100	80	84	68	72	75	80	97	71
Western Drama		100	64	79	50	64	69	73	108	83
Feature Film		100	72	76	67	82	83	85	62	52
All 7:30-11:00PM		100	72	77	60	76	75	78	80	57
LATE NIGHT (M–F)										
Tonight	(NBC)	100	62	73	33	64	66	73	87	5
Tomorrow	(NBC)	100	45	64	15	58	61	73	73	1FR
Late Movies	(CBS)	100	64	65	48	74	71	70	58	18
Wide World Myst.	(ABC)	100	59	64	48	80	73	71	48	20
Wide World Specials	(ABC)	100	74	40	82	78	86	66	14	

Source: Nielsen Nov. '74

SEASONAL FLUCTUATION IN VIEWING BY DAY PARTS (HOMES USING TV)

Each Quarter Indexed As Base Period

READ COLUMNS DOWN

Quarters	MORNING (10AM–1PM M–F) % HUT	JFM	AMJ	JAS	OND	AFTERNOON (1–4:30PM M–F) % HUT	JFM	AMJ	JAS	OND
JFM	24	100	109	104	104	32	100	114	114	107
AMJ	22	92	100	96	96	28	88	100	100	93
JAS	23	96	105	100	100	28	88	100	100	93
OND	23	96	105	100	100	30	94	107	107	100

Quarters	EARLY FRINGE (4:40-6PM M–F)	JFM	AMJ	JAS	OND	EARLY FRINGE (6–7:30PM M–F)	JFM	AMJ	JAS	OND
JFM	42	100	120	124	102	54	100	123	132	100
AMJ	35	82	100	103	83	44	82	100	107	82
JAS	34	81	97	100	83	41	76	93	100	76
OND	41	98	117	121	100	54	100	123	132	100

Quarters	LATE FRINGE (11-11:30PM M–S)	JFM	AMJ	JAS	OND	LATE NIGHT (11:30PM-1AM M–S)	JFM	AMJ	JAS	OND
JFM	46	100	105	107	105	27	100	100	104	104
AMJ	44	96	100	102	100	27	100	100	104	104
JAS	43	94	98	100	98	26	96	96	100	100
OND	44	96	100	102	100	26	96	96	100	100

Quarters	PRIME (8-11PM M–S)	JFM	AMJ	JAS	OND	WEEKEND DAY (1-4:30PM SUN.)	JFM	AMJ	JAS	OND
JFM	64	100	116	123	105	35	100	130	130	92
AMJ	55	86	100	106	90	27	77	100	100	71
JAS	52	81	95	100	85	27	77	100	100	71
OND	61	95	111	117	100	38	109	141	141	100

Source: Nielsen 1974

EXHIBIT 13–4 (concluded)

TELEVISION

SPORT EVENTS – AVERAGE RATINGS AND VIEWER COMPOSITION

	TV HH Rating	Total Men '000	% of Adult Viewers	Total Women '000	% of Adult Viewers	% of Total Men Viewers of T/C 18-34 (U.S. = 39%)	35-49 (26%)	50+ (35%)
FOOTBALL								
NFL Superbowl	41.6	24,240	61%	15,410	39	36%	28	35%
ABC-NFL	21.2	11,930	63	7,020	37	38	31	31
CBS-NFL	14.1	7,870	66	4,140	34	35	29	36
NBC-NFL	13.4	7,540	66	3,930	34	36	27	37
College Bowl & All Star	21.6	12,630	60	8,500	40	32	27	41
NCAA Reg-Season	12.2	6,250	63	3,640	37	36	25	39
BASEBALL								
World Series	30.7	15,610	54	13,130	46%	29%	27%	44%
All Star Game	23.8	13,260	60	8,940	40	35	22	43
Regular Season	9.0	4,310	59	3,030	41	28	20	52
HORSE RACING								
Kentucky Derby	16.5	6,730	45%	8,230	55%	20%	24%	56%
Preakness	14.9	7,620	56	6,090	44	39	18	43
Other Racing	5.2	1,560	46	1,850	54	19	29	52
BASKETBALL								
NBA Regular Season	9.3	4,930	67%	2,410	33%	47%	25%	28%
NBA Playoffs	13.5	6,670	61	4,330	39	41	26	33
NBA All Star Game	12.6	6,350	60	4,150	40	52	22	26
ABA Playoffs	4.3	1,380	57	1,050	43	36%	37%	27%
BOWLING								
Pro Bowl. Tour	9.0	3,940	51%	3,850	49%	31%	26%	43%
Brunswick Open	6.0	2,140	40	3,180	60	43	11	46
AUTO RACING	7.7	3,280	54%	2,780	46%	37%	26%	37%
GOLF								
CBS Golf Classic	4.1	1,760	57%	1,350	43%	26%	26%	48%
Tournaments	8.6	4,200	55	3,380	45	28	22	50
TENNIS								
CBS Tennis Classic	4.5	1,980	54%	1,690	46%	36%	26%	38%
Alan King Tennis	3.6	1,250	52	1,140	48	22	40	38
Family Circle Tennis	4.1	1,590	46	1,840	54	33	19	48
World Champ Tennis	4.7	2,090	59	1,460	41	38	26	36
Wimbledon	4.5	1,720	49	1,770	51	35	21	44
BOXING								
Madison Sq. Garden	5.1	2,720	65%	1,470	35%	35%	16%	49%
MULTI-SPORTS SERIES								
American Sportsman	9.4	4,560	61%	2,860	39%	40%	24%	36%
ABC WW Sports	11.6	5,520	59	3,760	41	40	25	35
CBS Sports Spectacular	6.4	2,970	54	2,490	46	35	25	40

Source: Nielsen

1975 NETWORK TV COSTS – 30 SEC. ANN.

		1st Qtr.	2nd Qtr.	3rd Qtr.	4th Qtr.
PRIME (Inc. Movie)	Est. cost	$ 29,000	$ 30,000	$ 24,000	$ 37,000
	Avg. Rtg	20.2	15.9	13.4	19.4
	CPM HH	$ 2.10	$ 2.75	$ 2.61	$ 2.64
DAYTIME	Est. cost	$ 5,000	$ 5,200	$ 4,600	$ 5,700
	Avg. Rtg	7.8	6.6	7.3	7.5
	CPM HH	$ 0.94	$ 1.15	$ 0.92	$ 1.05
EARLY EVENING NEWS	CBS Est. Cost	$ 11,200	$ 12,800	$ 9,500	$ 16,000
	Avg. Rtg	15.5	11.7	10.5	15.7
	CPM HH	$ 1.05	$ 1.60	$ 1.32	$ 1.41
	NBC Est. cost	$ 15,000	$ 15,000	$ 11,000	$ 13,500
	Avg. Rtg	13.8	12.2	9.5	14.6
	CPM HH	$ 1.59	$ 1.79	$ 1.69	$ 1.28
	ABC Est. cost	$ 10,000	$ 10,500	$ 8,000	$ 12,000
	Avg. Rtg	11.5	9.2	8.0	12.2
	CPM HH	$ 1.27	$ 1.67	$ 1.46	$ 1.36
TODAY SHOW	Est. cost	$ 6,000	$ 6,350	$ 6,350	$ 6,350
	Avg. Rtg	5.2	5.4	4.4	6.2
	CPM HH	$ 1.68	$ 1.72	$ 2.11	$ 1.42
AM AMERICA	Est. cost	$ 1,500	$ 1,500	$ 1,500	$ 1,500
	Avg. Rtg	2.5*	2.5*	2.5*	2.5*
	CPM HH	$ .88	$ .88	$ .88	$ .83
TONIGHT SHOW	Est. cost	$ 12,300	$ 13,700	$ 13,000	$ 14,300
	Avg. Rtg	9.1	8.9	9.5	9.4
	CPM HH	$ 1.97	$ 2.25	$ 2.00	$ 2.10
LATE EVENING MOVIE	CBS Est. Cost	$ 6,900	$ 8,000	$ 7,200	$ 8,200
	Avg. Rtg	7.4	6.1	6.1	6.6
	CPM HH	$ 1.36	$ 1.91	$ 1.72	$ 1.72
ABC WIDE WORLD OF ENTERTAINMENT:					
WIDE WORLD MYSTERY	Est. cost	$ 6,250	$ 7,500	$ 6,750	$ 8,000+
	Avg. Rtg	5.8	5.4	4.9	5.6
	CPM HH	$ 1.57	$ 2.03	$ 2.01	$ 1.98
WIDE WORLD SPECIALS	Est. cost	$ 6,250	$ 7,500	$ 6,750	$ 8,000+
	Avg. Rtg	4.6	5.4	6.6	5.0
	CPM HH	$ 1.98	$ 2.03	$ 1.49	$ 2.21
MIDNIGHT SPECIAL	Est. cost	$ 5,000	$ 5,300	$ 5,300	$ 5,300
	Avg. Rtg	5.0	4.0	3.4	3.5
	CPM HH	$ 1.46	$ 1.93	$ 2.28	$ 2.09
TOMORROW	Est. cost	$ 1,650	$ 1,650	$ 1,650	$ 1,650
	Avg. Rtg	2.6	2.8	3.0	3.3
	CPM HH	$ .93	$ .86	$ .80	$ .69

*As estimated By ABC network. (1st Qtr. Actual Rating 1.6) ABC guaranteeing equivalent of 3.0 Rating.

Source: ABC, CBS, and NBC as of January '75

8

TELEVISION

SPOT TV COST PER RATING POINT
(Base: ADI HH Ratings, Cost 30 Sec. Ann.)

TOP 50 MARKETS	Daytime M–F 9AM-4:30PM	Early Eve M–F 5-7:30PM	Prime All Eve. 7:30-11PM	Late News All Eve. 11-11:30PM	Late Eve M–F 11:30PM-1AM
1. New York	$ 60	$ 47	$ 214	$ 150	$ 65
2. Los Angeles	50	49	145	94	55
3. Chicago	36	37	100	79	43
4. Philadelphia	25	45	107	55	59
5. Boston	19	31	67	50	56
6. San Francisco	31	24	90	70	48
7. Detroit	20	23	64	40	28
8. Washington, D.C.	23	21	65	50	31
9. Cleveland	14	13	52	33	27
10. Pittsburgh	16	16	36	32	23
TOP 10 – Total	**$292**	**$306**	**$ 940**	**$ 653**	**$435**
Average	**$ 29**	**$ 31**	**$ 94**	**$ 65**	**$ 44**
11. Dallas-Ft. Worth	$ 15	$ 19	$ 50	$ 27	$ 22
12. St. Louis	13	15	37	31	21
13. Minneapolis-St. Paul	13	19	36	22	21
14. Houston	18	23	42	28	23
15. Miami	10	17	44	27	19
16. Atlanta	13	16	44	30	16
17. Tampa-St. Petersburg	11	11	30	18	18
18. Seattle-Tacoma	19	17	33	25	22
19. Baltimore	12	19	40	31	29
20. Indianapolis	10	11	30	17	11
TOP 20 – Total	**$426**	**$473**	**$1,326**	**$ 909**	**$637**
Average	**$ 21**	**$ 24**	**$ 66**	**$ 45**	**$ 32**
21. Hartford-New Haven	$ 17	$ 17	$ 45	$ 40	$ 15
22. Cincinnati	6	11	31	15	10
23. Kansas City	10	13	30	16	12
24. Milwaukee	9	14	24	15	17
25. Portland, Ore.	12	11	28	19	15
26. Sacramento-Stockton	7	11	29	14	18
27. Denver	10	15	26	22	19
28. Buffalo	10	14	31	20	16
29. Providence	9	11	17	12	13
30. Nashville	6	5	12	10	10
TOP 30 – Total	**$522**	**$595**	**$1,599**	**$1,092**	**$782**
Average	**$ 17**	**$ 20**	**$ 53**	**$ 36**	**$ 26**
31. San Diego	$ 12	$ 16	$ 22	$ 20	$ 16
32. Memphis	8	6	14	11	9
33. Columbus	8	9	17	10	13
34. Charlotte	8	6	16	11	16
35. Phoenix	13	16	18	20	17
36. New Orleans	*5	7	11	8	9
37. Louisville	5	5	16	10	11
38. Oklahoma City	7	8	12	9	9
39. Greenville-Spart.-Ash.	7	7	12	10	10
40. Charleston-Huntington	4	8	12	9	8
TOP 40 – Total	**$671**	**$688**	**$1,749**	**$1,211**	**$900**
Average	**$ 17**	**$ 17**	**$ 44**	**$ 30**	**$ 23**
41. Dayton	$ 8	$ 9	$ 16	$ 12	$ 11
42. Albany-Schenectady-Troy	5	7	11	6	
43. Grand Rapids-Kalamazoo	10	12	15	14	12
44. Orlando-Daytona Beach	8	10	13	13	14
45. Wilkes Barre-Scranton	5	7	11	7	8
46. Harrisburg-York-Lancaster	8	9	14	11	11
47. San Antonio	7	6	11	8	7
48. Birmingham	4	5	14	9	9
49. Norf.-Port.-Np.-Nws.-Hamp.	6	7	10	7	6
50. Toledo	6	7	15	9	7
TOP 50 – Total	**$678**	**$768**	**$1,883**	**$1,312**	**$994**
Average	**$ 13**	**$ 15**	**$ 38**	**$ 26**	**$ 20**

Source: Media Market Guide, Spring 1975(R)

ESTIMATED 4-WEEK REACH OF TV HOMES AT VARIOUS GRP LEVELS
(5 Sample Day-Part Combinations)

DAYTIME (100%) Wkly. Grp*	No. of Spots	# Stat.	4 WEEK REACH R	F
50	7	1	50 54%	3.8
75	11	2	64 68	4.7
100	14	3	71 75	5.3
150	22	3	77 81	7.7

DAYTIME (50% GRP) + EARLY FRINGE AND LATE NIGHT (50% GRP) Grp*	Day Spots	E.F. Spots	L.N. Spots	# Stat.	R	F
50	5				56 60%	3.8
75	5	1			63 67	4.6
100	7	1	2	2	73 77	5.3
150	11	4	7	3	80 84	7.4

PRIME TIME (100%) Grp*	No. of Spots	# Stat.	R	F
50	4	1	64 68%	3.3
75	4	2	71 75	3.9
100	6	2	78 82	5.4
150	8	3	82 86	6.9

PRIME TIME (1/3 GRP) + DAYTIME (2/3 GRP) Grp*	Prime Spots	Day Spots	# Stat.	R	F
50	1	8	2	60 64%	3.4
75	1	8	2	68 72	4.2
100	3	9	2	76 80	5.1
150	3	14	3	82 86	7.2
200	5	16	3	86 89	9.3

PRIME TIME (50% GRP) + EARLY FRINGE AND LATE NIGHT (50% GRP) Grp*	Prime Spots	E.F. Spots	L.N. Spots	# Stat.	R	F
100	2	2	4	2	71 75%	4.1
140	4	4	7	3	78 82	5.2
					83 87	6.9

*Based on a Daytime rating of 7, Early Fringe 10, Prime 18, Late Night 5.

Source: TELMAR SPOT TV R&F

9

EXHIBIT 13–5*

RADIO

NETWORK RADIO COSTS: 1 MINUTE/30 SEC RATES (1X-13WKS)

Network	#Stations	Drive Time M–F	Housewife MF	Scatter 7 Days	Week End
CBS	245	$1450/1100	$1450/1100	$1280/820	$1280/820
MUTUAL	633	$1200/840	$1050/740		$1200/840
NBC	230	$1525/1150	$1250/950	$1050/800	$1200/900
ABC		Fixed	ROS	ROS	ROS
Contemporary	328	$2200/1540	$1760/1230	$1760/1230	$1760/1230
Information	423	$1330/930	$1030/720	$1030/720	$1030/720
Entertainment	364	$1200/840	$ 960/670	$ 960/670	$ 960/670
FM	217	$ 600/420	$ 500/350	$ 500/350	$ 500/350

- **MUTUAL BLACK NETWORK:** Started in May of 1972, now totals 91 Stations; Programs news 10 MINS before each hour; written and voiced by blacks.
  16 Wk. Schedule 60 sec. $244/30 sec. $183
- **NATIONAL BLACK NETWORK:** Started in July of 1973; now totals 68 Stations; Programs News on the hour; written and voiced by blacks.
  15 Wk. Schedule 60 sec. $625/30 sec. $412

Note: (1) CBS's "Volume Plan" rates, 5-9 weekly, 13-25 weeks
      (2) NBC's "ROS" rates 13-25 weeks
      * Subject to Negotiation

Source: Rate Card Effective Jan. 1975

NETWORK RADIO AUDIENCE – CLEARED BROADCASTS
Average No. of Listeners per Broadcast (000)

	AM & PM Traffic 6-10AM	Mon.-Fri. 3-7PM	Afternoon 10AM-3PM	Night 7PM-Mid.	6AM-12N	Saturday 12N-7PM
	%	%	%	%	%	%
ABC - CONT.						
Men Total	801(35)	548(30)	602(33)	269(34)	773(32)	438(27)
18-49	603	477	506	234	597	398
Women Total	1060(47)	858(47)	967(52)	297(38)	1085(46)	834(51)
18-49	811	672	778	244	825	658
Teens	410(18)	414(23)	271(15)	222(28)	525(22)	371(22)
ABC-ENT.						
Men Total	878(36)	446(44)	784(41)	227(36)	558(38)	569(39)
18-49	642	336	533	196	334	313
Women Total	1383(57)	466(46)	1004(53)	320(50)	789(53)	703(48)
18-49	798	290	572	162	390	348
Teens	178(7)	110(10)	112(6)	90(14)	130(9)	185(13)
ABC-FM						
Men Total	255(41)	194(44)	165(34)	230(44)	322(40)	232(36)
18-49	153	178	142	186	322	210
Women Total	243(39)	163(37)	226(46)	148(29)	268(33)	283(45)
18-49	193	105	180	128	206	213
Teens	126(20)	86(19)	98(20)	138(27)	213(27)	119(19)
ABC-INFO.						
Men Total	723(42)	389(44)	729(45)	266(43)	496(35)	402(36)
18-49	494	269	371	155	260	251
Women Total	891(52)	419(47)	839(52)	301(48)	862(61)	591(53)
18-49	523	250	430	174	294	294
Teens	105(6)	78(9)	43(3)	55(9)	52(4)	116(11)
+ CBS						
Men Total	1448(48)	1048(55)	1192(48)	558(53)	904(44)	692(44)
18-49	861	565	738	311	493	402
Women Total	1440(48)	767(40)	1256(50)	415(40)	1112(54)	750(47)
18-49	689	314	529	132	450	306
Teens	101(4)	83(5)	38(2)	70(7)	30(2)	139(9)
MUTUAL BLACK NTWK.						
Men Total	167(38)	254(48)	262(47)	156(38)	196(42)	143(25)
18-49	148	150	222	126	161	100
Women Total	197(44)	172(33)	244(44)	148(36)	215(47)	224(40)
18-49	187	153	232	146	178	216
Teens	81(18)	101(19)	54(9)	110(26)	51(11)	196(35)
MUTUAL BROADCASTING						
Men Total	583(40)	417(42)	547(44)	173(34)	413(36)	378(35)
18-49	328	282	366	100	235	222
Women Total	542(42)	491(50)	630(50)	250(50)	588(52)	582(54)
18-49	419	275	357	162	306	369
Teens	116(8)	78(8)	79(6)	80(16)	138(12)	111(11)
NBC						
Men Total	685(39)	588(47)	621(42)	489(46)	396(39)	412(44)
18-49	384	352	363	326	190	241
Women Total	970(55)	524(42)	811(55)	400(38)	569(56)	464(50)
18-49	512	287	423	231	232	218
Teens	107(6)	145(11)	41(3)	171(16)	55(5)	56(6)
	M-F 10-11PM			Sat 10-11PM	Sun 10-11PM	
+CBS DRAMA						
Men Total	—	—	—	700(50)	391(49)	496(51)
18-49				494	170	298
Women-Total	—	—	—	508(41)	380(48)	415(43)
18-49				245	95	65
Teens	—	—	—	128(9)	25(3)	63(6)

% of Listeners 12 years +.

Source: Radar X

RADIO

SPOT RADIO COST PER RATING POINT
(Base: Metro Ratings for Top Stations M–F, 60 Sec. Costs)

TOP 50 MARKETS	6-10 A.M. Men Total	18-49	Women Total	18-49	10 A.M.-3 P.M. Men Total	18-49	Women Total	18-49	3-7 P.M. Men Total	18-49	Women Total	18-49
1. New York	$ 64	$ 74	$ 51	$ 67	$ 94	$105	$ 76	$ 64	$ 95	$115	$106	$115
2. Los Angeles	62	94	62	110	71	88	57	106	80	100	121	203
3. Chicago	46	52	51	52	53	57	61	61	64	61	75	79
4. Philadelphia	33	35	26	32	32	37	28	31	45	53	26	37
5. Boston	35	36	29	25	26	24	25	31	30	30	37	35
6. San Francisco	37	42	34	44	34	38	38	51	55	58	80	
7. Detroit	42	48	27	46	34	40	27	44	50	49	46	62
8. Washington, D.C.	32	36	37	36	39	37	27	31	33	34	39	44
9. Cleveland	21	23	28	23	28	26	15	17	24	26	21	23
10. Pittsburgh	18	18	13	16	12		13	12	20	17	25	
Total Top 10	$388	$457	$346	$457	$420	$469	$362	$436	$489	$563	$546	$723
11. Dallas	$ 21	$ 23	$ 21	$ 26	$ 28	$ 27	$ 33	$ 36	$ 29	$ 35	$ 33	
Ft. Worth	15	15	15	15	13	12	19	20	18	17	29	33
12. St. Louis	17	19	16	18	18	24	17	23	21	24	26	29
13. Minneapolis-St. Paul	15	17	12	15	18	25	11	16	18	21	20	22
14. Houston	21	22	18	19	15	19	20	21	24	20	25	24
15. Miami	15	20	14	15	17	24	14	16	20	23	16	20
16. Atlanta	18	25	13	18	24	31	23	26	20	27	20	22
17. Tampa-St. Petersburg	13	14	13	13	11	14	17	14	21	18	31	19
18. Seattle-Tacoma	13	14	13	12	10	11	11	7	15	15	19	14
19. Baltimore	13	13	10	11	12	16	12	16	15	18	20	21
20. Indianapolis	16	16	11	13	18	16	18	17	15	15	23	21
Total Top 20	$565	$655	$504	$631	$614	$694	$558	$645	$708	$790	$810	$981
21. Hartford	$ 6	$ 9	$ 6	$ 8	$ 10	$ 9	$ 18	$ 12	$ 15	$ 19	$ 16	$ 18
New Haven	7	6	7	6	8	6	5	7	8	7	8	9
22. Cincinnati	13	13	14	18	20	11	15	17	18	18	18	19
23. Kansas City	14	14	11	13	12	10	10	12	18	16	15	14
24. Milwaukee	17	14	14	17	19	19	13	15	20	25	23	26
25. Portland, Or.	12	13	10	11	16	14	10	8	15	13	15	12
26. Sacramento-Stockton	12	9	12	13	10	10	14	12	12	20	15	
27. Denver	15	17	13	13	15	12	10	10	20	19	18	16
28. Buffalo	17	19	14	17	23	28	16	19	21	21	21	24
29. Providence	11	10	8	9	8	7	6	9	9	9	9	9
30. Nashville	8	10	13	11	11	12	13	11	14	11	14	13
Total Top 30	$694	$798	$624	$762	$764	$850	$676	$772	$883	$960	$992	$1157
31. San Diego	$ 17	$ 15	$ 16	$ 17	$ 21	$ 17	$ 17	$ 15	$ 24	$ 18	$ 265	20
32. Memphis	8	9	9	10	11	8	8	11	17	12	17	12
33. Columbus, Oh.	14	14	14	13	14	12	17	17	17	14	27	24
34. Charlotte	15	14	9	10	13	14	9	8	16	16	12	20
35. Phoenix	14											
36. New Orleans	14	16	13	14	16	13	11	12	19	18	20	17
37. Louisville	12	14	10	10	13	12	11	11	15	14	13	13
38. Oklahoma City	7	8	6	8	9	7	6	8	11	11	13	9
39. Greenville	6	6	4	4	7	6	4	4	8	6	6	5
Spartanburg	4	4	3	3	3	2	1		2	2	2	2
Asheville	1	1	1	1	2	1	1		2	2	2	2
40. Charleston	5	4	4	5	7	6	5	8	8	9	7	9
Huntington-Ashl'd	6	5	4	4	7	6	6	9	6	9	6	7
Total Top 40	$817	$922	$728	$873	$901	$984	$79	$881	$1047	$1106	$1167	$1306
41. Dayton	$ 15	$ 15	$ 10	$ 9	$ 18	$ 18	$ 9	$ 11	$ 15	17	13	12
42. Albany-Schen. Troy	12	15	9	10	18	13	13	14	18	15	18	12
43. Grand Rapids	4	3	4	4	5	4	7	7	11	13	10	10
Kalamazoo	4	4	3	4	4	4	5	5	5	9	5	5
44. Orlando-Daytona	17	13	17	18	6	7	6	10	9	11	9	12
45. Wilkes Barre-Scranton	6	7	5	6	7	4	5	5	9	8	6	7
46. Harrisburg	5	5	4	5	6	5	3	3	7	7	4	4
Lancaster												
York	7	7	5	4	5	7	6	4	6	8	6	6
47. San Antonio	10	11	8	8	16	12	10	10	14	14	10	10
48. Birmingham	8	9	8	7	17	15	14	13	10	14	11	
49. Norf.-Port.-Np. News, Hamp.	10	10	6	8	16	9	8	14	13	12	10	
50. Toledo	10	10	8	7	17	18	16	9	8	14	12	13
Total Top 50	$930	$1040	$821	$972	$1037	$1107	$894	$981	$1188	$1243	$1302	$1424

Source: Media Market Guide, Fall 1974

ESTIMATED ONE WEEK AND FOUR WEEK REACH

	12 ann. per Station One Week		Four Weeks		24 ann. per Station One Week		Four Weeks	
Weekly GRP's	% Net Reach	Freq.	% Net Reach	Freq.	% Net Reach	Freq.	% Net Reach	Freq.
TARGET: Women 18-17 yrs. (All Day & Night)								
60	26%	2.2						
80	35	2.3	54	5.9				
100	43	2.3	65	6.1	30%	3.3	39%	10.0
120	50	2.4	71	6.7	36	3.3	44	11.0
140	56	2.5	76	7.4	42	3.4	49	11.3
160	64	2.5	79	8.1	47	3.4	55	11.5
180	69	2.6	83	8.7	52	3.5	62	11.6
200	71	2.8	85	9.4	56	3.6	68	11.8
250					66	3.8	76	13.1
300					74	4.1	83	14.4
TARGET: Men 18-49 yrs. (All Day & Night)								
60	32%	1.9	50%	4.8				
80	41	1.9		5.3				
100	50	2.0	70	5.7	39%	2.6	46%	8.7
120	57	2.1	78	6.1	45	2.7	54	9.0
140	63	2.2	82	6.8	52	2.7	60	9.4
160	69	2.3	86	7.5	57	2.8	64	9.9
180	74	2.4	88	8.2	61	3.0	69	10.5
200	79	2.5	89	9.0	66	3.0	73	11.0
250					73	3.4	82	12.2
300					77	3.9	90	13.3
TARGET: Teenagers 12-17 yrs. (Afternoon Drive & Night)								
60	31%	1.9	48%	5.0				
80	41	1.9		5.5				
100	46	2.2	66	6.0	37%	2.7	44%	9.0
120	52	2.3	73	6.6	43	2.8	51	9.4
140	55	2.5	79	7.0	49	2.9	56	10.5
160	60	2.7	84	7.6	54	3.0	62	10.4
180	64	2.8	89	8.1	58	3.1	67	10.8
200	69	2.9	92	8.7	61	3.3	71	11.7

Source: RAB

* *Ayer Media Facts,* 1975, pp. 5–11.

14

OTHER MEDIA FORMS

*A*lthough the four media discussed at some length in the two preceding chapters are major ones, there are a number of other important media available to the advertiser. This chapter will describe briefly the more significant aspects of the following media: direct advertising (direct mail); outdoor; transit; point-of-purchase; exhibits or trade shows; specialty advertising; screen; directories; sampling; house organs; packages; labels; and inserts. Some of these are usually classified in the area of sales promotion rather than in advertising; but, since they are important in the overall aspects of media planning in the advertising campaign, the authors discuss them here under the heading of media.

Direct advertising

Direct advertising is one of the oldest methods of reaching the consumer. It consists of printed matter that is sent by the advertiser directly to the prospect. This material is usually sent by mail, but it may be distributed by house-to-house or personal delivery, handed to passersby on the sidewalk, placed in automobiles, or stuck under windshield wipers of automobiles. That portion of direct advertising that is sent through the mail is called direct-mail advertising.

Direct-mail advertising differs from mail-order advertising in that mail-order advertising seeks to complete the sale entirely by mail, while direct-mail advertising is supplementary to other forms of advertising and selling. Direct mail is usually a part of the general marketing plan, whereas mail-order advertising is a complete plan in itself.

Direct advertising takes many forms, such as letters, postcards, announcements, catalogs, folders, envelope and package enclosures, novelties and goodwill reminders, cards, or blotters.

Use of direct advertising

One of the principal functions of direct advertising is to supplement general advertising in magazines, newspapers, television, radio, and other media. Proofs of advertisements that are to be used in mass media can be sent to dealers. Jobbers can be shown the advertising campaign in a broadside. Circular letters, folders, or postal cards can be sent to prospects, calling their attention to a specific advertisement.

Direct advertising may be used also to pave the way for salespeople. In most instances where a series of letters or folders has been sent before the salesperson's call, it takes less time and effort to complete sales. The retailer also can use direct advertising effectively. By the use of carefully planned material, the store can tie in its own appeal with the general advertising campaign of the manufacturer or wholesaler. The retailer may either mail, or distribute the direct advertising on a house-to-house basis. However, some cities forbid house-to-house distribution, so it is well to look into the local laws before adopting such a method.

Virtually all advertisers use some form of direct advertising. For many small firms, it is the only form of media used. Direct advertising is estimated to rank third among all media in volume.

Some idea of the specific objectives for which it is frequently used can be obtained from Figure 14–1.

Forms of direct advertising

A number of forms are significant to many advertisers and will be discussed briefly in the following paragraphs.

Form letters. In direct advertising, form letters are used most frequently. These are standard letters used alone or with other advertising matter, such as with catalogs, folders, or in answer to inquiries.

FIGURE 14–1
How is direct mail used?

To obtain orders by mail	14,813
To obtain prospects for personal contact by salesman	9,484
To obtain outlets, distributors, members or subscribers, or to keep them informed	5,468
To provide advertising literature for franchised or other dealers or outlets, mailed under permit number	3,425
To provide advertising literature for franchised or other dealers or outlets, mailed by those dealers or outlets	2,121
For general advertising purposes	33,043
To distribute (i.e., to move or to transport) the product	2,521
Other uses	9,795

Source: Department of Commerce survey of 56,417 users of bulk third-class mail.

No matter how attractively a catalog or booklet is prepared, its selling power is strengthened by sending a good form letter along with it, because a letter has a special appeal all its own. It may be used not only to give direction to the selling effort but to emphasize as well particular features of the product.

Circulars.   Circulars and leaflets, as defined here, include advertising literature not mailable under their own covers. These include dodgers, package inserts, bulletins, and pieces of printed matter that are not properly classified under any of the other forms.

The uses of circulars vary. They are not intended primarily as envelope enclosures, though they are often mailed in envelopes. Some circulars, for instance, may be given to workers as they leave the factory. They may be used to introduce a new product at a supermarket or even solicit votes for a certain candidate.

Circulars are also inserted in packages. For instance, in a cereal package an advertiser may put a circular advertising a brand of cakes. Circulars may be used by a manufacturer to inform the dealer about advertising plans or some other information of mutual interest, or for distribution.

Catalogs.   Catalogs are used as a source of purchasing information as well as to stimulate a desire for the goods described. In many instances, the products are illustrated in colors, and the catalog may carry a major share of the sales effort. Because the cover of a catalog is so important to its success, it is well to choose the cover with a great degree of care. It must be strong enough to go through the mails undamaged and last as long as the catalog is useful. It should also be designed to get attention as well as to convey the atmosphere of the goods advertised in the catalog.

Booklets.   In a catalog many items are listed, while in a booklet only a limited number of products might be explained.

Many manufacturers furnish booklets for distribution with or without the imprint of their local representatives. Special products, new lines, and services may also be treated effectively in booklets. In fact, in many national advertisements it will be suggested that the reader write for a booklet. Booklets are cheaper than catalogs and can be used as a supplement to give general information about specific requests.

Postcards.   The postcard is a widely used form of direct advertising, because it has high attention value and may be produced cheaply. It is intended to get direct and immediate action. When the article advertised is small and inexpensive, it pays to make ordering convenient by using a double postcard which may be detached easily and filled in with the name and address. Postcard messages should be brief and direct.

The postcard can be used effectively to call to the attention of customers other advertising material such as a catalog or samples, to give the date when salespeople will arrive, or announce such information as new dealers or new styles.

Broadsides.   Another form of direct advertising is a broadside, or a large advertising folder. It differs from the folder in that in a folder each page may be a separate unit, while a broadside when opened constitutes one advertisement. The large size of a broadside makes it possible to use a variety of typography and illustrations.

As one of the objectives of a broadside is to get immediate reaction, high attention value is important. For this reason, it is well to use more than one color.

Portfolios. A portfolio is a portable case for keeping, usually without folding, detached material or loose papers, prints, and booklets, and can be used effectively in direct advertising.

Manufacturers who advertise nationally, as an example, may send portfolios to the dealers to show the extent to which their products are backed up by advertising. Such portfolios will include full-page advertisements which have been run or are to be run in various publications, booklets, letters, folders, and all other forms of advertising employed.

The mailing list

The success of any direct advertising will depend primarily on having the material go to the right people—those who are potential customers for the advertiser's product or establishment.

In the case of direct-mail advertising, this list of names of prospects is called the mailing list. Ideally, the advertiser would like to have the list include all those people the firm wishes to influence with its advertisement—those who are prospects for its product or establishment —and no others.

There are a number of means of obtaining desirable mailing lists. For firms already in business, probably the best single source is the list of present (and past) customers of the firm. Retailers' lists should include both cash and credit customers. Names for the lists are often obtained from those responding to the firm's advertising, from coupons in advertisements inviting requests for information or booklets, from public records such as building permits, and directory membership lists and rosters of professional organizations.

A manufacturer can often obtain desirable names for its mailing list from its dealers and from its sales force. An advertiser who wishes to reach all the people in an area (rather than a selected group) can do so by addressing the material to the occupants of the street address in cities and boxholders on rural free delivery routes.

One of the principal means used by many firms to obtain lists is either to buy or rent them from list firms, to rent them from other business firms, or to exchange lists with appropriate noncompeting firms.

The most common way to obtain the ready-made lists is by rental. The advertiser never actually sees the list, but arranges for its use through a list house or a broker and is merely informed where to send his cards or envelopes to be addressed. Many classes of lists are available. For instance, Dartnell's *Directory of Mailing List Sources* has information on 1,200 lists that are available in 239 classifications. Probably the largest and best known of the individual list houses is R. L. Polk and Company.

For those compiling their own lists, it is very important that they be kept up to date and accurate. This means that the list must be checked constantly for the accuracy of names and addresses. This can be one of the costly aspects of direct-mail advertising.

Advantages of direct advertising

The advantages of direct advertising may be summarized as follows:

1. If the right list of prospects is secured, there is limited waste circulation; each prospect receives the material.
2. The potential consumers can be reached in a short period of time.
3. There is a personal touch in direct appeals. An advertisement on television or in a magazine is directed to a group; a letter or mailing piece is directed to one person either at home or in the office.
4. Through the more personal appeal of direct advertising, the advertiser can correlate the appeal in many ways to national, class, or trade advertising.
5. The sales campaign is hidden from competitors.
6. Advertising can be released at the right time; the advertiser can also take advantage of opportune markets, business conditions, or unusual circumstances of any kind.
7. Returns can be keyed more effectively than in general media because there is better control of the distribution of the material.
8. It is possible to divide the list into natural units and treat each unit separately.
9. It is the most selective of all media.
10. It is the most flexible of all media.
11. There is a wide variety of forms available to the advertiser.
12. It avoids distracting competition for attention from other advertisements and editorial material.

Limitations of direct advertising

1. In terms of the cost of reaching a thousand people, it is a high-cost medium. This feature can, of course, be offset by the careful selectivity of the mailing list and by the effectiveness of the results obtained.
2. If the mailing list is not carefully selected, there may be low readership and interest.
3. It is often difficult to obtain good mailing lists, and it takes a great deal of effort to keep a mailing list up to date and accurate.
4. Among some people, direct mail has a poor reputation and has been referred to as "junk" mail. This is usually the result of much direct mail being sent to people who are not good prospects for the item or service involved.
5. Direct mail also requires careful preparation in order to insure readership, since there is no editorial material or program to aid

in obtaining attention and interest. Thus, specialized skills are required by those preparing direct-mail advertising.

Outdoor advertising

Although outdoor advertising accounts for only about 1.1 percent of the U.S. advertising expenditures by media, it is an important form of advertising for many national advertisers and for many local firms. Its significance has been increased in the last decade with the great increase in the number of automobiles and the amount of driving that people do (both in everyday life and on vacation trips, despite the energy crunch), combined with the large suburban movement of the population and growth of suburban shopping centers. These trends have resulted in an increase in exposure of the potential customer to outdoor advertising.

Not all the advertising signs appearing along streets and highways are considered to fall into the category of outdoor advertising by the industry. Only those posters and painted displays that meet the standards set up by the industry, through the Outdoor Advertising Association of America, are considered as being part of the medium as such. Miscellaneous signs and posters not conforming to the organized industry standards are called *signs* and do not fall within the industry's technical definition of outdoor advertising. The most important aspect of this technical distinction arises in connection with the criticism of outdoor advertising and the attempts to legislate against it.

Types of outdoor advertising

There are a number of different types of outdoor advertising. Among the more important types are posters, painted displays, and electric displays.

Posters. The most important form of outdoor advertising is the poster which accounts for over 75 percent of the national outdoor sales volume. It consists of the advertisement lithographed, or otherwise printed, on sheets of paper, placed on a background.

The standard poster is known as the "24-sheet." This term is derived from the original unit of poster-size measurement. Copy area of the 24-sheet poster is 8 feet 8 inches high and 19 feet 6 inches long. The panels or structures on which the posters are placed are generally uniform and standard in size and construction. There are intermediate sizes, but 3, 8, and 24 sheets are the popular sizes. Three-sheet posters are used principally on the sides of retailers' stores. Eight-sheet posters are used mainly for theatrical signs, while the 24-sheet variety is the standard poster on which advertising may be placed along streets and highways.

The 30-sheet poster offers a display area 9 feet 7 inches by 21 feet 7 inches, although posted on the same size structure. New posting techniques now allow an even larger posting area, called a bleed poster, giving the advertiser approximately 40 percent more printed area than the 24-sheet poster copy. There is generally no additional space charge for the larger size.

Painted displays. Painted displays account for approximately 20 percent of the volume of all standardized national outdoor advertising and may be classified as bulletins or wall panels; these in turn may be either illuminated or nonilluminated.

Illuminated bulletins and wall panels are erected by the outdoor advertising companies who usually repaint them two or three times a year, with a change of copy at that time, if desired.

Nonilluminated bulletins and wall panels are of many types, and are placed on roofs, along highways, and on the sides of store buildings.

Painted displays are bought on an individual basis. The advertiser may order one display or many. The price varies with the size of the display and the position of the individual sign. Usually, these units are designed and built to fit the special requirements of a specific location, so they vary in size. The advertiser buys these on an individual basis, and the bulletin remains on display at the same location for the period of the contract. Each bulletin is priced on the basis of the merits of the specific location.

However, in some cases the bulletins are physically moved by the plant operator periodically to new locations in a market to give the advertiser wider coverage and the impact of the large printed display. This is called the rotary plan, versus the permanent plan described above.

Painted bulletins of both of these types are usually sold on a one-year (base rate) or three-year contract, the latter carrying a 10 percent discount. Shorter terms are available at higher monthly rates.

They can be individualized by using unusual designs, shapes, and sizes. By using cutout designs with the cutout feature extending in front or behind the surface of the bulletin itself, a third dimension can be added to increase its effectiveness and attention value, or to stress the product package or other features of the advertiser's message. The use of various special fluorescent and phosphorescent paints, beaded plastic, and black light enables the advertiser to achieve unusual and striking effects with painted displays.

One popular variation of the painted bulletin is known as "trivision," or "multivision." In this variation, a portion of the face of the bulletin is made up of vertical triangles which run at intervals, showing three different messages on the same panel.[1]

Electric spectaculars. Electric displays are individualized night spectacular bulletins with special lighting and action effects. They are erected at important traffic centers, such as Times Square, New York; Michigan Avenue, Chicago; Campus Martius, Detroit; the Public Square, Cleveland; on the piers at Atlantic City; on Canal Street, New Orleans; in Union Square, San Francisco.

Electric spectaculars are designed, erected, and maintained by out-

---

[1] "This is Outdoor Advertising" (New York: Institute of Outdoor Advertising, undated), pp. 11, 12.

door advertising companies. Space on them is sold usually for a period of from one to five years. Such displays are sold individually.

Characteristics of the medium

The outstanding feature of outdoor advertising is that it stands still and the reader is exposed to it as the result of being outdoors and traveling to some destination. Since the rate of travel of the potential viewer is determined by desire to arrive at a destination and not by the attractiveness of the various outdoor billboards, the outdoor advertisement must tell its story in the short period of time it takes the person to walk or ride past the poster.

Since virtually every person goes outdoors almost every day, outdoor advertising is truly a mass medium. In turn, it is difficult for the advertising firm using this medium to select its audience or to direct its advertising to a given segment of the market or type of consumer. Hence, it serves best for the national advertiser who has a product of wide appeal, or for local business firms that wish to reach a large share of the local market with their message. Outdoor advertising is flexible in that the advertiser can choose the areas or markets in which it wishes to advertise. The firm can easily adapt the use of outdoor advertising to meet the requirements of its particular distribution pattern and competitive conditions. Another feature of outdoor advertising is the penetration it can achieve by frequent repetition. If the advertiser uses a 100-showing in a market, most people will see the advertisement many times during the month, so that the number of impressions is great. A national study by Simmons revealed that in a 30-day period a 100-showing reaches 89.2 percent of all adults in the average market, with a frequency of 31 times.[2]

Outdoor advertising permits the use of color in a very effective manner. It enables the advertiser to reproduce the product or package exactly as it appears on the store shelf. The large size of the bulletin gives great impact and impressiveness to the advertisement. The message reaches the consumer on the way to the market and, hence, can influence him or her at a most important psychological moment. Since the advertisement is seen often by the dealer as well as by the consumer, outdoor advertising can be merchandised to the trade very effectively. It can be used effectively in cooperative advertising with local dealers by placing the name of the local dealer at the base of the bulletin.

Outdoor advertising has limitations. The message that can be included must be very brief, so the medium is not particularly appropriate for some advertisers and certain types of advertising. Normally, it is not suitable for telling a long story required to introduce a product, unless the advertiser might possibly use teaser type introductory ads. Basically, this requirement of such brevity of message makes the medium best for reminder type advertising. Thus, national advertisers generally use outdoor advertising as a supporting medium for their

---

[2] *O & M Pocket Guide to Media,* 1975, pg. 60.

campaigns using other media, or to get extra support in selected markets. The outdoor advertisement faces keen competition for attention from scenic attractions, traffic, buildings, and other billboards along the route of travel. And, of course, once the person has passed a particular billboard, he or she cannot possibly see the advertisement or read the message until they again pass that particular spot.

Outdoor advertising rates

In the case of posters, outdoor advertising is sold on the basis of showings. A 100-showing consists of that number of posters (strategically located in various parts of the city or market) required to give complete coverage of the market or to expose the advertiser's message to all the people in that market during a 30-day period. The number of posters required to constitute a 100-showing obviously will vary with the city. This is determined by the plant operator, and will depend on the population and area of the city, the arrangement or layout of the industrial, commercial, and shopping areas within the city, the pattern of streets and highways and the traffic flow thereon, the network of public transportation, and other factors. The actual number of posters in a 100-showing will vary from only one poster in a small town to 519 posters in the largest outdoor circulation market—Los Angeles Metro Area. Normally, there will be a number of 100-showings available in a market, each equal to the other not only in the number of posters (illuminated and nonilluminated) but also having such locations that an equal amount of traffic will pass during any given time.

The advertiser may also buy fractional showings if the firm does not believe it needs the intensity of coverage provided by the 100-showing. A *50-showing* is one in which the poster locations are as evenly distributed for purposes of covering the market, but with only one half the intensity of a 100-showing. The advertiser who wishes to saturate a market may buy a 150-showing which would provide one and one-half times the coverage of a 100-showing. Foster and Kleiser offers showings in the following intensities: 150, 100, 95, 90, 85, 80, 75, 70, 65, 60, 55, 50, 45, 40, 35, 30, 25, 20, 15, and 10. The charge for a 100-showing will vary from city to city. Figure 14–2 gives a few illustrations of the number of posters required for a 100-showing and the rates for such showings in selected markets. These rates are for the space only; they do not include the cost of designing or printing the advertisement.

Gross rating points. Presently, the outdoor industry refers to market showings in terms of gross rating points (GRPs), which are defined as a sum of the circulation of each of the panels in a showing, estimated from half-hour traffic counts. When an advertiser buys 100 GRPs, he is provided the boards necessary to give him in one day the number of exposures equal to the hundred percent of the population in that market. 75 GRPs provides 75 percent coverage.

FIGURE 14–2
Outdoor advertising costs—1975

Rank	Metro Area	100-Showing*		50-Showing*	
		Panels	Cost/Month	Panels	Cost/Month
1	New York	437	$ 80,507	275	$ 51,795
2	Chicago	360	52,190	241	34,594
3	Los Angeles	519	80,058	261	40,179
4	Philadelphia	314	41,162	163	22,860
5	Detroit	249	42,330	135	22,140
6	Boston	280	39,420	146	20,220
7	San Francisco/Oakland	176	28,266	88	14,133
8	Washington	77	10,849	40	6,155
9	Nassau-Suffolk	65	11,800	33	6,000
10	Dallas-Fort Worth	256	24,390	140	12,970
11	St. Louis	267	30,314	157	17,050
12	Pittsburgh	160	20,108	81	9,962
13	Houston	190	17,915	96	9,015
14	Baltimore	148	18,778	78	9,716
15	Newark	176	25,222	88	12,611
16	Cleveland	186	26,075	94	13,118
17	Minneapolis-St. Paul	263	34,268	150	18,555
18	Atlanta	155	18,325	80	10,011
19	Anaheim-Santa Ana	(Included in Los Angeles)		(Included in Los Angles)	
20	San Diego	86	12,390	43	61,950
Total Top	10 Markets	2,745	$ 412,003	1,529	$231,643
Top	20 Markets	4,315	608,833	2,364	334,441
Top	40 Markets	6,332	835,270	3,408	455,348
Top	60 Markets	7,778	993,965	4,287	543,310
Top	80 Markets	9,069	1,128,910	4,999	617,237
Top	100 Markets	9,939	1,120,179	5,513	664,899

* In some majors markets, poster panels are sold in terms of "GRP Packages". A 100 GRP Package usually contains more panels than the standard #100 Showing in the market.

A 100 GRP Package will provide enough panels to deliver in one day a number of exposure opportunities equal to 100 percent of the population of the market in which the panels appear. A 50 GRP Package will deliver daily exposure opportunities equivalent to half the population. (IOA)

Source: *National Outdoor Advertising Bureau,* 1975; quoted in *Ayer Media Facts,* 1975, p. 20.

Public relations problems of outdoor advertising

In addition to the usual criticisms of advertising, the outdoor field faces a serious problem in the criticisms leveled at it because "its signs mar the landscape, and hide scenes of beauty along the highway from the motorist." A second argument is that posters and bulletins are a traffic hazard. The claim advanced is that since drivers of automobiles must take their eyes off the road to see the outdoor advertisement, the posters and bulletins act as a distraction and will cause more accidents. Several studies have been made which indicate there is no evidence to show that outdoor advertisements do cause accidents and, in actuality, they may well reduce accidents.

However, despite these counterarguments, the trend has been for more legislation to be passed to restrict outdoor advertising. A provision was included in the 1958 Amendment to the Highway Revenue Act of 1956 (Highway Beautification Act), which provided additional federal funds to those states forbidding or at least severely restricting placement of outdoor advertising on highways constructed under the act. Some states have passed legislation restricting outdoor advertising in order to gain this additional federal support. In addition, many localities pass zoning ordinances that restrict the use of outdoor advertising markedly in certain areas of cities or counties.

Users of outdoor advertising

Outdoor advertising is used by both national and local advertisers. It is estimated that approximately 75 percent of the outdoor advertising is national and 25 percent local. Local advertisers use outdoor advertising often to remind people coming into the town to trade at the advertiser's establishment. In areas where tourist business is important, outdoor advertising strategically placed on all major approaches to the area constitutes an excellent way to reach tourists and inform them of the facilities available. Large local users of outdoor advertising include hotels and motels, restaurants, souvenir stores, garages, and resorts. In towns depending essentially on the population of the surrounding area, virtually all types of stores, entertainment, and service facilities may use outdoor advertising as a medium. National advertisers normally use outdoor advertising as a supplement to other media. The message type advertising will be carried in magazines or newspapers, on television, or radio, and outdoor advertising will be used largely in a reminder capacity. It may also be used to gain greater impact and penetration in selected markets.

Outdoor advertising is a good medium for widely used impulse-type goods which are already well known. It is used often by food manufacturers and soft drink firms to remind the housewife of their products when she is on her way to shop. Other heavy users of outdoor advertising are firms manufacturing products closely allied to highway use, such as automobiles, gasoline, or tires, and also breweries and distillers.

Traffic Audit Bureau. The Traffic Audit Bureau (TAB) has developed useful techniques for measuring the total circulation of a plant and what is called the "Space Position Value" of individual locations. The Traffic Audit Bureau does for outdoor advertising what the Audit Bureau of Circulations does for newspapers and magazines. The trade association of the standardized outdoor medium is the Outdoor Advertising Association of America. Its major function is to promote the use of outdoor advertising and represents the industry in legislative matters, besides handling the public relations program.

Another organization is the *National Outdoor Advertising Bureau* and it is cooperatively owned and used by the leading advertising agencies. It is involved in the creation, placing, buying, billing, supervising, and checking of outdoor advertising. The Institute of Outdoor Advertising is concerned with outdoor advertising research and dissemination of information.

Transit advertising

Transit advertising is the term used for all types of advertising signs on or in trains, subways, streetcars, buses, taxicabs, and other such public transportation vehicles, or the stations from which they operate. The volume of transit advertising is estimated to be approximately $40 million. Although people generally think only in terms of car cards when referring to transit advertising, there are actually three major basic types or forms of transit advertising. These are:

1. *Car cards.* These are the advertisements placed inside streetcars, buses, and the cars of subway, elevated, and suburban trains.
2. *Traveling displays.* These are the larger signs posted or painted on the outside of buses, streetcars, and cabs.
3. *Station posters.* These are the posters and displays of varied size which are placed inside bus and railway stations and airport terminals, and on station platforms.

There are also several miscellaneous types of advertising handled by the transit advertising companies. In a few instances, public transportation systems have their buses or streetcars equipped to broadcast radio programs and commercials in the vehicles received from a local FM broadcasting station. Some companies sell advertising space on dining car menus, on timetables, or spectacular displays on stations. Although in a few instances the transportation companies themselves sell the advertising space in their vehicles and stations, in the great majority of cases special independent transportation advertising companies buy an exclusive lease on the advertising space in, on, or around the vehicles and stations of the one or more transportation companies in the city, and then sell the advertising space. The advertiser using transportation advertising must supply the car cards and posters to the operator, as in the case of outdoor advertising (with enough extra copies to take care of normal replacement needs).

Transit advertising and rates

Car cards. Car cards are the most important form of transit advertising; the estimate is that about 70 percent of the volume of transit advertising is spent on this form. Car cards are sold on the basis of: (1) double run, which means two cards in each car; (2) a full run, which is one card in each car; (3) a half run, a card for every other car; and (4) a quarter run, which is a card for each fourth car. In some instances, the terms "showing" or "service" are used instead of run.

The standardization of card size has been accomplished to a considerable extent by the Transit Advertising Association, Inc. All car cards are now 11 inches in height. The length may be 14, 21, 28, 42, 56, or 84 inches. The most commonly used sizes are the 11 by 28 inches and the 11 by 21 inches.

As a rule, car cards are sold on a basis of six months to a year of service, the rates being discounted for longer contract periods. The contracts normally provide for the transit advertising firm to place, change, and maintain the cards in the cars, although the cards themselves must be provided by the advertiser.

Costs for reaching United States markets are shown in Figure 14–3 and costs for the Metro New York market are in Figure 14–4.[3]

FIGURE 14–3
Transit (buses)

| | Transit costs within the top 100 markets | | | |
| | Exteriors (30"X 144"— full service) | | Interiors (11"X 28"— full service) | |
Markets	# Units	Monthly cost	# Units	Monthly cost
Top 10	3,180	$137,324	22,865	$29,385
Top 20	4,400	182,053	28,150	39,293
Top 30	5,278	213,270	31,368	44,580
Top 40	5,728	229,610	33,024	47,022
Top 50	6,227	248,310	34,453	48,961
Top 60	6,729	266,654	35,713	50,743
Top 70	7,065	279,566	36,898	52,456
Top 80	7,241	286,518	37,288	52,951
Top 90	7,440	293,318	37,786	53,426
Top 100	7,675	301,414	38,206	53,880

Note: Transit Outdoor Advertising is Outdoor Advertising on the exterior sides, fronts and backs of buses. In-Bus Advertising is magazine-type advertising on cards inside buses. Half-service for Exteriors costs about half that of full service; for Interiors the cost is approximately 55 percent of full service.
Sources: SRDS Transit Rates, November 1974; Mutual Transit Sales, February 1975.

Advantages of car cards

1. Advertisers in cars and buses get the "last chance" at the buyer, because the potential customer can be reminded of the advertiser's product on the way to the store.
2. The cost is reasonable.
3. Cooperative tie-ins with local retailers can be arranged.
4. The car cards are before the prospects for a considerable length of time. Studies by the National Association of Transportation Advertising, Inc., point out that the average length of ride is over 25 minutes per one-way trip, and that the average rider will be in a position to see between six and fifteen cards during most of the trip.

---

[3] *O & M Pocket Guide to Media,* sixth edition, 1975, Figure 14–4, pp. 61, 62.

FIGURE 14–4
Metro New York—Major out-of-home media

Car cards—Combined IRT, BMT, and IND lines—12-month rates

	Standard size		Premium position	
	# Cards	Monthly cost	# Cards	Monthly cost
Full run.......	$12,000	$17,841	6,000	$26,761
Half run	6,000	9,812	3,000	14,719
Quarter run......	3,000	5,130	—	—

    Standard size = 11″ X 28″
    Premium position = 22″ X 21″ square end.

Station posters—Combined IRT, BMT and IND lines 12-month rates

	One-sheet (30″X 46″)		Two-sheet (60″X 46″)	
	# Posters	Monthly cost	# Posters	Monthly cost
Intensive........	1,200	$9,645	1,200	$16,533
Representative	600	5,306	600	9,093
Standard........	300	2,773	300	4,753

Commuter clock displays—Selected showings may be purchased for ethnic or specific distributional coverage. Copy is rotated periodically to other platform locations to provide greatest possible coverage.

	Costs and allotments based on the 12-month rate	
Citywide showing	# Units	Monthly cost
Saturation...............	200	$12,000
Intensive................	150	10,725
Representative	100	8,250
Standard................	50	4,675

Sources: New York Subways Advertising Company, 1976; Commuter Clock Advertising, 1976.

5. Small advertisers are not overshadowed by large competitors. A well-designed card, although there may be only one to each four cars, will not be overshadowed by a competitor who is using even two cards per car.
6. Readership of the cards is high. Dr. Frank J. Charvat, of Emory University, in an actual Georgia study found that 62 percent to 90 percent of the group studied, saw, read, and remembered the car cards included in the analysis.
7. Color can be used very effectively.

Disadvantages of car cards

1. Copy is limited. Ten to twenty words is about the maximum that should be used.
2. It is difficult to quote daily prices, because the copy usually runs for a period of 30 days.

3. Car cards are so numerous in each car and tend to look so much alike that they are confusing.
4. Automobiles are used by many potential customers in major markets. As a result, car advertising will reach only those who use public vehicles.
5. Shift of stores to suburban areas decreases the number of trips which the shopper makes to the downtown sections of the city.
6. Car cards are primarily an urban medium and are not effective in reaching rural and small-town areas.

Point-of-purchase advertising

The term is defined to include all advertising materials—signs and displays—placed in, on, or around retail stores (excluding the labels, packages, or containers of the merchandise itself). Various other terms are sometimes used such as dealer displays, dealer aids, and point-of-sale materials. Point-of-purchase is now the more generally used inclusive term, since it tends to put the emphasis on the consumer or buyer rather than on the dealer or seller. Also, the trade association of the industry uses the designation, Point-of-Purchase Advertising Institute, so we shall do so in this discussion.

In recent years the point-of-purchase medium has become increasingly important in the advertising picture. The trend to self-service and self-selection at the retail level has made it more important for the manufacturer to have some means of bringing its product to the attention of the consumer at the point where the final purchase is consummated. Since in many instances there is little or no personal selling, the manufacturer feels it must try to get its final suggestion or sales story to the prospective customer at the point where the buying decision is being made through some type of advertising display. Many studies have shown a great increase in impulse buying in recent years at the self-service outlets, and point-of-purchase materials can do much to stimulate impulse buying of a manufacturer's brand. With the increased competition of new brands and new products coming on the market, the manufacturer has found it increasingly necessary to devise some means to hold or enlarge its share of the market, and has found good advertising materials at the point of purchase to be an effective aid to sales.

The medium of point-of-purchase advertising has grown rapidly in recent years, and it is estimated that advertisers are now spending approximately $700 million annually for point-of-purchase merchandising materials.

Organization of the industry

The bulk of the materials included in the point-of-purchase advertising used by the retailer is provided by the manufacturers or advertisers of the products being sold by the retailer, although some of the display materials will be provided by the individual retailer, particularly in the case of the large department and specialty stores. In some instances, the agency or the advertiser plans the point-of-purchase materials and handles its production. However, much of the material is produced for the advertisers by firms specializing in the production of point-of-purchase display materials. Some 250 such firms are members of the Point-of-Purchase Advertising Institute (usually referred to as POPAI), and most of them are in a position to advise and aid advertisers in the planning of materials as well as in the actual production. Since the work of these firms is not commissionable, they usually try to work directly with the advertiser rather than through the advertising agency.

Forms of point-of-purchase advertising

A wide range of actual materials and devices, signs and displays are included in this medium—so wide as virtually to defy classification. They range from simple cardboard shelf strips to cloth banners to elaborate illuminated and animated spectaculars. They may be made of paper, wood, cardboard, metal, or plastics. Many are temporary in nature, such as paper banners and posters, while others are quite permanent, such as metal signs, self-merchandising display stands, and clock advertisements. Some are designed for exterior use and some for interior use. A list prepared by POPIA included 40 kinds.

Use of point-of-purchase advertising

Generally speaking, the advertising firm uses point-of-purchase as a part of its entire advertising and promotion program, to increase the sale of its brand of merchandise. But specifically the advertiser wishes to have this form of advertising in use so that it will remind the shopper of its product and brand at the moment he or she is in the store at the point of buying. A second basic purpose of point-of-purchase advertising is to stimulate impulse buying.

The third purpose the manufacturer has in mind in using point-of-purchase advertising is to influence the dealer to stock the merchandise and cooperate in increasing the sale of the merchandise through its effective display. In the same way that the advertiser's salesperson "merchandises" other media advertising when selling the retailer on why the store should stock the product, he or she uses the story of the good display material the firm furnishes and its influence in obtaining good sales and stock turnover to aid in getting the retailer to stock the product initially. Also, after the retailer has stocked the line, the salesperson uses the point-of-purchase materials to aid in getting better display positions, more display, and more pushing of the product by the retailer.

Considerations in creation and use of point-of-purchase advertising

One of the main problems the advertiser faces is to create point-of-purchase materials that will be effective in maintaining to the point of sale the message and the brand image created by the mass media advertising, and which will stimulate impulse and reminder buying by prospective customers. A number of factors should be considered in developing this material. These include:

1. The material must attract attention and must compete effectively in the store to catch a prospective buyer's eye and hold it. Design, shape, and color are methods which can be used in attaining this objective.
2. The material must build confidence. It must convey accurately the correct product image, and indicate that the manufacturer is reliable.
3. The material should give the product information briefly and succintly. The customer should be able to get in a glance all the information about the product.
4. The material should create the proper atmosphere for the product. It must be appropriate and suitable. Depending on the company whose products the point-of-purchase advertising is attempting to sell, it may be humorous or sophisticated, traditional or modern.
5. The appeal should create the impression that the product advertised is of good value. Buyers are trying to make their dollars go as far as they can. As a result, the appeal that stresses this fact will result generally in greater impulse sales.
6. The material must be attractive enough to deserve a preferred place in the store. Because of the competitive battle for space in the store, material that adds to the beauty of displays and the like is much easier to get into a position where it will have a maximum chance to be seen by the customers.

Exhibits and trade shows

The exhibit has two unique features as a form of advertising. It is the only one where the product can be made available for actual inspection and demonstration, and where the prospects come to the place of the advertising so the advertiser's salespeople can "sell" the product's features on the spot.

There are various types and categories of exhibits or trade shows. Some are designed for consumers, either to reach the general public or specific segments of the buying public. General type shows include the exhibits at county, state, and world fairs. Those aimed at special segments of the market include such exhibits or shows as automobile, boat, garden, hobby, and home furnishings shows.

However, a larger proportion of the shows are industrial, and restrict the attendance to people who are directly connected with that particular field. The bulk of these shows are in connection with the annual meeting of the trade association involved, and usually sponsored or run by the particular association. The limitation on attendance at these shows insures to the exhibitor that all who inspect the exhibit are potential customers. Thus in essence it is a form of controlled circulation for the advertising and sales effort.

The advertiser who plans to use the exhibit must plan the design of the booth in the exhibit with the thought of attracting the attention of those attending, and also maximizing the sales impact the exhibit will achieve. The exhibit may be very simple, consisting merely of tables with samples of the advertiser's product displayed, or they may be very complex and costly, with elaborate cutout working models of large pieces of equipment. Usually the advertiser will also have special sales literature and materials to hand out to those who stop and inspect the exhibit.

The exhibit can be a costly form of promotion. The exhibitor must pay rent for the space at the show, must pay for the design and construction of the booth and the contents thereof, and for moving the exhibit from one trade show to another, and also must consider the costs of providing salespeople and other people necessary to staff the booth during the show. Rental costs will vary from as little as $50 for a booth in a small local show to an average figure of $4.50 per square foot for a major industrial show. The cost of the booth and its contents will vary widely, but some exhibitors estimate that to do an effective job today involves costs varying from a minimum of $200 per running foot of booth frontage to $600 per running foot to do a creditable job of advertising. Most firms exhibiting in only a few trade shows will use the services of special companies specializing in the design and construction of exhibits. There are approximately 115 companies of this nature, most of which belong to the trade association of the industry, the Exhibit Producers & Designers Association. They usually work on a fixed fee basis.

Specialty advertising

As defined by *Advertising Age,* "An advertising specialty is a useful product with an advertising message imprinted on it. It is usually distributed to customers and prospects by businessmen to promote goodwill, with no specific obligation attached." It is always distributed free. The advertiser does hope, of course, that the recipient of the specialty will be influenced to buy its product in the future by frequently seeing the advertising message on the specialty. It is believed that over half of American business firms use some form of advertising specialty, and it is estimated that approximately one billion dollars is spent annually for specialties by these firms. All forms of advertising specialties are sold through advertising specialty distributors or firms, whose salespeople in the field vend this form of advertising in the same manner that other media have sales forces for their media.

The variety and range of items included or used as advertising specialties is virtually endless. However, we shall limit our discussion to three groupings—novelties, calendars, and executive gifts.

Advertising novelties

An advertising novelty is any relatively inexpensive item which is mass-produced for wide distribution as an advertising specialty. Literally thousands of items would fall into this category. Among the more common ones intended to be carried by the recipient are ball-point pens, bottle openers, coin purses, cigarette lighters, emery boards, key rings, pocketknives, and wallets. For use on the recipient's desk are such items as ashtrays, blotters, letter openers, pencils, pens, memo pads, and rulers. For use in the home are ashtrays, bottle openers, drink stirrers, pencils, ice picks, and thermometers. Every reader can think of many items used in everyday life that are such advertising novelties.

There are several reasons why advertising novelties are so widely used as a form of advertising. Since an object is normally a useful item, it cultivates goodwill for the advertiser, and it gives the recipient a value for looking at the advertiser's message. The novelty provides an excellent repetition of the advertising message, since the user of the item will be exposed to the message each time the article is used. For many novelties, this will be every day, and often many times each day. Another important feature of novelties is that they are inexpensive, and the cost per exposure is very small. The advertiser can select prospects, and use novelties in such areas and with such groups of prospects or customers as seem advisable. They fit in well with any regular campaign of advertising the firm may be using.

In selecting the novelty, the advertiser should be certain it is a useful item, one that the recipient will use or handle or consult frequently. The novelty should have a long life, to get the benefit of long use by the prospect to whom it is given. The item should be such that the advertiser's name and message can be displayed effectively on it. It should be so inexpensive that it is economical to provide all those prospects the advertiser would like to reach. The advertiser also should try to select a novelty that is appropriate, or one that ties in with the particular business. A bottle opener is good for the brewery; a key ring for car keys is particularly suitable for a service station or gasoline company.

Calendars

Calendars are the most commonly used of all forms of specialty advertising. A high percentage of individuals look at a calendar at least once every day of the year. Estimates are that from one third to one half of the money expended for specialty advertising is spent for calendars. Probably the most important problem facing the advertiser who decides to use calendars is the selection of an appropriate and attractive form and design for the audience to which the calendars are to be sent.

Executive gifts

Executive gifts is the term applied to advertising specialties that are expensive, in contrast to trinkets or inexpensive items that usually are classified as advertising novelties. In most instances, the executive gift is not imprinted with the advertiser's name or an advertising message. Hence, it probably should not be included as a form of advertising and not allocated to the advertising budget, although it frequently is so charged. The category is included here as an advertising specialty since it is usually so considered in the industry. And, of course, the gift often is designed or selected to be such that the executive will use it often, with the advertiser's hope that each time it is used or seen, a feeling of goodwill toward the giver will be generated, and that the recipient will tend to buy the advertiser's product. They are given in the industrial and commercial fields where the potential purchases by the recipient for the firm are appreciable in quantity, and so can easily justify a large expenditure per prospect.

There are crucial problems connected with the use of the executive gift—both moral and legal. For when an expensive gift is given to an executive who is in position to influence the purchases made by the firm, the question of commercial bribery arises. Hence, the advertiser may create more ill will than goodwill by offering such an executive gift. In many firms today, executives are prohibited by company policy from accepting gifts above a certain value.

Screen advertising

Some advertisers use short motion-picture films shown in regular movie houses as a part of their advertising program. Although theater-screen advertising is an important medium in many other countries of the world, it is only a very minor medium in the United States in terms of relative expenditures involved. While no comprehensive statistics are available, it is estimated that approximately 12,000 to 13,000 (including 4,000 drive-ins) of the some 16,000 movie theaters in the United States make their screens available for screen advertising.

Users of screen advertising

Screen advertising is used by both national advertisers and by local advertisers. National advertisers use it in manufacturer-dealer campaigns, in that the national advertiser produces and pays for the film advertisement, and the local dealer pays for the showing of the film, which includes a trailer identifying the local dealer as the place to buy the advertised product. The largest users of this medium on the above bases are the automobile manufacturers and the petroleum companies. Many of the local advertisers who utilize screen advertising do it as a part of their cooperative programs with their manufacturers. Among these are the automobile, petroleum products, and farm implement dealers. In addition, local service firms and retailers use screen advertising as an important medium for their local advertising. Among the heaviest users are banks and insurance agencies. Also, firms who naturally cater to after-theater business, such as restaurants, coffeehouses, pizza parlors, and ice-cream parlors are logical

users of film screen advertising. In some instances, these local advertisers may merely use slides rather than movie films to present their
advertisements.

Features of screen advertising

One of the major advantages stressed for screen advertising is that
it has great impact, due to the large size of the screen and the fine
picture presented to the viewer, and is able to use action and color, and
actually demonstrate the product in use.

In addition, it has the advantage of selectivity and flexibility. Another advantage of screen advertising is that almost everyone in the
audience for which the advertiser is paying is virtually certain to see
and hear the message. The disadvantage of screen advertising is that
some patrons of movie theaters resent the interjection of advertising
messages during the entertainment.

Costs of screen advertising

The charge for theater screen advertising is based on weekly showings in the various theaters. Rate books are published which show the
average weekly attendance for each theater, and the local and national advertising rates for a week. The actual rate on a cost-per-
thousand viewers basis would appear to be high, as compared with
other mass media, averaging in the neighborhood of $6 or $6.50 per
thousand (the range being from $5 to $7).

Directories

Another medium used to quite an extent by many advertisers is the
directory. There are more than 4,000 directories in current use in the
United States. These are published by directory publishers, magazines, trade associations, chambers of commerce, and city, state, and
federal government agencies. Most of these directories are published
to serve the trade, industrial, and professional fields. One of the most
widely used consumer directories is the classified section (Yellow
Pages) of the telephone directory. Yellow Pages usage is a direct outgrowth of telephone usage. The long-established habit of looking up
telephone numbers in the alphabetical (White Pages) directory carries over to the Yellow Pages when consumers are trying to find where
to call for a particular product or service. Companies that encourage
telephone shopping and use "tie-in" advertising (in which their TV,
radio, and print ads carry the "Find it in the Yellow Pages" reference)
reinforce the directory usage. To advertisers, one of the most significant features of the classified directory is that it is as available as the
telephone itself. Over 150 million Yellow Page directories are distributed each year, blanketing a large segment of the population. In
some large cities, because of size, the Yellow Pages forms a separate
volume. But in most cities, the White and Yellow Pages are bound
together. Every household or business having a telephone receives at

FIGURE 14–5
Telephone directory advertising

Telephone directory advertising				
Markets:	*1–10*	*1–25*	*1–50*	*1–100*
No. of directories.........	240	494	767	1,160
Directory-Area Population..	47,115	73,255	104,807	128,222
('000)				
Annual Cost:				
Bold listing..............	$ 7,075	$18,920	$ 19,765	$ 28,930
Trade mark ad...........	$30,200	$53,980	$ 79,380	$114,400
1/16 pg. display ad.......	$49,750	$88,530	$129,060	$184,870

Source: SRDS Oct. '74

Yellow Pages usage

Consumer: Seventy-six percent of the adult population (20 years of age and over)
consult the Yellow Pages. They refer to them an average of 40 times
a year. Eighty-nine percent of these references result in some form of
follow-up action.

Industrial: Ninety percent of the buyers in manufacturing firms use the Yellow
Pages. They refer to them an average of 86 times per year. Nine out
of ten of these references result in follow-up action.

Source: *Audits & Surveys*

Source: *Ayer Media Facts,* 1975, p. 20.

least one Yellow Pages directory. For those few persons without telephone, or those on the move, directories are available at public telephone locations.

The familiarity and availability of the Yellow Pages make it an
effective tool for the advertiser who seeks transient, seasonal, or infrequent customers, as well as general market customers.

For customers wishing to be represented in markets in a number
of geographic areas, the National Yellow Pages Service provides a
convenient way to order Yellow Pages advertising. One transaction
can provide for advertising in 5,000 Yellow Pages sections. Telephone
directory advertising may be in either alphabetical sections (White
Pages) or classified section (Yellow Pages). In the United States there
are approximately *4,200 local directories* with a combined *circulation
of 150 million.* They reach 83 percent of the households and every
business firm. (See Figure 14–5 for some Yellow Pages costs.)

Sampling

Sampling is a procedure by which a sample of the product is given
to prospective consumers so that they can test the product, on the
assumption the product "will sell itself" if once used.

There are four general types of sampling:

1. Delivered packages.
2. Delivered through cooperation with dealers.
3. Sent directly in answer to advertising coupons.
4. Sold through dealers and vending machines.

Delivering samples from door to door is one of the oldest forms of sampling. When advertising was not used to such a great degree and any new item distributed to the home was the center of a family discussion, almost any goods distributed from door to door received attention.

But with the change in living habits and the advent of laws and ordinances prohibiting the littering of streets, distributing samples from door to door has become less feasible. In addition to the cost of samples, delivery expenses tend to be high. It is sometimes advisable to use advertising to prepare a reception for the sample. Regardless of the cost, with many products like foods, house-to-house sampling can still be a profitable means of advertising.

One of the methods of sampling that has been tried in many different ways is that of supplying samples for retailers to give to their customers. This has been criticized because some dealers may sell the samples instead of giving them away. Some advertisers do not object to this. They say that the purpose of the campaign is attained, and perhaps those who pay for the samples use them with greater care and appreciation than if they were handed out gratis. Or, samples can be given out by demonstrators in the stores.

Another form of sampling which has worked out well in some fields is selling a small package of the product. Vending machines also may be used in a limited way to distribute sample package goods of low unit value. To arrange with dealers to redeem coupons which are used either in national or local advertising media is a common practice. In past years, a few advertisers have taken advantage of dealers by advertising that a dealer would supply a free sample or one at a reduced price on presentation of a coupon. However, the advertiser who uses this form of advertising should give the dealer sufficient notice so that he will be familiar with the campaign.

House organ

Another medium for a company to use is a house organ. This is a magazine or bulletin published by a company and sent to its dealers, customers, or employees for the purpose of promoting goodwill, increasing sales, or for molding public opinion. House organs are distinct from publications for which a subscription price is charged because they are sent without charge. While the mortality rate for such publications is high, they can render a real service to the company. A well-edited house organ can do much to get customers to feel they know the people who are in the company. Owing to the cost of editing, printing, and mailing, a first-class house organ is expensive and requires close attention if results are to be profitable.

House organs for customers

When the magazine is for the consumer or user, the material in it must be of a different nature from that of a publication intended for salespeople, agents, dealers, or employees. If house organs are sent to prospective consumers, it is important that the publication be interesting and informative. The prospective consumer does not have the same interest in the manufacturer that the employee has, and, therefore, the material must get attention and create interest if it is to be effective.

The house publication, when properly used, can be adapted to almost any business and is a valuable adjunct in building and maintaining goodwill.

Packages, labels and inserts

Although normally the package is considered as the container for the product (to protect it and to facilitate its handling) it also serves as a means for carrying a message about the product. Hence, in a sense, it is a type of advertising medium.

For best results, the advertising message on the package should be brief. A picture of the product, or the product in use, is desirable. The brand name and trademark should, of course, be prominent. Brief copy may include some information about the quality of the product, the contents and the methods of preparation. For food items, this may include recipes. If there is an inside container (glass bottle inside the cardboard box), the label on the bottle might have similar information on it.

Of almost equal importance is the package insert, often neglected by advertisers. Although it does not reach as many people, since normally seen only by the actual buyers and users, it still presents an opportunity to get a message across to the prospect. It is an inexpensive means of direct advertising to the prime prospects.

The insert can be used to convey various advertising messages. It can include more detailed information than the appeal on the package as how best to use, or care for the product, or, it can advertise other items in the firm's line.

Questions

1. It has been said that almost every business, regardless of size, uses some direct advertising. Do you agree? Explain.
2. With the recent criticism leveled at "junk" mail, and the advent of the consumers' movement, do you think the outlook for direct-mail advertising is bleak or promising? Explain.

3. Direct mail is often described as the most selective of all media. Is this true? Discuss.

4. Are specific forms of direct advertising more suitable for some retailers than others? Explain.

5. What are some of the recent trends and developments that have influenced outdoor advertising—some tending to increase its importance and some tending to diminish its use? From your analysis of these, what do you think the future holds for outdoor advertising? Why?

6. Are there any circumstances under which an advertiser might use outdoor advertising as his primary medium? Explain. If yes, give examples.

7. Is outdoor advertising suitable as a medium for reaching particular segments of the market? Explain.

8. For what types of products, and for what advertisers, do you think transit advertising is more appropriate? Why?

9. How important is transit advertising as a medium in your city? Why is this true?

10. Study the advertisements in the Yellow Pages of your local telephone directory. Describe what you consider the most effective ads you found there. For what types of advertisers do you think this medium is most appropriate? Why?

11. How often do you use the Yellow Pages as a source of information for shopping? Do you think this is really a good advertising medium? Explain.

12. For what types of products would you consider sampling a particularly good means of advertising? Discuss.

13. Visit one department store and one supermarket in your city. Describe the point-of-purchase advertisements you saw there. Which of the stores made more effective use of point-of-purchase materials? Describe what you considered the two best pieces of point-of-purchase advertising.

14. Why do you think it is becoming increasingly difficult for an advertiser to obtain wide use of his point-of-purchase advertising materials?

15. For what types of advertisers, and under what circumstances, are exhibits an important form of advertising?

16. Bring to class three examples of "specialty" advertising. Do you consider them effective advertising? Why?

17. Bring to class a package that you consider an effective advertising vehicle, and one you consider a poor one. Explain your selections.

Case **HENDERSON ASSOCIATES**
14–1 **Evaluating a marketing proposal**

Sybil Henderson, one of the most eminent writers in the food industry, has prepared a set of cookbooks which have proven to be not only an invaluable reference source for produce personnel and customers, but also a fine sales tool to help increase the volume and profits for produce departments.

Over three million of these books have been sold. Art Linkletter, Dinah Shore, Tom Frandzia, and *"Dial for Dollars,"* are only a few of the shows on which Sybil Henderson has appeared. She has written valuable booklets on many of the major aspects of flower and plant care.

The Henderson organization also has handled a number of food accounts for which it has planned and directed the marketing and advertising strategy. Henderson Associates prepared a marketing proposal for Granny Smith apples from New Zealand, which is given below.

Marketing proposal for Granny Smith apples from New Zealand

The following is a preliminary suggested promotional campaign for Granny Smith apples from New Zealand.

The increase from 3,000 boxes six years ago to 60,000 last year indicates the apple is of fine quality and is extremely competitive, especially because they are on the market during the soft fruit season in the United States.

A substantial increase in sales can be effected by making both the trade and the consumers much more aware of the fine qualities of Granny Smith apples.

These apples have exciting promotional possibilities—their freshness, compared with other storage apples on the market, their crispness and excellent flavor, their complete versatility and the romance of New Zealand are a few.

During the first year of promotion, the groundwork should be laid for a long, steady increase of sales of Granny Smith. Releases to food editors, business editors, and extensive information to the wholesalers and produce buyers will be delivered personally. The many years in promoting produce has given Henderson Associates an excellent reputation for accurate, dependable information, which serves to increase sales of produce. Henderson can bring this same capability into play for Granny Smith apples.

Henderson's specialty is taking small-volume items and building them into big ones. Its capabilities are regional and national in the United States, as well as international.

Introduction of Granny Smith

The ideal way to introduce a promotional program for a product is through a combination trade and media luncheon, presenting the product and the promotional campaign in an exciting, interesting and, in this case, tasty manner.

A lot of excitement can be generated about New Zealand—the growing areas surrounding the harbors, the ability to pack Granny Smith's very quickly after picking, and (perhaps) the fact that New Zealand also imports a great amount of apples and pears from the United States.

Granny Smith apples will be prepared in several different ways, showing the types of recipes which will be provided to the food editors for use in the food pages in their papers.

The name of the apple itself presents a number of possibilities for promotion. It certainly isn't a name that is easily forgotten—and one can have a lot of fun with it.

Different types of press and retailer kits will be made in advance so the information which is presented at the luncheon can be taken back to the office and used when needed.

Henderson Associates will have press photographers from the food trade magazines present so Granny Smith apples can get story coverage in the trade press.

There also is the possibility of working with the New Zealand Trade Commission on such a luncheon.

Basic program

Trade merchandising. Materials would be developed for the wholesale market and produce buyers, telling them about the background of Granny Smith apples, their availability, the volume the retailers can expect during the months that Granny Smith apples are available, and informing them about the promotional program.

This is an important function and should be done at least six weeks before the apples are available, in volume, for ads. Retailers are planning their ads considerably in advance and Henderson will want them to tie in with the food editor and the radio and television publicity.

Henderson's function is to encourage larger displays of Granny Smith apples at store level, as well as getting the buyer to promote them in newspaper ads.

The advantages of Granny Smith apples over other apples in the market at the time must be graphically pointed out. Inasmuch as apples now are available all year round, because of controlled atmosphere storage, it is very important that buyers are made aware of the freshness and added shelf life of Granny Smith apples.

It is equally important that this message get across to the produce man. The Washington State Apple Commission has year-round merchandising representation, and Henderson must make the produce manager aware of the advantages of Granny Smith during its season.

There are 44 chain store headquarters in the Los Angeles Marketing Area—and the potential volume of business to be realized in the future is great.

Food product publicity

There are two ways to approach the consumer in newspaper, radio, and television. One is through paid advertising, the other through food product publicity.

Henderson has found that recipes and photographs provided to the newspapers have resulted in as much as 100 times the space of an ad at a fraction of the cost to its clients.

Another advantage is that the consumer does not realize that she or he is being sold a product. It is written editorially, rather than being set up as an ad, and she or he accepts the story as such.

It is necessary to provide exclusive stories to the various papers, because one editor will not use any story used by another.

Henderson herself also makes personal appearances as guest on both radio and television programs. Inasmuch as Granny Smith apples are a variety and not a brand name, it opens more avenues for publicity.

Point-of-sale materials and recipe folders

Although more and more retail stores are refusing the average point-of-sale pieces, there is still a definite need for identification of Granny Smith apples. Too many people would just assume they are a pippin or a Gravenstein because they are green.

Recipes are an excellent way to increase sales. Retailers are always enthusiastic about them if they are distributed to the stores in an easy-to-use manner.

Henderson's policy is to work with the major retailers in advance, to see just what their current policy is before it goes to the expense of creating new point-of-sale material that may not get used. It is much too expensive to be wasted.

Printing the materials in New Zealand may be advisable and then ship this with the apples, depending on which would be more economical.

Because the major thrust is just for a two-month period, Henderson would want to get immediate distribution of any materials which were going to be used.

Other possibilities

Depending on budget, Henderson would suggest considering a display contest in some chains, possibly working with Air New Zealand on a trip to New Zealand for the grand prize.

Henderson would like to do some in-store demonstrations on a limited basis for two reasons: (1) to secure some specific data on consumer reaction and acceptance to Granny Smith apples, and (2) to use them as a tool to increase possibility of chain store ads.

Suggested budget

There are two general ways for arriving at a budget for produce promotion. One is a cents-per-box assessment, and the other a percentage of the dollar volume of the crop. Both are used successfully, but the dollar volume is the most realistic. An example is the California Avocado Advisory Board, which is on a dollar volume assessment of 5½ percent of gross receipts. Over the past ten years, the avocado advertising and promotion budget has remained almost the same, although the crop has fluctuated greatly from year to year. Many times a higher priced but smaller crop is more difficult to move than a larger crop whose lower prices alone help to sell the crop.

Whichever way the budget sum is arrived at, it should be sufficient to do the job necessary for the amount of produce to be moved.

The following is a prelimiary summary of a minimum budget that could get Granny Smith apples launched effectively in the Southern California market:

Henderson Associates:*	$ 5,000.00
Luncheon for trade and media....................	750.00
Trade-merchandising in-store calls and headquarters calls from April through mid-July	3,500.00
Food photographs, recipe development, and distribution of releases ....:	3,000.00
Travel, long-distance phone calls, and contingencies. . .	2,000.00
	$14,250.00

Demonstrations and point-of-sale printing are not included in the above budget. These items should be discussed based on materials already available in New Zealand.

* Consultation and recommendations for all phases of promotion, including working with the New Zealand Apple Board and the local brokers, to set up the program beginning as soon as possible and then continuing supervision through the month of July.

Case question

1. Evaluate the proposal for promoting Granny Smith apples.

Case
14-2
BERVEN CARPETS CORPORATION
Considering a cooperative advertising program

Philip Berven organized the company in San Francisco early in 1938. The operation was established as a decorator supply company—as essentially a sales organization catering to the carpet needs of interior designers. Also formed was the company's initial concentration toward that segment of the carpet business dealing with more highly styled, better quality goods.

As a result of material shortages caused by World War II, Berven's mill suppliers were unable to adequately supply the demands of its growing distributors' sales. Berven, therefore, first began to import oriental hooked rugs, but because of the continuing supply limitations, Berven entered carpet manufacturing with the purchase, in 1945, of a reversible chenille mill located in Fresno, California.

With the advent of a revolutionary carpet making process called "tufting" in 1950, Berven recognized that this was the most revolutionary change in basic carpet technology since the power loom was launched, and therefore in 1951 began to introduce carpets utilizing this process.

Berven's manufacturing presently encompasses three facilities, each separate and operationally independent, yet closely integrated. Viewing the operations individually, the Broadloom Mill accounts for the greatest percentage of sales and produces a selection of 35 qualities featuring a broad range of style offerings. There is an average selection of 17 colors in each quality.

In the specialty Carpet Mill Division, the company produces custom fabrics, i.e., carpet qualities produced to consumer specifications in size, shape, and color. In this phase of the operation, as a result of many years of special color dyeing services, the company now provides a library of swatches and dye formulas for approximately 50,000 color shades and blends.

The third facility is Varidye, which is Berven's trade name for a licensed yarn dyeing system enabling varied colors to be predictably spaced along a single yarn. While Berven instituted this dye technique initially to broaden its own style capabilities, a growing demand has taken place throughout the industry for pre-dyed yarn utilizing Varidye technology.

Berven places emphasis on manufacturing and flexibility, because the dominant influence in the industry during the past two decades has been technological change. In its Fresno headquarters and mills and the Dalton, Georgia, mill, totaling 1,185,000 square feet, the company ranks among the most modern and automated in the industry.

Sales

Berven's sales in the last fiscal year were $45,000,000. Its sales force markets the company's Berven of California trade-style products direct to retailers (better-quality department, furniture, and specialty floor covering stores) and is responsible for gaining product acceptance among architects and interior designers.

The company maintains showrooms for its Berven of California trade-style products in 25 major metropolitan areas throughout the country. A separate line of carpeting—bearing the Carriage Trade Mill trade-style, and marketed by a separate Berven sales division to stocking distributors—also is now being offered. To enhance its marketing power to supply total carpeting requirements of an installation, Berven distributes other complementary lines of carpet.

"Beautiful as all outdoors," is Berven's memorable and distinctive advertising phrase. Full-color pictorials of nature scenes, with Berven rugs and carpets as "The beautiful way to be practical," is used in the advertising in leading home and decorating magazines, such as *Sunset, Better Homes and Gardens,* and *House and Garden Decorating Guide.*

Consumer awareness of Berven carpeting is only one objective of the company's advertising. Promotional materials are provided to retailers, enabling them to promote Berven quality and to identify for the consumer those home furnishing specialists that carry Berven carpets in local communities.

Among the materials available to retailers are direct-mail advertising, point-of-purchase displays, copy and visuals for local radio and television spots, mats for local newspaper advertising, and informative pamphlets to give to prospects during sales presentation.

Contract carpet promotion is targeted through trade media, and

EXHIBIT 14–1

carpet for an interesting setting

Hopefully, our illustration suggests
the deep, textural luxury
of *Bridal Suite*,
by Berven Of California,
fashioned in lush,
plump nylon yarns.
Now imagine 23 lovely
tone-on-tone colors
featuring the important
return of *"the Naturals"* . . .
beautiful as all outdoors.
May we show you?

$00⁰⁰ sq. yd.

Devonshire Interiors, Ltd.

2345 BOREL AVENUE • GRAND JUNCTION • 338-6792

EXHIBIT 14–2

carpet for
an interesting room

We cannot hope to present in newsprint
the textural beauty and lustrous colors of lovely
Rondelure, by Berven Of California.
But, perhaps we can suggest the elegant taste with
which "pattern" returns to your floor.
Berven achieves it with a low,
dense-cut shag and loop pile combination
with 17 gently sculptured, multi-toned blends.
Definitely for an interesting room,
like all carpet from this talented Mill.
Do see.

$00.00 sq. yd.

Devonshire Interiors, Ltd.

2345 BOREL AVENUE • GRAND JUNCTION • 338-6792

EXHIBIT 14–3

carpet for
an interesting
person

This is *Make a Wish* by Berven Of California.
You'll find it a most interesting setting
to express your individuality.
11 color blends,
inspired by Nature hues,
are presented in an exciting
cut and loop pile Anso® nylon
you'll appreciate.
May we show you?

$00⁰⁰ sq. yd.

Devonshire Interiors, Ltd.

2345 BOREL AVENUE • GRAND JUNCTION • 338-6792

through selective direct mail to architects and interior design audiences.

Promotional strategy

The carpet industry underwent broad changes in raw materials and technology about 20 years ago, and as a result, the industry's approach to sales became strongly geared to emphasizing commodity and price. For the most part, it continues to be the same at present, and the promotional programs have been keyed toward stimulating greater consumer selling emphasis on the part of the retailers.

There continues to be retailer resistance to any sales or promotional program that deviates from the standard industry practice described above.

Berven sent each of its retailers a major promotional kit in which is included material for the various media which the retailer uses. As an example, in Exhibits 1, 2, and 3 the copy for suggested retail newspaper ads which feature the retailer's name is given.

Script for radio spots, TV spots, direct-mail brochures and other recommended approaches also are included. With the exception of the direct-mail brochures, all the materials contained in a major promotional kit are provided free of charge to Berven's retailers. Berven also maintains carpet specialists in each of its showrooms located throughout the United States, and these individuals serve as consultants not only to the retailers but, as well, to the customers who may visit these rooms.

Case question

1. Develop a cooperative program that Berven might consider using with its retailers.

Case **ANALYSIS OF THREE COMPANIES**
14–3 **Deciding on media**

Indicate the importance of using outdoor, transit, and direct mail in the selection of advertising media for each of the companies listed below and give reasons as to how and why they should or should not be used.

Direct Wholesalers, Inc.

The company's business consists primarily of the procurement, warehousing, and sale of groceries and nonfood items to independent supermarkets, discount stores, and neighborhood grocery stores. In 1961 the company instituted a method of selling which was unique at the time in the wholesale grocery business, and which is still followed by the company. At that time all salesmen were eliminated and today no salesmen are employed by the company. Instead, lists of products and prices are circulated weekly among the company's customers and potential customers, and orders are taken by telephone clerks and processed on IBM equipment. The company's business has approximately 5,000 active customers throughout the Eastern metropolitan area. Approximately 125,000 cases of groceries and nonfood items are moved in and out of the company's warehouse each week. Delivery is made in trucks leased by a company subsidiary, which leases trucks almost exclusively to the company. Sales are substantially on a cash basis, with accounts receivable collected within an average of three and one-half days after billing, which occurs one or two days before delivery of merchandise. The amount of the average invoice during the last two years was approximately $300. Most of the items distributed are nationally advertised brands and are purchased directly from manufacturers or through food brokers. The company believes it has adequate alternative sources of supply for such items.

Competition.   Since the company's business consists primarily of supplying independent retail outlets other than chain stores and cooperative groups, its success depends upon the ability of such outlets to compete successfully with chain stores, cooperative groups, and other independent operators.

The principal chain stores operating in the area served by the company are A & P, Grand Union, Food Fair, First National Stores, and American Stores. The company competes at the wholesale level with many other wholesale grocery distributors, independent and cooperative. The wholesale grocery business is thus competitive and has been characterized historically by narrow profit margins. Although comparative figures are not available, the company believes it is among the larger independent wholesale distributors of groceries in its area.

Discount Stores, Inc.

The company, a pioneer in the self-service discount department store field, opened its first store in 1950. This store has since been expanded and the company in 1977 operates a total of 12 stores with approximately 900,000 aggregate square feet of floor space in five states. Leases have been executed and construction commenced on three additional stores with approximately 325,000 aggregate square feet of floor space, one of which is scheduled to be opened later this year. The company's expansion program also contemplates the opening of additional stores.

Discount Stores, Inc., offers a wide range of first-quality, popular-to-medium-priced department store merchandise at discount prices. The following policies have permitted the company to reduce (and in some instances to eliminate) conventional retail operating costs and overhead.

1.   All sales are on a cash-and-carry basis, thus eliminating delivery, credit sale bookkeeping, and collection and accounts receivable financing expenses.

2. The company's "Unconditional Money-Back Guarantee" policy is intended to assure customer satisfaction.

3. Customers serve themselves by rolling conventional self-service shopping carts through aisles of merchandise and paying at check-out counters.

4. Merchandise is delivered directly to the stores by vendors. This eliminates warehousing and reduces inventory, stockroom, and merchandise handling costs, and facilitates more effective space utilization (i.e., greater selling space to total floor space ratio per store).

5. Simple self-service fixtures, which replace more costly counters, permit the display of a broader selection of merchandise and render it readily accessible to the customer.

6. Major thoroughfare locations in outlying, residential, or neighborhood shopping centers or areas result in more reasonable occupancy costs, better parking accommodations, and shorter travel time for customers within the trading areas served by the company's stores than for downtown stores. Only one of the company's present stores is located in a downtown area.

7. Single-story buildings eliminate elevator and escalator operating and maintenance costs, reduce housekeeping and merchandise handling expenses, and facilitate traffic flow within the stores. Customers are exposed to the merchandise from the moment they enter the store until they leave. Periods of nonexposure while in transit between floors, traffic congestion at elevators, escalators and stairs, and delays while waiting for sales clerks are thus eliminated. Counter and merchandise arrangements direct the traffic flow throughout the stores and facilitate both impulse and intended purchases (i.e., the merchandise "sells" itself).

8. Centralized planning, control, administration, and quantity buying for multiple operating units reduce overhead and unit merchandise costs, as compared with single-unit department store operations.

Besides the foregoing, all stores are well lighted, spacious, and are open from 10:00 A.M. to 10:00 P.M., six days a week. Two stores are open seven days a week. All stores are air-conditioned. Advertising has been conducted through all local media, including radio, television, newspapers, billboards, circulars, and transit.

Discount Stores, Inc., competes with all other national and local retail establishments which handle similar lines of merchandise within its trading areas, including conventional department stores, variety and auto accessory chains, clothing, drug, hardware, home furnishing, furniture and appliance stores, and specialty shops, as well as supermarkets, other self-service discount department stores, and some of their cotenants in residential shopping centers.

Lasting Paint Company

The company is primarily engaged in the manufacture and retailing of a complete line of paints for interior and exterior home decorating. The company also sells in its own retail outlets linoleum, floor tile, wallpaper, stepladders, rollers, brushes, and a line of accessories and items used in decorating the interior and exterior of residential and commercial buildings.

The company pioneered the principle of selling paint and decorating supplies directly to the public through large discount retail stores, and its sales have grown to $25 million in the last fiscal year. This method of merchandising results in operating economies by avoiding the expenses of a credit or mail-order department and shipping or delivery service, as well as the financing of customer receivables. This sales method has made it possible for the company to offer both the amateur painter and decorator paint supplies at prices which are lower than those of competitive products of the same quality. Although the bulk of sales is made to do-it-yourself householders, professional painters also make purchases in the company's retail stores. The company believes that its retail prices are lower than the net prices charged by most of the larger paint manufacturers to professionals after deducting a trade discount from retail prices. The company has continued to operate on this basis and presently operates 25 stores in the Midwest area, concentrating on catering to do-it-yourself property owners and tenants.

The paints sold by the company include interior and exterior oil base paints and enamels, rubber base paints, both oil and water emulsion paints and enamels, vinyls and acrylics, as well as varnishes, lacquers, and so on. Paints account for approximately 60 percent of the total sales of the company. Sales of various types of linoleum, tile, and other floor covering constitute approximately 25 percent of the sales of the company. Wallpaper, stepladders, rollers, brushes, and other lines of items and accessories, the sale of no one of which is significant in itself, constitute the remaining 15 percent of sales.

Competition

The paint industry is competitive and the company competes with a large number of major paint manufacturers and retailers and with the paint departments of department stores, mail-order, and discount houses. However, the company has concentrated its efforts in the field of paint and related products sold primarily to the do-it-yourself and amateur painter. The company is one of the largest in the country.

With respect to its floor coverings and other products, the company competes with numerous other merchandisers in its area.

Case   **MASTER FOOD, INC.**
14–4   **Considering promotional methods**

Master Food, Inc.'s products include beef stew, corned beef hash, chili with beans, ham salad spread, beans and bacon, beans and ham, and Vienna sausage. The products are sold under its brand name "Tasty Master" as well as the nationally known brand names of firms for which it custom-packs products. One third of Master's packs is sold under the company's brand name.

Master Food did only a limited amount of advertising in newspapers to promote the Master label. It relied primarily on the salesmen to get shelf space in order to retain the desired sales.

Recently, the Yancey Company, a large national firm, notified Master that it planned to purchase its products from another packer. In the past fiscal year, Master also experienced a decrease of 3 percent in sales of Tasty Master products. As a result, the company is faced with the problem of deciding whether or not to change its advertising strategy.

Process

Raw materials, consisting principally of meat, are readily available at commercial sources and, in order to alleviate the risk of market fluctuations, usually are procured upon the booking of orders. Except in a few instances, Master does not stock raw materials for which it does not have orders. The large percentage of meat is brought to the plant from packing houses located in the Midwest. Upon arrival, the raw materials, in the case of fresh meat, are placed immediately in freezer or cooler facilities preparatory to further processing. Depending upon the particular product, the meat is then ground, cut, or taken in its boneless state to batching areas where it is weighed according to predetermined formulas. Next, the meat is transferred to a processing area where other ingredients and spices are blended with it, according to specification, and it is precooked and preformed. Finally the entire formulation is transferred to mechanized canning lines (designed especially to accommodate the particular item being packaged), pressure-cooked, labeled with the respective customer's brand, packaged in cases, and stored preparatory to shipment.

Quality control

Master's plant operates under continuous inspection by the U.S. Department of Agriculture, Meat Inspection Division. The company maintains a separate department in which a quality control staff checks and tests products withdrawn from production runs to determine their compliance with predetermined quality control standards.

Research and development

Master maintains a separate research and development department at its plant. The department is engaged in developing and evaluating new food products and improving those presently produced both independently and in conjunction with customers.

Recommended strategy

The president of the company, Carl Grey, indicated that the company should not increase its general advertising, but should put more emphasis on increasing the shelf space for Tasty Master products. It was his opinion that among the reasons that Yancey discontinued buying from Master was because the executives of that company were disturbed because Master's own label was in direct competition with Yancey products. (Master's sales to Yancey had amounted to 2 percent of its total volume.)

While Master's president was concerned about the loss of the account, he believed that it was possible to offset this by increasing sales to its other accounts and, at the same time, increasing sales of Master's own brand.

The marketing manager, on the other hand, did not believe that more shelf space would build demand for Tasty Master products. He contended that Master's products were of the slower selling food varieties and would not respond economically to the effort that would be necessary to get more shelf space. He also stated that most supermarkets would generally not carry more than three brands of the items sold under Master's label.

Furthermore, he believed that the length of time between the purchase of Master's products was generally as long as two weeks or more. It was essential, therefore, in his opinion, that to increase sales of Master's products, one had to build brand loyalty through media, such as television, radio, and newspapers.

Need for shelf space. The president replied by stressing that purchase of Master's products was largely of an impulse nature. He stated, "Even with paper products it has been shown that two-thirds of these are bought on impulse." He went on to point out that it was his experience in merchandising that there was a direct relationship between shelf space and sales. He also argued that by Master's putting its promotional dollars into getting more shelf space, it would not alienate its other major customers.

Case questions

1. How important is the amount of shelf space which can be secured in the sale of Master's own brand?
2. If one found it was important to get shelf space, how should Masters attempt to service it?
3. Evaluate the comments of the president and marketing manager.
4. Should Masters plan its major promotional emphasis on securing more shelf space? Give reasons.

part six

Research techniques

15

RESEARCH TECHNIQUES

*A*s technical research has increased the number of new products being brought to market and has shortened their life cycle, as competition in the marketplace has increased, and as the sheer volume of advertising has made it more necessary and yet more difficult to make advertising effective, the need for and the importance of research in planning advertising has increased. Its use has grown markedly in recent years, as advertising people have found that in many cases research can be of real aid in arriving at the correct or best answer, or can at least develop a great deal of factual data to aid in reaching better decisions.

The need for research

In order to have advertising achieve its maximum effectiveness, it is necessary that the proper message reach effectively the greatest number of potential prospects at the minimum practical cost. This means it is of paramount importance to know the answers to such questions as who the prospects are, where they are located, what features they like in the product, what appeals will be most effective in inducing them to buy or in stimulating demand, what are the most effective means of presenting these appeals, when and how often advertisements should be run to maximize economical effectiveness, what media are best for carrying the messages to the prospects, and how much can justifiably be spent on advertising as compared with other parts of the marketing mix?

Changes are taking place so rapidly in the market today that determining the answers to the above questions by intuition or on the basis of the general knowledge and experience of the advertising man is virtually impossible. Even through the extensive use of research in its present stage, many of the questions cannot be answered. However, marketing research will almost always provide data that will enable the advertiser to arrive at a much better solution than would have been possible without such research.

Advertising research

In addition to these general types of problems that lend themselves to handling through marketing research, there are a number of problems, specifically in the field of advertising, that should not be answered by the advertising executive without using research to the extent that is deemed economically justifiable.

Among the specific advertising problems which research can aid in solving are the following:

1. What is the degree of consumer acceptance for the product?
2. At which market segments should the advertising be directed?
3. What should be the advertising strategy?
4. What appeals are best to stimulate demand among the various groups of prospects? What should be the campaign theme? What copy and headlines should be used?
5. What media will be most effective in reaching particular groups of potential customers?
6. In print media, what layout, illustrations, and size will be most effective in gaining consumer attention and in inducing effective readership of the advertisements? Should the ads be in color or black and white?
7. In radio and television, what program and copy will be most effective in obtaining listenership and viewing, and what message will be most effective in stimulating demand?
8. What timing and frequency of insertion will provide maximum return for the cost?
9. What tests can be made to predict the readership, listernership or viewing and effectiveness of the ads?
10. What should be the amount of the advertising budget?
11. How should the consumer advertising be merchandised to the advertiser's sales force, and to the trade?

General procedure in marketing research

Finding the answers to problems such as those listed above is the purpose of advertising research. Basically, marketing research is merely the application of the scientific method to problems in the field of marketing and advertising. In following such a systematic search for the facts and the solutions to problems, the researcher finds it advisable to follow a particular methodology which is designed to obtain accurate results. This treatment of the general procedure of marketing research is not intended to be an exhaustive analysis of the techniques of marketing and advertising research, but will be a brief discussion of the major steps involved in virtually every research project, regardless of its particular nature. Later in this chapter some of the specific tests and methods of research applicable to special problems in advertising will be discussed briefly. The student interested in research as a field should realize this presentation is merely an introduction to the subject and should consult the references in a good bibliography for further details on various phases of the subject.

Planning the study

The first step in any marketing research study is to define the problems accurately. To do this, the researcher should make a thorough analysis of the situation in order to define exactly the objective or objectives of the study. It is essential there be a clear statement of the objectives in order that the researcher can determine exactly what specific data is required. If the objective is not clearly defined at the start, much unnecessary data may be collected, while essential data may be omitted, resulting in an unsatisfactory study.

In making this analysis and definition of the problem, the researcher will conduct a background study, in which he will obtain basic information about the environment. With this the researcher is in a position to determine the real problem that should be studied. Although it may be believed that the problem is always obvious, this is not the case. In a number of instances, the apparent problem is found to be erroneous, and another aspect of the situation is the important one, the one that should be investigated. When the researcher has ascertained the real problem involved in the proposed study, he should write it down in a concise statement. For, unless the researcher can do this, it is evident that he does not have a clear understanding of the problem himself. Without an exact understanding of the problem he is to study, the researcher obviously has no clear objective for the further steps of his research work.

The preliminary investigation

The next step is to make the preliminary investigation (sometimes called the exploratory investigation or the informal investigation). The purpose of this step is to ascertain the possible solutions to the problem and to eliminate all except those that are the probable correct ones. If this is not done, much time and effort may be expended on possible, but improbable, solutions rather than concentrating all effort on the few most promising solutions to the problem. Also, in the conduct of this step the researcher obtains a practical familiarity with the actual conditions existing in the various areas on which his study will touch, eliminating the chance that his approach will be too theoretical and out of keeping with actual conditions.

In this preliminary investigation, the study is limited to matters pertaining to the specific problem as defined in step one. There is no formal outline of the procedures to be followed in making the preliminary investigation. The researcher must be flexible, for he is in reality an explorer attempting to find possible solutions to the problem he has defined. The usual search involves interviews with consumers (or industrial or commercial users) of the product involved, as well as with wholesalers and retailers who sell and service the product, specialists or experts in the field, and executives and personnel of the company involved in the study. In addition to such primary sources, this step will usually involve some limited evaluation of the secondary material in the field.

The interviews made in this step are not the formal planned interviews used in a regular field survey. The researcher usually will do the field work himself, and will merely talk to the above people. He normally will write up the results of each interview at its conclusion, and when he feels he has sufficient information, he will consider the ideas and suggestions contained in the individual interviews. It is then necessary to exercise judgment as to which of the original hypotheses seem to be pertinent ones. The final result of this study should be a clarification of the hypotheses and a list of the possible solutions that have real potential of solving the problem.

Execution of the research program

In general, data useful in solving the problems of marketing research may be said to be available from two main sources—primary and secondary.

Sources of primary data

The principal sources of primary data can be classified in the following manner:

Consumers. The people or firms who buy and/or use the product or service under study are usually the best sources of information. It is necessary to determine the extent to which the buyer differs from the user, which of the two is most significant for the problem involved, and who influences the decision to buy.

Dealers. In many instances the wholesalers and retailers who handle the product are good sources of data regarding their own particular operations, reactions, and opinions. The salesmen also may be a good source of information about buyers.

Specialists. For certain types of research studies, various experts and specialists in the field may be a good source of data bearing on the solution of the problem. They are used more frequently in the preliminary and background phases of the study than in the final collection of data.

Sources of secondary data

There are many kinds of secondary data and sources from which it may be obtained. Here, only a few points will be made to indicate leading sources of data. A frequently used distinction of types of secondary sources is that of *internal data* and *external data.*

Internal data refers to information found within the records of the company itself. Sometimes the proper organization and manipulation of information contained in the accounting and sales records of the firm provides the answers to some of the research problems. Figures such as sales by type and size of product, prices, sales by consumers and classes of customers, sales by territories, and selling and advertising expenditures are indicative of the type of data that may well be analyzed in the study of a problem involving some facet of marketing. In some instances, important qualitative information may be obtained from customers' correspondence, salesmen's reports, and analysis of adjustments and complaints.

External data refers to materials that have been published in some form or that are compiled and sold by various types of organizations. It includes both writings of all types and statistics that have been compiled by government and public agencies, associations, and private firms of various types. The research man should know the general sources of marketing information and how to locate and evaluate the information acquired from such sources.

The main sources of secondary data are the following:

Libraries. One of the first places to look for published data is the library. Most public libraries contain a great deal of business information and many business publications, and contain the various indices and source books that make possible an organized search for available material on the subject under study. Most universities and many large business firms and institutions maintain libraries that contain good collections of materials on business in their special field of interest. The addresses and descriptions of the collections in special libraries may be found in *Special Library Sources,* available in any good public library.

Reference bureaus. There are also certain other institutions that function to provide business information. One of the most useful is the "Inquiry Reference Service" of the U.S. Department of Commerce in Washington, D.C., which will provide service on specific requests from business firms. The Department of Commerce also maintains field offices in the principal cities which keep stocks of the department's literature and publications and also offer reference assistance on request.

Federal government. The largest collector and publisher of information in the world is the United States government. It is a source of much valuable information for the researcher, since its data are comprehensive and impartial and are available in many instances free of charge, or otherwise for a nominal cost. The researcher should familiarize himself with the types of data available from the federal government and the different publications and sources of government publications. Lists of such publications may be obtained from the Superintendent of Documents in the Government Printing Office in Washington, D.C., or from the special government agency involved.

The following government departments are among the major sources of data valuable to the field of marketing research:

Department of Agriculture:	Bureau of Agricultural Economics
	Production and Marketing Administration
	Office of Administration, Research and Marketing Act
Department of Commerce:	Bureau of the Census
	Bureau of Foreign and Domestic Commerce
	Bureau of Standards
Department of Labor:	Bureau of Labor Statistics

Federal Communications Commission
Federal Reserve System
Federal Power Commission
Federal Trade Commission
Securities and Exchange Commission

State governments. Various agencies of state governments are engaged in gathering data on subjects of interest to the researcher, usually covering only the state involved. Data are particularly good in the fields of agriculture, retailing, and labor. Information on the data published by the states can be obtained through the *Monthly Check List of State Publications,* published by the U.S. Government Printing Office.

Publishers. Some of the large publishers of general magazines and newspapers have been active in conducting marketing research studies and collecting data. This is usually done to serve their advertisers, but much of the information is valuable for the researcher and can usually be obtained on request. Publishers of the many magazines in the industrial and trade publication field are specialists in their fields of interest, and valuable information in the technical and business fields often may be obtained from such trade publications. A well-known and widely accepted source of secondary data for use in estimating territorial market potentials is *Sales Management* magazine's "Annual Survey of Buying Power." This index is designed to reflect the relative buying power of the counties and cities of the United States, and is based on the area percentage of national disposable personal income (weighted 5 times), national retail sales (weighted by 3), and national population (weighted by 2).

Trade associations. Virtually every important field of business has its own trade association, and most of them collect statistics in their field. The pertinent trade association should always be contacted for data and can be located through the comprehensive directory published by the Department of Commerce, entitled *National Associations of the United States.* Somewhat similar in nature are the chambers of commerce of states and cities which often have local current data on activities in their areas.

Private sources. There are a number of specialized marketing research and statistical collection agencies that make a business of compiling information, and charge a fee for providing the data. The charges may seem high, but often it is less costly to buy the information desired from such firms, if they have it available, than to collect it firsthand, and it usually is much less time consuming. Some of these are:

Source	*Data*
A. C. Nielsen Company, Chicago	Current sales in retail stores for various drug and grocery products by brands, etc.; index of television and radio listening.
Daniel Starch and Staff, N.Y.	Magazine and newspaper readership surveys.
F. W. Dodge Corporation.	Statistics on actual and contemplated construction.
Dun and Bradstreet, Inc.	Credit ratings and information about companies.
Gallup Robinson, Princeton.	Magazine and television impact ratings.
Market Research Corporation of America, New York	Continuous consumer panel data, showing purchases by brands of selected commodities.
R. L. Polk Company.	Auto registrations and mailing lists.
Audit Bureau of Circulations	Paid circulation data on newspapers and magazines.
Standard Rate and Data Services.	Advertising rates and publication data for all publications and stations of the major advertising media. The SRDS Consumer Market Data provide estimates on population, number of households, consumer spendable income, and retail sales for counties and standard metropolitan statistical areas.
Publisher's Information Bureau.	Monthly expenditures by advertisers in various magazines and in radio and television.
Media records.	Newspaper advertising linage by advertisers.

Great care should be taken in selecting and using data from secondary sources, since the researcher is depending on other people's having done accurate and unbiased work in the collecting, compiling, and reporting of the data involved. The data must be very carefully evaluated before being accepted and used as the basis for solving the problem under study. Usually it is better to use the figures compiled in a study than to use the findings and conclusions which may have been drawn from them. A few of the things to keep in mind in evaluating secondary data are: the character and integrity of the organization collecting the data or making the study, the objectives of the study, the research methodology employed, the definition of terms used, and the time covered in the study.

Methods of collecting primary data

After the researcher has determined what data is available from secondary sources and, thus, what further data must still be obtained from primary sources, he must decide what methodology to employ. Basically, there are three methods of obtaining primary data. These are the observational method, the experimental method, and the survey method. These techniques vary in their approach and, in cases, in the accuracy of the data obtained. Since in some instances any one of the three could be utilized, it is necessary for the research man to decide which one is best in the particular conditions of a specific study.

Observational method. The observational method is having an observer (a person or a machine) watch what is taking place and record it. If the observer perceives accurately what is taking place and records it accurately, this method will obtain factual data. Obviously, only overt behavior can be studied in this manner. But, in those instances where it can be used, it has the advantage of greater objectivity than surveys, and so there are many valuable applications of this technique in marketing research.

An example might serve to clarify what is meant by the observational method. If a hat manufacturer desired to know just what the average retail clerk said and did while waiting on a prospective customer for a hat, he would post an observer in the store and have him record what the retail clerk did and said while waiting on the hat customer.

The observational method is more objective and accurate than the survey method. It eliminates the human element of the respondent which is uncontrolled in the survey method, and although usually the observer is human, he is one that is trained and controlled to a high degree by the researcher. However, he can observe only what people actually do, and this is sometimes not sufficient for the researcher. Also, this method is usually much more costly than the survey method. Further, it is not applicable at present in many instances. But when it is applicable, the researcher should give the method serious consideration because of its objectivity.

In some cases the observing is done by a machine. For example, the sales talk may be recorded by tape or wire recorder; traffic may be counted by one of several electric devices; and the users of radio and television sets may be recorded by the "audimeter" of the A. C. Nielsen Company.

Experimental method. The experimental method is, in essence, the procedure of carrying out, on a small scale, a test solution to a problem; so this method is used primarily to determine whether the tentative conclusions reached will prove to be right in actual conditions. It is essential that the conditions in which the test is conducted be essentially the same as the conditions that will be found in the total operation to which the conclusions are to be applied. In the conditions normally holding for marketing research, it is obvious that the environment of people, and market conditions, are ever changing and cannot be controlled by the researcher. However, by conducting the experiment simultaneously in different conditions and by repeating the test in rotated conditions of the different sets of variables, it may be possible to isolate the effect of different factors. Also, the experiment is used to try out different selling, advertising, and promotion programs in small areas, where the conditions of the test are selected to be as near those of the entire market as possible.

An example of the experiment would be the following procedure. If a package for a soap product has been selected, and it is decided that either blue or pink is the desirable color, an experiment might be used to select which of the two colors is best. Putting up equal displays of the two colors of packages in a carefully selected sample of stores, a record would be kept of the actual sales of the two colors of packages. At the end of the selected period, the color which had sold most in actual conditions would be presumed to be the better color from a sales standpoint.

Survey method. In marketing research terminology, the survey method refers to all methods of obtaining information through asking questions of others. Because a series of questions, when combined, is called a questionnaire, this method is sometimes referred to as the questionnaire method. The essential element in this method is that the information is furnished by an individual or respondent in a conscious effort to answer the questions. An example of the survey method could be given by referring again to the problem of selecting the preferred color of package, blue or pink. In the survey method, investigators or interviewers would show a blue and a pink package to a sample of people and ask each, "Which color of package do you prefer?" The survey method is probably the most widely used of all research techniques, since much more information can be secured by this method than by the others. Attitudes, motives, past actions and experiences, and much factual information that cannot be observed can be obtained only by the survey method. Two significant factors affecting the survey method should be mentioned here. First, the questions must be worded in such a manner as to obtain the desired information in an accurate and unbiased form. Also, the person giving the information, usually called the respondent, must be able and willing to give the desired information in response to the questions asked, accurately and without bias.

There are three principal methods of conducting the survey insofar as reaching the respondents are concerned, and when electing to use this means for gathering primary data, the researcher must plan on which of these three methods to employ. The three methods are by mail, by personal interview, and by telephone. The two most widely used are by mail and by personal interview. Each of these has its advantages and disadvantages, and they should be understood so that the preferred method can be used for the particular study involved.

1. The mail survey. The mail survey has several important advantages. It eliminates the personal element and possible bias introduced by the field investigator or interviewer. The entire country can be covered even though respondents are spread all over the country and in remote areas, all at the same cost per respondent. It may be possible to reach people by mail who would be very difficult to find at home or in the office for personal interviewing. Since the questions appear in print, they are the same in every questionnaire. The respondent may take more time in preparing answers to questions, will be able to confer with others if he so desires, and may hence take more care in his responses. The respondent is anonymous and may feel freer to give frank and confidential information.

This method has some serious disadvantages. There is always grave danger of having the returns represent an invalid and biased sample. It may be difficult to obtain a truly representative mailing list. The persons who return the questionnaire often represent a highly selective group of those receiving it, which results in a distorted sample. Often only a small percentage of the questionnaires mailed out are returned completed, so that the assumed low cost becomes an actual high cost per usable return. It is difficult to plan the timing for a mail survey. Since respondents may take some time in returning the completed questionnaire, often it takes more time to complete a mail survey than one using the personal interview method. It is impossible to observe anything about the respondent and his surroundings. Also, for obtaining information that requires extensive discussion and some probing, personal interviews have great advantages. And, if a specific order of questions is essential for obtaining the desired information, this cannot be achieved by a mail survey.

2. The personal interview. In general, the advantages and disadvantages of the personal interview method of making a survey are the opposite of those just enumerated for the mail survey. The sample can be much better controlled in the personal interview method. The interviewer can obtain the required number of interviews within the time limits set, so that work can be completed quickly if that is necessary. The interviewer can observe the person and his surroundings, and so obtain much significant information not included in the actual questionnaire. The interviewer can explain questions if doubt arises in the respondent's mind, can probe for further information, and can stimulate the respondent into supplying further information. The interviewer asks the questions in the desired order and records the replies in a standardized and clear manner, simplifying greatly the editing and tabulating of the data.

This method does have limitations that must be considered when determining which survey method should be used. The personal bias of the interviewer cannot be avoided. And the mere presence of a person may cause some respondents to alter their answers to avoid embarrassment or to try to please the interviewer. If it is desired to include remote areas in the study, the costs of using interviewers may be prohibitive. It is very difficult to find some people at home or at the place of the interview, and this either results in higher costs for return calls or distortion of the sample for the final study. People may refuse to answer questions of a highly personal nature when asked in person. The interviewee may be in a hurry, or in a state of excitement, and this may prevent him from giving accurate replies to the questions.

3. *The telephone survey.* Use of this means of obtaining information by the survey method has increased greatly in recent years. The chief advantage of this method is that it is possible to obtain a large number of interviews quickly and at a relatively low cost. It may be possible to reach people who would not care to be interviewed personally, and also at times when interviewing might not be feasible.

One of the most significant disadvantages of this method is that it is limited to telephone subscribers, which is a selective group, with different characteristics than that portion of the population without telephones. Generally speaking, only a relatively small amount of information may be obtained from answers to questions of a simple and nonconfidential nature. It is virtually impossible to obtain vital classification data about the respondents. It is difficult to get the cooperation of the respondent, since setting up a desirable rapport between the unseen respondent and the interviewer is most difficult. Recently, with so many firms using the telephone for direct selling, it is becoming more difficult to obtain the cooperation of selected respondents. Usually, due to the cost and time involved in attempting to place toll calls to outlying areas, the method is confined to urban areas and ignores outlying areas. For most survey purposes, the disadvantages of the telephone method far outweigh its advantages, so its use is confined to special types of studies and information.

Executing the collection of primary data

After the method of collecting the primary data has been selected, the actual execution of the plan may begin. Several aspects of such execution will be discussed briefly.

Sampling. Since in most studies it would be virtually impossible from a standpoint of time, cost, and practicality to interview (or observe) every individual person, firm, or household possessing data involved in the study, in most instances only a sample of the total number of people or firms, known as the universe or population involved, is contacted. Sampling is the science of selecting a relatively small group from a larger group in such a manner that the small group accurately represents the larger group from which it is drawn. A good sample must fulfill two basic requirements: It must be representative of the population from which it is drawn; and it must be reliable, or adequate.

The sample is representative when its characteristics provide an accurate cross section of the characteristics of the entire population from which it was selected. Within limits, the larger the number of cases included in the sample, the greater the accuracy of the results.

The reliability of a sample can be controlled by taking a sufficiently large sample and by using proper sampling techniques. In marketing research, usually the researcher has made some decision about the degree of accuracy that he requires in his study. On the basis of sampling theory, it is known that there is a sample size which will yield accurate results about the entire population within stated limits of error. To use a sample larger than one that will yield the required degree of accuracy is wasteful for the researcher, since it reduces the chances of error more than is necessary for his particular study, and the costs of increasing the size of the sample increase much faster than does the increase in accuracy of the results obtained.

Preparing questionnaires and forms. The design of proper forms and questionnaires to be used in the field work is of great importance. Properly designed forms insure that the proper data will be collected, and that it will be recorded in an accurate and readily usable form. Generally the forms for observation studies are not unduly complicated or difficult to design. Their functions usually are to provide or indicate exactly what is to be observed, to provide a standardized and simple manner of recording the observations, and possibly to facilitate the tabulation of the results obtained. Normally the form should make provision for identifying the observer and the place and time the observations took place. Such a form should be well pretested before the final collection of data begins on any large scale.

Questionnaires. The questionnaire (the term for the form used in the survey) involves considerably more problems than the usual form for observation studies. For, in addition to having the functions of the form noted above, it includes the problem of asking the right questions in the correct form and in the sequence that will result in maximizing the amount of accurate information obtained. And the proper arrangement of questions and their correct wording is one of the most difficult arts of marketing research.

Basically, the questionnaire will consist of three parts: the identification information, including usually the name and address of the respondent and the name or initials of the interviewer; the classification data, including descriptive information about the respondent (such as age, sex, income); and the actual questions designed to obtain the information bearing on the problem under study. The questions should be relevant, clear, specific, and arranged in proper sequence. Care should be taken to word questions in such a manner that they do not induce bias. Proper design of the questionnaire is a difficult art, and experience is more important than following any set of rules that might be listed. It is important to pretest the questionnaire prior to its use, to eliminate as many weaknesses as possible.

Interviewing. With the sample selected and the questionnaire designed, the next step is the actual interviewing. In outline form, the important steps here include the following:

1. Providing an adequate number of well-qualified and well-trained supervisors.
2. Selecting and training a good staff of field investigators or interviewers.
3. Providing complete written instructions for the guidance of the interviewers.
4. Adequate supervision of the work of the interviewers.
5. Checking of the work of the field staff.

Tabulation and analysis. When the completed questionnaires are received, the first step is to edit them carefully. This involves checking carefully the reports of each interviewer to appraise the accuracy of his work, checking for inconsistent answers within the questionnaire, rejecting obviously inaccurate replies, standardizing answers involving units of measurement, filling in incomplete answers where possible, and sorting general answers into the desired classifications. Then the answers from the questionnaires are tabulated; that is, all the answers in the same classification are consolidated into totals and summarized in orderly tables. The data is then in shape for analysis. This involves studying the data and arranging it in such ways as to make its nature and relationships clear. It is often helpful also to summarize the data by applying appropriate statistical measures, such as computing measures of central tendency and dispersion.

Interpretation. At this point, the researcher must study the data obtained above, including the various statistical measures that have been computed, and draw from them their meaning with regard to the specific problem under study, and decide what conclusions can be drawn from the data. Usually this would involve deciding which of the original hypotheses set up as possible solutions for the problem was the correct one. This step calls for clear logical thinking, the use of judgment, and a constructive imagination.

Presentations of the findings. The final step is to present the findings of the study to the responsible executives involved. This may be done orally or in writing. There are a number of somewhat different types of reports, depending on the person or persons for whom the report is intended. Regardless of the type of report, those intended for the sponsors of the research must be well presented, otherwise the results may be ignored regardless of their accuracy and value. In a very real sense, research results must be "sold" if action based on the findings is to be taken.

Some special forms of research

The above discussion has in a brief manner discussed the general field of marketing research and its methodology. The attention of the reader now should be drawn to certain special fields or types of research, which are of special interest to advertising.

Motivation research

The general marketing research survey study is designed to determine many facts about the characteristics of the present or potential customer, such as how many and what kind of people buy a certain brand or product, where they buy, and where they live. However, it has long been realized that this type of survey did not obtain accurate answers to such questions as: "Why do people buy my product?" and "Why do they act as they do?" A new type of research, known as motivation research, has been developed in recent years which attempts to discover and explain why the consumer behaves as he or she does, and what appeals and sales programs will best influence his or her decision to act and buy.

Motivation research has been defined as "the use of psychiatric and psychological techniques to obtain a better understanding of why people respond as they do to products, advertisements, and various other marketing situations."[1]

The two main groups of social scientists contributing most to the development of motivation research are the psychologists and psychiatrists, who basically study the personality of the individual as such, and the sociologists and anthropologists, who study the social framework or environment in which the individual lives. Its principal use to date has been to aid the advertising man in selecting the best appeals and the best words, symbols, and concepts with which to influence the consumer. However, since motivation research ascertains the basic needs and desires (conscious or unconscious on the consumers' part) which are most important in influencing buying decisions, it can aid in many business decisions. Hence, this type of research should prove to be of great value not only in determining the proper promotional and sales programs and the proper advertising appeals, copy, and advertising presentation, but also should prove of great value in product planning and design, in packaging, and in the selection of brand names and trademarks.

Motivation research basically is the application to the specific problems of business of the theories and generalized observations developed by social scientists about how individual consumers and groups in the society behave, and why they behave as they do. On the basis of this knowledge of why people act as they do, and about their feelings, wants, and motives, the motivation researcher narrows the marketing or advertising problem to a manageable set of hypotheses. After this has been done, the researcher determines what field study may be necessary to determine the correct hypothesis or answer to the particular problem. It is then necessary to decide which of the several techniques of motivation research will provide the information needed to solve the particular problem. This aspect of motivation research is stressed here because so often discussions of the field place so much stress on the unusual techniques of this method, such as depth interviews or projection tests, that readers come to believe these techniques constitute motivation research.

The projective test. The use of this technique involves stimulating the interviewee to project himself or herself into an artificial or ambiguous situation. For example, if the researcher wanted to learn about women's attitudes toward shopping in a supermarket, the procedure adopted might be to show the woman in the testing sample a picture of a woman shopping in a supermarket and then ask her to tell a story about the shopper in the picture. Without realizing it, the interviewee normally will weave into the story she tells her own feelings, attitudes, and values. There are several types of projection tech-

---

[1] Charles J. Dirksen, Arthur Kroeger, and Lawrence C. Lockley, *Readings in Marketing* (Homewood, Ill.: Richard D. Irwin, Inc., 1963) p. 439.

niques, including the picture (projective) response, free-word association, and sentence completion.

Depth interviewing. In contrast to the regular interview, no formal questionnaire normally is used in the depth interview. Instead, the interviewer, who must be a highly trained person, merely asks questions to encourage the interviewee to talk as freely as possible about the subject in question. Rather than trying to solicit factual information, the interviewer merely is asking questions to draw out the emotions, the feelings, the opinions of the interviewee, and develops the pattern of questions as the interview proceeds in such a way as to bring out the interviewee to the maximum extent possible. The interview will normally last from one to two hours. The information gathered in such interviews must be analyzed and interpreted by a highly trained social scientist. Usually only a rather limited number of interviews is sufficient for the motivation researcher, since the studies are more qualitative in nature than quantitative, as is true of the ordinary surveys.

Motivation research has now become an important form of consumer research done by most agencies, advertisers, and marketing research firms. It is especially valuable for discovering and identifying the "subconscious" or hidden attitudes, feelings, and motives of the consumer. Hence, because it can be used to bring out the inner determinants of proper behavior, it is most useful and valuable for determining alternative appeals which can be used as the theme for an advertisement or a campaign.

Use of mathematics in the decision-making process

It is apparent from the above discussion that the ultimate object of all marketing and advertising research is to aid the executive in making sounder decisions. In recent years rapid developments have taken place in the application of various tools of mathematics to the decision-making process, including the fields of marketing and advertising. And, although a certain amount of quantitative analysis has always been involved in marketing and advertising research, it usually involved only basic statistical applications. Currently, far more sophisticated methods of quantitative analysis are being developed and applied in advertising to aid in making better decisions.

A good discussion of the techniques involved, some applications, and the implications involved in a more quantitative approach to decision making are included in the article by Philip Kotler which appears in the October 1963 issue of the *Journal of Marketing.* If the student will read this article carefully, while keeping in mind that the general concepts as applied to marketing can be applied equally well to advertising research and advertising decision making, he will gain a good idea of the possible use of quantitative methods and mathematical models in advertising. If more information is desired, recently published books on quantitative methods and marketing research should be consulted.

Testing advertising effectiveness

Due to the large sums of money invested in advertising, and the highly competitive nature of today's market, media owners and advertising agencies are all vitally interested in determining the effectiveness of advertising.

Because of the complexities of testing advertising effectiveness, many advertisements are not tested. That is, some people engaged in advertising doubt the validity of tests designed to measure advertising effectiveness. Or they feel the qualities of advertising that can be tested do not truly measure the value of the advertisement to achieve its ultimate goal, the sale of the product or service, and so it is not worthwhile to test. Some feel that the creation of good advertisements is an art, not a science, and the use of tests and research tends to stifle the creativity of advertising people. Others feel the costs of good testing outweigh its value. On occasion, due to the pressures of time, testing and research may be omitted because good research does require adequate time and cannot be rushed. Some advertising people are confident they have the ability and experience to create effective advertising without measurement or testing.

However, the use of testing and measuring of advertising effectiveness has increased in recent years due to several factors. One is the increased interest of top executives of advertisers in getting the best possible results with the larger advertising appropriations required today, so that they support expenditures for testing. The development of scientific methods of testing has also helped in getting more agencies and advertisers to budget sufficient funds for the proper testing of a good share of their advertising.

Most advertising people will agree that it is wise to make judicious use of testing. They would agree that all methods of testing do have certain limitations. However, they believe that careful and adequate use of testing can be a real aid to producing better advertisements and advertising. Also, it should be stressed that generally speaking it is not always possible to measure the effect of an advertisement or advertising on sales and profits of a company (because of the difficulty of isolating the effects of advertising from the effects of all the other elements of the marketing mix). Hence it is usually necessary to establish other criteria of effectiveness for advertising, and test these. Other objectives may be established for advertising and tests are devised to measure the effectiveness of advertising in achieving these more specific and narrower objectives. Among these objectives are the extent to which print advertising is noticed, seen, or read, the extent to which the message is understood, the extent to which it is believed, and so on.

Some tests are designed to determine the effectiveness of advertisements prior to running them, and are known as "pretests." Other tests are designed to evaluate advertisements or campaigns while they are being run or at completion of the campaign. The major forms of both these types of tests will be discussed briefly in the following paragraphs.

Consumer jury test

This is a type of pretest designed to determine the effectiveness of an advertisement before it is run, and is known as a form of copy testing, a general term used to describe tests designed to evaluate advertisements before they are run, or measure expected results from an advertisement. The consumer jury test obtains the preference of a sample of typical prospective consumers of the product for one advertisement or some one part of an advertisement out of several being considered by the advertiser. The prospective consumer, or juror, rates the advertisements, the headlines, or the theme, by direct comparison. Since the advertisement is designed to influence the prospective consumer of the product being advertised, it is believed that he or she is in a better position to determine what advertisement or message will influence him or her than is a member of the general public or the advertising expert.

In the case of advertisements designed to be run in print media, the test usually is conducted in the following manner. A small group, or sample, of people, considered to be typical prospective buyers or users of the product to be advertised, is selected to serve as the "jury." This jury should be representative of the consumers or prospective consumers for the product. A group of advertisements is prepared which are based on different themes, or in which the headline or some other part of the advertisement is varied. These advertisements are then shown to the individual jurors, and they are asked to express their preference for the different advertisements by answering such questions as the following:

1. Which of these advertisements would you notice first?
2. Which of these advertisements is most interesting to you?
3. Which of these advertisements is most convincing to you?
4. Which of these advertisements would be most likely to cause you to buy this brand?

The juror may be shown all the advertisements being tested in turn, and asked to rank them in order of relative value or merit. This method is known as the "order-of-merit" rating technique. The weakness of this technique is that it is quite difficult for any person to rank more than five or six advertisements consistently in the same order, although with less than this number jurors can rank rather accurately. The other technique for juror ranking is the "paired-comparison" method, in which the juror will be asked to rate or compare only two advertisements at a time. Every possible combination of advertisements is paired, so that an opinion is obtained from each juror regarding each pair of advertisements. Although this method produces more accurate and consistent rankings of advertisements, it poses a serious problem if there is a large number of advertisements to be tested, since the number of combinations then becomes very large.

It is desirable to control closely the circumstances or conditions in which the juror rates the advertisements, as in such matters as the length of time they are permitted to see the advertisements. If the juror is permitted too long a time to make his decision, it is believed he or she is apt to assume the role of a critic and try to determine what he or she thinks other people would think or like rather than to give their own first reaction.

There are several variations in the handling of juries and in the techniques used in this test. In most cases, the advertisements are shown to jurors as individuals. However, in some instances, researchers attempt to obtain suggestions and ideas regarding a group of advertisements by presenting the advertisements to be tested to groups of jurors, usually ranging from six to ten people. The group is permitted to discuss the advertisements and express their opinions and ideas regarding them, with the interaction and stimulation of discussion among the jurors supposedly providing better results than those obtained from the members acting purely as individuals.

Since the usual method of rating advertisements by jurors, the comparative ranking of the advertisements, gives no indication that any of the advertisements is really good or effective, or any indication of the relative superiority of the preferred advertisement, some researchers use attitude scales. This technique obtains the absolute score or opinion of the juror regarding the advertisement's effectiveness.

Although usually the consumer jury test is conducted by personal interview, it is sometimes conducted by mail. Some firms conducting this test include with the advertisements being tested one or two old advertisements which actually have been run before, and for which they have some measure of effectiveness, to serve as control advertisements and thus measure the relative quality of the advertisements selected by the jurors.

The consumer jury method also is used to pretest radio and television commercials. They can be shown to individuals or to groups (studio audiences) very much in the same manner as print advertisements. Frequently commercials are pretested simultaneously with the testing of programs, using the studio audience approach. The concept here is the same as with print media advertisements, the difference being in the methods required to run the actual testing procedure.

Problems in conducting consumer jury test. Among the problems connected with the use of the consumer jury method of testing advertisements are the following:

1. Selection of a valid sample of "prospective consumers" for the product being advertised.
2. Preparation of the advertisements so that only one element or concept is tested at one time.
3. Proper wording of the questions to be asked the jurors.
4. Handling the showing of advertisements, the time they are shown, and the instructions to the members of the jury to maximize the probability of obtaining the personal reaction of the juror, rather than his or her idea of what the reaction should be.

Evaluation of consumer jury test. This method of testing can be done in a short time, usually requiring less than two weeks to complete. It can be done at relatively low cost, since it does not involve actually running the advertisements in some medium. The advertisements often can be prepared in rather rough form and still obtain desired results. It does not require a particularly large sample, the usual size ranging from 50 to 200 people. The test is fairly easy to conduct. It can be used to test a number of different features or aspects of advertisements. There are no "outside influences" to distort results, such as position of the advertisement in the medium. It is generally conceded to be of real value in separating the very strong from the very weak advertisements. It is believed valid for determining such things as whether the advertisement is interesting to the juror, whether the juror believes the claims made for the product, and whether the advertisement's copy stimulates the juror's desire for the product.

There are several criticisms leveled at this method of testing. The chief one is that the entire test is somewhat unrealistic in nature. The juror cannot be a "normal" prospect, but tends to place himself or herself in the position of a critic or expert. The advertisement is not being viewed as it would be under normal real-life conditions. If the juror is asked, "Which advertisement would attract your attention first in a magazine," or "Which advertisement would most likely cause you to buy the product?" the answer is purely hypothetical. Some critics of the consumer jury test believe jurors try to please the person conducting the test, vote for the advertisements they feel they should like rather than ones they actually like personally, prefer advertisements that resemble others they have seen before, and seldom vote a preference for advertisements based on a negative appeal or containing very "hard-sell" copy. Also, this method of testing gives no indication that the advertisement selected by the jury as best is really good or effective (unless control advertisements are included among those tested), and no indication of the relative superiority of the preferred advertisement over others (unless some scaling technique is used in the testing program).

The inquiry test

The inquiry test is another method of copy testing which may be used to check the relative effectiveness of several advertisements by running them on a limited basis, or to test the reaction to one of a series of advertisements on a comparative basis. The method used is to include in the advertisement an offer to send something to the reader if he will write for it—hence, the name inquiry test. The offer stimulating the inquiry may be made by including in the advertisement an actual coupon which can be cut out and mailed in, by giving the offer a prominent position in the headline or copy of the advertisement, or by a "hidden offer," that is, an offer included in the body of the copy with no unusual stress on it so the offer will not be noticed by a casual reader but only by a careful reader of the larger part of the copy. Frequently, in order to discourage so-called professional coupon clippers, children, and those only casually interested in the product, the offer may require sending in a nominal sum of money with the inquiry. By coding the coupons and advertisements in appropriate ways, the advertiser can determine which of the different advertisements obtained the responses.

If the test is being used to determine the relative effectiveness of one or more variations of a single element of an advertisement, such as the headline or illustration, the other elements must be the same in each of the advertisements.

Split-run tests. Since one of the main problems in conducting the inquiry test is that returns may be influenced by such factors as the position of the advertisement in the publication, the amount of competing advertising, the editorial content of the publication, the time of appearance of the publication, and other variables, some newspapers and magazines will divide their pressrun to enable the advertiser to use a different advertisement in each of the splits or portions of the printing. If the portions of the printing containing the different advertisements being tested are then distributed alternately among subscribers receiving the publication, all the above variable factors are eliminated, since the two advertisements being tested appear in the same position, with all other conditions being the same for each.

A relatively fast and inexpensive manner of conducting the inquiry test is by direct mail. Obviously, this method is best when used to test advertisements to be used in direct-mail advertising. However, it is sometimes employed when the advertisements are to be run in magazines and newspapers, even though obviously the conditions in which the advertisements are exposed to the reader are different than if they were run in the publication. In this direct-mail method of inquiry testing, the advertisements are prepared as though for publication, then mailed to comparable groups of people, preferably a sample of the readers of the publications in which the advertisement is to appear. Again, the advertisement eliciting the greatest number of responses is considered the best.

The inquiry test also, of course, can be used with radio and television. The above discussion of the inquiry test in published media would apply to these media, except that no actual coupon can be used. It is possible to use the split-run technique on cable television.

Evaluation of the inquiry test. The inquiry test is rather easy to execute, and the conditions in which the reader responds to the advertisement are comparable to those in which the reader normally will be exposed to the advertisement. However, it does involve the actual running of the advertisements in the media and, hence, may be somewhat costly and require a considerable amount of time. Unless the split-run method can be used, it is very difficult to control, or allow for, the variables that may influence the returns from the different advertisements being tested.

The chief criticism of this test is with regard to its basic validity. It is generally conceded the test is quite valid when testing advertisements that are intended to bring specific and immediate results, such as mail-order advertisements actually selling by means of the advertisement. However, when the purpose of the advertisement is indirect in nature, to achieve sales results over a period of time, or to stimulate primary demand for the product, or to build the prestige of the brand, there is considerable difference of opinion as to whether or not inquiries actually measure the effectiveness of the advertisement to achieve its purpose, or merely measure the ability of the advertisement to obtain inquiries.

The sales-area or sales-results test

The sales-area test can be used as another pretesting form which involves the experimental method of research. The basic concept involved in this test is to run an advertisement or campaign (or several different ones) on a small scale to determine effectiveness before running the campaign over the entire marketing area with its attendant large costs. The test can be used to evaluate different themes or various different copy techniques.

The procedure is to run the advertisements with different appeals (or copy or headlines) or the different campaigns in separate comparable markets, usually cities, for the determined desirable period of time. By comparing the actual sales to consumers taking place in the different markets through the retail stores, the more effective appeal (or copy or headline) or campaign is selected. The test is only valid for advertising designed to obtain immediate sales responses and for items that are bought frequently, where the influence of advertising can exert itself quite quickly.

In the actual conduct of the test, the advertiser, who, it is assumed, is interested in testing the effectiveness of a completely new appeal as compared with the one now being used, would first select the test areas. Normally, these would be two groups of cities, as comparable as possible in all respects influencing sales of the product (and also representative of the whole market in which the advertising is to be run later). One of these groups of cities would constitute his "control" group of cities, and one his "test" group of cities. The control group will provide the data which will serve to measure the influence of the factors other than the advertising on sales, while the new appeal advertising will be run in the test group to provide the data which will serve to measure the influence of this new type advertising. Normally there should be at least three cities in each group, so that if some unusual event occurs in one city, the results of the test will not be spoiled. The usual advertising (and other selling efforts) would be continued in the control cities, while the advertising with the new appeal would be run in the test group of cities (where, again, all other selling efforts would be continued in the same manner as formerly). If two different appeals are being tested, usually three groups of cities would be used, one for control, two for testing. In this case, the advertising in the two test groups of cities would be run in the same media, the same size of advertisement, the same frequency of insertion, and so forth; that is, all conditions other than the appeal in the advertisements would be kept comparable. Sales in the control group of cities will indicate what sales are during the period in the usual conditions which exist during the period, while the sales in the test group (or groups) of cities will reflect the difference in sales resulting from the new or different advertising appeals.

Usually the test period is divided into three periods, with the first period being a pretest period. During this time, sales are checked in the several groups of cities to determine sales in normal conditions and to note any trends in sales. The test advertising campaigns are run during the second or actual test period. The third period is a posttest period, and sales are checked during this period to ascertain the carry-over effect of the advertising. The minimum length of time for each of the three test periods is one month; usually two months for each is preferable, and in some cases researchers advocate three to six months each, or nine to eighteen months for the whole test. Various factors influence the preferred length of time, although the rate of frequency of purchase and repurchase of the item being advertised is probably the most important factor. The more frequent the normal purchase of the item, the shorter the test periods that can be used safely. Sales are measured for each of the three periods by checking the retailers' stocks and purchases at the beginning and end of each period. Every effort should be made to maintain "normal" conditions in all retail outlets in the various cities, since variations in display, promotion, and selling price can influence sales markedly. When interpreting the results of the test, it is important to check carefully for any outside factors that may have unduly influenced sales in any of the cities included in the study. If the factors appear to have been comparable in the various sets of cities, they can be ignored. If, however, some outside factor or factors appear to have unduly influenced sales in one or more cities, either a correction must be made for the effect of the outside factor, or if this does not appear feasible or if only one city is involved, the results from the unusual city should be discarded in making comparisons of sales.

Virtually all advertising people agree that the sales-area test provides authentic results when properly conducted, since it does measure actual sales under actual market conditions. However, it is a difficult test to conduct properly. The selection of cities to be included in the test, maintaining comparable conditions in the various groups or cities, and applying the proper corrective allowances when conditions do vary, all pose very serious problems. It should also be noted that this test takes a long period of time (in addition to three to six months of actual testing time, considerable time also would be consumed by the other phases of the entire test, such as planning the project, selection of the cities, and tabulation of data and interpretation of results). It is also very costly. It can be used only for certain types of products, and can use only local media. Another serious problem is that competitors are alerted to the activities of the advertiser. They may then vary their promotional activities in order to create unusual or changed conditions in the test markets, hoping to cloud and confuse the test results. In some instances, they have been known to buy large quantities of the test item, both for analysis and to create confusing sales totals. This is especially significant if the test is being run in small markets, where such purchases can seriously distort the sales figures. A still more serious danger is that a competitor will copy the test product, or even improve on it, and still bring it to market ahead of the original testing company. Some of the largest companies have been known to send research teams into another firm's test markets, and conduct surveys to measure the results of the test, using such test results in aiding their decisions. Hence other methods usually are used if they will give results sufficiently accurate for the advertiser. Often other tests are used to screen appeals for campaigns or the concept to be tested, then the sales-area test is used as the final check on the advertising selected by means of the other tests.

The systematic rating list, or checklist

Another method of evaluating advertisements before they are run is the rating scale or checklist. Although this is not actually a method of testing advertisements, it is an evaluation method and should be mentioned here. The concept involved is to develop a list of qualities which the advertisement should contain, or a list of questions to be asked about each advertisement being evaluated, and then to check the advertisement against the list to ascertain whether or not it contains the features enumerated, or to rate the advertisement on each of the features listed. Usually, the lists include such factors as attention and interest value, although there are checklists designed to ascertain such features as the readability or understandability of the advertisements. The checklist method was given its greatest initial impetus by the Townsend Brothers, who developed a checklist of some 27 items, with a value assigned to each item, which was designed to enable one to determine the effectiveness of any advertisement in only a few minutes.

This method of testing has one real value. It does allow the one using it to be certain no important element has been omitted from the advertisement through oversight. In addition, this method is simple to carry out, takes very little time, and the cost is minimal. However, there are real problems involved in evaluating advertisements with this technique. What items or values should be included in the list? What relative weights should be assigned to each item or quality? In practice, different people usually score the same advertisement quite differently. A major criticism is that no one checklist can be appropriate for all types of advertisements, for different products, with different objectives.

Post-testing methods

There are several other tests quite widely used, normally to test advertising while it is being run, or campaigns after they have been completed. Among these are the recognition or readership test, the recall test in various forms, and attitude and opinion tests. In these tests, the objective is not to determine the selling effectiveness of the advertising directly but to measure whether the respondents have read the advertisement, what impression the advertising has made on them, or the attitude resulting from the advertising.

The recognition or readership test.   This is a test conducted after the advertisement has been run to determine the number of readers of the publication who have seen and read the specific advertisements being tested. By analyzing various advertisements so tested over a period of time, the advertiser can determine to some degree what features of the advertisements result in increasing the number of readers who see and read the advertisements. Such information can then be utilized to improve future advertisements by incorporating the features that will obtain this higher seeing and reading.

The techniques used in this test can be illustrated by discussing how it would be applied in the testing of an advertisement appearing in a given magazine. Interviewers would call on a representative sample of the readers of the particular magazine at an appropriate period of time after the publication date and ask if the interviewee has read that particular issue of the magazine. If so, the interviewee is asked to go through the magazine page by page with the interviewer and to indicate which of the advertisements he or she has observed or seen and how much of the copy was read. Various influencing conditions, such as the order of going through the magazine, are controlled by the interviewer. This test of the number seeing and reading the advertisement is not so significant from the standpoint of the actual score made by the particular advertisement as it is from a comparative standpoint; that is, for comparing the figures for advertisements run in the magazine over a period of time, and with the figures of other similar advertisements for the same category of product run in the same issue of the magazine.

Probably the best-known organization using the recognition test is Daniel Starch and Staff which conducts the Starch Advertisement Readership Service, covering all advertisements one-half page or larger in many national magazines and a number of newspapers. This service provides considerable information on recognition of the advertisement, including categories they term "noted," "seen-associated," and "read most," as well as for various component parts of the advertisements; and comparisons of these figures for various sizes of black-and-white and color advertisements, the readers per dollar for the advertisement, and the cost ratio for the various advertisements checked.

As a rule, the term "noted" includes all those respondents who tell the interviewer they remember seeing the advertisement in the particular issue of the magazine or copy of the newspaper involved. The "seen-associated" category includes all the respondents who have seen or read enough of the advertisement, such as the trademark or company name, to enable them to know the product or the advertiser involved. To be classified in the "read most" category, the respondents must say they have read 50 percent or more of the reading material in the advertisement.

Since one of the basic criticisms of the recognition test has been that although it might measure the attention value of the advertisement and the number of people who read it, this did not measure the value of the advertisement in selling the product, the Starch Service now attempts to measure the extent to which the readership of the advertisements has influenced the reader to buy the product. This is done by ascertaining the percentage of readers and nonreaders of an advertisement who have bought the product within a certain number of days prior to the interviewing. The difference between the percentages (when corrected for the greater readership of advertisements about a product by those who are interested in and loyal to it) measures the effectiveness of the advertisement in stimulating the purchase of the product by the reader.

Another weakness of the recognition test is the so-called confusion factor. That is, when a proposed advertisement that closely resembles an advertisement already run is being tested, many of the respondents may claim sincerely to have seen the advertisement in the particular magazine or newspaper being checked, when, in actuality, they had seen the very similar advertisement in this or another publication. Also, some respondents may claim to have seen advertisements they did not see.

Some research people using the recognition test attempt to correct for this confusion element by showing to a sample of interviewees several advertisements prior to their having appeared in any publication. The percentage that claims to "recognize" the unpublished advertisement is then applied as a reduction factor to the results obtained in the regular running of the test. No technique has been developed to correct for the understatement of recognition.

Considerable debate exists among researchers relative to the validity of readership tests in general. Some researchers have conducted tests attempting to duplicate the methods used by organizations such as Starch in obtaining their readership ratings. Some of these researchers feel that readership scores are influenced more by the respondent's imagination than by actual readership of the advertisements, some that the scores are unduly affected by the number of multimagazine readers included in the samples, while others believe that the readership scores are more a measure of reader interest in the product than of the ability of the ad to obtain readership and remembrance of the advertisement.

Recall tests. The recall type of test, like the recognition test, is based on the memory of the respondent, and is designed to measure the positive impression created by the advertisement on the person being interviewed. Probably the best known of the recall tests are the "impact" studies of magazine and television advertisements of Gallup-Robinson. The test can be probably best illustrated by describing the Gallup-Robinson recall studies of magazine advertisements. The interviewer first ascertains that the respondents had seen the issue of the magazine being studied by showing them the cover of the magazine, but not opening it, and then ask's" the respondents to name all the advertisements they can recall having seen in the magazine. If the respondents have seen or can correctly identify at least one item in the magazine, they are handed a set of cards carrying the names of advertisers or brands appearing in the issue, are asked how many of these they remember having seen, and are then asked to tell the interviewer everything they can remember about each of the advertisements they can identify, including the appearance of the advertisement, what it said about the product, and the main message of the advertisement. This test measures the impression the advertisement made on the respondents and the meaning it had for them. What the respondents say they remember of the advertisement and its message enables the researcher to analyze the effectiveness of various parts of the advertisements and the ideas it contains. The number of respondents who can remember the advertisements under this test is normally lower than the number of readers under the Starch type of recognition test. It is believed the Starch type recognition test is more effective in obtaining quantitative data on readership, but that the recall methods will obtain more qualitative material from those few who can remember the advertisement.

The *"triple-associates"* test is another form of recall test. It was developed by Henry C. Link, and is used to test the effectiveness of a campaign rather than individual advertisements. In it, the interviewer asks the respondents what brand name or advertiser they associate with the product and theme or slogan which the interviewer names for him. For example, the interviewer will ask the respondent, "What brand of cigarette (product) is advertised as '———Tastes Good Like A Cigarette Should' " (slogan), or "What brand of cigarette is the cigarette that 'tastes good like a cigarette should?' " The correct answer to this would be Winston, of course.

Two organizations, Gallup-Robinson and Young and Rubicam advertising agency, publish special testing magazines to pretest advertisements. The magazines contain editorial matter, advertisements to be tested, and a number of control ads (these have previously been tested in regular consumer magazines). Copies of the magazine are distributed to a sample of homes and the people are asked to read it as a regular magazine. The following day the interviewer conducts an aided recall test as with a regular magazine.

This method has the advantages of control of conditions surrounding the test, using an exposure method fairly near normal conditions, although its weakness is that the reading of the magazine and, hence, responses are somewhat forced.

Several organizations conduct either telephone or personal interviews with samples of consumers in certain major markets, to determine what television programs the respondents viewed, what products they saw advertised, and what they remember of the commercials.

These recall tests thus measure not only that the respondent has seen or read some of the advertisements (which is measured by recognition tests, too) but also measure the lasting impression the advertisement has made on the reader, and to some extent the meaning the advertisement conveyed to the respondent.

However, the tests do not indicate whether or not the respondent will buy the product because of recalling the advertisement and its message, or even whether the respondent actually believes the advertiser's message, even though he or she may remember it.

Attitude and opinion testing

Many studies are made to measure the attitudes and opinions of customers or potential customers toward a firm's advertising, its branded products, and toward the company and its policies in general —or to measure the brand or company image. These studies are designed to measure the effectiveness of both the firm's product advertising and its institutional and public relations advertising.

The methods used in these studies include both opinion polls and surveys and consumer panels. Measurement may be made by using single spot surveys or by a series of periodic studies. The recurring study pattern has the real advantage of reflecting changes in the attitudes or opinions of consumers over time. The results of such attitude and opinion surveys enable the advertiser to plan his advertising program to offset any unfavorable attitudes and develop favorable ones. Additional follow-up studies enable him to ascertain the degree of success the changed advertising program is achieving.

Measuring scales. Direct questioning of people regarding their attitudes is not too effective, since many are not aware of their attitudes or have difficulty in formulating a statement of their attitude, which consists of a complex of many feelings. To date no standardized measuring scale or device has been developed to measure attitudes. The process of developing measuring devices that are used to measure attitudes is called scaling. These scales may be either ordinal or interval scales. The ordinal scale serves to rank correspondents according to some characteristic, such as liking or disliking a certain commercial, or to rank items, such as advertisements or brands, in order of preference. Such scales do not measure the degree of liking of the different rankings. Interval scales do measure the distance between such positions in equal units, in addition to separating the items by rank order.

A commonly used type of scale is one in which the respondents are asked to rank themselves by checking the point most descriptive of their attitude on a scale running from one extreme of the attitude being measured to the other. For instance, if the researcher were determining attitudes toward a picture to be used in illustrating a certain advertisement, he could ask respondents to check the box most nearly expressing their feelings about the picture:

Dislike intensely	Dislike considerably	Dislike moderately	Neutral	Like moderately	Like considerably	Like intensely
☐	☐	☐	☐	☐	☐	☐

or

Dislike					Like
☐	☐	☐	☐	☐	

FIGURE 15–1
Specific product image

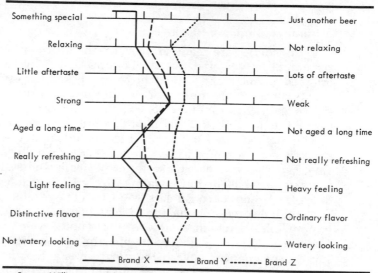

Source: William A. Mindak, "Fitting the Semantic Differential to the Marketing Problem," *Journal of Marketing,* Vol. 25 (April 1961), p. 31.

FIGURE 15–2
Company image

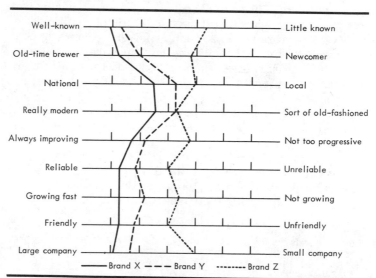

Source: William A. Mindak, "Fitting the Semantic Differential to the Marketing Problem," *Journal of Marketing,* Vol. 25 (April 1961), p. 31.

Graphic scales of this type can be constructed to fit the needs of the particular study and are relatively simple and easy to use.

Another of the attitude-scaling systems used is known as the "semantic differential." In this case, the researcher sets up a series of scales with extremes of positive and negative values which he or she obtains from preliminary investigation of the subject. The respondents are asked to check on each scale a point that most nearly expresses their attitude or opinion of the subject under study. This method has been used mainly in company and brand image studies, since it enables the researcher to develop descriptive profiles to use in comparing the firm with competitors. An example of the application of this method is shown in Figures 15–1, 15–2, and 15–3 which

FIGURE 15–3
Advertising image

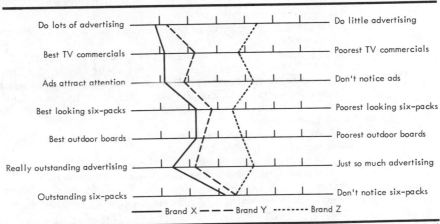

Source: William A. Mindak, "Fitting the Semantic Differential to the Marketing Problem," *Journal of Marketing*, Vol. 25 (April 1961), p. 31.

show the profiles obtained in a study whose "purpose was to determine beer drinkers' reactions to the personalities of three local brands of beer (and specifically Brand Y). . . ." "Various facets of this image were to be explored, such as specific characteristics of each brand, the attitudes toward advertising, the image of the company. . . ."[2]

The "semantic differential" is being adopted to a considerable extent because it is the simplest of the scaling methods and is believed to produce attitude measurements comparable with other more complex methods.

Questions

1. Why do some advertisers not use testing to determine the effectiveness of their advertisements?

[2] William A. Mindak, "Fitting the Semantic Differential to the Marketing Problem," *Journal of Marketing*, Vol. 25 (April 1961), pp. 28–33.

2. If you were an advertiser, would you insist that all of your advertising be tested? Why?

3. Do you think testing effectiveness will eventually replace the advertising man's reliance on experience and judgment?

4. Do you think the attitude toward testing advertising for effectiveness varies among advertisers, media owners, and advertising agency executives? Explain.

5. Why are direct measures of the sales effectiveness of advertisements seldom used?

6. Is it worthwhile to test ads for attention value, readership, effect on attitude, etc., when the usual objective of the advertisement is to sell the product? Discuss.

7. How would you proceed to determine whether or not the advertising effectiveness test itself is accurate and impartial?

8. Is it really important, in the use of the consumer jury test, to use in the sample only those people who have a distinct interest in the product? Why?

9. Evaluate the consumer jury test.

10. For what type of advertising is the inquiry test a valid measurement of effectiveness?

11. What is a split-run inquiry test? What variables that might influence results of the test are controlled by the use of the split run?

12. "Virtually all advertising people agree that the sales-area test provides authentic results when properly conducted, since it does measure actual sales under actual market conditions." If this is so, why are such tests not used more frequently?

13. For what types of products is the sales-area test of advertising effectiveness most suitable? Why?

14. Compare the recognition test with the aided-recall test with respect to information obtained and the usefulness to the advertiser.

15. Briefly describe how you would conduct an inquiry test to determine the relative effectiveness of two different magazines as media for your product ads.

16. Evaluate opinion and attitude tests.

Case **JACKSON PAPER COMPANY**
15–1 **Use of copy testing**

Jackson is engaged in the manufacture of paper towels, tissues, household wax paper, and industrial cleaning tissue, and in the production of wood pulp. Finished paper products are distributed by Jackson throughout the United States and to a comparatively limited extent in the foreign market.

Of the net sales of Jackson, sales of tissues amounted to 41 percent. No other product accounted for as much as 18 percent of such sales.

Jackson's products are sold to more than 3,000 direct purchasers, primarily wholesale distributors, chain stores, department stores, and jobbers in the grocery, paper, drug, hardware, and janitor-supply trades.

The paper industry is highly competitive, and Jackson would be considered one of the four leading U.S. producers in tissues, paper towels, and household wax papers. Sales of the company average about $50 million per year.

Copy testing

The advertising director of the Jackson Company, although he used marketing research extensively, did not put much faith in copy testing. He stated:

> There are so many variables involved in making a test of the copy that I do not believe the results warrant the cost involved. I have tested a number of our advertisements and have found that the correlation between what people say about the advertisement and how they will react at the store is relatively low. Therefore, I have been hesitant to ask our agency to make any such studies, although I do from time to time make some copy analysis.

Recently, the company shifted the appeal for its tissue advertising from an emphasis on color to one of softness. Jackson used a six-month-old baby as a pseudotrademark in the new series of advertisements. In the advertisements, the baby was pictured on a towel. The caption stated: "Your Baby Deserves the Best." The copy which followed compared the softness associated with a baby to the softness and purity of Jackson's tissues.

Copy testing study

Because the results of the campaign could not be measured satisfactorily, the director of research suggested that a "readership" test be made of the series.

The approach followed was to have the interviewer ask a number of persons selected at random which magazines they read. If the answer given included a magazine in which a Jackson advertisement had run, the interviewer then asked the person to check the magazine from cover to cover and indicate which advertisement had been read or noticed.

The results of the study showed that readership of the advertisements ranked high. The baby had won the public's heart. However, most of the people did not know what product was being advertised. Many stated that it was a towel advertisement. Some correctly said it was a tissue advertisement, but only a few related the baby with the Jackson Paper Company.

The advertising director indicated that, while the results of the study were somewhat different than he had expected, he believed that copy testing was too inexact to be used on a large scale by a manufacturer in the paper business.

The research director pointed out that the many methods of copy testing (consumer jury, split run, checklist, psychogalvanometer, and readership method, to name a few) are divided into two categories: those which are used to test the advertisement before it appears, and those which are used after the advertisement appears.

Recognizing the problem of convincing the advertising director of the value of copy testing, the research director suggested that the company use the inquiry method to make a study of two appeals that were being considered for the next campaign.

The inquiry technique, in his opinion, eliminated many of the variables that exist in other methods, because the results are based on actual returns received by people who have read the advertisements. He also felt that burying the free offer in the copy in the same place in the advertisements would discourage the "free-sample hounds" and children from writing for the samples.

Case questions

1. How important is it, in your opinion, for the Jackson company to test the copy in its advertisements?
2. Recognizing that the company is selling a product in which 65 percent of sales are made on impulse, if you were to use copy testing, would you put the emphasis on pretesting or posttesting?
3. Do you believe the research director was wise in recommending the inquiry test approach? Why or why not?
4. What method of pretesting copy could the company have used to determine "brand recognition" in the "Your Baby Deserves the Best" series?

Case 15-2 ROANOKE FOOD COMPANY

The Roanoke Food Company processes raw potatoes into a variety of convenient products for the retail, restaurant, and institutional markets. These products are precooked and are designed to simplify final preparation.

Sales in the past three years had begun to level off, and the vice president in charge of advertising was interested in ascertaining whether or not it would be advisable to subscribe to the National Food Survey at an annual cost of $50,000.

The National Food Survey would provide a bimonthly report of sales data pertaining to the competitive standing of the Roanoke brand. These data were developed from 2,500 selected retail stores located in 750 cities which were chosen from the census reports to provide an adequate cross section of the buying habits of the people in the United States.

The sample provided basic information about sales to consumers, purchases by retailers, retail inventories, stock turn, average order size, displays, retail gross profit, and total sales. These figures were then broken down into brands, store sizes, territories, size of packages, and cities.

Products

Frozen French fries were introduced in 1956 and the frozen potato line has since been expanded to include shredded potato patties (introduced in 1957), crinkle-cut French fries and hash brown potatoes (introduced in 1961), and cottage fried potatoes and small whole peeled potatoes (introduced in 1963).

The company also produces instant mashed potato flakes, which are prepared by adding milk and boiling water, and sells fresh potatoes in limited quantities.

The company seeks, through its product development program, to further expand its product line by the addition of other easy-to-prepare potato products. The company also has from time to time processed limited quantities of other vegetables, which include frozen whole kernel corn and corn on the cob.

During the last fiscal year the company's sales were divided approximately as follows:

Frozen French fried potatoes	55%
Crinkle-cut French fried potatoes	30
Instant mashed potato flakes	3
Other potato products	7
Corn products	5

Sales

During the last year the company made food product sales to approximately 1,500 different customers, no one of which accounted for more than 5 percent of total sales. During the year sales for the retail market accounted for approximately 80 percent of frozen potato product sales, and restaurant and institutional sales accounted for the balance.

The company's food products are sold nationally through a food sales management company. This company supervises approximately 70 independent local food brokers who cover the major marketing areas in the United States. The Sales Management Company also advises Roanoke on its advertising program, provides sales projections, and performs other services related to sales.

Shipments are made from the company's cold storage warehouses or from inventories maintained in approximately 200 public warehouses throughout the country. Shipments from the company's plants to the public warehouses are made either by refrigerated trucks owned or leased by the company or by public or contract carriers.

During the last fiscal year the company marketed approximately 60 percent of its potato products under its own brand names and the balance was packaged for sale under buyers' labels.

The company competes with a number of other processors of frozen potato products and, in a general way, with processors or distributors of other food products. Among the company's competitors are potato-processing divisions of several substantially larger food processing companies.

Sources of supply

The company has in the past purchased substantially all of the potatoes required for processing operations from growers in the area of its plants. The company contracts in advance of the growing season with growers and growers' associations for a major portion of its potato purchases. Under such contracts, the company generally agrees to purchase at a basic price all of the potatoes meeting certain grading requirements grown on specified lands. The company works closely with growers to assist them in the application of modern planting, growing, and harvesting techniques, and sells to the smaller growers most of their seed potato requirements.

Potato planting normally is started in April, and the harvest period extends from August to mid-October, when raw potato inventories reach their peak. The company has been able to obtain short-term bank loans by pledging raw potatoes in storage and processed product inventories, and considers such banking arrangements adequate for carrying these inventories.

Statement of income

The statement of income for the last three years is given below:

| | Year ended December 31 (in thousands of dollars) | | |
	Year A	Year B	Year C
Income:			
Net sales	$21,000	$21,100	$20,000
Other income	450	600	700
Total income	$21,450	$21,700	$20,700
Less:			
Cost of sales	$17,000	$17,500	$17,000
Selling & general expenses	2,800	2,900	3,000
Interest	300	350	360
Total expenses	$20,100	$20,750	$20,360
Net income before provision for income taxes	$ 1,350	$ 950	$ 340

Advertising

Approximately 2 percent of the planned sales was spent each year by the Roanoke Food Company on advertising. With this amount the vice president in charge of advertising directed the advertising primarily to the major urban areas, through national magazines, radio and television spots, point-of-purchase material, and newspapers.

The company had made a number of general market surveys about the consumers and their buying habits. It had relied on its sales figures to provide the necessary data for making marketing plans.

Because the advertising that the company had used was of a general nature which emphasized the appeals of the ease of preparing the Roanoke potatoes and the high quality of its brand, the vice president was of the opinion that it was not possible to test effectiveness of these appeals.

While the Roanoke line of frozen potatoes had been dominant in the market for the ten prior years, the company believed that it was losing ground to the private labels. A number of the brokers and salesmen also reported that the retailers were not providing as much freezer space and these same retailers were using more and more of the space for their own private brands of frozen potatoes.

Case questions

1. Should the company subscribe to this $50,000 service? Why? Or why not?
2. What other methods might the company use to check the effectiveness of its advertising?
3. Is there other information that the company should attempt to secure about its market? Buying motives of consumers?
4. What precautions must Roanoke keep in mind about any research program that it might use?

Case 15–3   ROSE OVENWARE COMPANY
The pretesting of advertisements

The Rose Ovenware Company, a large manufacturer of pottery ovenware of such various types as casseroles, baking dishes, bean pots, and custard cups, had developed recently a new type of glazed china ovenware, which had a much finer appearance of quality and style than did their traditional lines of pottery ovenware, because it could be manufactured in much lighter weight and could be designed along smarter and finer lines. At the same time, it was equal to the old lines of ovenware from the standpoint of durability and quality of its baking results. The company selected the name "China Roseware" for the new line.

The company had decided to do a thorough job of pretesting its advertising and promotion program for the new line before beginning its national advertising campaign and marketing program.

The company marketed its regular lines nationally through hardware stores, department stores, and houseware specialty stores. It was a leading firm in the field and had very good distribution through most of the leading stores of the above types.

The Rose Company planned to market "China Roseware," through the same types of stores, although it was thought adding gift shops might be advisable as a channel for the company's new line, since it was believed that the smarter appearance and better styling would make "China Roseware" very attractive for wedding and shower gifts, as well as for Christmas gifts, as was true of the traditional lines.

In the regular lines of ovenware, Rose Company sales records indicated two retail sales peaks—one during the last part of November and in December before Christmas, and the second (a slightly smaller sales peak) in April and May. The company had for many years carried on a consistent program of advertising in national magazines, using women's service magazines primarily, and the appeal of "the finest quality in ovenware" as the major theme.

Rose Company's advertising agency had from time to time made surveys to determine consumer usage of Rose Company's products and the opinions of Rose ovenware. These surveys had indicated that Rose ovenware enjoyed a fine reputation among most housewives, who considered it one of the finest quality lines of ovenware on the market.

While discussing plans for marketing the new "China Roseware" line, the advertising agency recommended the Rose Company conduct an area sales test to select the advertising approach to use in the national campaign. Since Rose Company planned to invest several million dollars in promotion of the new line during the next few years, the agency deemed it advisable to protest the main advertising theme. The agency had developed three different copy approaches from ideas submitted by various members of the agency.

The three themes developed by the agency were: copy theme 1, stressing "the beauty and style of China Roseware"; theme 2, "the convenience and attractiveness of serving food at the dining table directly from the utensils in which the food was cooked"; and theme 3, "the better baking results from China Roseware." Although the Rose Company advertising manager was somewhat dubious about the ability of any firm to conduct a really sound area sales test, because of the many problems involved, he finally approved the plan for the agency to conduct such a test.

For the test, the agency selected nine cities (as nearly comparable as possible for all important factors), all of which met the usual criteria for good test cities. The Rose Company had very good distribution of their regular lines in all these nine cities. In the two months prior to the conduct of the test (July and August), a team of three Rose Company salesmen covered the nine test cities with an intensive sales effort, and were able to get over 90 percent of all the company's regular outlets to stock the new line of ovenware, with only very minor variations among the nine cities in the percentage of stores stocking the China Roseware line.

For the test, the advertising agency developed three sets of advertisements, each set based on one of the three copy themes. The sets of advertisements were considered comparable in quality and attractiveness. In conducting the test, the advertisement series 1, using the theme "the beauty and style of China Roseware," was run in cities A, B, and C. The second series of advertisements, based on theme 2, "convenience and attractiveness of serving food at the dining table directly from the utensils in which it was cooked," was run in cities D, E, and F. The third series of advertisements, based on theme 3, "the better baking results from China Roseware," was run in cities G, H, and I. Sales in all the hardware and department stores in all the nine cities were audited weekly for a period of six weeks before the advertisements were run, and for the six weeks of the actual advertising campaign. Since the new ovenware was fair-traded, no cut-price sales took place during the period of the test, and no unusual promotions were held by any of the stores which were audited. Half-page advertisements were run twice a week for the six weeks in the leading evening newspaper published in each of the nine cities, always in preferred positions in the women's section of the paper, and on the same day of the week.

Sales results for the two periods involved were as shown in Exhibit 15–1 below.

The agency was very pleased with the results, which indicated all three appeals were very good. Although the agency believed the results were sufficiently significant to make advertising theme 3, "the

EXHIBIT 1

	Sales, 6-week period preceding advertising, Sept. 1– Oct. 15	Sales, 6-week period of advertising, Oct. 16– Nov. 30	Percent of increase due to advertising
Cities A, B, & C. Advertising theme 1, "The beauty and style of China Roseware"	2,000	3,000	50
Cities D, E, & F. Advertising theme 2, "The convenience and attractiveness of serving food at the dining table directly from the utensil in which it was cooked"	1,800	2,800	56
Cities G, H, & I. Advertising theme 3, "The better baking results from China Roseware"	1,600	2,600	62.5

better baking results from China Roseware," the obvious theme to use, they decided to follow the sound procedure of double testing, so obtained the approval of the Rose Company's advertising manager to run an inquiry test to check the results of the area sales test.

For this purpose, they decided to use the Chicago *Bugle* (a fictitious name) a newspaper which provided facilities for running a three-way split-run test. In its Sunday edition, the *Bugle* published a "local news" section, varied for different areas served by its circulation. This section had excellent readership in all areas, and had often been used by food and drug companies for inquiry tests, with excellent results in the way of response. The *Bugle* showed them the results of several of these tests, and the enthusiastic letters received from the agencies which had conducted them.

For the inquiry test, the agency prepared new and improved advertisements, using the same three basic appeals which had been tested in the area sales test previously. The same sized advertisement, in the same position on the same page of the special section, was inserted for each appeal. The advertisement using advertising theme 1, "the beauty and style of China Roseware," was run in the section of the paper which went to the North Side. The advertisement using theme 2, "the convenience and attractiveness of serving food at the dining table directly from the utensils in which the food was cooked," was run in the section which went to the South Side, and the advertisement using theme 3, "the better baking results with China Roseware," appeared in the section distributed in the towns and rural areas of downstate Illinois. Although the circulation varied slightly for the three areas, the inquiry results were corrected to allow for this discrepancy. The offer, a recipe book (*One Hundred Delicious Casserole Dishes*), was in the form of a buried offer, and was equally prominent in all three advertisements. The advertisements all appeared on Sunday, January 8, since it was believed housewives spent more time reading the newspaper on Sundays.

The corrected results of the inquiry test were as follows: advertising theme 1, using "the beauty and style of China Roseware," 127 inquiries; advertising theme 2, stressing "the convenience and attractiveness of serving food at the dining table directly from the utensils in which the food was cooked," 108 inquiries; and advertising theme 3, incorporating the idea of "the better baking results from China Roseware," received 181 inquiries.

Since this test so definitely marked advertising theme 3 as the superior appeal, and also confirmed the results of the first test, the agency now was positive it had the best appeal, and recommended to the advertising manager of the Rose Company that he authorize them to plan its campaign around advertising theme 3, the appeal of "the better baking results from China Roseware."

Case question

1. If you were the advertising manager of the Rose Company, what would be your reaction to the agency's recommendation, and how would you evaluate the testing procedures used?

Case   **B. F. GOODRICH COMPANY**
15–4   **Pretesting advertisements**

The B. F. Goodrich Company plans to use the advertisements in Exhibits 15–2 and 15–3 in its "straight talk" campaign for passenger tires.

Exhibit 15–2 ("Can you trust us with your wife on tire-buying day?") is scheduled for *Sports Illustrated, U.S. News & World Report,* and *Newsweek.*

Exhibit 15–3 ("Are four-ply tires going the way of inner tubes?") is scheduled for *Business Week.*

EXHIBIT 15–2

Can you trust us with your wife on tire-buying day?

Absolutely.

You say she doesn't know anything about cords and plys? You say she can't tell a retread from a radial?

Fine. We say she doesn't have to. (Neither do you, if you'd rather keep the dubious pleasure of buying tires all to yourself.)

Because, at B.F.Goodrich, we talk straight talk. Not a lot of technical tire gibberish.

All you've got to know to get the right tires from us is a few simple facts about how you drive. How much, how far, how fast and so on.

Then you reach for one of our BFG Tire Value Calculators. Feed it the facts, as you know them. And it will tell you which BFG tire will suit you best, cost you least.

Would we try to sweet-talk anyone into buying the wrong tires?

Nope. We're the straight-talk tire people.

The straight-talk tire people. **B.F.Goodrich**

Courtesy B. F. Goodrich Company.

EXHIBIT 15–3

Are four-ply tires going the way of inner tubes?

It looks like it. Almost all the tires we ship to car makers now are two-ply rather than four-ply. Matter of fact, nearly all new cars have come with two-ply tires for the past three years.

But we've been asked: How can we take something out of a tire and make it better?

People asked the same thing when B.F.Goodrich introduced tires without inner tubes: How could they be as strong? But they were. Today almost every car rides on tubeless tires.

Sure, two-ply tires have only two plys (layers) of cords while four-ply tires have four. But every cord in two-plys is twice as big and twice as strong as the cord in four-plys. So, two-ply tires are every bit as tough as four-plys. And, in some ways, they're better. They run cooler. And give a softer ride.

Who says so? Test experts on car-proving grounds. And millions of car owners who've racked up billions of miles on two-plys.

Next time you need tires, ask a BFG dealer about two-plys. He'll give you straight talk. It's a specialty of the house.

The straight-talk tire people. **B.F.Goodrich**

Courtesy B. F. Goodrich Company.

Case questions

1. Recommend a plan for pretesting the two advertisements. Describe the size and composition of the sample and how you would obtain the information.
2. To what extent would your procedures be changed, if B. F. Goodrich asked you to compare the effectiveness of the "straight talk" appeal to one which emphasized some other appeal, such as safety or durability?

part seven

Advertising management

16

THE ADVERTISING BUDGET

One of the basic advertising, financial, and control devices is the budgeting process. This activity involves a planning and control system because it provides a continuing process throughout the year for checking on all phases of the advertising program. While some executives may look upon the very concept of a budget as a straitjacket type of control, it is important to keep in mind that budgeting is not synonymous with forecasting as such. Budgeting involves not only the planning activity, but also the controlling function, in order to maximize the chances of achieving the objectives.

Management indeed wants to know if its advertising program is effective, and that it is making adequate use of this instrument of survival and growth in competitive markets. It is clearly the prerogative of management to set the framework within which these discussions will take place. Persuasion within an orderly framework is essentially negotiation. Recognition that the budget-making procedure is basically a process of negotiation should put it in a better perspective than any of the attempts to reduce it to a mechanical formula.

Management is not a passive customer waiting to be sold. There are management functions to be served through budgeting if the initiative comes from the top. A full awareness of these functions should favor a more constructive outcome of the annual negotiation concerning advertising expenditures.

The goals of management

Discussion of an annual budget provides a channel of communication concerning goals and the means of attaining them. It may be used by top management to communicate an understanding of com-

517

pany objectives and what selling and advertising are expected to contribute. There is a great deal of lip service for the so-called "objective and task" method of determining advertising expenditures. This doctrine often means little in practice since the task cannot be defined in the absence of a clear statement of objectives. Management in some companies may prefer to have the advertising department present a budget based on its best guess as to what the objectives are. The program as presented can then be criticized in terms of the undisclosed objectives. Considering the amount of effort which goes into the preparation of a detailed budget, it is recommended that short range objectives at least should be defined by management in advance of the budgeting procedure.

The starting place for management in considering advertising is *long-range objectives,* whether these are fully disclosed or interpreted for the benefit of subordinates. These underlying objectives might be grouped under the headings of *growth, profits, investment, and personnel development.* More than advertising is involved in these objectives, but the preparation of the advertising budget provides the occasion for reviewing them in relation to the entire marketing program.

Sales growth is a basic goal for most companies which advertise. The desired rate of growth is dependent in part on management's estimate of competitive developments. *Not only the rate of growth but the direction of growth* may be a part of company goals. Management wishes to broaden its product line for the sake of stability, to make better use of projected additions to plant capacity, or to add items which will strengthen its position with its marketing channels. *One of the uses of advertising is to accelerate trends in demand.* Bringing about changes in demand, or adjusting to them as they occur, are perhaps the most basic of all long range company goals.

The goal of greater profits can be served either by increasing sales or by decreasing costs. Advertising is often more economical than other means of selling, as well as being more effective. The total amount of distribution costs including wholesale and retail margins may be reduced through a shift to advertising. Profits are both the result of continuing growth and the necessary condition for further expansion. Management upon occasion does an admirable job of explaining its need for net revenue and the uses to which it will be put. An advertising program acquires greater point and urgency when it is visualized as a means of seeking these goals of growth and profits.

Next to producing adequate sales revenue, management is most concerned with finding investment dollars. Growth must be financed through retained earnings or new issues. Either way, advertising makes it easier to obtain the needed funds. Present stockholders are willing to see profits go into retained earnings rather than dividends if they believe in the appreciation of the company's equity values. New investors will buy the company's securities on a favorable basis if they appear to represent an attractive combination of risk and return over a period of years.

The future of a company depends in large measure on the quality of its personnel. The successful company must equal or excel its competitors in attracting good men and in holding them. Advertising which carries conviction about the present and future strength of a company can facilitate recruitment. It can also help to maintain morale of existing staff and inspire loyal and competent performance. Dealers and distributors are often considered a part of the organization for this purpose. Advertising cannot be aimed primarily at the company's own personnel, but the influence on morale is a very important side-effect to be considered in making a budget.

Here are the objectives which should shape the advertising tasks. They must be weighed by management and assigned relative priorities. Otherwise, the advertising department is likely to define its own tasks only in terms of short-run sales goals. It can make its program sound very concrete and practical, but it may not be on the target in terms of a broader perspective. Disclosure of what management is really after does not provide an automatic solution for advertising problems but it at least makes it possible to state them.

Sales planning and advertising results

There has been a good deal of debate in advertising about the respective merits of what are called "the breakdown method" and "the build-up method" of preparing an advertising budget. Neither of these terms accurately describes a negotiational approach to the budget in which top management makes the first move. It does not start out with a statement of what is available to be spent, as in the breakdown method, but with a specification of the goals to be achieved. It does not assume that management will remain passive until a budget has been prepared and presented for approval, as in the build-up method. Negotiation inside a company, like negotiation between independent agencies, moves toward an exchange of commitments. Such an exchange between any subordinate group and top management involves a commitment on one side to attain the specified goals and on the other side to provide adequate resources for the purpose. Questions may arise during the process as to whether the goals are feasible at any cost or whether the company can afford what seems to be required to achieve them. When the budget is finally approved it represents a working agreement about what can and should be done.

A commitment to perform the task assigned by management should rest on something more than the energy and optimism of the sales and advertising departments. Top management is entitled not only to an assurance that it can be done but to some indication of how it is to be done. If the results required are greater than those of the past year, the presentation of the sales plan should indicate the ways in which the program should be changed to achieve these results. Top management cannot afford the time for a detailed review of every sales plan if the company is advertising a long list of products. There is scarcely any substitute for going over plans for selected products and demanding assurance that other plans are equally detailed.

A judgment of whether advertising dollars will be well spent can best be made in terms of how advertising is expected to fit into the total sales effort. Will it open doors for salesmen? Will salesmen use it to get wider distribution or better representation in retail displays? Will the advertising of an industrial product stimulate direct inquiries or is it calculated to bring pressure on purchasing agents from others in customer companies? Will a proposed campaign with an institutional slant make the company better known to investors or to other target segments of the public?

General budget concepts

The process of setting the advertising budget involves four fundamental management requirements: anticipation, coordination, control, and payout evaluation. These requirements mean that advertisers are faced with the problem of anticipating customer requirements, product changes, and competitors' strategies. They must coordinate all phases of their advertising plan in order to have such details as the store displays and general promotion tie in with the advertising. At the same time all facets of the program need to be controlled, and, in the final analysis, payout evaluation will give management the information required to determine whether or not the objectives of the advertising have been attained.

The aim in setting the amount of money to be spent on advertising is to spend enough to attain the objectives of the advertising campaign but not to waste money by spending more than is necessary.

The determination of this optimum amount to spend on advertising is a problem that plagues virtually all advertisers. That is, although they may have decided on the amount of advertising which has obtained good results, from the overall marketing and profit standpoints, there still remains unanswered the question, "Would some other amount, either larger or smaller, have obtained even better results, or equally good results?"

This is true even of the major firms that plan their advertising very carefully and establish specific objectives to achieve with their expenditures. As an example, consider a national organization which sells its products on a national basis and distributes them through wholesalers to retailers to the consumers. This company uses national, regional, and local media as well as various forms of cooperative and point-of-purchase advertising. It also has a staff of missionary salesmen who advise the retail stores, besides a regular sales staff which handles the wholesale accounts. As a result of the variety of selling methods employed in moving the products, it is difficult to appraise the results of advertising.

On the other hand, a company which does all its business on a mail-order basis will find it easier to appraise the results of its advertising because it can correlate its sales to the advertising used. This can be done by observing the changes in sales where immediate increases in sales can be expected from advertising, or by counting the number of inquiries when the advertising was aimed at securing requests for information.

In other instances, however, the primary aim of advertising may be to develop favorable attitudes or to communicate an idea. One might expect that building acceptance in increasing awareness will be reflected in future sales. These results must be measured over long periods of time and are difficult to determine because there are factors other than advertising which may influence them.

This chapter will discuss some of the facets of setting the advertising budget, methods in common use for establishing this amount, and some aspects of allocation and control of advertising expenditures.

Forming the budget expenditure

A number of considerations are involved in the problem of determining the amount of the funds to be appropriated for advertising. These include: the sales forecast, the general marketing plan, customer density, customer size, product profitability, product popularity, channels of distribution, competitors' strategies, quantity sold, unit price, objectives, trading area, end use of product, and general economic conditions.

Time of establishing the appropriation

In actual practice, most firms that have been operating for a period of time establish the entire advertising appropriation for the coming year at one time, several months prior to the beginning of their budget year. This is done on the assumption that all marketing plans, both for old, established products and any new ones to be launched on the market during the coming year, are reasonably well known at the time. This, of course, also means that the executives must have developed their tentative advertising programs or campaigns for each of their products and for their institutional campaign (if any) by this same date and, hence, are able to recommend the desired amount for each of the advertising campaigns to form the basis for the entire advertising budget.

Other firms, which may be on a different budgeting period basis, such as semiannual or quarterly, would establish their advertising appropriations on a comparable time basis. It should be noted that such firms must, however, make plans for individual campaigns sufficiently far in advance to meet their particular needs and, hence, may find it necessary to set tentative advertising appropriations for such campaigns for longer periods of time than that noted. And many small firms do not have definitely established budgets for their operations or advertising and will establish the amount for each individual program or campaign as it is developed. Even for such firms, it is most important to devote care to the setting of the appropriation for a campaign early in its planning stage.

Flexibility of the budget

A firm that sets the amount one year in advance will do well to permit a certain amount of flexibility in its budgeting for advertising.

Even when setting the appropriation for a shorter period, or for only one specific advertising campaign for an individual product, a certain amount of flexibility is necessary in order to meet changing and unforeseen conditions in the market. In the case of the firm establishing amounts a year in advance, a number of conditions may make it desirable to spend a smaller or larger sum than originally planned.

During the year, the general economic climate may change completely, and an unpredicted slump or rise in general economic activity may occur. A marked change of this type may call for a considerable change in overall marketing plans and strategy, with a resulting effect on the amount of money believed necessary for the advertising program. The objectives of the firm may well change due to such conditions, or it may become evident that more or less money will be required to achieve the desired objectives. For example, a manufacturing firm may have a maximum capacity of, say, 100,000 units of its one product. It has set up a marketing plan involving an advertising campaign designed to achieve sales of that 100,000 units in view of certain anticipated general economic conditions which it judges will enable the industry to generate total sales of that product of 1 million units, with its taking 10 percent of the market. If, fairly early in the year, general conditions change so that the rate of sale of the product is much greater than had been anticipated, and it becomes obvious that the firm will be able to sell its entire output with a considerably modified advertising and sales program, it would be questionable to continue with the original extensive program. In these conditions, the firm might revise its budget downward. Should the reverse have been the case, the firm probably would, and should, expand its advertising appropriation, if such is believed desirable to attempt to achieve its sales of 100,000 units.

In addition to general economic conditions, other changes may occur. The firm itself may decide to change general plans upon which the budget was based. It may decide that it should enter new markets, or due to some unforeseen developments, it may decide to expand its product line, or add new products to its line. Such changes would undoubtedly call for increases in advertising.

By the same token, decisions to drop lines or products or to retrench the market area might call for decreased sums for advertising. Advertising plans are usually predicated on certain assumptions regarding the competitive activity in the field. Should the competitive situation change markedly during the budget period, it may be decided that different sums will be necessary for advertising in order to achieve the desired objectives. It is also possible that changes will occur in the media situation, with regard to availability, rates, or desirability, which would indicate a need for varying expenditure. Conceivably, sudden changes might occur in the dealer picture that would call for increases or changes in the dealer phase of the advertising campaign.

Whatever the reason, it is clear that changes may occur indicating that either more funds will be needed to achieve the original or changed objectives of the firm or that the objectives can be achieved with a smaller expenditure than originally planned. Obviously, it is merely good business to change the planned budget to meet such changed conditions, assuming, of course, that the financial position of the firm makes it feasible. The budget may take care of normal, unexpected changes by including in the original allocation a certain amount for contingencies which is not budgeted for any specific purpose. If changes call for increased spending, such could be taken care of out of this contingency reserve. Other means for providing flexibility are to have a periodic and reasonably frequent review of the budget, to compare expenditures with original appropriations, and to check the results in relation to established objectives.

Some considerations influencing the size of the allocation

The most important factor influencing the amount of the appropriation is the general marketing mix of the company for the particular product involved, which in turn is determined by the type of product, the differentiating features involved, the appeals available, the volume and margin, company strategic considerations, company policy, and related factors. If the product is one for which a strong consumer demand can be stimulated, so that the pull strategy of marketing can be used effectively, the budget for advertising might constitute virtually the entire marketing cost and the firm show a profit even though advertising costs would run 40 percent of sales—as is true for some home-remedy type medicinal products with a wide margin of selling price over production costs. On the other hand, for some standardized basic products or materials, advertising may play a virtually negligible part in the marketing strategy, and it might be advisable to use other means.

Items to be charged to advertising

Obviously, the amount of money appropriated will be influenced also by the nature of the items to be charged to the budget. Policies and practices as to what items are properly to be charged to "advertising" vary considerably among companies. Some firms charge to this budget any sales promotion type expenditure or goodwill type expenditure which cannot easily be allocated to any other account presently set up in the budget. Some firms are also prone to charge to advertising such miscellaneous expenses as the cost of Christmas presents for employees, contributions to the community chest and other charitable organizations, tickets to the police ball, and costs of entertainment at sales conventions. Since there was no account to which such expenditures seemingly could logically be charged, the advertising account became a sort of catchall account for many charges that were not too closely related to advertising itself.

Printers' Ink developed a recommended list of items that are unquestionably chargeable to advertising and a list of items that are borderline (their gray list) and should or should not be charged to advertising depending on the method used in carrying on the activity under question. The magazine also has what it terms a "black list" of

FIGURE 16–1
Printers' Ink guide to allocation of advertising appropriations (sometimes called the "white, black, and gray list")

White list (*these charges belong in the advertising account*)

Space	Catalogs	Administration	Mechanical
(paid advertising in all recognized mediums, including:)	Package inserts (when used as advertising and not just as direction sheets)	Salaries of advertising department executives and employees	Artwork
Newspapers			Typography
Magazines	House magazines to dealers or consumers	Office supplies and fixtures used solely by advertising department	Engraving
Business papers			Mats
Farm papers	Motion pictures (including talking pictures) when used for advertising	Commissions and fees to advertising agencies, special writers or advisers	Electros
Class journals			Photographs
Car cards			Radio & TV production
Theater programs	Slides	Expenses incurred by salesmen when on work for advertising department	Package design (advertising aspects only)
Outdoor	Export advertising		Etc.
Point of purchase	Dealer helps	Traveling expenses of department employees engaged in departmental business	Miscellaneous:
Novelties	Reprints of advertisements used in mail or for display		Transportation of advertising material (to include postage and other carrying charges)
Booklets	Radio	(Note: In some companies these go into special "Administration" account)	Fees to window display installation services
Directories	Television		Other miscellaneous expenses connected with items on the white list
Direct advertising	All other printed and lithographed material used directly for advertising purposes		
Cartons and labels (for advertising purposes, such as in window displays)			

Black list (*these charges do not belong in the advertising account, although too frequently they are put there*)

Free goods
Picnic and bazaar programs
Charitable, religious, and fraternal donations
Other expenses for goodwill purposes
Cartons
Labels
Instruction sheets
Package manufacture
Press agentry
Stationery used outside advertising department
Price lists
Salesmen's calling cards
Motion pictures for sales use only

House magazines going to factory employees
Bonuses to trade

Special rebates
Membership in trade associations
Entertaining customers or prospects
Annual reports
Showrooms
Demonstration stores
Sales convention expenses
Salesmen's samples (including photographs used in lieu of samples)
Welfare activities among employees
Such recreational activities as baseball teams, etc.
Sales expenses at conventions
Cost of salesmen's automobiles
Special editions which approach advertisers on goodwill basis

Gray list (*these are borderline charges, sometimes belonging in the advertising accounts and sometimes in other accounts, depending on circumstances*)

Samples
Demonstrations
Fairs

Canvassing
Rent

Light
Heat

Depreciation of equipment used by advertising department
Telephone and other overhead expenses, apportioned to advertising department

House magazines going to salesmen
Advertising automobiles

Premiums
Membership in associations or other organizations devoted to advertising
Testing bureaus
Advertising portfolios for salesmen

Contributions to special advertising funds of trade associations
Display signs on the factory or office building
Salesmen's catalogs
Research and market investigations

Advertising allowances to trade for cooperative effort

This chart is based on the principle that there are three types of expenses that generally are charged against the advertising appropriation.

The first charge is made up of expenses that are always justifiable under any scheme of accounting practice. These have been included in the white list of charges that belong in the advertising account.

A second type consists of those charges which cannot and should not under any system of accounting be justified as advertising expenses. These have been placed on the black list.

There is a third type of expense which can sometimes be justified under advertising and sometimes not. Frequently the justification for the charge depends upon the method used in carrying on a certain activity. These charges have been placed in a borderline gray list.

The chart is the result of the collaboration of the editors of *Printers' Ink* and several hundred advertisers. It has been revised for a third time with the aid of advertising and accounting men. It may be considered, therefore, to represent sound, standard practice.

items that should not be charged to advertising, even though in practice they often are. This list from *Printers' Ink* is shown in Figure 16–1.

The four major types of charges that are properly allocated to the advertising appropriation are the media costs, production costs of the advertising, advertising research, and administrative costs.

Methods of establishing the appropriation

Although various studies of methods for setting the advertising appropriation may list anywhere from two to 24 ways of setting the appropriation, there are three basic bases for establishing budgets. These are the percentage of sales method (and its variations), objective-task method, and the competitive parity method.

The percentage of sales method

This is generally considered the most widely used method of setting the appropriation, although its use has declined in recent years. There are several variations in the actual application of this method. The percentage may be based on the past year's sales, on estimated sales for the coming year, or on some combination of these two. A variation of this method of setting the budget that basically involves the same philosophy is that of setting a certain per unit sum for advertising and multiplying that sum per unit by sales in units (past or estimated) to give the total advertising appropriation.

The wide use of this method can probably be explained on several bases. It is a relatively simple method to apply. Most companies relate the various items of cost in their operating statements by means of computing them as a percentage of sales, and have come to think of their advertising expenditures in terms of a certain percentage of sales. The overall operating budget is based on the sales volume, the margins available, and the profits to be realized. The advertising appropriation must fit into this budget which normally must show a profit for the firm. Also, usually in the overall marketing plan of the company the advertising is assigned a fairly fixed portion of the marketing task or marketing mix. If, on the basis of experience, a certain percentage of the marketing budget assigned to advertising has resulted in a profitable operation, it may be the best thing to do to continue assigning that part of the marketing budget to advertising. Then the question remaining is to decide how best to spend that amount of money to get the most from the advertising. When the method involved uses future sales, the method appears reasonably logical. If it normally takes a certain amount of advertising effort to move a number of units of merchandise or to achieve a certain dollar volume of sales, then appropriating that sum per unit or that percentage of sales for advertising for next year should result in achieving the projected volume of sales. In other words, a certain relationship exists between sales and the amount of advertising expenditures required to obtain such sales.

In practice, this method, when based on estimated future sales, may often actually work quite well. If virtually all conditions in the firm's market, including the general economic conditions and the competitive activity, remain rather constant, then it is quite possible that the same correlations will remain between the advertising and other sales and promotional activity expenditures and the resulting sales volume. Using future sales does overcome to a large extent the argument most frequently advanced against the use of a percentage of past sales, which is that such a method ignores the fact that advertising should precede and is an important factor in stimulating demand and obtaining sales, and is not something that follows sales. In other words, advertising should be considered the "cause" and not the "effect" of sales.

In actuality, of course, few firms ever face such a situation of "all other things remaining equal." The amount of advertising required to achieve a given level of sales in the coming period will be influenced by many factors which often change, such as the general level of income; changes in the firm's and competitors' products and prices; and changes in competitive marketing and selling, promotional, and advertising activity. Dynamic conditions change the relationship between the sums spent on advertising and the sales resulting therefrom. Hence, even the use of projected sales does not make this a truly sound method of establishing the appropriation.

Also, if a firm is using only a limited amount of consumer advertising primarily for the purpose of influencing the trade, the mere fact that consumer sales will be up next year does not mean that there is any real basis for increasing the number of advertisements being run to influence the trade. Or, if a good job has been done in the past on dealer advertising and promotion, it may not be necessary to increase this portion of the budget just because it is believed the consumer sales of the product will increase in the year ahead.

The objective-task method

The objective-task method is coming into wider use as it provides a more logical basis for establishing the advertising appropriation to meet the dynamic conditions facing marketing today. It directs attention to the objectives to be attained by the marketing program, the role that advertising is to play in attaining such objectives, and definitely recognizes the fact that advertising plays a vital part in stimulating demand and creating sales, and is not the result of a certain sales volume.

When the objective-task method is used, the first step is to set the objectives of the program for the coming year or budget period. There may be one or several objectives, such as obtaining a certain volume of sales, obtaining a larger share of the market, entering a new area, obtaining additional dealers, or launching a new product. Next, on the basis of experience or research findings, it is determined just what specific means will be necessary to achieve these objectives, or the task involved. Then it is necessary to determine how much and what kind of advertising will be required to accomplish the tasks established in the first two steps. At this point it may be advisable to take another step. The proposed appropriation for advertising is considered in light of the overall budget and financial position of the company. If the amount involved appears to be excessive, in view of the firm's financial position and overall budget situation, it may be necessary to reconsider both the objectives and the proposed advertising plans, and modify them so that they will fit into the overall situation of the company. In theory, this would appear to be the best method of setting the advertising appropriation. It does not rely on any specious fixed relationship between advertising and sales. It is not bound by historical precedent. In deciding how much and what kind of advertising will be necessary to achieve the objectives, full consideration can be given to the ever-changing conditions in the market as discussed earlier. It definitely relates the amount of money to be spent to the specific tasks required to achieve the established objectives.

In practice, there is one serious problem involved in the use of this method of setting the appropriation. That is, how does the advertiser determine just how much advertising and what type of advertising will be necessary to achieve the objectives as established? With the present available methods of measuring the effectiveness of advertising, it is difficult to say with any real certainty just how much and what kind of advertising is required to achieve a certain result. Although the experienced advertiser using the best research methods available can ascertain general answers to these questions, one still is not certain that he has selected the optimum expenditure. Until he has much better methods of determining the effectiveness of advertising, he will be faced with this problem of not knowing just what is the ideal amount of money needed to achieve certain tasks and objectives.

It is interesting to note that the various advertising objectives have been measured, in part at least, by some company or research organization. Among the objectives which have been measured are:

1. Changes in sales
2. Changes in extent and nature of attitudes of the consumers
3. Changes in product usage
4. Increase in consumers' knowledge of the company or its product
5. Correlation of a purchase to the effectiveness of advertising
6. Impact of advertising on salesmen and outlets
7. Importance of advertising in the sale of a product
8. Development of a company or product image

The competitive parity method

Although few executives would indicate that this method is the one they use in setting their appropriation, many do, in practice, actually follow this procedure. In essence, this method consists of setting the appropriation by relating it in some manner to the expenditures of the firm's major competitor or competitors. This may be a matter of matching the actual expenditures of the major competitor, or attempting to maintain some set relationship between the expenditures of the firm and the competitor. In other instances, this method may involve using the average percentage of sales spent by the firms in the entire industry, and then applying that percentage to the firm's sales to establish the appropriation. The basis for the use of this method is probably that since advertising is a major competitive weapon, it is necessary for the firm to match its competitors' advertising if it is to hold its share of the market against such competitors.

Another rationale is that, since the firms in the industry are successful, the average of their expenditures is a figure that achieves relative success in sales and profits, and is an expenditure with which the firms can live and be successful. The average represents, in a sense, the combined thinking of all the advertising experts in the industry, and should normally be better than the thinking of any one man. And, since in many areas of business it is common to compare the firm's operations, as percentages of sales, with industry average figures to ascertain their relative efficiency of operations, it is easy to see how the advertising executive might come to think of the industry average as a sort of standard for that type of business and, hence, one that he should follow unless he can find a very good reason for varying from the standard.

However, there are weaknesses inherent in this method. The industry average or expenditures of major competitors need not have any relationship to the objectives or problems of this particular company. Not all companies use the same marketing methods, nor do they operate in exactly the same conditions from the standpoint of such things as brand reputation, entrenchment in the market, and cumulative effect of past advertising. Hence, no one figure is sound for all firms with their varying problems, varying marketing strategies and methods, and varying objectives and long-range goals. Also, there is not a valid basis for assuming that the competitors are setting their appropriations on a sound basis, or that they are attaining the same quality of advertising with their advertising dollar.

From a practical standpoint, using the competitive parity method generally means using historical figures or past advertising appropriations of the competitor or industry, since it is difficult to obtain such figures in advance.

In setting a budget under this method, however, it is important to consider the amount of advertising which the leaders in the various industries are using. Figure 16–2 gives, by industry, the advertising as percent of sales for leaders on the basis of their total advertising expenditures. One finds that the percent of the sales dollar devoted to advertising is the highest among the drugs and cosmetics industry where 15 of the 22 drug and cosmetic companies listed spent over 17 percent of their sales dollar for advertising.

FIGURE 16–2
Leaders' advertising as percent of sales (covering total ad expenditures; including measured and unmeasured media)

AD RANK	COMPANY	ADVERTISING	SALES	ADV. AS % OF SALES	AD RANK	COMPANY	ADVERTISING	SALES	ADV. AS % OF SALES
	Cars					**Beer**			
2	General Motors Corp.	$173,000,000	$20,733,982,000	0.8	36	Jos. Schlitz Brewing Co.	35,000,000	324,043,086	10.8
4	Ford Motor Co.	116,500,000	11,537,789,264	1.0	38	Anheuser-Busch Inc.	34,200,000	553,509,809	6.2
9	Chrysler Corp.	80,000,000	5,299,934,803	1.5	73	Pabst Brewing Co.	17,750,000	253,585,672	7.0
59	American Motors Corp.	22,500,000	990,618,709	2.3	83	Falstaff Brewing Corp.	16,500,000	228,150,782	7.2
77	Volkswagen of America Inc.	17,000,000	500,000,000*	3.4	92	Carling Brewing Co.	14,741,000	400,931,310*	3.7
	Food					**Oil**			
3	General Foods Corp.	120,000,000	1,381,049,000	8.7	53	Standard Oil Co. (Ind.)	23,500,000	3,063,161,000	0.8
17	National Dairy Products Corp.	56,927,000	1,815,489,000	3.1	60	Standard Oil Co. (N. J.)	22,242,500	12,493,031,000	0.2
22	General Mills Inc.	49,000,000	524,678,315	9.3	74	Shell Oil Corp.	17,500,000	3,104,918,000	0.6
24	Kellogg Co.	46,000,000	366,000,000	12.6	101	Mobil Oil Co.	12,708,000	5,517,426,000	0.2
25	Campbell Soup Co.	44,000,000	712,785,000	6.2	106	Gulf Oil Corp.	12,000,000	4,185,253,000	0.3
28	Standard Brands Inc.	40,500,000	727,801,679	5.6	113	Texaco Inc.	11,000,000	4,008,053,779	0.3
32	National Biscuit Co.	38,300,000	627,300,000	6.1					
41	Corn Products Co.	32,000,000	552,774,000	5.8		**Soft Drinks**			
43	Borden Co.	31,000,000	1,385,518,426	2.2	16	Coca-Cola Co.	64,000,000	518,424,872*	12.3
45	Pillsbury Co.	27,000,000	470,046,502	5.7	30	PepsiCo Inc.	39,500,000	509,950,282	7.7
47	Quaker Oats Co.	25,500,000	360,000,000*	7.1	74	Canada Dry Corp.	17,500,000	170,856,000	10.2
49	Ralston Purina Co.	24,500,000	954,770,923	2.6	81	Seven-Up Co.	16,908,000	40,000,000*	**
55	Carnation Co.	23,000,000	539,924,018	4.3	94	Royal Crown Cola Co.	14,125,000	53,422,325	26.4
63	Pet Milk Co.	21,000,000	431,271,000	4.9					
66	Armour & Co.	20,500,000	2,064,847,000	1.0		**Paper Products**			
77	Swift & Co.	17,000,000	2,750,956,717	0.6	55	Scott Paper Co.	23,000,000	460,982,000	5.0
85	Nestle Co.	16,200,000	231,000,000*	7.0	77	Kimberly-Clark Corp.	17,000,000	622,529,000	2.7
90	Continental Baking Co.	15,275,000	524,936,394	2.9					
95	Hunt Foods & Industries	13,500,000	445,649,000	3.0		**Liquor**			
102	H. J. Heinz Co.	12,500,000	620,262,649	2.0	21	Distillers Corp.-Seagrams Ltd.	50,098,000	844,932,000	5.9
121	California Packing Corp.	9,000,000	478,972,000	1.9	52	Heublein Inc.	23,609,000	328,000,000	7.2
123	Morton International Inc.	8,000,000	123,018,781	6.5	54	Schenley Industries Inc.	23,252,000	460,762,963	5.0
					62	National Distillers & Chemical Corp.	21,370,000	829,031,000	2.6
	Soaps, Cleaners (and Allied)				68	Hiram Walker-Gooderham & Worts	19,775,000	529,014,945	3.7
1	Procter & Gamble	245,000,000	2,243,177,000	10.9					
6	Colgate-Palmolive	95,000,000	400,130,000	23.7		**Appliances**			
7	Lever Bros. Co.	90,000,000	456,300,000	19.7	10	General Electric Co.	75,000,000	6,213,600,000	1.2
50	S. C. Johnson & Son	24,250,000	175,000,000	13.8	20	Radio Corp. of America	50,700,000	2,057,117,000	2.5
111	Purex Corp.	11,500,000	176,123,729	6.5	40	Westinghouse Electric Corp.	32,773,000	2,389,909,000	1.4
					88	Sunbeam Corp.	15,500,000	306,758,854	5.1
	Tobacco								
12	American Tobacco Co.	71,000,000	1,231,628,708	5.8		**Chemicals**			
13	R. J. Reynolds Tobacco Co.	70,000,000	1,639,148,320	4.1	18	Du Pont	56,400,000	2,665,000,000	2.1
27	Brown & Williamson Tobacco Corp.	40,612,000	634,575,000	6.4	23	American Cyanamid Co.	46,785,000	708,528,000	6.6
31	Philip Morris Inc.	39,000,000	577,726,080*	6.8	51	Union Carbide Corp.	24,000,000	2,063,901,000	1.2
33	Liggett & Myers Tobacco Co.	37,000,000	478,261,072	7.7	67	Monsanto Co.	20,000,000	1,468,147,000	1.4
34	P. Lorillard Co.	36,460,000	479,046,310	7.6	87	Olin Mathieson Chemical Corp.	15,800,000	874,244,000	1.8
113	Consolidated Cigar Corp.	11,000,000	165,204,868	6.7					
123	General Cigar Co.	8,000,000	213,416,000	3.7		**Metals**			
					99	Aluminum Co. of America	12,982,000	1,165,596,256	1.1
	Drugs and Cosmetics				118	Reynolds Metals Co.	10,400,000	739,796,000	1.4
5	Bristol-Myers Co.	108,000,000	391,433,053	27.6					
10	American Home Products Corp.	75,000,000	627,579,550	12.0		**Airlines**			
15	Warner-Lambert Pharmaceutical Co.	64,500,000	383,837,000	16.8	72	Pan American World Airways	17,800,000	669,000,000	2.7
35	Alberto-Culver Co.‡	36,000,000	88,855,898‡	40.5	93	United Air Lines	14,622,000	792,759,000	1.8
36	Sterling Drug Co.	35,000,000	161,958,000	21.6	96	Eastern Air Lines	13,300,000	507,524,000	2.6
39	Miles Laboratories Inc.	33,000,000	137,557,638	24.0	97	Trans World Airlines	13,200,000	672,787,000	2.0
44	Johnson & Johnson	27,500,000	431,009,367	6.4	113	American Airlines	11,000,000	612,435,000	1.8
48	Revlon Inc.	25,200,000	206,703,003*	12.2	125	Delta Air Lines	7,915,000	257,460,000	3.1
58	Carter-Wallace Inc.	22,750,000	83,747,472	27.2					
69	Smith Kline & French Laboratories	18,500,000	202,446,000	9.1		**Photographic Equipment**			
71	Chas. Pfizer & Co.	18,000,000	287,598,000*	6.3	26	Eastman Kodak Co.	43,000,000	967,485,000	4.4
74	Chesebrough-Pond's Inc.	17,500,000	83,941,000	20.8	106	Polaroid Corp.	12,000,000	204,003,000	5.9
77	Richardson-Merrell Inc.	17,000,000	213,401,000	8.0					
82	Shulton Inc.	16,591,000	63,157,500*	26.3		**Others**			
84	J. B. Williams Co.	16,350,000	50,000,000*	32.7	8	Sears, Roebuck & Co.†	86,000,000	6,390,000,312	1.3
88	Plough Inc.	15,500,000	64,107,033	24.2	14	American Telephone & Telegraph	69,900,000	11,323,000,000	0.6
91	Block Drug Co.	15,000,000	36,000,000*	41.7	19	Gillette Co.	52,000,000	339,064,000	15.3
98	Avon Products	13,000,000	282,189,000	4.6	55	Stanley Warner Corp.	23,000,000	190,817,000*	12.1
100	Mennen Co.	12,800,000	52,000,000	24.6	61	Columbia Broadcasting System	22,200,000	699,732,483	3.2
102	Lehn & Fink Products Corp.	12,500,000	66,702,978	18.7	86	Armstrong Cork Co.	16,000,000	374,678,000	4.3
110	Noxell Corp.	11,600,000	31,226,014	37.1	104	American Can Co.	12,345,000	1,265,062,000	1.0
111	Norwich Pharmacal Co.	11,500,000	63,723,531	18.0	105	General Telephone & Electronics	12,129,000	2,035,621,000	0.6
122	Beecham Products	8,280,000	215,670,000	3.8	106	Philadelphia & Reading Corp.	12,000,000	288,366,000	4.2
					109	3M Co.	11,650,000	1,000,261,000	1.2
	Gum and Candy				116	Mattel Inc.	10,500,000	100,686,000	10.4
63	Beech-Nut Life Savers Inc.	21,000,000	201,000,000*	10.4	119	Eversharp Inc.	10,000,000	53,424,708	18.7
63	Wm. Wrigley Jr. Co.	21,000,000	128,555,210	16.3	120	International Telephone & Telegraph Corp.	9,095,000	449,800,000*	2.0
116	Mars Inc.	10,500,000	125,000,000*	8.4					
	Tires								
29	Goodyear Tire & Rubber Co.	40,000,000	2,226,256,469	1.8					
42	Firestone Tire & Rubber Co.	31,400,000	1,609,756,478	2.0					
46	U. S. Rubber Co.	26,800,000	1,225,516,000	2.2					
69	B. F. Goodrich Co.	18,500,000	980,122,000	1.9					

*Domestic sales estimated by AA. **No % of sales figures is listed, because the ad total is for Seven-Up whereas the sales estimate is for sales of the basic extract only, which is all the company sells. †Percentage shown would be more than doubled if Sears' $131,971,000 in local advertising were added to the $86,000,000 national ad total. ‡Sales for 10 months ended Sept. 30, 1965.

Note: All ad totals are domestic. Wherever possible, AA has reported the company's domestic sales figure in this table, although for some companies only a worldwide sales total was available.

Source: Reprinted by permission of the copyright holder, *Advertising Age*.

Finalizing the advertising budget

As noted through this chapter, there are a number of ways in which firms set their total advertising budgets. In deciding on this budget, however, it is important to consider the following points:

1. General business conditions.
2. Capacity of the plant involved.
3. Past sales of the article to be advertised and sold.
4. Number of competitors in the field.
5. Share of market for the company.
6. Present distribution system.
7. Importance of advertising in sale of product.
8. Price of the product and profit margin.
9. Amount of money which might be allocated for advertising.
10. The stage of the product cycle for the article.
11. Effectiveness of available appeals.
12. Possibility of measuring advertising results.

Checking the above list indicates that it is a complex problem to establish the advertising appropriation. As a result, most executives do not have a satisfactory basis for answering the question, "How much should we spend for advertising?" Although they may know, quite effectively, how to allocate the available advertising funds to various media and products, they are still seeking reliable techniques for determining accurately the overall effects of any campaign, or for measuring the effectiveness of their advertising in the total marketing mix of the firm.

Recommendation

Although the authors recognize the complexity of setting a satisfactory advertising budget, they have found the method listed below to be quite satisfactory for most organizations.

1. Analyze the sales of the prior comparable periods. The first step in planning advertising is to secure the sales figures of prior periods. A retail store might get an insight into the importance of the month's sales potential to annual sales volume. A company selling air-conditioning units might get its information on a seasonal basis. A company selling industrial equipment might find it more advantageous to use a yearly basis. Break this information down for the periods in the following manner:

    a. Actual sales in units.
    b. Average prices.
    c. Actual sales in dollars.

2. Set the period's planned sales goal. Appraise the unit and dollar market potentials and set the justifiable unit and dollar volume at which to aim for the period.

3. Decide on the amount which is needed for advertising. This amount will vary widely depending on such factors as line of business,

intensity of competition, broad goals, image of the company, and the like.

4. Set the period's total advertising media budget. Having established the period's planned sales goal and the amount to be spent for advertising, one is now ready to set the media budget. Put down the cost of television, radio, magazine, newspaper, direct mail, and all other advertising in an advertising budget as shown in Figure 16–3.

5. Allocate the amount among the company's products. Having decided on the total media budget, one must decide on the emphasis to place on the various commodity groups if the company sells a number of different products.

FIGURE 16–3
Advertising budget (summary)

Summary page no._____of_____   Budget page no._____
Company_____   For year_____
Date_____

Advertised products.	Market data—totals (*in company sales territory— for all industries*)		
		Last year	This year
	1. Potential units 2. Potential-dollars 3. Co. sales goal-units 4. Co. sales goal-dollars 5. %-adv. to sales goal		

Advertising program

Acct. Activity No. Units or media	Item totals		Activity totals	
	Last year	This year	Last year	This year
1–1 Newspapers 2–1 Television 3–1 Radio 4–1 Magazines 5–1 Customer service items 6–1 Direct mail 7–1 Paid space 8–1 Services from outside agencies 9–1 Exhibits 10–1 Display material 11–1 Art & engravings administration Total				

6. Decide how the media can be used most effectively throughout the period. The size of the media budget and the selling opportunities will be important factors in determining the timing of specific appeals and the general frequency pattern used.

7. Set up controls to show the actual record of use of advertising for the period in the media.

8. Provide some means of checking on the effectiveness of the advertising. This might include:

   a. Observing changes in sales.

   b. Counting number of inquiries.

   c. Measuring changes in attitude of customers.

While partial measurement of results is nearly always possible, one seldom is able to measure all of the effects of advertising. As an example, in a Fort Wayne, Indiana, study conducted by the Harvard Graduate School of Business it was pointed out that the consumer's image of a product is likely to be more influenced by actual usage than by any amount of advertising exposure. Yet, when advertising stops, awareness of a product decays. The study also indicated that "repetition of a message may heighten awareness of a new product without improving its image proportionately."

Progress being made in research would seem to indicate that within the next decade it will be possible to predict to a greater degree the effect of advertising on profits, and that it will be possible to use such predictions to design efficient advertising programs.

How much should be spent for advertising?

The total amount of the appropriation is the biggest question to be answered each year. There is no way of obtaining a precise answer as to what is the right amount. There is a great deal of confusion as to means of getting even an approximate answer. The most hotly debated issue is between the use of a fixed percentage of sales and the objective and task method. Both have some merit as a way of setting limits, but neither defines an optimum expenditure.

The percentage of sales method is responsive to several considerations. It recognizes that money spent for advertising eventually must come out of sales revenue, and that it must bear some relation to current sales, since advertising in legal and accounting terms is defined as a current expense. It may give expression to a desire to spend at the rate that is current among competitors. Most basically, it is a way of expressing what management thinks it can afford in relation to all of the other claims on current revenue.

The objective and task method rests on the assumption that the advertising department should determine what it needs, and that management should be willing to grant this amount after reviewing the evidence of need. It may be significant that this term generally gets abbreviated to the "task method" in conversations among advertising men. In any case, the great hazard is that the objective will be lost from sight. The fact tends to become obscured that it is the privilege and responsibility of management to set the objective and hence to determine the task. It is the proper function of sales and advertising executives to define the subobjectives for each product or market. These limited goals must be properly related to the overall marketing objective and this, in turn, to other objectives of management, such as those concerned with production, product research, and finance.

Economic theory as applied to advertising still provides the best conceptual framework for determining how much to spend, even though it is not possible to get an exact solution of the mathematical problem posed by theory. Simply stated, the principle is that the advertising budget should be raised to the exact level where the last dollar of advertising just pays for itself in additional profit. In practice it is not easy to locate this optimum point. It is usually possible, however, with respect to any given level of advertising to make a reasonable judgment whether returns from advertising would be increased or decreased by changing the amount. Logically, advertising expenditures should go up as long as they are in the range of increasing returns. If this can be accomplished product-by-product or market-by-market in combination with the rudiments of distribution cost analysis, the trend for the whole appropriation will be in the right direction. As in most other aspects of practical affairs, rational conduct does not lie in waiting for a perfect answer, but lies in constantly working for a better answer through step by step improvement. This approach to the determination of the advertising appropriation is consistent with the negotiational approach to budgeting.

Conclusions

1. The most important factor influencing the amount of the appropriation is the general marketing mix, which in turn is determined by the type of product, appeals available, the volume and margin, company policy, and related factors.

2. A good system of advertising budgeting is a two-sided affair that provides for a formal planning process which leads to an overall goal, with control procedures that enable management to assure that the objectives become results.

3. There is need for straighter, more businesslike thinking from minds freed from tacit acceptance of certain stereotypes of long standing, about so-called methods of setting appropriations that are not real procedures but merely formalized labels used and reused. These include average industry ratios used as standards in spite of faulty averaging, and ratio data that are questionable and not comparable.

4. Decide on the source of advertising funds. Is it feasible—and really worthwhile—to separate costs of advertising into (a) what produces goodwill, and (b) what helps produce actual sales volume and profits? If these can be separated, should they be separately charged— the goodwill producing a capital charge, the sales producing an annual cost out of income?

5. It should be decided whether the advertising appropriation should be for a fiscal period or a continuing period.

6. Distribute between advertising costs and direct selling costs the items on the border line to be sure of having an overall schedule with no item missing and with each allocated to one or the other.

7. For this overall budgeting, and particularly for selling and advertising expense budgets, any business is likely to benefit from techniques not implicit in the appropriation way of operation. Correlation, mathematical or graphic, and estimating equations are two ways of approximating these optimum ratios; and learning these ratios may lead to even more far-reaching changes in advertising and selling.

8. Some of the new techniques in program evaluation and review techniques offer advertisers great promise for the budgeting and control of advertising.

Questions

1. One plan for setting the advertising appropriation includes the following steps:
   a. Determine the objectives for the period.
   b. Plan the sales goals.
   c. Determine the percentage of sales that will be invested in advertising.
   d. Set the total advertising budget.
   e. Divide the amount among the different items.
   f. Decide on how this is to be spread among the media.
   g. Set the time periods for the advertising to appear.
   What recommendations would strengthen the above plan?

2. Many companies have a tendency to curtail advertising expenditures at the first sign of a depression or recession. Because of the reluctance of many firms to increase advertising appropriations at such times, it has been suggested that advertising reserves should be set aside in profitable years to be spent during such periods of depression. Comment.

3. Compare the objectives, control, and setting of a budget for a young married couple with that of the advertising budget for a corporation.

4. A local department store had used all its allocated budget for the period in question when the merchants' association of the city in which the store was located decided to hold some special sales days. What should the store do?

5. "In setting the appropriation, the firm should allow for a certain amount of flexibility." What is meant by this statement?

6. If you were requested by a client to let him know how much should be budgeted to introduce a new cereal on a national basis, what procedures would you adopt to give him an answer?

7. Why do you believe the drugs and cosmetics industries spend such a high percentage of the sales dollar for advertising?

8. At what time should the advertising appropriation be determined? Discuss.

9. The average selling cost (percent of sales) and percent of sales expended for advertising in a number of lines of business are listed on page 536:

Line of business	Average selling cost (percent of sales)	Percent of sales expanded for advertising
Automobile dealers	8.25	2
Burglar alarm services	5	2
Men's clothing	19	3.5
Electric heating appliances	9	3.5
Building materials	19	0.25
Office appliances	30	2.2
Grocery specialties	15.5	4
Proprietary medicines	15	10
Shoes (women's)	11	0.5
Shoe polish	25	10
Store fixtures	40	5

Indicate how the above percentage figures in the above lines of business would affect the setting of the budget.

10. An accounting executive made the following statement: "An advertising budget is best controlled through a job-costing procedure under which allowances, commitments, and actual costs are broken down and recorded by jobs or projects." Comment.

11. Under what conditions should an advertising budget be built for each unit of the company?

12. What advantages are gained by applying standard advertising budgets, which are developed by trade associations, to specific companies?

13. How does the organization structure of a company offset the placement of responsibility for the development of the advertising budget?

14. What administrative expenses would you recommend be included in the advertising budget?

15. Describe a procedure in determining an approximate break-even point for an advertising budget, when data are not available to calculate it mathematically.

Case   **LEO ELECTRIC COMPANY**
16–1   **Considering a detailed appropriation**

The Leo Electric Company had followed the policy of allocating 1 percent of planned sales as the lump sum to be spent on advertising each year, and had given the advertising department the responsibility for allocating this amount to individual projects.

This budgeting policy had been followed for the past ten years. However, about six months ago, John Gift was appointed treasurer of the company. Mr. Gift decided to adopt a new budget procedure and requested that the head of the advertising department submit a detailed appropriation prescribing the manner in which it would be expended.

Mr. Gift also asked the advertising head to indicate what percentage of the cost of the next year's advertising appropriation should be considered as a deferred expenditure. Mr. Gift believed that the next year's advertising and promotional campaign would benefit future periods and a part of these expenditures should, therefore, be charged against these periods. He wanted to correlate the advertising expenditures with the particular revenue secured from the advertising. "Otherwise," he said, "the advertising expenses for next year will be overstated, and the advertising expenses for future years will be understated."

Products

The Leo Company designs and manufactures both lighting fixtures which are directly connected to the permanent wiring system of a building, and lamps which serve the function of lighting fixtures but which can be plugged into existing outlets. The lamps manufactured by the company include desk, pinup, wall, pole, and tree lamps. The line of lamps consists of 150 designs and accounts for 52 percent of the company's sales. Most of the company's sales are concentrated in the medium-price field, although the line includes items which retail for prices ranging from $5 to $250.

Leo places great emphasis on styling and design, and emphasizes the development and use of interchangeable components which can be incorporated in many different styles of fixtures and lamps.

Marketing

The Leo Company sells most of its products in 15 eastern states. This is the company's principal market, and in the past fiscal year accounted for approximately 75 percent of sales.

The company has 15 full-time sales employees. Also serving the midwestern states which account for 20 percent of sales are 12 independent sales organizations employing 30 salesmen. All salesmen are paid a base salary plus commission. The independent sales organizations are compensated on a commission basis.

Leo's lamps are sold primarily through department stores, furniture stores, and lamp stores. The lighting fixtures are carried primarily by lighting fixture dealers and electricxal jobbers. In the last fiscal year, the company made sales to over 4,000 customers, none of whom accounted for more than 2.5 percent of its sales. A substantial portion of Leo's lighting fixtures is used in new construction. The company plans to place greater emphasis on the replacement and redecorating market in order to protect itself from any general decline in new construction which would adversely affect its sales and earnings.

The statement of income for the three years ending June 29, 19— is given on page 538:

Statement of income (year ending June 30)

(in thousands of dollars)

	Year A	Year B	Year C
Sales.............................	$5,500	$6,500	$8,200
Cost of sales	3,300	3,700	5,100
Gross profit	$2,200	$2,800	$3,100
Selling and admin. expenses..........	1,600	1,800	2,200
Income from operations	$ 600	$1,000	$ 900
General and other expenses..........	$ 100	$ 125	$ 125
Net income before federal income tax	$ 500	$ 875	$ 775

Competition

The lamp and lighting fixture industry is highly competitive. In the states where the company markets its products, it competes with a substantial number of larger manufacturers and numerous smaller companies.

As a result of this competition, the treasurer believed that a detailed appropriation for the advertising budget would help the company study and set its advertising objectives on a firmer basis. In order to accomplish these goals, he gave the advertising director the budget form in Exhibit 1, and asked him to complete it.

The advertising director disagreed with the concept of developing such a detailed budget. He emphasized that the cost and effort required in the preparation of such a budget would be excessive for any benefit which the company might realize.

He was afraid that once the budget was set it would become too inflexible, and shifting one specific appropriation to another use would be too difficult. In discussing the matter with the treasurer, he said "the competition in the industry is so intense that it just isn't realistic to firm in advance the exact percentage we are going to spend in each medium. Conditions change so rapidly in the industry and in specific markets that we are forced to place greater emphasis from time to time in an area to meet the competition. As an example, we had to give the retailers special cooperative advertising allowances last year in four Eastern cities because of special concessions our competitors had begun to offer."

The advertising director also disagreed with the treasurer's plan of deferring the cost of advertising. He stated, "there is no question that the current advertising will benefit future periods and should constitute an expense for these future years. However, I do not see how I can correlate a particular advertising expenditure with the revenue resulting therefrom. I believe the practical difficulties of setting a reasonable basis of amortization are too great to make it worthwhile for us to attempt this."

EXHIBIT 16–1
**Advertising budget report (classification for six-month period Jan. 1, 19—
to June 30, 19—)**

	Lamp division	Lighting fixture division
1. Administrative expense		
a. Salaries		
b. Traveling expenses		
c. Telephone and telegraph		
d. Supplies		
e. Postage		
f. Association dues		
g. Miscellaneous		
2. Consumer contacts		
a. Newspapers		
b. Magazines		
c. Radio		
d. Television		
e. Direct mail		
f. Outdoor		
g. Car cards		
h. Other		
3. Dealer helps		
a. Store and window displays		
b. Dealer signs		
c. Stationery		
d. Imprinting		
e. Electros and mats		
f. Other		
4. Trade contacts		
a. Trade papers		
b. Dealer house organ		
c. Direct mail		
d. Postage		
e. Other		
5. Mechanical		
a. Artwork, photographs		
b. Typography		
c. Engraving		
d. Other		
6. Miscellaneous		
Totals		
7. Percent of appropriation to be charged against the expenses of the following years:		
1974		
1975		
1976		
1977		
1978		

Case questions

1. Should the Leo Electric Company adopt the recommendations of the treasurer?
2. What are the objectives of advertising control?
3. Is a policy of allocating a percentage of planned sales to be spent on advertising realistic?
4. What method of accounting and appropriation should Leo company use for its advertising budget?
5. When is a policy of deferred advertising expense realistic?

Case
16–2

RULES, INC.
Planning a budget

Rules, Inc., is in the business of selling fashion wearing apparel and sportwear for adults by direct mail. For 55 years Rules has operated a specialty mail-order business. Rules serves selected customers, most of whom live in or near large metropolitan areas throughout the United States, and has over seven million customers who have purchased merchandise from it in recent years. In the last fiscal year, Rules had a sales volume of $86.5 million.

Products

Rules confines its merchandise offerings to men's and women's apparel, and present sales volume is divided almost equally between the two. The women's items include several types of dresses, knit suits and pant suits, casual fashions, sports outfits, nylon stockings and panty hose, bonded slacks, nightgowns and pajamas, jackets, coats and raincoats. Men's garments include a diversity of slacks, dress and sport shirts, sweaters, sport coats, car coats, raincoats, ties, socks, underwear, and shoes. Rules endeavors to maintain its styles and colors in keeping with current fashions and to make available a broad range of sizes. It follows a policy of offering quality merchandise at attractive prices.

All merchandise is designed and manufactured to Rules' specifications by a number of independent suppliers located throughout the country. Rules does not have any long-term contracts with its suppliers and is not dependent upon any single supplier. Company stylists and merchandising staff collectively review fashion submissions from apparel manufacturers and, working closely with these suppliers, assist in the design of the offerings that eventually reach the customer. Selections and specifications are set and deliveries of finished garments are planned to coordinate closely with these suppliers and the arrival of customer orders.

Marketing and distribution

Over the years Rules has developed its own customer lists. These lists are maintained with source and experience data in its computer system. The locating, testing, and developing of lists of new customers is a continuing activity of Rules.

All selling is done by means of carefully prepared direct-mail letters, colorful folders, and individual order forms which offer Rules merchandise. Each mailing presents a limited number of items. Rules does not issue catalogs.

Rules also offers its customers a seven-day free trial of all merchandise ordered. Full payment for the merchandise is due at the end of the free trial period. If payment is not made, Rules initiates a series of payment request letters and eventually places unpaid accounts into collection.

While Rules has experienced increased collection activity in recent years, due to its expanded sales volume, such increase has not been material and Rules' collection experience has been satisfactory over the years.

Rules maintains its own in-house direct-mail advertising department which creates, designs, writes, and directs the preparation of all selling material. Photography, artwork and printing are produced by outside suppliers. All orders are received at, filled, and mailed from, Rules' central facility and warehouses. Mail preparation—addressing, collating, enclosing, sealing, tying into bundles, sacking, and transporting to postal trucks for nationwide distribution—occupies a large number of people even though mailing operations are highly mechanized.

Rules maintains an extensive system of electronic data processing equipment for control functions in order processing, payroll, receivables, handling, inventory control, and other functions designed to reduce costs and provide improved customer service.

It has been Rules' practice to pay postage and handling costs on orders accompanied by full payment for the merchandise ordered, whereas such costs are borne by the purchaser if the merchandise is paid for after delivery. The Federal Trade Commission advised the company that it believes that, under these circumstances, the postage and handling costs constitute "finance charges" within the meaning of the Truth in Lending Act and the regulations thereunder, and Rules should make the disclosures required by those regulations and the act.

Postage rates

Rules uses the U.S. mails extensively, and its postage costs exceed $10 million per year.

Competition

Rules business is highly competitive, as it competes with other direct mail and catalog businesses, retail department and specialty stores, and discount stores, many of which have significantly greater financial resources than Rules.

Future plans

It was the opinion of the executives that Rules had reached its maximum sales potential with its current method of using direct mail as the major media. They also believed that the postal rates would continue to rise. As a result, they decided that they should consider setting up an advertising budget in which other media would be utilized.

The most difficult phase of the planning of the advertising budget was to determine the income from sales using the new media. This appeared to be quite complex to the executives because it involved unknown and imponderable factors. There was no past history of sales volume which could be used; yet, they did not want their estimates to be too conservative or too optimistic.

One of the executives recommended that they project the demand for their products which would result from the use of the new media over a five-year period. Another recommendation was to have each one of the executives prepare estimates of the volume which they believed might be received. While such a method is a composite guess, it was believed that these pooled estimates would be quite dependable.

It was the belief of another executive that the "batting average" of most forecasting is notoriously poor, and, as a result, he believed that they should simply allocate a given amount for the next year, and then try to determine from internal records what the results were.

Lastly, the controller recommended that Rules should set an objective of getting $5 million in sales from orders received from other media advertising and then arbitrarily allocate 10 percent of expected sales for general media advertising.

Case questions

1. How might Rules use economic and market forecasts in developing its media budget?
2. Who should be responsible for firming the marketing plan?
3. Should the advertising budget for the general media be fixed or variable? Give reasons.
4. For how long a period of time should the general media budget be set?
5. Establish a budget for Rules' general media and indicate what techniques you recommend to control it.

Case **HEURISTIC, INC.**
16–3 **Analysis of a budget**

The Heuristic Department Store is located in a city of 250,000 people and is one of the five major stores. Heuristic carries the classes of merchandise usually handled by such stores, including men's, women's, and children's wearing apparel and accessories, home furnishings, housewares, and appliances.

Heuristic does business on both cash and credit bases, and in the prior fiscal year, of the $9.65 million sales, 28 percent were cash sales and 72 percent were sales on credit.

The general character of the business done by Heuristic had not changed in the past three years. However, the company had an average increase in sales each year of about 2 percent during this period.

While it was the policy of Mr. Frank Anthony, the advertising manager, to work closely with each department head in planning the advertising appeals for the various departments of the store, it was his opinion that he had to decide on the amount that was to be allowed each department.

EXHIBIT 16–2
Heuristic, Inc. sales (by merchandise lines, 19—)

Sales by merchandise lines	Actual sales last fiscal year
Upstairs departments..........................	$ 500,000
Piece goods and household textiles	500,000
Small wares	1,000,000
Women's and misses' ready-to-wear	1,700,000
Accessories............................	1,800,000
Men's and boys' clothing and furnishings	1,000,000
Home furnishings........................	1,950,000
Miscellaneous (candy, books, etc.)..........	800,000
Basement store	900,000
	$9,650,000

Furthermore, he believed that he was best qualified to determine what media should be used.

Mr. Anthony followed the procedure of setting up the planned advertising budget for each department in the store about 45 days prior to the first business day of the month in which the advertising was to be placed. He then presented the recommended budget to the store manager for his general approval. After the budget was approved by the store manager, Mr. Anthony then consulted the department heads to determine what appeals they wished to use for their departments in the period under consideration.

In the middle of September, therefore, Mr. Anthony began to work out the planned advertising budget for the month of November. In Exhibit 2 the actual sales by merchandise lines, are given for the last fiscal year. In Exhibit 3 the expenses, by expense centers and by natural division, are given for the same year.

The store manager informed Mr. Anthony that he has set a goal for the current year to increase sales by 3 percent for the store and hopes to plan for 12 percent to be secured in November.

EXHIBIT 16–3
Heuristic, Inc. expenses (by expense centers and natural divisions)

Expenses by expense centers

Fixed and policy expense	$ 600,000
Control and accounting	100,000
Accounts receivable and credit	240,000
Sales promotion	395,000
Building operations	310,000
Personnel and employee benefits	265,000
Material handling	215,000
Direct and general selling	965,000
Merchandising	500,000
Total	$3,590,000

Expenses by natural divisions

Payroll	$1,820,000
Real estate costs	325,000
Advertising	270,000
All other	1,175,000
Total	$3,590,000

Case questions

1. Set up an advertising budget, by merchandise lines, for Heuristic for the month of November.
2. Divide this budget for each merchandise line into the following media:
    a. Newspapers.
    b. Direct mail.
    c. Television.
    d. Radio.
    e. Miscellaneous.
3. What controls might Mr. Anthony adopt to see that the advertising budget for each merchandise line will be properly used?
4. How might the procedure which Mr. Anthony follows be improved?

17
PLANNING THE CAMPAIGN

The advertising campaign is comprised of the correlation and combination of all the advertising and related efforts on behalf of a product or service, during a given time frame, and directed toward the attainment of one or more predetermined objectives. It is the long-range overall plan usually made up of a number of short-range plans or programs and goals.

The advertising campaign also can be considered as the cumulative sales effort; it should be consistent in all aspects throughout the time period in which it is used.

A campaign must be coordinated with the various parts of the marketing program if it is to be successful. That is, the various parts of the overall plan, such as consumer advertising, trade advertising, dealer cooperative advertising, and dealer point-of-purchase displays, must be carefully meshed with all other types of sales effort to attain full effectiveness. This means that the campaign must be correlated with the personal selling activities of the sales force, those of the various distributors of the product and their salespeople's activities, and with the various other promotional efforts which may be a part of the marketing mix.

Thus, in the broad sense, planning the advertising campaign is but one phase or part of planning the total marketing effort. And because any marketing plan must have definitely established goals and purposes, so also must the campaign be designed with certain definite goals or purposes in mind. The objectives of the campaign may be quite broad in scope, or may be quite specific. The purpose may be to stimulate primary demand for a product, or to build a brand preference. On the other hand, the program may be designed to educate customers to a new use of a product, to stimulate dealers, to teach consumers the correct pronunciation of a brand name, to elicit inquiries, or one of many other possible objectives that fits into the company's marketing strategy.

545

FIGURE 17–1
Illustrative ad

The Mercedes-Benz 280.
This year, some new American cars
look surprisingly like it.
On the outside.

56.7"

108.3"
195.5"

The original: the Mercedes-Benz 280 Sedan. Inspiration for other manufacturers' imitation.

The "Look-alikes" are here…sedans whose shapes and sizes are remarkably close to that of the Mercedes-Benz 280. It was bound to happen. We expected it. The silhouette may look the same, but that is where the similarity ends.

You simply can't make a car into a Mercedes-Benz by imitating its appearance. Or its interior. Or any other single element. You, the driver, can prove this to yourself. Test drive a 280 Sedan. Then put any of the newcomers through the same demanding test. The difference will be driven home. The *engineering* difference.

We don't fault others for trying to follow the lead of the 280. In fact, we applaud the move toward sensibly sized sedans. That's progress. But we really must question the idea that another car is like a Mercedes-Benz

Mercedes-Benz 280 grille.   *American "Look-alike" sedan grille.*

because it has a grille like one. Or a silhouette like one. An automobile either is a Mercedes-Benz, or it isn't.

The Emperor's new clothes

Look beyond the new suits of clothes that the imitators are sporting. It's the same old story.

Take the engine. You'll find little that's new. These cars may still offer you engines designed long ago. That may be hard to believe, but it's an engineering fact.

It's a different story with Mercedes-Benz. The contemporary engine in the 280 Sedan was designed specifically for the 280 Series; designed as an integral part of the automobile.

This modern, twin overhead camshaft engine directly meets demands of today's driving. It gives you fuel economy without sacrificing performance. No "Look-alike" domestic sedan has anything like the engine in a Mercedes-Benz 280. You'll instantly feel the difference on your first test drive.

No place to compromise

Look closely at the rear suspension on any of these "all-new" domestic sedans. They still feature simple wagon axles. The axles are one-piece and suspended by groups of leaf springs. When one rear wheel hits a bump, the other is jolted too.

Now look at the Mercedes-Benz 280. Its rear suspension is completely different. Each wheel has its own independent suspension system. That way, each wheel reacts to the road surface independently. This design—fully independent suspension—is also a safety feature. It gives you the security of control because it helps the standard radial tires stay on the road, where they belong.

Although 4-wheel independent suspension is far more expensive to engineer into an

automobile, it is the no-compromise way. And at Mercedes-Benz, we don't feel suspension and handling are places to cut corners.

The only way

The same can be said for brakes. Certainly no area to compromise. Here is one area where American sedans have made great strides. The "Mercedes-style" new cars you will see in 1975 will probably have disc brakes. But where? On the front wheels. Why are disc brakes confined to their front wheels?

We have no answer to that question. At Mercedes-Benz, we have designed 4-wheel disc brakes into all of our automobiles for years. Every wheel on every Mercedes-Benz has a disc brake to stop it—4-wheel disc brakes. We wouldn't engineer an automobile without them. At Mercedes-Benz, it's the only way.

You get what you pay for

To be sure, a Mercedes-Benz 280 is more expensive than the domestic newcomers that will try to challenge it. Consider the basic

The 280: independent rear suspension so a bump on the right can't jounce the wheel on the left.   *The "Look-alike:" wagon-type rear suspension so a bump on the right must jounce the wheel on the left.*

differences already mentioned. Add some others like safety engineering, resale value and the Mercedes-Benz commitment to quality. These are fundamentals you can't just "add on." In a Mercedes-Benz you get what you pay for.

More and more you hear about cars that have this or that "just like a Mercedes-Benz." But you don't make a Mercedes-Benz by just trying to copy it. The Mercedes-Benz 280 Sedan. Test drive one. See why a Mercedes-Benz has become the standard other manufacturers measure by.

Mercedes-Benz ⟨logo⟩
Engineered like no other car in the world.

The Mercedes-Benz 280 Sedan:
the standard the others measure by.

©Mercedes-Benz 1974

In Figure 17–1, Mercedes-Benz uses this ad to explain why its car is superior to those American cars that have copied its styling.

Factors influencing the planning of the campaign

Many factors influence the planning of the advertising campaign. While these are, of course, factors that are included in planning the overall marketing program, they also influence the advertising strategy. The exact sequence in which these factors should be considered will vary depending on individual circumstances. Some will even be evaluated simultaneously, since they are so closely interrelated, and should not be handled as independent variables.

Among the most important of the factors are:

1. *The organization:* its reputation, position in the market, financial strength, etc.
2. *The product:* the type of product, whether it is new or already established on the market, its differentiating features, the package, the product line
3. *The market:* the number and types of potential customers, their location, the total potential volume
4. *The competition:* number and strength of competitors, their advertising and marketing strategy
5. *The price:* absolute price of product, relationship to competitive prices
6. *The channels of distribution:* the number and types of distributors, their location, degree of cooperation currently obtained from them
7. *The sales force:* brochures and kits to be supplied, their activity in merchandising the advertising to the trade
8. *The budget:* the amount of money needed, the amount of money available
9. *The advertising theme:* the various appeals that might be used, the one appeal that will best meet the needs of the objective, the campaign keynote theme or idea
10. *The media:* the various media that would reach the potential market, the most appropriate type of media to use for this particular product and purpose, the appropriation to be allocated to various major media, the specific publications and radio and television stations most appropriate
11. *The advertising schedule:* the timing of ads, the frequency and size of ads to be run
12. *The dealer program:* the cooperative advertising, the point-of-purchase display materials, merchandising tie-ins, reproductions of ads to be supplied to dealers
13. *Correlation* of all phases of the program so that materials will be in the hands of retailers before campaign breaks, etc.
14. *Coordination* of all phases of program so the dealer and consumer advertising is properly timed, the advertising materials

will be provided salesmen and dealers when needed, and merchandise is in hands of retailers before campaign breaks
15.   *Government regulations and controls*

Planning the campaign

The actual planning of the advertising campaign for major companies will be a joint effort of the advertiser and an advertising agency, since the agency usually works very closely with the marketing division of the client, through the client's advertising manager. This is particularly true if the product is a new one being introduced to the market or is a product to be advertised extensively by the client for the first time.

So the advertiser, working with the account executive and the various appropriate people in the agency (such as the merchandising director, the research director, the production manager, the media director, and the head of the creative department)—possibly organized into some sort of plans board to handle the particular account —will begin by collecting and organizing all available data about the product and the market.

In small-sized companies, the proprietors can often get help from the media and agencies which specialize in smaller accounts. They may also get advice from suppliers, trade associations, and the like. Regardless of the size of the firm, however, the general procedures in planning the campaign will be somewhat similar.

Much information about the firm, the product, the competition, and the channels of distribution can be supplied by the company, although it may be necessary to obtain some information from other sources. In any event, the data on the 15 factors listed above will be collected and organized in such a manner as to throw the maximum amount of light on the problem at hand.

The market

Before any real planning can take place, many questions about the market or potential market for the product must be considered. It will be necessary to determine who the potential users of the product are and how many there are. If a new product is involved, the advertiser will want to know who will buy the product, who will use the product, and who will influence the decision to buy the product; just how the customer might use the product, and, hence, which features of the product are important to the customer; if the potential customers are men, women, or children, or some combination thereof; if age is of significance, and whether marital status has any importance. Will the product be bought only by people in high income brackets, or in specific occupations, or in various social strata? And finally, the advertiser will want to determine how often they may buy and whether they buy all during the year or only during one season of the year. If a product is already on the market, the advertiser will want to know the above information and, in addition, how competitors' brands share in the market.

The objectives of a campaign

Although, as noted earlier, it is difficult to give an exact sequence in which the individual decisions regarding the various factors involved are made, because of the close interrelationships of all facets of the campaign, it is probable that at this stage the advertiser would decide the objectives or purpose of the particular campaign. That is, it would be decided just where the advertising was to fit into the overall marketing program, and just what purpose the campaign was designed to accomplish. It is vital to determine quite early in the planning stage the specific objectives of the advertising program, since so many of the later decisions depend, to such a significant degree, on this factor.

Also to be noted is that in setting the objectives there is, in many instance, an underlying assumption that the maximization of profits through increased sales is the major purpose of the advertising campaign. However, there may be other objectives of even greater importance for a specific campaign. Listed below are some objectives which a company might wish to consider for a campaign.

1. Stimulating demand for the product through:
   a. Appealing to the person who buys the product.
   b. Appealing to the person who influences the person who buys the product.
   c. Emphasizing new uses of the product.
   d. Emphasizing more frequent use of the product.
   e. Attracting a new class of consumers.
   f. Providing better services.
   g. Extending the territory in which the product is sold.
   h. Offering combined sales with other products.
   i. Developing new distribution techniques.
   j. Giving easier credit terms.
2. Building a "family" concept for the products which the company manufactures.
3. Using the "hitchhiker" tactic for a new variety of a product debuting under an old, established brand name.
4. Extending the brand image of the company.
5. Meeting the strategies of competitors.
6. Influencing the dealers to "push" the product more extensively.
7. Changing the buying season for a product.
8. Developing a new image for the company.
9. Educating the public about the product use.
10. Building a broad general public relations program.
11. Informing the public what the actual product being sold is.

While these are only a few of the various objectives which the advertiser might set for a campaign, they indicate a number of the types of goals which various companies have set.

There are, of course, parameters on such goals—set by company tradition, product mix, competitive position, and just plain consumer habit—which place limitations on the possible scope of these. There is a fundamental marketing maxim in this sort of strategy of brand-image-sales management objectives: When consumer tastes are changing, the product itself must change with them, but the established image must be revamped in such a way that the changes appear to be only normal evolution.

It is generally more effective for the advertiser to limit the campaign to a specific purpose. By pinpointing the advertising efforts to one objective, the firm will be able to control the advertising and, at the same time, be able to measure the results of the approach that has been used.

Setting the budget

In general it is advisable when the study of the market has projected the scope of the task involved, and the purpose indicates just what is to be done by the advertising, to determine at that time how much money will be required to do an effective job and how much money may be available for the program. It should be kept in mind that the amount of money appropriated will be influenced by many of the other factors involved in planning the campaign, and at the same time will, in turn, influence many of the other decisions, such as the media to be used, the number, frequency, and size of advertisements, and other related factors. Thus again, the close interrelationships of the decisions on each phase of the campaign planning become evident; hence, the difficulty in setting up a specific sequence of steps to be taken in the planning of the campaign.

The appeal or theme

Once the objective and the budget have been determined, the advertiser should review the data collected on the various factors discussed up to this point. Then, on the basis of all the known information about the product, the market, the customers, and the objectives, the advertiser would consider just what appeal or appeals would be the most effective in achieving the desired results. It is quite probable that a study would be made using motivation research, since this method is a satisfactory one to use in determining just why people buy certain products or brands and, hence, makes it possible to determine an effective appeal in stimulating sales.

It should be stressed that the research study will not actually produce the campaign theme or keynote idea. Research will produce the basic information regarding possible appeals or themes that could be effective in stimulating the consumer. But the actual selection of the theme, as well as putting it in its final form, is the work of the creative thinking of one or several people, often the copywriters, who devote much of their effort to creative thinking in order to evolve new and effective themes. For instance, one of the interesting copy themes which American Telephone and Telegraph Company uses for its Yellow Pages is "Let Your Fingers Do The Walking." This keynote concept gets the message across in a challenging manner and has been used effectively in both print and broadcast media.

In a similar vein, it will be noted that a successful advertising campaign is built around one central idea, or theme, which is normally carried throughout all the advertising, whether printed or broadcast, all promotional materials, and usually is also the main theme of the salesmen's presentations.

In other words the "one sell" concept requires a single basic selling proposition that can be treated visually and audibly so as to enable it to be used in other marketing areas, such as equipment, packaging, public relations, promotion, and sales. At the same time this basic idea should be of such a nature that it can be supported by subordinate concepts and presentations which will make it more motivating and more acceptable.

Listed below are examples of some keynote ideas which have been used in various campaigns:

1. *Get as close as you want.*
        Polident
2. *Where the future is now.*
        Metropolitan Life
3. *If you don't have the blades, you don't have the shave.*
        Gillette
4. *We believe quality can be beautiful.*
        Whirlpool
5. *The night time pain reliever.*
        Excedrin P.M.
6. *We've got your plug.*
        Champion
7. *Built better, not cheaper.*
        Kitchen Aid
8. *Maybe we can help.*
        The Travelers
9. *It gives you back your smile.*
        Dentu-Creme
10. *Extra care in engineering makes a difference.*
        Dodge
11. *The friendly skies of your land.*
        United Airlines
12. *The typewriter of the cartridge age.*
        Smith-Corona
13. *For virtually spotless dishes.*
        Cascade
14. *Does she or doesn't she?*
        Miss Clairol Cream Formula
15. *You've come a long way, baby.*
        Virginia Slims

16. *People you can count on.*
    Mutual of Omaha
17. *In more cars, on more corners.*
    Delco Batteries
18. *Progress for people.*
    General Electric
19. *We're looking for a few good men.*
    The U.S. Marines
20. *The quality goes in before the name goes on.*
    Zenith
21. *See how much car your money can buy.*
    Toyota
22. *The dependability people.*
    Maytag
23. *Creators of the indoor world.*
    Armstrong
24. *The best part of a puppy's day.*
    Purina Puppy Dinner
25. *The anti-gas antiacid.*
    Di-Gel

The media

On the basis of the knowledge obtained previously about the market to be covered, the people to be influenced, the funds available, and the appeal to be used, the advertiser should be able to determine what media will be best for this particular campaign. Since the relative advantages and disadvantages of the various media and the general principles governing the selection of media have already been discussed at some length in prior chapters, they need not be discussed further here. At this point, the types of media to be used will be determined, and the allocation of appropriated funds to each type of media will be decided. After the media have been selected, the specific media must be chosen. That is, if the major media are to be magazines and newspapers, the advertiser will determine which particular magazines and newspapers will best meet the needs of the particular campaign.

The schedule

When the media have been selected, the advertiser should then proceed to draw up a detailed schedule for each of the individual media involved to submit to the account executive for approval. In planning the schedule, a number of variables must be considered. Among these are such factors as coverage of the particular publication or station, size of the advertisement, frequency with which advertisements will be run, and timing.

These must be considered not only for each specific medium being used but also as related to the various other individual media that may be in use, and, of course, always with relation to the specific purpose of the particular campaign being planned.

One of the most difficult problems in scheduling the advertising for a specific medium, say a magazine, is that of the relation of the size of the advertisements and the frequency with which ads shall be run, or space size and frequency of insertion. The space size is significant from the standpoint of impact of reader impression; while frequency is important from the standpoint of the continuity of reader impressions. Although larger space usually obtains a stronger short-run visual impact, it often does not obtain an increase in attention proportional to the increased size. And, of course, the larger the space taken for the individual insertion, the less frequency of insertion that can be obtained with the amount of funds appropriated for the particular medium. The advertiser must, therefore, attempt to obtain the best compromise between size and frequency for his particular campaign.

In reaching this compromise, the advertiser must consider virtually every factor that enters into advertising, including object of the program, appropriation, nature of the medium, characteristics of the readers, kind of product, degree of acceptance of the product, competition, and planned duration of the campaign. For example, if the purpose of the campaign is the speedy introduction of a new product, it is probable that best results will be obtained by the use of large space at the beginning of the campaign in order to obtain strong initial impact. But if the purpose is to stimulate repeat purchases of a well-known convenience good that is bought very often, frequency of insertions might be more important than large space for impact.

The other main problem in scheduling is that of timing the advertising. Timing includes the selection of the months, weeks, or seasons of the year when the advertisements will be run; and the days of the week for the advertisements to be used in newspapers, radio, or television. Here again, many factors, such as the objective of the campaign and the buying habits of the customers for the particular product, will influence the strategy of timing the advertising.

If the product involved has definite seasonal peaks in sales, such as the graduation gift period and the Christmas gift period in the case of watches, much of the advertising might be concentrated in the weeks ahead of these two periods, with the appearance of the advertisements so timed as to achieve maximum cumulative effect for these two heavy buying periods. And if the product has differing sales periods in different parts of the country, due to the influence of weather, the timing would involve running the advertisements at different times in the various parts of the country. Thus, if the campaign for a lightweight suit was being run in newspapers, the advertising might appear considerably earlier in the southern part of the country than in the Midwest or in the New England states. And the advertiser of a food specialty product would face the problem of whether to have the advertisements appear on the same day of the week as the heavy supermarket advertising appears, or to run them on the alternate days when the advertisements would not compete with so much price advertising.

The competitive situation also may influence the timing of a campaign, since if most competitors have developed a particular pattern of timing an advertiser may elect, for strategic reasons, to adopt a somewhat different timing pattern, such as starting the campaign earlier in the season, or allocating some of the funds to an off-season program of advertising.

It must be remembered that the buying periods of dealers usually are several months ahead of buying periods for consumers. Thus the timing of the advertising directed to dealers should take this factor into consideration. The advertising directed at the dealer must appear sufficiently ahead of the consumer advertising to achieve its desired effect of having the dealer stock the item, or the entire consumer campaign may well be rendered ineffective.

When the above decisions regarding the scheduling of the advertising have been worked out, the advertiser will draw up a detailed media schedule. This would show in detail the names of the specific media to be used, the size of the advertisements to be run (or length of time periods for broadcast media, or duration of showing in the case of outdoor signs or car cards), the dates on which the advertisements are to appear, the costs, and any other pertinent information. After this detailed schedule has been approved, the actual insertion orders can be prepared and the work of preparation of individual advertisements can begin.

The dealer program and promotional activities

During the period when the above decisions on media and allied problems have been under consideration, the advertiser should be making decisions regarding the details of the dealer portion of the campaign. Decisions should be made on whether or not dealer cooperative advertising will be a part of the campaign, what advertising will be directed at the dealers, what types of point-of-purchase display materials are to be provided for the dealers, whether reproductions of media advertisements will be utilized in dealer display materials, what brochures or kits of advertising materials are to be provided for the salespeople to use in their activities, what materials will be provided for dealers' salespeople, and whether any direct action stimuli (such as sampling, premiums, introductory price offers, or contests) are to be used in the marketing campaign. For example, if the advertiser's salespeople are to use kits of advertising (including the detailed schedules of appearance of the advertisements and actual reproductions of the advertisements to appear in national magazines, as is often done), in their selling program to obtain stocking of the product by the dealers before the consumer advertising appears, it will be necessary to have the detailed advertisements created very early in the program. Thus the time at which the artists and copywriters must finish their work, and the production department of the agency must have advertisements actually produced, will depend on the decisions regarding salesforce activities and use of advertising reproductions.

Summary

In summarizing some of the concepts involved in campaign strategy, the authors wish to emphasize that there are a number of important factors which must be considered.

As an example, Company X makes men's dress shirts and sport shirts along with pajamas, underwear, and sweaters. The company is one of the three largest sellers in the shirt field, uses national distribution, and concentrates its advertising on dress and sport shirts.

The consumers recognize that Company X offers good quality, style, and value. For many years, the officers believed that by adding more style, they could provide the glamorous image that would reflect product improvements. However, the growth of consumerism (in which such features as tumbled dry, durable press, and other features have become more important) has changed the situation so that the short-term and long-term objectives have become more divergent.

To set the campaign strategy Company X should evaluate the following factors:

1. Study the products and determine what characteristics or features to emphasize. (Should company emphasize contemporary styling, durable press, color combinations?)
2. Evaluate the market conditions and decide who the buyers of the product are and who influences the buyers. (To what extent do the wives influence their husbands in the purchase of shirts? How would this be decided if the emphasis is on color combinations?)
3. Look at how the product is being distributed and consider the best ways of utilizing the channels of distribution. (To what extent are the shirts presold? How effective can the salesmen in the retail store be in reaching the buyer?)
4. Determine what the plans of competition will be for the ensuing period, but do not allow this competition to dominate your planning. (Will the competition emphasize style and color?)
5. Ascertain in what stage of the product cycle the product is at the current time. (The changes in style are still somewhat limited. Company X's products are in competitive stage.)
6. Review past advertising, sales figures, and market trends.
7. Correlate the planned campaign objectives with the long-term goals of the company.
8. Set the advertising budget on the basis of the objectives or purposes of the campaign.
9. Decide on the keynote appeal for the campaign.
10. Check on the media that can be used for the campaign.

Questions

1. In evaluating the strategy to use in an advertising campaign, one finds that few competing brands and products spend their advertising media allocations in the same proportions. Indicate how this should be considered.

2. A major advertising study concluded that the customers harbor resentment when they are subjected to information which carries no useful meaning for them. How might this conclusion affect the planning of a campaign?

3. What is the relationship of the advertising campaign to the marketing plan?

4. Contrast the planning of a campaign for a product with that of a political campaign.

5. How would the planning of a campaign for a local retailer differ from planning a campaign for a manufacturer distributing a product on a national basis?

6. From a current issue of a general magazine find five advertisements which contain keynote ideas revealing strong creative insights which you believe are effective for a campaign.

7. An executive, in planning strategy for a campaign, recommended to the advertising department that it use a simulation method. It was his opinion that mathematical techniques could be applied to sift through the many different strategies which might be used. Comment.

8. Since the attitudes which people form toward products seem to be more dramatically influenced by actual usage and experience, it is difficult to develop a scientific approach to planning campaign strategy. Comment.

9. Develop a step-by-step procedure that you believe an advertising agency should follow in planning a campaign for a product.

10. How should a company decide whether or not it should vary the keynote theme in a campaign?

11. Assume that you are the account executive for a major advertising agency handling the following accounts:
    a. Polident (a preparation for cleaning dentures).
    b. Eversharp (new safety razor blades).
    c. A patent medicine.
    d. A major piece of industrial equipment which is manufactured on order and will cost from $100,000 to $200,000 per unit.
    Indicate what procedures you would recommend that the advertisers use to plan a campaign for each of these products including the selection of the keynote theme.

12. Although advertisers can use past experience, the way in which this can be correlated to the planning of current advertising strategy may be difficult to attain, because present problems are unique to the product, the company, and the competition. Comment.

Case **CARRIER CORPORATION**
17–1 **"City Lights" case history**

The largest division of the largest corporate complex in the air-conditioning industry, Carrier Air Conditioning Company, markets total comfort. The product mix is the diverse—room air-conditioners, residential units, furnaces and related products, large refrigeration systems for commercial applications, and gigantic systems for skyscrapers and superstructures. Of these, the residential division has the largest consumer advertising program. Attention is focused on a single product—the Round One (a central air-conditioning unit for the home).

Carrier manufactures the only round central residential condensing unit in the industry, and since the time of its introduction it has given the owner four important benefits: (1) it is economical to operate, (2) it is efficient, (3) it blows the hot exhaust air upwards instead of across the lawn, thus not killing the grass and shrubs, and (4) it is unusually quiet.

In the spring of 1973, with the advertising program just getting under way, the Carrier advertising and marketing departments scheduled meetings with its agency, N. W. Ayer, to structure the strategy for 1974.

The agency assignment was as follows (excerpts from the Marketing Report from the agency to the company):

"(1) Identify Carrier as the manufacturer of the highly-efficient Round One in a way which separates it from competition in the consumer's mind.

(2) Provide a means of provoking consumer contact with Carrier dealers.

"That is the assignment. Our purpose: to position Carrier's Round One as highly efficient. As for programming, we propose an expanded television campaign for 1974 to carry the main advertising burden for the "Round One." And we will back this up with a print program with strong merchandising pluses for the distributor/dealer trade.

"For the Round One, we are preparing one 30-second TV commercial which will be delivered over all three major networks a total of 28 times during the Spring [see Exhibit 17–1]. That same commercial will also be made available to some 5,000 Carrier dealers in a form that identifies each as the soure of the unique Round One.

"This is the way national and local advertising work best—together. The national program puts the Round One into the mass mind with a very special idea. The local one seizes upon that special national advertising idea and identifies the individual dealer by name and location as the one man to call. This is the way leads develop. And leads are the life blood of every dealer's business. [Two examples of local advertising on the national theme are given in Exhibits 17–2 and 17–3.]

"We are also preparing two four-color print advertisements on the Round One for use in a selected list of magazines.

"In addition to TV and magazines, we will produce a special radio commercial on the Round One, set to music, which dealers can adapt with any special offer they want.

"The 38GS Compact unit [a price-oriented builder model] will get some limited support in print advertising during 1974.

"This is part of the marketing plan to inform consumers that Carrier has equipment to meet every family budget.

"Our advertising thrust with the Compact will be confined to magazine appearances. And our creative strategy will be to offer it as an efficient, Carrier-quality unit at surprisingly low price."

In support of the program, three storyboards were submitted to the advertising department. Of the three, the most dramatic was one featuring the efficiency of the Carrier round unit in terms of the amount

EXHIBIT 17–1

N W Ayer ABH International

1345 Avenue Of The Americas, New York, N. Y. 10019

CLIENT	CARRIER AIR CONDITIONING DIVISION	PROGRAM	SPORTS & NEWS
PRODUCT	"ROUND ONE" RESIDENTIAL UNIT	FACILITIES	NETWORKS
TITLE	"LIFE OF THE PARTY"	DATE	SPRING,
NUMBER	XCLX0076 FOR PRODUCTION	LENGTH	30 SECONDS

VIDEO		AUDIO	
1.	OPEN ON NIGHTTIME PARTY SCENE VIEWED THROUGH SLIDING GLASS DOORS. SPOKESMAN OPENS DOOR AND STEPS OUT ONTO PATIO. CAMERA PULLS BACK AS HE WALKS FORWARD TO STAND BESIDE CARRIER'S AIR CONDITIONING UNIT, "THE ROUND ONE."	1.	SFX -- PARTY SOUNDS, MUSIC ANNCR: (O.C.) Want to meet the real life of the party? It's right here . . . Carrier's Round One . . . the most attractive central air conditioning unit you buy . . . and one of the most efficient.
2.	CUT TO CU OF SPOKESMAN AGAINST NIGHT SKY.	2.	Fact is, if all the others in the country ran as efficiently as this one . . .
3.	CUT TO SPOKESMAN AS HE TURNS AND WALKS TO EDGE OF PATIO WHERE WE SEE THE LIGHTS OF LOS ANGELES SPREAD OUT BELOW HIM.	3.	there would be enough electricity saved this year, we estimate, to power Los Angeles every night for six months. To find out what the Round One can save you,
4.	SUPER LOGO -- "Carrier -- Number one air conditioning maker" -- OVER SCENE OF CITY LIGHTS AND HOLD.	4.	(V.O.) call your Carrier Dealer.

F-440

s1/1464

---

of electricity that could be saved to light the city of Los Angeles; it was referred to as the "City Lights" commercial.

The Carrier national print ad was scheduled to run in the *National Observer, Time, U.S. News, Sports Illustrated,* and *Newsweek.* (See Exhibit 4.) It was conceived entirely by the creative department at

EXHIBIT 17–2

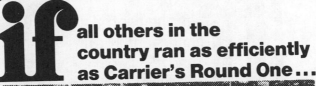

EXHIBIT 17–3

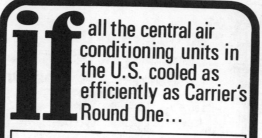

if all the central air conditioning units in the U.S. cooled as efficiently as Carrier's Round One...

CENTRAL AIR CONDITIONER

Carrier

we figure that enough electric energy would be saved this year to power the city of

day and night for the next

months

Start today to beat the high cost of living and call us for a free survey.

JONES AIR CONDITIONING

1001 MAIN STREET
Phone: 8143696

Insert your city photo here

Insert city name here

 years

Insert number of months or years here

Put your name, address & phone here

EXHIBIT 17–4

If all others could
cool as efficiently
as this one...

If all central air conditioning systems used to cool homes in the U.S. could only cool as efficiently as the Round Ones, by Carrier, there would be enough electric energy saved this summer to light the city of Los Angeles...every night...*for six months!*

That's a point worth considering when you weigh the merits of air conditioning your home against rates for electric power and surcharges for additional uses.

The long-term savings built into the Round One look better and better as the economic climate changes.

It still makes sense to air condition your home...perhaps more than any other home improvement you may make. It's a high return investment rather than an expense. But just make sure to consult a local expert—your Carrier Dealer. His free home survey alone is an important first step to having the most comfortable house on the block, and electric bills you can live with.

You'll find him listed in the Yellow Pages.

Number One
Air Conditioning
Maker

Carrier

Division of Carrier Corporation

N. W. Ayer. The Carrier advertising manager discarded the other two commercials, presented the commercial to Carrier management, and finally to corporate management where it was approved in September. The agency bid out the job and the production company scheduled the filming for October. Los Angeles was selected because it has a stable climate for the fall production schedule. The first TV appearance was scheduled for early March. However, between those dates, the President appeared on television twice telling the American people that the energy problem was now an energy crisis and that we, as Americans, had become much too dependent on such luxuries as air-conditioning. This specific reference to air-conditioning as a luxury and, indirectly, the inference that it was a heavy user of energy alarmed Carrier Corporation management enough that in December, the day the shooting was completed, they withdrew their support of the program in the belief that the commercial, instead of persuading, would produce a negative impact and could be a political football, thereby damaging not only the company but the entire industry. The Carrier advertising manager adopted a wait-and-see policy to determine whether this decision would be sustained leaving the company with no alternative.

Early in February it became apparent that decision would stand, therefore a substitute commercial was produced and a new print campaign was hastily submitted and approved. The kickoff TV appearance was not color corrected and, of course, the dealer support commercials were offered to the field too late to be useful.

In May 1974, the big news was Watergate and the energy crisis had reverted to an energy problem again and, although the situation was still critical, the ominous overtones faded away. Therefore, the agency recommended that since efficiency was still a sound story Carrier should use the City Lights commercial as the focus of its 1975 advertising program. There would be an adaptation of the commercial available to be used locally on TV and in newspapers. (See Exhibit 5.) Both managements concurred and the program was implemented. A formula was worked out by the Carrier engineering manager of consumer products in conjunction with a representative of a national utility research group. This formula was to allow the Carrier dealers around the country to tie into the national advertising program with a local savings and efficiency story inasmuch as both would vary with the district.

Probably the most unique part of this program, besides the White House influence on the direction of an advertising program, was the development of the formula dramatizing the efficiency of the Carrier round units. Accuracy was essential not only to meet the internal critical standards at Carrier but also for the networks and clearances, and to answer any questions from investigative agencies. The steps, briefly, were as follows:

a. Ayer creative took the ARI* directory and classified all residential central air-cooled units into five groups according to capacity.
b. ARI estimated the total number of units in each of these groups

* American Refrigeration Institute.

EXHIBIT 17–5

Date: 3/14/75   Subject: 1975 CONSUMER NATIONAL ADVERTISING   Dept: ADVERTISING
LOCAL TIE-IN PROMOTIONAL PROGRAM

Number: Author: THOMAS CAMPBELL

To help you tie-in locally with our 1975 Consumer National Advertising, we're making available the following items:

(1) AD REPROS

    (A) <u>Localized "City Lights" Ad</u> (5 columns X 9-1/8 inches)

        This ad repro is a local adaptation of the "City Lights" ad currently running in leading consumer publications (<u>The National Observer</u>, <u>Newsweek</u>, <u>Time</u>, etc.). You simply insert the name of your local city along with the number of months (or years) of electricity that can be saved. Use the formula we provide to compute the amount of power savings for the city you want to use.

        We recommend that the photo you show in this ad be a night scene of the city with an easily identifiable landmark. Check with the Chamber of Commerce, local newspapers, or photo studios for such a photo. If you cannot find an appropriate photograph, you can use a night shot of any large city or even adapt the photo from the existing consumer ad.

        You may also wish to make this repro a dealer listing ad and add a paragraph or two at the end about the Lions Share Promotion.

    (B) <u>Smaller "City Lights" Ad</u> (2 column X 9-1/8 inches)

        This is a smaller size version of the ad repro described above, and the same instructions apply. We suggest you run this ad a number of times in order to achieve maximum impact.

    (C) <u>"House Lights" Ad</u> (2 column X 7 inches)

        This ad is a print adaptation of our current "House Lights" TV commercial. The point made in this ad is that Carrier's Round One can save enough electricity cooling a house all day to pay for the lights burned in the house at night. You may wish to run this ad as an extension of Carrier's "House Lights" TV commercials, or independently as part of your local power-saving story.

(2) FORMULA SHEET

    An instruction sheet, this explains in detail how to compute the energy savings for any city in the United States. Just follow the instructions step-by-step, and coming up with the correct energy saving figures for your area should be just a matter of arithmetic.

M616 (6/74)

EXHIBIT 17–5 (*concluded*)

1975 CONSUMER NATIONAL ADVERTISING

(3)   NATIONAL AD

    This is a facsimile of the consumer print ad, "City Lights," currently running in leading national consumer publications.

(4)   TV COMMERCIAL SCRIPTS

    (A)   One script of the 30-second "City Lights" ("Life of the Party") TV commercial.

    (B)   One script of the 30-second "House Lights" TV commercial.

(5)   "CITY LIGHTS" RADIO SCRIPTS

    Copies of suggested 30- and 60-second radio commercials tied in with and patterned after the ad repros mentioned above. As with the ads, you simply insert the name of your local city along with the number of months (or years) of electricity saved. Ten seconds are left at the end of each script to include your own local dealer tag.

(6)   NATIONAL ADVERTISING SCHEDULE

    A handy chart listing Carrier's 1975 National Consumer Advertising Schedule for both print and TV. Refer to this schedule regularly to tie-in your local promotional campaigns with the national ones.

That's the entire local tie-in promotional program in a nutshell. All that's needed now to make it successful is your personal expertise and hard work. And to add extra strength to the whole program, there are two television commercials available now in Literature Distribution. The dealer version of the network commercial, "City Lights," and a special one created for local use called, "House Lights." Each is 30 seconds long and allows a full 7 seconds of dealer identification at the end. The commercials are on separate reels and are priced at $10 each, subject to co-op. Order numbers are 838-129 for "City Lights" ("Life of the Party") and 838-130 for "House Lights."

TC/jm^c v

Thomas Campbell

shipped between 1963 and 1973 from an estimated 3.1 million total units in the United States.

   c.   Again using the ARI directory, they determined the actual wattage rating of the best unit within each capacity group built by each of 53 competitors.

   d. These numbers were averaged and then compared with the average wattage of the top ten Carrier round ones within the same capacity groups.

   e. As an example, in the 22,000 to 28,000 BTU† group, the top competitive units averaged 3,175 watts; the average for Carrier's top ten was 2,230 watts. The difference obtained for that size group is 927 watts.

   f. It was then determined by a combination of U.S. Air Force figures and the comfort indices for major cities compiled by the U.S. Weather Bureau that these units operated an average of 1,200 hours per year, but that figure was lowered to 1,000 to be on the conservative side.

   g. The final input came from the Los Angeles Department of Water and Power. It estimated that the total amount of power needed to run the city from 6:00 A.M. to 6:00 P.M. for six months was 3,614,630 KWH.

   h. It was possible to establish that if all the central residential units in the country operated as efficiently as the Carrier round one, there would be 7,917,200 KWH of power saved—enough to run the city of Los Angeles for one year. It was decided, however, to use only six months—partly for conservatism so as not to overstate and run the risk of losing some credibility, but also if there were a miscalculation, to err on the safe side.

Case question

1. In a down year for building construction and business recession, evaluate the theme and the program in maintaining Carrier's position and share of market.

Case   **STERLING DRUG INC.**
17–2 **Responsibility in advertising**

   Sterling Drug Inc. was started on May 14, 1901, under the name The Neuralgyline Company. Its first employees were the two founders; now there are more than 15,000 men and women on the Sterling payroll. The first year's sales amounted to $10,000; sales today are in the vicinity of $300 million a year.

   The founders were young men who pooled their talents, resources, enthusiasm, and hopes. W. E. Weiss, a pharmacist, and A. H. Diebold, his friend from high school days in Sistersville, West Virginia, started—appropriately as history was to prove—with a pain reliever called Neuralgine as their only product.

   In the first year, Neuralgine was promoted by means of roadside signs nailed to fences and trees in the Wheeling area. In 1902, the management adopted an advertising budget of $10,000, an amount equal to the entire sales volume of 1901. Virtually the entire advertis-

---

† British Thermal Unit.

ing appropriation was earmarked for expenditure in mass media in the form of two Pittsburgh newspapers. Sales increased, and the market was expanded from a local community affair into one of national dimensions and, decades later, of world scope.

The years went on and the business prospered. In 1917, the Neuralgyline Company name was dropped, and the business became known as Sterling Products Incorporated, the Sterling name, incidentally, coming from Sterling Remedy Company, one of the enterprises acquired in the early years.

When the United States entered World War I, the Alien Property Custodian seized the properties of enemy aliens. Among these properties were the shares of the Bayer Company of New York, Inc., which were owned at that time by aliens who had sought to establish a business in the American market.

A month after the 1918 Armistice, the government offered the Bayer stocks for sale at public auction to the highest American bidder. To the successful bidder would go a large plant, a relatively little known product called aspirin, a substantial number of physicians' drugs, and a line of dyestuffs.

Many American firms were interested in acquiring Bayer, including Sterling, which saw in Bayer aspirin a product of genuine promise. Moreover, the Bayer business could provide the vehicle for diversification into the pharmaceutical field. The management asked itself: How much could Sterling afford to pay for Bayer? In their earlier years, the founders had had the courage to invest almost half their capital to acquire a business, now entirely forgotten, and to create an advertising budget equal to the previous year's entire sales. Now they decided to bid, if necessary, as much as their own business had earned in the almost 18 years of its existence up to that time.

More than 100 American firms participated in the bidding, which started at $1 million. When the auctioneer for the U.S. government finally banged his gavel as he said, "going, going, gone," Sterling had acquired the Bayer Company for $5.31 million, a figure which was only about $1 million less than the company had earned from 1901 through 1918.

Although the sales of aspirin were small, a separate Sterling subsidiary, also called The Bayer Company, was organized to market the product. An entirely new corporation, Winthrop Chemical Co., Inc. (now Winthrop Laboratories), was formed to handle the pharmaceutical preparations, and the dye division was sold outright to another company.

That period, 1919–41, was an era in which the mission of the company—Sterling's business is everybody's health—began to be clearly defined. The business in Bayer aspirin moved forward rapidly in response to the therapeutic magic of the product and the thrust of advertising in its behalf. In the United States, other products identified by honored names were added to Sterling's consumer lines—Phillips' Milk of Magnesia, Fletcher's Castoria, Haley's M-O, Dr. Lyon's Tooth Powder, Z.B.T. Baby Powder, Energine cleaner and lighter fluids, to mention a few. In addition, the business spread beyond U.S. boundaries—to Canada and Latin America in the western hemisphere, and overseas to the United Kingdom and as far away as the Philippine Islands. Today, the largest Sterling facility outside the United States is the manufacturing plant in the United Kingdom of Sterling-Winthrop Group, Ltd.

Year after year the advertising appropriations grew larger as sales increased. With the advent of radio, the management foresaw the extraordinary impact of this medium of communication and made the company a major radio advertiser. Such programs as the "Bayer Album of Familiar Music" and "Manhatten Merry-Go-Round" helped to raise the level of musical appreciation in the United States. The company also used the soap operas, which morning and afternoon brought to the busy housewife stories that evoked gentle tears and happy endings.

Winthrop brought Sterling into the pharmaceutical field with a list of renowned preparations. One was Luminal, the original phenobarbital. Others were Salvarsan and Neo-Salvarsan, the first effective drugs in the treatment of syphilis. To bring these drugs into the widest possible use in the shortest time, the company collaborated with government agencies and with local clinics in giving to physicians demonstrations of the techniques of treatment with the famed "magic bullet" invented by Ehrlich.

The sulfa drugs represented still another advance in chemotherapy in the 1930s. Winthrop introduced Prontosil, first of the sulfas, to the American medical profession.

Winthrop made other significant contributions, notably in anesthesiology. Through Novocain and later Pontocaine, a new technique in anesthesia was unveiled.

Winthrop not only offered these anesthetics to the medical profession—it organized medical teams to work with anesthesiologists in clinics to perfect techniques in basal, intravenous, infiltration, and spinal anesthesia. Thereafter, Winthrop produced motion picture films demonstrating these specialized techniques, which were projected to tens of thousands of doctors and medical students.

Sterling products are available today in 123 countries. They can be found in the family medicine chest. Many are particularly useful in hospitals to save life, to relieve pain, to facilitate diagnosis, to build tissue, to control infection, to produce anesthesia, even to curb colds, clear stuffy noses, and eliminate sniffles. Also useful in their relation to health are other Sterling products, such as animal vaccines and vitamins for food enrichment; disinfectants, insecticides, and rodenticides; even optical brighteners in laundry detergents. One more recent discovery is not a product but a process—the Zimmermann Process—which makes a significant advance in sanitary engineering through its efficiency in disposing of industrial and community stream-polluting wastes.

More than a thousand Sterling products—professional, consumer, and industrial—are identified by brand names and trademarks. Brand names enable the consumer to reward the producer by buying his product again when it gives satisfaction, or to punish him by not buying again if the product fails to deliver value. The goodwill which brand names symbolize is what makes tomorrow's business more than an accident. And perhaps most important of all, brand names encourage the pursuit of excellence in the marketplace.

Glenbrook Laboratories is a division of Sterling Drug Inc. engaged in the manufacture and distribution of medical preparations advertised to the public and available without prescription.

The executives of the Glenbrook Laboratories believe their expenditures for advertising represent investments to help insure the continuity of the company, not alone in the present but also into the future. This objective conditions all their business judgments, including those related to the selection of advertising media.

The products which Glenbrook advertises—such as Bayer Aspirin and flavored Bayer Aspirin for children, Phillips' Milk of Magnesia both regular and flavored—are in most of the medicine chests in America. As part of its total marketing concept, Glenbrook advertises in newspapers, magazines, radio, professional and trade publications, and television. (See Exhibits 6, 7, 8.) As to television network shows, its advertising participation is directed to those shows which will give it maximum advertising impact and the kinds of audiences indicated for each of its advertised products.

Glenbrook is a participating advertiser on television shows and a participating advertiser on nighttime and daytime television network shows with other advertisers.

Generally speaking, the selection of network television shows into which Glenbrook buys reflects, in a major degree, the recommendations of Dancer-Fitzgerald-Sample, its advertising agency associated with it for three decades of Sterling's growth. Neither Glenbrook nor the agency chooses any show because it happens to fall into a particular category—i.e., mystery, situation comedy. Their selections are made solely on the basis of specific shows which, in their judgment, reach in each case the kind of audience appropriate to Glenbrook's products. The agency's recommendation is made on the basis of a pilot film of a specific show. This permits the agency to form a judgment as to the type of audience the show is likely to attract, how the audience fits into its overall marketing program, and, hopefully, the size of the audience.

The agency receives advance scripts of various shows. Primarily, the agency examines each script from the viewpoint of insuring that it reflects the character of the show that Glenbrook bought into, as that character was projected in the pilot film. Glenbrook makes no attempt at censorship. It has no list of "musts" or "must-nots."

Glenbrook believes that an American business enterprise has a responsibility to serve a social as well as economic function. It acknowledges a social responsibility to the television audience, which it exercises by associating Glenbrook only with those shows that, in its judgment, are fit to be seen in the American home.

Insofar as television advertising—and all other activities—are concerned, Glenbrook believes it has economic and socioeconomic responsibilities to sections of the American audience: to its sharehold-

EXHIBIT 17-6

HOW TO BE SURE

your youngsters take the laxative they need

**Give them Mint-Flavored Phillips' Milk of Magnesia. They'll like
the taste. And it's the kind of laxative doctors recommend.**

Mint-Flavored Phillips' tastes so good, children and grownups
alike take it happily. What's more, when the makers of Phillips'
Milk of Magnesia asked thousands of doctors, "Do you ever recommend milk of magnesia?" the overwhelming majority said,
"Yes."

Phillips' Milk of Magnesia brings really complete relief because
it is both a laxative and antacid, so it relieves both constipation
and the acid indigestion that so often accompanies it. Get Mint-
Flavored Phillips' Milk of Magnesia for your family. Also still
in regular form. Get Phillips' today.

Courtesy Glenbrook Laboratories Division of Sterling Drug, Inc.

EXHIBIT 17–7

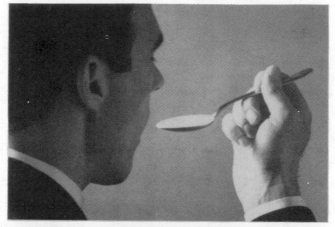

When you've got acid indigestion...

"Boy, what a difference Phillips' Milk of Magnesia makes!"

That's the feeling of Phillips' Milk of Magnesia! As soon as you take it, Phillips' liquid action goes right where the trouble is, to relieve upset stomach, heartburn, queasiness, and other discomforts of acid indigestion *in seconds!*

Many people like the feeling of Phillips' Milk of Magnesia even better in its refreshingly tangy mint-flavored form. Either way, Phillips' is one of the fastest and most effective stomach acid neutralizers known to medical science.

Next time you suffer from upset stomach, heartburn, or other discomforts of acid indigestion, take Phillips' Milk of Magnesia and feel better *in seconds!*

Courtesy Glenbrook Laboratories Division of Sterling Drug, Inc.

EXHIBIT 17–8

The most important minutes of your summer day

When hot weather makes you feel tense, irritable, headachy, two Bayer Aspirin and a short rest can help you feel better fast!

It happens to most of us on a hot, humid summer day, when the pressures of daily living mount up. By mid-afternoon we feel so head-achy and edgy that we're in no mood to enjoy life or the company of others.

Here's how to turn that mood around: just take two Bayer Aspirin for your headache, sit down for a few minutes and re-lax. These few minutes can make a world of difference in the way you feel and act. You'll enjoy being with people, and they'll en-joy being with you.

When you get headachy and out of sorts on a hot afternoon, set aside a few minutes for Bayer Aspirin and a brief rest. These can be the most important min-utes of your day.

Courtesy Glenbrook Laboratories Division of Sterling Drug, Inc.

ers, in providing a fair return on investment in the company; to employees, in assuring continuing job security at good pay and in working conditions that meet today's standards; to the 19 communities in 14 states in which Sterling's facilities are located, in contributing to job opportunities for local residents; to the retailers of America who have invested capital, time, skill, and energy in its products, in helping them to move Glenbrook's goods off the shelves into the medicine chests of America.

Beyond these responsibilities, Glenbrook is mindful that Sterling's business is everybody's health. It hopes, therefore, that the total operation, including advertising, prospers so well that it will be in the future, as it is today, in position continually to expand its research looking to the development of new and improved products that will contribute to the preservation of life and the protection of health.

Case questions

1. In your opinion, does Glenbrook plan its advertising programs effectively?
2. What changes would you suggest, if any?
3. Should advertising inform the public not only about the products but also about the principles, goals, and objectives of the Glenbrook company?
4. How can Glenbrook maintain or improve its image through advertising?
5. What other policies should Glenbrook consider in advertising its products?

Case **HUBBARD COMPANY**
17–3 **Deciding on strategy for a technical product**

The Hubbard Company manufactures dies, tools, and plastic molds. In addition, the products of these tools are carried through the manufacturing process to the production of finished pieces or completed instrument assemblies.

The work, composed of both industrial and consumer items, is largely on a job-order basis. The company employs from 100 to 125 people and has been able to diversify its production quite satisfactorily.

Recently a designer, retained by the company on a consultant basis, designed a production tool that was accepted by the company on a royalty basis. The company decided to manufacture and sell this tool. The tooling and manufacturing problems were routine matters because of past experience in this work. However, the article to be made was the first product that the company planned to sell itself; therefore, it had to set up a marketing program. None of the company executives had had any marketing experience. This new tool, a unique electric soldering iron, was considered an advance in the soldering iron field. Because of the nature of the commodity, it was necessary to sell these irons through industrial outlets.

Twelve such outlets were obtained to cover all sections of the United States. Industrial trade papers and magazines carried full-page advertisements of the iron. The initial response was favorable and indicated that there was a potential demand from foreign as well as domestic markets.

At this time, a marketing research firm was engaged to analyze the sales possibilities of the iron. Although some attention had been given to marketing, it was easily apparent that it had been rather broad in nature and had extended mainly to plans on paper. The actual field work had not yet been undertaken.

As the field work was started, the advantages of the iron were studied:

1. The soldering iron's copper tip had a special plating which was good for approximately 400 hours of use. Because of this plating, it was not necessary to clean the tip.
2. The tip always maintained its original shape. This would offset at least $21 of the hidden costs in tip maintenance of ordinary irons.
3. A precise measurement of the amount of solder to be used was possible by adjusting a micrometer screw feed.
4. The plug-type tip was recessed so that the heater element was inserted into the tip. This was an important improvement because other irons on the market merely conducted heat from the element to the tip by a butt contact. Higher temperatures were possible with decreased wattage.

The research also revealed that:

1. The soldering iron was attractive to a wide market. Both skilled and unskilled persons expressed interest in the iron because of its simplicity of operation.
2. Factory personnel were difficult to train in new lines. Although the iron reduced the job of soldering to pulling a trigger, it would be difficult to train personnel to know what to solder and how to do it.

The research firm found that in a number of cases customers who had used the iron were not always pleased with the results. The follow-ups that were made showed that the difficulty came about primarily through improper use of iron and ignorance of the principles of soldering. On the basis of its study, the research firm concluded that Hubbard Company must educate the trade in soldering techniques and in the adaptation of these techniques to its electric soldering iron.

To help solve this problem, the company began to send to all customers a monthly bulletin in which suggestions were included about the techniques the company desired its customers to use.

After the analysis, it was decided to use manufacturers' representatives, granting them the right to handle not more than three lines from three different companies. This policy was selected so that the representatives would have an adequate number of products to make their operations profitable; yet, at the same time, they would not spread their efforts among too many items. The representatives, in turn, selected distributors carrying both electrical and industrial items for the purpose of *demonstration selling only.*

Case question

1. What strategy should Hubbard plan for its campaign?

Case **BUDGET, INC.**

17–4
Budget, Inc., sells fabrics and sewing notions through 175 retail stores in 22 states. The company estimates that approximately 70 percent of its sales were fabrics and that the balance of such sales were sewing notions. Budget merchandise is in the medium price range and is sold primarily to housewives, schoolgirls, and working women for use principally in making women's and children's clothing. All stores are operated by Budget in leased premises located primarily in shopping centers and also in downtown business districts. Stores serve populations of at least 25,000. Budget does not franchise any of its operations.

Retail stores

Each store carries a large selection of fabrics, including cottons, rayons, silks, synthetics, woolens, and laces. These fabrics are first quality merchandise and do not include factory remnants, mill ends, or irregulars. Each store also sells notions, including threads, zippers, patterns, buttons, sewing accessories, and ornamentations. Approximately 75 percent of the yardage carried by each store is basic nonseasonal merchandise, and the remainder is for the spring and fall seasons. Seasonal fabrics are not carried over to the next season, but are reduced in price until sold.

A typical store consists of 4,500 square feet, of which approximately 90 percent is sales area. Most stores are air-conditioned, similar in physical layout, and contain fixtures made to Budget's specifications. Annual rent averages about $12,000 per store.

Each store has a manager, an assistant manager, and an average of four full-time sales clerks. Each store manager reports to a district manager, who is responsible for supervising a maximum of ten stores and who in turn reports to one of the area supervisors.

Suppliers and distribution

Budget has no long-term contracts for the purchase of merchandise and purchases no more than 10 percent of its merchandise from any one supplier. Budget has never experienced difficulty in obtaining satisfactory sources of supply.

Budget purchases substantially all of its merchandise directly from manufacturers. Most of the fabrics are delivered in bulk to Budget's distribution center and are unrolled, cut to 20- or 30-yard lengths and then double rolled on fabric boards labeled with its trademark. Merchandise is shipped from the center directly to its retail stores.

Up until two years ago, Budget's new stores were opened in major regional shopping centers. At that time, however, Budget began opening 50 percent of its new stores in neighborhood shopping centers, thereby broadening locations for expansion.

Budget plans to operate approximately 40 new stores in the current year. The average cost of opening a new store is $60,000, of which $45,000 is for merchandise inventory and the balance for fixtures. In recent years, a number of stores have been remodeled at a cost of approximately $15,000 each, and Budget plans to remodel approximately 20 additional stores within the next two years.

Budget is continuously seeking new store locations and reviews proposed sites for store locations recommended principally by shopping center developers and its own area supervisors and district managers.

Competition

The retail sale of fabrics and notions for home sewing is highly competitive. Budget's stores compete with large chain department stores, many of which have greater financial resources than Budget, and with independent and chain retail fabric stores. Budget believes that the variety of fabrics and notions it offers is greater than that generally offered by its competitors, and that its experience, volume purchasing, and specialization in the sale of fabrics and notions enable it to compete favorably with its rivals.

Case question

1. Suppose you are an account executive in an advertising agency and have been assigned the job of developing the advertising strategy for Budget. Outline the strategy that you would adopt, taking into consideration:
   a. Nature of the product.
   b. Consumer and market segment to be sought.
   c. Distribution policies.
   d. Buying motives and consumer behavior.
   e. Pricing policies.
   f. Marketing mix strategy.
   g. Advertising budget.
   h. Media selection.
   i. Competition.
   j. Economic effects.

Case **ARTHUR FOOD COMPANY**
17–5 **Planning a new special campaign**

Arthur Food Co. and its domestic and foreign subsidiaries are engaged in the manufacture, packaging, and sale of an extensive line of food products. As a result of some test market studies the company has decided to offer a new line of prepared ready-to-serve foods.

The decision to offer prepared products of this type was based on the data of other firms in the field. The companies showed that they could provide better and more nourishing meals at lower costs to school districts, restaurants, hotels, airlines, and hospitals, than these organizations had been able to do.

Marketing

Arthur sells directly to chain, wholesale, cooperative, and independent grocery accounts, to distributors, and to institutions, including hotels, restaurants, and certain government agencies, and sells indirectly through brokers and agents. In the United States, the company has sales offices in most principal cities and distributes its products to approximately 10,000 customers. Arthur has a domestic sales force of approximately 750 employees who call on special customers and retail service stores.

Arthur uses advertising and sales promotional programs as important marketing tools. Almost all types of advertising media are used on both a national and local basis. During the last fiscal year consolidated expenditures for advertising and sales promotional activities were approximately 10 percent of consolidated sales.

Raw materials and supplies

Arthur manufactures its products from a wide variety of raw food products. Preseason contracts are made with farmers for a substantial portion of such raw materials as tomatoes, cucumbers, onions, potatoes, corn, and other vegetables. Such materials as fruits, dairy products, meat, sugar, and flour are purchased on the open market. Fish is obtained through direct negotiations with boat owners, at auctions, by posted offers, by periodically negotiated contracts, and by bid-and-ask transactions with suppliers. The cost of purchasing and processing seasonal materials necessitates borrowings which generally reach an annual peak in November.

Manufacturing processes

Substantially all the Arthur's products are manufactured and packaged ready to serve. Most products are prepared from recipes developed in the company's research laboratories and experimental kitchens. Ingredients are carefully selected, washed, trimmed, inspected, and passed on to modern factory kitchens where they are processed; after which the finished product is filled automatically into containers of glass, metal, plastic, paper, or fiberboard; which are then closed, sterilized (where appropriate), labeled, and cased for the market. Finished products are processed by sterilization, freezing, or pickling so that they will keep a reasonable length of time.

Tomato, potato, cucumber, and some other fruit and vegetable products are manufactured primarily on a seasonal basis. Many other products are produced throughout the year including baby foods, tuna and other fish products, beans, cooked spaghetti, soups, mustard, salad dressing, sauces, relishes, and vinegar.

Arthur has participated in the development of much of its food processing equipment, certain of which is patented.

Quality control and research

Arthur pioneered in the development of quality control in the processed food industry. Quality control staffs in the factories aid the manufacturing staff in obtaining the required degree of quality and uniformity of the finished product. Arthur also maintains an active research program, including research and development of mechanical harvesting methods and crop research, which has been successful in increasing the disease resistance, quality, and yields of tomatoes, cucumbers, pineapples, and other crops.

Agricultural specialists, working in association with personnel from universities and government, furnish contract growers for Arthur with new and improved tomato, cucumber, and potato and other plants and with advice about fertilizer technology and crop protection. Arthur also experiments with new methods of food processing and the development of new food products.

International operations

Arthur carries on extensive international operations. The major portion of Arthur's foreign sales is made in the United Kingdom, Canada, Italy, Australia, Mexico, Peru, Venezuela, the Netherlands, and Portugal, where processing facilities are located. Sales are also made in many other countries in Europe, South and Central America, Asia and Africa. Arthur's United Kingdom subsidiary accounted for 19 percent (no other foreign subsidiary accounted for as much as 10 percent) of the company's consolidated net sales. It is the intention of the Arthur Food Company to continue its policy of development of international markets. Financing needed to carry out this policy is generally sought in the countries concerned and from the cash resources of the company's subsidiaries involved.

Income from international operations is subject to fluctuation in currency values, export and import restrictions, and other factors. From time to time exchange restrictions imposed by various countries have restricted the transfer of funds between countries and between Arthur and its subsidiaries. The Arthur executives believed that because the other major competitors had set up subsidiaries to manage the food services on a professional basis, they would limit the market segment to working women and housewives for the prepared puddings, rices, fruit cups, and dinner items which they planned to offer.

Suggestions for advertising

The advertising agency account representative prepared the recommendations listed below:

Target audience to be reached. Working women (or housewives whose schedule doesn't leave time for preparation of meals) of middle-class (or higher) income status.

Advertising message. These products are part of an exclusive new line that—

    a. Is fast, easy and convenient to prepare.
    b. Offers a variety of delicious dishes.
    c. Contains special, high quality, expensive ingredients not normally found in products of this type.
    d. Can be used to complement a special meal, enhance everyday meals, or be a complete meal.

Media used and reasoning for same. Sunday supplements, women's service magazines *(Better Homes & Gardens, Sunset, McCall's, Ladies Home Journal, Woman's Day),* plus *TV Guide.*

    1. High quality reproduction will be necessary to bring across the message of quality, to show the ingredients in an appetite appealing way and to highlight usage.

    2. Sunday supplements and women's magazines will be the most effective print media available to reach target consumers, in terms of readership and cost per reader. *Life* and *TV Guide* also will be included to gain immediacy of impact, especially in the introductory coupon ad. All other publications used will be monthlies, except for Sunday supplements.

    3. A limited budget will not permit effective usage of broadcast media.

Sequence of advertisements.
The first ad should:

    a. Illustrate that these products met a specific consumer need,
    b. Make the consumer aware that these are exclusive products and part of a new line,
    c. Emphasize the quality ingredients used which mandate a higher price.
    d. Have considerable appetite appeal,
    e. Entice the consumer to try the product.

(Since the products are more expensive than competitors', it is believed that a reduction in cost might stimulate initial trial. Therefore, a coupon will be added to the original ad. Although this coupon covers part of the list of ingredients, which were vital to the advertising message, it is considered to be important to initial usage, even though it detracted from the appetite–appeal objectives.)

Subsequent ads should:

    a) Emphasize individual products in the line.
    b) Introduce the consumer to various uses of the products.
    c) Be appetite appealing.
    d) Include the fact that these products are part of a new product line and that other products of this nature are also now available for a variety of new, good-tasting, meal-enhancing dishes.

The vice president in charge of marketing believed that the campaign recommendations were satisfactory and indicated that Arthur Foods Co. should proceed. However, the president was not too satisfied with this approach. He stressed, "The approach is the same old stereotyped one that does not excite the housewife. I think it is essential for us to make a big splash in the announcement and the only way that this can be accomplished is with broadcast media with a dramatic appeal. If we follow the plan of the agency representative, we are not going to be able to get the consumer even to try the product. The industry is too competitive for us to enter what I know are the highest quality products in the market with this old establishment plan."

Case questions

1. Evaluate the suggested campaign as outlined by the advertising agency.
2. How important is it for Arthur to make a dramatic entry into this product field?
3. To what extent should information, argumentation, and motivation be used in appealing to the consumer for these products?
4. Do you believe the company should pinpoint the advertising to the female segment of the market? Why not put emphasis on men? On school children?
5. How will Arthur be able to get the stores to give adequate shelf space for the products?

Case   **JACK DANIEL DISTILLERY**

17–6   Jack Daniel Distillery, founded in 1866, is the oldest nationally registered distillery in the United States. It is still located in Lynchburg, Tennessee (population 361), where Jack Daniels got started near a limestone cave spring where the water is excellent for making whiskey, flowing all year at 56°F and not carrying a trace of iron.

Its product has won many national and international awards, the first of them being a gold medal at the Louisiana Purchase Exposition at the World's Fair in St. Louis, Missouri 1904–05.

The major functions of the distillery process are as follows:

The first step in the manufacture of sour mash whiskey is to cook the cornmeal, which is ground a little coarser than that used for making bread, to the boiling point. This cornmeal mash is then cooled to approximately 156°. At this point, the proper amount of rye is added, which yields more starch and flavor to the mash. The mash is then cooled again until it reaches 146°. The barley malt is then added. (Barley malt is barley grain that has been processed by sprouting and drying and allowing it to produce enzymes necessary to convert starch to fermentable sugars.) After the malt has been added to the mash and the conversion has taken place, then the mash is transferred from the mash cooker to the fermenter. The yeast is then added, along with strained stillage from a previous fermenter. Fermentation immediately takes place and continues until most of the sugar is consumed by the yeast leaving an important byproduct—alcohol.

The beer (fermented mash) is ready for distillation. The still is a tall copper column sectioned with plates, down spouts, and trays, and so designed as to allow the beer coming down from the top to be cooked into a vapor form by steam coming in from the bottom. The vapor travels from the top of the still to a doubler, which is another distilling process, then to a condensor. The condensor consists of copper tubes inside a copper tank that is continually cooled with cold water. After the vapor is condensed into liquid form it is now ready for the charcoal mellowing process.

The charcoal mellowing process which helps give Jack Daniel's its distinctive flavor takes place in a building full of wooden vats filled with the finely ground sugar maple charcoal. This charcoal has been packed into the 12-foot-high vats in order for the whiskey to seep slowly down through the charcoal on its way to the cistern room, where it will be put into new charred white oak barrels and transported to a warehouse for aging.

The charcoal mellowing is the leaching process that makes this whiskey so expensive. It was once called the "Old Lincoln County Process" (Lynchburg was in Lincoln County until 1872, when it became the county seat of Moore County). The process by tradition was handed down by slaves who made whiskey in the hills. Leaching through charcoal removes the corn taste from the whiskey and makes it the true "Tennessee Whiskey," never called bourbon. A taster samples every vat, rolls the liquid around in his mouth. If the taste is not right, the charcoal is replaced and the liquid is run through again.

After the leaching process the liquid is run into government receiving cisterns, where it is drawn off into barrels, properly gauged, given a serial number and date, and put in the bonded warehouses. It is in these warehouses that the clear spirits change to the beautiful red color in the oaken casks as the change of seasons works its magic for as many years as the distiller requires to perfect his certain brand of whiskey. (Bonded whiskey must stay for four years.)

Advertising

Jack Daniels places its major advertising emphasis in the media of magazines and direct mail. The programs in both markets are closely related, and, in many cases interrelated.

The magazine ads are identified as "Jack Daniel's Silver Cornet Band," "Some of the Boys," and "Folks Who Tour." The "Band" ad, of course, was inspired by a photograph which was made around the turn of the century. In the photograph the names of the members were typed under each individual in the picture (see Exhibit 9). In many cases, their descendants still work at the distillery or in the town of Lynchburg. The copy in the ad relates to how Mr. Jack Daniel used the band to promote his whiskey. The inset at the base of the picture in the ad explains how an individual may acquire a copy of the record reproducing the fine music from the turn of the century.

The "resurrection" of the band required some three years. The stereo recording in 1974 culminated in a live performance at Opryland

EXHIBIT 17–9

If you can't find this record, Herb Fanning has it for $5.98 plus 35¢ postage at the Lynchburg Hardware & General Store, Box 239, Lynchburg, Tennessee 37352.

JACK DANIEL'S SILVER CORNET BAND reached its peak in 1894. Thanks to Paramount Records, you can still hear their music today.

Jack Daniel started the group to sell whiskey at saloon openings and political rallies. Today, we've dusted off some of their old-time sheet music and carefully recreated a sound that hasn't been heard for 75 years. (Finding these old-style mellow conical horns took us from an antique dealer's attic in Nevada clear to Paris, France.)

The result is a Paramount Records' album that's available wherever good records are sold. If the music inspires a sip of Jack Daniel's, don't be surprised. That's *just* what Mr. Jack intended it to do.

CHARCOAL MELLOWED
◊
DROP
◊
BY DROP

Tennessee Whiskey • 90 Proof • Distilled and Bottled by Jack Daniel Distillery
Lem Motlow, Prop., Inc., Lynchburg (Pop. 361), Tennessee
*The first Distillery placed in the National Register
of Historic Places by the United States Government.*

EXHIBIT 17–10

SOME OF THE BOYS who make Jack Daniel's Whiskey during the week make a good brand of music on weekends.

Ray Rogers and his group play pig roasts, benefits and country jamborees throughout Moore County. Here in our Hollow, they handle an assortment of jobs to help smooth out our whiskey. And they take equal pride in this line of work. You see, Ray says the country is filled with men who can make music. But there's only a handful who can make Jack Daniel's.

CHARCOAL
MELLOWED

◊

DROP

◊

BY DROP

Tennessee Whiskey • 90 Proof • Distilled and Bottled by Jack Daniel Distillery
Lem Motlow, Prop., Inc., Lynchburg (Pop. 361), Tennessee
*The first Distillery placed in the National Register
of Historic Places by the United States Government.*

in Nashville, Tennessee, in February. The band plans to make selected concert appearances during the next few years, which will be part of the distillery's Bicentennial contribution. The ad entitled "Some of the Boys" (see Exhibit 10) reflects continued use of the distillery personnel in telling the story of Jack Daniel. With the exception of historic photos or distillery visitors, all of the people in the ads are employees. Since the company enjoys 70–80,000 visitors a year to its distillery, this adds credence to its advertising.

"Folks Who Tour" (see Exhibit 11) is one of a series of magazine ads which appears annually in all national, regional, and local magazines—inviting people to visit the distillery. Each visitor or family, several weeks after leaving Lynchburg, receives a letter from the president and a small gift.

The format of the newspaper advertising has been altered for improved readability. The copy is much shorter and larger because of the voluminous amount of advertising that appears in newspapers in general (see Exhibit 12). Another reason for deviation in the copy format is that effective readership of liquor advertising in newspapers is about 25 percent that of magazines.

Brochures are given to visitors at the distillery, made available in airport displays and to liquor stores, and sent to many of the company's friends who write to the distillery. The *Tennessee Historical Quarterly* contains an article entitled "Jack Daniel Distillery and Lynchburg: A Visit to Moore County, Tennessee," which was written by a prominent Tennessee genealogist, Jeanne Ridgway Bigger. Through the auspices of the Tennessee Historical Commission, Jack Daniel Distillery was nominated and placed in the National Register of Historic Places on September 14, 1972. The reproduction of the *Quarterly's* article is sent as part of the direct-mail program, with a letter from one of the guides as a result of a request to an offer from one of the national magazine or local newspaper ads.

In the newspaper ad depicting the old bottles (see Exhibit 13), the one in the center foreground is the Maxwell House bottle. On the neck of each Maxwell House bottle it is indicated that there is limited distribution throughout the United States. When a Jack Daniel's customer purchases this bottle and directs the request to the company to register his bottling number, a letter, certificate and metal neck band are sent. This again is part of the combined advertising and direct-mail program.

The advertising budget for 1975 was divided as listed below:

Magazine	$1,250,000
Newspapers	300,000
Direct mail	25,000
Brochures	10,000

EXHIBIT 17–11

FOLKS WHO TOUR Jack Daniel Distillery say there's no other tour quite like it.

No loudspeakers. No standing in line. No concession stands. And no charge. But unfortunately, no free samplings of whiskey. (You see, the very county in which we make Jack Daniel's is dry.) Still, we think you'll enjoy a leisurely stroll through the buildings and grounds of our Hollow. And we're certain you'll enjoy a sip of Jack Daniel's, in countless counties where the law is allowing.

CHARCOAL
MELLOWED

DROP

BY DROP

Tennessee Whiskey · 90 Proof · Distilled and Bottled by Jack Daniel Distillery
Lem Motlow, Prop., Inc., Lynchburg (Pop. 361), Tennessee
*The first Distillery placed in the National Register
of Historic Places by the United States Government.*

EXHIBIT 17–12

These men are retired
now from Jack Daniel's,
but our whiskey
is the same
as the day
they began.

CHARCOAL
MELLOWED

DROP

BY DROP

TENNESSEE WHISKEY • 90 PROOF
DISTILLED AND BOTTLED BY JACK DANIEL DISTILLERY • LYNCHBURG (POP. 361), TENNESSEE

© 1972, Jack Daniel Distillery, Lem Motlow, Prop., Inc.

EXHIBIT 17–13

For special occasions we've changed the shape of our bottle. But never the smooth, sippin' whiskey inside.

CHARCOAL
MELLOWED

DROP

BY DROP

TENNESSEE WHISKEY • 90 PROOF   © 1972, Jack Daniel Distillery, Lem Motlow, Prop., Inc.
DISTILLED AND BOTTLED BY JACK DANIEL DISTILLERY • LYNCHBURG (POP. 361), TENNESSEE

Case questions

1. Evaluate the approach which Jack Daniel uses in its advertising.
2. Develop an advertising campaign for Jack Daniel, indicating marketing strategy and media one would recommend.
3. What are the motives that stimulate consumers to purchase Jack Daniel?
4. List ten appeals that Jack Daniel might use for advertising in *Sports Illustrated* and give reasons why you believe these would be good ones to use.
5. Should these appeals be used in a factual or exaggerated manner? Why?
6. Select one appeal and indicate in what different ways it might be presented.

18

EXECUTION OF CAMPAIGN

The successful execution of an advertising campaign depends upon the alertness with which the advertiser senses the consumers' desires and the speed exercised in satisfying them. This is because the market conditions are dynamic and the nature of the buying process is subject to rapid variations. As a result, the proper timing of a campaign can be even more important than the development of the keynote idea and the selection of the media.

As an example, studies have pinpointed that advertisers can speed up fashion movements, but they generally cannot profitably move styles as they wish. The woman wants what she wants at the time when she wants it. When a high percentage of men decided to stop wearing hats, the industry advertised to convince them how they might profit by wearing hats. However, the advertising did not convince them to change their habit and the negative shift in the demand curve for hats continued.

For an advertising campaign to be successful, the advertiser must evaluate not only all the major campaign decisions which should be made so the details of the program will be carried out, but it is also critical to be sure that the timing of its execution fits market conditions.

Kinds of campaigns

The following are a few of the principal bases of classification of campaigns usually used. Frequently, the basis will be the audience to be reached and influenced by the campaign, such as consumer, trade, or industrial campaigns.

The media may be the basis, such as direct-mail, magazine, newspaper, outdoor, radio, or television campaigns. At times, the function

588

or objective may be the basis, as in the case of primary demand or selective demand campaigns, institutional campaigns, or introductory or continuation campaigns. One of the more important bases of classification is geographical, or that of the territory involved, in which instance the usual division is that of local, zone or regional, and national campaigns. In the local and zone campaigns, the advertiser selects a restricted or limited geographical area and concentrates advertising efforts in that particular area. The national campaign is broader in scope and is directed to consumers in several regions or throughout the nation. The chief differences lie in the size of the territories covered, the media used, and in the fact that for the local and regional campaigns such types of advertising as direct-action advertising may be used to a greater degree than in the national campaigns.

Local campaigns

Local campaigns are those that are confined to a single trading area. Most such campaigns are those of retail stores, although some wholesalers who limit their distribution primarily to one large trading area may use local campaigns. Also, some small manufacturers with a strictly local market use this type of campaign for promoting their products. In certain circumstances, large manufacturers that normally use national advertising may also use the local campaign. For example, they may use such a campaign in testing proposed advertising programs designed for later use on a national scale. However, since most local campaigns are retail campaigns, the discussion will be centered on them.

The retailer should plan the store's advertising program with the same care as was outlined above for the national advertiser's campaign. The retailer should think in terms of what image it is trying to create for the store, the present and potential customers, the objectives or purposes of the coming period's advertising, the media available and best suited to its needs, the necessary budget, the coordination of all phases of the advertising and selling activities, and other necessary considerations.

The retailer should plan the desired amount for institutional advertising, the regular merchandise advertising in terms of items and departments of the store, the holiday promotions pertinent to its line of merchandise, and the special promotions and sales that are planned for the year. Funds must also be allocated to the various media.

Most retailers rely heavily on newspapers, types of shopping news publications, and direct-mail media, although some may make fairly heavy use of local radio and television, and of transportation and outdoor advertising. For any seasonal or special promotion, there should be close coordination of the media advertising and the displays, and salespeople should be trained to gear their selling efforts into the promotional activities.

The retailer can obtain aid in the planning of advertising programs from materials and information provided by national trade associations, such as the National Retail Dry Goods Association, or by local media, such as local newspapers. They normally will provide a *Retail Planning Guide,* which will list such dates as all-important national holidays, "weeks," as well as special local events, conventions, and activities that may provide the occasion for special promotions. Many national advertisers provide their retail outlets with advertisements in the form of mats, point-of-purchase materials, spot announcements, and proposed advertising schedules for the coming six months or year that are geared into their national advertising program. Thus, although the retailer may have many more short-term, special-event promotions than the national advertiser, which require, to a degree, a special advertising theme or program, it is important to keep in mind that there must be an underlying basis or purpose for the entire advertising program.

The zone or regional campaign

The zone or regional campaign is one that is limited to a geographical region with several trading areas. It might be a portion of one state, or include a whole area, such as the New England states. Distributors and wholesalers whose distribution is limited to such a region, retail chain organizations with outlets covering only a limited area, and manufacturers whose distribution is geared to a particular area—all use the zone type of campaign. National advertisers also may use the zone campaign in various circumstances. For example, a manufacturer of lightweight suits might regularly launch advertising at different times in various regions of the country to take full advantage of the beginning of warm weather. The firm also might wish to vary its advertising by regions to meet area differences in buying habits and living conditions, to satisfy unusual trade conditions in the area, to meet the competition of a strong regional brand, or to bolster sales in regional zones in which it has traditionally been weak.

The regional campaign may be used by the national advertiser for testing purposes rather than restricting it to a local campaign. In this manner any faults, weaknesses, or omissions in the advertising and selling methods can be uncovered, without the risks involved in a national campaign. Probably the most frequent use of the regional campaign is for the introduction of a new product. In the first instance, the regional method of introduction not only enables the firm to test its product before launching the program nationally, it also has advantages in facilitating the starting of regular plant production and the training and supervising of the sales force for the introductory program.

For example, a major soft-drink bottler used the zone campaign approach to introduce its product. It faced strong competition from established brand names, like Coca-Cola. These other soft drinks could be bought throughout the country, had gained general acceptance on a national basis, and were advertised heavily on a national scale. To sell its product on a national scale, the company would have been required to spend millions of dollars in advertising to stimulate demand. To minimize its risk and to facilitate its operational efforts, the firm decided to follow the zone campaign method of marketing in introducing its product. Its first zone embraced only a small area—a few counties around Dallas, Texas. Intensive advertising and selling efforts resulted in intensive distribution, good sales, and a satisfactory profit from operations. Additional areas were added, until the firm attained national distribution and could use national advertising. In this manner, the firm was able to develop its national market with a relatively small amount of invested capital, and with a minimum of risk.

In most respects, the planning and execution of the zone campaign are similar to the strategy discussed earlier for a local campaign. Here again, the main difference arises in the media to be used. Zone campaigns can use newspapers, local radio and television, direct mail, and transit, outdoor, and point-of-scale materials. Today, magazines can also be utilized effectively, because it is possible to buy space in the geographic and/or demographic editions of most national magazines that match the advertiser's distribution. Media must be selected carefully to obtain adequate coverage of the zone involved at a reasonable cost per thousand potential customers.

The national campaign

The national campaign is one involving a number of zones or regions, or the entire country. It is used by the manufacturing firm that has become so well established that it has distribution of its product or products in a number of regions or nationally. And it is used by the new manufacturer when it has obtained satisfactory distribution in a number of areas and wishes to use a single campaign to bolster its zone campaigns and to cover gaps between the zones that may not be covered satisfactorily by the individual zone campaigns. Occasionally, a national campaign is used by a new manufacturer entering the market, as was true of the introduction of a number of brands of cigarettes. Some of the large national firms introduce new products to the market with national campaigns. An example would be the introduction of new razor blades by the Gillette Company.

The introduction of a new product by means of a national advertising campaign and marketing plan calls for expenditure of a major sum of money and for considerable skill in coordinating all parts of the overall marketing plan. An example of a campaign is that developed by a national advertising agency for an ice cream company, when its ice cream was to be marketed nationally (after having been a successful regional brand for a number of years and distributed in a limited Eastern area).

The company was renowned in this area for its high quality. An important part of the initial promotional campaign was a trade advertising campaign directed to the retailer. These ads told the retailer how to maximize profits from his freezer space. The agency created a floor plan showing how much cabinet space should be given to this ice cream, and to other ice creams, including private brands. The advertising promoted it as the one and only "All Innate" ice cream—a product claim made several years before naturalness became a buzz word. The "All Innate" story was told in a series of eight TV spots. In its advertising, the agency met the question of high price for the ice cream head on—"It costs more, but then all natural ingredients cost more than the artificial kind." The unique positioning and pricing was successful when the product was test marketed in Miami, an area outside its old market area. The distribution of the brand was then expanded rapidly into other markets.

The main theme of the advertising is still the "Innate" theme. "All [our] ice cream still untouched by artificial ingredients. Ice Cream made in cooperation with nature." And the most recent commercial, to distinguish it from other ice creams, now stresses the "pure and simple" theme. They tell viewers that "there is still one ice cream so pure and simple that it contains only four ingredients—milk, sugar, natural flavoring, and thick milk cream." The ads were run on television in all the areas into which this ice cream was being introduced, some 80 markets. Between 1971 and 1975 sales volume quadrupled and this became the second largest selling ice cream in the United States, and is fast closing in on number one.

Another example of executing a successful campaign was that for a brand of ice milk. The product had a lot going for it when it was introduced in 1968—a noticeable product superiority, unique positioning as the ice milk with the taste of ice cream but only half the fat, and, of course, the family name.

Four years later, however, competitive products with improved quality, similar names and product claims, and lower prices were beginning to catch up. With this change in the market, it was time to take a long, hard look at what the consumer wanted. The company and its agency first conducted a telephone "attitude and usage" survey reaching 1,200 families in 25 markets. That information was supplemented by in-depth "focus group" interviews with both ice milk users and nonusers.

Analysis of research results revealed that the ice milk market is relatively small—more than seven out of ten families never buy ice milk—because the consumer generally regards it as poor in quality, compared to ice cream, with flaky texture and an artificial taste.

To convince the consumer that this brand of ice milk is really different, the company and its agency decided not to compare it with other ice milks at all. Knowing that both its name and the term ice milk communicated the low-fat story, they focused in on a closer direct comparison with ice cream.

Positioning it as "the *Ice Creamy* Ice Milk," the ad campaign emphasized exciting new flavors—natural, of course—its smooth texture and rich taste, dropping the low-fat claims altogether. The new ads, new flavors, and even new packaging were all parts of a campaign calculated to focus on the quality—as good as ice cream and well worth its premium price.

To get the message across, two TV spots were tested in 1973 and then rolled out in the entire market area in May 1974.

In the first spot a beautiful woman simply gazes into the camera and says, "How could anything like Carmel Nut, Toffee Crunch, and Vanilla Bean . . . Lemon Chiffon and Banana Strawberry Twirl be Ice Milk? How could anything called Ice Milk taste as thick and creamy as Ice Cream . . . ?"

Playing a vital supporting role in communicating this new image at the point of sale is new packaging. The packaging is outstanding in every sense of the word. Unlike the nondescript packaging of other ice milk on the shelves, the packages catch the consumer's eye with strong graphic treatment which, focusing on the natural ingredients, puts the emphasis on flavor where it belongs and gives the package a bold, clean look. Wrap around supergraphics provide powerful flavor identification and a standout package when viewed from any angle. "The main thing is that the look of the packaging was built off the advertising concept and reinforces the idea that this is a high quality product."

The quality message delivered by the advertising campaign and the packaging had a tremendous impact on the ice milk market when it was test marketed, according to an advertising awareness study conducted at that time.

"Unaided advertising awareness had almost tripled and sales had more than doubled in the test markets," reported the tests.

Total combined sales volume of the ice milk in the test markets was up by 102 percent, compared with a 6 percent increase in the rest of the area.

Preliminary results of the ad roll-out to the entire market area indicate that the average sales increase has been over 100 percent.

Spectacular results by any standards, they indicate the success of the TV spots and of the packaging and the print ads as well—the total marketing program!

Campaign execution

The details of the execution of the campaign will vary depending upon whether the campaign is one for: a consumer product; an industrial product; a product which will be pushed or pulled through the channels of distribution; a product that is being introduced into the market for the first time; a shopping good; or a fashion good. The size of the budget, the length of the campaign, and the economic conditions that exist are also factors which must be taken into account.

The coordination of the execution of the campaign generally is the responsibility of the company's advertising manager. That is, the advertising manager must work closely with all parties involved to see that the preparation of the advertisements and the materials meets the scheduled planned programs for the salespeople, middlemen, retailers, and consumers.

When an advertising agency is used, the agency team for the account normally would take over the details of executing the direct facets of the campaign. The account executive and the account group (usually including representatives of the copywriting group, research department, art department, and media department) would take over the responsibility for seeing that the advertisements are produced and published or broadcast on schedule. This is true for all the advertisements to appear in media that are to be directed to the consumer, as well as for those directed to various levels of the trade, which include display materials, salespersons' aids, publicity releases, and any other materials to be used in merchandising the advertising.

In addition to the above, the advertising manager must control the advertising budget. The manager must handle the approval and payment of the invoices for the advertising materials and services involved in the campaign, and must be sure that all people involved economically use the budgeted advertising dollars. Periodically the manager should review the advertising expenditures to date, and analyze and evaluate the advertising done and the results obtained, in terms of such factors as sales volume, share of market, competitive marketing activity, status of general economic conditions, and profit. This evaluation, in turn, should be reviewed by the top marketing and financial executives of the firm, and consideration should be given to several questions, including:

1. Are the basic economic conditions on which the campaign planning was done still in existence?
2. Are we presently within our budget, and shall we stay within it?
3. Are our tests of advertising effectiveness indicating that our campaign is accomplishing the objectives we established? If not, why is it failing?
4. In view of the results achieved to date, is there any reason why we should decrease or increase our advertising effort? If so, what changes should be made?
5. Have any new and unexpected developments taken place, either internally or externally, that would call for changes in the planned campaign?

Other aspects of coordination

In the actual carrying out of the campaign, the advertising manager and the agency account executive must work together to see that all facets of the program are properly coordinated. Also, if the advertiser has a number of divisions or product lines with individual advertising programs, the advertising manager must check closely to see that all the individual campaigns are coordinated and compatible in terms of objectives, and that there is consistency in the appeals and copy of the advertisements.

It also is the responsibility of the advertising manager to insure that other departments of the company are notified in proper time of the advertising program, so that they can carry out their obligations. This is especially true of the production departments and the sales departments. If, for example, a special promotion and intensified advertising campaign is to be carried on for a certain period, the production department must be able to plan to have adequate stocks available, and the sales force must have notice so they will be sure all retailers and wholesalers have adequate stocks on hand prior to the anticipated sales increase.

The salespeople should also be informed about the trade advertising which is being done to pave the way for sales calls. Such trade advertising normally tells the dealers (or industrial users) how they will gain by stocking or purchasing the advertiser's product. The salespeople then can coordinate their sales approach with the advertising message.

For these reasons the sales force should know the underlying basis for the campaign, the basic theme of the advertising (and the reason for its adoption), the type of ads to be used, the media to be used, and the schedule of advertising. This information can be given to them in various ways—through letters, sales meetings, films, brochures, closed-circuit television presentations, and so on. In many cases, firms also provide the salespeople with portfolios containing samples of national consumer ads to be run, the media schedules, and samples of materials available to the retailer.

Since display materials frequently are distributed to dealers through the sales force, it is important that the advertising manager work closely with the sales manager to see that the salespeople give proper push and stress to obtaining wide use of these items. It usually takes aggressive and enthusiastic support from the sales force to achieve good distribution and use of such point-of-purchase materials. As noted elsewhere, there is such keen competition for shelf space in the retail store today that it takes unusually effective personal selling to achieve reasonably satisfactory use of an advertiser's point-of-purchase materials. In some instances, in order to obtain dealer support in the form of display and push of their advertised product, advertisers pay the retailer for preferential display or shelf space. Since this is a form of advertising allowance, the manner in which such allowances are made available is covered by the provision of the Robinson-Patman Act. In essence, this act states that such advertising allowances are discriminatory, and thus illegal, unless made available on proprotionately equal terms to all competing customers.

As part of the overall program to achieve effective marketing of its product, the advertising firm may wish to have the retailer promote its product through the use of dealer cooperative advertising (also known as manufacturer's cooperative advertising, or vertical cooperative advertising). This is the policy on the part of the advertising firm to make an allowance to the retailer for a part of the cost of advertising its product on the part of the retailer. For example, the company might adopt a policy of paying one half of the space cost of any advertising of its product done by the retailer. The manufacturer may have a number of policies regarding the type and amount of advertising which will qualify for the allowance. The firm may specify that only certain media be used. It may insist that the advertisement itself meet certain specifications, such as: it must be devoted exclusively to the manufacturer's products, it must be regular price advertising of the merchandise, it must contain certain copy appeals, and so forth. And it may place restrictions on the total dollar amount that will be paid, such as a certain percentage of total purchases of the product by the retailer.

Putting the campaign to work

As an example, consider the problem of a major bus company which had centered its appeal on "cheapest way to get there." As a result of improvement in equipment and in types of travel service offered, it wished to change its image and attract customers who would appreciate the "fun" of traveling by bus. The company believed that it had much "happy travel" to offer. It was now able to preplan vacations, and it had slumber-stop service, through-express schedules, and a fleet of long-distance coaches, all available at low cost.

Its preplanned vacations include transportation, hotels, and sightseeing tours. The vacations are entirely flexible and may be shortened or lengthened to fit the traveler. Slumber-stop service means that the traveler can go by bus from New York to San Francisco with a hotel reserved automatically along the way every night. Through-express buses operate from principal cities. The scenicruiser and highway traveler buses include wide-view picture windows, air-conditioning, roomy, adjustable seats, and an air-suspension system which consists of flexible rubber-nylon air bellows that take the place of conventional metal springs. In addition, the scenicruiser has a unique two-level seating arrangement for passengers. The upper deck seats 36 passengers who ride "above the traffic." Complete washrooms are also a part of each bus.

The strategy that was selected in the campaign was to concentrate on the "happy travel" connotation that would be associated with the fun of traveling by bus.

In putting this campaign into action, it was necessary for the company to take this general appeal and correlate it to the media (radio and television spots, magazines, transit advertising, outdoor boards, and such point-of-sale material as folders, quarter cards, posters, and window banners) that were selected, as well as to get the message to the traveling public through club and school lectures, guest appearances, and radio and television interviews.

The company also recognized that it had to do a thorough training job with its sales personnel because it had found that agents and ticket clerks can convince the traveler to buy round trip tickets by asking, "Round trip?" instead of simply taking an order.

The company recognized in setting up the campaign that it not only had to do a broad promotional job with the general traveling public, but also had to get full participation from its employees if the campaign was to be successful.

Conclusion

An advertising campaign is a complex plan and must be kept fluid enough to meet the shifts in consumer demand and the intensification of competition. Decisions for the campaign must also be made in the light of both the long-run effects as well as the attainment of short-term objectives. How will a campaign emphasizing price affect a long-range guide to action of producing high-quality products for a small segment of the market? How will giving "free samples" of candy affect the sales of a high-quality candy manufacturer?

As a result, within the framework of the basic marketing strategy, the details of the campaign must be constructed and executed. The basic activities are listed below, although it must be kept in mind that they will vary depending upon such factors as objectives, budget, and schedules.

1. Review the long-range marketing strategy and objectives of the company.
2. Set reasonable and, whenever possible, measurable objectives for the campaign.
3. Evaluate the timing strategy that will be adopted.
4. Determine the budget that will be needed to attain the objectives which have been set.
5. Firm the pricing strategy.
6. Design the package and trademark when necessary.
7. Select the media and firm the time and space schedules.
8. Develop the copy, scripts, etc. for the advertisements.
9. Establish the controls so that all phases of the campaign will be completed on schedule.
10. Develop the dealer merchandising plan that will be used.
11. Keep other departments of the company informed of what advertising is to be done for what products, and of the implications thereof for the department.
12. Work with the sales department to insure proper correlation with the use of trade advertising, consumer advertising, and cooperative advertising.
13. Control the advertising budget.
14. Evaluate the results of advertising as rapidly as possible after it is run, and assess the implications of findings.
15. Modify plans as is indicated by unexpected results of advertising or changes in actual conditions from those conditons assumed when plan was designed.

Questions

1. Discuss what you consider to be the important differences in executing an advertising campaign for a retailer and a national advertiser.

2. What are the distinctive features of a regional campaign?

3. Under what circumstances might a manufacturer with national distribution and advertising of its products utilize a regional campaign?

4. Do you think a large manufacturer of food products with national distribution and advertising (such as General Foods or General Mills), would ever use a local campaign? If so, under what circumstances?

5. One advertising manager states: "Recent changes in media arrangements are such that the choice of media for use in a regional campaign do not differ materially from those available for a national campaign." Would this statement be accurate for the geographical region in which you are living? Explain.

6. What are the responsibilities of the company's advertising manager in connection with the execution of the advertising campaign?

7. Which aspects of campaign execution normally would be handled by the agency account executive?

8. What do you understand by the statement: "It is the advertising manager's responsibility to exercise financial control of the campaign."?

9. As the advertising manager, what should you cover when you make your periodic review and evaluation of your advertising campaign?

10. Why is it important for the advertising manager to work closely with other departments of the company in the execution of the advertising campaign?

11. Explain how the advertising manager should work with which other departments of the company to assure success of the advertising campaign.

12. Assume you are the advertising manager for a large food products manufacturer, with national distribution, a sales force of 240 people organized in 24 districts, running campaigns for 11 major product lines, with a total budget of approximately $50 million, some $500,000 of which is budgeted for trade advertising, some $3 million for point-of-purchase materials and promotions, and about $2 million budgeted for dealer cooperative advertising:

     a. To what extent do you think your department should work with the sales department?

     b. Explain how you would go about working with the sales department to assure maximum effectiveness for your advertising campaigns.

13. As the advertising manager, how would you try to assure effective use of your dealer cooperative advertising budget?

14. Visit a local supermarket or department store and determine their use of, and attitude toward, dealer cooperative advertising. What do they think are the good features and the weaknesses of such programs? Evaluate their comments.

15. Discuss what you consider to be the key aspects of executing the advertising campaign.

Case   **THE FIRESTONE TIRE & RUBBER COMPANY**
18–1

The Firestone Tire & Rubber Company is a worldwide organization which manufactures and markets not only 7,900 different sizes and types of tires but nearly 40,000 other products in the fields of rubber, metals, plastics, textiles, and chemicals.

Steady growth has marked the company's history since its founding by Harvey S. Firestone in Akron, Ohio, on August 3, 1900, with assets of $20,000 and a tire-mounting patent. Sales for the year 1901 amounted to $110,000.

In fiscal 1974, sales reached a record $3,674,890,000. Net earnings of the company in 1974 were $154,025,000, a return of 4.2 percent on sales.

Firestone products are sold to the public through thousands of independent dealers and distributors and a network of more than 1,300 company-owned stores in the United States.

The creative approach, and why

Of prime importance in approaching the consumer with the Firestone Steel Radial 500 tire is the clear establishment of the *value* and *advantages* of the tire. While this may sound fundamental, both the economy and the radial market put special pressure on a tire maker to find ways to effectively emphasize those points in his product.

For number one, the consumer is confronted with an uncertain economic climate, in which tire makers are asking him not only to buy a more expensive type of tire but to buy one with construction and handling features with which he is not familiar at all. And secondly, many tire makers are approaching him in various ways to convince him that their brand is best.

The result: a somewhat unsure product arena in a somewhat unsure economic climate.

The Firestone creative platform was therefore to be one of ASSURANCE; to assure the consumer that the purchase of the Firestone Steel Radial 500 was a wise and safe one from the standpoints of both economic climate and consideration of all available brands.

The approach to the advertising was to combine all the product propositions of the tire to create an overwhelming argument for the Firestone brand by matching or exceeding competitive offers. And also to feature certain monetary assurances and safeguards to justify making the purchase in an unsound economic climate. The 40,000 mile warranty, the seven-day test ride, and the gas-saving proof all add to the value and/or implied return on investment offered by this more expensive tire.

The combination of all these features seemed to be best expressed in a phrase many people often use to describe any very good value— "just too much to turn down." Thus—"It's too much tire to turn down." (See Exhibit 18–1.)

The headline on this particular ad was written to give further assurance beyond the guarantees and product features, for research shows that "previous good experience with the brand" is a strong motivating factor in a purchase. Thus to remind people that many, many others are purchasing or have purchased the product serves to further assure them that the brand must be performing well on the road.

EXHIBIT 18–1

Go out and compare the new Firestone Steel Radial 500 with any other radial tire...

1. The Proven Gas Saver This is the tire that earned the name *Gas Saver.* When run at steady highway speeds against our original equipment belted bias tire, it saved up to thirty miles per tankful, important savings at today's gas prices.

2. 7-Day Test Ride and Handling Warranty We're so sure you'll like the smooth ride and quick, positive handling of the Steel Radial 500™ that you can buy them, drive on them for seven days, and get every cent back if there's anything you don't like. Does any other tire company offer you that?

3. New Water Squeezer Tread Firestone's amazing new Water Squeezer Tread actually pushes water out the sides of the tread to help keep water from getting between the rubber and the road. And the big, wide, Steel Radial 500 footprint puts a lot of tread under you to help hold tight to wet pavement.*

4. Steel Between You and Tire Trouble Two belts of steel cord under the new Water Squeezer Tread help protect your tires from chuckholes and roadjunk* that you can't always steer around. They also hold the tread firmly to cut down on "tire squirm" that causes wear.

5. 40,000 Mile Warranty If the Steel Radial 500 doesn't give you 40,000 miles of normal passenger use on the same car, any Firestone Store or participating Dealer will give you a new one, charging you only for the mileage received plus Federal Excise Tax. A small service charge may be added.

*Don't forget, the safety of your tires is also affected by air pressure, wear, load, and operating conditions.

It's too much tire to turn down

Broadcast advertising

Firestone also developed an interesting strategy for broadcast, particularly television. Because of the overwhelming acceptance of 30-second commericals and a favorable cost relationship between a 30 and a 60, the company developed a series of five 30-second commercials, each one featuring one of the reasons to consider the Steel Radial 500. (See Exhibit 18–2.)

Because much of its television is bought with the idea of achieving product exclusivity on a sports program, Firestone frequently has four or six 30-second messages within a 1½ to 2½ hour presentation. By featuring one specific product advantage in each commercial, the company is building an accumulative effect of all of the many reasons why the viewer would want to investigate its product before making a decision on a replacement steel belted radial tire.

Early history

Highlights of the early history of Firestone were the introduction in 1900 of the solid rubber sidewire tire as one of the company's first products; development of the first mechanically fastened, straight-side pneumatic automobile tire in 1904; introduction in 1906 of the universal rim to accommodate either the straight-side or the clincher tire; development of the first commercial demountable rim in 1907; and the introduction of the first angular nonskid tire tread in 1908.

The first experiments in the use of cord fabric for automobile tires as a replacement for square-woven fabric were conducted by the company in 1915.

Firestone perfected a method of insulating tire cords against internal heat by its now famous "Gum-Dipping" process in 1920; and in 1922 developed the industry's first low-pressure balloon tire.

Harvey S. Firestone was a leader in many different movements to aid his company, the industry, and the general public. He organized the "Ship by Truck" movement in 1918 to encourage use of trucks for the transportation of food, machinery, and other goods, and led the "Good Roads" movement.

He initiated the now popular one-stop service store program in 1926; and he inaugurated the first commercially sponsored network musical radio program, the "Voice of Firestone," in 1928.

In 1922 Mr. Firestone began his campaign, "Americans Should Produce Their Own Rubber," in protest against the Stevenson Rubber Restriction Act that caused a rise in the price of natural rubber. Carrying out his program, Firestone began its own plantation operations in Liberia in 1924. Today the Liberian plantations cover 90,000 acres, and Firestone also operates plantations in Brazil, Ghana, the Philippines and Guatamala.

One of Mr. Firestone's achievements was his start of the campaign to "Put the Farm on Rubber" with the development of the first practical low-pressure farm tractor tire.

Mr. Firestone, a farmer's son, was aware of the shortcomings of

EXHIBIT 18–2

VIDEO:	AUDIO:
OPEN ON KEVIN IN YARD BETWEEN A FOUR YEAR OLD CHILD AND AN EIGHT YEAR OLD.	*KEVIN O. C.:* One reason Firestone's new 40,000 mile Steel Radial 500 is too much tire to turn down is because they'll last about four years on the average family car . . .
	. . . That's the difference between 4 year old Jody here and eight year old Mike.
KEVIN WALKS FROM CHILDREN TO CAR IN DRIVEWAY AND KNEELS DOWN TO TIRE (SR-500).	And another good reason is two belts of steel cord to help protect the tires on the family car from damage by road hazards.
KEVIN STANDS BY TIRE, CHILDREN REJOIN HIM—CAMERA PULLS BACK. SUPER: The 40,000 mile Firestone Steel Radial 500 Too Much Tire To Turn Down	Forty thousand miles. Another reason why the new Firestone Steel Radial 500 is just too much tire to turn down.

VIDEO:	AUDIO:
OPEN ON DRAMATIC SHOT OF KEVIN STANDING BY SAWHORSE WITH BLINKING ROADWORK WARNING LIGHTS AROUND HIM. HE LIFTS HAND WITH STEEL AROUND IT THEN, HE POINTS TO CHUCKHOLE WITH STEEL. CUT TO FULL SHOT OF KEVIN WALKING OVER TO CAR WITH SR-500's ON IT.	*KEVIN O. C.:* One Reason Firestone's new 40,000 mile Steel Radial 500 is too much tire to turn down is because of two belts of steel cord right under the tread to help protect your tires from chuckholes like this.
HE TOUCHES SR-500 AGAINST THE STEEL CORD. MOVE DOWN FOR CLOSEUP OF TIRE. SUPER: LEGAL DISCLAIMER	Of course—the safety of your tires is also affected by air pressure, wear, load and operating conditions.
KEVIN KNEELING WITH TIRE.	But remember. Firestone *Steel*—Another reason why the 40,000 mile Steel Radial 500 is just too much tire to turn down.
SUPER: 40,000 Mile Firestone Steel Radial 500 Too Much Tire to Turn Down	

steel wheels, and in the late 1920s he started to develop a rubber tire for the farm. He took the balloon tire principle of low pressure and wide area and to it added a chevron tread design. As time went on, the tread design was recut to a wider, deeper chevron for greater traction, alternative bars were connected, and the series of Ground Grip tires was launched in 1932. The Thirties, despite their economic stresses and strains on business generally, were years of substantial growth for Firestone. Products were improved and diversified. Old plants were expanded and new plants were opened. Sales and profits increased.

In the early 1930s, Harvey S. Firestone also started a retail store program for two reasons: to increase the number of Firestone outlets for its products and, of equal importance, to use the stores to test the salability of specific products and methods of merchandising them. These stores have become a vast merchandising laboratory, and practices that are successful in the stores are passed on to Firestone's independent dealers.

From 1933, when Firestone scientists started their research in synthetic rubber, their ultimate goal was to produce a rubber that would have the desirable properties of natural rubber. Twenty years later they succeeded and called the new rubber Coral. It was established that the new rubber had the same X-ray crystalline pattern and molecular structural features to be found in natural rubber. In addition, more than a half-million miles of truck tire tests proved that this new synthetic rubber was outstanding in its resistence to cracking, and the tread wear was about the equivalent of natural rubber. Coral eventually could be a complete replacement for natural rubber.

Numerous other developments were made by Firestone in the synthetic rubber field, including: the perfection, in 1948, of a "cold" process for the manufacture of synthetic; a new synthetic rubber tread compound which practically eliminates "squeal" in tires and gives a soft, smooth ride; and hundreds of synthetic compounds to meet various product specifications.

Tire developments

An intensive research program for the development of a tubeless tire was put into effect in the late 1940s. In January 1951 the company announced that a premium-priced tubeless blowout-safe and puncture-proof tire had been added to the company's line. In February 1954 the "DeLuxe Champion" tubeless tire was offered to the automotive industry without a premium price tag on it. Thus, Firestone became the first in the rubber industry to produce a tubeless tire that could be sold for no more than the price of conventional tire and tube.

As a result, the tubeless tire became standard equipment on 1955 passenger cars. In March 1953 the company announced the development of the first tubeless truck tire in the rubber industry.

Another truck tire offered during 1960 and 1961 was a new single truck tire to replace duals on tractor trailer rigs. Called "Duplex," the unusual tire was nearly twice as wide as conventional truck tires and its load carrying capacity exceeded that of the two tires it replaced.

Production of radial ply tires for truck and compact cars was started by Firestone in 1964. Several types of tire cord, including steel cord, are used in these tires which offer longer tread life, lower fuel consumption, quicker steering response, and better cornering than conventional tires offer.

In 1968, Firestone announced a new tire and wheel concept, called the LXX—tire for the '70s. It was heralded by the automotive press as the "forerunner of the next generation in tire safety" and the "most outstanding product breakthrough in the tire industry in 25 years." The new tire has a low section height and fits on a narrow, larger diameter rim.

The development of a liquid molded, cast tire made without cords or plies was announced in 1970. A new manufacturing process and the development of improved synthetic rubber compounds enabled the company to produce this exceptional tire. To produce the tires, heated liquid rubber is squirted into a mold and minutes later a finished tire is removed. The tire was cited by Industrial Research Inc. as one of the "100 most significant technical products of the year."

Another Firestone tire development—the Town & Country All-Position tire—made its debut in 1970. The tire, which has an asymmetrical tread design, provides greater traction and maximum pulling power and is practical on all four wheels of an automobile.

The steel belt radial tire was the first U.S. made tire of this type to be approved by the auto industry. Now called the Steel Radial 500, the tire became standard equipment on many new cars. Since 1972 the demand for radial tires has continued to grow, and the company has announced several production breakthroughs in radial tire manufacturing.

The Radial V-1, made with the new method, and the Steel Radial ACT, a tire with run flat capabilities, were also developed. The LXX Mach 1 aircraft tire was put into service by two U.S. airlines.

Diversification

Tires are Firestone's principal product, but the company is a leader in several other fields.

Firestone is the world's largest manufacturer of rims for trucks, buses, and tractors. In addition, its metal products divisions manufacture such widely diversified metal products as beer barrels, farm wagons, stainless premix and postmix containers, stainless and chromeplated parts, and trim for automobiles, color television, and other home appliances.

It is a producer of air springs, hose, V-belts, and a great variety of miscellaneous extruded, calendered, and molded rubber products used in many industries.

The Coated Fabrics division produces fuel cells, inflatable dams, and collapsible containers, which are used to store fuel or other chemicals and products used in pollution control.

In 1967, Firestone acquired a group of seat belt companies, thus widening its diversification. The Hamill Manufacturing Company, now a division of Firestone, has plants in Michigan and in Ontario, Canada.

Firestone's chemical and raw materials divisions make a wide variety of products, including polyvinyl chloride resins, film, and sheeting; vinylidene chloride; nylon filaments and resins; and polyurethane foam.

The company also makes a large part of its tire cord and fabric requirements in its textile plants, and it sells various types of textile yarns to other manufacturers. It is also active in producing polyester yarn and tire cord, as well as steel cord for use in tires.

The company is a major producer of synthetic rubber and a number of specialty rubbers that are widely used in paints, carpet backings, coatings, and in fabric and paper treatment. Firestone also makes a rubber additive to increase the durability of asphalt used in the paving of highways; a rubber material that adds resilience to asphalt playground surfaces; and special coating materials of various kinds.

In the early 1970s the company broadened its diversification by establishing Bank Firestone, Ltd., in Zurich, Switzerland. Firestone stock is listed on the London, Frankfurt, and Geneva stock exchanges.

Firestone tires were on the winning car in the first race at the Indianapolis Motor Speedway in 1909. In 1911, the first 500-mile Sweepstakes was held there, with the winner on Firestone tires. On this great proving ground, Firestone tires have been on the winning cars in the annual Memorial Day event 48 times.

The company announced, in 1967, that it would not enter into any new contracts with racing teams for using Firestone products. Firestone racing tires, however, were available for purchase by any race car owner or driver who elected to use them. In 1974 the company announced that it was phasing out the development, production, and servicing of USAC Championship and Formula race tires because of the high costs.

Firestone has set up an organization to study environmental problems and to work for solutions to eliminate them. The company continuously initiates new programs, processes or projects aimed at achieving its goal of excellence in environmental engineering.

Case question

1. Develop a campaign for the Firestone Steel Radial 500:
    a. *Definition of the market. Describe clearly the market you are going to try to influence with your advertising campaign.* What type of person is your best prospect—income, occupation, social status, and the like. How many of him or her are there? Where do they live—national or regional; urban or rural? Where do they buy this type of product? When and how often? Do others influence buying decisions, and if so, are you going to address some of your copy to them? *What is your target?*
    b. *Objectives.* An early step in planning the complete campaign for the next year should be the setting of an objective (or objectives). *State such an objective.* It need not be identical with, or similar to, the advertiser's objectives in recent years.

c. *Appropriation and budget.* You are now in a position to proceed with advertising plans for the next year. At some point, obviously, you must arrive at a figure representing your total advertising appropriation. For the present, *set a tentative figure.* While this seems to be contrary to the ideal "research-objective" method of determining the appropriation, it is neither an impractical nor an unwise way to start. In the light of the past experience of the company, and the objective of the next year, you can set a figure which seems reasonable.

d. *Appeal to be emphasized.* Now you must decide upon the appeal or appeals you are going to emphasize. *Present the appeal or appeals and the reasons for their selection.* If you feel a test is necessary to check the wisdom of your selection, *describe the test you would recommend.*

e. *Types of media.* Next, proceed to consider the types of media which seem likely to serve your purposes best. *List the types of media you plan to use.* State clearly why you include each type. Explain the exclusion from your list of any of the major media—newspapers, magazines, radio, direct mail, transportation, outdoor, and window display. Think in terms of "impressions per dollar" or some other useful standard.

f. *Advertising schedules.* With one eye on your advertising appropriation and the other on the buying motives, buying habits, reading and listening habits of your customers and potential customers, as well as on the advertising of competitors, you can now determine the size (or length) of your advertisements and the frequency of their appearance.

g. *Checking effectiveness of the advertising.* Most large advertisers, and many small ones, attempt to measure the effectiveness of their advertising efforts, within reasonable cost limits. *List and describe briefly the nature of the pre- and post-checks you would use in attempting to measure the effectiveness* of your recommended advertising.

h. *Differentiating ideas.* Not every advertising campaign succeeds in the competitive selling job for which it was planned and executed. It is not easy to reach and influence favorably potential customers. In this final section, point out and comment on the particular features of your campaign which endow it with adequate selling power.

Case **RYDER SYSTEM INC.**
18–2

Description of the business

Ryder System provides a wide range of truck transportation services through its truck leasing and rental, its networks of truckstops, and its specialized motor carriers. Its sales for 1974 were $512,000,000.

Full-service truck leasing and rental are the foundation of its business, accounting for 77 percent of the company's continuing revenues for the year, and for 47,500 vehicles operated by Ryder in its continuing operations.

A prime reason for Ryder's number-one position in the truck leasing and rental market is its geographic coverage: 429 service locations and 1,300 dealerships throughout the United States and Canada. The company also has an expanding and profitable truck leasing and rental operation in the United Kingdom.

Ryder has built its Truckstops of America into a substantial grow-ing chain, with 22 locations in 12 states and two new units under construction.

The specialized motor carriers consist of a large automobile hauler serving Chrysler as well as other operating companies, which main-tain custom-designed truck transportation systems for a variety of manufacturers and distributors.

Truck leasing and rental

The highest lease sales in history were achieved by the company's basic business of truck leasing and rental in an unsettled year that was plagued by inflation, energy shortages, record high interest costs, and a steadily deteriorating economy.

In 1974, truck leasing and rental had an over all 24 percent increase in revenues to $396 million from 1973's previous high of $319 million.

Lease sales, including new and increased contracts, were a record $74 million, up 21 percent from the prior year. A better job than ever in servicing and retaining existing accounts was done, and there was an improvement in the ratio of accounts lost to new business sold. Consequently, the year's net gain in new lease sales was 37 percent, from 39 million to $53.3 million.

Two basic problems confronted truck leasing and rental all year. One, beyond its control, was the high cost of money. With revenues up 24 percent, interest expense increased more than 60 percent from the year before. The second problem, against which aggressive and resourceful measures were taken, involved rising operating expenses, and a softening of the commercial rental market with its effect on utilization of Ryder's large fleet of rental vehicles.

From mid-year on, when the general business slowdown shrank the rental market served by Ryder and its competitors, a resulting over-supply of vehicles brought about a more competitive situation. Strin-gent steps were taken to reduce the Ryder rental fleet. As substantial reductions were made, tighter controls were established to balance fleet size with constantly changing market conditions.

Where the worsening economic climate affected commercial rent-als adversely, it had a somewhat opposite effect on Ryder's "Rent it here . . . Leave it there" one-way dealer-rental business. Revenues from dealer rentals were up 11 percent on approximately the same number of trucks in service as the year before, to $48 million from $43 million, as more Americans than ever moved themselves and their belongings across town or across the country.

Fleet Services

The Fleet Services division continued to expand its Truckstops of America chain in 1974, closing the year with 22 modern full-service facilities in operation along some of the nation's key interstate high-ways.

There were four additions during 1974: at Lodi, Ohio, and Harrisburg, Pennsylvania, both new constructions, and at Gallup, New Mexico, and Summit, Utah, which were acquisitions. Two additional truckstops were opened at Knoxville, Tennessee, and Maybrook, New York.

Net sales of the division increased to $79 million, from the prior year's $63 million, a 25 percent increase.

Custom Foods Management Services, Inc., operates restaurants at 18 Ryder truckstops, as well as 12 family-style restaurants in New York state. Custom Foods' sales continued to grow through the year, as did those of the division's Fleet Control Services, a fuel-purchasing control program for truck operators.

Ryder's Truckstops of America facilities, with their wide range of services for the professional trucker, have become pace setters for the truckstop industry. And motorists as well as truckers have come to look upon Ryder truckstops while traveling as places to refuel, dine, and shop, and to rest overnight.

Specialized transportation

M & G Convoy, Ryder's largest continuing specialized motor carrier, had an operating loss in 1974. It transports new automobiles for Chrysler and certain foreign car makers, and its loss on sharply lower revenues was the result of 1974's depressed conditions in the automobile industry.

Ryder's other continuing specialized transportation operations had healthy growth in 1974. Their revenues were up 80 percent over 1973, to $6 million, with profits in line with the business increase. Auto parts delivery operations for General Motors, Chrysler, and Ford, and equipment and produce delivery operations for Southern Bell and Swift & Co., were expanded. New carriage operations were begun for DeSoto, Inc., a large national furniture, paint, and home accessory manufacturer, and for the Miami (Florida) *Herald and News* newspapers.

Through 1974 Ryder transportation specialists were active, performing transportation studies for major concerns, designing new highway transport systems, and implementing certain of those systems with elements of the Ryder service line.

Insurance management

Southern Underwriters, Inc., the company's subsidiary which serves as the managing general agent in Florida for a group of property and casualty insurance companies, had another excellent year, with premiums written, revenues, and earnings at new high levels.

Discontinued operations

At the end of 1974, Ryder recognized the impracticability of being able to continue to expand its truck leasing market and to support all of its ancillary operations. Management carefully analyzed all of the company's operations and considered various options available to them. It was decided that if the company was to maintain its number-

EXHIBIT 18–3

Introducing The Short Lease. For companies who don't want long-term commitments.

Now you can lease Ryder trucks, tractors and trailers for 30 days, 60 days, six months, you name it. At very attractive rates. So you get the advantages of leasing without any long-term commitment. Including a GMC, Chevy or other fine truck that's exactly right for your needs. Including all maintenance and repairs, 24-hour road service throughout the U.S., replacements if needed. In short, everything you need except the driver.

Ryder has many ways to help you stay loose in today's tight economy. Call (800-327-7777) toll-free and ask about our Short Lease or mail this coupon now.

Ryder, tell me more about your Short Lease.

NAME/TITLE

COMPANY NAME

ADDRESS

CITY/STATE/ZIP

PHONE   W3

Ryder Truck Rental, Inc., Mr. Joe Claster, P.O. Box 520816, Miami, Florida 33152.

Ryder. The best truck money can lease.

one leadership in the truck leasing field, it was necessary to focus all of its financial resources on the truck leasing operations. Ancillary operations that complemented the truck leasing operations and were able to support themselves would be kept. In line with this, it was decided to dispose of Miller Trailers, Inc., Complete Auto Transit, Inc., Toro Petroleum Corp., Ryder Schools, Inc., and Ryder Littlease, Inc. Toro Petroleum was sold on December 30, 1974, at a profit. It is the intent of the company's management to dispose of the other discontinued operations.

Short lease program

Because of the confusing and uncertain economic forecasts, it appeared that businessmen were unwilling to make long-term commitments in an atmosphere of uncertainty.

As a result, the company believed that it would be opportune to publicize the fact that a prospect could lease Ryder trucks, tractors, and trailers for 30 days, 60 days, or for any period the customer wanted, at attractive rates, and the prospect would enjoy the advantages of leasing without having to make the long term commitment. (See Exhibit 18–3.)

The ad was placed in the *Wall Street Journal* and in *Business Week*. These have continued to be the two basic media for reaching commercial truck lease and rental prospects. Media analysis has continually demonstrated that Ryder can achieve its reach-and-frequency objectives better with this combination than with any other combination of general business or trade magazines affordable within its budget. The advertisement ran twice in both publications.

The response from the sales force was good because the program gave them an opportunity to talk to a prospect with much more flexibility. Ryder cannot break out its "Short Lease" sales or revenue, since it does not believe it important enough or worth the trouble to set up a whole accounting system to handle it.

However, general results indicated that Ryder was on the right track and subsequently advertised a "Trial Lease" alternative, whereby prospects signed up for the long-term lease but with a specific period, usually 90 days, wherein they can cancel the lease with no penalty. Because they make a long-term commitment on good faith, Ryder also offers even better long-term rates and more flexibility.

Case questions

1. Evaluate the current advertising program that Ryder is using.
2. Develop other appeals which Ryder might use.
3. At what market targets should Ryder project its comparison?
4. Set up an advertising campaign including media and timing of the advertisements.

Case   **TIFFANY & COMPANY**
18–3   **Developing a campaign**

For over a hundred years, Tiffany & Co. has been recognized for leadership in the design and manufacture of silverware to the most exacting standards of excellence. It has also sold more diamond engagement rings than any other organization in the world, besides being leader in quality for jewelry, watches, silver, china, crystal, and stationery items.

Its product lines include prices that range from $2, for a crystal goblet, $5.25 for a silver key ring, to diamond rings and other products that are marked for over $250,000.

The store was founded by Charles L. Tiffany in 1837 and was first opened in the name of Tiffany & Young (a partnership). This name was changed to Tiffany & Co. in 1853.

In the early days the store purchased almost all of its silverware from John C. Moore, who had begun the manufacture of silverware in 1827 and who was later joined in business by his son, Edward C. Moore. Just about all of the silver made by the Moores was sold to the Tiffany jewelry firm.

In 1868 Tiffany was incorporated and the silverware factory of the Moores became part of the organization, with Edward C. Moore becoming one of its directors and officers. From then on, and until Mr. Moore's death, the silverware made in the factory bore not only the mark "Tiffany & Co.," but also the letter "M." Ever since then, both the name Tiffany & Co. and the initial of the company president appear on all Tiffany-made silver.

During the 1850s the firm led in the introduction in this country of the English standard of sterling silver 925/1000 fine.

Heavier weight

Tiffany silver is of noticeably heavy weight, with more silver per unit than is generally used. Tiffany teaspoons, for instance, weigh from 14–17 ounces per dozen spoons, luncheon forks from 20 to 26.5 ounces. By comparison, many other makes have only 10-ounce teaspoons and 14-ounce forks, per dozen. It takes more time and skill to produce articles from the extra-weight silver used by Tiffany, and this means superior construction and quality. Although Tiffany sterling flatware is slightly higher in price than most sterling, the value is there.

The salad fork, for example, is a full-size fork. The knife has a true hollow handle. There is no need for filling to achieve balance, or for dent resistance. The bowl of the iced tea spoon is round, making it a good mixing spoon (one that gets to the bottom of the glass). It can also be used as a parfait spoon.

The beautiful soft finish on Tiffany sterling is justly famous. A considerable portion of the price of fine silverware is represented by the time and effort spent in securing a proper finish. It is attained by the complete removal of all the marks of working, such as hammer marks, filing marks, and any other irregularities in the surface, as well as the discoloring oxides of copper, known as "fire." The unusually smooth surface achieved by Tiffany silversmiths requires many operations, which may include stoning by hand with pumice and bluestone, as well as sand bobbing, brushing, and buffing. Only in this way is the surface ready for final polishing, which results in bringing out the fine color and luster of the metal.

Butler finish

Tiffany silver has what is called the "butler" finish, a "beautiful soft luster characteristic of silverware which has been cleaned and polished at home by years of hand-rubbing, as was done in the past by experienced butlers."

The Tiffany silver factory is located in a suburb of Newark, New Jersey. The vault containing old flatware dies is probably one of the most extensive of its kind in this country, and it would be difficult to place a valuation on the collection of dies in this repository.

Tiffany craftsmen melt and alloy their own sterling silver and each lot is assayed in its own laboratory under the supervision of one of the best metallurgists in the industry.

Where soldering is required, only silver solder (which is hard solder) is used. This means added strength and insures an almost invisible joint. Solder of this kind has a higher melting point than "soft" solder, which is used by many silver manufacturers. Soft solder is used by Tiffany only in rare instances when it is required by the nature of a special order.

In hollow ware, where the silver must be rolled against itself to form a decorative border, as at either a top or bottom edge, the seam is closed with silver (hard) solder. This guarantees an airtight seam not only stronger, but which prevents liquids entering interior surfaces with resultant unsanitary conditions.

Joints between component parts of an article are carefully cleaned of all excess solder, whether the joint is normally visible or not. Furthermore, the bottoms of flat pieces, such as trays and waiters, are stiffened by planishing. This is a hammering operation which increases their rigidity. Not until these hammer marks have been removed, by hand rubbing abrasive stones across them, are the final finishing operations undertaken.

Tiffany & Co. currently merchandise 29 sterling silver flatware patterns. The oldest in the line is the "Beekman," which was introduced in 1869. The newest member of the family is "Provence," brought out in 1961.

English patterns

The firm for many years has handled English sterling silver. One flatware pattern much in favor is the "Rat Tail." It is a Tiffany exclusive and bears the registered English hallmark of Tiffany & Co. "Rat Tail" has regulation size spoon bowls and fork tines. The customer who is partial to English silver has a choice of three or four tined luncheon and dinner forks. The knives are available with plain or octagonal pistol handles and slipper-shaped or pistol blades.

Recently the silver department of the store issued a release on the care and treatment of stainless steel knife blades. These blades are manufactured by the Northampton Cutlery Company. The complaint about staining and pitting is an old one which has plagued manufacturers for years.

Staining and pitting could not occur without contact with certain food acids. Vinegar, mustard, sauerkraut, mayonnaise, and ordinary table salt are the worst offenders. Tiffany & Co. recommends washing silver immediately after use or as soon as possible, contending that if this is done, corrosion will not occur. Notice was also given at the time that the blades would no longer be refinished or replaced free of charge.

To meet the ever-growing demand and competition in award and presentation silver, Tiffany has also established a Corporate Gift department. The price list for some of Tiffany's sterling flatware patterns is given in Exhibit 18–4, which follows.

Diamond rings

Every Tiffany diamond ring is an entire Tiffany product. From the time the diamond is selected to the time it is purchased as a finished jewel, the diamond never leaves the premises. The stones are graded and sorted to exacting standards, and are set in rings designed and made in the workrooms at the Fifth Avenue store.

Diamonds are pure or nearly pure carbon. Millions of years went into the formation of a diamond, and during that time three extraordinary things happened.

First, it was given its unique powers of light refraction and dispersion, enabling it to gather light within itself and send it back in a shower of fire and brilliance.

Second, it was given a purity unmatched by any other gemstone. It is as clear as a dewdrop.

Third, it became the hardest substance known to man. Diamonds are 120 times harder than the next hardest substances known, rubies or sapphires. Steel cannot cut a diamond. The only material that can cut a diamond is another diamond.

Four points to remember when choosing a diamond

The four factors determining the price of a diamond are referred to as the four Cs: cutting, color, clarity, and carat weight.

Cutting. The only thing man can do for a diamond is cut it—nature has done the rest. The diamond's optical system is in two parts: the lower part, the pavilion, which acts like an automobile headlight, gathering the light and forcing it out the top in a concentrated beam; and the upper part, called the crown, which acts as a series of prisms on the light beam, dispersing it into a myriad of dazzling colored flashes.

There are 58 tiny facets on the diamond that should be thought of as mirrors, and it is necessary for the cutter to place each of these facets in exact geometric relation to one another, in order to achieve maximum fire and brilliance.

EXHIBIT 18–4

Individual Pieces	Faneuil	Flemish	Provence	Hampton	Shell & Thread	English King	RATTAIL Plain Pistol Knives	RATTAIL Octagonal Pistol Knives
Bouillon Spoon	$16.25	$ –	$ –	$21.50	$21.50	$22.00	$22.00	$ –
Butter Spreader, Flat	12.00	14.75	16.50	16.50	18.00	19.00	19.00	–
Butter Spreader, H.H.	18.00	20.50	24.50	24.50	26.00	26.00	26.00	30.00
Cocktail Fork	16.00	–	–	21.50	21.50	22.00	22.00	–
Coffee Spoon	9.25	13.00	14.75	14.75	15.00	16.00	16.00	–
Cream Soup Spoon	21.50	26.00	30.50	30.50	30.00	33.00	33.00	–
Dessert Fork	20.50	–	–	27.00	27.00	28.00	28.00	–
Dessert Knife	20.50	–	–	26.00	27.00	27.00	27.00	31.00
Dessert Spoon	22.00	24.50	32.00	32.00	30.50	33.00	33.00	–
Dinner Fork	26.00	30.50	38.00	38.00	38.50	39.00	44.00	–
Dinner Knife	23.50	26.50	32.00	32.00	30.50	32.00	32.00	36.00
Fish Fork	24.00	–	–	30.00	29.50	32.00	32.00	–
Fish Knife	22.00	–	–	28.00	27.00	27.50	27.50	31.50
Fruit Spoon	–	–	–	–	–	–	23.50	–
Iced Teaspoon	16.00	–	–	26.00	29.50	26.50	26.50	–
Luncheon Fork	20.50	24.00	29.00	29.00	30.50	30.50	31.50	–
Luncheon Knife	19.75	22.00	26.50	26.50	26.50	28.00	28.00	32.00
Salad Fork	20.50	24.50	29.00	29.00	29.50	30.50	31.50	–
Steak Knife, Ind.	27.00	30.50	33.00	33.00	33.00	33.00	33.00	37.00
Teaspoon	15.00	19.00	21.50	21.50	21.50	23.50	23.50	–
Serving Pieces								
Berry Spoon	62.00	–	–	–	–	–	77.00	–
Butter Server	24.50	–	–	–	–	–	33.00	37.00
Cake Server	44.00	53.00	57.00	57.00	57.00	57.00	57.00	61.00
Cheese Server	29.00	30.00	32.00	32.00	33.00	33.00	33.00	37.00
Cold Meat Fork	52.00	61.00	67.00	67.00	67.00	70.00	70.00	–
Flat Server	65.00	–	–	–	–	–	78.00	–
Gravy Ladle	44.00	56.00	61.00	61.00	60.00	61.00	61.00	–
Jelly Spoon	33.00	–	–	–	–	–	42.50	–
Salad Serving Fork	68.00	–	–	–	–	–	88.00	–
Salad Serving Spoon	68.00	–	–	–	–	–	88.00	–
Sauce Ladle	29.50	38.00	39.50	39.50	39.50	41.00	41.00	–
Serving Fork	44.00	56.00	60.00	60.00	58.00	60.00	60.00	–
Sugar Spoon	22.00	30.50	33.00	33.00	33.00	33.50	33.50	–
Sugar Tongs	20.50	29.50	30.50	30.50	32.00	32.00	32.00	–
Tablespoon	30.50	39.00	48.50	48.50	50.00	50.00	50.00	–
Vegetable Spoon	60.00	73.00	73.00	73.00	74.00	79.00	79.00	–

Carving Pieces

	Salem	Hamilton	Castilian	Windham King William	San Lorenzo Richelieu	Audubon	Olympian	Chrysanthemum Feather Edge
Roast Carver	56.00	65.00	68.00	68.00	68.00	68.00	68.00	72.00
Roast Fork	56.00	65.00	68.00	68.00	68.00	68.00	68.00	72.00
Steak Carver	33.50	—	—	—	47.00	—	49.50	53.50
Steak Fork	33.50	—	—	—	47.00	—	49.50	53.50

Additional Pieces

	Salem	Hamilton	Castilian	Windham King William	San Lorenzo Richelieu	Audubon	Olympian	Chrysanthemum Feather Edge
Afternoon Teaspoon	13.25	—	—	—	—	—	21.00	—
Ice Tongs	83.00	—	—	—	—	—	—	—
Lemon Fork	15.25	—	—	—	—	—	—	—
Olive Fork	19.50	—	—	—	—	—	—	—
Individual Salt Spoon	9.25	—	—	—	—	—	—	—

Individual Pieces

	Salem	Hamilton	Castilian	Windham King William	San Lorenzo Richelieu	Audubon	Olympian	Chrysanthemum Feather Edge
Butter Spreader, Flat	$13.00	$16.75	$16.75	$19.00	$19.00	$20.50	$24.00	$24.00
Butter Spreader, H.H.	19.50	24.50	24.50	26.00	26.00	29.00	35.50	35.50
Cocktail Fork	16.75	20.50	—	22.00	—	24.50	—	28.00
Coffee Spoon	10.75	14.75	14.75	16.00	16.00	16.75	19.25	19.25
Cream Soup Spoon	24.50	29.50	29.50	30.50	30.50	33.00	39.50	39.50
Dessert Spoon	24.50	30.50	30.50	32.00	32.00	35.00	41.00	41.00
Dinner Fork	30.50	38.00	38.00	38.50	38.50	41.00	48.00	48.00
Dinner Knife	26.00	30.50	30.50	30.50	30.50	35.50	44.00	44.00
Iced Teaspoon	19.25	24.50	—	26.00	—	29.00	—	33.00
Luncheon Fork	24.00	28.00	28.00	30.50	30.50	33.00	39.00	39.00
Luncheon Knife	22.00	26.50	26.50	27.00	27.00	33.00	38.50	38.50
Salad Fork	23.50	28.00	28.00	29.50	29.50	33.50	38.50	38.50
Teaspoon	16.25	20.50	20.50	22.00	22.00	24.50	29.50	29.50

Serving Pieces

	Salem	Hamilton	Castilian	Windham King William	San Lorenzo Richelieu	Audubon	Olympian	Chrysanthemum Feather Edge
Cake Server	48.00	57.00	—	57.00	—	67.00	—	77.00
Cold Meat Fork	56.00	65.00	65.00	67.00	67.00	77.00	85.00	85.00
Gravy Ladle	47.50	58.00	58.00	59.00	59.00	70.00	74.00	74.00
Serving Fork	47.50	58.00	58.00	59.00	59.00	68.00	74.00	74.00
Sugar Spoon	24.50	33.00	33.00	33.50	33.50	36.00	41.00	41.00
Tablespoon	36.00	47.00	47.00	48.50	48.50	54.00	61.00	61.00

Few diamonds are properly cut. The vast majority are "spread." This means that the cutter has compromised the ideal proportions and has cut the stone to weigh more than it should, thereby sacrificing brilliance for size. In addition, the customer is *paying* for this *extra padding.* The vintner who waters wine and the grocer whose thumb occasionally rests on the scales are similarly taking advantage of an unknowing public.

Tiffany makes no compromise in this crucial matter. Tiffany customers are offered only diamonds cut with ideal proportions and exquisitely polished, thereby giving the customer a much sounder investment for his money.

Color. Diamonds occur, by rare accident of nature, in pink, green, red, blue—more frequently in yellow and brown. But the traditional engagement diamond is a clear dewdrop white.

Although these diamonds may appear colorless to the untrained eye, the majority contain varying tints. The more colorless the diamond, the greater the rarity and value. Tiffany diamonds are graded in three color categories, *all well above* colors usually available elsewhere.

"Extra River" is its stone of highest quality color. "River" is only slightly less fine. "Fine White" diamonds are again a little lower than River stones. This category makes possible the selection of a stone of good color for the customer seeking a larger stone for a more modest price.

On extremely rare occasions Tiffany finds a stone worthy of being classified Extra, Extra River or even Extra, Extra, Extra River, and their rarity, beauty and value, as their name implies, is extraordinary.

The fact is, a diamond's value increases with each increase in color quality. Such differences may run to hundreds, or even thousands, of dollars per carat, depending not only on the difference in color, but on the size of stone.

One word of caution: be wary of the term "blue-white" diamond. This term has been so indiscriminately used to describe inferior stones that few reputable jewelers still use it.

And be especially cautious of bluish light or any attempt to demonstrate "blueness." Almost any diamond will flash back every color of the rainbow, including blue.

Clarity. Flawless diamonds are extremely rare. If magnified highly enough, it is possible to find in most diamonds tiny carbon spots, feathers, or faint flaws. These are called "inclusions."

A diamond is said to be "flawless" if no inclusions can be seen when the diamond is magnified ten times by the usual jeweler's loupe. This has the disadvantage of allowing the use of only one eye when examining the diamond. Tiffany, however, uses a binocular microscope to magnify each of its diamonds. This allows its experts to use both eyes and to inspect for inclusions far more critically. Tiffany was the first to use the binocular microscope for the purpose of grading diamonds.

Carat weight. The word "carat" is derived from the carob tree, the seeds of which were so uniform in weight that they became the standard for measuring the weight of gems in ancient India. One one-hundredth of a carat is referred to as a "point." So Tiffany's smallest diamond ring, 15 points, would be .15 of a carat.

However, the size of a diamond alone is almost meaningless unless one takes into account the other qualities: cut, color, and clarity.

In fact, it is just as ridiculous to say a painting by an unknown artist is more valuable than a Rembrandt because it is twice as large.

Size, however, does increase the value of a good diamond, for the simple reason that large stones are rarer than smaller ones, and a two-carat diamond is thus worth more than twice as much as a one-carat stone of the same quality.

History of the diamond engagement ring

Although the ancient Egyptians wore a bridal ring on the third finger, left hand, it was not until the 15th century that the diamond was first recorded as a bridal jewel.

This was in 1477, when the Archduke Maximilian of Austria ordered two rings for his bride-to-be, Mary of Burgundy. One was a diamond engagement ring, the other a wedding band of gold.

Because of their rarity, diamonds for engagement rings were for centuries limited to only brides-to-be of the aristocracy. However, in 1870 the vast diamond deposits of South Africa were discovered, and for the first time diamonds became available to brides-to-be the world over.

During the 1870s the Tiffany Setting was created. Since then its setting of prongs, which lift and hold the stone away from the ring to expose greater brilliance, has become the standard against which all engagement rings are judged. From the beginning of Tiffany & Co., diamonds have been personally selected by a senior officer of the company.

Seasonal business

Sales of Tiffany & Co. have increased from $15,993,562, with net earnings of $918,075 in 1965 to $34,879,564, with net earnings of $2,-067,766 in 1974. Selling, general, and administrative expenses amounted to $10,390,322 in 1974.

Sixty percent of Tiffany's business is done in the eight weeks before Christmas in its New York store. Thirty-five percent of the volume comes from out of New York. Tiffany also has established branches in San Francisco, Beverly Hills, Chicago, Houston, and Atlanta.

Case question

1. Develop the annual advertising campaign for either flatware sterling silver or diamond rings. Include in the campaign long-range marketing strategy and objectives, budget planning, appeal to use, merchandising plan, and media selection (time schedules, and the like).

Case   **INTERNATIONAL DRUG COMPANY**
18–4   **Handling cooperative advertising allowances**

The International Drug Company, faced with aggressive competition in a number of its key markets, decided to liberalize its cooperative advertising allowances to the retail outlets in these areas.

It, therefore, contracted with a number of the chains and retail drugstores last year and offered allowances for special services:

1. Paying money amounting up to 5 percent of purchases of International's products in consideration of these customers paying said money to its salesclerks in the form of "push money" to promote the sale of the products.
2. Paying 5 percent of net purchases in consideration of these customers maintaining a permanent daily counter and window display.
3. Making available a cooperative newspaper advertising agreement under which these customers were reimbursed for the cost of advertising International's product. These advertisements were run as a listing with the customers' own advertisements.
4. Paying to these customers certain allowances for radio, TV, and direct-mail advertising.
5. Encouraging both the large and small retailers to engage in joint price advertising. In some cases, special consideration would be given to the large retailers in the area.

For the first six months after the cooperative advertising allowances were given, International Drug's sales increased 7 percent in the market in which these were granted.

The executives were pleased with results and were planning to extend these allowances on a national basis when their attorney called to their attention the various interpretations the Federal Trade Commission had made in the use of cooperative advertising.

Joint advertising

The right of retailers to engage in joint price advertising is questionable. The Federal Trade Commission warned that joint ads involve antitrust violations. However, the antitrust division of the department declared that FTA has given retailers some bad advice.

The particular dispute rates as one that veteran observers find most difficult to comprehend. To help eliminate uncertainty, the FTC offered to give advance advisory opinions to businessmen concerned about the legality of their activities.

Among the first in line when FTC's advisory opinion service got under way were representatives of retail drug organizations. Some of these organizations had recently submitted to antitrust consent settlements which involve heavy penalties for future price-fixing activity. They wanted assurance that their plans for joint advertising activity would not lead to new antitrust trouble.

Some of the sponsors of specific plans had had indications from the

Department of Justice and FTC that their particular plans were doubt-ful. FTC's staff seemed to be convinced that the co-op plans that were submitted would represent price fixing. But as a special service they took the proposals to the Department of Justice.

The commission claimed the ban on joint advertising was inescap-able, and that the Department of Justice agreed. While the ruling indicated that plans had been submitted, it stated, "that no prices, terms, or conditions of sale of any kind should appear in the advertis-ing."

It is interesting to note that in the testimony, it was stated, "the fact that prices are quoted in joint ads has not in the past, and is not now, regarded as conclusive proof of price fixing."

This testimony, however, did not appear to be fully adequate. A member of the FTC majority suggested that the differences are more than semantics. This member emphasized that the drug industry plans which were before the committee involved an arrangement whereby a committee of retail druggists selected the items to be fea-tured and the prices to be listed. The mere existence of this mech-anism to select items and designate a price represents the essential ingredients of illegal price-fixing arrangements.

To some, the existence of a mechanism to select items and desig-nate price is per se an offense. But, to others, the existence of the mechanism is meaningless, unless the result is a binding arrange-ment which results in a restraint of trade.

On the other hand, a House committee reviewed the ruling and decided that it does not mean what it says. The House Small Business Committee said that it is legal for independent retailers to pool their funds and purchase joint advertising. It also asserted that the advertis-ing could include prices of products shown. It was the opinion of the committee that the independent retailer generally is too small to take full advantage of these cooperative allowances unless joint advertis-ing is allowed.

Cooperative advertising for apparel makers

The Federal Trade Commission listed 163 wearing apparel manu-facturers who have promised not to give discriminatory allowances in the future, and 76 others who face complaints for failing to reach agreement with the commission.

The report involves the first public identification of the wearing apparel industry members whose cooperative advertising payments were challenged in the commission's industry-wide attack on coopera-tive advertising arrangements in the apparel industry. Earlier, the commission announced that about 250 companies had been given an opportunity to sign standard consent settlements to discontinue dis-criminatory payments which had been turned up in an investigation of apparel industry suppliers and retailers.

In its announcement, FTC warned that the companies which refused to accept the opportunity for a standard consent settlement will face "appropriate action" on "a priority basis." FTC said some large stores received "thousands of dollars," and it is also reported to be preparing cases against retailers who solicited discriminatory payments from the suppliers.

The investigation included sworn reports by mail from scores of leading department stores and apparel shops, which were required to list all the advertising allowances they received from suppliers. Later, the reports from the retailers were matched against similar reports obtained from several hundred suppliers.

An initial FTC effort to induce about 150 suppliers to accept a standard consent settlement bogged down when industry leaders protested that the commission was punishing some suppliers and failing to enforce similar restraints on their competitors. FTC subsequently enlarged its investigation and brought charges against 100 additional suppliers.

Case questions

1. Is International's cooperative plan a good one? Why, or why not?
2. How should the cooperative advertising plan be implemented?
3. What problems may the company encounter with its plan?
4. Do the terms of International Drug Company's cooperative advertising plan fall within the area of activity allowed by federal regulations?
5. How can International modify its cooperative advertising plan to comply with the existing regulations?
6. What procedure should International adopt when it extends its cooperative advertising on a national basis?

Case **MELVILLE SHOE CORPORATION**
18–5 **Considering a promotional campaign**

Melville Shoe Corporation, a leading manufacturer and merchandiser of footwear, apparel, cosmetic, and health products is faced with the problem of developing an advertising campaign.

The Melville Shoe Corporation became an official entity in 1916 and by the early 1920s was a recognized leader in the industry.

As a result of the combination of Frank Melville's desire to work out a new and different arrangement for marketing a good quality, low-priced, mass-produced shoe, and his son, Ward, urging him to consider further expansion, the two began working out plans for a new Melville chain. The idea—developed with leading New England shoe manufacturer J. Franklin McElwain—was to establish a new kind of relationship between a manufacturer and a retailer. It guaranteed the manufacturer a steady market for his output and enabled the retailer to rely on a steady supply of good quality shoes manufactured to his specifications at reduced costs that allowed a low selling price, giving better value. J. F. McElwain Co., as the manufacturer, shared in the Melville profits, while Melville shared in the manufacturing profits. This arrangement, which is said to have been sealed with a simple handshake, continued until J. F. McElwain Co. became part of Melville in 1939.

On the retailing end, the Melvilles envisioned a chain with a standard store format that would be recognizable across the country and a brand name that could be considered truly national. Ward Melville, who had long been interested in architecture, played a major role in the development of the familiar "white front" Thom McAn store with the name attached in large script to the storefront itself. It is believed that this was the first time in the history of retailing that the store sign had been made a part of the storefront.

Ward Melville was also responsible for the name of the new chain. He found the original name in a roster of Scottish golf pros, added the *h* to "Tom" and took an *n* and a *c* out of the "McCann" and capitalized the *a*. The net result was to give the name novelty and brevity as well as projecting an image of quality and thrift. Originally, there was a picture of Thom McAn used in the firm's advertising, but it is said that the picture was actually a sketch of a Bowery bum who had agreed to pose for the artist.

Today, Thom McAn—"the best selling shoe in all America"—is sold through 900 Thom McAn stores located in 44 states and Puerto Rico. Mostly because of Thom McAn's domination of the low-priced shoe field—as the Model T dominated the low-priced automobile field— Melville kept on growing and making a profit during the Depression years. The worse things got, the more men turned to the shoe into which Melville had packed so much quality. Customers got their $4 worth—and then some—when they bought Thom McAn shoes.

Through the 1930s and 1940s, until the end of World War II, the combination of good quality and low price attracted the buyers. But to the men coming back from the war, a "good bargain" wasn't enough. After years of wearing combat boots, the veterans wanted a little flash, a little style. They wanted barge toes and more bounce to the ounce.

Unfortunately, Melville, geared up as it was to the "You can have any color you want as long as it's black" philosophy, went right on grinding out the shoes that, as events proved, nobody wanted. There was also another trend running that by-passed Melville. This was the flood tide of the residential flow from the cities to the suburbs.

The combined effect of Melville's failure to get with the style trends and its missing of the commuter train to the suburbs, cut heavily into the company's profits and put it in near jeopardy in the middle 1950s. Fortunately, there proved to be a way—in fact, three ways—out.

The first was a mass shift of Thom McAn stores from downtown to the suburbs. In this crash program—under the able leadership of Robert C. Erb, who was president of Melville from 1956 to 1964—the company closed the old, unprofitable downtown stores and opened new suburban ones as fast as it possibly could. In ten years between 1955 and 1965, Melville closed 278 stores and opened 417. When it finished this restructuring of its retailing operations they were located where the people were once again—at the very core of the population explosion with millions of shoe-buying young families at their door.

Second, Melville stopped thinking of itself as being in the shoe business, and started thinking of itself as being in the fashion business. It stopped concentrating on selling what it made, and started concentrating on making what it could sell. It turned its whole operation around and looked at it from the marketing, rather than the manufacturing, end of things. It came to view its stores as profit centers and the factories as cost centers. The company came to realize that the way to make money was to appeal to customer wants, not by cutting prices, or leather, in a different way.

In the third place, there were strong currents of change running in the marketplace itself. The most important of these—besides the shift to the suburbs and the new demand for style and variety in footwear—was the steadily dropping median age of the population.

However, knowing there was an expanding youth market and getting the young people to buy Melville's product instead of those of its competitors were two entirely different propositions. How was the company going to bridge not only the generation gap but the marketing gap? How was it to get the youngsters to come into Thom McAn stores?

As it often happens, the answer came almost by accident and from a highly unlikely source—in the person of a young singer named Chubby Checker. He set off what was probably the biggest rage of the 1950s—a dance called The Twist.

As most rages do, The Twist started with the teen-agers and spread to the adults; and Melville was lucky enough to catch up with both the dance and Chubby Checker in the early stages. It signed Chubby Checker to promote Thom McAn shoes well before he hit his peak. By using his name and picture and by calling just about every pair of shoes "Twisters," Melville began selling a lot of shoes to teen-agers.

The company found that the best way to reach the youngsters was through their sense, or lack of sense, of hearing. The young people don't always listen to their parents, but they do listen to "sound radio" and its blasting of the airwaves with the "top 40" hits.

From practical experience, Melville became an expert in what in the early 1960s was the relatively new art of teen-age marketing. It tied shoe styles into all kinds of teen fads and favorites—the Pontiac GTO car, surfing, rock bands, the Monkees, Indian music, motor bikes—and got its shoes associated with the teen way of life. At the same time, in appealing to the adult market, it advertised heavily on television. Some of the ads, such as the famed "Man in the Shoe" commercial, became classics. Moving into the latter half of the 1960s Melville's combination of the accent on youth, shopping center concentration, and "excitement" selling resulted in the best growth record in the shoe business. It seemed that Melville's only remaining challenge was to expand its position as a leader in footwear.

Operating in the front lines of change, however, the modern retailer must be a man in constant motion, detecting and reacting to change not on a 10 or 25-year basis, as used to be the case, but rather on a year-to-year, or even month-to-month time scale.

In Melville's case, as it moved to shoes, to footwear, to fashion, and into apparel, it became apparent that as well as it did in these areas no one of them actually defined its business. Rather, it was pretty obvious that merchandising was its business, and a very special kind of merchandising at that.

Determining what kind of business a company is in, with things changing as rapidly as they are today, is not nearly so easy as it sounds. Not only is it not easy, but the price of miscalculation in making this determination is inordinately high, often adding up to the difference between success and failure. There are a number of industries today that have found themselves in this dilemma. The railroads, for example, failed to realize that transportation was their business. Steel did not see that materials was its field. The oil companies were slow to recognize that they were in the energy business.

Melville acknowledged that merchandising was its game. But, again, given the incredible rate at which conditions in its operating environment change, it knew that it could not sit back and contemplate its accomplishments even at this level of the company's evolution. As a result, in further refining its role, the company now sees itself as a specialty merchandiser. In recent years, rather than responding to the pressures of a technologically oriented mass society by lining up like automatons, and thinking, dressing, acting, and buying with unvarying sameness, consumers have been "doing their own thing." Perhaps, because they want to feel different to emphasize their individuality, today's consumers like to shop in stores that cater to them in a special way. To a retailer, this means being small enough to treat the customer as someone important, yet, as the result of specialization, being able to carry a much more complete line within a given product area. This also means better, more personal service all around. Most importantly, it means more sales.

Specialty markets have developed out of increased education, sophistication, affluence, and leisure time. People today have an interest in more things, are active in more ways, have better developed and more specific tastes, have more time to spend doing more things, and, to top it off, have more money to spend in a discretionary way. All this adds up to a wider ranging, more demanding consumer, who is an "expert" purchaser and wants to deal with an "expert" seller who is interested in giving him complete "customer satisfaction."

As the result of these factors, people buy for different reasons than they used to buy. As professor Theodore Levitt of the Harvard Business School has put it, rather than buying a product itself, today's consumers buy "with an expectation of benefits." Their purchasing decision is not determined by the simple, straightforward reasoning that they need a pair of shoes to keep their feet warm and dry, but rather because the shoes are going to help them make a good social impression, or help them "feel better" in a number of ways.

The term "product augmentation" has replaced the emphasis on product characteristics. This has grown to some extent out of the fact that almost any competent company in a given field can manufacture a product that is as good as his competitor's and can usually meet his competitor's price. The competition begins, and is decided, at the "value satisfaction" level. As Charles Revson, president of Revlon, has expressed it, "In the factory we make cosmetics. In the store we sell hope." In retailing, "product augmentation" means a good shopping environment, created by a conducive store format. It also means a high degree of personal involvement on the part of both buyer and seller. It means a complete in-depth coverage of a given product line.

In a way, the trend toward specialty merchandising represents a return to the small, intimate shops characteristic of Europe and of this country in its earlier days. How then can it be possible for a company the size of Melville, that has gotten where it is primarily through the mass merchandising of a single product line, to provide the kind of intimate, concentrated merchandising involved here?

Melville has answered this question by becoming a company made up of a number of retail chains in a variety of fields. Each chain specializes in its area, providing the kind of concept, store format, merchandise, and service that add up to specialty merchandising.

While such a course may seem an abrupt turning from Melville's past, it is actually, in many ways, a logical extension of many of the elements that have contributed to its progress in recent years. Thom McAn, with its emphasis on the teen-age and young family market, has been a specialty merchandiser to some extent.

Miles has been developing into a specialty chain with its new small and intimate stores. Designed to appeal to the young woman, these new Miles shops feature soft lights, bright colors, and pleasant background music. Low pads have replaced the customary chairs and Miles advertising and promotion is keyed to what the young people are thinking about and talking about.

In March 1968, Melville made its first completely new move into specialty merchandising, when it opened the first store of Chess King teen-male apparel chain. Created for the 12- to 20-year-olds, Chess King exemplifies the "product augmentation" theory of specialty merchandising.

Chess King merchandise has special appeal for the market—bell bottoms, white jeans, necklaces, Marlene Dietrich hats, and incense. The store environment literally makes shopping a "happening" for the youngsters. On special occasions, rock bands blare forth from a permanent raised platform at the back of the store. Shopping at Chess King is so much fun for the kids that the stores now rival the drugstore as the favorite teen hangout in today's shopping centers.

The launching of Chess King marked Melville's first expansion outside the shoe field. In December 1968, Melville purchased Foxwood Casuals, the fast-growing young women's sports apparel chain. Foxwood fit perfectly into the specialty merchandising concept, with a recognizable store format designed to appeal to the suburban young woman along with clothes consistent with her active, informal lifestyle. It is the girl's own Chess King.

In still a third move into specialty merchandising, this time completely outside both the footwear and apparel business, Melville acquired a health and beauty aid chain, New England-based Consumer Value Stores, specializing in a complete line of cosmetic and health products bought primarily by the young woman. The Consumer Value acquisition gave Melville a good foothold in a fast-growing field that will almost certainly grow bigger with each passing year.

More important, the Consumer Value acquisition gave Melville another unit to use in making its specialty merchandising concept a practical reality. Specialty merchandising is much more than a merchandising theory with Melville, it is a plan of physical action with the goal of establishing a half-dozen, or even more, Melville stores in as many shopping centers as possible.

This means that with a multiple chain approach, with each unit designed to fit into the shopping center mix on its own, Melville multiplies the number of shopping centers with each new chain it creates or acquires. With one brand name chain, the expansion of a retailing organization is limited by the number of new shopping centers constructed. With six or more chains, shopping center representation is increased sixfold. In implementing its specialty merchandising program, Melville expects to open about 1,000 new stores and leased departments within the next three years which would give the company a total of 2,400 outlets. Melville's sales are about $500 million. The company is the largest combined retailer and manufacturer of footwear, which it sells through its Thom McAn and Miles stores, and its Meldisco division, which operates leased departments in discount stores.

In recent years Melville has, for the first time in its history, expanded beyond the footwear field. In March 1968, Melville started the Chess King chain of young men's apparel stores, and in December 1968, it acquired the Foxwood chain of young women's sportswear stores. It has 1,600 stores, 15 factories, 12,000 employees, and 18,000 stockholders.

Advertising expenditure

Melville spends somewhere between 2 percent and 3 percent of gross sales for advertising and 1 percent to 1.5 percent for window and store display material. The actual percent will depend on the autonomous decision of the president of each Melville division.

Advertising policy

Each division of Melville sets its own advertising strategy. This approach of autonomous decision is necessary and efficient when one considers that each Melville division presents entirely different product lines to entirely different customer groups. However, it is generally true that all Melville divisions have taken up the general direction set by Melville management of creating a feeling of *excitement and fun* in advertising and display.

In Exhibit 18–5 is an advertisement that was placed in such newspapers as the *Albany Times Union, Boston Globe, Hartford Times, Charleston News-Courier, Honolulu Star Bulletin, Kansas City Star, Seattle Times,* and *Washington Post.* Exhibit 18–6 is another advertisement in the Thom McAn promotion of its children's shoes.

EXHIBIT 18–5

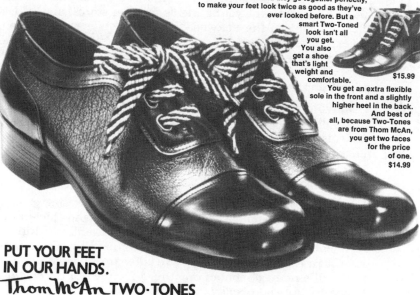

ARE YOUR FEET TWO-FACED?

They will be when you put on a pair of Two-Tones. Because Two-Tones have two different faces, each one made of rich leather. One is rugged and grainy in texture, the other is slick and smooth and takes a terrific shine. And they go together perfectly, to make your feet look twice as good as they've ever looked before. But a smart Two-Toned look isn't all you get. You also get a shoe that's light weight and comfortable. You get an extra flexible sole in the front and a slightly higher heel in the back. And best of all, because Two-Tones are from Thom McAn, you get two faces for the price of one. $14.99

$15.99

PUT YOUR FEET IN OUR HANDS.

Thom McAn TWO-TONES

EXHIBIT 18–6

"If you can't find anything wrong with our shoes within 30 days, they're yours."

"We make Thom McAn shoes for children and we honestly believe they're the best you can buy.

But we don't expect you to go along with that just because we say so.

We think you should have a chance to make us prove it. And that's just what you're going to get.

From now on, when you buy a pair of our boys or girls shoes, we're going to give you thirty days to put us to the test.

If, during that time, you are dissatisfied with our shoes for any reason whatsoever, bring them in and we'll buy them back from you.

Or give you a new pair, if that's what you prefer. And we'll do this with no questions asked, and no rigmarole to go through.

You just give us back our shoes and our sales slip and we'll give you back your money.

You may be wondering how we can afford to do something like this and still stay in business.

Well, we couldn't if we didn't make such good shoes. But we test and retest all the leathers and other quality materials we use at our Melville Testing Labs.

We test and retest the stitching and cementing that holds our shoes together.

And we test and retest everything else that goes into the making of a fine shoe.

So when you buy Thom McAn shoes for your son or daughter, we're pretty sure you'll be happy with them.

And we don't think very many of you will be back to complain or ask for your money back.

But we still feel obligated to give you that opportunity. Because we believe that any shoe company that isn't willing to buy their shoes back, shouldn't sell them to you in the first place."

Lawrence E. McGourty
Lawrence E. McGourty
President of the Thom McAn Shoe Company

Thom McAn Children's Shoes $5.99–$9.99

Infants' shoe sizes 2 to 8, Girls' 8½ to 4, Boys' 8½ to 6

Case question

1. Develop a campaign for Thom McAn children's shoes in which you will define the market, set the objectives, firm the budget, decide on the appeal, and select the specific media.

Case **MARSHALL FIELD & COMPANY**
18–6 **Deciding on customers of a store**

In the course of its long history, Marshall Field & Company has been engaged in a wide variety of activities that have included retailing, wholesaling, manufacturing, and real estate. Until about 40 years ago, it was principally a wholesale operation. Since 1953, it has confined itself almost entirely to the operation of retail stores. It now has ten of these. Much the most important, both in sales and earnings, is the main store in downtown Chicago. Second in importance is the main Frederick & Nelson store in Seattle.

The Chicago operation includes branches in Evanston, Oak Park, Lake Forest, Skokie, Oakbrook, Calumet City, and Park Forest, all suburbs of the city, and in Wauwatosa, a suburb of Milwaukee. The Seattle store has three suburban branches.

It is an ironic fact that the founder, Mr. Marshall Field, is remembered mainly as a great retail merchant. Throughout his life dry goods wholesaling was the principal part of his business, and his interest in retailing was distinctly secondary, particularly in the early years of his career.

Mr. Field arrived in Chicago from Pittsfield, Massachusetts, in 1856. He was 21 years of age and had been reared in a strict New England farm family. After four years as a clerk in a country store, he decided to head west with his savings of something less than $1,000.

His brother Joseph helped Marshall obtain employment as a clerk in the largest wholesale dry goods house in Chicago—Cooley, Wadsworth and Company. His salary was $400 a year. He slept on the premises and at the end of the year had saved $200.

As a result of his seriousness of purpose, his selling skill, and his keen interest in merchandising, young Field progressed rapidly, becoming a partner in 1860. In 1863, the firm name was changed to Farwell, Field & Company, John V. Farwell having become a partner some years earlier. Also in 1863, Levi Z. Leiter joined the firm.

Two years later both Field and Leiter left Farwell, Field & Company and bought into the dry goods store of P. Palmer, changing its name to Field, Palmer and Leiter. In 1867, the two men bought out Potter Palmer and his brother, and the firm name became Field, Leiter & Company.

Potter Palmer had come to Chicago from Lockport, New York, in 1852. He established a dry goods store on Lake Street with his $5,000 capital. At this time Chicago had a population of 40,000. Its streets were unpaved. Its sidewalks were of wood, many of them on stilts. It was indeed a rough frontier town.

Potter Palmer was the first to bring quality and fashion to the city. He branched out into the wholesale business and introduced many innovations in advertising, personnel, merchandising, and customer relations. His business grew rapidly and was profitable. At the time he sold out to Marshall Field and Levi Leiter, its sales volume approximated $8 million, nearly as much as the combined sales of its two leading competitors.

The center of Chicago's dry goods trade was then on Lake Street near Clark. State Street was a narrow road flanked by rows of more or less dilapidated shacks. In the mid-1860s, Palmer came to the conclusion that State Street could be made into a more satisfactory retail center than Lake so he quietly began buying property on the street. In due course he owned most of it. He then proceeded to move the buildings back far enough to allow for a street 100 feet in width. With this project completed he constructed a six-story building at the corner of State and Washington, and the first Palmer House a few blocks south.

With the signing of a lease by Field, Leiter & Company on Palmer's new building, State Street was on its way to becoming one of the great shopping streets of the world. With the leading dry goods firm in the city located there, most of its competitors were soon forced to follow.

The decade of the 1870s proved to be a period of great trial for Field, Leiter & Company. Its beautiful new store on State Street was totally destroyed by the great Chicago fire in 1871; it was caught in the financial panic of 1873; its State Street store again burned to the ground in 1877.

The 1871 fire, on October 9, devastated practically all of the central business district. After the fire the only evidence that a store had stood on the corner of State and Washington was a crude sign reading: "Cash Boys and Work Girls will be paid what is due them Monday 9 A.M. Oct. 16th at 60 Calumet Ave. Field, Leiter & Co."

Three weeks after the fire, the company reopened its business in an old car barn at 20th and State Streets. Meanwhile, it had decided to construct a building on Madison Street just west of the present Loop in which to house the wholesale division. This building was completed in March 1872. For the first time the wholesale and retail branches were housed at different locations.

The retail division moved back to its old site at State and Washington on the second anniversary of the fire, October 9, 1873. It occupied a new and somewhat larger five-story limestone structure leased from the Singer Company, which in turn had bought the land from Potter Palmer.

In 1873, the country entered a severe depression which lasted six years. Despite a decline in the price level, Field, Leiter & Company maintained its dollar sales volume during the period. Its earnings averaged nearly a million dollars annually on a capital investment of between $2.5 million and $4.5 million.

In November, 1877, a second fire destroyed the new State Street store. Thirteen days later the company was open for business in an exposition building at Adams Street on the lakefront. In March 1878 it moved once again, this time into a row of buildings on Wabash Avenue, near Madison.

In the meantime, the Singer Company had proceeded with the construction of a new six-story building on the old site at the corner of State and Washington. Mr. Field and Mr. Leiter offered $500,000 for the property but the Singer Company refused to sell for less than $700,000. During this impasse the building was leased to an important competitor, Carson Pirie Scott & Company. Faced with this dilemma, Mr. Field and Mr. Leiter bought the building for $700,000 and paid Carson's $100,000 to cancel its lease. Field and Leiter then proceeded to lease the building to Field, Leiter & Company. The new store opened for business in April 1879. The company's main store has been at that corner ever since.

Despite two devastating fires and a serious depression, the company not only survived the 1870s but in 1880 was a flourishing and highly profitable enterprise. While Mr. Field was its dominant figure, he had shown great skill in the development of younger men, several of whom had become junior partners. However, serious differences had arisen between Mr. Field and Mr. Leiter. Field therefore agreed to buy Leiter's interest in the firm or offered to sell his own interest to Leiter. Since the junior partners were clearly loyal to Field, Leiter had no choice but to sell. The transaction was consummated in 1881 at a price of something over $2 million. Thus Marshall Field became practically sole owner of the business. Thus, too, there came into being for the first time the name Marshall Field & Company.

During the next 25 years, the company enjoyed a remarkable growth. Sales increased from $25 million to $73 million. Retail sales, which in 1882 had been 16 percent of the total, increased to slightly more than one-third in 1906. Annual net profits in the 25-year period increased from $1.7 million to $4.8 million.

The steady growth in sales of course necessitated the acquisition of additional space. In 1887, the wholesale division moved into a new building constructed on the block bounded by Adams, Quincy, Wells, and Franklin Streets. In 1893, the retail division was enlarged by the construction of the building which still stands at the northwest corner of Washington and Wabash, adjoining Holden Court on the west. In the years between 1893 and 1914, Mr. Field or his estate acquired the entire block bounded by State, Wabash, Washington, and Randolph. New buildings were constructed from time to time as the business grew, until in 1914 the main store occupied the entire block. Also, the old Singer Building, built in 1878, had been replaced in 1907 with a modern structure. The building housing the Store for Men, across Washington Street from the main store, was completed in 1913.

Since 1914, there have been no basic changes in or additions to the downtown store properties in Chicago. They have been kept in excellent physical condition, however, through the expenditure of many millions of dollars on maintenance and modernization.

Harry Selfridge was hired by Mr. Field in 1879 as a stock boy in the wholesale department. Four years later he was transferred to the retail division and in another four years was its general manager at the age of 29. Selfridge was a man of terrific energy and soaring ambition. He was extremely creative and imaginative. He also possessed great promotional skill. He more than anyone else deserves credit for transforming the retail dry goods store into a full-line department store, by adding many lines of merchandise not previously carried.

Mr. Selfridge's personal ambition probably was responsible for his departure from the company in 1904, and, two years after the departure of Selfridge came the death of Mr. Field. He had been one of the great businessmen of his day. Coming to Chicago as a youth with less than $1,000 in his pocket, he died a multimillionaire. Not only did he build a great commercial enterprise but in his mature years he played an active role in the affairs of numerous other industries, notably transportation, steel, banking, and real estate. Without question he was one of the most influential and powerful men in Chicago.

It might be useful at this point to examine the principles and policies which Mr. Field applied to his business. One of these had to do with integrity. He would tolerate no deception of any kind in his relationships with customers and employees. His extremely liberal treatment of customers is reflected in the well-known phrases: "Give the lady what she wants" and "The customer is always right." In practice this meant that the customer could return merchandise for full credit for practically any reason whatever.

Mr. Field had several very strong convictions with respect to merchandising. He constantly stressed quality and would have nothing to do with cheap or shoddy merchandise. He was a pioneer in the field of fashion, something which Chicago women had hardly heard of prior to the days of Potter Palmer. He believed in assembling the widest possible assortments of merchandise not only from domestic sources but from countries around the world. He was a pioneer in the establishment of European buying offices, having opened the first such office in Manchester, England, in 1871. Mr. Field also was one of the first to offer merchandise for sale at only a single clearly marked price.

Mr. Field probably had as much to do with the development of the customer service concept in retailing as any merchant in America. He employed good people and saw to it that they were thoroughly trained in the art of courtesy in dealing with the public. Full satisfaction was to be given to all customers regardless of the nature of their requests.

As a result of his emphasis on service to the public, the company was among the first to make available to its clientele many facilities not usually then found in retail stores: tearooms; waiting, writing, and rest rooms; nurseries; information desks; theatre ticket offices, travel bureaus; and numerous other conveniences.

Finally, Mr. Field believed in providing his customers with the most attractive physical facilities obtainable. He felt that people responded to beauty and good taste in the design of buildings and interiors just as they admired beauty and good quality in merchandise.

Meanwhile, back in 1901, the company had begun to interest itself in manufacturing and converting. Between that year and 1929, some 30 mills were acquired, most of them producing or converting textiles.

Much of their output was sold to wholesalers, and for a time, the company undoubtedly gained important advantages from this course of action. However, as the wholesale trade started its long decline in 1924, the ownership of the mills presented the company with many new and serious problems. All the mills eventually were sold or liquidated.

The decade between 1920 and 1930 was marked by four important events: the purchase of the Davis Store on south State Street in Chicago in 1923; the opening of three suburban stores in the Chicago area in 1929; the purchase of Frederick & Nelson in Seattle in the same year; and the building of the Merchandise Mart in 1929–30.

The Evanston, Oak Park, and Lake Forest stores were among the first department store branches built in this country. They were successful from the start and still are.

The company had entered the Depression of the early 1930s a sprawling enterprise comprising a group of retail stores, a wholesale operation, an assortment of mills, and the largest commercial building in the world. One of the stores—the Davis Store—the wholesale division, the Merchandise Mart, and at times the mills, were all sources of substantial operating losses. In fact, through a period of eight years starting in 1930, these losses approximately offset the rather satisfactory earnings of the Marshall Field and Frederick & Nelson stores.

The process of transformation began with the liquidation of the wholesale division. Some of the mills and converting operations were disposed of at about the same time. The wholesale had been on the decline since the early 1920s, due mainly to the growth of retail chains and the practice of direct buying. Its liquidation was recommended by a business consultant, James O. McKinsey, who was elected chairman and chief executive officer of the company in 1935. The Davis Store on south State Street was also sold during the McKinsey regime, which was terminated by his sudden death in late 1937.

By 1943 the feeling was beginning to develop that the company should confine itself to the operation of quality department stores. To this end, it began to work toward the sale of the Merchandise Mart. This was accomplished in 1945 and resulted in a substantial strengthening of the working capital position.

The Merchandise Mart had been conceived in the early 1920s as a grandiose scheme to save the wholesale division. Not only the company's own wholesale unit but competitive establishments as well were to be housed in one gigantic center. The plan has never been realized to this day, due in part to the Depression, but mainly because of the continued rapid decline of the wholesale dry goods industry.

The last of the mills were finally sold in 1953. The mills were originally acquired as important sources of supply for the wholesale division. Following the disposal of the wholesale, the relationship of the mills with the rest of the company was of negligible importance. It was believed that the capital derived from the sale could be put to excellent use in retail expansion.

With the company once again in strong financial position due in part to improved earnings in the 1940s, it was able to move forward aggressively on the retail front. Up to this time the reputation with the public had rested largely on the State Street store in Chicago and the Frederick & Nelson unit in Seattle. True, it had opened three rather small suburban stores in the Chicago area back in 1929, but they were no longer adequately serving the suburban market. The population explosion into the suburbs was already well under way.

Despite this fact, the company still regarded the two main stores as the principal bulwarks of the business. In the years following the war, therefore, it spent many millions on improvements in the State Street store and on the modernization and enlargement of the Seattle store, the latter alone at a cost of $10 million.

Meanwhile, the company again turned its attention to the suburban problem. The first modern shopping centers had begun to spring up in the late 1940s, and automobile transportation was well on the way toward revolutionizing customer buying habits. While the downtown stores were doing well, and still are, the only way to maintain or improve its position in the market was to expand further in the suburbs.

The first move in this direction was the opening of a small store at Bellevue, east of Seattle, in 1946. This was replaced by a much larger unit in 1956, which was expanded in 1964. A second suburban unit, Aurora Village, was opened in 1963, and the third Frederick & Nelson suburban store, Southcenter, opening in 1968.

In 1950 the company completed the acquisition of over 100 acres of land in Skokie, north and a bit west of downtown Chicago. It then undertook to create what it hoped would be the most beautiful shopping center in the world, Old Orchard. The company store in that center opened for business in 1956, and has been very successful. The store was enlarged in 1963 and again in 1967.

In the meantime, in 1955, the company had opened a somewhat smaller store than Old Orchard in Park Forest, south of Chicago. This unit also has proved to be successful and was enlarged in 1957.

In the mid-fifties, the company decided to go into the Milwaukee market and opened a store in the new Mayfair center in Wauwatosa in 1959. This store is approximately the size of Old Orchard. After a slow start, it has grown rapidly.

Oakbrook Center, in the western suburbs of Chicago, was paterned after Old Orchard and was ready for business in March 1962. The size of this unit was increased in 1964 and again in 1968. Many people now regard Oakbrook, with its gardens, trees, and fountains, as the most attractive shopping center in the country.

In 1966 another Chicago suburban unit was added. River Oaks, located southeast of the city in Calumet City, is similar in design to the Oakbrook and Old Orchard stores. With the opening of this store the ring of regional shopping centers north, west, and south of the city was complete.

Mr. James L. Palmer stated the following principles of the company: "In all of our business relationships, we believe in integrity of the highest order. We believe in rendering the finest possible personal service to our customers. We feel that our main function is the assembling, from all corners of the globe, of the widest, deepest, and newest assortments of quality merchandise to be found anywhere. We believe in the fair and generous treatment of our employees, and as a matter of policy, we pay higher wages and grant more liberal benefits than the average firm in our industry. Finally, we believe in operating only full-line, quality department stores so designed and equipped as to achieve the maximum in beauty and good taste."

Case questions

1. In what ways do the customers of the branch stores of Marshall Field & Company differ from the customers of the main store in Chicago?
2. Would you find the same kind of quality merchandise in Marshall Field's as you would be able to secure in high-price specialty shops?
3. What classes of customers does Marshall Field attempt to reach?
4. To what extent should department stores be leaders in fashion?
5. How should Marshall Field & Company plan its advertising strategy?

19

ORGANIZATION FOR
CONTROL

The advertising for an organization may be handled in one of several different ways. It may be shared by the company and an advertising agency, it may be assumed fully by the advertiser, or the full responsibility may be delegated to an advertising agency.

There is no rigid rule which can be set to determine which is the best procedure. This is determined by such factors as the size of the organization, the objectives of the company, the type of product, the nature and extent of the market, and the nature of the advertising job.

Regardless of what method is used, the primary purpose of the advertising organization is to provide the means by which the advertising job will be done on an efficient, systematic, and economical basis. As a result, in some companies the entire job may be done by one person. In other concerns, it may require a complex structure. Two companies of the same size may not handle the advertising in the same manner. Even companies selling competitive products may use different organizational structures and different approaches to the handling of their advertising.

Location of advertising department within the company

A study of a number of American companies conducted by the Association of National Advertisers indicated that there are a number of different places within the company organizational structure to locate the advertising department. Which location is best depends on a number of factors, including: the size of the company; the general task that will be assigned to advertising in the company's marketing program; the amount and type of advertising the company plans to use; the general type of market in which the firm competes; and the

635

extent to which top management is involved in the planning and handling of the advertising function.

There are six basic ways in which the advertising department is positioned within the company. These six ways are:

1. Advertising is one of several functions reporting to the chief executive of the company. (See Figure 19–1.)

FIGURE 19–1
Advertising reports to the chief executive of the company

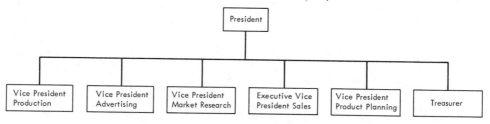

2. Advertising is one of several marketing functions reporting to the chief marketing executive.

3. Advertising reports to the chief sales executive (or in some cases at a level below the chief sales executive).

4. In a multiple-division company advertising is a centralized operating department.

5. In a multiple-division company advertising is decentralized, operating at a division level. (See Figures 19–2a and 19–2b.)

6. In a multiple-division company advertising is decentralized at the operating division level with a central advertising staff to aid, coordinate, and supplement the work of advertising in the various divisions.

"There are, of course, variations of the above, but by and large the companies studied fall into one of these basic types."[1]

In answer to the question, "Which type of organization is best?", the only sensible answer to this question is: Best for what purposes? The A.N.A. studies of organization plans and practices concluded that there are no two companies which are organized exactly alike just as there are no two human physiognomies exactly alike.

Obviously no company should attempt to adopt an exact carbon copy of another's plan of organization. Common sense dictates that the shoe wouldn't fit. But this does not mean that *certain features* of a plan of organization cannot be adapted to the needs of another company."[2]

The following questions should be considered in reviewing advertising's position in the company organization structure.[3]

---

[1] Association of National Advertisers, Inc., *Practical Guide and Modern Practices for Better Advertising Management,* Vol. II, *Advertising Organization* (New York, 1957), pp. 8–9.

[2] Ibid., p. 21.

[3] Ibid., pp. 22, 23.

FIGURE 19–2a
General Electric Company marketing organization at corporate level

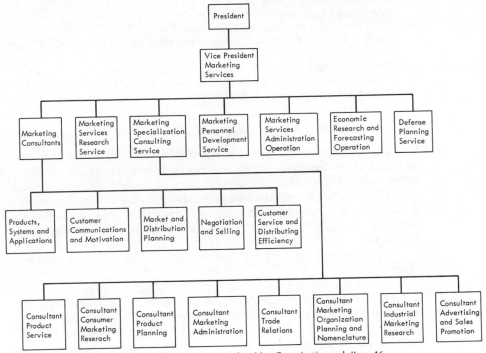

Source: Association of National Advertisers, Inc., *Advertising Organization,* vol. II, p. 16.

FIGURE 19–2b
General Electric Company typical operating department

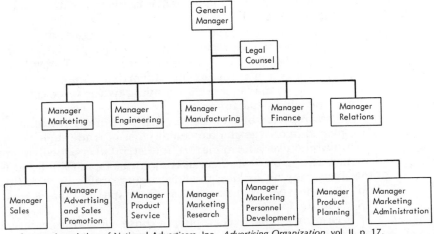

Source: Association of National Advertisers, Inc., *Advertising Organization,* vol. II, p. 17.

1. To what position should advertising report?
    How important is advertising to the company?
    What is advertising's prime job?
    Who makes key *marketing* decisions?
2. What functions should advertising encompass?
    What is the company's definition of advertising, sales promotion, public relations?
3. Should advertising be centralized or decentralized?
4. What are the pros and cons of the product-manager type of organization?
5. What relationships are required between advertising and other functions?

Organization of the advertising department

The organization of the advertising department itself within the company is influenced also by several factors, such as the position of advertising within the company, the number and types of activities included in the advertising function, and the extent to which the various functions and responsibilities of advertising are performed in the advertising department or are carried out by the advertising agency and other outside agencies.

There are five basic ways of organizing an advertising department. These are:

1. Organization by subfunction of advertising. In this type of organization, the director of the department would have reporting to him personnel in charge of national consumer advertising, sales promotion, advertising production, copy, and media. This form would be used by firms doing a large amount of their own production of advertising, and sales promotion work. (See Figure 19–3.)

2. Organization by media. This form of organization would involve having skilled personnel who are specialists in divisions handling such areas as magazine advertising, newspaper advertising, outdoor advertising, radio and television advertising, direct mail, etc. There is generally a "counterpart" specialist on the agency side, and the company media supervisor works with the agency specialist in this area in adapting the company's advertising to the particular medium. (See Figure 19–4.)

3. Organization by product. This form of organization has become a very popular one in recent years for large advertisers of a line of consumer products. Organization by product will vary from companies having two or three product advertising managers reporting to the advertising manager to those having two or three echelons within the advertising department.

4. Organization by end user. In this type of organization managers are placed in charge of a particular class of trade such as consumers, institutional users, farm market, industrial users, medical profession, babies, and so on. A number of companies have found that while the products may be similar, the advertising problems of telling a story to different types of users may call for a special type of organization. (See Figure 19–5.)

5. Organization by geography. In those companies where there are

FIGURE 19–3
Organization by subfunction

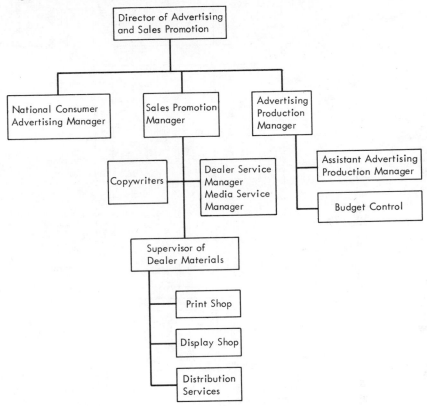

decided geographic differences in customer tastes and habits, organization of the advertising department along geographic lines may be indicated. In such cases, there will be divisional advertising managers located in each of the firm's sales divisions. For example, one large brewing company has advertising operations centered around "divisional advertising managers" located in each of the firm's seven sales divisions, with each division advertising manager having a staff of two or three field representatives to work closely with the distributors and with local media.

In few of the cases studied is an advertising department organized purely according to a single method; most companies have evolved a combination of two or more methods which, together, suit the advertising needs and purposes of the company.

It should be pointed out that in many companies the advertising department may consist of the advertising manager with perhaps a few people to handle stenographic, clerical, and layout work. This is by no means confined to smaller advertisers; a number of very large

FIGURE 19–4: Organization of advertising division, marketing department, ESSO Standard Oil Company

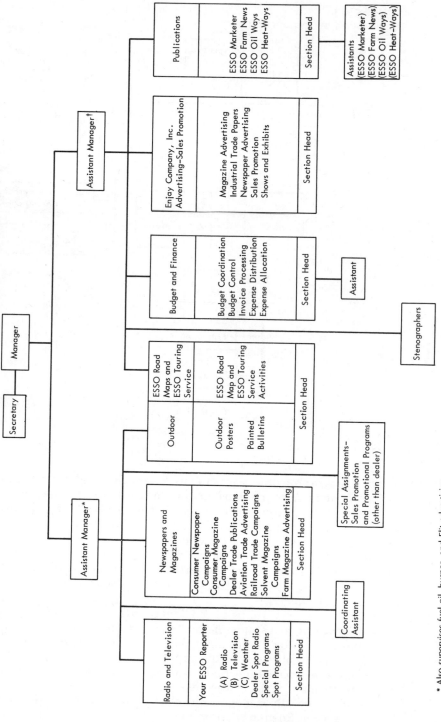

* Also supervises fuel oil, burner, and Flit advertising.
† Also supervises Penola and Essotane advertising.
Source: Association of National Advertisers, Inc., *Advertising Organization*, vol. II, p. 67.

FIGURE 19–5
Organization by end user

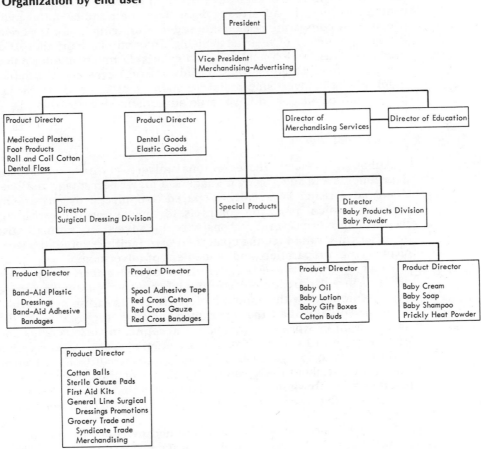

advertisers operate on the philosophy of a very minimum of experienced "professional" advertising personnel in the company, looking to the agency for such high level talents.

Size of the advertising department

The size of the department and the number of people in the department need bear no particular relationship to the size of the company
or of its advertising appropriation. The advertising departments of
national advertisers literally may vary in size from one individual to
departments employing several hundreds.

The size of the department is related primarily to the extent to
which the company relies on its advertising agency or agencies for the
creation and production of its advertising. It is also influenced by such
factors as the amount of advertising, the type of advertising, the number of products and brands advertised, the market and its nature, and

the philosophy of the company management. For instance, in tobacco companies, which are large advertisers in terms of dollars and percentage of sales, the advertising departments tend to be quite small, because the companies rely on their agency or agencies for the creating and producing of their advertising. In contrast, many industrial products firms (which tend to spend relatively much smaller dollar sums and percentage of sales on advertising) create and produce much of their advertising material, such as brochures, direct-mail pieces, and catalogs, and have large advertising departments.

Why advertisers use agencies

Although, as noted above, national advertisers have advertising departments and advertising managers, a major percentage of all national advertising is actually prepared and placed by advertising agencies, which make the contracts for space and time with the media. There are several reasons why the advertisers normally use agencies rather than relying upon their own facilities for all the work of planning, preparation, and placement of advertising.

Among the factors causing advertisers to believe agencies are more effective are: the greater objectivity and independence of an outside agency compared with an internal department; the fresh approach of an outside organization; the experience and advantages gained by the agency from its work on a number of accounts in various fields and industries, resulting in the cross-fertilization of ideas; the motivation of the agency to do a good job of planning and executing the advertising in order to hold the account; the ability of the agency to bring together a highly skilled group of specialists that only a very few of the largest advertisers could possibly afford to do for themselves in a department.

Under the present widely used method of compensation of the agency, many of the services which the agency performs for the client in essence cost the client nothing, since the agency's compensation is obtained in the form of commissions from the media used. However, if the company established a house agency it is now possible for this agency to receive the equivalent of the commission which the media grant to independent agencies.

Another reason sometimes advanced favoring the use of agencies to handle the advertising is that it is much easier to change agencies if the company becomes dissatisfied with its advertising than it would be to eliminate its advertising department.

Selection of the agency

Making the right selection of an agency is a very important decision for the company, to insure obtaining good service. The general approach to the selection of the agency would be similar to that used in the selection of any other professional type service. First the company should determine the nature of the advertising "job" the agency is expected to do for the company. On the basis of this job description the firm should set up the criteria for selection. Then it should draw up a list of possible or prospective agencies. The criteria listed earlier should then be applied to this list of possible agencies, and the agency best qualified to provide the effective counsel and services as described by the standards set up should be selected.

The first step in this selection process should involve the preparation of a written statement covering in detail the exact type and extent of the services which the agency will be expected to perform, and which functions the advertising department of the firm will perform. Some companies want their agency to perform "full service" (which means everything, including marketing plans, research, copy, art, production, media selection and placement, publicity, sales promotion materials, and so forth), while others desire only a very limited number of services from their agency.

On the basis of this statement of agency services desired, and the company's general philosophy, criteria should be established for the selection of the agency. Some of the factors that are usually considered in establishing the list of criteria are the following:

1. Advertising philosophy. Unless the general attitudes of the firm and the principals of the agency toward advertising and its place in the marketing program are similar, the probability of the relationship's being a happy one are remote.

2. Size. This is important from the standpoint of the advertiser in several ways. A large advertiser needs an agency of sufficient size to be in a position to handle all its work and services satisfactorily. A small advertiser wants an agency that will take a deep interest in it, and fears that if it is relatively too small an account, the large agency may not give it such interest. The thinking is: "It is better to be an important account to a small agency than just another account to a large agency."

3. Services rendered. The important question is whether or not the agency has facilities and manpower to render all the services the client will need. Special service requirements should be included here.

4. Experience. The advertiser is interested in the types of accounts the agency is handling, and what products it now handles that are comparable from a marketing and advertising standpoint to its own. Other questions raised under this topic would be how long the agency has had its accounts, its familiarity with the advertiser's industry, and its record of success with other accounts. Some firms also would include here questions relating to the agency's record with various types of media.

5. Personnel. The ability and background and experience of the agency principals, top creative and account personnel, as well as the ability and records of the executives who would actually be assigned to the advertiser's account. If the firm has some special requirements relative to personnel for their account (for example, a woman copywriter), they should be considered here.

6. Method of compensation. Since there are differences in the manner in which agencies do handle charging for research and certain other services, it should be ascertained in advance just what services the agency would render for the normal commission, which services would be charged for (whether at cost or cost plus usual markup), or, if a smaller account, details of the fee system proposed. Details of method of compensation should be carefully agreed upon beforehand.

7. **Location.** Although this would not be significant for most large national advertisers, in some instances firms insist that the agency have an office in the same city as their head office. And, many smaller firms using small agencies will desire to use an agency in a convenient geographical location.

In selecting the agency, the advertising manager (and other involved executives) should consider the above factors and any others that seem pertinent in a particular situation. The list of agencies to which these considerations would be applied can be compiled in a number of ways, depending on circumstances. At times some one key criterion will be the basis for compiling the list; for example, if the company has made location a key criterion, then all agencies with offices in its home city might be listed. Major criteria are then applied, eliminating agencies as they fail to meet the standards. Information for checking against criteria can be obtained through the use of mailed questionnaires, and is sometimes done by personal interview. After the list has been winnowed down to those who meet all criteria acceptably, the advertising manager would usually have at least one meeting with the executives of the agency and would probably also visit some of the clients of the agency. This final group of agencies may or may not be requested to make a "presentation" to the key executives of the firm.

Working with the agency

Below are a few rules that have been evolved by advertising managers and account executives to help maintain good relationships with the agency and enable the firm to get the best results from its advertising agency:

1. The company should have in writing clear marketing objectives and goals and clear marketing plans for each major product line. This will enable the advertising agency to know what the advertising goals and objectives should be and how to plan the advertising to fit into the overall marketing plan.

2. The company should have a clear working arrangement with the agency, in writing, as to just what the responsibilities of the agency are, what the company expects of the agency, what the agency will do in the way of service for its 15 percent commission (or, rate per hour fee charge), and what the company will do. The channels of communication, the contact person, and the method of approval between firm and agency should be clearly spelled out.

3. There should be very close cooperation between the advertising manager and the account executive in planning and executing the work of the agency. The firm should give the agency full and complete information. For example, research findings of the firm should be

made available to the agency to aid it, and not used to "trap" the agency.

4. There should be an attitude of mutual confidence and trust. The agency should be encouraged to participate fully in the planning and be expected to contribute ideas and make suggestions or recommendations, although on major areas such as the budget, major media, and a campaign theme, the company should have the final decision. However, normally the firm should then permit the agency to carry on with its creative work, and with details of media selection, with a minimum of interference. The company, of course, should feel free to contribute creative ideas when it has them, and the agency should be happy to accept and consider such. The firm's executives should learn that creative people want to be "appreciated" and "respected." A little of this appreciation may help in getting much extra effort from the creative staff of the agency.

5. The firm should set up criteria for evaluating the agency and its work in light of the original objectives that were established in the plan.

If, in general, the company executives will work with the agency people as though they were partners in the marketing program, sharing information, ideas, trust, and confidence, they should get a maximum amount of effective advertising from their agency and have a happy working realtionship.

Evaluation of agency performance

After the agency has been selected and the bases for a good working relationship evolved, the advertiser has the task of carrying out the last of the rules for insuring effective advertising on the part of the agency, namely, the evaluation of the work of the agency. If there were some sound and reliable basis for obtaining accurate measures of the effectiveness of advertising, the problem of evaluating agency performance would be much easier than it now is. Since it is not possible to attain such accurate measurement for most types of advertising, the advertiser must use other criteria.

Although such performance standards can be developed for the advertiser's particular situation, it is still difficult to judge performance against these criteria. Some standards should attempt to evaluate the quality of the creative work performed by the agency, and the quality of the planning work of the agency. If any standards have established quantitative measures (such as increasing brand awareness in a new territory by x percent), these should be included in the quality evaluation. Some evaluation should also be included of such factors as the technical aspects of the advertising work of the agency, including art, layout, and production. Some firms also place some emphasis on the actual quantity of work performed by the agency, including the number of advertisements produced and the number of pieces of sales promotional material produced. However, most agree that major emphasis should be on the results of the advertising, to the extent this can be evaluated.

The retail advertiser

Since as a rule the retail store does not handle its advertising through an advertising agency, a large percentage of its advertising is done locally by retail organizations; and, since virtually every retail store does advertising in some form, a few words will be devoted to the different aspects of the retail advertising picture.

Retail advertising organization

As a rule, the small retail store does use less advertising as a percentage of sales than the larger store. In many of these cases, the store owner or manager also acts as the advertising manager. He may have a small advertising department to assist in the planning and preparation of the advertising, or no advertising department. In either event, he usually will obtain a great deal of assistance from several outside sources. The local media (newspapers, radio, and television stations) have people who will help in all facets of the advertising, from the planning of the campaign and establishing the advertising budget to the actual preparation of the individual advertisements, including the selection of items to advertise, the layout, the writing of copy, and the supplying of illustrations. Suppliers (manufacturers of branded items) will in many cases furnish recommended guides for advertising schedules, mats for newspaper advertisements, film, and transcriptions for broadcast media, inserts for direct mail, as well as point-of-purchase display materials. The small retailer also may obtain assistance from trade associations, since most of these provide suggestions for advertising programs, scheduling of advertising, and ideas for the details of individual advertisements.

The large store will have a complete advertising department, with almost all the same specialists found in the advertising agency. In a large department store, the advertising generally is under the control of the advertising or the sales promotion manager, who usually reports either to the general manager or to the merchandising manager. The sales promotion manager will normally have his division divided into three departments: advertising, display, and publicity or promotion. The completeness of the work of the advertising department will be evident from the typical department store organization chart of the advertising department shown in Figure 19–6.

The department plans all advertising, in cooperation with the general merchandising manager, and has the task of the actual preparation and production of all advertising and display and the selection of media and placement of the advertising. They normally do not use an agency for their advertising, although in some instances they will use an agency for certain special parts of their advertising, such as the production of television programs or advertising placed in national media. And, in the case of the large national chains, which now are doing a good deal of national advertising in magazines and television, they are handling this through advertising agencies.

FIGURE 19–6
Department Stores, Inc., organization chart: Advertising division

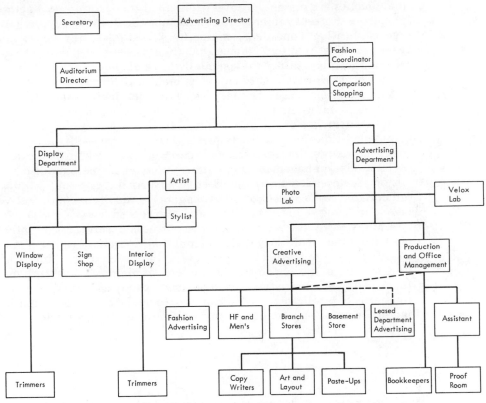

Why retailers normally do not use agencies

Although virtually all general advertisers use advertising agencies, as discussed earlier in this chapter, very few retailers do. Large retailers typically plan and prepare their own advertising in their own internal advertising departments, and small retailers usually utilize the assistance of media and the manufacturers who supply their merchandise. The following factors are most significant in the nonuse of advertising agencies in the planning and preparation of retail advertising:

1. By far the largest share of retail advertising is placed in newspapers at "local," or retail, rates. These normally are considerably lower than national rates, and the newspaper does not grant a commission to an agency for placing such local advertising. Hence, if the store were to use an agency to handle its advertising, it would probably have to pay the agency a fee, since generally newspapers will not grant a commission to the agency.

2. The retail store normally works on a very close time schedule. That is, although the general program of the advertising and the strat-

egy is planned well in advance, the actual individual advertisement is often written "against time" or "against a deadline." Frequently the final touches are put on the advertisement at the last minute. Factors in causing this delay in preparation include the desire to take advantage of weather conditions, competitors' activities, and consumer reactions. Most retailers believe that their internal department can handle these last-minute revisions better and more easily than an outside organization, regardless of its technical competence.

3. The average retail store handles a large number and wide variety of products, many more than the average national advertiser. In a large department store, several dozen of these items may be advertised on any single day and hundreds over a period of time. With the department in the store, the creative people can work closely with buyers and merchandise managers to obtain information on the merchandise and customers necessary to create effective advertising. It would be quite difficult for the account executives of agencies and the agency creative people to know so many products and markets so well.

4. Many retailers obtain a great deal of free counseling and creative work from the media they use and from their merchandise suppliers. Closely related to this feature is the fact that much of the help from their sources of merchandise is in the form of mats (or transcriptions) furnished by the manufacturer to be used exactly as furnished if the retailer is to be eligible for the cooperative deal (in which the manufacturer usually pays for at least one half of the cost of the media space or time).

The advertising agency

The advertising agency is a unique type of business organization that has over the past century played a significant part in the development and growth of advertising as a part of the American economy. The standard Directory of Advertising Agencies lists about 5,000 national advertising agencies. It is estimated that they prepare and place about 75 percent of the national and regional advertising.

Definition[4]

An advertising agency is—
1. an independent business organization
2. composed of creative and business people
3. who develop, prepare and place advertising in advertising media
4. for sellers seeking to find customers for their goods and services.

An agency may do things related to advertising and to help make the advertising succeed, but if the agency does not prepare and place advertising, it is not an advertising agency.
1. Independent

An advertising agency is an independent business organization—in-

---

[4] Reprinted with permission of the American Association of Advertising Agencies, Inc., 420 Lexington Avenue, New York 17.

dependently owned and not owned by advertisers or media or suppliers—

   a. independent so as to bring to the clients' problems an outside
      objective point of view made more valuable by experience with
      other clients' sales problems in other fields;

   b. independent of the clients so as to be always an advocate of adver-
      tising (seeking to apply advertising to help clients grow and pros-
      per);

   c. independent of media or suppliers so as to be unbiased in serving
      its clients (the sellers of goods and services).

2. An advertising agency is composed of creative and business people.
   They are writers and artists, showmen and market analyst, media
   analysts and merchandising men and women. They are research
   people, sales people, advertising specialists of all sorts, but with all
   this, they are business people, running an independent business, fi-
   nancially responsible, applying their creative skills to the business
   of helping to make their clients' advertising succeed.

3. These people develop, prepare, and place advertising in advertising
   media.

      Advertising agencies seek in every way they can to apply advertis-
   ing to advance their clients' businesses. Everything that goes before
   and everything that comes after the advertisement is preparation for
   the advertising or follow-up to help make it succeed. To prepare and
   place advertising—successful advertising for the advertiser—is the
   primary purpose of the advertising agency.

4. The agency does this, not for itself, but for sellers seeking to find
   customers for the sellers' goods and services.

Agency organization

A typical organization chart for an agency, showing the functions
performed, is shown in Figure 19–7.

Types of agency organization

Agencies are organized in many ways—no two, perhaps, in exactly
the same way. Management may elect to organize the larger agency
in either of two major ways—as a group agency or as a departmentalized or concentric agency.

In a group agency (and these are usually larger firms), the group
handles the contact, planning, and creative work for one or more
clients or products. Similar groups handle other accounts. Each group
does its contacting, works out the plans (subject to check by the agency's planning board or its chief officers), writes the copy, and makes
the illustrations. Parallel to that group, another does the same for
other accounts. Usually all groups use the centralized research, media,
print production, and accounting departments. All have the benefit of
a general planning board.

The second type of agency, the departmentalized or concentric, is
completely departmentalized by the functions performed. Each department serves all clients. The account executive calls on the copy

FIGURE 19–7

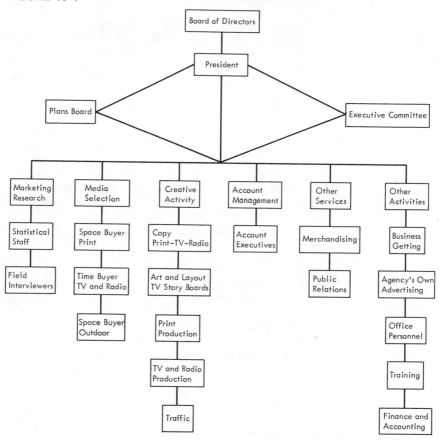

department for the copywriting for his accounts, on the art department for the layouts and illustrations, and so on.

Some agencies are a mixture of the group and departmentalized types, incorporating certain features of each. There are many possible variations.

Agency jobs

For a view of agency organization and work, it is usually best to consider the various nonadministrative jobs, treating each one as a separate function.

The account executive's job (which is usually a combination of contact, plans, and merchandising work) is one of the top positions in the field. As liaison between the advertising agency and the client whose product is being advertised, the account person must have a good general knowledge of all phases of advertising, merchandising, and general business practice. In many cases, he must also be a creative man, able to aid in the building of plans for a campaign and to suggest solutions to the client's special advertising problem.

Copywriting furnishes jobs for another large group of people in the agency business, and several thousands more for people in firms that produce at least part of their own advertising or help others to advertise. One point usually overlooked is that the copywriter often does more than write headlines, copy, captions, and the rest. He frequently is called on to produce the entire idea for an advertisement, or a complete plan, and to have a hand in planning the layout and illustration for his written copy.

Art and layout personnel, working with the advertising manager, account executive, or copywriter, establish the layout for advertising copy and see that proper artwork is prepared.

Research people provide the facts on which advertising can be built. They carry on the kinds of research discussed in Chapter 15. Mechanical production men and women have the task of translating artwork and copy into the mechanical materials used in reproducing the finished advertisement. A wide knowledge of engraving, lithography, typography, electrotyping, and many other technical processes is needed to see that the most effective work is done as economically as possible. Responsible for coordinating the flow of advertising materials to publications, the mechanical production people often oversee the flow of work (traffic) through their agencies as well.

Radio and television production personnel put on the shows that go over the air. Working closely with the directors of the shows, they see to it that casts are hired, physical properties procured, and the other problems solved that lie behind even the simplest radio or television performance.

Media selection is the job of finding the best possible places for the advertiser to present the message. Hundreds of magazines, each with a different combination of characteristics; thousands of business publications serving different business fields; thousands of newspapers, daily and weekly, each serving its geographical area; the national television and radio networks and the hundreds of television stations and thousands of radio stations serving local areas; outdoor plants where traffic congregates; car cards in buses, subways, taxicabs, trains, and stations; all these and more—windows and store displays, direct mail, premiums, and sampling—all are included in what agencies need to know about the available media and means which can be used to carry their clients' messages to potential customers or trade factors.

Media also are changing constantly, and require continuing study by hundreds of agency specialists and researchers who do nothing else.

Elements of agency service

"Agency service," as defined by the American Association of Advertising Agencies, "consists of interpreting to the public, or to that part of it which it is desired to reach, the advantages of a product or service." This interpretation is based upon:

1. A study of the client's product or service to determine the advantages and disadvantages inherent in the product itself and in its relation to competition.
2. An analysis of the present and potential market for which the product or service is adapted:
   a. As to location.
   b. As to extent of possible sales.
   c. As to season.
   d. As to trade and economic conditions.
   e. As to nature and amount of competition.
3. A knowledge of the factors of distribution and sales and their methods of operation.
4. A knowledge of all the available media and means which can profitably be used to carry the interpretation of the product or service to consumer, wholesaler, dealer, contractor, or other factor. This knowledge covers:
   a. Character.
   b. Influence.
   c. Circulation:
      Quantity.
      Quality.
      Location.
   d. Physical requirements
   e. Costs
5. Formulation of a definite plan, and presentation of this plan to the client.
6. Execution of this plan:
   a. Writing, designing, illustrating advertisements, or other appropriate forms of the message.
   b. Contracting for the space or other means of advertising.
   c. The proper incorporation of the message in mechanical form and forwarding it with proper instruction for fulfillment of the contract.
   d. Checking and verifying insertions, display, or other means used.
   e. The auditing, billing, and paying for the service, space, and preparation.
7. Cooperation with the client's sales work, to insure the greatest effect from advertising.

These are the elements of agency service, whether all the above functions are shared by a few persons, or each function is carried on separately by a specialized department. Into this pattern fit account executives who contact the client, art directors, copywriters, space and time buyers, research workers, mechanical production and radio production people, and so on.

Additional agency services

In addition to advertising service there is a willingness among many agencies today to assist the client with other activities of distribution. They do special work for the manufacturer in such fields as package designing, sales research, sales training, preparation of sales and service literature, designing and production of merchandising displays, public relations, and publicity. The agency, however, must justify such work by doing it more satisfactorily than can either the manufacturer himself or a competing expert.

Sources of agency compensation

Nearly all major media—newspapers, magazines, television, radio, business publications, outdoor plant owners, and transit advertising companies—allow commissions to advertising agencies, which they recognize individually.

The commission is usually 15 percent of the medium's published rate, although outdoor plant operators pay 16.66 percent.

The medium will bill the agency for the gross cost of the space (or time). In this instance assume the space cost is $10,000. The medium will allow an agency commission of 15 percent, or $1,500, so the agency would owe the medium $8,500. Since most publishers (but not broadcasters) also grant a 2 percent cash discount for prompt payment, the actual amount the agency would pay the medium would be $8,500 less $170, or $8,330. The agency would in turn bill the advertiser for the full gross amount of the space bill, $10,000, less the $170 cash discount for prompt payment.

This medium commission normally covers the planning and creative work of the agency, and the selection and placement of advertising in media, but does not cover the production costs involved for many of the materials involved. Suppliers of artwork, typography, and plates for print media, and transcriptions for television, do not allow an agency commission. The agency normally will bill the client for such production costs and, depending upon its agreement with the client, usually will add its own service charge of 15 percent or 17.65 percent (to equal 15 percent on the "selling price" of the service) to the amount of the bill for each expenditure made on behalf of the client for production.

In some cases, and for some services, the agency may work on a fee basis. This may be the case for a market research study, the preparation of direct-mail or dealer displays, or for retail or industrial accounts.

Larger advertising agencies receive, on the average, about 75 percent of their income in the form of commissions allowed by advertising media, 20 percent from the agency's own percentage charges on purchases (which they specify and/or supervise for their clients), and 5 percent in fees of various kinds for special services. Among medium-sized agencies, the corresponding figures are 70 percent, 20 percent, and 10 percent, and among smaller agencies 60 percent, 25 percent, and 15 percent.

There are a limited number of advertising agencies which have shifted from the commission basis and bill all clients on a strictly fee basis. These agencies return the equivalent of the media commission which they are given to the clients. Agency service charges and fees are arrived at individually by agreement between each agency and client.

Agency recognition

In order for an agency to qualify to receive media commissions, it must be "recognized" by the medium involved. The procedure generally followed is that no person or firm should be able to receive the commission until the agency has satisfied the medium that it is qualified to provide the services required to "earn" the "functional discount" the medium grants the agency. The services listed below are what media say agencies do for them:

1. The advertising agency develops new business.
2. The agency reduces the hazards of advertising, and thereby the mortaility rate in the medium's business.
3. The agency advocates the idea of advertising.
4. The agency creates the advertising messages which are an essential element in the sale of the space or time which media wish to sell. This is the conversion of white space or blank time into advertising influence.
5. The agency develops and improves advertising techniques, and thereby increases the productivity of advertising.
6. The agency simplifies the medium's credit operations and reduces the cost of these operations.
7. The agency carries the cost of credit losses.
8. The agency simplifies and reduces the medium's cost in the mechanical preparation of advertising.
9. The agency reduces the medium's cost in following up advertising schedules to meet publication or broadcasting deadlines.

The requirements that an agency must meet to qualify for the commission are:

1. To have sufficient personnel of ability and experience to serve properly general advertisers.
2. To have sufficient financial resources to meet obligations it might incur with media.

It should be noted that, prior to 1956 (the year a consent decree was entered into by the Justice Department, the American Association of Advertising Agencies, and the media associations, restraining these organizations from enforcing uniform standards for "recognition" and from withholding commissions from agencies not recognized by the associations), a requisite for recognition was that the agency not rebate any commissions to clients.

Since then, recognition is strictly a medium decision. Media still grant the commission only to recognized agencies. However, so-called "house agencies," controlled by an advertiser, may be recognized and granted commissions by media. But there has still been no major shift away from the usual commission method of agency operation.

The commission system

There has been criticism of the commission system of payment of advertising agencies for many years. For example, why should an agency still be paid by the medium instead of by the client? (in contrast to the early 1900s when, in essence, agencies were sales organizations for the print media). Does this arrangement serve as an inducement for the agency to recommend more expensive media? Does it cause agencies to recommend larger budgets, to increase media expenditures? Is agency compensation correlated with services rendered? That is, it may not take a great deal more agency time and effort to produce the full-page advertisement to run in a consumer publication whose page rate is $60,000 per page than for the advertisement to run in an industrial trade magazine whose page rate is $300. But, the agency receives $9,000 commission in the first instance, and only $45 commission in the second.

Another argument advanced is that there is no established rule for what services are included in the 15 percent commission. Hence, either the advertiser may be paying for "free" services he docs not want and would not order if he were controlling payment arrangements, or else he is paying fees for services that should be included in the commission.

Some of the main arguments for the commission system are: It is a simple system that the industry has learned to "live with" over the years and that has worked reasonably well; it eliminates the need to haggle over rates of compensation, and puts agency competition on nonprice factors, such as creativity and service; it is a fairly flexible system, in that agencies may give more "free" services to large and profitable accounts, and put the top people and more time on the advertisements of the major accounts.

Most agencies, media, and advertising managers still consider the commission system a satisfactory one, although approximately one-third of the advertising managers are of the opinion that some fee system would be preferable.

The agency industry

In 1975 there were approximately 4,750 agencies in the United States, employing an estimated 75,000 people. Of these, 707 agencies billed a combined total of $14.6 billion in 1975. There were 77 agencies which billed $25,000,000; another 108 agencies billed between $10-

FIGURE 19–8
Top ten agencies on basis of total billings, 1975* (U.S. agencies: Billings in millions)

Rank and agency	1975	1974
World billings		
1 Walter Thompson Co.	$900.1	$846.9
2 Young & Rubicam Int'l	800.9	750.5
3 McCann-Erickson	775.1	689.5
4 Leo Burnett Co.	623.0	587.1
5 Ted Bates & Co.	604.0	565.8
6 Ogilvy & Mather Int'l	581.6	523.0
7 BBDO	525.0	512.9
8 Grey Advertising	399.3	387.5
9 Foote, Cone & Belding	396.4	339.8
10 D'Arcy-MacManus & Masius	329.5	314.0
U.S. billings		
1 Young & Rubicam Int'l	$476.6	$468.9
2 J. Walter Thompson Co.	432.8	415.4
3 Leo Burnett Co.	400.0	366.1
4 BBDO	369.8	373.9
5 Grey Advertising	287.0	286.5
6 Ted Bates & Co.	280.2	255.1
7 Foote, Cone & Belding	275.3	238.0
8 Ogilvy & Mather Int'l	266.1	223.3
9 D'Arcy-MacManus & Masius	234.0	222.0
10 McCann-Erickson	230.8	212.8
Billings outside U.S.		
1 McCann-Erickson	$544.3	$476.7
2 J. Walter Thompson Co.	467.3	431.5
3 Young & Rubicam Int'l	324.3	281.6
4 Ted Bates & Co.	323.7	310.8
5 Ogilvy & Mather	315.5	299.7
6 Leo Burnett Co.	223.0	221.0
7 SSC&B	179.0	174.0
8 BBDO	155.1	139.0
9 Norman, Craig & Kummel	140.6	130.3
10 Foote, Cone & Belding	121.2	101.8

* *Advertising Age,* February 23, 1976, p. 1.

$25,000,000; 139 agencies had billings in the $5-$10,000,000 classification; and, 112 agencies reported billings under $1,000,000. J. Walter Thompson Co. was first in world billings with a volume of $900.1 millions; Young & Rubicam Int'l. was first in U.S. billings with a volume of $476.6 millions; and McCann-Erickson was first in billings volume outside the United States with $544.3 millions. (See Figure 19–8.)

Questions

1. What is the best procedure for a company to use in handling its advertising?

2. What factors should be included when studying the problem of where to place the advertising department in the company organizational structure?

3. Discuss briefly the six basic ways in which the advertising department is positioned within American companies.

4. Can you give a categorical answer to the question, "Which positioning of the advertising department within a company is best?" Why, or why not?

5. What are some of the key questions to consider in reviewing advertising's position in the company organization structure?

6. What factors influence the internal organization of the advertising department?

7. What are the five basic ways of organizing the advertising department? Discuss each briefly.

8. Why do advertising departments of companies, spending about the same amount of dollars on advertising, vary so in terms of size and number of employees?

9. Why do industrial product firms, which normally spend relatively far less on advertising than consumer product firms, often have larger advertising departments?

10. Do you agree with the reasons given for "why most large national advertisers use advertising agencies"? Explain.

11. If you were a large national advertiser whose present agency had just "resigned" your account,
    a. How would you proceed to select a new advertising agency?
    b. What criteria would you establish for selecting the agency?
    c. Who in the company should make the final decision on the agency? Why?

12. As an advertising manager, how would you work with the agency to get maximum results?

13. If you were the advertising manager for a large national firm, how would you evaluate the work of your advertising agency?

14. Some large national advertisers with wide lines of products use four or five different advertising agencies, giving each certain products. Why do you think they do so? Do you think this is a good policy? Why?

15. Why do retailers seldom use advertising agencies? Do you think this explanation is valid? Why?

16. Explain the commission system of compensating agencies. Why has this system been questioned in recent years?

17. What method of compensating agencies do you think is best? What method do you think will predominate in the future? Why?

18. Do you think an agency should have to turn down an account because it already has a competitive account? Why?

19. Do you believe it is advisable for a company to have an advertising department and also hire an advertising agency? Give reasons.

20. A large manufacturer recently announced a change in its advertising agency. For a period of 15 years, Agency A had represented the company, and during that period of time the company had become one of the three

leaders in its field. Sales had been increasing each year, and current-year figures indicate that sales should exceed last year's volume by 5 percent. The relationships between the company and the agency were of the best. However, the president of the company stated that it was for the best interest of both parties to make a change. Give your reasons.

Case 19–1   NORTHERN ELECTRIC COMPANY
Location of advertising function

The Northern Electric Company has expanded its operations into new product lines to try to stabilize its sales, which have fluctuated widely during the past five years. As a result, the company is faced with the problem of developing a new organizational structure.

Northern began its operations by manufacturing audio recording-reproduction equipment which was used primarily for recording and reproducing music, voice, and other program material for radio and television stations, recording companies, and allied groups.

In the initial stages of the company's development, its products were handled by an exclusive distribution agency. The company's organization structure at that time appears in Exhibit 19–1.

EXHIBIT 19–1

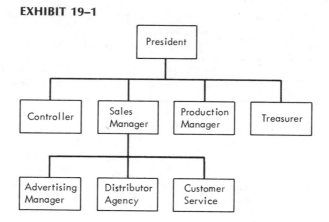

Later the company engaged other distributors, and then established distribution through nonexclusive local distributors. However, the organizational chart of the company was not changed, and the sales manager remained responsible for directing all the advertising of the company.

By modifying and extending the range of its audio receivers, the company was able to record measurement information and control information on tape. As a result, whole new markets of specific applications in the use of the equipment for telemetering, securing data on aircraft performance, shock and vibration control opened up for the company. In order to handle the new markets, the company decided to change its method of distribution and set up its own sales staff, and, at the same time, changed the responsibility and authority of the sales manager. (See Exhibit 19–2.)

The sales manager argued against the new organizational structure. He emphasized that the objectives of the sales department were centered on providing the means to sell the goods. In the new structure, he no longer directed the advertising of the company. He also believed that there might be a tendency to place too much emphasis on general advertising and overlook the use of advertising as a selling tool.

The advertising manager did not agree with the sales manager and believed that the new organizational structure would provide a satisfactory supporting arrangement so that each function could work

EXHIBIT 19–2

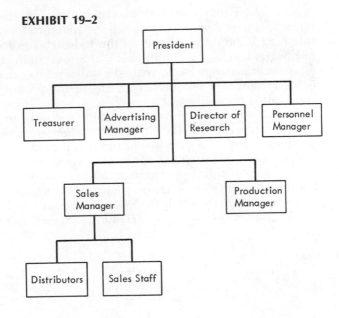

most effectively and in balance with the other functions. It was his opinion that the advertising function had to be considered in a context broader than that of a strictly selling function. He considered that advertising is both a line and staff operation. On the one hand, he stated that he advised, assisted, and counseled both the president and his staff on broad matters which would affect the long-term image of the company, and, on the other hand, he was directly concerned with carrying out the necessary creative work which the sales manager required for securing adequate sales.

In the organizational structure recommended in Exhibit 19–2, he believed that he had the authority and responsibility to handle the advertising function in the manner that this activity demanded.

The sales manager did not agree and contended that in the new structure he would not have control over the complete sales activity of the company.

Case questions

1. What organizational structure should Northern Electric adopt?
2. Where should the advertising function be placed in a company?
3. What effect will a change in organizational structure have on the individuals involved?

Case 19–2 **DAJ PAPER COMPANY**
Recognizing the advertising function

The DAJ Paper Company manufactures and sells industrial and household paper products through the company's salesmen to wholesale distributors and jobbers in the industrial grocery, paper, drug, hardware, and janitor supply fields. The advertising has been handled on a decentralized basis, with the sales manager of each division being responsible for the advertising of the products which he was responsible for selling.

The company has expanded rapidly and only recently purchased a competitor, the CIV Industrial Paper Company, in order to be able to offer a more extensive line of industrial products. The advertising and sales organization has not been changed for a period of 20 years and, as a result, has developed a number of overlapping functions between the different sales divisions. (See Exhibit 19–3.)

The industry in which DAJ Paper Company is engaged is highly competitive. There are specialized firms as well as national concerns

EXHIBIT 19–3

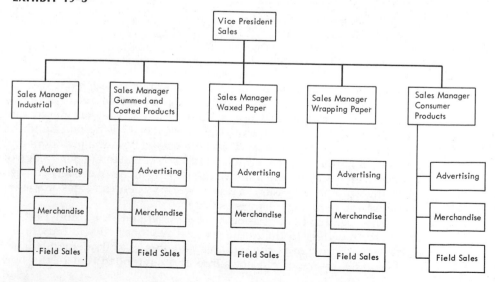

which compete in the market for each product that the company sells. Two of the national brands are backed with heavy national advertising and the local specialized firms have developed strong customer preference and loyalty over the years.

The company has five sales divisions: industrial, gummed and coated products, waxed papers, wrapping papers, and consumer products. The sales organuzation plan of the company resulted in the salesmen from the different divisions calling on the same distributors and customers in many instances. The salesmen and agents of the company were located in the cities as given in Exhibit 19–4. The agents operated on a 5 percent commission and originally had been used by the company to contact distributors prior to the period when the company extended its sales force. These agents had done a satisfactory job in building demand and had been allowed to continue to be credited for the business which they secured.

EXHIBIT 19–4

	Industrial agents	Industrial salesmen	Gummed and coated products Pacific Coast salesmen	Waxed papers salesmen	Wrapping papers salesmen	Consumer product salesmen	Total salesmen
Seattle	2	1	1		1	1	4
Portland.	2				1		1
San Francisco . .	3	2	1	1	2	1	7
Los Angeles. . . .	3	2	1	1	2	1	7
Salt Lake City . .	2				1		1
Denver	2	1			1	1	3
	14	6	3	2	8	4	23

Shortly after the purchase of the CIV Industrial Paper Company, the vice president of sales retired and the sales manager of the Consumer Products Division was promoted to the vacated vice presidency. He wanted to reorganize the sales force and centralize the advertising function to eliminate as much duplication in sales promotion and sales coverage as possible and to make his salesmen more effective. He also wanted to eliminate 11 of the 14 industrial agents to whom the company paid a 5 percent commission, because cost of sales by the company's salesmen was only 2 percent. These agents were competing with the company's salesmen for the same accounts.

Total sales of the company were divided as follows:

To wholesale grocers and cooperatives	20%
To paper wholesalers	30
To wholesale drug companies	5
To industrial users.	45

The vice president's problem in reorganizing his sales and advertising was further accentuated when a large eastern manufacturer built a mill on the West Coast. This manufacturer advertised its products nationally and followed a policy of selling directly to chain stores, wholesale grocers, and cooperatives. The company did not sell an industrial line but put its full efforts on resale outlets. As a result, both the products and brand names of this eastern manufacturer were well established in the consumer market. This company sold 60 percent of its volume to chain stores and 40 percent to wholesale grocers and cooperatives.

The vice president pointed out that he was planning to centralize the advertising function for the following reasons:

1. To consolidate the function so that one person would be responsible for the total advertising.
2. To have a unified advertising program.
3. To purchase advertising space more effectively.
4. To coordinate and guide all the activities.
5. To stimulate more aggressive selling.
6. To relieve the sales managers of the responsibility of placing advertising.
7. To make all the divisions more profit conscious.
8. To meet the sales challenge of the national firm that has invaded the market.
9. To improve the corporate identity.
10. To have the sales managers specialize in sales and general merchandising functions.

When the sales managers were told about the plan, a number of them objected and indicated that they would not be able to perform their jobs as effectively. Among the reasons which they emphasized were:

1. Under decentralization, the advertising decisions could be made more speedily.
2. The divisions of the company were unique and each division had specialized advertising problems.
3. Since they had the responsibility for making the quotas that were assigned, they should have the authority to decide what type of advertising should be used.
4. The sales managers had the background and experience to shoulder the responsibility of deciding on the advertising.
5. Each division of the company had been making satisfactory progress and during the last ten years, sales of the company had increased faster than those of its competitors.
6. The sales managers were closer to the market and had a better insight as to the kind of advertising that should be used.
7. Decision-making power should be given as close to the place where the action takes place as is feasible.
8. There would be danger of too much image-building advertising which might clash with the assignment of responsibility and au-

thority of the sales managers who need these funds for increasing sales of their divisions.
9. It would take away the initiative of the sales managers.

Case questions

1. Evaluate the reasons which the vice president and the sales managers gave for and against the centralization of the advertising function.
2. What are some of the major functions which the central advertising department might perform that are not being done on the present decentralized basis?
3. What other factors would determine whether or not the DAJ Company should centralize its advertising activities?
4. Do you believe it requires a different type of person to handle the advertising for each of the product divisions of the company?
5. What advertising organization plan would you recommend for the DAJ Company?

Case 19–3 **MYERS CANDY COMPANY**
Importance of using an advertising agency

In June, Carl Myers, president of the Myers Candy Company, called his two sons into his office. He asked them to consider if it would be advisable to check with an advertising agency about handling the advertising for the company.

The Myers Candy Company was located in New York City and had built a premium business for its high-grade candy in the city. All its candy was manufactured and packaged on the second floor of the New York building which the company owned. The first floor of this building was used for the sale of candy and for restaurant purposes.

Myers' candy was considered to be one of the premium products in the area, and, as a result, the company charged a price which averaged about 50 percent above prices at which nationally advertised boxes of candies were sold.

With continued growth of the suburbs and the development of large shopping areas, Myers had found that its candy sales had continued to decrease each year during the last five years. (See Exhibit 19–5.)

EXHIBIT 19–5
Myers Candy sales

Year	
A	$265,000
B	232,000
C	212,000
D	195,000
E	194,000

Sales operations

Until Year E, all the candy had been sold through the Myers store in the city of New York. In June of Year E, however, the company had leased space for a candy department in a department store in a major shopping center outside New York City. It had been selling candy in this new department for three months in Year E. While the sales in this outlet had not reached the level which was hoped, nevertheless, Myers was optimistic about the long-term potential of this department.

Curve of seasonal influence in the company's candy sales is approximately as follows: Peak sales occur at Christmas, Valentine's Day, Easter, and Mother's Day, with a declining trend during June to October and a rise thereafter to the peak period.

All candies are sold under Myers' trade name. The trademark of the company is registered.

Advertising

Two New York newspapers and one radio station had been used in advertising the company's candies. The advertising always had been written by Mr. Myers. He believed in a personalized type of message which he featured in each advertisement. As an example, he had a special portrait sketch made of himself, and this was used with the copy he wrote. He generally tried to emphasize the reasons why Myers' candy was the finest candy that could be purchased. He pointed out the great care he took in buying the ingredients. In other instances, he would include letters he received from some distinguished person who wrote to him and stated how much he had enjoyed Myers' candy.

General comment

After an analysis of the company's sales, the sons recommended that Myers go after selective distribution on a more extensive basis in the New York area. It was their opinion that Myers had adequate production facilities to increase its output by about 40 percent. However, they questioned the need for hiring an advertising agency because they believed that the advertising would have to be concentrated in the local newspapers and other media of this nature. They doubted that an advertising agency would be of much help in working with a company that sold only in a very limited market.

Case question

1. What advantage would it be for Myers to use an advertising agency?

Case **R & J DRESS MANUFACTURER**
19–4 **Selecting an advertising agency**

The R & J dress manufacturer is engaged in the design, production, and sales of a diversified line of misses' casual dresses which are sold in the budget departments by department stores and specialty shops.

R & J introduces four seasonal lines each year, with transitional lines added periodically. The dresses produced by the company are sold to about 2,000 department, specialty, and women's apparel stores through its own officers, salesmen, and sales representatives. It has a sales office and showroom in New York.

All advertising has been handled by its own staff because R & J has not attempted to build a national brand appeal, but has depended on its styling, price, and service to sell the stores.

The women's apparel industry is highly competitive, and no one company accounts for more than a small part of the national output. Sales of the company had increased to such a degree that the officers decided to try to create a demand for the R & J brand. As a result, the company asked several advertising agencies to present information about their experience. One of the agencies, the KD & A Agency, presented the following material:

Introduction

KD & A Advertising Agency is a flourishing and expanding one, and has been in the advertising business for more than 40 years. In this period, it has catered to the needs of advertising programs for various types of clients from all over the United States. However, more of the advertising business of this agency is concentrated on the East Coast. It is interesting to note that the ownership of this agency has remained with its employees.

In order to understand better the workings of an advertising agency, it is deemed important to discuss in brief the development and concepts of advertising in general.

What is advertising?

A great many marketing transactions involving both the transfer of ownership and physical movement of goods take place in this country daily. Most purchases of goods—whether by manufacturers for use in their factories and offices, by wholesalers and retailers either for equipment purposes or for resale, by consumers for household or personal use, and others—are the result of some sort of selling effort on the part of vendors. Advertising and personal selling play an indispensable role in our economy. Advertising has become an integral part of present economy.

Modern advertising is a recent development, its growth having come in less than a century—the period of the industrial development of this nation. At the close of the Civil War, the American economy was predominantly agricultural, characterized largely by small communities. Now the country has a highly advanced industrial economy in which large-scale producers of a great variety of products sell on a nationwide basis. Advertising has played a major role in this development into an industrial economy, the annual national expenditure on advertising rising to $12.5 billion in 1962.

Advertising must be viewed in perspective as constituting only a part of the whole selling process, and, as such, its effectiveness must be evaluated.

What is an advertising agency?

Advertising agencies play an important part in conducting the advertising of most manufacturers today. The advertising agency is a firm, specializing in advertising, which provides counsel relative to the advertising and allied operations of its clients, and actually prepares, buys space and time for, and places a large part of the advertising of its clients. In addition, it may perform other services, such as conducting market research, preparing sales promotional materials, counseling on public relations, preparing and distributing public relations messages, and so on.

Since the turn of the century, with the general agency plan crystallized and with agents more and more accepting responsibility for offering full plans and preparing as well as planning advertisements, the trend has become strong for agencies to offer more service and to become not just advertising counsels but also marketing counsels. The number of services offered and the competency in the services vary, of course, among agencies, and so do their internal organizations.

There are account executives who contact the clients, and there are art directors, copywriters, space and time buyers, research workers, mechanical production workers, and so on. The problem of effective organization of an agency, particularly a large agency, is not an easy one. An advertising agency is a collection of advertising and marketing specialists—specialists in planning, advertising, and selling, in copywriting, in layout and typography, in production of advertisements, in production of radio and television shows, in marketing research, in consumer research, and so on. To service a client well calls for the assignment of competent men to the account and good coordination of the work of the various types of specialists.

KD & A advertising agency

A. Location. The advertising agency's main office is located in New York, and it has offices in San Francisco, Chicago, and Washington. The company runs its business in this nation through its four offices, but a major portion of its business activity is located on the East Coast.

B. Personnel. This company has 84 employees running the various activities of the agency.

C. Structure. The stockholders of this company elect the board of directors, which in turn elects the chairman of the board and appoints the president, who is the executive head of the company. Four executive vice presidents and 15 other vice presidents are in charge of specific operations of the company in all its offices. Each of the offices is in charge of the manager, who is a vice president. The accounts function is carried out mainly at the New York office. Other important office bearers are production manager, who is in charge of the mechanics of advertising; media manager, who is concerned with buying space and time in the media; television and radio director; creative director; and research director.

D. Clients. KD & A has clients with various types of products such as apparel, groceries, building materials, home equipment, travel, and others such as insurance, department stores, and cosmetics. However, apparel and food products have been the important advertising clients. The agency enters into a contract with its clients to offer its services demanded by clients under the general contractual arrangements.

E. *Current Business.* KD & A reports billings of $8,645,000, of which $2,750,000 was in capitalized fees and $100,000 in billings outside the United States. Billing breakdown by percent was: Newspapers, 22.1; magazines, 31.1; radio, 1.1; television, 15.1; outdoor, 19.1; business papers, 10.1; and point of purchase or sales, 2.1.

F. *Agency Services.* The agency envisages in its field of operations the services described below:

1. A study of the product or service in order to determine the advantages and disadvantages inherent in the product itself and in its relation to competition.
2. An analysis of the present potential market for which the product or service is adapted; as to location, the extent of possible sale, season, trade and economic conditions, nature and amount of competition.
3. A knowledge of the factors of distribution and sales and their methods of operation.
4. A knowledge of all the available media and means which can profitably be used to carry the interpretation of the product or service to consumer, wholesaler, dealer, contractor, or other factor.

    This knowledge covers: character, influence, circulation (quantity, quality, location), physical requirements, costs. Acting on the study, analysis, and knowledge as explained in the preceding paragraphs, recommendations are made, and the following procedure ensues:
5. Formulation of a definite plan.
6. Execution of this plan:
    a. Writing, designing, illustrating of advertisements or other appropriate forms of the message;
    b. Contracting for the space or other means of advertising;
    c. The proper incorporation of the message in mechanical form, and forwarding it with proper instructions for the fulfillment of the contract;
    d. Checking and verifying of insertions, display, or other means used;
    e. Auditing, billing, and paying for the service, space, and preparation.
7. Cooperation with the sales work, to insure the greatest effect from advertising.

Conclusion

The President of R & J decided in favor of the KD & A Agency, and gave the following summary to his board:

1. KD & A is a relatively small agency and will have a personal interest in our account.
2. The agency has had experience in the apparel field.
3. The agency is in a sound financial position and has been in business for over 40 years.
4. The agency has offices in several states and will be able to make market studies for us in a number of areas.
5. The agency has handled a variety of products.

Case question

1. What additional information should R & J have considered before selecting an advertising agency to handle its account?

Case   **BENTON & BOWLES**
19–5   **Launching a new house campaign**

Benton & Bowles, one of the largest advertising agencies in the United States, had billings of $315,800,000 in 1974. Of this amount, domestic billings were $181,300,000 and international billings were $134,500,000. Benton & Bowles has been recognized as one of the more creative agencies in the use of broad marketing techniques in correlating appeals to media. It employs about 800 persons in its offices in the United States. Like all agencies, it is important for Benton & Bowles to maintain the highest quality services. Yet, it is complex for an agency to use appeals and techniques that will reach the users of its services on a professional level.

The approach that the executives of Benton & Bowles decided that they would use was an institutional campaign. In the campaign they wished to create the "image" that the agency was both a highly creative one as well as one having the professional capability to meet the diverse challenges which both new and old accounts had to resolve.

The agency decided that an effective approach was to launch a major print campaign on its own behalf. Twelve black-and-white advertisements, to appear throughout the fall and winter, focused on B&B's agency philosophy, "It's Not Creative Unless It Sells."

The initial advertisement in the campaign was an all-copy explanation of Benton & Bowles' creative philosophy (Exhibit 19–6) and appeared in *Advertising Age,* the *New York Times,* and the *Wall Street Journal* during the week of October 28, and in the November issue of *Fortune.* Subsequent ads, which ran in the same four publications, displayed the slogan, "It's Not Creative Unless It Sells," in over-sized lettering, each ad with a small line drawing representing one of B&B's advertised products and services. The first two ads featured the Gillette Safety Razor Company's Trac II Shaving System (Exhibit 19–7) and General Foods Corporation's Cool Whip (Exhibit 19–8).

The president of the agency states, "The words 'It's Not Creative Unless It Sells' represent the philosophy that guides every facet of B&B advertising activity." The president further explains, "There can be no other meaning to the word 'creative' in this business." Steps are now being taken to register the phrase as a B&B service mark.

Complementing the new house campaign are lapel buttons and embroidered samplers displaying the words "It's Not Creative Unless It Sells" (Exhibit 19–9) and a specially designed postage meter mark with that phrase, which is now being stamped on all outgoing B&B mail.

EXHIBIT 19–6

It's not creative unless it sells.

If anything came out of the so-called creative revolution of the 60's and the recession of 1970, it was a clearer understanding of what advertising is and what it isn't.

By the time that era was over, many advertisers and their agencies had been painfully reminded that advertising was not an art form but a serious business tool. And that "creative advertising" really was advertising that created sales and not just attention.

You might say creativity grew up in those years. And one would think that the mistakes made then would never again be repeated.

Yet here we are, a scant half-dozen years later, and like war and politics, advertising seems to be repeating itself. You need only look at television and pick up a magazine to see the frivolities and ambiguities that are passing as creative selling.

Once again many advertisers are learning— the hard way—what some of us have always known:

Not an entertainment medium.

During those crazy 60's, the ambience of television rubbed off on the advertising message and more and more advertising tried to become as entertaining as the programming in which it appeared—very often at the expense of the selling idea. One can still see a plethora of imitative commercials following the advent of popular new television programs and feature films. Remember all those "Bonnie and Clyde" commercials or the dozens of "Yellow Submarine" animated spots that followed that feature film? And how about the recent rash of "Gatsby" takeoffs?

Awards for what.

Awards for creativity conferred by juries of advertising people often have nothing to do with advertising that sells. Certainly, in recent years, the importance of advertising awards has diminished. Their value seems to have decreased in direct proportion to the proliferation of festivals. At the same time, many began to question the worth of honors bestowed out of context of sales results.

But as long as advertising will continue to be written by people, people will continue to give each other awards. And that isn't all bad. George Burns once said of Al Jolson, "It was easy enough to make him happy. You just had to cheer him for breakfast, applaud wildly for lunch, and give him a standing ovation for dinner."

You don't have to be loved.

Criticism of an advertising campaign has little bearing on selling effectiveness. There are many examples of advertising which are disliked by the very people who are reacting to the message.

By the same token, much advertising that is beloved by the critics and consumers alike fizzles badly.

This is not to suggest that advertising need be grating or irritating or hated to be effective. Wouldn't it be great if we could always write advertising that would win awards, that people would love and talk about, and that would sell the product, too?

But, alas, this magic combination is very elusive. And remember, the main objective is not to win awards, not to get people to love your advertising, but to get them to act upon it. In the process of meeting that objective, you may not endear yourself to some consumers but you may become very popular with your stockholders.

Watch out for distraction.

A selling idea runs a very real risk of being swamped by its execution. It's a cliché of the advertising business, but how many times does someone describe a commercial to you almost verbatim and then fail to remember the product? Humor is most often involved. A good joke, a funny piece of action, a great punch line—all can undermine the strongest selling idea. And yet humor, judiciously used, can uplift a piece of advertising, increasing its chances of being remembered while actually enhancing the selling idea. A good test: Is the humor relevant to the message?

Explore the alternatives.

There is no sure way to sell anything. There are many ways to approach the sale of a product— strategically and executionally. Some ways are better than others and you really don't know for sure which is best until you copy test and market test.

The time is long past when an ad agency can deliver a single advertising campaign to a client without examining and presenting alternatives. Every client has the right to take part in the selection process that an agency goes through in leading up to a creative recommendation.

And the most creative campaign is the one that ultimately proves itself in the market.

Don't overshoot the audience.

A lot of words have been written and spoken about advertising catering to the lowest intelligence level of its prospects. That of course is as untrue as it would be unwise.

But equally ridiculous is advertising that wafts over the head of the prospect. We still see and hear commercials and ads that are so cleverly obtuse that they reflect no more than the private narrow world of their creators. For every potential customer who reacts to such "sophisticated" advertising, there are countless others who just don't get it.

There is no "soft sell."

The one factor that did more to end the creative revolution and topple the "creative crazies" from power was the recession of 1970. It was a very sobering experience for many high-flying businesses and advertising agencies.

Creative philosophies seemed to change overnight. "These are hard times that call for hard sell" became the watchword.

But the truth of the matter is: All times are hard times and all times call for hard sell. Hard sell meaning the presentation of a cogent, persuasive idea, stripped of any distracting or irrelevant elements, that will convince people to buy a product. Is there any other kind?

There can be no doubt that advertising today must be more intrusive, more imaginative, more innovative than it has ever been. In a business riddled with sameness and clutter, there is a great virtue in being "creative."

Yet, if ever a word was subject to misinterpretation and confusion, it is the word "creative."

To some it means advertising that wins awards. To others it is advertising that makes people laugh. And there are those who think to be creative, advertising must be talked about at cocktail parties and joked about by comedians.

But "creative" can also mean dramatically showing how a product fulfills a consumer need or desire. Or it can be something as simple as casting the appropriate person for a brand. A unique demonstration of product superiority can be creative. So, of course, can a memorable jingle.

There are probably as many opinions of what is creative as there are people who conceive and judge advertising.

But no matter what your interpretation of the word, one thing is irrefutable:

It's not creative unless it sells.

That, in six words, is the philosophy that guides Benton & Bowles.

Benton & Bowles
909 THIRD AVENUE, NEW YORK, N.Y. 10022. (212) 758-6200

Amsterdam · Antwerp · Barcelona · Bilbao · Brussels · Buenos Aires · Frankfurt · London · Los Angeles
Madrid · Munich · New York · Paris · Port of Spain · Toronto · Turin · Vienna

EXHIBIT 19–7

Benton & Bowles

It's not creative unless it sells.

You start with a good product. Without it, advertising really doesn't pay.
But given a fine product like The Trac II® Shaving System and a sound marketing strategy, it's not enough
just to be clever in your advertising or to be entertaining.
It's not enough to be talked about or to win awards for creativity. Advertising cannot be called creative unless it sells.

The closest thing to a perfect shave.

EXHIBIT 19–8

Benton & Bowles

It's not creative unless it sells.

You start with a good product. Without it, advertising really doesn't pay.
But given a fine product like Cool Whip and a sound marketing strategy, it's not enough
just to be clever in your advertising or to be entertaining.
It's not enough to be talked about or to win awards for creativity. Advertising cannot be called creative unless it sells.

The great fresh taste tells you it's Cool Whip®

EXHIBIT 19–9

BENTON & BOWLES, INC.

Case question

1. Evaluate this approach that Benton & Bowles has used.

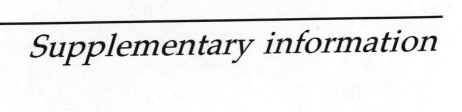

Supplementary information

SOURCES OF SUPPLEMENTARY INFORMATION

Periodicals

Since advertising is a field of rapid change and development, students will find it interesting and worthwhile to follow current happenings by reading the periodicals, which cover the field quite well. The following list includes the leading magazines in the major areas of advertising believed to be of most value to students.

General advertising periodicals

Advertising Age, 740 Rush Street, Chicago, Illinois 60611
Industrial Marketing, 740 Rush Street, Chicago, Illinois 60611
Journal of Advertising (official publication of the American Academy of Advertising), University of Georgia, Athens, Georgia 30602
Journal of Advertising Research, Advertising Research Foundation, Inc., 3 East 54th Street, New York, New York 10022
Journal of Marketing, 230 N. Michigan Avenue, Chicago, Illinois 60601
Journal of Marketing Research, American Marketing Association, 222 South Riverside Plaza, Chicago, Illinois 60606
Sales and Marketing Management, 633 Third Avenue, New York, New York 10017

Specialized advertising periodicals

Broadcasting, 1735 DeSales Street, N.W., Washington, D.C. 20036
Incentive Marketing, 111 Fourth Avenue, New York, New York 10036
MAC, MAC Publications Inc., 6565 Sunset Boulevard, Los Angeles, Ca. 90028
Media Decisions, Decisions Publications, Inc., 342 Madison Avenue, New York, New York 10017
Reporter of Direct Mail Advertising, Direct Marketing, 224 Seventh Street, Garden City, New York 11530

675

Advertising associations

Some of the more important advertising associations that are good sources of information about advertising are listed below.

The Advertising Council, 825 Third Avenue, New York, New York 10022

Advertising Research Foundation (ARF), 3 East 54th Street, New York, New York 10022

The American Advertising Federation, 1225 Connecticut Avenue, N.W., Washington, D.C. 20036; and 50 California Street, San Francisco, California 94111

American Association of Advertising Agencies (AAAA-the 4 A's), 200 Park Avenue, New York, New York 10017

American Marketing Association (AMA), 222 South Riverside Plaza, Suite 606, Chicago, Illinois 60606

Association of Industrial Advertisers (AIA), 41 East 42nd Street, New York, New York 10017

Association of National Advertisers (ANA), 155 East 44th Street, New York, New York 10017

Audit Bureau of Circulations (ABC), 123 North Wacker Drive, Chicago, Illinois 60606

Business Publications Audit of Circulation, (BPA), 360 Park Avenue, South, New York, New York 10010

Center for Marketing Communications, (CMC), P.O. Box 411, Princeton, New Jersey 08540

Council of Better Business Bureaus (CBBB), 1150 17th Street, N.W., Washington, D.C. 20036

Direct Mail Marketing Association, Inc. (DMMA), 6 East 43rd Street, New York, New York 10017

Institute of Outdoor Advertising (IOA), 625 Madison Avenue, New York, New York 10022

International Advertising Association (IAA), 475 Fifth Avenue, New York, New York 10017

Magazine Publishers Association (MPA), (Marketing Division, and Publishers Information Bureau), 575 Lexington Avenue, New York, New York 10022

Marketing Communications Executives International (MCEI), 2130 Delancey Place, Philadelphia, Pennsylvania 19103

National Retail Merchants Association (NRMA), 100 West 31st Street, New York, New York 10001

Newspaper Advertising Bureau, 485 Lexington Avenue, New York, New York 10017

Outdoor Advertising Association of America (OAAA), 625 Madison Avenue, New York, New York 10022

The Point-of-Purchase Advertising Institute (POPAI), 60 East 42nd Street, New York, New York 10017

Premium Advertising Association of America, Inc. (PAAA), 420 Lexington Avenue, New York, New York 10017

Radio Advertising Bureau, Inc. (RAB), 555 Madison Avenue, New York, New York 10022

Specialty Advertising Association, International (SAAI), 740 North Rush Street, Chicago, Illinois 60611

Television Bureau of Advertising, (TvB), One Rockefeller Plaza, New York, New York 10020

Traffic Audit Bureau, Inc. (TAB), 708 Third Avenue, New York, New York 10017

Transit Advertising Association (TAA), 1725 K. Street, N.W., Suite 414 Washington, D.C. 20006

Western States Advertising Agencies Association (WSAAA), 5900 Wilshire Boulevard, Room 1402, Los Angeles, California 90036

Special reference services

The special references listed below are also of importance in securing specific information.

Advertising Checking Bureau, Inc. (ACB), 434 S. Wabash Avenue, Chicago, Illinois 60605

Ayer, N. W., & Son's Directory of Newspapers and Periodicals (Annual), N. W. Ayer & Son, Inc., West Washington Square, Philadelphia, Pa. 19106

Broadcast Advertisers Report, Inc. (BAR), 500 Fifth Avenue, New York, New York 10017

Broadcasting Publications, Inc., 1735 DeSales Street, N.W., Washington, D.C. 20036

Broadcasting Yearbook, Broadcasting Publications, Inc., 1735 DeSales Street, N.W., Washington, D.C. 20036

Leading National Advertisers, Inc. (PIB), 347 Madison Avenue, New York, New York 10017

Lloyd Hall Reports (Magazine Editorial Reports), Lloyd H. Hall Co., 261 Madison Avenue, New York, New York 10016

Media Records, Inc., 370 Seventh Avenue, New York, New York 10007

Newspaper Circulation Analysis (Annual), Standard Rate & Data Service, Inc., 5201 Old Orchard Road, Skokie, Illinois 60076

Standard Directory of Advertising Agencies, National Register Publishing Co., Inc., 5201 Old Orchard Road, Skokie, Illinois 60076

Standard Rate and Data Service, Inc., 5201 Old Orchard Road, Skokie, Illinois 60076

Survey of Buying Power (Sales Management), Sales Management, Inc., 633 Third Avenue, New York, New York 10017

Television Digest, Television Digest, Inc., 1836 Jefferson Place, N.W., Washington, D.C. 20036

INDEX OF CASES

INDEX

*This book has been set in 9 and 8 point Primer,
leaded 2 points. Part numbers are 32 point Compano italic and part titles are 24 point Compano
italic. Chapter numbers are 54 point Palatino
italic and chapter titles are 18 point Optima.
The size of the type page is 26 x 48 picas.*